Washington's TOP
Fishing
Maps

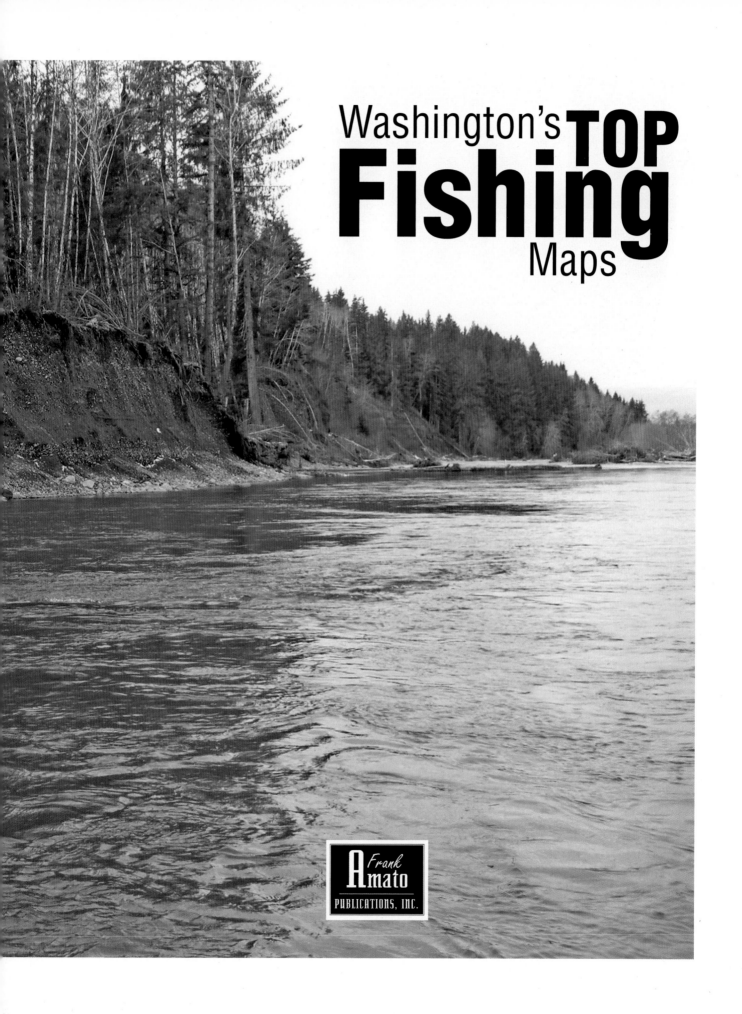

Washington's **TOP** Fishing **Maps**

Frank Amato
PUBLICATIONS, INC.

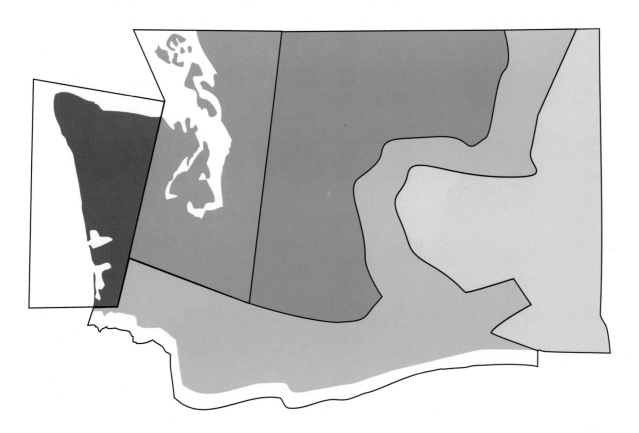

■ **Columbia River Waters**

■ **Puget Sound Waters**

■ **Olympic Peninsula & Coastal Waters**

■ **Central Washington Waters**

■ **Eastern Washington Waters**

■ **Canada Waters**

All inquiries should be addressed to:
Frank Amato Publications, Inc. • P.O. Box 82112 • Portland, Oregon 97282
503-653-8108 • www.amatobooks.com

ISBN-10: 1-57188-471-8
ISBN-13: 978-1-57188-471-8
UPC: 0-81127-00311-2
Printed in Singapore

Table of Contents

Introduction 7

▮ Columbia River Waters

Salmon

Columbia River: Longview to Camas 9
Buoy 10 11
Bonneville 13
Cathlamet Channel 15
Cowlitz River 18
Dalles Pool 20
Drano Lake 23
Hanford Reach 25
Kalama Bar 27
Kalama River 29
Lewis River 31
Lower Yakima River 35

Steelhead

Cowlitz River 38
Drano Lake 42
Kalama River 43
Lewis River 46

Trout

Big Sheep Creek 50
Omak Lake 51
Quail Lake 53
Riffe Lake 54
Sun Lakes Chain 56
Naches River 58
Kettle River 60
Yakima River 62

Bass

Burbank Slough/Paterson Slough 65
Horn Rapids 67
McNary Dam/Paterson Slough 69
Okanogan River 71
Priest Rapids 73
Potholes Reservoir 75
Riffe Lake 77
Silver Lake 79

Wanapum Lake 81
Washougal River 83

Walleye • Shad

Lower Columbia 85
McNary Dam/Paterson Slough 87
Moses Lake 91
Potholes Reservoir 93
John Day Dam 95

▮ Puget Sound Saltwater

Salmon

Elliot Bay 98
Hat Island 100
Hood Canal 102
Jefferson Head 103
Point Defiance 105
San Juan Islands 107
Tulalip Bay 109
Whidbey Island 111
Marine Area 8-2 113
Marine Areas 8-2, 9 116
Marine Area 10 118
North Sound 120

Trout

Hood Canal 123
Puget Sound 125

Halibut • Lingcod • Crab

Admiralty & Mutiny Bays 128
Strait of Juan De Fuca 130
Marine Area 9 132
Hood Canal 134
South Puget Sound Crabbing 136

▮ Puget Sound Freshwater

Salmon

Lake Cushman 139
Green River 141
Snohomish River 143
Lake Washington 148

Table of Contents

Steelhead

Sauk River 151
Upper Skagit River 153
Skykomish Chinook 157
Snoqualmie River 159

Trout

American Lake 162
Cranberry Lake 164
Emerald City Lakes 165
Lake Stevens 167
Lake Washington 168
Upper Snoqualmie 173

Bass • Crappie • Perch

Emerald City Lakes (Bass) 164
Lake Cassidy 177
Lake Sammamish 178
Lake Stevens 180
Lake Washington (Bass) 182
Westside Lakes (Crappie) 186
Lake Washington (Perch) 188

Olympic Peninsula & Coastal Waters

Salmon

Grays Harbor 191
Humptulips River 193
Umatilla Reef 195
Willapa Bay 297

Steelhead

Olympic Peninsula 200
Bogachiel River 202
Grays River 204
Hoh River 206
Satsop River 208
Sol Duc River 210
Wynoochee River 213

Halibut

Neah Bay 215

Central Washington Waters

Trout • Bass • Walleye • Kokes

Alpine Lakes Wilderness 223
Banks Lake 226
Lake Chelan 230
Fish Lake 233
Mineral Lake 235
Palmer Lake 237
Rufus Woods Lake 238

Eastern Washington Waters

Steelhead • Trout • Bass • Crappie • Walleye

Snake River 242
Rock Lake 246
Sullivan Lake 248
Williams Lake 250
Long Lake 251
Twin Lakes 252
Grande Ronde River 254
Spokane River 255
Sprague Lake 259

Canada Waters

Steelhead

Northern BC: Babine, Nass, Skeena River 262
Vedder River 264
Vancouver Island 266

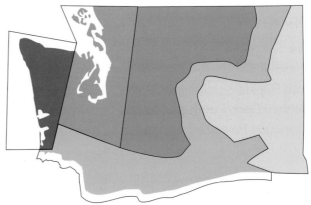

Introduction

Getting Started!

Planning and anticipating future fishing trips is half the fun, but with so much information out there it can become overwhelming quickly. Thousands of lakes and streams, fresh and salt waters, and numerous fish species—Washington's angling opportunities are endless.

Buying this book was a great start, *Washington's Top Fishing Maps* makes it a whole lot easier to plan and organize your upcoming adventures. The fishing information in this book comes from the long-time top rods in each area, this guarantees you the insider's scoop and puts you ahead of the game—even if you've never been there before. You will find everything you need: local accommodations and services, directions, fish species and where to find them, run timing, productive techniques, bank and boat access, guides, hottest tackle, and more.

It's time to call some buddies, pick a spot out of *Washington's Top Fishing Maps*, and start planning the fishing adventure of a lifetime!

Businesses and fishing regulations change frequently,
confirm the information online before you finalize your plans.

Always Important Around Water!

- ALWAYS wear life vests when boating (legally required for children).
- Read CURRENT regulations book or check online.
- Haul out more garbage than you brought in.
- Look out for others and offer to help folks.
- Keep boat lines clear of objects.
- Never drag your anchor in a current on a short line.

This book and its maps are NOT FOR NAVIGATIONAL PURPOSES. All bodies of water are subject to change from strong currents, wind, erosion, soil deposition, etc. ALWAYS view maps with a critical eye!

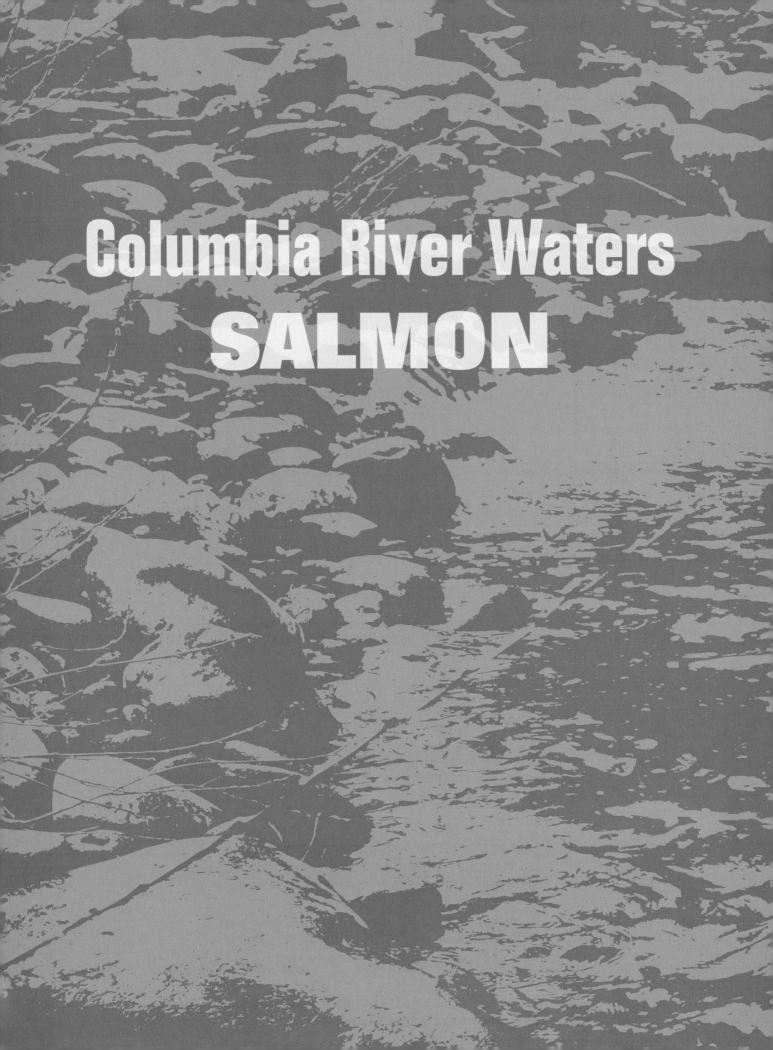

Columbia River Waters
SALMON

Mid-March signifies *real* start of springer season

LONGVIEW

by Joel Shangle

THOUGH THE RUN has been slow to build this year, the Columbia from the mouth of the Cowlitz up to Kelly Point, and on to Camas, should be decent bet for springers starting in mid-March. Don Dupois hooked this 19-pounder on the big river near the mouth of the Lewis.

I f the Columbia River spring Chinook fishery were analogous to a meal, you'd consider the February and early March fisheries the appetizer. Action comes in little bite-sized flurries, with a fish or two from Clifton Channel, a fish or two from Multnomah Channel, some more onesy-twosy bites around Willow Grove and Puget Island.

But come mid-March, when the Big C opens from I-5 up and local salmon hunters start to descend in increasing numbers upon the fishery, it becomes time to belly up to the table for the main course. You'll start to see sharpies like Eric Linde at Linde's Sportfishing (360-607-6421), Rich Mercado at Rich's Northwest Guide Service (253-376-8004), Terry Mulkey at Mulkey's Guide Service (503-803-1896) and Jack Glass at Hook Up Guide Service (503-666-5370) — guys who make their living catching salmon — out on the water daily between Longview and Portland to welcome the first significant runs of the spring Chinook class of 2005.

"I don't get serious about springers on the Columbia until after the third week in March," says Linde. "By that time, there'll be better numbers of fish in the system and you can start to realistically expect to catch fish."

And while guides like Linde and Mercado will definitely be part of the Bonneville Dam anchor-drop crowd later in April, they'll spend much of their time between Longview and Vancouver during the first two weeks of the month — targeting the biggest concentration of fish in the total run of 400,000-plus spring Chinook bound for the Columbia and tribs this spring — before following the runs up to Camas and Bonneville.

"The way I look at it, I want to stay down where the most fish are," Mercado explains. "You have a huge number of fish coming into the Willamette, you have good numbers coming back to Lewis, you have good numbers coming into the Cowlitz, you have fish headed for the Kalama. If you fished up above those areas, look at how many fish you're not even touching. You're talking about several thousand fish that you wouldn't even see if you stayed up by Camas or Bonneville before the dam counts started to pick up."

Hoglining: Much of the fishing between Longview and Portland is done in hoglines, with boats anchoring up in dozens of established spots off wing dams and river mouths during the outgoing tide, rolling out curtains of plugs and spinners and waiting for a buried rod to interrupt the cigar smoking, beer/soda drinking and socializing.

"You go over the Lewis & Clark Bridge when the season is going hot and heavy and look upriver, and you'll

AT a GLANCE

What: Spring Chinook fishing on the Columbia River.

Where: Between Longview and Camas.

When: Best fishing here is in early to mid-April.

Why: With big numbers of fish headed back to the Willamette, Cowlitz, Lewis and Kalama rivers, your best shot at the highest concentration of springers is in this section of the river.

How: Troll spinners and/or herring on the incoming tide, anchor up and hogline with plugs on the outgoing tide

Guides: Rich Mercado, Rich's Northwest Guide Service (253-376-8004); Eric Linde, Linde's Sportfishing (360-607-6421); David Perez, Hooked on Fishing Guide Service (360-993-5843); Jeff Williams, Black Dog Outdoors (360-751-9095); Tim Marisch, Northland Guide Service (360-560-0156); Brad Shride, Onco Sportfishing (877-483-0047); Josh Frederick, Big Fish Guide Service (541-380-1415); Gimme A Go Fishing Adventures, Jon Ball (503-539-1576); Eli Rico, Hotshot Guide Service (425-417-0394); Terry Mulkey, Mulkey's Guide Service (503-803-1896); Jack Glass, Hook Up Guide Service (503-666-5370); Clancy Holt, Clancy's Guided Sportfishing (360-262-9549); Erik Brigham, Erik's World Class Fishing Adventures (360-513-1331); Mike Kelly, The Fish Reaper (509-243-3474).

Info: Fisherman's Marine (503-557-3313) in Oregon City; Fisherman's Marine (503-283-8310) in Portland; Bob's (360-425-3870) in Longview; Fishermen's Depot (360-225-9900) in Woodland.

see hogline after hogline," says Mercado. "It's actually a pretty cool thing to see. There are a ton of different places where you'll find hoglines — basically anywhere you find a wing dam, you'll find a hogline."

The bite in a hogline can be a mercurial thing, with one boat in a line of six knocking 'em stiff for a couple of hours, and another boat sitting 10 feet away, not getting a single bite in that same time frame. Positioning yourself in line is akin to drafting and passing at Daytona, because every hogline on the river will be set up over some sort of trough or channel that funnels fish through. If you can position yourself to take advantage of a slot or channel, you're ahead of the game.

"If you have a hogline of six boats, it's not uncommon for them to be fishing at depths that differ from 10 to 20 feet in the space of a few yards, and sometimes only two boats in an entire line will catch fish," says Mercado. "Say you're in a spot where the bottom drops from 18 to 20 feet — there'll be a trough there that fish will naturally move into. They'll usually lay in the deep side of any trough or channel."

But you're not absolutely out of it if you arrive at your favorite hogline and find that you're boat No. 5 in a line of seven.

"When the tide first starts to move out, the guy on the inside of the line might be doing really well, but those fish will move as the tide goes out further and the water drops," Mercado says. "Sometimes being the fourth boat over gives you a better position in the tide because fish will move out to you. Put in your time in there, wait for those fish to slide out into your groove, and get on 'em."

Trolling: The drill on the incoming tide is to troll, pulling Fish Flashes ahead of herring or spinner blades. It's a good idea to run some of both, at least until you figure out a definite bite pattern on one or the other.

"I use a lot of spinner blades when I'm trolling, but I'll never troll without a couple of rods set up with herring," says Mercado. "I'll put the top two rods out with herring, one rod rigged with a spinner, and then maybe another set up with herring. That spinner is going to create a noise in the water, and if they can hear or feel it and it helps them find the bait, you're going to catch them."

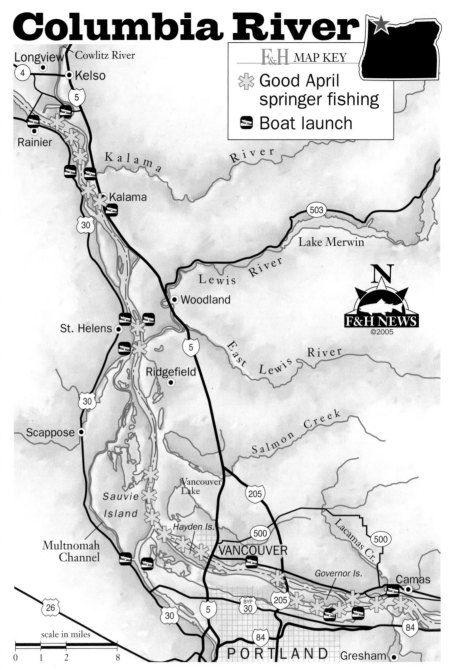

Columbia River

F&H MAP KEY

✳ Good April springer fishing

⛴ Boat launch

Trolling, hoglining hot spots: Some of the long-established, most consistently productive hogline and trolling locations between Longview and Camas include:

• The mouth of the Cowlitz River, on the Washington side

• Prescott Beach, near Rainier on the Oregon side

• Mouth of the Kalama River, near Kalama on the Washington side

• Mouth of the Lewis River, on the Washington side

• Mouth of the Multnomah Channel/Warrior Point, near St. Helens on the Oregon side

• Mouth of the Willamette River, near Kelly Point on the Oregon side

• The lower end of Government Island, on the Washington side

• The upper end of Government Island, on the Oregon side

• Just below Lady Island, on the Washington side

• Mouth of the Sandy River, on the Oregon side.

Tides dictate your effort for Buoy 10 salmon

ILWACO

by Lance Fisher

THAT'S 24 POUNDS of BBQ fodder hooked by Edward Gallagher, fishing near Baker Bay during an August Buoy 10 assault.

August and September is probably the pinnacle of the fishing calendar here in the Pacific Northwest because over the next two months large numbers of fall Chinook and coho will be swimming past Astoria and Ilwaco on their way up the Columbia River.

This fishery has it all: knuckle-busting action, water that keeps you on your toes and some very large, hot fish. I've looked forward to this fishery since I left it last September, and all I can say is, Thank God it's finally here!

Here's the drill: Buoy 10, the marker defining the outermost deadline for anglers fishing in the river has, over the years, transcended into the entire Lower Columbia fishery. For those of you new to the area, if someone tells you they're heading down to Buoy 10, they could be fishing anywhere from the ocean to well above Tongue Point on the Oregon side. Where to fish at certain points in the run — and even more specifically, during specific parts of the tides — is the question, and people who are dialed into the migration patterns of these fish do extremely well.

Kings and coho began staging heavily off the mouth of the Columbia in the first part of July. During that time, fish work the ocean currents in search of the anchovies and herring that so conveniently arrive about the same time. Anglers tend to fish in the ocean until about the second week in August, when large concentrations of fish begin to work their way into the river.

Fishing the salt: The saltwater fishery here encompasses a vast area, and fish will move around regularly depending on the currents and the water temperatures. The CR Buoy is a popular area, but only because I think people feel comfortable fishing around the marker and the crowds of people that are drawn to it.

Typically, I will start in the area around Buoy 4 and work my way out with the current. At some point along the way, I'm generally going to run into a school of fish, at which time I hit the "man overboard" button on my Garmin 2010c and proceed to work the area until my fish box is full.

I think the most important thing in fishing the ocean is patience. The fish are out there, and sometimes it might take some time to find them. On a particular day last year, we started in about 100 feet of water and didn't find a big pile of fish until we were in 550 feet of water about 8 miles northwest of the CR Buoy. We would get bit here and there along the way, but it wasn't until temperature and current lined up that we were really into the fish.

The lower river isn't like the ocean where you'll fish many different depths. Generally speaking, coho will be found in the upper 20 feet of the water column and the Chinook below that. Simply stagger your rods and keep an eye on your fish finder. You will eventually find the fish and all the fun that accompanies them.

Moving upriver: Sometime during the middle of August, large numbers of fish will begin to work their way into the river with the incoming tides. Buoy 10 is a popular area to ambush these fish because it represents the first place they'll see bait in the river. The area is heavily fished, and if you're not used to

AT a GLANCE

What: Buoy 10 kings and coho.

Where: At the mouth of the Columbia River, from the ocean upriver to Tongue Point.

When: Best fishing at Buoy 10 generally starts in the middle of August.

Why: This is the first interception point for Chinook and coho coming in from the Pacific Ocean. Consequently, it's typically loaded with fish on the incoming tides.

How: Troll herring, changing your location according to the tides.

Rules, regs: The daily bag limit at Buoy 10 is two salmon, only one of which may be a Chinook. Coho must be fin-clipped. Each angler aboard a vessel may continue to use angling gear until the daily limit for all legally licensed anglers and juvenile anglers aboard has been achieved.

Information/bait: Free Willy's Bait and Tackle (503-861-1201) in Hammond, Ore.

Guides: Lance Fisher, Professional Fishing Guide (503-936-4774), Hooked on Fishing (503-997-2279); Onco Sportfishing (877-483-0047); Fish Hawk Adventures (503-349-1411)

running a boat in a hard current, I would discourage getting right into the mix of the area. When a good push of fish does come in, the area can turn into utter chaos, with fish on everywhere and boats trying to maneuver in the hard-ripping tide. When fishing among this mass of humanity and you do hook-up, please don't just cut your motor and float sideways up the river with your fish. People will have a hard time getting out of your way, and you'll end up crashing into people. Slowly back your boat down the river after the fish with your net in the air. This will give the boats down-tide from you ample opportunity to get out of the way. A little common sense and courtesy goes a long way.

Usually the Buoy 10 area will fish pretty well through the first couple hours of the incoming tide at which point I will move upriver and try to get in front of the mass of fish that has moved in. This is the part that gets a little tricky, and having a few fishing buddies with cell phones will go a long ways.

As you move up, the river is divided by Desdemona Sands. The Washington side of the sands has the Church Hole and the area above the Astoria-Megler Bridge; both produce good catches. The Oregon side has the Green Line, a series of buoys in about 40 feet of water that runs down the length of the sands. In years past, the Washington side of the river has produced better early in the season, with the Oregon side picking up pace as the run progresses in late August.

Changing tides, techniques:
The tide will eventually slack and start moving out at which time I will simply work my way back towards the ocean in search of pockets of fish that are either trying to fight the tide upriver, or backing their way back out to the ocean.

There are many different opinions on which tide is more productive, but a majority would probably say that the outgoing is the better of the two tides. There's also an ongoing debate as to whether trolling with or against the tide is more productive, and I guess I'd have to say that I like trolling against the mild part of the tide and trolling with the harder part of the tide.

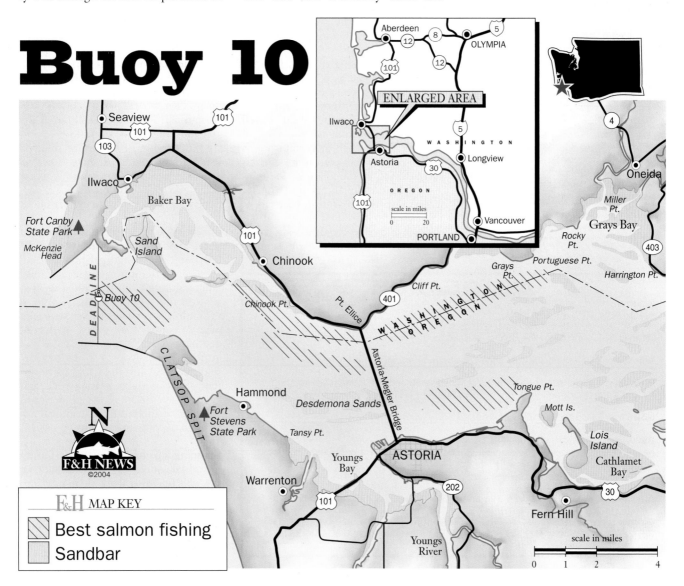

Buoy 10

ENLARGED AREA

MAP KEY
Best salmon fishing
Sandbar

Dam counts, water levels dictate Bonneville bite

NORTH BONNEVILLE

by Joel Shangle

BY BOAT or bank, Bonneville's a good area for springers. While sleds run plugs, spinners or bait, use Spin-N-Glos and sand shrimp from shore. Ken Malueg, Jr. and daughter Katie used the latter tactics and nailed a pair of Chinook below Bonneville Dam in early March 2003.

Numbers don't lie. They can be fudged, padded, twisted, juggled and skewed, but in the end, they're indisputable.

Or are they?

Perhaps moreso than any other fishery in the Columbia River spring Chinook lineup, the annual April attack on springers between Rooster Rock and Bonneville is very clearly defined by one number: the adult Chinook passage count past the fish ladder at Bonneville Dam.

History indicates that, if the number is low — as has been the case through much of the 2005 springer season so far — the year's class of upriver fish haven't moved out of the lower river yet. For obvious reasons, those low dam counts often keep the bulk of the springer boats grouped around lower-river tributary fisheries, like the mouths of the Lewis, Cowlitz and Willamette rivers.

But when that same ladder count gets really high on a consistent basis, usually in May, the fish are moving out of the Bonneville area and into upriver fisheries, like the Wind River, Drano Lake and the mouth of the Deschutes.

But doesn't it seem like there should be a middle ground somewhere, when counts are high enough to indicate that a fishable portion of the run has made it past the lower river tributaries, yet still low enough to indicate that fish are still hovering below the dam?

With the traditional April pressure peak barreling down on us, we asked a handful of the best rods on the river to give us the "magic number" — the number they'll use to gauge this year's Bonneville fishery.

Turns out that numbers might not tell the whole story this season.

"To be 100 percent honest with you, I don't know how much attention I'm going to pay to the dam counts in April," says Eric Linde at Linde's Sportfishing (360-607-6421). "I've had killer days when the dam count was dismal, where fish were stacked up below the dam before they moved over. The guys at the Wind River and Drano wait until there's 1,500 fish a day over the dam before they get serious, but I'm not so sure it's going to matter as much below the dam this year. Bottom line: If I can fish it, I'll be there the first week in April, no matter what."

There *is* numerical reinforcement to Linde's early-April reference: The 10-year average indicates that April 2 is the day the first four-figure number is recorded at the Bonneville fish ladder. Those counts traditionally climb through the first two weeks of the month — building to 2,000 a day by April 6 and 3,000 a day by April 11 — before arriving at the one date that you should absolutely pay attention to this year, come Hell or low water: April 15.

As in Tax Day.

"From April 15 on is slay time," says Linde. "If the dam counts aren't good by then, they won't be good all season. It won't take a huge dam number to get the fishing good up there, although, I guess it'd be nice to have that reassurance (of strong counts). But even if we never do see those numbers, I'll still be up there the third week in April."

AT a GLANCE

What: Spring Chinook fishing below Bonneville Dam.

Where: Between Rooster Rock and the deadline at Bonneville Dam.

When: Open Sunday, Monday and Tuesday only from Rooster Rock to the deadline. Peak of the fishery is from April 15 on.

Limit: One king per day, fin-clipped hatchery fish only.

How: Bonneville is a spinner or plug anchor fishery, but back-bouncing eggs might be the ticket this year, if the lower-river bait bite is any indication.

Guides: Rich Mercado, Rich's Northwest Guide Service (253-376-8004); Eric Linde, Linde's Sportfishing (360-607-6421); David Perez, Hooked on Fishing Guide Service (360-993-5843); Jeff Williams, Black Dog Outdoors (360-751-9095); Tim Marisch, Northland Guide Service (360-560-0156); Brad Shride, Onco Sportfishing (877-483-0047); Josh Frederick, Big Fish Guide Service (541-380-1415); Dan Ponciano, Ponciano's Guide Service (360-573-7211); Gimme A Go Fishing Adventures, Jon Ball (503-539-1576); Eli Rico, Hotshot Guide Service (425-417-0394); Terry Mulkey, Mulkey's Guide Service (503-803-1896); Jack Glass, Hook Up Guide Service (503-666-5370); Clancy Holt, Clancy's Guided Sportfishing (360-262-9549); Erik Brigham, Erik's World Class Fishing Adventures (360-513-1331); Mike Kelly, The Fish Reaper (509-243-3474); Scott Warter, Warter's Northwest River Guides (253-279-1944).

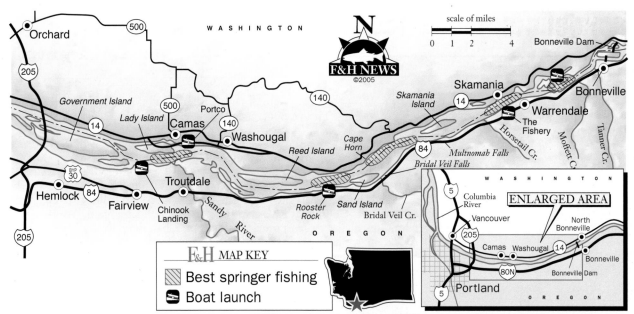

Bonneville springers

Fear factors: As late March, the year-to-date Bonneville counts were a dismal 4 percent of the 10-year average. Late March is still much too early to be sending up alarm flares, but the inordinately low counts coupled with an equally inordinate lack of water has the Columbia springer corps shifting uncomfortably in their deck seats.

"I think everybody is a little concerned with the numbers," Linde says. "The one thing that could throw a giant monkey wrench into it is the low, low, clear water. It's way, way low. I mean, pretty damn low. We had clear water in 2001, which was the last low-water year, but it wasn't quite as low then as it is now. I think everybody is waiting to see what happens on the next good set of tides, waiting to see if all Hell breaks loose finally."

March's slow showing is even more troubling in light of the age-class breakdown of the 2005 run, which is comprised mostly of early-running 5-year-olds. And yet another potential cause of heartburn for Bonneville sport anglers: a second consecutive over-forecast, which would ultimately cost recreational anglers time on the water during the traditional late April peak.

"The gillnetters net according to the preseason predictions," says Linde. "If those predictions are off and there's a midseason adjustment, it'll cost the sport guys, not the gillnetters. They'll already have their fish."

Here's hoping: All that said, you'd be crazy not to plan for Bonneville in April. Harvest figures indicate that the biggest number of fin-clipped spring Chinook hit the decks when the Columbia is open between Rooster Rock and the deadline at Bonneville, and this year's fishery — despite a limited Sunday, Monday, Tuesday opening — will provide plenty of April action.

"Oh, we'll get our fish," says Linde. "I'm going to remain optimistic until I'm proven wrong, but I think we'll have a good fishery at Bonneville. We'll see how the whole thing plays out, but I'm betting on it being a good place to be in April."

Low-water tech tips: Take some advice from the guys who have been banging away at fish below I-5 for the past month and a half: The 2005 bite is different than the 2004 bite.

The class of 2004 went on a wicked split plug/spinner bite that matched the early-season bite in the lower river, but the spring of 2005 is shaping up to be a stronger year to run bait.

"It sure seems to be more of a herring bite than a plug bite this year, at least down low," Linde says. "The really good bait trollers are doing a lot better than the pluggers. What'll that mean when I fish Bonneville? Well, I'll still fish Kwikfish and spinners, but I'll think a little more about putting out bait."

That means breaking out the cannonballs and back-bouncing big gobs of eggs. And regardless of whether he's fishing bait, plugs or spinners, you'll likely find Linde's "Blue Jewel" hovering over deeper water this year.

"The last couple of years, I'd have told you to fish shelves, ledges and bars, but I can tell you one thing for sure this year: They're running deeper," he says. "Typically I'd tell somebody to target 13 to 20 feet, but I'm finding fish a lot deeper this year. I'd be looking more at 20 to 30 feet."

The thinner water will also translate into tighter fishing conditions than last year, so be prepared to fish in a crowd. "There's definitely less water this year, which means that it'll be bumper-to-bumper in some spots," says Rich Mercado at Rich's Northwest Guide Service (253-376-8004).

Best dam fishing spots: You'll find the right combination of fish-holding structure and depth throughout the Rooster-to-Bonneville stretch, but here are a handful of spots to focus on:
• Rooster Rock;
• The flats above Cape Horn;
• The Fishery;
• The Culvert Hole, which lies just below the deadline;
• The Shad Rack;
• As long as you're fishing in the area, also try the mouth of the Sandy River.

Channel your springer energies at Clifton, Cathlamet

CATHLAMET

by Joel Shangle

It only rang up to "12," but the numbers on the digital scale at Fisherman's Marine & Outdoor in Oregon City verified what Washington and Oregon anglers had been waiting for: The first springer of the year. It was caught by a plunker on Jan. 21, a tidy little 12-pounder that interrupted the usual routine of winter steelhead at Meldrum Bar. Confirmed reports of a half-dozen fish in Oregon City followed, then rumblings of fish in Portland Harbor, a few in Multnomah Channel and even one all the way upriver in the Cowlitz.

By the time you read this in late February, the first waves of springer fever will have pushed Beaver and Evergreen State plunkers, herring-trollers and hogliners out onto the lower Columbia River in search of the forerunners of the spring Chinook class of 2005, which is projected to be somewhere north of 400,000.

It won't be lights-out action yet, but it'll be springer fishing, by God, and that's enough to satisfy some of us until things really get cooking around St. Patrick's Day.

"You're not going to see any real numbers of fish until the third week in March," says longtime Columbia guide Clancy Holt at Clancy's Guided Sportfishing (360-262-9549; *clancys-fishing.com*). "Until then, the fishery appeals to two kinds of people: the party of two who doesn't mind that they're only going to catch two, maybe three fish; and people who come on a guided trip to learn how to catch springers so they can fish the rest of the season in their own boats."

A springer refresher course with an old hand like Holt is definitely a smart idea, but there's another reason why a late February or early March focus on the lower Columbia could pay big dividends: There'll likely be some 5-year-old Willamette River fish rolling through Clifton Channel, around Puget Island and past Cape Horn at that time.

TROLL HERRING or spinners, or anchor and run plugs for springers in Clifton and Cathlamet channels. Anglers Fred, Jim, Rod and Gary wailed on the Chinook there last year while fishing with guide Dan Heasley.

Springer spinner tech talk

COME MARCH and April, when the fishing gets good, there's a fair chance that you'll find the Eric Linde's Pabst-emblazoned North River running spinners out back.

"Last year, the plug bite was a little sporadic at times," says Linde "For whatever reason, they bit spinners better. I just find that it's a real effective technique."

Like clockwork, you can count on one or two new spinner colors lighting it up every year. And although it may take awhile for the spinner sharpies to figure out the hot color of the season, Linde is partial to a basic arsenal of Luhr Jensen Clearwater Flashes in four colors: 3152 (chartreuse/blue/brass with red beads); 3135 (charteuse/green/metallic gold with green beads); 3154 (blue/green/chartreuse/white); and 0858 ("Fire & Ice"). He'll run

No. 6 or 7 blades on anchor, and size up to 7 or 8 when he trolls.

"You can't go wrong with chartreuse, but throw in a blue and pink tip rainbow and you have the color spectrum covered," Linde says.

Other options include No. 5 or 6 Blue Fox, FlashGlo, Lucky R, Backmore or Cascade blades.

Linde runs 54 inches of 40- to 60-pound Big Game leader ("They're not leader shy," he says), 4 to 8 ounces of lead on a slider (24-inch dropper) and 50-pound Spiderwire mainline. He'll go heavy on his rod and reel, with the same 8½-foot rod and levelwind reel he'd use for running plugs. "When they hit, you want them to bury that hook," he says.

Linde typically fishes spinners in 12 to 20

feet of water, either on an inside turn or at a spot where the river narrows, but won't hesitate to move into deeper water.

"There were times last year when fish were running in 25 to 30 feet of water," he says. "If 20 feet isn't working, don't be afraid to try something different. I'll fish shallower in the morning and then move deeper in the afternoon, especially on sunny days."

This being a low-water year, you probably won't need an 8-ounce weight in most spinner spots, but it's critical to use enough lead to maintain contact with the bottom.

"Don't cast your rig out, because it'll just get tangled," Linde says. "Just bounce it behind you, and make darn sure it's always on the bottom."
— J.S.

"We do catch some big fish early," Holt confirms. "In 2003, my first fish of the season weighed 38 pounds, and I caught quite a number of 25- to 30-pound fish early last year too. (ODFW and WDFW) are saying that almost 80 percent of the Willamette fish are going to be bigger 5-year-old fish this year, and those fish always get here early."

Looking further into March, you can expect fish — including the meat of the abovementioned run of some 87,000 Willamette 5-year-olds — to be spread from the Lewis River down to the estuary. And while pressure points will include spots as far upstream as the mouth of the Lewis and as far downstream as Rice Island, the stretch of water between Skamokawa and Longview/Rainier is an excellent place to start the springer Chinook hunt of 2005.

Clifton Channel: The Oregon side of Tenasillahe Island is, according to Holt, "just one of those places where boats congregate."

"It's not necessarily better than any of the other spots close by, but you do run into fresh fish there because it's

downstream enough that they haven't been fished for very much," he says. "One thing about that area is that it's a pleasant place to troll. The depth is even, it's not very snaggy, and there's a nice, long piece of water to troll."

Clifton is one of the few spots on the lower Columbia where you'll see trollers on the move through both

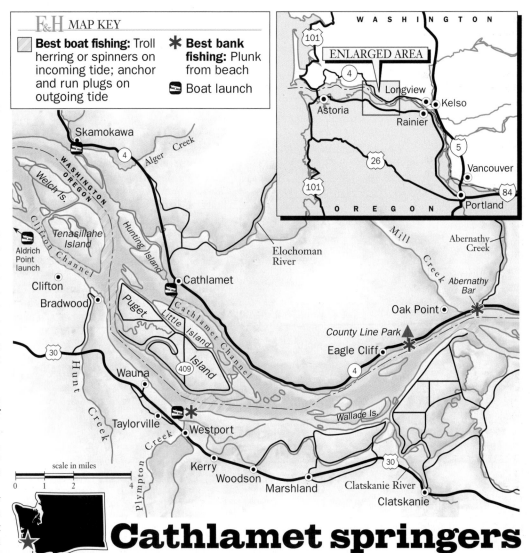

Cathlamet springers

AT a GLANCE

What: Lower Columbia River springers.

Where: Between Skamokawa and Longview/Rainier. Key spots for boaters include Clifton Channel, Puget Island, the Oregon shoreline between Rainier and Puget Island. Best bank fishing spots include Jones Beach, County Line Park and Abernathy Bar.

When: Fish are already being caught on the Columbia, but you won't see significant numbers of them until the third week in March.

Why: A class of more than 87,000 5-year-old Willamette River fish will be among the first runs to enter the river. These fish, some of the biggest in the run, will be around before the middle of March

How: Troll herring or spinners on the incoming tide; anchor up and fish plugs on the outgoing tide.

Who to call: Clancy Holt, Clancy's Guided Sportfishing (360-262-9549); Eric Linde, Linde's Sportfishing (360-607-6421); Rich Mercado, Rich's Northwest Guide Service

(253-376-8004); Brad Shride, Onco Sportfishing (877-483-0047); Jeff Williams, Black Dog Outdoors (360-751-9095); Tim Marisch, Northland Guide Service (360-425-1411); Terry Mulkey, Mulkey's Guide Service (503-803-1896); Jack Glass, Hook Up Guide Service (503-666-5370); Erik Brigham, Erik's World Class Fishing Adventures (360-513-1331); Mike Kelly, The Fish Reaper (509-243-3474); David Perez, Hooked on Fishing Guide Service (360-993-5843).

stages of the tide, but Holt — like most other vets — does his trolling on the incoming tide and into the very early stages of the outgoing, and then finds an anchor spot and rolls out the plugs through the outgoing tide.

"There are several pilings you can tie up behind, or find a place to anchor and fish Kwikfish in that channel," he says.

Tenasillahe Island (Washington side): As is the case on virtually the entire stretch of the Columbia from Longview to the head of Rice Island, the sandy flats along the north side of Tenasillahe are good places to anchor on the outgoing tide.

"You can anchor in water from 8 to 25 feet deep there, basically anywhere you can find the right depth along with a sandy bottom," Holt says. "There's also a row of pilings right at the head of the island and some further down on the Washington side that you can tie up to."

Puget Island: This is where you'll start to notice the influence of the Willamette, as fish almost routinely tuck into the channel on the south side of the island on their way upriver.

"Fish travel on that side more, especially early in the season," Holt says. "I'm pretty sure the smell from the Willamette pushes them over to the Oregon side, and they'll definitely follow that smell up that side of the river."

You can fish a handful of different locations around the perimeter of the island:

• The pilings that run along the entire lower end, out slightly into to the channel between Puget and Tenasillahe, on the Oregon side.

• The pilings located above the Wahkiakum County Ferry landing, on the Oregon side.

• Jones Beach, on the Oregon mainland near Westport, where you can plunk from the beach.

• On the Washington side, above the bridge to Cathlamet.

Willow Grove to Puget Island: Fish will continue to favor the Oregon side of the Columbia as they continue upriver toward Longview, with proven interception points for boaters at the

Ammo Dump (a series of docks and pilings across the river from Mill Creek) and good plunkers' spots at County Line Park and Abernathy Bar on the Washington side.

"I'd say that 75 to 80 percent of the boat fishing between Willow Grove and Puget Island is on the Oregon side," says Holt. "That's especially true early in the season. A little later in the season when fish are spread out a little bit more, you can move to some of the pilings over on the Washington side above Puget Island and do OK."

Net effect: Commercial nets will be in the lower Columbia Tuesdays and Wednesdays early in the season, and don't be terribly shocked if ODFW and WDFW allow additional fishing days during the week.

"It'll be pretty tough fishing when the nets are in," Holt says. "It's my guess that (the commercial fleet) will get some more days than just Tuesdays and Wednesdays, but we'll just have to wait and see. Either way, fishing will be a lot better when those nets are out."

The lower Columbia will typically be net-free Friday, Saturday and Sunday.

9 hot spots for bankbound Cowlitz springer anglers

— LONGVIEW

by Tim Deaver

With this spring's on-again, off-again Chinook fishery on the Columbia, many anglers are turning to other rivers to fill the void. Few offer as much public bank opportunity as the Cowlitz.

Not only is one of the largest springer runs in years projected to return to this big southwest Washington river, you'll also find sporadically good early summer-run steelhead action too.

Plunker power: If you're new to bank springer fishing, the primary method is plunking. A standard rig consists of a Spin-N-Glo or Cheater attached with a heavy enough weight so the setup will not drift but stay in place (this usually includes a 5- to 8-ounce pyramid sinker). In fact, it's the sound of the heavy weight hitting the water that gave technique its name.

The rest of the setup is as follows: From your fishing rod, run 15- to 25-pound mainline then two 8mm beads up your line; Tie a size 3 or larger swivel, a 36-inch piece of 30-pound mono (this is your "shock cord"); Run up a large slider followed by two more 8mm beads and then another size 3 swivel; Tie on another 36-inch leader, but with a little lighter line of 15- to 20-pound test; Run a Cheater or a size 2 Spin-N-Glo with two 5mm red beads and a double 2/0 solid tie, which is attached a sand shrimp.

It is important to note that the shock cord must be at least 30-pound line; otherwise when you hook a large fish, the force of the heavy weight sliding back and fourth will break your line.

Once you've cast out, take another 36-inch leader (usually the same weight as your Spin-N-Glo leader) and tie on a Brad's Wiggler or a Fatfish in blue or green pirate. On the other end tie on a size 7 Sampo snap swivel, snap this on to your main line and let it go down to the water. The force of the plug diving against the current will send it down to the top swivel two beads, where it will stop.

As far as a rod is concerned, a heavy- action 9-footer like you'd fish on the Columbia River isn't necessary. In fact, I see lots of guys doing quite well with 7½-foot back-bouncing rods. The shorter rods actually allow them to fish areas that have quite a lot of overhanging brush. Also there are few holes that require casting much further than 6 to 12 feet from shore.

Go with a reel capable of holding at least a 150 yards of 20-pound mono.

For bait, stick with fresh sand shrimp or pink and cerise prawns smothered in Mike's shrimp gel. Also remember, springers are very scent-sensitive, so wash your hands in a scent-removing soap before baiting up.

Another final tip is that a lot of anglers are switching to a spectra line like Power Pro. Its low diameter allows for less line drag, which allows for a lighter weight. Also, spectra lines have 2-percent stretch, which allows for instant hook-ups. My personal favorite is 65-pound test Power Pro, which has the diameter of 15-pound and virtually no drag.

STANDING ON THE BEACH and plunking bait is the primary way to hook springers on the lower Cowlitz River.

AT a GLANCE

What: Lower Cowlitz bank springers.

Where: From the Olequa Gravel Bay down to the Slaughter Hole, near Gearehart Gardens on the lower river. Hot spots include the Slaughter Hole, Rocky Point Hole, Hoyer Road, Camelot, High Bank, the Car Lot Hole, the Garbage Dump, mouth of the Toutle, Olequa Gravel Bar.

Why: No opportunity on the mainstem Columbia, but the Cowlitz is scheduled to see one of its best salmon runs in recent years. Throw in early summer steelhead for good measure.

How: Plunking bait from the bank. Gear up with a 7½-foot back-bouncing rod, a reel that'll hold 150 yards of 20-pound test, and basic gear including Spin-N-Glos, Cheaters, beads, hooks and bait (prawns flavored with Mike's shrimp oil)

Information: Bob's Sporting Goods (360-425-3870); Four Corners (360-274-8111) in Castle Rock.

Banking options: Most of the bank fishing is done from Kelso north, with the best holes as follows:

• Slaughter Hole: Take exit 36 off I-5, cross over the Cowlitz River bridge, then take the immediate left to Gearehart Garden Road and boat ramp. Follow the road until you come to a gate and walk in about 200 yards to the hole.

• Rocky Point Hole: Located off Highway 411 (the West Side Highway) at the Lexington dike north of Kelso. This hole is one of the few where the further you cast, the better. This is also an excellent sturgeon hole.

• Hoyer Road: Also off 411, take Hoyer Road down to the river. This section of river offers a ton of bank fishing and fairly light pressure, and has lots of room for the family.

• Camelot: Another 411 spot, this is an area with lots of room for the family. There's also a nice place to launch a boat off the sand.

• High Bank: Located across from Delameter Road just below Four Corners, this is one of the best holes on the river, and, consequently, the most crowded.

• Car Lot Hole: Located in downtown Castle Rock, this hole is steep and rocky.

• Garbage Dump Hole: North of Four Corners off 411 just below the mouth of the Toutle River. Take Chapman Road to the old county dump parking area. This hole is a heavily fished by the locals, so make sure not to crowd other anglers.

• Mouth of the Toutle: Located on the east side of the river, take I-5 exit 49, head east and take the first left, which is a frontage road. Travel about 2 miles to the parking area above the train bridge at the Burlington Northern-Sante Fe gate. Unfortunately, the gate is locked so be prepared to pack light and walk down the road about a ½ mile to the hole.

• Olequa Gravel Bar: Off I-5 at the Barnes Road exit, head west about 3 miles until you come to the boat ramp sign. Follow the sign to the boat ramp and gravel bar. If you've got 4-wheel drive, you can actually fish from your truck.

One final note: Make sure to remove all trash, even if it's not yours, or we may lose most of this bank opportunity.

Lower Cowlitz River

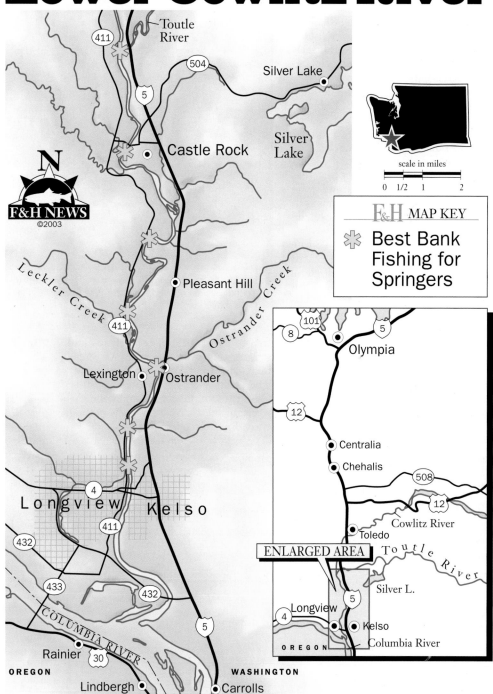

scale in miles

0   1/2   1   2

F&H MAP KEY

✳ **Best Bank Fishing for Springers**

ENLARGED AREA

OREGON

WASHINGTON

Explore unpressured Dalles Pool for springers

THE DALLES, Ore.

by Joel Shangle

It's not that Eli Rico is a loner. Actually, the Seattle-based guide is one of the most personable guys you'll ever meet. But Rico, owner of Hot Shot Guide Service (206-469-0567), gets a semi-cagey, semi-delighted look in his eye when he talks about a fishery that, through late March and early April, has been his personal spring Chinook playground.

"I can go up there right now and pop a fish, and there won't be a lot of pressure," says Rico. "As a matter of fact, where I fish, I don't even see another boat. I'm out there all by myself."

He's talking about the virtually unexplored springer opportunity that lies between The Dalles Dam and John Day Dam, a fishery that, until this year, had been the property of walleye and bass anglers in April and May.

If Portland-, Spokane-, Tri-Cities-, Seattle-, Anylittlepodunkville-based springer hunters are smart, all those bass and walleye boats armed with crankbaits and bottom bouncers will be joined over the next month by jet sleds loaded with Kwikfish, FlatFish, spinners and bait.

"The upriver springer count is 440,000," says Rico. "I hear that roughly 300,000 of those are headed past The Dalles. Even if that's not the exact number, there are still a lot of fish heading upriver. There aren't a lot of

GUIDE ELI RICO prepares to release a picture-perfect wild springer, estimated to weigh 40 pounds. It was hooked a quarter mile below the mouth of the Deschutes with a spinner/bait setup late last month.

fish up there yet, but once the counts start getting into thousands — where there are 1,000-plus fish going over The Dalles — that's the time to fish it. Once those numbers are good and the weekend pressure on Drano is getting crazy, I'm fishing above The Dalles."

The fishery: Rico's familiarity with The Dalles-to-John-Day springer fishery came from several years of fishing the same body of water for walleye and bass. And while it's relatively new territory for many salmon anglers, this might be the perfect time to get buddy-buddy with veterans of the pool's spinyray fishery.

"If you know where to catch walleye up there, you know where to catch springers," Rico says. "People who have caught springers incidentally while fishing for walleye know what I'm talking about. That's how I found that fishery, fishing plugs at high speed for walleye. I'd be trolling and *boom*, there's a springer. And then *boom*, another springer. I started to figure out that it wasn't a fluke. That's how I learned the travel lanes, and where they hang."

The key to the springer fishery is to know salmon-holding structure when you see it.

"The fish finder is a vital tool," says Rico. "You're fishing a lot of breaks,

AT A GLANCE

What: Springers between The Dalles and John Day dams.

When: Open now, but fish numbers over The Dalles will build through April. The best fishing will start around the third week in April. Watch for 1,000-plus fish a day over The Dalles Dam for prime fishing.

Where: Areas to hit include the mouth of the Deschutes River, Browns Island near Avery, above Maryhill and below John Day.

Techniques: Pull plugs, backbounce shrimp and eggs, fish spinners. Plugs are the best choice early in the season.

Tackle/Supplies: Available at Dint's Market in Biggs Junction, Ore.

Lodging: Lyle Hotel (509-365-5953)

Information: Eli Rico, Hot Shot Guide Service (206-469-0567)

looking for shelves that drop 10 to 30 feet. It's a lot of structure fishing, working close to shorelines where you'd normally find walleye. You want to find staging areas where fish hold up, and travelling lanes where fish will move through."

Rico's structure-finding routine is simple: He'll idle downriver in quarter mile stretches, watching the finder for concentrations of fish either holding on structure or travelling thorough.

"If there are fish there, we'll stop and work for them," he says. "If we're not marking anything, I'll keep moving until I find fish."

Where to start: Starting just above The Dalles and moving upriver, here are some spots to start your search:

Browns Island: Launch in Avery on the Washington side (off Highway 14 west of Maryhill) and work around the island for travelling fish.

"Fish seem to hold around the island overnight and then travel it during the day," says Rico. "It's fairly shallow there, so they seem to use it more as a travelling lane."

Deschutes River/Miller Island: Look for fish to start heading into the

Deschutes in viable numbers around the third week in April.

"I usually start looking around the Deschutes when numbers of fish aren't moving over John Day," says Rico. "That means that fish are holding between the dam." Look for breaks and channels from the mouth of the Deschutes downriver about an eighth of a mile. You'll find two main channels ranging from 15 to 40 feet, where fish will lay in deeper water before moving up onto the edges to travel during the day.

Maryhill: Fish from the Highway 97 bridge up to the island roughly a mile upstream from the Maryhill State Park launch.

"You're mainly fishing travelling lanes above Maryhill," says Rico. "Get on your fish finder and find the structure there. When you see that they're moving upriver, move up with them."

RAY BOJORGES came up from San Jose, Calif., and hooked this mid-Columbia keeper above The Dalles Dam. Hatchery fish will be scarce in this fishery, but available through the next month.

John Day: Work both sides of the river from the deadline (roughly a quarter mile below the dam) down to

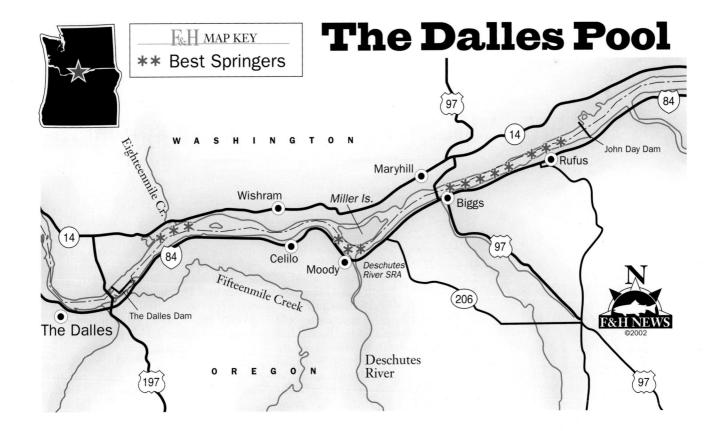

F&H MAP KEY

** Best Springers

The Dalles Pool

WASHINGTON

97

14

84

Eighteenmile Cr.

John Day Dam

Rufus

Maryhill

Wishram

Miller Is.

Biggs

14

84

Celilo

Moody

Deschutes River SRA

97

206

Fifteenmile Creek

The Dalles Dam

The Dalles

N

F&H NEWS
©2002

OREGON

197

Deschutes River

97

the big island, looking for travelling lanes on the Oregon side and holding pockets on the Washington side.

"There's a lot of deep structure on the Washington side, definitely deeper water and holding areas," says Rico. "The Oregon side is more open, with flats. You're looking for breaks that fish might be travelling on."

However, the Oregon side closest to the deadline above the John Day ramp is loaded with deeper holding structure.

Techniques: Bring your downriver setups with you: The Dalles-to-Day fishery is a plug-pulling, bait-bouncing, spinner-fishing show.

"Plugs are the way to go through the first part of the season," says Rico. "I'll go to spinners later in the season. And if you can find a travelling lane where you're marking a lot of fish, anchoring up and backbouncing shrimp and eggs along the bottom can be killer."

The same fluorescent red, silver/green plugs that work on Drano/Wind fish are applicable here, although Rico will switch to a clear plug in clear water.

"If I have 15 feet of visibility, I want that plug to look as small as possible," he says.

Standard setup is a 6-foot, heavy leader with a 2-foot dropper and enough weight to keep you on the bottom.

"My springer setup last year was 14-pound mainline and 20-pound leader, but I've gone to 40-pound leader and 50-pound mainline this year because the fish are significantly bigger. If you're

fighting a big, strong 20-pound fish, you need to get it under control. There's no time to play."

Rico advises switching the standard plug treble to a single octopus hook.

Best backbouncing setup includes the same three-way dropper system and shrimp or eggs loaded on small (2/0) hooks.

Don't come upriver looking to stuff your freezer with fillets — the ratio of hatchery-to-wild fish will ride in the 2:8 range.

"To me, the fishery is like fishing for trophy steelhead on the Olympic Peninsula," says Rico. "If you're set on retaining fish, go to the Wind or Drano. The upriver springer fishery is definitely geared for the guy who can enjoy catching and releasing for sport."

Smallies too: Oh, and just in case you left a spare spinning rod and some crankbaits, spinnerbaits or plastics in the boat, put them to good use. The waters above The Dalles Dam on the Washington side is bronzeback country.

"The first mile above the dam, on the Washington side, has a lot of structure," says Rico. "You're fishing water from 1 to 30 feet deep, casting plugs, fishing spinnerbaits. It's excellent smallmouth fishing."

On the other end, cast cranks and plastics off the banks between the ramp and deadline below John Day, and area that's loaded with bassy structure on both the Washington and Oregon sides.

Watch dam count for trib springers

HOME VALLEY

Be prepared for the springer fishery to move above Bonneville this month as fish make their way into the Wind River and Drano Lake. Both these fisheries are solid late April and May bets.

"If the count over Bonneville Dam is around 2,000 (a day), the Wind and Drano will be smokin'," says Rich Mercado at Rich's Northwest Guide Service (253-376-8004). "Those fish come in little bunches — sometimes you'll catch three, boom, boom, boom, and then have to work for the next fish. Daylight seems to be good, and then again later on in the afternoon."

Fish the trough along the buoy line at the Wind, and hit fish as they come

around the corner out of the Columbia into Drano Lake.

Standard gig is to troll a red Mag Wiggle Wart, herring or spinner and prawn with the rest of the sleds and odd Clackaweld. Run plugs on top early, and then watch your graph and adjust lure depth through the day.

Our ace Drano spy Chris Spencer reported seeing four caught there March 29 — one hefty 30-pounder from the bank and three in boats — in six hours of fishing.

For updated daily fish counts at Bonneville, The Dalles, etc., go to *www.cqs.washington.edu/dart/adult.html.*
— *Joel Shangle*

Drop bait, pull plugs for Drano Lake springers

WHITE SALMON

by Joel Shangle

Following is a highly detailed, step-by-step process for catching Chinook salmon this spring on Drano Lake: 1) Bring your plugs; 2) turn left.

OK, so maybe it's not quite *that* simple to find a two-fish limit at Drano, but the bottom line is that the very straightforward technique of trolling plugs accounts for the great majority of springers on this Columbia River tributary.

AT A GLANCE

What: Drano Lake springers.

Where: Between Stevenson and White Salmon in the Columbia Gorge.

When: Best fishing is in May, but fish will start to slip in out of the Columbia by early April.

Why: Strong runs of hatchery fish destined for the Little White Salmon Hatchery are expected (enough to *possibly* warrant a four-fish limit later in the season).

Regulations: Open to fishing six days a week. Tribal nets go in on Tuesday, and it's closed to all fishing the following day. Two-fish limit.

Techniques: Magnum Wiggle Warts in pink, orange and red are the go-to method. Troll them moving counterclockwise from the Highway 14 bridge up to the launch and back down along the north shoreline. Dropper lead and cut-plug herring is a good way to go when fish are running deep. Smaller lead and cut-plug herring is another way to target suspended fish.

Supplies: Main Street Convenience Store (509-427-5653) in Stevenson carries plugs, bait, etc.

Information: Clancy Holt, Clancy's Guided Sportfishing (360-262-9549); Rich Mercado, Rich's Northwest Guide Service (253-376-8004); Eli Rico, Hot Shot Guide Service (206-469-0567); Rich Bogle, Rich's Fishing Guide Service (360-983-3608); Roger Smith, Cowlitz/Columbia Guide Service (360-438-1979)

"I'd say that 90 percent of the fish caught in Drano are caught on fluorescent red, orange or pink Magnum Wiggle Warts," says Clancy Holt at Clancy's Guided Sportfishing (360-262-9549). "You might see plugs shaded with yellow or green, but usually it's just a Wiggle Wart in some shade of red."

The standard Drano plug rigging and trolling routine are just as simple: Tie 16- to 20-pound mainline directly to the plug (via a duolock snap), keep the lead in the box (the plug will dive deep enough on its own), toss out an average cast behind the boat and join the cadre of other boats winding their way around and around and around the western fringe of the lake.

"Some guys will troll here and there scattered all over the lake, but most of the boats will go in a circle from the ramp to the bridge, trolling counterclockwise," says Holt. "It's kind of an organized thing where you just get in line with all the other boats and troll at the same speed as the boat in front of you. You don't want to try to go clockwise."

Why Drano? Trolling around in circles for hours on end might sound like sheer monotony, but the payoff is well worth it: Like nearby Wind River, Drano will be juiced with a significant run of springers this year, thanks to an aggressive hatchery program.

"A good portion of this record Columbia River run is coming out of Drano and the Wind River — we need to take our hats off to the managers of those two hatcheries," says Holt. "I expect a good season on both Drano and the Wind — matter of fact, I'd imagine that (Washington Department

THE REWARD for trolling around in circles for hours, fighting howling winds, manuevering in tight quarters, dodging hurled Mag Warts? Only the tastiest fish around, Drano springers.

of Fish & Wildlife) will bump the average to four fish up there before the season is over."

A slightly rearranged tribal netting schedule on Drano should also benefit anglers come late May and early June, when the fishery has historically been shut off to sport fishermen.

"We can fish it six days a week this year," says Holt. "The Yakama tribes net it every Tuesday night, so it's closed to all fishing on Wednesday. In previous years, (WDFW) would close it to sport fishermen the third week in May and the tribes went in after that and netted it every night. The way it's arranged now, we should be able to have it stay open until June. Those nets will affect it early in the season, because they take a lot of fish, but fishing should still be pretty consistent in May and June."

Where/When? For Drano newbies, finding where the fish run from the Columbia up to the Little White Salmon hatchery is a simple matter of getting in step with the rest of the troops as they make their way out of the ramp and head north toward the rocky point/island, west towards the Highway 14 bridge and back east towards the ramp.

"Fish come in off the Columbia and run into a big, deep hole at the bridge before it starts to shallow up as it gets closer to the point where the bankies fish," says Rich Mercado at Rich's Northwest Guide Service (253-376-8004). "(Fish) turn back around that point heading to the hatchery, and I think that's a staging area for them coming in off the Columbia."

Prime time for fishing is in May, but you'll find fish washing into Drano in force by mid-April.

The alternatives: Salmon running into the Drano fishery will cruise from 8 to 18 feet, hence the use of the ubiquitous Magnum Wiggle Wart, which runs down to 15 feet. Mercado recommends trying different shades and colors occasionally as a changeup.

"Those fish see 15,000 pink plugs," he says. "I wouldn't be afraid to mix it up a little. Go ahead and fish the regular plug, but put something different on one of your rods."

Plugs, though, aren't the only way to catch Drano springers — matter of fact, learning and utilizing alternate techniques (and we've heard our share of 'em, trust us) can be the difference between a two-fish day and a four-fish day.

"My thought is that those fish are looking for something to eat, coming out of the Columbia," Mercado says. "I'll always fish bait on one of the rods, no matter what. I know it's a Wiggle Wart show, but those plugs can only dive so deep. If fish are running in 18 feet of water and you're pulling a plug at 15 feet, you're not even fishing. You have to adapt to different ways to get the bait to the bottom. If you see that fish are suspended, go ahead and run plugs or cut-plug herring with 2 ounces of lead."

"But if they're deeper, you see guys scratching their heads because they're not catching anything, but it's because they're not diving deep enough to get to where the fish are."

One proven alternative is to bounce dropper lead and cut-plug herring or a spinner, a la Tillamook Bay. Because of the traffic-jam nature of the fishery, though, running a dropper and bait set-up correctly is absolutely crucial.

"You want to run enough lead to keep the line right at the back of your boat," Mercado says. "You can't longline anything or you'll get in trouble. Try to keep the rods real close to the boat — I run short Loomis 930s, just trying to

A SELECTION OF popular plugs for Drano Lake springers. Actually, while many anglers will troll red Wiggle Warts — and catch fish — switching colors or running a spinner-prawn rig on a dropper is effective as well.

keep everything as close to the boat as possible so I don't interfere with anybody else."

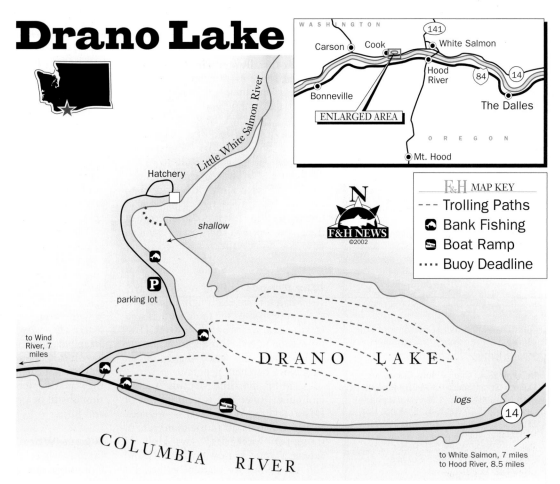

Drano Lake

WASHINGTON

Carson Cook 141 White Salmon

Hood River 84 14

Bonneville

ENLARGED AREA

OREGON

The Dalles

Mt. Hood

Little White Salmon River

Hatchery

shallow

N
F&H NEWS
©2002

F&H MAP KEY
- - - Trolling Paths
- Bank Fishing
- Boat Ramp
···· Buoy Deadline

parking lot

to Wind River, 7 miles

DRANO LAKE

logs

14

COLUMBIA RIVER

to White Salmon, 7 miles
to Hood River, 8.5 miles

Hit Reach for summer kings moving through

by Dusty Routh

Here's an irony that won't be lost on hard-core Columbia River salmon anglers: there are thousands of summer kings coming up the river through the Hanford Reach on their way to the Okanogan River. Huge fish, and lots of them.

But there are very few anglers out hunting them down.

That's because of several reasons. First, the Columbia ran high and nasty for most of June through this area. There was so much milfoil and other grunge in the water, and so much current and murky water, that anchoring up or even plunking was almost impossible.

As if that wasn't enough to deter even the most dedicated salmon anglers, these fish are going somewhere, on the move all the time. They are migrating well past the Reach, and that means fishing can be a real hit-or-miss proposition.

To put that in perspective, fall kings that come into the Reach have reached their destination, they're spawning in the same area where you're fishing. That concentrates the fish in a big way.

"When the fall-run kings are in, you'll go from having three fish in a hole, to 30 fish, to 300 fish," says Phil Motyka of Motyka's Bait and Tackle (509-375-6028) in Richland. "That increases your odds astronomically."

But these summer fish have an agenda all their own, and it typically doesn't involve stopping at the Reach to lollygag around.

How it's done: You really have three ways to go for these kings. One is to fish for them further north, up near the Okanogan, where they'll slow down.

The second is to anchor up and fish like they do just below Bonneville, with heavy (6- to 8-ounce) cannonball weights, long leaders and banana plugs or big audacious chartreuse/rainbow spinners. Spinners seem to be the key this year; they walloped the springers, and they're doing a number on the summer kings too.

Lastly, if you're shorebound, you can plunk with a Spin-N-Glo.

Reach defined: The Hanford Reach officially starts in Richland and goes all the way up to the Vernita Bridge. But unofficially most anglers who fish here will tell you it goes from Ringold to the Vernita Bridge. Ringold is about 11 miles up the river from Richland by boat, or 25 miles by truck.

There are makeshift launches at Vernita Bridge, downstream at White Bluffs and down at the Ringold Hatchery. There's also some nice concrete launches in the Richland area, like at Columbia Point.

"Personally," says Motyka, "I think summer-run salmon are tougher to catch than springers. Of course, the easiest fish of all are the fall fish that are destined to only reach the Hanford Reach and no further."

These summer fish are also referred to as June hogs.

"Those are the fish that start up around the first week of June, and then come pouring over Bonneville. They can be big fish," Motyka says. "Sometimes they're 5-year fish, so they're bigger. A lot bigger. Others are 4-year fish, but they're still big."

Motyka says the summer run usually peaks by the middle of July, and there can be a lot of fish in the river.

"See, with the spring fish, 80 percent go up the Snake, and only 20 percent come up the Columbia this far," he says. "But then in the summer it reverses itself, with something like 75 percent coming up here and only 25 percent going up the Snake. Most of these fish are all going up to the mouth of the Okanogan, and when it opens up there they'll do well, just about what they did last year."

For the time being, Motyka points out the river hasn't been cooperative.

"There's hardly anyone fishing because the river is just unbelievable," Motyka says. "It's screaming and full of milfoil, it's absolutely ridiculous. You can't keep a line in the water, and it's very difficult to anchor up. But it'll subside. As soon as the flows start going down, the fishing should be great just below Priest Rapids Dam."

Don't forget fall fish: Motyka was a guide in this area of the Columbia River for nearly 25 years.

"The fall fish usually start up the day after Labor Day," he says. "You fish for them like you do at Bonneville. Anchor up in hoglines, or plunk."

Pikeminnow money: Motyka says he hasn't spent much time chasing kings this year, however.

"Ever since they upped the ante on the northern pikeminnow bounty, I've been fishing for them," he explains.

That bounty now starts at $6 a fish, which isn't bad money for a day of fishing if you can get into them.

"I drift fish for them, using a heavy lead weight with a double-hook set-up and worms, or I'll power troll with plugs," Motyka says.

"You can also just baitfish for them, using nightcrawlers, crickets, chicken livers, chicken skins, cheese or shrimp. As the water starts to recede and the spills aren't so strong, as the river goes down, the big fishing will start on these pikeminnows. You can sometimes find big schools of them spawning."

Motyka bounty fishes in the Hanford Reach area, up the Snake and down

---

AT a GLANCE

What: Fishing for summer kings on the Hanford Reach, as well as for pikeminnows and smallmouth.

How: Plunk and hog-line for the kings, drag the bottom with bait for the pikeminnows, fish grubs for smallies.

When: The summer run peaks around mid-July. Look for them to get further upriver, to the mouth of the Okanogan, soon after.

Where: From Priest Rapids Dam down to Ringold.

Who to call: Motyka's Bait and Tackle (509-375-6028) at 1939 Saint St. in Richland, open Mon.-Fri., 9-6, Sat. 8-5.

near McNary.

"I don't go lower, like down to Granite, where they're really catching them," he says.

The tackle shop owner says some anglers who know what they're doing are catching 30 fish a day.

"Some guys are pretty good at it and making some dough, they devote their time and energy to it," Motyka says. "I went to McNary the other day and caught 22 of them, some real monsters, and the smallest was 20 inches. Some of those fish will tear you up. They'll tear the rod right out of the holder. But they're like walleye. They give up right away."

Bass too: Motyka says the smallmouth bite this year has been fantastic.

"It's just been unbelievable, they're catching a lot of fish just about everywhere — on the Yakima, the Snake, over at Irrigon," he points out. "It's been very good, very good this whole year. Grub sales are hot."

WAYLAY UPRIVER-BOUND summer kings in the Hanford Reach with banana plugs or spinners. They'll be moving through in good numbers this month to Brewster, where Cindy Williams hooked this one last August.

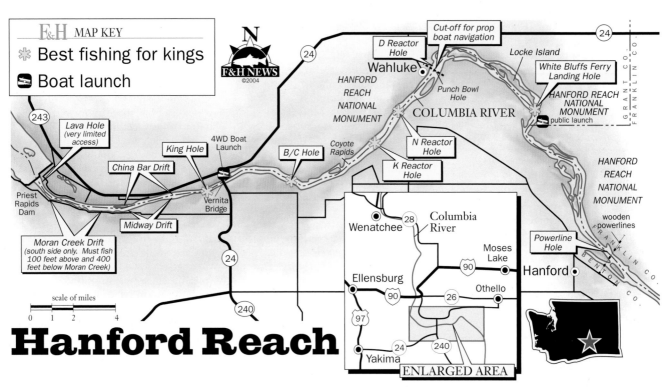

F&H MAP KEY

✳ Best fishing for kings

🛥 Boat launch

Hanford Reach

ENLARGED AREA

Intercept URBs at Cowlitz mouth, Kalama Bar

LONGVIEW

by Dusty Routh

FISH KALAMA BAR — where the Hills of Snohomish nailed these four brights — or the mouth of the Cowlitz for upriver kings and coho. Marty, Alan and Jeremy used green wobblers to fish up the quartet last September.

September. The very word calls up great memories and images for sportsmen. This transitional month between the dog days of August and the cooling days of October kicks off all kinds of things on a sporting calendar. Football starts up. Bird hunting gets into swing. Trout fishing picks up. Baseball games take on some meaning. And salmon fishing intensifies to the point where work and other modern-day obligations seem to be a hindrance.

In other words, if you're ever going to be unemployed for any length of time, let it happen in September.

That's because one of the real highlights of this month is the extraordinary salmon fishing you'll encounter on the Columbia River. For starters, of course, down low in the river at the mouth and the fabled Buoy 10 fishery, there are hordes of big silvers and fall Chinook just waiting for you to pick a fight with them. When the fishing here gets hot, it's about as good as it gets anywhere in either Oregon or Washington.

Even better, those fall Chinook are split into two separate groups of fish: the great, white-meated tule salmon, which appear copper-colored and full of fight, and the even greater chrome-bright fish, the upriver brights, heading east to the Hanford Reach and on up the river as far as Idaho. The genetics of URBs are such that they retain their bright color for much of their upriver migration, and the fillets from these magnificent animals are firm and red, even after they've been in warm, fresh water for a prolonged period of time.

URB 101: Upriver bright salmon are not hard to understand or difficult to figure out. Their patterns have been known for decades, and this year's run up the Columbia should be no different.

Unlike spring Chinook, URBs have a well-known propensity for running up the river in deep troughs and along deep shelves, with 40 to 50 feet of water just about right for intercepting them. While prime springer water is as shallow as 8 to 15 feet, that water just doesn't suit these fish that are flying so far up the river. For them, colder, darker and deeper water provides their primary migratory highway.

In terms of timing, URBs are making their appearances now.

"The fishing should start real soon; they're coming in now as we speak," says Mitchell Johnson, one of the fishing pros at Bob's Sporting Goods (360-425-3870) in Longview. "It's been a little spotty here recently, but it should really crank up in the days ahead."

URBs move quickly, preferring not to tarry too long in the lower river. Early to mid-September is the prime time to intercept them, though the fishing can hold up until the end of the month in some years, depending on conditions.

AT a GLANCE

What: Hammering upriver bright fall Chinook (URBs) in the lower Columbia River.

When: Now is the time. Fish started nosing in at the end of August, and mid-September should be peak time.

How: Anchor up and fish with spinners and wobblers. Use wobblers on a hard, outgoing tide, and spinners for all other tides. You can troll, also. But fish deep, 40 to 55 feet.

Where: The mouth of the Cowlitz is the hot spot, followed by the Kalama Bar.

Guides: Jon Ball, Gimme A Go (877-347-4662); Eric Linde, Linde's Sportfishing (360-607-6421); Rich Mercado, Rich's Northwest Guide Service (253-535-0403); Clancy Holt, Clancy's Guided Sportfishing (800-871-9549).

Info: Bob's Sporting Goods (360-425-3870)

Columbia URBs

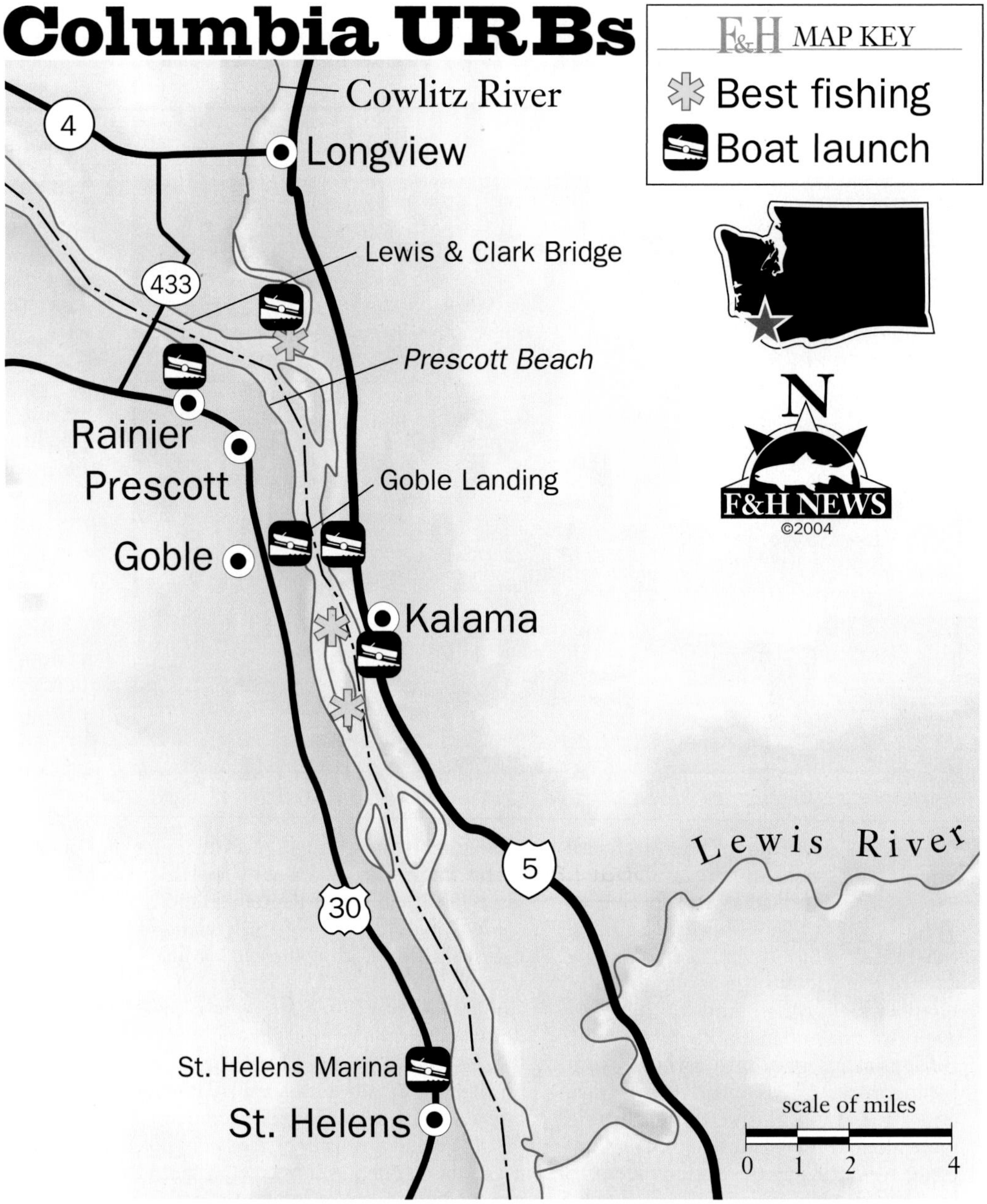

Map labels:
- 4
- Cowlitz River
- Longview
- 433
- Lewis & Clark Bridge
- Prescott Beach
- Rainier
- Prescott
- Goble
- Goble Landing
- Kalama
- 5
- 30
- Lewis River
- St. Helens Marina
- St. Helens

N

F&H NEWS
©2004

scale of miles
0   1   2   4

Wobbler delight: While springer anglers ply the water with spinners and banana plugs, URB hunting is more of a big wobbler and spinner deal. Says Johnson, "Your best bet is to fish the wobbler on a hard, outgoing tide. That imparts the most action to the lure."

You can anchor up, again in 40 to 55 feet of water, if your boat is equipped for hard-current, deepwater anchoring (an EZ Anchor System is a must for this kind of boat maneuver in the Columbia). Or, you can elect to troll, adjusting weight to get down close to the bottom where these monsters like to hang.

When the tide is running hard out, rig up with a spreader bar. Run a 5-foot leader to your wobbler, and a 5-foot dropper line to your lead weight. Again, adjust the weight to the current so you're just ticking bottom as you back-bounce your line out.

Wobblers come in lots of sizes and varieties. Popular models include Brad's Wobbler, the Brad's Mini-Extreme, the Clancy and, the all-time favorite, the Alvin Wobbler. If you haven't fished with these before, they're great big, wide pieces of metal with a sashaying back-and-forth wobble (they work well as kokanee dodgers too). Guide Eric Linde with Linde's Sportfishing (360-607-6421) likes an Alvin Wobbler in chrome with dark blue tape.

However, if the tide isn't going hard out, it's coming in or it's at slack low or slack high, switch out the wobbler for a big spinner. Douse it with scent, or do as Jon Ball with Gimme A Go Fishing Adventures (877-347-4662) does, and make sure to wash your hands with a scent-cleansing fisherman's soap. This helps remove tobacco, gasoline, and other human odors from your lure, which Ball believes salmon can detect.

He likes to use a rainbow-colored No. 3 spinner. Rig this on a similar rig to the wobbler set-up.

Where to fish: When the fish are in, it's not hard to determine where they are. Simply look for all the boats. The hands-down favorite is the mouth of the Cowlitz River, where 200 to 250 boats at a time can be parked to intercept these fish.

"Those URBs, those are the nice ones that everyone wants," says Johnson. "So they really crowd in there. With the average being about 15 pounds, that's a lot of good eating."

The Cowlitz mouth fishery is a hogline fishery, so be prepared to deal with the crowd and exercise patience and river courtesy (not to mention safety) as you fish there. If you haven't experienced this fishery before, going with a guide is one of the safest and most effective ways to learn it.

Another popular spot on the lower river is the Kalama Bar, which is Johnson's favorite spot to fish. He's fished this bar for years for these big URBs.

"The Kalama Bar isn't exactly the mouth of the Kalama River. It's just off the mouth, in deeper water," he says. "It's a good hole to fish."

Jam to the Kalama for summer steelhead, Chinook

KALAMA

by Tim Deaver

There are very few who would challenge that the Cowlitz is king among salmon and steelhead rivers, but if that's the case, then the Kalama River should be the prince. The Kalama has two excellent hatcheries that help it produce some of the most consistent numbers in the state. Add to this such famous holes as Million Dollar Rock, Saddle Rock, Round House and, of course, Beginners Hole, and this river just plain reeks of salmon and steelhead.

Summer-runs: Steelhead begin trickling into the Kalama about the last week in May and really peak about July 4. August and September are slightly slower but usually produce much bigger fish. Best early fishing will be from the first hatchery down to Camp Kalama at the I-5 bridge.

Boat anglers, you will have best fish-

ing early but low water usually runs most boats out by July. Run Wiggle Warts, Brad's Wigglers and Hot Shots in size 35 or smaller in blue and green pirate, metallic pink and rocket red. Also try slow-rolling size 4 Blue Fox and Mepps spinners in metallic blue and green.

As for bait, leave the divers at home and drift small shrimp or eggs with about 4-foot leaders and 8-pound mono.

If you're bankfishing, spend most of

Kalama River

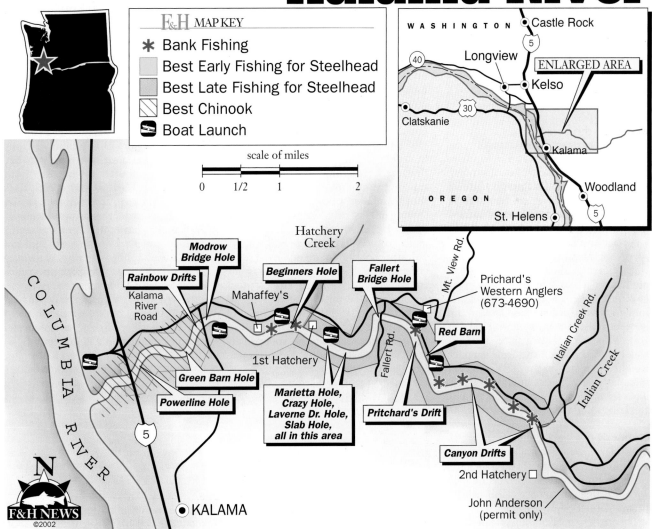

F&H MAP KEY

* Bank Fishing
  Best Early Fishing for Steelhead
  Best Late Fishing for Steelhead
  Best Chinook
  Boat Launch

scale of miles

0   1/2   1   2

WASHINGTON
Castle Rock
5
40
Longview
ENLARGED AREA
Kelso
30
Clatskanie
Kalama
OREGON
Woodland
5
St. Helens

Hatchery Creek

Modrow Bridge Hole

Rainbow Drifts

Kalama River Road

Mahaffey's

Beginners Hole

Fallert Bridge Hole

Mt. View Rd.

Prichard's Western Anglers (673-4690)

Red Barn

Italian Creek Rd.

Green Barn Hole

1st Hatchery

Fallert Rd.

Italian Creek

Powerline Hole

Marietta Hole, Crazy Hole, Laverne Dr. Hole, Slab Hole, all in this area

Pritchard's Drift

Canyon Drifts

2nd Hatchery

John Anderson (permit only)

N

F&H NEWS ©2002

KALAMA

COLUMBIA RIVER

5

your time at the Hatchery Creek Hole located above Beginners Hole, Beginners Hole and the tailout of Beginners that runs into the Willow Hole behind Mahaffey's Campground.

The hottest bait going the last couple years has been steelhead jigs like Fish Doctor's Nightmare and Daymare and Hurley's shell pink and cerise. These jigs are best fished with Mike's shrimp oil and a small pinch of sand shrimp. Bobber lengths should be anywhere from 2 to 8 feet. If you driftfish, use small baits and light line.

As summer moves on, you should too. By mid-July migrate upriver from Pritchard's to the deadline located just below the second hatchery.

Best late-season holes are Deadline, Saddle Rock and Italian Creek. Fish typical lower river rigs with the addition of spinners in size 3. Also the canyon, as its called from Italian Creek to Deadline, is an excellent spot to do some fly fishing. A 6- to 8-weight fly rod loaded with a Cortland 444 sinking steelhead line and about 75 yards of backing with an 8X tippet will work quite nicely. Fish egg imitations, black and green Woolly Buggers and Muddler Minnows.

Kalama kings: The Kalama's great summer-run fishing gives way to a fairly good Chinook fishery in mid- to late August with nice Chinook to 30 pounds caught every year. Most of the best fishing takes place below Modrow Bridge in tidewater to the mouth. Drift a bobber and large bait of eggs or toss size 6 spinners. You can also do quite well plunking glow balls and eggs at night until night fishing comes to an end Sept 1. Boat anglers can get some limited access on high tide around the state boat launch on the west side of I-5. This is a great place to troll weighted spinners with no dropper weight and magnum Brad's Wigglers in metallic greens, blues and rocket red. This fishery will stay strong till the last week in September.

Coho: The Kalama's silver fishery has been red hot the last couple of years and this year's run should be good. Silvers can be caught as early as Sept 1, with the first run of early fish usually peaking about Sept. 15.

This fishery is also a lower tidewater show with massive runs of silvers stacking from Camp Kalama to the mouth.

Run bobber and quarter-sized gobs of eggs or No. 4 Blue Fox spinners in green and chartreuse for early-run fish.

From a boat, fish below the lower boat launch in the deep holes down by the mouth. Troll at high tide with Brad's Wigglers in black, green pirate and rocket red, and plunk Corkies and eggs at low tide.

Around Oct. 1 the late run of silvers starts to show, with the peak coming by the end of the month. Usually by this time we will have had some pretty good rains and the fish will be scattered through the system.

Best fishing will be from Modrow Bridge up to Pritchard's early then moving up to the canyon area towards the end of the month. Also the fly fishing only hole opens up to bait fisherman on Nov. 1, and that's usually pretty hot when it opens.

Pitch size 4 spinners, drift Corky, egg and yarn combos or pull plugs.

Fly fishing: In my opinion the best fishery of all is the Sept. 1-Nov. 1 fly-fishing-only season. It encompasses the Kalama from the lower hatchery intake down to the pipeline at Mahaffey's Campground. This pretty much gives you the best of the best as far as salmon are concerned. The best two holes will be the Hatchery Creek Hole and Beginners Hole. It's not uncommon to see several thousand fish staging in these two holes waiting for a good rain.

Bring at least an 8-weight rod loaded with a fast-sinking fly line like a 300-grain Deep Water Express and a heavy 10X tippet. Also dud up in a good set of chest waders. Most anglers like to wade across Hatchery Creek Hole tailout which gives a better approach to Beginners Hole just below. Also the tailout of Beginners, which leads into the Willow Hole, can be accessed; this spot usually

SUMMER-RUNS are one of the Kalama's best fisheries, but Chinook aren't far behind.

holds lots of late summer-runs taking advantage of the spawning salmon.

Best salmon patterns will be large Teeny Nymphs in orange, green and cerise and any and all Egg-sucking Leech patterns. Best steelhead flies will be small Teeny Nymphs and tiny egg imitations.

Camping: The Kalama River is located 5 miles south of Longview of I-5 at the Kalama River Road exit. The river has two major campgrounds: Camp Kalama located at the I-5 exit, and Mahaffey's about 4 miles east of the interstate up Kalama River Road. Both have RV hookups and their own private river access, which is an added bonus. Also anglers have some limited camping at Rainbow Park located off Modrow Road about 2 miles east up Kalama River Road. This private park also has a small $2 fee-fishing area that gives you access to about a quarter mile of river bank at the top of tide water. This area can be excellent fishing in low-water summer months on a high tide.

AT A GLANCE

What: Kalama River summer-run steelhead, Chinook and coho.

Where: Southwestern Washington, 5 miles south of Longview, just off I-5.

When: Summer steelhead peaks in July, but can continue well into September. Chinook fishing gets good in August. Watch for early-run silvers to peak by Sept. 15, with late-run fish peaking at the end of October.

Information: Bob's Sporting Goods (360-425-3870); Mahaffey's Campgrounds (360-673-3867; camping@mahafferysrv-campground.com); Pritchard's Western Anglers (360-673-4690).

Lewis mouth, upstream holes good Chinook fisheries

WOODLAND

by Terry Otto

The Lewis River is one of the most popular spring Chinook fisheries, and for good reason. Success rates on the southwest Washington river tend to be high, and a good portion of the returning salmon end up in some fishermen's cooler.

Last year was a banner year for springers here, and there are reasons for genuine optimism this year as well. According to Dan Mahitka, a long-time salmon and steelhead guide (360-673-1523) on the river, you can expect this year to be pretty much like last year.

"More than 7,000 springers are headed back to the Lewis this year, so we expect to catch a lot of fish," says Mahitka.

Last year's actual return topped 10,000 salmon, after a preseason projection of 5,400. Could we get lucky again, and get even more fish back then predicted? It certainly is possible.

Timing: The Lewis run usually arrives on the tail of those early-returning Willamette fish, with peak numbers in late April. However, early April can yield some good results too, especially at the mouth of the river.

AT a GLANCE

What: Spring Chinook fishing in southwest Washington.

Where: The Lewis River, from just off its mouth up to Merwin Dam.

When: From early April on; best is late in the month/early May.

How: Troll plug-cut herring off the north bank of the river near the mouth; side-drift bait or back-bounce from the Meat Hole down; plunk, drift bait on bottom or under a bobber or toss spinners from shore.

Info/gear: The Fishermen's Depot (360-225-9900) in Woodland;

Guides: Dan Mahitka (360-673-1523); Jeff Williams (360-751-9095).

"A lot of springers that are heading further up the Columbia will dip into the mouth and check it out," Mahitka explains, "and the guys that are out there early catch a lot of those fish."

The best fishing at the mouth will be during the last week of April and the first week of May. After that the best bite will shift to the state-run hatchery, and the fishing should stay good there all the way to July, when the summer steelhead start to arrive.

Mouth bite: The mouth of the Lewis has always been a consistent and popular fishery, even back when anglers were refused the Columbia. Now that the big river is open more often, the fishing pressure at the Lewis has dropped off a little. This gives anglers a little more breathing room, and a better shot at the fish. Fishermen can also fish further out when the Columbia is open, allowing them to troll out to the edge of the shipping channel.

The most popular bait is plug-cut herring, with most anglers choosing either blue or green label. Some fishermen prefer to troll sardine-wrapped plugs such as the Kwikfish. Favorite sizes run from 13 to 15, and the most popular colors include silver and chartreuse.

The most common rig consists of a 24- to 30-inch lead line, rigged with a slider, and about 8 feet of leader with a chain swivel halfway to the herring. Two to 4 ounces of weight is usually sufficient.

Since the water in the Lewis is typically much clearer than that of the Columbia, use lighter leaders than usual. While a 20- or 25-pound leader is good for most situations on the Columbia and elsewhere, old-timers on the Lewis often use 10- or 12-pound test instead, and their success rates are hard to argue with. With patience, you can land 30-pound fish on the lighter line, and you will definitely hook up more often.

Also, because of the water clarity, flashers are rarely used or needed, so most fishermen troll without them. If the water does turn turbid following a spring rain, try a red or green flasher in place of the chain swivel.

APRIL SHOULD BE a solid month for spring Chinook on the Lewis River. The author shows off one he caught right along the edge of the shipping channel while trolling herring last season.

As in any spring Chinook fishery, scents play a big part in catching the fish. Most savvy fishermen carry a wide selection of different kinds of scents, and they keep changing them until they find one that works. Sometimes certain combinations of different scents can also trigger a fish to strike. Experienced anglers also brine their herring. This adds salt scent to the bait, and makes it firmer so that it stays fresh longer on the hook.

Where to troll: Most of the trolling takes place between the private launch and the shipping channel in the Columbia. Depending on tide stage, most of the water is 12 feet deep or less. There is a channel along the north bank of the Lewis from the boat ramp up to the railroad bridge is also a good bet, especially on rising tides. There are some very shallow mud flats along the south banks of the Lewis, so boaters should stay to the north. Bank anglers often plunk from Austin Point, and they also do well. When there is a strong ebb tide, some fishermen will hog line in the channel just inside Austin Point.

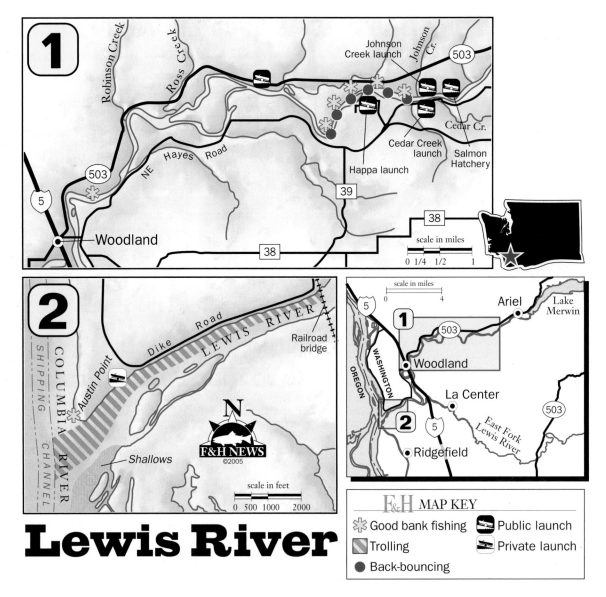

Lewis River

Most fishermen launch their boats at the private boat ramp and RV park just off Dike Road. The cost is $4 to launch, and $2 for parking any additional vehicles.

Upstream action: Once the action shifts upriver, the best place to catch fish is at the Meat Hole near the hatchery. This is where the fish stage in schools below the hatchery trap inlet. Boat and bank anglers both do well here, but are forewarned; the fishing pressure can be fierce.

"When they close the Columbia, this is where everybody heads to," says Mahitka, "and the guys will be doing the bumper-boat thing."

He also points to some other good upriver spots.

"The first four or five holes below the Meat Hole are pretty good, as well as the rapids in the town of Woodland."

Most fishermen in the Meat Hole are side-drifting eggs or egg and sand shrimp combinations. Prawns are also a good bet.

According to Mahitka, another good way to approach the river below the Meat Hole is back-bouncing.

"Most guys use 2 to 4 ounces of lead, and bounce that bait back through the good water. It's a good way to fish the Lewis."

Shore options: Bank fishermen usually fish with bait as well, either below bobbers, or by drifting. Salmon eggs are the preferred bait, but the egg/shrimp combo is also popular.

Springers can be caught on spinners as well, especially when they are migrating. Target tail-outs and shallow rapids with Blue Fox Vibrax in sizes 4 or 5.

There is good bank access near the hatchery and on the north bank near the boat launch. There is also good bank access at the riffles in Woodland. Some springers are taken all the way up to the deadline at the Merwin Dam, but that reach is often closed or restricted to bank fishing until the hatchery gets its allotted escapement, so check before fishing there. This reach is accessible by drift boat, and holds some good back bouncing water, too. However, most springers will stay lower in the system, and your best chance to intercept them remains below the hatchery.

Toss hardware to Lewis River summer-runs

by Terry Otto

Throwing Stee-Lees on the Lewis River is always a good bet when bank fishing for steelhead, but the bright summer fish that hammered my second cast caught me off guard. With that big lure in its mouth, it took to the sky and then charged downstream too fast for the plunkers below to react. It raced under their lines and jumped again. Somehow, it avoided all the lines in the river and eventually came to the bank. A chrome bright summer steelhead is always a pretty fish, and this

10-pounder was no exception.

Summer steelheading is heating up on the Lewis River, and you can expect it to get really hot by the Fourth of July. Fish managers expect a good run this year, although last year's three-fish limit won't be happening again. Although it may seem slow compared to last year's bumper crop, returns are already on pace for an above-average run. Fish culturists at the Lewis River are seeing lots of returning fish, including a lot of big three-salt fish.

These are the remaining fish from the last year-class of steelhead, and you

should catch some of these. Lewis fish run much bigger on average than summer-runs returning to streams further up the Columbia River, but those three-salt fish will be rod-busters into the upper teens. Two-salt fish will run from 8 to 12 pounds.

Independence Day fireworks:
Aaron Roberts of the Lewis River Hatchery says that the peak of the return is Independence Day, but the fishing will remain hot all through September. In fact, as the river levels drop later in the year, fishing can

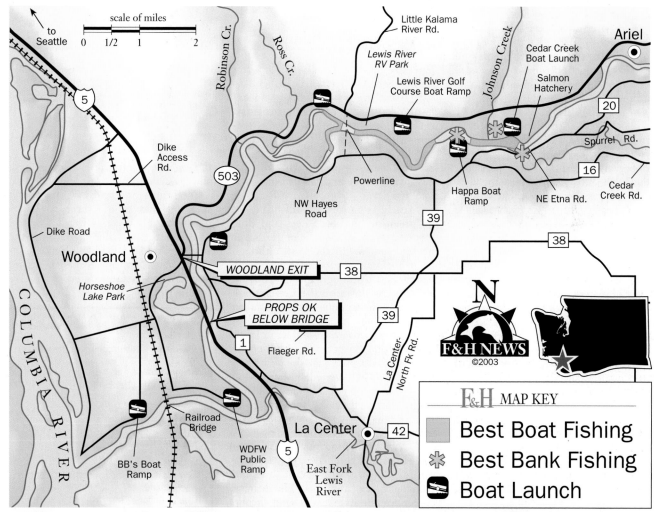

North Fork Lewis River

actually heat up as fish concentrate in the riffles and faster water, making them easier to find consistently. However, in June and July, the fish are spread through the system, mostly from the Lewis River Golf Course to Merwin Dam. It's easier to get a strike from these fresh fish, but they are tougher to land as well.

Tee it up: Kevin Clark, WDFW fish culturist, says that lots of anglers will look for these fish at the Golf Course Hole.

"It's probably the most productive hole on the river," says Clark, "and it's good from the bank or from a boat."

You can launch at the golf course itself, although the ramp is a rough one. Most guys put in at the Island Ramp and run up.

Most popular method is boondogging, or free-drifting roe. Sand shrimp also account for a lot of fish.

There are good areas for pulling plugs as well. Clark says that the most popular plugs include Hot Shots and Brad's Wigglers; he prefers the mini sizes. Good patterns include blue pirate and the Michael Jackson.

On foot you can access this reach by taking the gravel trail that is at the eastern end of the golf course.

There is good water for drifting or bobber fishing, but please pack out your trash. If fishermen abuse the privilege of access here, it could be closed.

Also be aware that on busy weekends there will be a lot of passing boat traffic, and that can make for tough fishing.

Other productive runs: Additional good access points include the Lewis River Hatchery, or Cedar Creek, and Merwin Dam. Both points have boat launches, and the run from Merwin down to Cedar Creek is popular with drift boaters. There is some excellent steelhead water along the 4 miles of river that separate the two.

With the springer run winding down, you can expect to see a drop in pressure at the hatchery, both from boat and bank, although on weekends it gets busy.

If you're walking the bank, concentrate your efforts at the hatchery and the dam. Both locations can get crowded at times, but the river is big enough to accommodate. Fish a jig and bobber, or drift bait and yarn.

There is a long glide just upriver from the boat launch site that is excel-

lent steelhead water. In high water (more than 3,000 cfs), it's difficult to fish, but it's very productive. As water levels drop this section can provide fast action. Locals prefer to drift this section with Cheaters and yarn or bait, and they do very well. Favorite colors are red, pink, orange and pearl. The best baits are roe and sand shrimp.

When levels drop, try hardware in this reach. I've taken a lot of fish there on green or blue Stee-Lees and Blue Fox spinners in sizes 3 or 4. Silver blades seem to do the best, although bronze can be a good color on really sunny days. Although spring Chinook are winding down on the Lewis, there may be a few bonus springers taken here as well.

As summer progresses and water levels bottom out, target the deadline at Marmot Dam. You can do well from shore and boat here. Many boaters tie up to the deadline cable itself and fish plugs. Many of them also throw a jig and bobber, which is a very successful tactic in this water. I've taken quite a few steelhead here by floating small pink jigs in the current. There is good water for drifting Cheaters with bait or yarn, and plunkers score well too. The bait of choice for the plunkers is sand shrimp and a Spin-N-Glo. Once again, bring some hardware with you. It may come in handy when the fish get finicky. Late in

A NUMBER of three-salt summer runs will be mixed in the North Fork Lewis River this year. Braden Segundo, 12, caught this 10-pound two-salt there last July. He was fishing with his grandpa Tom.

the year these fish really pile up in here, and the action can be fast.

Conditions on the Lewis are pretty stable, thanks to the three reservoirs upstream. However, water levels can change often, and that can change the way steelhead respond to offerings. It's a good idea to call ahead and get an idea of river levels before you go.

AT a GLANCE

What: Lewis River summer steelhead.

When: Best fishing is from the Fourth of July through the summer, but you'll often catch fish well into the fall.

Where: Near Woodland.

Hot spots: The Golf Course, the Hatchery Hole.

Information: The Fishermen's Depot in Woodland (360-225-9900); Lewis River Hatchery (360-225-7413).

Guides: Jon Huston of Huston's Guide Service (360-896-5946).

Walk bank, drift Yakima River for spring Chinook

YAKIMA

by Jim Pearson

WITH THIS YEAR'S slightly later run, you should see Yakima River springers like this beauty in force from mid-May on. Selah's Bob Graf holds a plug-caught king he hooked with a casted orange Wiggle Wart last May 11.

Last year on May 9, I had my daily limit of two Yakima River spring Chinook in the boat at 8:25 a.m., so I got to row the rest of the day. Two days later, a friend and I boated three more.

If history is an indicator, you should be fishing the Yak this month.

After being gone approximately 40 years, Yakima springers are back in fishable numbers thanks to a state-of-the-art fish hatchery belonging to the Yakamas. It is located near Cle Elum and spawns only native fish that are trapped at Roza Dam. That insures that all hatchery fish are no more than one generation away from free-spawning parents.

The river is open from the State Route 223 bridge at Granger to the closed-water boundary line 3,500 feet downstream of Roza Dam in the Yakima Canyon. That's a lot of water, and it's a whole lot more river than it was last year because it's carrying much more water.

We fish from a drift boat simply because we get to see more river, but on several occasions last year, shore fishermen outdid us. They pulled off I-82, walked to the river and began fishing, mostly with eggs. They used a slip bobber with a glob of cured eggs dangling below. They cast upstream, watched the bobber to the end of the drift, picked it up and cast again. Plugs take fish too, but shore fishermen didn't use them. If I were shore fishing, I would also try using a side planer with

plug, or side planer, diver and eggs. However, the latter method wouldn't be usable if the shoreline is crowded with other fishermen.

Some bank anglers are making good use of the Greenway Pathway, a paved pathway following the west side of the Yakima and Naches rivers for several miles. They take a rod and net aboard mountain bikes and pedal to where they want to be. They park their cars in the lot at the Selah boat ramp or in the lot alongside the river where the bridge crosses headed to Moxee, unload their bike and begin pedaling and fishing.

From the drift boat, we fished plugs and roe. Red or orange Wiggle Warts or the same color Hawg Bosses worked nicely, but the man running the oars must pay attention to the rod tips. They best indicate if the plugs are working properly and whether he needs to let the boat move faster or whether he needs to reposition it for more or less current. U-20 FlatFish or its equivalent in Kwikfish also work well if the current is slower.

From anchor, we cast roe below a slip bobber or cast the plugs like a bass fisherman. I also ran eggs behind a diver as the boat moved down the river. One day we drifted by two guys who had anchored their boat in one of the slower stretches. Their rods nestled in holders while the FlatFish did their thing. As you can see, fishing from a boat does offer more options, but it is not without problems.

Where to launch: Boat launches are unavailable above the Selah launch, although friends of mine slid their boat across dry land north of Selah, launched and caught fish. From I-82, you can see a boat ramp on the east side of river just below Union Gap, but don't launch a drift boat there. Two dams are directly below you. Downstream a mile or so from the Parker dam, you will see a parking lot and toilet on your right as you drive down the freeway. You can launch there and take out at the Zillah bridge. That's an all-day float if you stop at anchor very long. So is the drift from the Zillah Bridge to Granger. Both those spots have good launch ramps.

Downstream from Granger, there are

AT A GLANCE

What: Yakima River spring Chinook.

When: Now until June 16.

Where: Open water on the Yakima from Granger (Highway 223 bridge) upstream to the deadline 3,500 feet below Roza Dam.

Access: Foot access via Highway 82, the Greenway Pathway.

Launches: Selah, Zillah, Granger bridge, east of Mabton.

Techniques: Best bets from shore or drift boat are plugs or roe.

Tackle and Supplies: Grumpy's South First Surplus (509-452-0868); Chinook Sporting Goods (509-452-8205)

boat ramps on both sides of the river at the bridge east of Mabton, but remember, if you use Yakama Indian Reservation land to launch or to fish, you need a $25 reservation permit. It's the same one you need for hunting the reservation, and I consider it a bargain considering what I get in return. Permits are available in Yakima at both Bi-Marts (509-457-1650; 457-5175) as well as Chinook Sporting Goods (509-452-8205). From there to the deadline at Prosser is approximately 8 miles, and any take-out spots down there are unimproved.

Water to fish: From shore or boat, fish the deeper water where the springers don't have to fight to move upstream. We call the real slow spots frog water — places where you can fish

a bobber for five minutes before having to retrieve and cast again. Salmon move into that kind of water to rest. Frog water is often on the inside of turns; it doesn't have to be deep to hold fish.

For whatever reason, bank guys seldom take advantage of frog water. Last year, we saw one exception. We were anchored and throwing plugs into slow-moving water 3 feet deep when a bank fisherman showed up and tossed out a slip bobber with eggs. He made two casts, caught two fish, and went home.

So who needs a boat? Well, we do. Like Huck Finn, we enjoy drifting down a river fish or no fish, but be warned: If you use a boat, at least in the stretch of river from the deadline below Roza Dam to Granger, make it a drift boat. You will be sorry if you attempt it in

your 12-foot cartopper, and you will have some very upset bank fisherman when you begin bouncing off the rocks in front of them.

Some things have changed since last year. This year you may keep only fin-clipped fish and you must use a single barbless hook with a gap from point to shank of a half-inch or less. Those changes were made to protect the larger but more scarce Chinook headed for the Naches or American rivers. Last year, a wild fish I took weighed 15 pounds, but most of the hatchery fish are in the 7- to 11-pound range. Because the wild fish are being protected, John Easterbrooks, WDFW fish biologist for Region 3, tells me the season will probably be longer this year. Still, it may end early if too many fish are caught.

Lower Yakima River

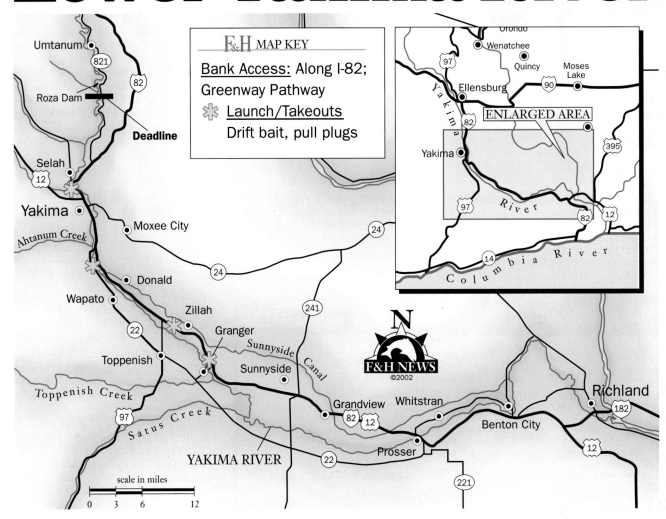

Columbia River Waters
STEELHEAD

Cowlitz steel: December 'best month on the river'

— TOLEDO

by Dusty Routh

In the world of steelhead fishing, there are bad rivers, good rivers and excellent rivers, in terms of your chances of putting steelhead in the boat. The Cowlitz River in southwest Washington falls into the latter category, easily. It has a continuous flow of incoming hatchery steelhead from Thanksgiving into January and February, with enough fish that a lot of experienced anglers and guides have multiple-fish days all the way through winter with no problem.

What's more, this month is considered by many to be the very best for Cowlitz River winter steelhead. One of those proponents is Rich Mercado of Rich's Northwest Guide Service (253-535-0403).

"The Cowlitz stays good all the way," Mercado says. "It's got a continuous flow of fish, and I think December is the best month to be on the river. I really fish it hard in December, and again in January."

He pounds the river hard in these two months for a variety of reasons. "It typically kicks off around Thanksgiving," he says, "there's fish in there by then. But the fishing doesn't get hot until December. But I also like that month because with the holidays and everything else going on a lot of guys aren't on the river. And I like January too, because a lot of the guides who work the Cowlitz are off it, doing the sportsman shows. The fishing can stay hot all the way through the end of January."

Delayed fish: It used to be on the Cowlitz — like a lot of other big steelhead rivers in the state — that all the fish tended to show up at once, and for a two- to three-week period the fishing would be red-hot, then it would die off and slow to a crawl. But WDFW and the Blue Creek Hatchery now has a delayed planting schedule, which means returning fish are more spread out.

"We used to get just a big bulk of fish all at one time," Mercado says. "And everyone banged on the fish real hard and then it would slow down. But the way they do the delay plant thing now, it's a longer season. You have to work a little harder for your fish, but at least you have fish for a lot longer period of time."

Almost the entire winter run is made up of hatchery steelhead heading to the Blue Creek Hatchery. But every winter Mercado says he encounters a few "wild" fish, which he's sure are hatchery fish that didn't get fin-clipped.

"You can definitely tell they're hatchery fish," he says. "They're all real cookie-cutter, about 10 to 12 pounds. But all the hatchery fish in the winter tend to be nice fish, bigger than the summer-runs."

And not all of them fit into that 10- to 12-pound category. "Occasionally we'll hit a fish that's 18 to 20 pounds. Last season we got some 16s and 17s. And I had a

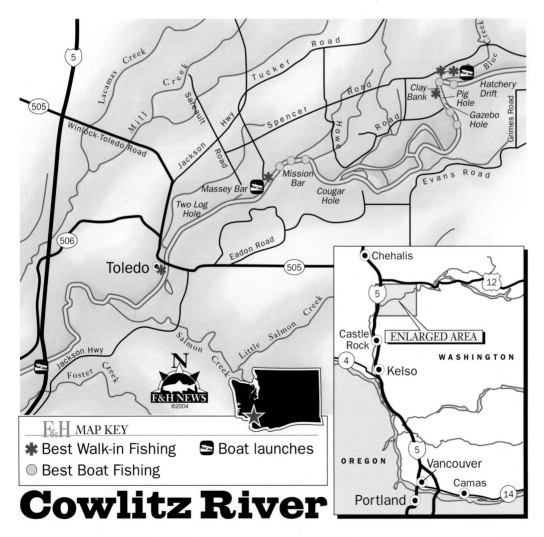

Cowlitz River

F&H MAP KEY

✳ Best Walk-in Fishing   🛥 Boat launches
◯ Best Boat Fishing

client that got back-to-back 20s, two 20-pounders from the same hole. He hit the first one behind a big boulder in the boulder garden right near Blue Creek. So we ran back up and on the third drift he got the second one," Mercado says.

Favorite haunts: For Mercado and a lot of the other guides who jet-sled the river, the best way to fish is to launch at the ramp at the hatchery on Blue Creek, and go around the corner into the mainstem of the Cowlitz. Work that water really well, then continue to slide down the river as far as the Mission Bar. Or if you want to encounter fewer people, fish from the Mission Bar on down towards Toledo and the I-5 bridge.

Boondogging nirvana: You can pull plugs on the Cowlitz, of course, but this is a river that's absolutely made for side-drifting, and it's an incredibly effective technique. Mercado uses 10½-foot Lamiglas LLS spinning rods, outfitted with Shimano Stradic spinning reels. He spools up with 10-pound mainline, and uses 8-pound fluorocarbon leaders. He uses two No. 4 Gammy hooks, a small Corky and a small gob of cured eggs.

Corky colors include red, red/orange, green, red or clown/chartreuse, and peach/orange. In the summer, Mercado recommends using a really small gob of eggs, about the size of a dime, but in the winter he ups the size to about a nickel or quarter size, depending on the water flow. Mercado's side-drifting platform is a new 25-foot Alumaweld with a 200-hp tiller Mercury and an 8-hp, 4-stroke kicker motor.

Mercado says the best way to learn how to sled or drift the Cowlitz is to go on the river when the water's down. "Go when it's low and look at the water and see what the structure is," he says. "Then you know what's down there, and you'll know what to expect when the water's high, because you know where everything is, like logjams and rocks."

What you're looking for in December are current seams. "I'll really key on fishing the different current structures there, that's how I typically fish it," Mercado says. "Because that's where the fish are going to be. And they tend to be in the same spots, so if you catch fish in one hole, come back in a week and there's fish in that same hole again."

Mercado tends to work his favorite places over and over again, because of the propensity for different steelhead to use the same places in the river. "If I've caught fish in that place before, I'll pound it pretty hard. But sometimes you don't want to move around a whole lot, because at certain times in certain places, there's a bite that's going to happen, maybe a 10-minute or a 5-minute bite. If you're gone looking for new places and new fish, you may only get two fish that day because you missed the hot bite in some of those other places where you know there are fish."

Anchor or drift? The Cowlitz used to have more drift boats on the river than sleds, but that ratio is changing. The question then becomes, is it better to anchor up and work an area thoroughly, or drift through it and run back up to it?

For Mercado, free-drifting, or boondogging, is so effective that it's his numero uno preferred way to work the river. "If you do anchor up," Mercado warns, "just be careful of what's up above you. Some of those rock walls along the river have caved in before, that's how that guy got killed a few years ago on Super Bowl Sunday. When we have freezes and thaws, and rains, you get a lot of erosion, and stuff comes down, like trees and rocks. What happened there was the hillside caved in, and guys went in the water. So you don't want to be anchoring underneath big cliffs with trees hanging over you."

Watch out for others: Anchoring makes it hard for the boats that are free-drifting, and free-drifters can get in the way of boats that are anchored. The Cowlitz has gotten to be a very busy place in the winter, with wading anglers, drift boaters and sledders all sharing the same water.

"You have to just be courteous and patient," Mercado says. "Some guys in their brand new boats are running the river at mach speed, and you really don't need to be doing that. There's too many people on the river, especially drift boats that can't maneuver out of your way. So everybody just has to cut everyone else some slack, and they'll have a better and safer time of it."

THEY DON'T SIDE-DRIFT so everyone gets a nice view of the scenery on the Cowlitz, they do it because it's the best way to thump winter-runs on the Southwest Washington river. Marc Davis shows off a pair caught in 2003 on eggs fished from a sled.

AT a GLANCE

What: Powerfully productive winter steelhead fishing on one of the best metalhead rivers in the Northwest.

Where: The Cowlitz River in Lewis County. From Blue Creek down to Mission Bar is the river's best steelheading water.

When: Things get cooking in late November, and by December the river has plenty of steelhead in it.

How: Pulling plugs will work, but side-drifting eggs and Corkies on long, noodle spinning rods is ultra-deadly here.

Contacts: Rich Mercado, Rich's Northwest Guide Service (253-535-0403); Onco Sportfishing (877-483-0047); VLT Guide Service (253-639-1644); Brett's Salmon & Steelhead Guide Service (360-403-8477).

Gear up for Washington's best winter steelhead river

CHEHALIS

by Dusty Routh

The Cowlitz River likely conjures up a variety of images for you, depending on your experiences with this popular southwest Washington river.

If anything, if you've fished this river before, you likely have some memories of big fish hooked — the Cowlitz can really kick out monsters. You might also have memories of catching a lot of fish. The river's famous for the quantity of sea-run cutthroat, steelhead and salmon that return to it every year.

But you might also have memories of shoulder-to-shoulder fishing, crossed lines, bank anglers shouting at boat anglers, drift boaters cursing at sled boats, and one big, fine mess at combat fishing areas like Blue Creek.

Your experiences on the Cowlitz, while not uncommon, confirm that this river is a waterway of sharp contrasts. There are areas of the Cowlitz where you'll encounter more humans than fish, while there are other areas where you'll find a quiet, pristine, Northwest river full of big steelhead, SRCs, coho, fall and spring Chinook, and even smelt.

Flowing out of the Cowlitz Divide southeast off Mount Rainier, the Cowlitz River provides water to two impoundments: Riffe Lake, formed behind Mossy Rock Dam at nearly 1.6 million acre-feet at full pool, and Mayfield Lake, formed behind Mayfield Dam, at a modest 21,380 acre-feet.

Below Mayfield Dam, the Cowlitz flows past the Cowlitz Salmon Hatchery, down past the Cowlitz Trout Hatchery, past Toledo and Castle Rock, through Kelso and into the Columbia River.

As the calendar turns toward late November and early December, coming up from the Columbia will be a healthy run of winter steelhead that can keep rods jumping all the way to spring.

How good is good? Even though it's a solid 2- to 2½-hour drive from Seattle, a number of Emerald City-area fishing guides call the Cowlitz their

SLAB HATCHERY STEELHEAD like these twin hogs are what make the Cowlitz River the best winter-run fishery in the state. Carl Huswick of Lake Stevens yanked the pair out of the Blue Creek area.

home river. While steelhead fishing around the Northwest can be notoriously fickle, guides consider the Cowlitz a can't-miss, go-to place where they can take paying clients to consistently score fish. This river fishes that good.

Rich Mercado with Rich's Northwest Guide Service (253-376-8004) says the winter-run fish usually show up in good numbers by December. Mercado fishes the Cowlitz all winter long.

"The fishing is real good for winter-runs," Mercado says. "The Cowlitz holds up really well."

Summer to winter: Summer steelhead fishing on the Cowlitz generally kicks off in May, with bright fish showing up well into August. The summer-runs can be fun, fun fishing, accompanied by warm weather and lots of cooperative hatchery fish.

As with other Westside rivers, though, the winter metalhead season starts around Thanksgiving as the weather turns nasty. Winter-runs provide excellent action all the way to March.

The peak of winter fishing on the Cowlitz really depends on weather-rainfall particularly. In drier years, the winter fish run can stretch out over a longer period, while a winter that dumps a ton of rain early on can bring fish in early. Overall, however, the Cowlitz is one of the most dependable steelhead rivers in Washington for winter fish.

Get away: If you haven't fished the Cow before, be prepared to be patient. The boat ramps at the hatcheries can get busy and crowded, especially on weekends. From the upper ramp at the Salmon Hatchery to below Blue Creek, bank anglers crowd in pretty tight. After that, for the first few miles below Blue Creek, you'll find lots of drift boats and sleds.

However, as a rule of thumb, the further you slide down the river, the more river you'll have to yourself. Fishing on a Saturday in mid-fall just above the Toledo Bridge, for example, our boat drifted through long stretches of lonely river. After negotiating the gambit at Blue Creek, it was heaven.

Get on 'em: You'll see just about every conceivable steelhead fishing method used on the Cowlitz, and for all intents and purposes just about all methods will work at one time or another. But, just as some fishermen are more equal than others, some methods will do better than others.

Most of the sled boaters and guides swear by free-drifting, and this is one river where it's relatively easy to do and incredibly effective. Free-drifting is where your lines are out in front of the boat at 45-degree angles. As the boat drifts downstream, keeping on pace or slightly slower than the current, your offering is drifted along the banks and through slower water on both sides of the boat.

The typical Cowlitz rig for free-drifting is a short ½-ounce pencil weight, a 5-foot leader, small baithook(s) with yarn (pink or fluorescent), and a cluster of eggs or a piece of sand shrimp. Your sinker should be tick-tick-ticking the bottom as you drift downriver. Most guides will use long "noodle" rods with ultra-sensitive tips for this kind of fishing. Main line can be up to 12-pound test, with leaders anywhere from 10- down to 6-pound test.

Mercado uses Lamiglas steelhead rods with either Shimano or Ambassadeur baitcasting reels. Spinning reels will also do the trick. You could put the rods in rod holders, but for free-drifting it's better to hang on to 1) lift the weight free of any obstructions as it drifts downriver, and 2) to feel that elusive "inhalation" from a steelhead when it takes.

Drift boat anglers often pull plugs, like Tadpollies and Wiggle Warts, throw spoons like Steelees, or spinners like Blue Foxes. Drifters also often anchor up and plunk, or peel off line to get their plugs into holes. Another method you might see is called "hover" fishing, where anglers use a heavy weight to keep their offering right on the bottom as they slowly — very slowly — move the boat downstream.

Bank anglers plunk with Spin-N-Glos and shrimp or eggs, throw spoons and spinners, cast plugs, and drift egg and shrimp combinations.

You'll also see a fair number of fly-rodder on the Cowlitz, throwing steelhead flies on sinking tip lines.

However, for winter-run fish, bait seems to be the key.

"That's all I use on the Cowlitz for winter fish," says Kyle Ward of Kyle Ward Guide Service (425-334-3988). "Eggs mostly, sometimes sand shrimp, but always bait."

Recycles: Once steelhead successfully negotiate their way upriver to the hatchery, surplus fish are often trucked back downstream and released. You'll know these fish by the round hole punched on their gill plates by hatchery personnel. Regulations can vary

too, depending on how many fish make it to the hatchery. If an abundance shows up, regulations may be changed to offer a larger daily limit. On the other hand, daily limits can also be ratcheted down, again all depending on the return numbers. Be sure to check the regs for the time period in which you're fishing.

Go-to: The whole of the Cowlitz below the dams will fish good for steelhead and salmon. Upriver close to the dam, the area around Blue Creek, Gazebo Hole and the Pig Hole are sure-fire areas to try. As you go downriver, Mission Bar has earned a reputation for excellent fishing. And Two Log Hole is an often undisturbed section that will hold fish.

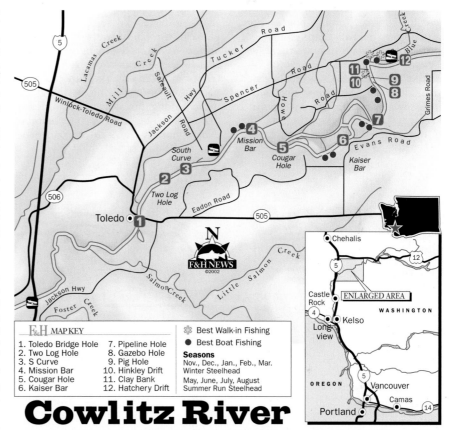

Cowlitz River

AT A GLANCE

What: Winter steelhead fishing for lunker Cowlitz River metalheads.

When: Kick-off is around Thanksgiving, with strong months in December and January, lasting to March.

Where: Below Mayfield Dam and Blue Creek. The lower river is productive all winter.

How: Bobber and jig, plunk, or drift Corkies/yarn/eggs or sand shrimp. Spinners and spoons will also work.

River conditions: Contact Tacoma Power's Fishing Line (888-502-8690).

Guides/information: Rich Mercado, Rich's Northwest Guide Service (253-376-8004); Mike Sexton, Mike's Guide Service (360-864-6665); Dave Baugh, XLT Guide Service (253-639-1644); Kyle Ward, Kyle Ward Guide Service (425-334-3988); CML Guide Service (866-262-3474); Set The Hook Guide Service (253-709-4294); J&L Guide Service (206-920-2428); DJ's Fishing Adventures (360-886-2128); Let's Fish Guide Service (360-458-8847); JR's Guide Service (360-262-9584); Fishquest Guide Service (425-255-0552).

Three ways to nail Drano Lake steelies

by Scott Small

From the parking lot, Drano looks too easy. Steelhead rolling up the Columbia River enter the lake through a deep, narrow passage and congregate in a small, 410-acre holding pool. There are plenty of fish, and you've got three distinct ways to hook them.

First way to whack a steelie is to troll them up. The most productive lure on my recent trip was a small crayfish plug, 50 feet behind the downrigger, which was set between 15 and 20 feet deep. Lots of folks were pulling pink Wiggle Warts, perhaps hoping to catch an early-season salmon.

Traditional Drano trolling patterns are counterclockwise loops, either between the launching ramp and the bridge, or out in the main body of the lake. My observation was that people trolled all over the lake, but the only place they hooked fish was the steep trench along the north shore of the main lake. The Little White Salmon and Columbia flows interact to produce a mild vortex in that area, which apparently attracts fish. So unless the quantity of boats on the water necessitates a lockstep trolling pattern, I'd spend extra time working just that trench.

Second way to catch metalheads is anchor up where the Little White Salmon enters the northwest corner of the lake and fish with bobbers. Rig a red or purple prawn below your float, add a couple of split shot to take the bait down and toss the whole set-up behind your boat. Use a highly visible float, and set the hook hard at the first sign of a strike. Watch the sonar and make sure your float is set to dangle the prawn at the exact depth where fish are holding.

Finally, the stretch of river below the hatchery is prime real estate for bank anglers who like to plunk bait and wait. It looked crowded but congenial, with anglers gladly netting fish for each other.

Bobber and bank fishing are an all-night party at Drano. While I was retrieving my boat at dusk, I saw quite a few people getting ready to launch for the night shift. I'd give this fishery a low rating on the peace and solitude scale, but when it comes to hooking hatchery steel, it's at the top of the list.

Drano Lake

N

F&H NEWS
©2004

WASHINGTON

Carson   Cook   White Salmon   141

Bonneville   Hood River   84   14

ENLARGED AREA

The Dalles

OREGON

Mt. Hood

F&H MAP KEY
- Bank fishing
- - - - Especially good trolling
- Anchored bobber fishing
- Jig for salmon
- Boat ramp
- · · · · Buoy deadline

Hatchery

Little White Salmon River

shallow

parking lot P

to Wind River, 7 miles

DRANO LAKE

14

COLUMBIA RIVER

to White Salmon, 7 miles
to Hood River, 8.5 miles

Easy access, abundant fish for Kalama steelheaders

—————————————————————————— KALAMA

by Trey Carskadon

There are few rivers in the Northwest as fun to fish as the Kalama for summer steelhead. Having caught my first steelhead on this river 35 years ago, it holds special prominence for me, although I'm sure within your first few casts you'll be taken by this river as well.

The Kalama, if you haven't yet experienced it, is a bank angler's dream, with lots of productive water to fish without the physical expense tolled by other rivers. It's a great early-season summer steelhead river that gets going in June but holds up well through July, with fresh summer fish taken into August.

You can see the first couple holes right from I-5, with Beginner's Hole — one of the big name drifts — just a stone's throw from the interstate. From there it's just a parade of fishable water as you go upstream. Kalama River Road follows the river most of its 45 miles, allowing premium access much of the way. There's plenty of water that requires an investment of sweat equity, but there's also plenty of fish-holding water that's surprisingly close to the road.

Tech tips: Go to the Kalama with versatility in mind. In other words, bring the tackle box and be prepared to try a variety of presentations. Jigs in black/red or pink/red are always a great choice on this river and account for lots of fish. Spinners, spoons and drift rigs are also productive and add a refreshing change of pace to a day on the river.

When you're fishing spinners and spoons, remember to keep them close to the bottom. Quarter cast (45-degree angle) upstream, allow the spinner to drop to the bottom, give the rod a good snap to start the blade rotating and follow the drift of the spinner near the bottom. Try keeping your rod at a 2 o'clock position, you'll find it will give you more control over your presentation as you bump into rocks. Removing the treble hook and replacing it with a siwash will help to prevent snags and improve your landing percentage. The same is true for spoons.

Some favorite spinners include size 3 and 4 Metrics with a flame blade or nickel blade and black Vibrac Rooster Tails in assorted sizes. Remember to try different size hardware. Some days summer fish like small presentations; other days they like something a bit more substantial.

There's also some very productive fly-only water above Summers Creek all the way to the falls.

The real charm of this river, other than spectacular drifts and productivity, is its accessibility. It's perfect for a quick after-work or half-day getaway.

Who to call: Prichard's Western Anglers (360-673-4990).

Kalama River

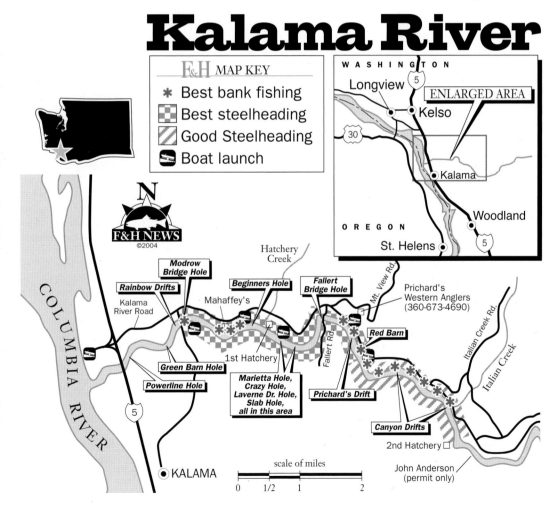

F&H MAP KEY
* ✳ Best bank fishing
* ▨ Best steelheading
* ▨ Good Steelheading
* ⛴ Boat launch

WASHINGTON
Longview
Kelso
ENLARGED AREA
30
Kalama
Woodland
OREGON
St. Helens

COLUMBIA RIVER

N
F&H NEWS ©2004

Kalama River Road

Modrow Bridge Hole
Rainbow Drifts
Mahaffey's
Beginners Hole
Fallert Bridge Hole
Hatchery Creek
Mt. View Rd.
Prichard's Western Anglers (360-673-4690)
Red Barn
Green Barn Hole
1st Hatchery
Powerline Hole
Marietta Hole, Crazy Hole, Laverne Dr. Hole, Slab Hole, all in this area
Prichard's Drift
Fallert Rd.
Italian Creek Rd.
Italian Creek
Canyon Drifts
2nd Hatchery
John Anderson (permit only)

KALAMA
5

scale of miles
0   1/2   1   2

Winter-runs now joining mix on Kalama River

KALAMA

by Joel Shangle

FISH AND MOVE for Kalama steelhead. The southwestern river offers plenty of bank access and boat launches. Steve Houston nailed this winter-run on a drift last February.

Given the attention paid recently to Mt. St. Helens, you may have forgotten about one of the southwest's best salmon and steelhead streams. That's perfectly fine with the regulars on the Kalama River.

While the big volcano sputtered and spewed through September and October, Kalama flyrodders merrily hooked Chinook, coho and steelhead in the "fly-only" waters between the lower hatchery and Mahaffey's Campground (360-673-4488), and bank-standing gearbangers tied into the same mix of kings, silvers and metalheads on the upper river.

Sorry you missed it, but don't spend too much time fretting about missed opportunity — one of the greatest things about the Kalama is that there's always a fresh run of fish coming in, and by the time you read this there'll be a fair number of early winter steelhead pulling in from the Columbia.

"When do first winter steelhead get here? Two weeks ago," cracked Mahaffey's owner Wayne Orzel in early November. "We have a whole lot of water this year. On a normal year, we'd have about a quarter of the water we

have now, but this year, these guys are booking right upriver, man."

By "these guys," Orzel is referring to a mix of B-run coho and early winter steelhead. The Kalama's second-run silvers, bound for the higher of the two hatcheries on the river, will normally trickle in through October and November. They're usually joined by the first winter-runs shortly after Election Day, but it's safe to say that the winter metalhead season on the Kalama has already begun.

"The B-runs will usually hold out in the Columbia a little, take their time and come in here with a red stripe, but this year, they came in brighter than hell," Orzel says. "Same with the steelhead. They're not waiting around much this year. They're here."

Konkering the Kalama: The Kalama is easily one of *F&H's* "most-mapped" rivers, and for good reason. No matter your level of experience and technique preferences — and regardless if whether you have a boat or not — there's a place for you here. Matter of fact, there are *several* places for you here, and that's especially true during winter steelhead season.

"I always tell people that the gener-

al mentality on the river is 'Don't think you're steelhead fishing,'" Orzel says. "Approach it like you would for trout: Go to one spot and try it, and it's not working out for you, go to another spot and try that. Part of the beauty of this river is that there are so, so many good spots to fish."

Getting the drift? Novice drift boaters, take note: the Kalama is your kind of river. Unlike the rock gardens of the Olympic Peninsula and the boat-bashing sweepers of rivers like the Sauk, the Kalama is defined by mellow drifts from top to bottom.

"There are only two places that take any skill whatsoever," says Orzel. "The highest is Weber's Drift behind Prichard's, where you just have to stay to the left third of the river. If you go down the middle, you'll get wet. The other is coming around toward Fallert Bridge. All you have to do is pull the bow of the boat toward the rock in the river, stroke back a couple of times, and you'll scoot right around. The rest is a piece of cake, but if you're worried about your skills at all, just put in at the Slab Hole just above the lower hatchery."

From top to bottom, the put-ins (all accessible from Kalama River Road, exit 32 off I-5) are as follows: Red Barn (5.5 miles upriver); Prichard's Western Anglers (4.9 miles upriver); Slab Hole (roughly ¼-mile upriver from the first hatchery); Beginner's Hole (just upriver from Mahaffey's, which lies 2.5 miles off the freeway) and Modrow Bridge (just over 1.3 miles above I-5). There's also a take-out below I-5.

Every bit of that water is virtually void of pressure during the week and fishable with a number of techniques, but you'll see many of the regulars backing divers and bait, tossing spinners or fishing jigs.

"Best way to go is a diver with sand shrimp, but this is one helluva spinner river and it's become real popular with the jig fishermen," Orzel says. "You'll see some guys drifting shrimp and eggs too. Hell, man, whatever you like to fish, bring it. It'll work."

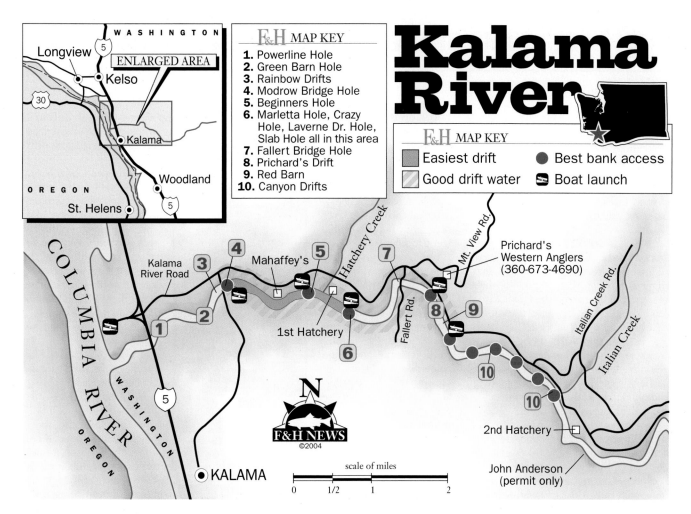

Kalama River

F&H MAP KEY
1. Powerline Hole
2. Green Barn Hole
3. Rainbow Drifts
4. Modrow Bridge Hole
5. Beginners Hole
6. Marletta Hole, Crazy Hole, Laverne Dr. Hole, Slab Hole all in this area
7. Fallert Bridge Hole
8. Prichard's Drift
9. Red Barn
10. Canyon Drifts

F&H MAP KEY
- Easiest drift
- Good drift water
- Best bank access
- Boat launch

Bank on it: What makes the Kalama so attractive come winter steelhead season is the amount of bank access from top to bottom. Unlike the cramped quarters of Blue Creek on the Cowlitz and Rieter Ponds on the Skykomish, the Kalama serves up literally miles of foot access to good steelhead spots, starting in the Canyon below the upper hatchery and extending all the way down past Red Barn to the Prichard's storefront. Below Prichard's, bank anglers can toss spinners, float jigs and drift eggs or shrimp at the Hatchery Creek Hole, Beginner's Hole and Willow Hole (which runs right behind Mahaffey's), and just above the bridge at Modrow.

Water worries: The Kalama will stay fishable through much of the winter, with occasional one- or two-day blowouts that clear just as quickly as they came.

"General rule is that, if it takes a day to blow out, it'll take a day to come back in," Orzel says. "Even if we get rain here, it doesn't all come down the river in a big deluge. Pay attention to the snow level here — if it gets down to 2,000 feet, a lot of that water will get dispersed by snow in the mountains. It doesn't all come into the river at once."

Still, when water is high, fish high: Hit the Canyon or Red Barn first and move downriver as the water drops.

AT a GLANCE

What: Kalama River winter steelhead.

When: Winter-runs are already here (along with a mix of B-run coho). Expect the fishing to build through late November and December.

Why: The Kalama serves up a mix of easy drift boat water and bank access, where several different techniques work.

How: From a drift boat, back bait divers, drift bait, fish bobbers/jigs or pull plugs. From the bank, float jigs, drift bait or toss spinners.

Where: Boaters have five put-ins (all off Kalama River Road): Red Barn, Prichard's, Slab Hole, Beginner's Hole, Modrow Bridge. There's also a last-chance takeout below I-5. For bank anglers, access is abundant from the upper hatchery/Canyon down to Prichard's. You can also fish just below the first hatchery, Beginner's Hole/Willow Hole behind Mahaffey's and at Modrow.

Information: Call Prichard's Western Anglers (360-673-4690) for recorded updates on river conditions; Mahaffey's Camp Store (360-673-4488).

Target both forks of Lewis for early winter steelhead

WOODLAND

by Terry Otto

Savvy steelhead anglers know that both forks of the Lewis River are great places to hook the first winter steelhead of the year, and forecasts look rosy. Here is what to expect this winter on both of these fantastic fisheries.

NORTH FORK

Early fish: Southwest metalhead anglers are dreaming about that first winter run of the year, respooling their reels and thinking about the Lewis River. Vets know that by the traditional Thanksgiving weekend kickoff of steelhead season, the North Fork Lewis is already red-hot, and has been for almost a month. According to Tom Moat, fish hatchery specialist at the Lewis River Salmon Hatchery, this run of winters has always been earlier than most.

Moat expects a good run this year, especially after this year's fantastic summer run. Almost 15,000 steelhead returned to the hatchery this year, with an expected return of about half that for the winter run. Most of these fish will range from 7 to 10 pounds, and will be very fresh after their relatively short run from the Columbia River Bar.

AT A GLANCE

What: Lewis River winter steelhead.

Where: Near Woodland.

Why: Both the East and North forks of the Lewis provide excellent early steelhead opportunity. Bank fishing opportunity is excellent on both too.

Tactics/techniques: Bank anglers should stick to baits (sand shrimp, eggs, prawns) early in the season, when fish are fresh in the river. Fish baits with Corkies or under bobbers. Switch to spoons and spinners when fish have been in the river awhile.

Information: Lewis River Hatchery (360-225-7413); Bob's Sporting Goods (360-425-3870) in Longview.

Guides: Mike Sexton (360-864-6665); Harvey Van Brunt (888-750-8707).

Bank on it: Moat says that this fishery is mostly a bank fishing situation, although some boat anglers score well above the forks. Below that, it's hit and miss. The best fishing is definitely right at the Lewis River Hatchery, especially when the river runs above 5,000 cubic feet per second.

The river tends to stay high this time of year as water is dumped from Merwin Lake to make room for the winter rains. When the water does run lower, consider fishing right at the deadline below Merwin Dam. The crowds will be smaller, and the fishing can be very good, especially later in the run. In both situations, target fast water near the bank when the river runs high, and try the main riffles when the water drops.

Fish bait early: When these fresh steelhead first come in, they will key right in on bait, with sand shrimp faring the best. Eggs and prawns are also popular. Try drifting the bait with Corkies in pink or orange when the water is clear, or when you're fishing fast water. Some anglers like to drop bait below a bobber in the slower, deeper drifts. Both methods work well. Lots of the locals like to plunk the shoreline, and they often score well early on.

Switch it up: Don't be afraid to experiment, because sometimes the fish can be finicky. After the fish have been in the river awhile they are less apt to strike bait. When this happens I switch to Corky and yarn, leaving the bait at home. Pink and orange Corkies work best. And don't forget to try a little hardware too: Steelies work well in green or blue, and Blue Fox in sizes 3, 4 and 5 score with the same colors.

Remember, the higher the river level, the shallower the fish will be. Try to be considerate when fishing the high water.

LEWIS RIVER VETS know that this southwest system gets an early run of metalheads. Both the East Fork and North Fork are productive from bank and boat.

It's really aggravating to try to drift in 2 feet of water when the guy above you insists on longlining, and letting his drift cut you off.

The upper Lewis River is controlled by three dams, and the reservoirs help settle turbidity out the water. This means that it rarely blows out to where it is unfishable. It does get really high in wet years, sometimes to the point that shoreline access is restricted. However, when this happens the water level pushes the fish right to the bank. The result can be some fantastic steelhead fishing.

As December gives way to January, wild fish will start to enter the river. These fish will be there through March, and sometimes into April. If the water stays high all year, they can be difficult to catch. However, if the water drops below 5000 cfs, the fishing for these catch-and-release bruisers can be some of the best of the year.

Get there: To reach the hatchery and Merwin Dam, take Highway 503 north from Woodland, and follow the signs. For more information, call the Lewis River Hatchery (360-225-7413)

EAST FORK

The sleeper fork: This smaller tributary of the Lewis is a little-known secret across the state when it comes to steelhead, but savvy local fishermen have long known about the East Fork and the great fishing it has to offer. However, hatchery stockings are coming to an end on the East Fork, and soon it will be a wild-fish-only river. Stockings still continue, with 125,000 winter steelhead smolts planted in 2001, so there are still a few years of hatchery harvests left.

Bank on it: This river is a bank angler's dream, with lots of access and room to move. Look to Lewisville Park in Battle Ground to start, and you will find long stretches of water that can be waded easily. Another favorite access point is Daybreak Park. In both stretches you can find water to yourself, if you are willing to walk a little ways. This stream is smaller and easier to fish than the North Fork.

Tough drifts: Moat says that although it can be difficult, the East Fork can be drifted, and he suggests the drift between Lewisville Park and Daybreak Park. The best launch is at the Highway 503 Bridge, and you will have to drop the boat with a rope. The first 300 yards are the most difficult, then things get a lot easier.

Moat suggests banking the boat and drift-fishing the holes and pockets. Then put the boat out and pull plugs down through the same water.

Bait to artificials: Once again, bait works the best when the fish have just come in. As they stay in the river for a while, the bite will switch more to artificials. It's always a good idea to pack some hardware for when the bite gets tough. The same colors and sizes that work in the North Fork will also work here.

The East Fork does not have any dams or flood control, so it blows out easily. It's always a good idea to check conditions before you go. A rise in the water level isn't always a bad thing, as the steelhead will often bite the best when the river is coming up.

Get there: Lewisville Park can be accessed from Highway 503 in Battle Ground. Daybreak Park can be reached by taking N. E. 82nd Street south to N.E. Daybreak Road.

For more information, call the WDFW Region 6 headquarters (360-696-6211).

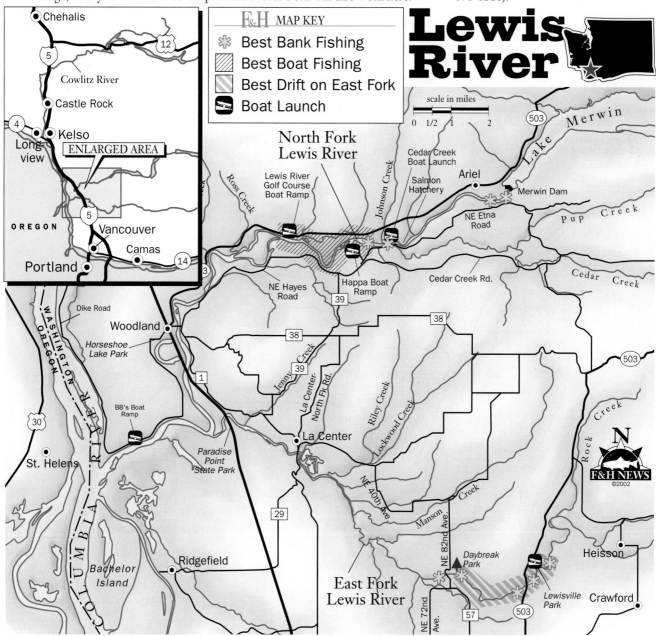

Lewis River

F&H MAP KEY

✳ Best Bank Fishing

▨ Best Boat Fishing

▨ Best Drift on East Fork

🚤 Boat Launch

Lewis steel: hatchery down now, Merwin down later

WOODLAND

by Terry Otto

The North Fork Lewis River has had some really great summer steelhead runs during the last few years, and there is no reason to expect anything different this year. Local anglers know that the summers will start to enter the river in good numbers in June, and when July arrives, the fishing will get red hot. Expect it to stay that way into September, but the action will shift as the water temps warm up and the river starts to drop.

These Skamania-strain fish run big: 10-pound steelhead are common. The Lewis usually sees some really big ones too. It's a rare year that doesn't see a few steelhead boated over 20 pounds.

Golf course and up: The middle river is the place to be early in the run. Look to the holes near the Lewis River Golf Course, and up to the hatchery. While there is some limited shore access at the golf course, most of this reach is best fished from a boat.

There's a launch at the golf course, but it is pretty rough. Most anglers launch at the Island Ramp and run up, and most of this water lends itself well to fishing jig and bobber. However, side-drifting and free-drifting with sand shrimp is effective too. If you prefer to pull plugs, the best patterns are blue pirate and Michael Jackson.

Bank on it: From the bank, concentrate your efforts at the hatchery. The steelhead will pile up below the entrance to the hatchery ponds and in the long glide just above the Meat Hole. This is good drift water, but anglers here increasingly are turning to jig-and-bobber presentations, and their success is hard to argue with. The best colors to use are red, pink and orange.

Movin' on up: As the water drops later in the summer, steelhead will congregate in the faster water and riffles. That's the time to fish the reach from Merwin Dam down to the hatchery. The warmer water makes the bite a little tougher, but the fish are easier to locate, and are bunched up.

This is a good time to use hardware and other baits that the fish have not seen a lot of. My own favorite is a green or blue Stee-Lee. Fish them in the fastest water and be prepared for some vicious strikes.

Who to call: Fisherman's Depot (360-225-9900) in Woodland.

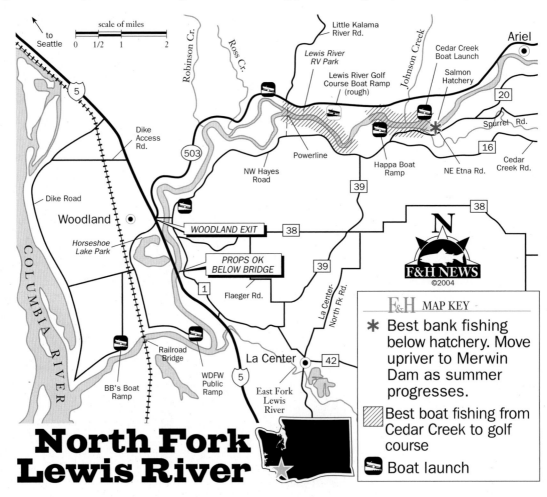

North Fork Lewis River

F&H MAP KEY
* Best bank fishing below hatchery. Move upriver to Merwin Dam as summer progresses.
▨ Best boat fishing from Cedar Creek to golf course
⊟ Boat launch

Columbia River Waters
TROUT

Out of the way Big Sheep Creek: brookies, rainbows

by Lou Bignami

You could make a case that Big Sheep Creek is the most remote spot to fish in Stevens County. Tucked tight to the Canadian border on the north side of the Columbia, it's the spot I go over holiday weekends to escape mobs. This year I'll be in Central America so it's all yours.

You get two species (brook trout and rainbows) and four creeks (the American Fork, Little Sheep Creek, West Fork and Big Sheep Creek) for the drive, plus assorted tributaries to fish, besides the excellent brown trout action usually fit in on the nearby Colville River at dawn and dusk. Do check Colville on the way up for road and fishing reports.

Think of the creeks as a "W" with an extended leg dumping out on the Columbia River across from Northport and just east of Steamboat Rock. Highway 25 runs up to Canada along lower Big and then Little Sheep Creek and, while it's got the same mix — brook trout high and rainbows low — it gets more fishing pressure than other forks. Most trout run in the 8- to 10-inch range. There's camping here at Upper Falls and Sheep Creek Falls, and the frisky might fish up Boundary Creek towards the Canadian border too.

The stretch between Upper Falls Campground and the point on Big Sheep Creek where the road returns to the water offers a couple of hours decent action too.

Big Sheep Creek turns west away from Highway 25 just past the campground, so you need to backtrack east past the old Speedway and follow Sheep Creek Road up to its namesake creek.

A number of springs feed the upper creek, and as the water cools and white-water stretches that hold rainbows change to meadow meanders and brushy banks, rainbows start to thin out and brook trout take over. Turner Creek, a small tributary on the north side about halfway to the American Fork, is another good bet for those who like to walk to catch small, tasty brook trout out of tidy waters.

At this point the banks change and brush takes over long stretches. About a mile above the mine entrance on the south bank the creek swings away from the road. That's a good spot for a drop-off and bank fishing up to the junction of the American Fork a couple of miles up and you return to the road. There are a lot of frisky small brook trout in this section and in the upper American Fork too. There's a chance at a 16- or 17-inch brook trout here.

Note this road runs on up Elbow Lake on the seldom-fished hiker's West Fork of the American Fork. Follow the road east and you end up back on Highway 395.

There's nothing special needed in the way of tackle or techniques in any of these creeks. Last visit I tied on a No. 14 Elk Hair Caddis and only replaced it when it was chewed to bits. My wife prefers to fish what she calls "finger-nail" spinners in ⅛- to 1⁄16-ounce sizes and has not so far found a color that won't work.

Information: Republic Sport Shop (509-750-3040)

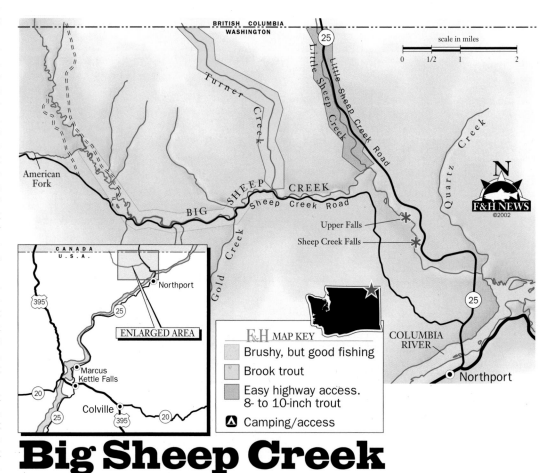

Big Sheep Creek

Does another state-record cutt lie in wait at Omak?

by Joel Shangle

In the early 1990s, Omak Lake came screaming onto the Washington cutthroat fishing scene, hurdling into the pantheon of nearby Lake Lenore as The Place To Catch A Big Cutthroat. Funny what a couple of state records will do for your image.

You can trace the birth of Omak's big fish mystique back to 1992. That's when Pateros' Dan Beardslee boated a 15-pound Lahontan cutt while trolling a J-Plug at midlake. That record lasted all of a year . . . when Beardslee brought in a hook-nosed cutt that tipped the scales at an eye-popping 18.4 pounds. But this monster was just one of several chunky cutts that Beardslee has hooked in 8 years of fishing on the 3,000-acre reservoir — and it may not be the biggest that this fishery ultimately produces.

"That *can't* be the biggest fish in there, can it?" Beardslee wonders. "I mean . . . could I have possibly caught the single biggest fish in that lake? It's a huge lake. It's hard to imagine."

What *isn't* such a stretch is the possibility of Omak kicking out the state's third-straight state-record Lahontan. Hey, 20-pound trout are stupendously rare anywhere, but . . . well it *could* happen. Couldn't it?!?

"Oh, I think there may be fish in excess of (18.4 pounds) in the lake," says Kirk Truscott, a Colville Confederated Tribe fisheries biologist. "I've never actually had one in hand, but every spring when we trap fish in the shallows, we see fish in the 15- and 16-pound class. And we by *no* means see all the fish in the lake."

BIOLOGY 101: When Omak was first stocked with hatchery Lahontan cutts in 1968, Colville Confederated Tribe biologists hoped that the fishery would respond like the species' natal populations in Heenan and Summit lakes in north-central Nevada. Well-adapted for survival in the highly alkaline waters of well-known cutt producers like Pyramid Lake near Reno, the Lahontan cutt seemed like a natural fit at Omak.

"They had tried other salmonid stocks, but hadn't had much success," Truscott says. "They stocked it with rainbows and even brook trout in the '50s, but (the fish) couldn't withstand the alkalinity of the lake."

Because there are no adequate free-flowing streams available to Omak's cutts for spawning, recruitment is supplied by the Colville Tribal Hatchery, which loads the lake with 60,000 to 100,000 fingerlings a year. Those fish go into the water in the spring, and enter the fishery the following year.

BIG ONES NOW: The catch-and-keep season at Omak ends Feb. 29, with a catch-and-release season in effect through June to preserve fish as they move in to try to spawn. As Omak tails out toward catch-and-release season, big fish will start relating to shallower waters and catches of 4- to 8-pound cutts will start to become common.

KEVIN ERICSON (left) of the Outdoor Channel hooked this 10-pound Omak cutt trolling with Dan Beardslee, who's holding the state-record 18.4-pounder below.

"Your typical strongest class of fish now is in the 21- to 25-inch category," says Truscott. "But the spawn-age class of fish that moves into shallow water in the spring — 60 percent of those fish will be in the 4- to 6-pound range."

ON THE FLY: A funny thing happens in downtown Omak from March to June: The town starts to see a steady procession of Oregon license plates passing through, heading to the lake. The skinny on Omak's catch-and-release fly fishery has made it over the border to a growing crowd of Webfoot flyrodders, some of whom migrate north annually to take advantage of the opportunity.

"You see more people from Oregon on that lake in the spring than people from Omak," says Dick Caryl of Cascade Outfitters (509-826-4148). "There's a pretty good group of Oregon fly fishermen who fish it every year."

Our advice to Evergreen State fur-n-feather folks who think that Lenore is the king: Give Omak a shot.

"By the middle to end of March, when the fish move into the shallows to try to spawn, you're fishing shallow water," says Caryl. "It's a maximum of 15 feet up to 3 feet. That's when the fly fishing starts to get really good."

You can get as techno-dweeby as you want with your patterns . . . but a Woolly Bugger, Muddler Minnow or Sculpin is really all you need.

A SHORE THING: Not a member of the

AT A GLANCE

What: Lahontan cutthroat at Omak Lake.
When: Good fishing year-round, but best shot at big fish from the bank comes in spring, when fish head into shallow water to spawn. Trolling is best late in the summer and into fall.
Limit: Two fish over 14 inches
Season: Catch-and-release from March 1 to June 30.
License: Located on Colville Confederated Tribe land. You must have a tribal license to fish Omak. Licenses are available at most sporting goods stores in the area.
Directions: Take Highway 155 east out of Omak for roughly a mile, then head south on Omak Creek Road for another 5 miles. The pavement runs into a dirt road, which leads straight to Beer Can Beach.
Special Regs: Mission Bay, the northernmost embayment, is closed to fishing March 1 to June 30.
Information: Dick Caryl, Cascade Outfitters (509-826-4148); Colville Confederated Tribes, Fish & Wildlife (509-634-2110).

Orvis crowd? Not a problem. Spincasters tossing diving plugs and spoons off the banks will have no trouble getting into the shallow-water bite.

"There are so many ways to catch fish in that fishery," says Caryl. "Diving-type plugs and spoons in the shallow bays are just as effective as fly fishing."

You can try anything from a Rapala to a Cruise Minnow, but my personal favorite for Lahontan cutts is a Luhr Jensen Power Dive Minnow (blue and silver are key colors), cast out and cranked back hard enough to bump the nose of the bait into the bottom. Repeat this process several times on the retrieve. It's a killer.

WHERE: The bite for shore anglers will come from the bays and along the shoreline on the northern side of the lake. Starting at Beer Can Beach on the far northern end all the way down to the far end, hit the big bay at midlake and the bay out of Poison Oak Creek.

This side of the lake is almost all walk-in access, except for a rough 4-wheel drive road that runs from the south end just past Poison Oak Creek.

PUT IN, TAKE 'EM OUT: Boaters hitting Omak over the next couple of months will see the bite moving out of the 80-foot depths toward the shallows. Find the right depth, set your downriggers and skirt the shoreline with U20 FlatFish (blue and silver), Tor-P-Dos (black and white, chartreuse and red or pink and black), Needlefish (frog colored or red/pearl head), Apex, Rapalas, broken-back Rebels or any wobbling spoon or minnow imitation.

"These fish are *not* hard to catch," says Beardslee. "Once you locate them, you can put a beer can down there with hooks and they'll bite it. It's a matter of finding the thermocline — figuring out where they are vertically and horizontally."

Mission Bay, the northernmost embayment on the lake, is closed to fishing through the catch-and-release season to allow gathering of spawners.

STORE THIS AWAY: The trolling gets noticeably better on Omak in the late summer and into the fall, when a hard thermocline develops and fish, looking for cooler water, keg into a relatively limited space. Beardslee swears by fishing the thermocline, and his logic is hard to refute.

"If you can find the thermocline, you've just eliminated 95 percent of the water," he says. "You've just reduced the lake down to 110 acres instead of 8 miles. If you can manage to get a handle on the thermocline, you have 80 percent of the battle won."

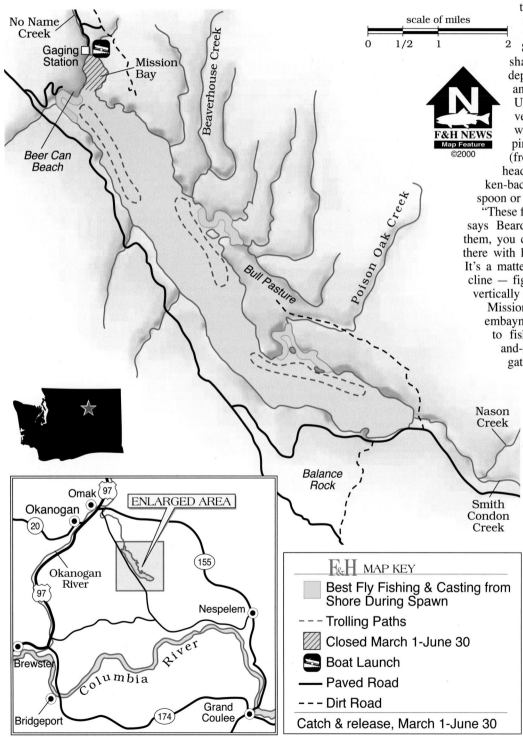

F&H MAP KEY

Best Fly Fishing & Casting from Shore During Spawn

- - - Trolling Paths

Closed March 1-June 30

Boat Launch

Paved Road

- - - Dirt Road

Catch & release, March 1-June 30

Midges key fly action at Quail Lake

OTHELLO

by Lou Bignami

For big fish in shallow water, you can't beat the fly-only catch-and-release fishing at Quail Lake, part of the seep lakes south of Potholes Reservoir. In fact, you can take some nice fish without casting by simply dragging a dark Woolly Worm or Woolly Bugger on a sink-tip line along the outside edge of weedbeds on a fairly heavy leader.

However, you can do far better with midges on days when calm water gets sprinkled by the rain-like riseforms that indicate a midge hatch. But you'll need to use at least a 10-foot leader tapered down to 5X or even 6X or you won't be in the successful group. These are Ph.D.-level trout, fished over by some of the most expert casters in Washington.

On days with no rises, try pupal midge forms, the classic Eastern Washington chironomids that come in more colors than Joseph's Coat (except, of course, the color you need) and in sizes from about 10 down to "can't see to tie them."

As an alternative try ridiculously large black, sable or purple Wooly Buggers (we've tried streamers but they apparently don't work well) or whatever big dark nymphs you have left from Montana trips.

There doesn't seem to be any real hot spots in the lake because the big trout cruise around a lot. So we normally anchor out with two anchors off likely beds, get the Fishing Buddy in operation and either cast to risers, or to fish we see underwater. I've given up blind casting.

While you can fish off the bank if you don't mind spending lots of time removing weeds from your fly, the best bet is fishing the outside of weedbeds. I prefer to do this with a canoe or Porta-Bote. It's only about a ½ mile in and you can roll in a canoe or Porta-Bote with portable wheels.

If there are no risers on Quail, we simply stick the canoe back on the wheels and roll on to Pit, North or South Teal or back to the car by way of Lyle Lake. There are four or five dozen seep lakes and canals to fish in here,

Some are CNR only, some are not. All are interesting spots to fish spring and fall. Come summer you fry and the snakes come out, and winter's blasts don't make for comfortable conditions either.

To get to Quail, go north from Othello, west on McManamon Road past Thread Lake to the trailhead.

Try Mar Don Resort (509-346-2651) for info.

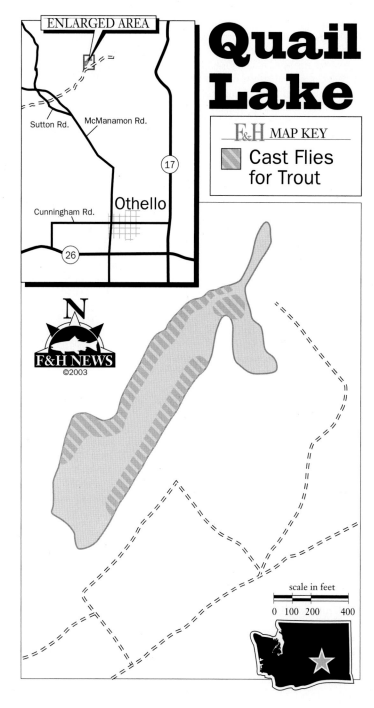

ENLARGED AREA

Sutton Rd.   McManamon Rd.

17

Othello

Cunningham Rd.

26

N

F&H NEWS
©2003

Quail Lake

F&H MAP KEY

Cast Flies for Trout

scale in feet

0   100 200   400

Best silver fishing in the state at Riffe Lake? Maybe

MOSSYROCK

by Dusty Routh

The first thing that's important in any discussion about Riffe Lake in southwest Washington is to first come to friendly agreement about how to pronounce the name. Some anglers refer to this wildly productive reservoir as "riff" like a guitar riff, while others have been known to add an extra "ey" at the end to make it sound like "riffey."

But the official pronunciation of this rich impoundment of the Cowlitz River is "Rie-ff," with the "i" pronounced like a hard vowel rather than a soft vowel. The name comes from the small settlement that was flooded when the reservoir was formed.

If all this grammatical gobbledygook and history reminds you of grade school and wretched memories of exacting teachers exasperated at your consistent use of the words "ain't" and "gunna" as in "I ain't gunna sit here and listen to this crap anymore, 'cause I'd rather be fishin' at Riffe Lake," well, then, my earnest apologies.

On to more important lessons ...

Big water and lots of fish: At full pool Riffe is no tiny pond. It cradles a whopping 12,000 surface acres of water, and ranges as deep as 360 feet. All that water means, of course, that there's tons of shoreline — 52 miles of it to be exact. Surprisingly for such a big lake, the boat launches are really limited in number. There's a good one that works at most all water levels at Mossyrock Park (888-502-8690), and another at the far northeastern end of the lake known as the Kosmos launch. There is also a launch at Taidnapam Park, also on the east end, but more towards the south.

Mossyrock Park is an excellent place to camp if you plan an excursion to the area, incidentally. The park offers terrific amenities, with 60 main sites, 24 sites with water/electricity, 24 sites without hookups, and 12 walk-in tent sites. There are 40 more sites in the lower overflow area, and 33 sites in the upper. There are showers, a summer-season store, picnic tables, grassy lawns, fish-cleaning station, and so forth. It's nice digs.

OWEN "BUGSY" BURGER holds a pair of silvers he caught while fishing at Riffe Lake with his dad Brian Burger and buddy Gary Hurt in June. He was trolling a Flash Lite and red Wedding Ring midlake on the east side at 25 feet.

Riffe is a utility reservoir managed by Tacoma Power and Light. They also manage nearby Mayfield Lake, and of course other water bodies in the state like Lake Cushman near Hood Canal. Riffe is considered to be at full pool once it hits 778 feet. As of mid-August, it was sitting at a very comfortable 771 feet, so it's quite practically full.

All that water adds up to a pretty good assortment of fish, and Riffe doesn't disappoint. The lake is probably most famous for its landlocked coho (not sockeye), locally known as just plain ol' "silvers."

Frank Abbruzzese with the Fish Country Sport Shop (360-985-2090) is quick to point out that a lot of people believe these are regular kokanee, as in landlocked sockeye, but instead these are resident coho stranded in the reservoir when the Cowlitz was dammed.

Silver slammin': Fishing for Riffe's silvers kicks off early in the spring, with fish close to the surface and close to the shoreline. Most anglers fish for them with prawns and eggs under bobbers, between 7 and 10 feet deep. As summer wears on, like now, the silvers go deeper, and then trolling with leadcore and off downriggers is the norm, at depths exceeding 50 feet. It's tough to beat red Wedding Rings and flies trolled just behind dodgers or a gang troll for these delicious coho, some of which can reach decent size.

You can also still-fish late in the summer and into early fall, using a slip-bobber and fishing deep, but deepwater trolling is really the most effective way to go this time of year. Limits can be pretty much the norm once you're dialed in.

Rainbows too: Riffe also has a generous amount of rainbows, some of which can top 20 inches, but most of which are in the 10- to 15-inch range with an average of about 12 to 14 inches. And there are plenty of them. These are planter fish from WDFW, but the lake is so large that a lot of carryover happens and bigger trout are known to happen. The rainbows can be taken on the same gear as the silvers, along with spoons and fur spinners like Panther Martins and Rooster Tails. Fishing the bottom with nightcrawlers and marshmallows will also produce.

There are also rumors of some monster brown trout in Riffe. Fish Country says that browns to 9 pounds have been caught. Trolling for these early and late in the day along the rocky shorelines with leadcore line and super-long leaders, pulling big bodybaits like jointed Rapalas (in the German brown color, of course) is the ticket. Big browns are largely nocturnal, with most of their activity happening just before and during first light, and again right at dusk.

Last but not least of the coldwater species, the big lake also has cutthroat trout that thrive in all that cold, deep water.

Bass and spinyrays: Riffe is also a darn good smallmouth bass lake. We fished the eastern edges of the reservoir not long ago and cleaned up on the bass. All the smallmouth were relatively small, under 2 pounds, but they're plentiful, and exceptionally aggressive. The usual assortment of goodies will take them, including crawfish-colored crankbaits, grubs and even topwater baits late in the day towards evening on shallow flats. The best fishing for smallmouth is at the warmer, more shallow eastern end. We can't emphasize enough how well small, deep-diving crawfish crankbaits work here.

Riffe also has an assortment of spinyray panfish, including perch, crappie and bluegill.

AT a GLANCE

What: Excellent fishing at 12,000-acre Riffe Lake in southwest Washington, an impoundment of the Cowlitz.

When: Now is an excellent time to score on trout, silvers and smallmouth bass. The reservoir is currently at near-full pool.

How: Troll deep for the silvers, fish shallow flats with crawfish-colored crankbaits for the smallmouth, and troll the middle depths for trout with spoons, flies, and spinners.

Where: The eastern end of the reservoir is excellent for smallmouth, and so is the far western end near the dam. Rainbows and silvers can be caught at both ends. For browns, fish the north and south shorelines away from civilization early and late in the day.

Contact information: One of the best sources of information, tackle, bait, and supplies is at the Fish Country Sport Shop (360-985-2090), located along Highway 12 in the small burg of Ethel. Mossyrock Park can be reached at (888) 502-8690. This is also the number to call if you want information about Riffe's lake level. While it will be at full pool through the summer, the water will start going down soon to make way for winter rains and for next spring's snowmelt.

Riffe Lake

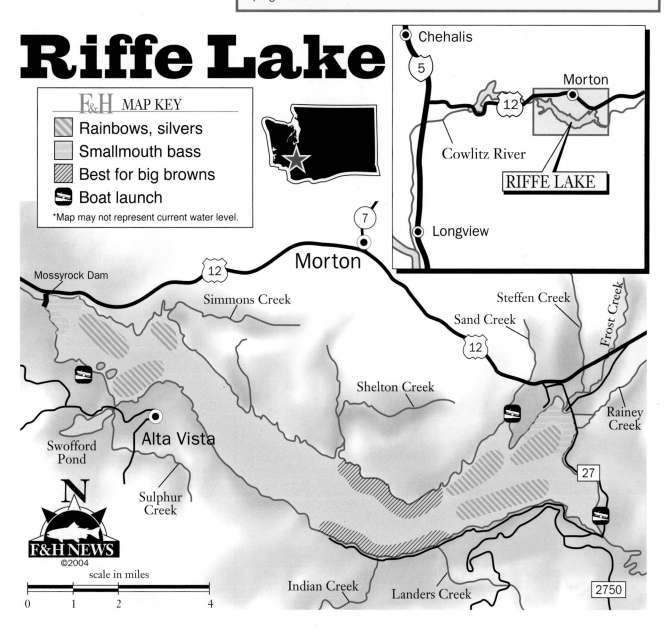

F&H MAP KEY
- Rainbows, silvers
- Smallmouth bass
- Best for big browns
- Boat launch

*Map may not represent current water level.

N

F&H NEWS
©2004

scale in miles

0   1   2   4

Sun Lakes Chain still Basin's go-to spot in April

COULEE CITY

by Leroy Ledeboer

Simply drive Highway 17 past the Sun Lakes Chain on the late April opener and you might believe you're seeing a record crowd. Somewhere around 4,000 anglers will be along the shoreline or boating on the two big lakes, Park and Blue.

However, even this figure is a real drop from the heyday of these two lakes, when more than 9,000 would crowd along those banks and clog every boat ramp. Illegal plants of spinyrays initially retarded the trout catch in the early 1990s, and although both lakes were rehabbed and had good years in the late '90s, they've never totally regained their popularity.

Once again, though, the trout in both Blue and Park could be losing out to the spinyrays, mainly perch and large-mouth bass.

"Yes, this could be a pivotal year for Blue and Park," says Region II fish biologist Jeff Korth. "Last year both lakes were still fairly productive, at least in part because we propped them up with substantial plants of catchables. But also the fingerlings we planted the fall before had a much better survival than I expected."

"This year we're having to spread our catchables around to more lakes, so there won't be as many for those two," he says. "Last March we put 55,000 catchables in Blue, 35,000 in Park. This time Blue got 25,000, Park 17,000 — roughly half. Between these and the survivors from our fingerling plant, hopefully we'll have decent fishing, but it may again be time to look at rehabbing both lakes."

Blue and Park will still be nice family lakes, though, if fishing is at least decent. Boat anglers do have an advantage, but there is plenty of shoreline access on both, starting right along the highway, where plunking dough baits, worms, etc., is still popular. Take the access roads along their eastern shores and you'll run into some more fishable spots.

In their best years, trolling over deep water with small FlatFish in colors from black and dark green to bright red or yellow was a guaranteed way to catch quick limits, and it should still be effective. Blue may have a slight edge here, but I wouldn't guarantee it.

Fishing from an anchored boat is also productive. Just move into the shallows, testing depths from 10 to 20 feet until you find the rainbow comfort zone, and plunk your favorite bait. As we move into midspring to the real heat of summer, look for the 40- to 50-foot holes.

Late April might still be too early to fly fish on Blue or Park, but by mid-May the shallow ends of both lakes will start having huge bug hatches and are definitely worth exploring with a float tube, mainly early in the morning and late evening.

Targeting either lake's German browns on opening weekend is tough, but once that crowd thins out, work the rocky shorelines along the highway. Browns were planted in these waters to control sculpin, their natural prey, so try plastics or cranks that simulate these ugly little fish, and work them right off the rocks in anything from 6 to 15 feet of water.

If there's anything good about those illegal spinyray plants, it's that at least some of these fish are now decent sized. Even two years ago I saw some 8-inch perch taken along private docks and just off the weedlines. If you get into perch, take as many as you're willing to fillet. If you get into bass, go ahead and keep a limit. There's no reason to practice conservation here. Within the next couple of years, rotenone will turn all of these fish into seagull food and lake fertilizer anyway.

THE SUN LAKES CHAIN opener has long been a fave of traveling anglers, thanks to generally sunny weather, excellent shoreline access and, of course, good plants of fish. Joe Buss of Seattle caught this 7½-pound brown trout at Park Lake on April 30 last year.

AT a GLANCE

What: Trout fishing in lower Grand Coulee.

Where: Six lakes along Highway 17 just south of Coulee City — Blue, Park, Vic Meyer, Perch, Dry Falls and Deep.

Why: Blue and Park offer good odds of opening-day stringers; Vic Meyer and Perch hold surprising numbers of fish for their size; Deep can produce limits after the opener and kokes in June; Dry Falls is just cool to fish.

How: Plunk baits off the shore for Blue and Park stockers, or troll plugs, spinners, etc. Plunk at Vic Meyer, Perch and the east shore of Deep, or troll Deep with Wedding Rings or FlatFish. Work leech, mayfly and chironomid patterns at Dry.

Regs: Blue, Park, Vic Meyer and Deep all open April 30 and fall under statewide regulations; Dry Falls was set to open April 1 and is selective gear only, daily limit one.

Contacts: WDFW Ephrata (509-754-4624); Big Wally's (509-632-5504) in Coulee City; Blue Lake Resort (509-632-5364) on Blue Lake; Soap Lake Liquor and Variety (509-246-1432).

Sun Lakes Chain

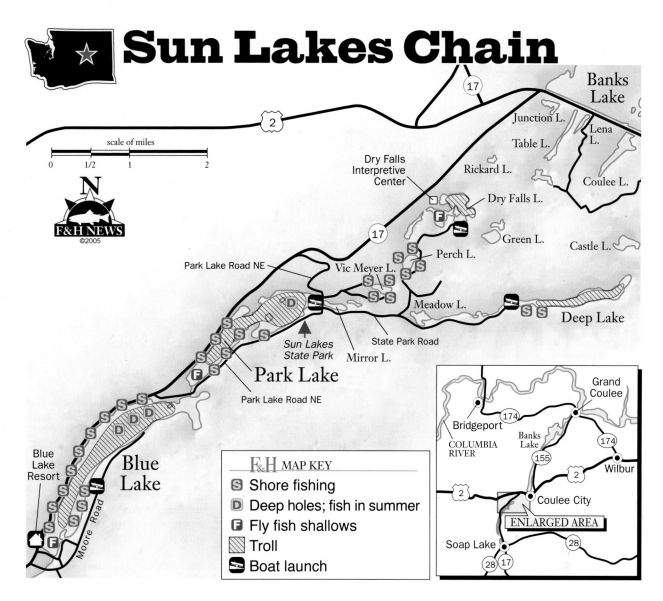

F&H MAP KEY
- **S** Shore fishing
- **D** Deep holes; fish in summer
- **F** Fly fish shallows
- ▨ Troll
- ◧ Boat launch

Perch Lake and Vic Meyer are both tiny, but year after year these two ponds offer good bank angling for about the first two weeks of season. If their opening day crowds are too intense, it's difficult fishing, but that wasn't the case when I checked them out two years ago. They weren't being ignored, but there was still plenty of available shoreline.

Deep Lake, at the upper northeast end of the chain, is one of my favorites, but the narrow road in and the launching area can create opening weekend headaches. After that, Deep is a quiet and scenic fishing water, where in May you can usually troll up a limit of 'bows on anything from FlatFish to worm-baited Wedding Rings. Around the first of June the kokanee kick in, making white corn on Wedding Rings a better

choice. I've seen plunkers work the east shoreline, but my impression is that trollers do much better.

Don't go to Deep looking for any real trophies. The lake trout that were once planted here have all but disappeared, and I've never seen a real slab of any kind. It's simply a beautiful canyon lake, where both the kokes and the trout will run 9 to 11 inches, with an occasional 14- to 16 inch carryover.

Dry Falls may be the chain's biggest disappointment the year. The selective gear lake, once a real jewel for this state's fly fishers, was scheduled to open April 1, but WDFW personnel didn't have high expectations.

"We weren't getting real positive feedback from Dry Falls in '03 and last year was much worse," biologist Jeff Korth

admits. "It's not a deep lake anyway, and right now the water level is down at least a couple of feet. But that doesn't really explain why it's so unproductive. We've planted quite a few triploids in the last three years, so I'd expect a few anglers to get into real monsters. But overall, the trout fishing has really dropped off."

If Dry Falls does prove worth fishing, April and early May flyrodders usually do the best with bigger patterns such as black leeches, but this lake is so shallow that the chironomids can kick in fast. Some anglers do fish from the shoreline, but a float tube gives you real advantages. First, you can quickly hit the 10-foot depths with a sinking line and wet fly, or if there's topwater action, it's much easier to roll-cast into those shallows from the lake side.

Naches, Tieton offer excellent small-stream trouting

YAKIMA

by Rob Phillips

Take a quick look at a map of Eastern Washington and you may be reminded of something. Blue lines everywhere, just like Aunt Mildred's legs. No, wait, that's not it. It should remind you that there are literally dozens of streams throughout the region, with each of those blue lines representing a fishing opportunity.

And during early fall, the opportunities are never better. Besides the fact that the weather couldn't be more perfect for a day of fishing, most trout anglers have stored their rods and reels for the year and are now concentrating on hunting or watching football or something else.

Which is a shame, because the trout fishing in many of the streams in the east slopes of the Central Cascades is excellent during the last days of summer and into early fall. Stream temperatures are starting to cool, which in turn means that trout are putting on the feedbag in anticipation of the cold months ahead.

This has been a particularly dry year and many of the smaller streams may be *very* low, but that doesn't mean they are unfishable. And the rivers, which are mainly controlled by the reservoirs in the Cascades, should be flowing

THE SMALL STREAMS of western Yakima County offer fine autumn fishing for trout. Use flies or small plugs and spinners on light-action rods.

fairly consistently.

Specifically there are a few rivers and creeks in Yakima County that can provide some dazzling fishing and some breathtaking scenery in late September and early October. The leaves are changing color daily and the fish, which have been in a hot August funk, are now getting active.

Yakima: Of course everyone knows about the Yakima River. This blue-ribbon trout stream offers some fabulous fishing in the fall. Fly anglers from all over come for an Indian summer afternoon of wading and double hauls.

What people tend to forget is that the Yak above the Rosa Dam is not just a fly fishing river. If you prefer to fish with ultralight spinning gear, you can have just as much fun. Just make sure your lure has a single hook and is barbless and you're as legal as the next guy.

You might get some funny looks and even hear a snide remark now and again from the guys with the wading vests and wood nets dangling from their necks, but fishing the

Yakima with a small spinner can be extremely fun and productive for catch-and-release rainbow up to 20 inches in length.

Naches: Other rivers in the area are totally underfished. The Tieton and the Naches may not be quite up to the standards of the Yakima, but when you have hole after hole to yourself, who cares!

The Naches runs from high in the Cascades to the city of Yakima. The best fishing is found higher up, along Highway 410. And because the river follows the road almost its entire length, there are many, many spots to stop and wet a line. Above and below Whistlin' Jack Lodge, near Cliffdell and down to Horseshoe Bend, there are all kinds of holes where you can work a fly or a small lure.

Even higher up 410, the Little Naches has several holes that see way more hunters than anglers during this time of the year, even though it can provide some quality fishing.

Near the Nile on 410, Rattlesnake Creek feeds the Naches. A walk

AT a GLANCE

What: Fall trout fishing in the streams of the east slopes of the central Cascades.

When: Now through Oct. 31, when all streams except the Yakima River above Rosa Dam close for the year.

Where: The Yakima, Naches, Little Naches and Tieton rivers, and Rattlesnake Creek; all west of Yakima in Yakima and Kitittas counties.

How: Flies, small plugs, spinners in the many holes available along each river. Public access is not a problem through U.S. Forest Service lands and campgrounds.

Info: WDFW Yakima (509-575-2740).

upstream on the Rattlesnake can also be productive for both brook and rainbow trout. The fish aren't big, but they are certainly feisty.

Like the Yakima, the regs on the Naches, the Little Naches and Rattlesnake Creek say no bait, and only barbless, single-hooked flies and lures may be used.

Tieton: A jump over to the White Pass highway puts you right next to the Tieton River. Depending on how much water they are dumping out of Rimrock Lake, the Tieton can be fit more for rafting than fishing. But the heavy water flow lasts only a few weeks and usually by mid-October the river drops into great fishing shape.

Highway 12 follows the river for miles and miles and with most of the adjacent lands being Forest Service, access to fishing holes is almost unlimited.

Above the small village of Rimrock Retreat (used to be called Trout Lodge), there are some very nice spots to work a topwater fly or a small spinner.

And below there, all the way down to where the Tieton meets the Naches, there are holes at almost every turn of the river. The same selective-gear rules are in effect on the Tieton.

Small-stream tactics: A friend of mine, Kevin Herald of Naches, is one of the best stream anglers I know. He uses a super-long, super-light spinning rod which he uses to work small lures in hole after hole on the Naches and Tieton with craftsman-like efficiency.

One of his favorite lures is a small F3 or F4 FlatFish. You can also use a Kwikfish. With a small split shot added just up the line, Herald will drop the little lure into an undercut in the bank or behind a big rock and just let it wiggle in the current. Fish just seem to appear out of nowhere to whack the small lure.

If the plug isn't working, he'll try a small spinner like an ⅛-ounce Rooster Tail or a Mepps. Again, he drops the spinner right into the hole and lets it work in the current until a fish hits.

With both the plug and spinners, Herald will try different colors, but most of the time he stay with the basics like black, brown, green or white.

You can have equal success off a fly rod on these streams. Another friend of mine will take his fly rod up the Tieton and without so much as a cast, will hook trout after trout. He likes to "walk" a small surface fly on top of the water, just flipping it out and letting the fly skim along the surface in the current. It is a blast to watch the trout splash after the fly that looks like it is swimming upstream.

On most of these streams, whether you are fishing flies or with spinning gear, long precision casts are just not needed. A flip here and a toss there is normally plenty to get you where you need to be.

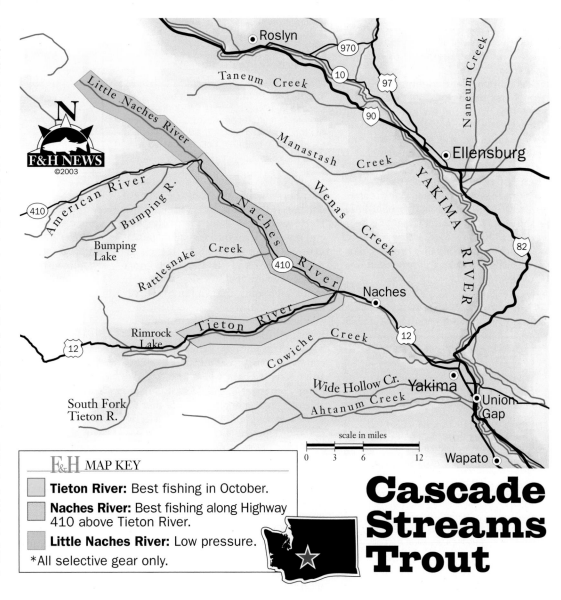

MAP KEY
Tieton River: Best fishing in October.
Naches River: Best fishing along Highway 410 above Tieton River.
Little Naches River: Low pressure.
*All selective gear only.

Cascade Streams Trout

Expect Kettle to start cooking early this year

by Dusty Routh

If you're one of the rare regulars who fishes the Kettle River a few times each summer, you're likely sitting back and waiting for it to drop into shape. That usually takes place around the first week or so of July, sometimes even later, after most of the snow up in Canada has melted off and sped on down the river.

But don't let the Kettle catch you napping this year.

Due to unseasonably warm weather hitting this region early, a smaller amount of spring rain than usual and a smaller snowpack up north than in most years, the Kettle will likely be ready to receive the trout faithful by as early as mid-June.

"It's running hard right now," Gary Dougherty of the Republic Sport Shop (509-775-3040) told us in mid-May. "But the water's pretty clear for this time of year. I called and checked with my source up in Curlew, and he agrees this year is definitely going to be different from last year. It will probably be fishable by the middle of June, which is pretty early. I'd say it's going to be a little high then, but the water should be clear enough to fish."

If you like throwing flies in wild country for wild rainbows and browns, this is your bell ringing.

Where to fish the Kettle: The Kettle River flows down out of Canada

THE KETTLE RIVER flows south out of Canada near where Toroda Creek dumps in (above). It features brown trout that routinely top the 4-pound mark all the way to where it ducks back into British Columbia at Danville.

AT a GLANCE

What: Earlier than usual action on Ferry County's Kettle River for scrappy rainbows and hidden browns.

When: While this river is usually high with snowmelt through June, expect it to be fishable by mid-June.

How: These trout love flies, including dry flies, hopper patterns and weighted nymphs fished deep.

Where: From the Canadian border south and east to Curlew, and then north again to the Canadian border.

Information: Gary Dougherty, Republic Sport Shop (509-775-3040).

into Ferry County west of the town of Curlew. It flows south and then east to Curlew, where it hangs a dogleg left and goes back up into Canada again at Danville along Highway 21. It then re-enters the U.S. to the east, near Laurier, where it flows almost directly south and joins the Columbia River near Kettle Falls.

Where's a good place to start your early-season trout quest?

"West of Curlew, where the river comes down from Canada," says Dougherty. "That's where you'll find a lot of slack water in that stretch. There's at least a dozen good holes from there to Curlew, with good road access. There's not much private property. You'll find some good spots to pull out and fish."

Even better, as the river moves north past Curlew and bends back into Canada, Dougherty says there's good fishing opportunities in this stretch, more so than in the run of river to the west of Curlew. But, "In order to fish that, you almost have to have a canoe, a boat, a raft, a belly boat," he advises. "There's private property and tough access. But if you can find a way to get

on the water, you can have some pretty good fishing. There are good opportunities and holes in that stretch, but there's really no way to access it without floating it."

Dougherty reports that you can camp at an unimproved dry camp 8½ miles north of Curlew near Lone Ranch Creek, which is just south of Danville.

"You can put in upriver and put a spare rig down there," Dougherty says.

From Lone Ranch Creek up to the Canadian border, Dougherty reports there are a couple of hot spots where you can wade in.

"You can walk in from the bank in a couple places, and there are some pretty fair holes to fish," he says. "That's the important part to finding fish in the Kettle. Find the holes."

A fine Kettle of fish: Most of the action on the Kettle is going to be for rainbows, particularly if you don't know the river well. The rainbows are spirited and cooperative, and fairly easy to convince with an assortment of standard trout flies ranging from beadhead nymphs to dries like Royal Wulffs and

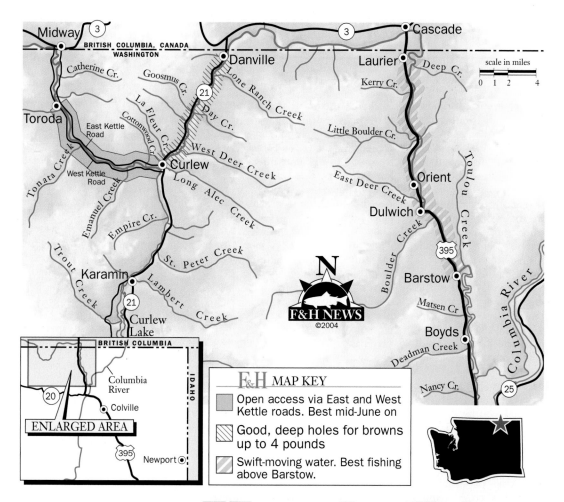

F&H NEWS ©2004

F&H MAP KEY

Open access via East and West Kettle roads. Best mid-June on

Good, deep holes for browns up to 4 pounds

Swift-moving water. Best fishing above Barstow.

Kettle River

Stimulators. Later in summer, hopper patterns are killer.

But for a greater challenge, spend some time targeting the Kettle's brown trout. These fish are legendary for their spooky prowess and ability to hide in the Kettle's obstructions — logs, rocks, grasses and deep pools.

"You won't see too many browns during the daytime," says Dougherty. "I think they're a nocturnal fish. But if you know where to look and how to catch them, you're in for a treat."

These browns can get big: up to 4 pounds or more. Fishing "deep" is the way to get to them. That is, fish with sinking lines in the deepest pools you can find, some of them bottoming out as much as 15 to 20 feet down.

"Muddler Minnows are the ticket," Dougherty reports. "Grizzly or yellow colors. You can also throw green, brown, or black Woolly Buggers. But you've got to fish them deep. These browns will go 3, 4, 5 pounds. And there's some browns in there that will scare you."

Most fly anglers never see them because they don't target them.

"Most people don't rig right for them," Dougherty confirms. "They'll run you to your backing and spool you. But you've got to nymph in deep pools in order to reach them. You've got to get down to where you can hook one of those big boys, down there in the deeper spots with brush, logs, and rocks. Sometimes you might find a brown out of shallower, faster water, but not very often."

Water an issue: Because of its location, the Kettle typically starts to run pretty skinny as summer wears on.

"Water really becomes an issue as early as the end of July," Dougherty explains. "It will start to flatten out and shallow up, depending on rain and how much snow is left in Canada. Normally, you aren't fishing until the first of July,

but this year it might be that it will be best from mid-June to mid-July. By August, it should be way down. You can fish it then, but you're really looking for the pools then in order to find fish."

Kettle docket: From the Barstow Bridge near Roosevelt on upstream, the Kettle is open June 1-Oct. 31 under selective gear. There's a two-fish daily limit, minimum size 12 inches.

Where to stay: Curlew Lake State Park has good facilities but they do not accept reservations, so it's first come, first serve. There's also Fisherman's Cove Resort on Curlew Lake (509-775-3641), and Black Beach Resort (509-775-3989). You can also try the Curlew Motel (509-779-4260) or the Curlew RV Park (509-779-4864). There are also good national forest campgrounds to the west of the Kettle.

Weather, water, hatch factors lead to hot Yak summer

ELLENSBURG

by Joel Shangle

These kinds of alignments of natural factors come along for the average blue-ribbon trout fly fishery about as often as a solar eclipse (which is to say *not very damn often*): light snowpack, minimal runoff, unseasonably low water flows and cooler-than-average summer temperatures. All of which contribute to strong hatches, easy wading and fabulous fishing.

Welcome to the Summer of 2001 on the Yakima River. You may not see this kind of cosmic alignment of water and weather again in years, so take advantage of it while you're still young enough to wade the boulder fields throughout the Canyon.

Summer slowdown: "What we're hearing is that flows between Ellensburg and Roza will be down to about 60 percent of normal this summer, so between 2,000 and 3,000 cubic feet per second," says Jack Mitchell at Evening Hatch Guide Service (509-962-5959). "The kind of conditions we're seeing right now are awesome. Usually we'll have water ripping through the Canyon so hard you'd be crazy to try to wade it. I'm a little concerned about what it's going to look like in September, but as long as it doesn't get too hot later this summer, we should have a pretty darn good fishery."

July on the Yak: A typical July on the Yakima involves fishing high, above Thorp to Cle Elum, but this year's low water will bring the lower Canyon into play more then usual. Hatches are normally lighter during the heat of the summer, occurring in the morning and evening, but if forecasts of overall cooler summertime temperatures prevail, look for hatches of Yellow Sally stonefly, summer stonefly, caddis, baetis and Drake (see fly box info below) from top to bottom.

Lower Canyon: Stretching from Wilson Creek/Ringer Road to Roza

UPPER CANYON rainbow for Brad Raymond of Bellevue, who tossed a golden stone nymph this spring to attract the 22-inch beauty. Look for July hatches of mayfly, stonefly, caddis and terrestrials from Ellensburg to Roza Dam.

Dam, the lower Canyon is loaded with two things: access and boulders. State Route 821 (Canyon Road) parallels the river from Ringer down, offering easy walk-to access to the water, but the lower river's boulder-garden composition makes it tough to wade, even in good low-water conditions.

"It's tough, tough wading because of the boulders," says Mitchell. "It's bad enough that you might consider knee pads. You have a streambed full of rocks — there are some areas that are relatively easy wading, with easy, flat bars, but generally it's slow going over boulders."

Still, the lower Canyon is attractive because of the wide-open access, and because of a proliferation of bugs.

"Boulders hold lots of bugs," says Mitchell. "There are also a lot of sculpin, a lot of feed down in those rocks. That's fishy stuff."

Best fishing is usually in the morning and evening, starting at the foot access area just below Ringer Road and extending down past Umtanum Creek and Squaw Creek to Roza.

Good float from Umtanum Creek to Roza.

Farmlands: From Wilson/Ringer upstream to the Diversion Dam in Thorp. Hatches are the same as the lower canyon, but wading access is

AT A GLANCE

What: Yakima River fly fishing.

Where: From Cle Elum to Roza Dam.

Why: Expect lower-than-average water flows and cooler temperatures this summer. Light snowpack and minimal runoff mean slower water in the Canyon. Cooler weather encourages bug hatches.

Species: Wild rainbows, cutthroat.

Regulations: Selective gear, catch-and-release, no bait.

Access: Open walk-to access via State Route 821 (Canyon Road) from Ringer Road to Roza. Access is spotty above that (private from Rinehart Park in Ellensburg to Ringer).

Hatches: Caddis, stonefly, terrestrials, baetis, Drake.

Info: Jack Mitchell, Evening Hatch Guide Service (509-962-5959); Steve Worley, Worley Bugger Fly Co. (509-962-2033); Red's Fly Shop (509-952-6043); Gary's Fly Shoppe (509-972-3880); Creekside Angling Co. (425-392-3800)

Web sites: Check out The Evening Hatch's site (<www.theeveninghatch.com>) or Worley Bugger Fly Co.'s (<www.worleybuggerflyco.com>) for exhaustive information on hatches, water conditions, links to water flows. Also, if you want to book a guide for a day, these guys are the ones to call.

much more limited. This is good drift boat territory, specifically from Rinehart Park in Ellensburg to Ringer.

"There are a lot more bars and braided channels up there than in the lower Canyon," says Mitchell. "There are some logjams and sweepers, but it's floatable assuming you're a good oarsman. Remember, things change. There's a lot of cottonwood in there that can fall into the river and change things up. You just have to be alert to conditions."

Those cottonwoods lining the bank contribute to excellent terrestrial fishing late in the summer.

"You have a lot of trees and a lot of terrestrials falling off them," says Mitchell. "It's still a little early for the terrestrial thing to really get going, but

it'll be picking up in August."

Upper Canyon: From the Thorp Diversion Dam up to Teanaway. This section of river is where many flyrodders spend the majority of their summer hours, drifting from the WDFW

access above the town of Teanaway, down to the Thorp bridge takeout below Swauk Creek.

Flatlands: Short stretch of water between Teanaway and Cle Elum, but good fishing in the middle of summer.

YAKIMA FLY BOX: *What do the guides carry in their fly boxes on the Yakima River? We asked Jack Mitchell to detail the river's summer hatches and give us some suggestions for patterns. Here's what he gave us:*
"In July, there's typically a lack of overall insect hatches, but if the summer's cooler than normal like they're predicting, we should have some good hatches."

Yellow mayfly: Fish a Pale Morning Dun (14-18) or a Pale Evening Dun (14-18).

Stonefly: Run a Yellow Sally (16) now, then switch to orange or yellow Stimulators (8) in late July when the summer stones come off.
"Sometimes they want to eat yellow, sometimes they want orange, tan or brown. Hard to predict, but carry a handful of different colors."

Caddis: Comes off in the evening. Tie on a tan, gray or peacock Elk Hair Caddis (12-18), X-Caddis (12-18), emergent sparkle pupae.

Baetis Hatch in the slower water above the canyon. Fish a grey Parachute Adams (20).

Drakes: These mayflies were prolific in June, Brown Drakes (10) will come on and off through the month.

Terrestrial: Not much terrestrial activity until August. Fish black ants (14-18), black beetles (12-20), yellow and cream hoppers when they start falling into the water.

Streamers: Always a good idea to pack along black, olive, grey, peacock Woolly Buggers, Zonkers, Muddler Minnows, Bunny Leeches, all in sizes 4 to 8. Smolt patterns are also worth a shot on the lower Canyon because of all the salmon smolt.

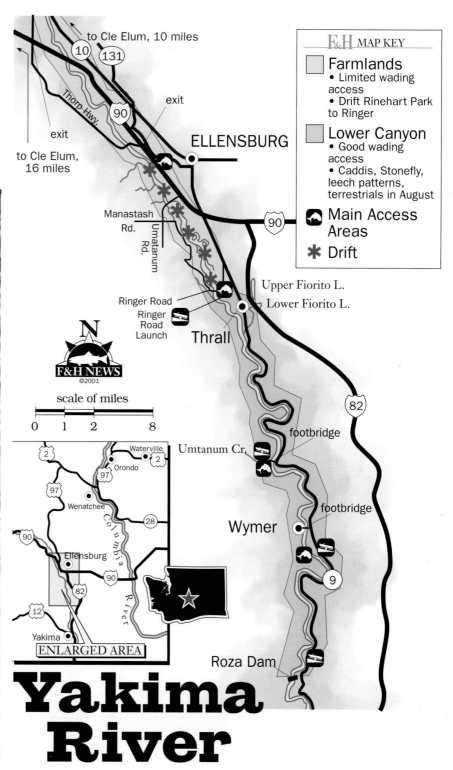

Yakima River

Columbia River Waters
BASS

Bass bite amping up in Tri-Cities area

by Pete Berry

With the longer days and warmer temperatures, the bass have really turned on in the Tri-Cities area. There have been a few tournaments recently that have produced outstanding numbers of fish, and there is no let up in sight for the next few months.

Anglers have a load of options to choose from during this time of the year, including the Yakima River, the Columbia River and the lower Snake River. Bass are feeding heavily and are very aggressive at this time. As the summer comes and goes, the bass will continue to be catchable as long as you adapt your techniques to the changing conditions.

ADJUST YOUR TECHNIQUE: There are opportunities all season long for the bank angler, as well as the boater. A number of different baits can be used depending on the situation. Grubs, crankbaits, live rubber jigs, spinnerbaits and topwater baits all have applications in certain settings or under certain conditions.

Topwater baits fished in the early morning or in the evening as the sun is setting can be a highly effective way to catch aggressive bass. Rebel Pop-Rs, Tiny Tor-P-Does, Zara Puppys and floating Rapalas are all excellent topwater baits.

When choosing a color for a bait fished on the surface, my only concern is whether it is white or black on the bottom. The bottom of the bait is the only thing the fish are going to see, and having white on the bottom of the bait during a bright day is not going to be the most effective. This is why white-bottomed baits work well in the low light conditions of early morning and evening.

It can be tough to find baits with black on the bottom, but there are paints available, and it can prolong the topwater bite for you if you have a few dark-colored baits in your box.

We came, we saw, we caught fish

SMALLMOUTH ACTION CONTINUES to be hot despite the Columbia River's cold water. With water temperatures still in the low 50s, smallmouth bass were still in a prespawn mode at the May 13 American Bass Association (ABA) Team tournament held out of Tri-Cities. Twenty-five limits were brought to the scales, with the winning weight taken by Lew Sprengel and Paul Nixon, who amassed an amazing 22.65 pounds of smallmouth (five fish). Their biggest smallie weighed 5.41 pounds.

ON THE SCENE

The heaviest bass live in the Hanford Reach, and they are now accessible as the water level is up. That is, *if* you know where the rocks are! The Reach is very dangerous to navigate and is not recommended for the inexperienced. But if you know how to get there in one piece, it is an amazing smallmouth fishery that gets little pressure, especially since water levels drop in the summer, making it inaccessible to normal bass boats.

If you don't know how to safely maneuver the Reach, don't feel slighted. Partner Bob Sweeney and I culled out a nice limit of smallies below Tri-Cities, proving that they are also on the bite outside the Reach. Our limit weighed 13.60, which was good for 11th place and a check. We were fishing a submerged railroad bed that topped off in 2 feet of water and had 5 to 6 feet of depth on the sides. We took nice keepers off of VPR-Pro white spinnerbaits, SnakeBite 4-inch MegaCurl grubs on Mojo Rigs (Marc's Green Envy color), Carolina-rigged Yamamoto Hula Grubs in color No. 176, and crankbaits as well. Start off fishing the top of the railroad beds and then work the sides and bottom as the sun comes up.

These Columbia smallmouth are heavy with eggs and are moving to the spawning beds now. Look for hard bottoms out of heavy current, especially into the mouths of sloughs off the main river. These fish are very aggressive first thing in the morning when hitting reaction baits, but after the sun is up pay close attention or you will miss the bite on soft plastics. For some reason these smallies are just ticking the bait; daydream and you just missed your chance.
— *Marc Marcantonio*

F&H NEWS bass columnist Marc Marcantonio with a pair of fat smallmouth pulled off of a submerged railroad bed below Tri-Cities. (**F&H News** photo by Marc Marcantonio)

STARTING IN THE YAK: The Yakima offers bank fishermen lots of opportunities, from the mouth up to the town of Benton City. Just about any place that you can get to the river, there are holes to fish and bass to catch.

My favorite baits for the Yakima are 3-inch Kalin grubs in dark colors such as smoke with red flake or pumpkin pepper.

If I want to cover more area, or fish some of the slower-moving water, I will throw a Luhr Jensen Speed Trap or a Floating Rapala. If there are no weeds in the hole you are fishing, a spinner can be very effective.

One of the most productive areas to fish is the stretch of river just below Horn Rapids Dam. Be careful to fish below the boundary signs because this rule is strictly enforced.

At the mouth of the Yakima River, anglers fishing from a boat can find action in some of the backwaters or around some of the islands between the main river channel and Bateman Island. Be careful in this area because the water can get really shallow really fast.

HITTING THE COLUMBIA: The Columbia is best fished from a boat, with the exception of a few spots around Paterson or Burbank. Boat anglers should spend their time around the Burbank Sloughs, the Hanford Reach or the mouth of the Yakima River. Crankbaits, jigs and 5-inch grubs make up the list of the most popular baits. Jigs tipped with pork trailers are excellent for fishing the edges of some of the deeper water that is adjacent to the weedbeds and flats where fish would generally move in to feed. If the fish are on the flats and feeding, ripping a crankbait will cover a lot of water in a short amount of time.

Casey Pond on the downriver side of the Burbank Peninsula is a great place to find largemouth bass hanging out off the edges of the grassy banks, and in some of the shallow backwaters. There are also some excellent submerged rockpiles in the middle that can be dangerous to run through in a boat, but are great places to crank a Luhr

STRATOS PROSTAFFER Stan Scott and partner Kalle Hyrkas, both from Tri-Cities area, show off a tournament-winning quad of smallies and largemouth taken in the Tri-Cities area in April.

Jensen Speed Trap over for smallmouth.

Bank fishermen can get access to some of the largemouth spots by walking in on the Burbank Peninsula, or they can find some good smallmouth fishing on the south end along the railroad riprap near Quarry Pond.

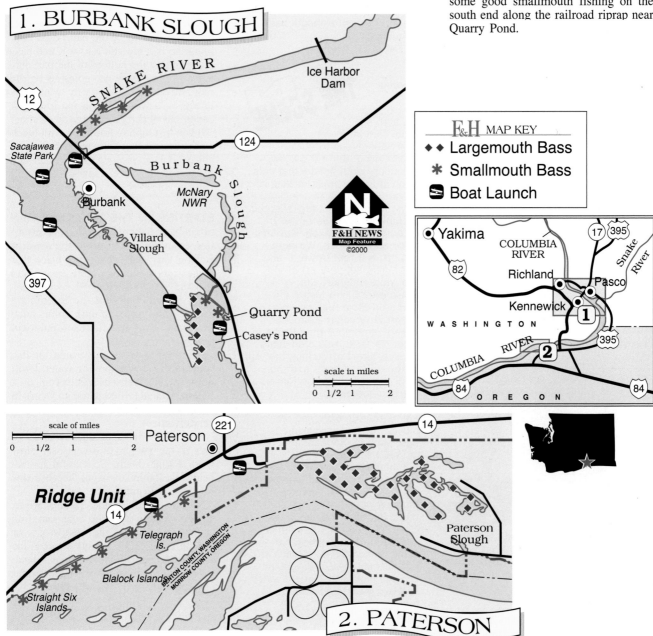

Horn Rapids offers unpressured bass, cats

by Jim Pearson

"Uncrowded Bliss" — that's what some would call it, but I call it Horn Rapids and so do the maps. It's a crooked section of the Yakima River downstream from Benton City, and a crooked river means slow waters and deep pools. That, my friend, also means catfish. But in the same area are riffles and rocky, brush-shaded shore-lines, and that means smallmouth.

And how would you like to fish it? From a boat? From the shore? Want to float it in a canoe, drift boat or rubber raft? All right, you can do any of those.

Want to camp 300 yards from your fishing spot in a park with acres of lawns, water and electrical hookups? No problem. You might even have the park to yourself because the place is undiscovered.

Drift away: Once you're settled into camp, take your watercraft up to Benton City and launch it off the gravel bar below the bridge. I keep two rods rigged when I do that, one for catfish, one for smallmouth. If I'm after whiskerfish, I anchor the boat above a deep hole and sink a two-hook setup on the bottom below the boat. The hooks are baited with worms, stew meat or fresh cut bait — sucker, preferably. If I don't get a bite right away, I pull anchor and it's down the river I go.

I can fish the riffles for smallmouth from the boat, but most of the time I stop and cast a spoon or a spinner. A black Vibric Rooster Tail with a silver blade is one of my favorites. A No. 4 Mepps Black Fury is also a favorite, but the truth is this: a smallmouth bass is a pugnacious fish that bites things when he isn't even hungry because he's a schoolyard bully without fists.

The drift will take you most of the day if you do much stopping, but the take-out is easy when you get back to camp. The ramp is good, and if you've got your polarized shades on, you will see lots of 2-inch smallmouth swimming across the top of the concrete slab.

Powered up: If it's a powerboat you have, launch and park in the middle of

FROM BANK OR BOAT, the Horn Rapids area of the lower Yakima offers bass and catfish. This 4½-pound smallie hit a surface plug there early in the morning.

the river out from the ramp. Drown a gob of nightcrawlers and you catch smallies or catfish on the same bait. But a word of warning: have a large enough anchor to hold your boat in the current and be sure the motor runs. Horn Rapids Dam is a ½-mile downstream. It's an irrigation conversion dam and it's only 3 or 4 feet high — probably not enough to kill you if you go over it. It probably won't even total out your boat, but what it will do is ruin your day.

Bank on it: If bank fishing is your game, you're in the right place. You can

do it two ways: from a lawn chair with the bait on the bottom, or patrolling the shoreline and casting. Either way is productive. In fact, I've seen a guy set his lawn chair up in the middle of the boat ramp and fish from there. Why not? More than likely, no one will be using the ramp anyway.

Bait and switch: If sedentary fishing is your game, the baits I've mentioned above work just fine. Some guys have a favorite catfish bait they like to bring along — shad preserved in some manner or another, hot dog chunks soaked in various types of nectar, salmon belly meat. The list goes on and on, but I'll still lay my money on fresh-cut sucker being best and stew meat being nearly as good. There are scrap-fish in that part of the river, of course, so sometimes you bring in a chisel-mouth, a squawfish (northern pikeminnow), or a bugle-mouth bass (also known as carp). As I drifted that part of the river one time, I watched a shore fisherman battle an obviously large fish. Just as he got it to shore, it broke off. The angler made a headlong dive into the river and came up with a carp that was in the 10-pound range. I hope it was tasty because he earned it.

The scrapfish are especially likely to hit worms. Do that with me and they're liable to wind up as fresh cutbait, something whiskerfish are especially fond of.

Bank patrol: If patrolling the bank is your thing, try downriver from the launch ramp. It's good all the way down to the dam that is a ½-mile from the launch. It's even better below the dam where you need to cross a footbridge to get to the river shore. Otherwise, an irrigation canal blocks your way. You will see an Indian dip-net platform built there, and the water is rocky and fairly shallow, but don't forget to cast under the weeds right by the shoreline. Feisty smallmouth lie in those places practically on the shore waiting to ambush their prey.

My favorite way to fish that kind of water is with a small surface plug early in the morning. If anything is more fun than catching smallmouth on surface plugs, I couldn't write about it on these pages. I have several surface plugs I use for smallmouth, but the only ones I know the names of are the Rapalas. I like a silver-sided one with a gray back, but it must have red on the bottom — not a lot of red, but red is a requirement. Bass fishing pro Bill Roberts told me that a long time ago, and he's right.

A fishing friend likes a Hula Popper. It has a big metal cup on the mouth and every time he twitches the rod, it goes "blurp." Bass love it.

If I have a good-looking smallmouth plug that doesn't have some red on the bottom, I paint some there. Whatever it is, throw it out there and let it lie, giving it a tug occasionally. If a bass swirls by it but doesn't strike, throw your plug back to the same spot and do the same thing. Pretty soon Mr. Bass gets mad and whacks it a good one. Let the fun begin!

Fly flinging: If fly fishing is your thing, you can do that. Local fly fishing guru Jack Luther drifted from Benton City to Horn Rapids a couple years ago and caught lots of bass. He used poppers — the cork-headed kind, and red and white seemed to be the preferred color.

I fly fish only if it's the best way to catch fish or if it's required on a particular water, so I'm still sticking with spin and baitcasting rigs in the Yakima.

Limits/regs: There is no limit on the number of smallmouth less than 12 inches, but you may keep only one over 17 inches and nothing between 12 and 17 may be kept. The powers that be wrote that in order to protect smolt from smallmouth predation. Does the slot limit mean bass longer than 12 inches don't have a taste for smolts? That regulation is ridiculous to the extreme.

Now for the good news: catfish regulations are simple and straightforward. There is no season or size limit of any kind. That's the way it should be for smallmouth too, at least in the Yakima River. It wouldn't damage the fishery at all.

Horn Rapids

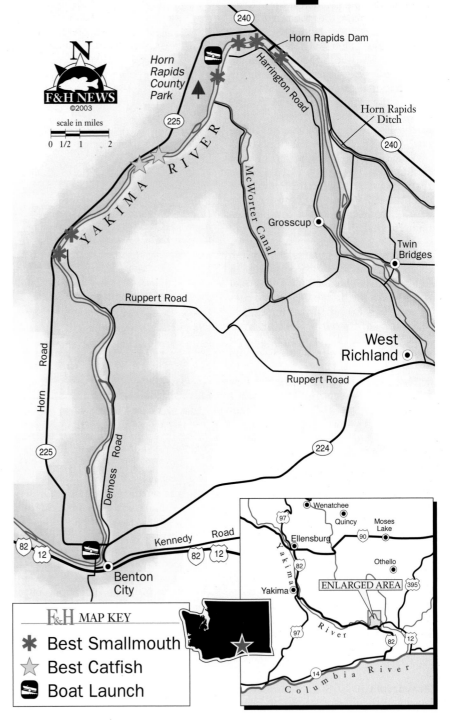

AT a GLANCE

What: Smallmouth bass and catfish.

Where: The Horn Rapids section of the Yakima River downriver from Benton City.

When: From now through October.

How: Drift it, still-fish it from an anchored boat, or cast from the shore. Use bait for catfish and smallmouth, or small surface plugs for bass.

Camping: Camp at Horn Rapids Park. Tent sites are $10. Campers with electrical and water hookup cost $20.

Information: Grumpy's South First Surplus (509-452-0868) in Yakima.

MAP KEY

✳ Best Smallmouth
★ Best Catfish
🚤 Boat Launch

McNary opportunity: bass, walleye, sturgeon, panfish

TRI-CITIES

by Pete Berry

The stretch of the Columbia below McNary Dam has a lot of different opportunities for the recreational and tournament angler. There are bass, walleye, sturgeon and panfish to be found here, and fishing can be red-hot if your timing is right. This area has something to offer throughout the year, but the primary season for catching all of the species mentioned above would have to be between April and August. Bass and walleye tournaments are regularly held in this area, and some of the tournament-record stringers for our region have come from here.

Walleye: The walleye revolution around the Tri-Cities started more than 20 years ago and has turned our area into one of the best walleye destinations in the country. The location that was first thought of as a walleye "hot spot" was just downriver from McNary Dam, adjacent to the Paterson Slough. This spot has produced on a consistent basis since it was found, and is still hot.

During the first part of spring, the preferred method is using a controlled drift to slowly present grubs tipped with nightcrawlers to prespawn walleyes. These fish are still a little lethargic, and they will be right on the bottom, so working your jig slowly is the key to success. Fish in 15 to 25 feet of water, and look for temperatures between 40 and 45 degrees. The drift just downriver from Plymouth State Park is excellent for early walleye action. You can also find quite a few fish in the Glade Creek area just downriver from the Ridge Unit HMU at Paterson.

When the weather heats up in June and July, the fish are starting to rebound from the spawn and are extremely aggressive. Drifting worm harnesses off a bottomwalker, or power trolling plugs is an excellent way to cover a lot of water. The goal of the angler when the fish are biting on a consistent basis is to present your bait to as many fish as possible, and these techniques are both good for this.

Look for fish to be a little shallower during the summer months, when you can usually find them from 8 to 20 feet deep. Fish in the same areas that you had success in during the early spring, but move in toward the bank a little to find the shallower shelves.

Sturgeon: Because it is so productive, sturgeon fishermen look forward to the McNary Dam fishery turning on every year. The best spots are found between the dam and the bridge. There are some huge fish in these holes, but they can be tricky to land when the flood gates are open because of the strong current. The fishing has been good since the first week in March this year and will continue through the end of the summer.

There are a few special items needed when planning on fishing this area for sturgeon: a heavy duty anchor with chain (one-half the length of your boat), a stout rod and reel with at least 250 yards of 40-pound test, and a variety of baits to offer these fish. Baits that I would not be without include pickled squid, Roll Mop herring, eel and salmon. These should be rigged on 8/0 to 10/0 barbless hooks, in pieces that

FAT LARGIES are the target of bass anglers working the edges and beaver huts throughout Paterson Slough.

are about the size of a thumb. Run the hook through the bait, and use elastic thread to attach the bait to the hook. A large Corky or two just above the hook will keep the hook from dulling on the rocky bottom.

The weight needs to be at least 8 ounces to hold on the bottom, and if the current is running fast you might need to go as high as 16 ounces. When casting, throw slightly upstream to give the weight an opportunity to hang up before getting behind the boat.

Another thing to keep in mind when trying to anchor is to not put your anchor above the deadline indicated on the bank just below the dam. The game department will issue tickets if you are caught above it, or if your anchor is above it.

To choose which spot to anchor, keep courtesy in mind and consider how close you want other anglers getting to you.

Most of the water in this stretch will hold sturgeon, but what I look for is a change in depth just off of the main current flow that goes from about 15 feet to 40 feet quickly. Being out of the main current is not necessary, but it can make it easier to anchor, and the fish don't have to work as hard to sit in areas like this. If you get too close to

AT A GLANCE

Where: McNary Tailrace.

Species: Walleye, sturgeon, smallmouth bass, largemouth bass, panfish.

Where: Fish between the dam deadline and highway bridge for sturgeon. For walleye, look downriver from Plymouth State Park, through the Ridge Unit, and along rocky break areas. For bass, work the edges of Paterson Slough or around the beaver huts.

When: Prime fishing for postspawn walleye starts in June. Bass fishing is good now and will continue through May.

Information: Critters Outdoor World (509-543-9663)

the bridge on the Washington side of the river, there is a cable near the bottom; it can cause problems with anchoring and with fighting large fish.

Bass: The bass fishing in this stretch is also well worth the trip. Paterson Slough is an excellent place to spend the afternoon casting plugs, grubs and spinnerbaits for largemouth or smallmouth. There are so many different ponds and backwaters in the slough that it would take a few days to cover all the water. If the water is down, not all of the areas will be accessible, but do pay attention to the structure that is exposed for future reference.

There are a lot of beavers in the Paterson area, and they have done some extensive construction in a lot of the backwaters. One of the best techniques when you find a beaver hut is rolling a spinnerbait down the side. This can be deadly on largemouth when the water first starts to warm up. The other thing to look for when fishing around beaver huts is the channels that are used by the beavers to get from spot to spot. They will be a foot or two deeper than the surrounding water, and these can be good spots to catch a big smallmouth loafing. Try fishing grubs and crankbaits in these channels.

Panfish: Panfish can be found in this stretch of the Columbia as well. Perch, crappie and even bluegill can be found in any of the slower-moving or still waters. The Ridge Unit HMU and any of the boat basins or launches are good places to find panfish.

Perch can be located by fishing with worms under a bobber, and then using mini-jigs tipped with smaller pieces of worm. If you are after crappies, target the deeper water around boat launches and fish mini-jigs without a bobber. There are also a few crappie spots that can only be accessed by foot. There are some old gravel pits and beaver ponds in the Paterson Slough that from time to time have large numbers of crappie in them.

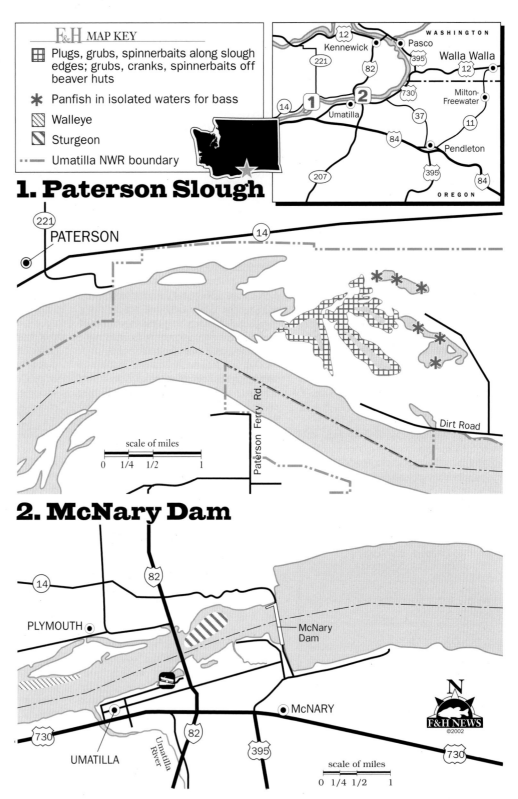

F&H MAP KEY

- Plugs, grubs, spinnerbaits along slough edges; grubs, cranks, spinnerbaits off beaver huts
- * Panfish in isolated waters for bass
- Walleye
- Sturgeon
- ·—··— Umatilla NWR boundary

1. Paterson Slough

2. McNary Dam

Okanogan River an undiscovered gem for smallies

— OMAK

by Dusty Routh

You don't hear a lot about it. It's not like the other famous smallmouth rivers in the state, places like the Snake River, the Columbia below McNary or The Dalles, or the Grande Ronde.

But if you're an admirer of what smallmouth bass represent, one of the greatest and most spirited of all the game fishes, and if you think their pale honey color in spring and their dark bronze and black vertical striping in summer are a natural wonder, you surely must have heard of the Okanogan River.

Some people say it might be the best smallmouth stream in Washington.

A long way out: The Okanogan has tons of bass. But as for getting press, glamour and the attendant pressure that often comes with that, this river has none of it.

The fact that the Okanogan is a long way from nowhere helps considerably. You don't just casually fish this river. First, you have to get there. Secondly, while bank access is available in places, this is a river made to be floated. If river angling in the Pacific Northwest has

RIVER SMALLIES are slowly but surely waking up in the Okanogan River. That's right, we said "Okanogan River." This piece of water represents some truly underfished bronzeback potential.

schooled us in anything, it's that water has to be cherry-picked. And that's best done by boat. So you either raft the Okanogan, sled it or drift boat it. You can also get a prop boat in from the mouth near Brewster up to about the town of Malott.

The lay of the land: The Okanogan flows south out of Osoyoos Lake near the Canadian border close to Oroville. Osoyoos, straddling the Canadian/U.S. border, is a massive lake that's considered a terrific warmwater bass destination in its own right. Late evening topwater fishing can be excellent here in the summer.

The river then flows south, following Highway 97 past Tonasket, where it then separates from the highway. It rejoins 97 near Riverside, and continues south through Omak, down past Okanogan and Malott. It then empties into Lake Pateros (the Columbia River) just east of Brewster.

The Okanogan is subject to swelling when ice and snow melts in the spring, particularly with water coming in from the Similkameen River up near

Oroville. May and June can often produce tumultuous, unfishable flows.

"The smallmouth fishing kicks off right after the water comes up from spring runoff," says Okanogan smallie sharpie John Truex. "When it comes back down, usually in June, you can start fishing."

Truex says he thinks the Okanogan is a world-class fishery.

"There's 6-pounders in there, but there's hardly any fishing pressure," he says. "People don't realize what's in there."

Where to fish: A lot of the locals like to fish the Okanogan from shore, plunking with everything from nightcrawlers to freshwater mussels. Prop boats can fish the lower river up to Malott, but above there it shallows up with lots of rock structure.

One good drift is to put in at the Omak Stampede Grounds and float down to the city of Omak or down to the town of Okanogan.

"That's about a 5- to 8-mile float," Truex says. You can also put in up near Riverside and float down to Omak.

There are hard falls between Tonasket and Riverside (about 4 miles above Riverside), so you need to launch below there.

Seasonal behaviors: Though they're prevalent in rivers, smallmouth are still a warmwater species. In winter they keg up in the deepest holes in the river, bunched together and lethargic, the size classes mixed, their metabolism and digestive systems slowed to a crawl. As spring comes on and water temps get into the 40s they begin to disperse and divide by size. The first to become active are the big females. That's why early fishing in June tends to produce not quantity but quality.

Most river fish begin prespawn feeding and related activity when water temps hit 45 to 50 degrees. This is when the fish feed more aggressively, as shallow parts of the river start to warm and forage becomes active. Spawning can happen anytime in the 50- to 55-degree slot. Catch-and-release fishing during this phase can be awesome.

AT a GLANCE

What: Superlative smallmouth fishing a long way from anywhere. Expect good action without a lot of company.

When: Right after spring runoff, usually starting up in mid-June.

Where: Boat the lower river from the mouth up to the bridge at Malott. Or float the upper river between Riverside and Omak or Okanogan.

How: Throw grubs, Rapala stickbaits, crankbaits, and Carolina-rigged finesse worms or drop-shot finesse worms.

Bonus fishery: The lower river near Pateros offers good walleye fishing.

Info: Cascade Outfitters (509-826-4148); WDFW fish biologist Art Viola (509-665-3337). For lodging, try the Ponderosa Motor Lodge (509-422-0400) in Omak.

Like largemouth, postspawn small-mouth get picky and sulky, requiring you to slow down your presentations and wait out big fish in likely areas. This is when drop-shotting finesse worms can pay huge dividends.

After spawning and runoff is done, usually by early July, the summer bite comes on and bass spend the rest of the season attacking everything that crosses their path. They will prowl the haunts of scattered chunk rock. They will feed down the sides of gravel bars. They will gravitate to the lee side of current seams to feed on freshwater mussels from the bottom.

On bigger rivers, like the Columbia and Okanogan, when the water warms up bass will often school and hunt in wolf packs using complex interdependent behaviors, corralling lesser baitfish into the shallows. Bassmen on the Columbia, for example, have seen vast schools of 2-pounders passing under their boats as they hunted.

Where to find them: Early in the season look to the bottom in deep holes for big fish. Backwater eddies with some depth are ideal. Ply these with crankbaits, suspending and diving stickbaits, leadhead jigs and grubs, and Carolina-rigged finesse worms. Fish slow and deliberately through June.

By early July, look for fish on gravel bars, on the insides of current seams, along cutbanks, in sloughs off the river and in back eddies. Drifting the river and throwing grubs to the banks is an ideal way to get into fish.

By July, after the river has settled into a summer pattern, you can throw just about anything in your tackle trays, including topwaters, flies, black Rooster Tails, grubs, stickbaits, cranks, spinnerbaits — smallmouth aren't choosy once the water warms up enough.

"Look for the deep holes," Truex advises "By June, the river is gin-clear. It gets to be a smallish stream. It's real slow and flat in the lower river, there's a lot of wasted water there. Fish up above in deep, rocky areas."

Regs: From the mouth of the river at Pateros up to the Highway 97 bridge at Malott, bass fishing is open year-round. From that bridge up to Osoyoos, season is June 1-Aug. 31. The area ¼ mile just below Zosel Dam at Osoyoos is closed to all fishing. Trout fishing is closed year-round on the entire river.

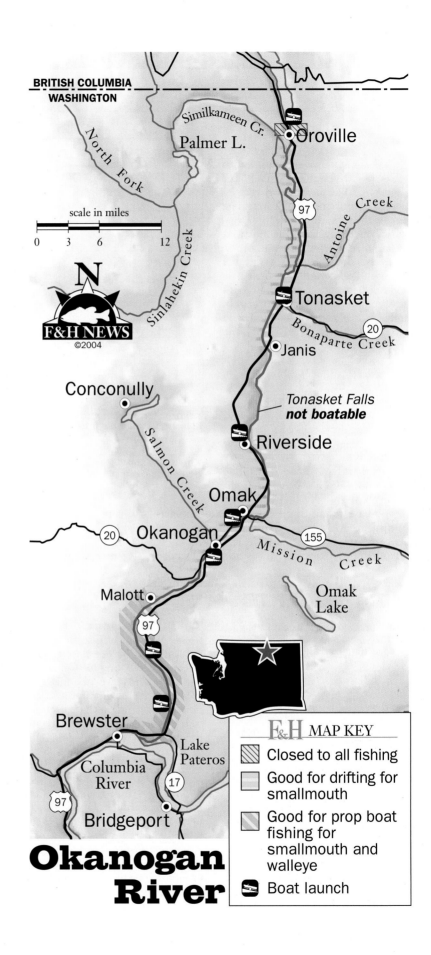

Okanogan River

F&H MAP KEY

- Closed to all fishing
- Good for drifting for smallmouth
- Good for prop boat fishing for smallmouth and walleye
- Boat launch

Time to fall in love: Priest Rapids smallies make anglers dizzy *by Jim Pearson*

YAKIMA

In the spring when the water begins to warm up, dedicated smallmouth fishermen head for the Priest Rapids pool because they know it's bronzeback time at Buckshot.

Asking a guy to choose one game fish as his favorite is unfair. It's like asking a guy to choose only one girlfriend and name her as his all-time favorite. Neither question is fair. But one time up in Oroville many years ago, a pretty girl asked me to take her riding in my Buick convertible. I declined because I was on my way to fish for smallmouth below Zosel's dam. I liked girls very much, but that afternoon I preferred smallmouth, and that love hasn't faded. I don't chase girls any more, but I still go after smallmouth — most of the time in the Columbia River.

The Columbia holds bronzebacks in selected areas from the Canadian border all the way down to Portland, but that's too big a map, so let's confine this discussion to the stretch between Priest Rapids and Wanapum dams. That's approximately 17 miles of river, but only selected spots are prime smallmouth water.

The action starts first at Buckshot because the water is more shallow and warms earlier. Two miles north of Desert Aire on Highway 243, you will see the WDFW signs. Sloughs and shallow back waters run north and south from the parking area. To explore them properly, you need hip boots or waders. And the farther you get away from the parking lot, the better the fishing.

TACTICS: I always start with a 1/6-ounce flame coachdog Rooster Tail, but a friend swears by the same lure in black with silver blade. Rubber grubs will work, too, but some scent is a big plus. One time Norm Lehmann and I had a thousand bites down there on unscented grubs, but they would spit the hook so fast we never took a fish. The next day, a guy was there with a shad-scented grub just nailing them. Several flavors of commercial scents would probably work, but I know shrimp juice does. The

LANDON ADAMS, Yakima, with a 3-pound smallmouth he took while fishing from the shore at Buckshot. Adams was using a Rooster Tail.

next time your wife makes a shrimp salad, save the juice and dip your rubber baits in them. It works.

Another gangbusters method at Buckshot is a nightcrawler. That's all — just a nightcrawler. You need a light spinning outfit because you're casting only the weight of the worm. The fish don't slam a worm the way they do spinners. The just glom on and move slowly away. I use fusion or braided line because it floats. As the crawler is drifting toward the bottom, I watch the line. Count slowly to five when you see the line moving out slowly, then set the hook and hang on.

Crawdads are excellent smallmouth bait — for that matter, they're excellent bait for a number of different game fish. Lenny Frasure told me that he turns over rocks in the Snake River

AT a GLANCE

What and where: Smallmouth bass on the Columbia River in the Priest Rapids pool.

When: Right now until the water gets cold. Sometimes it lasts until the middle of November.

How: Use bait or artificials. Smallmouth will slam a lure to defend a territory or suck in a worm because they're hungry.

while he's scuba diving in order to collect some crawdads for bait. He says smallmouth will crowd up to him almost touching his shoulders as they wait for a crawdad lunch. But, he says, the fish leave the big old grandaddy crawdads alone. Bass don't like to get pinched, I guess.

ACCESS: A boat launch is at the Buckshot parking lot, but be careful after you've launched. It's a wide channel leading out to the river. It's shallow all the way, especially if they're spilling water over Priest Rapids. Hug the left shoreline getting out to the main river, and then be careful even when you're in the river. It's easy to lose a prop. I know and that's why I run a jet pump.

After the fish have spawned, they move back out into the main river, but smallmouth are temperature sensitive. When you begin catching bronzebacks, check the water temperature. Then, as you move up and down the river, try to find water of that same temperature, or nearly so.

In June, Rollie Heiser, Tom Perry and I were above Buckshot on the east shore catching a few smallmouth, but only in one small area. I thought is was just a favorite area for the fish, but Tom pointed out that the temperature was warmer there than any other place we had been on the river that day. A small stream fed into the river and warmed the water up a few degrees. That's all it took.

I took the first two fish, but then the action stopped and we began changing lures. Tom switched to a broken-backed Rapala and started taking fish again. It was the one with a silver belly and a dark blue or black back. It didn't take Rollie and I long to follow suit.

Across the lake on the west side, the water stays colder later into the season. If the shoreline is rocky, it holds small-mouth. I troll along over there using the MinKota auto troll casting toward the shore — casting the same old stuff except I occasionally snap on a Mepps Black Fury. It's a deadly lure on all spiny rays and seems to be a favorite of walleye. I've taken a few of them in front of the site of an old railroad bridge, but they were all small.

Three other boat landings are on this stretch of river. One is at Desert Aire and it's a beauty, but it does have a $4 launch fee. Choose that site if you're going to fish south down to the dam. Again, the shallow, warmer water is on the east side of the river. The west shoreline is rockier and deeper.

Another launch is just below Wanapum Dam on the east side of the river. Another, unimproved launch is just above the

railroad bridge 2 miles south of the dam. Avoid the unimproved launch of it's a windy day, and remember, this stretch of river can get very windy. I've never been blown off, but I have scooted my hiney back over to the east side near the launches when the wind cranked up a bit. When it's whitecapping on the lake, it's usually fairly calm and easy to retrieve a boat at any of the three improved launches.

SIZE: Three quarters of a pound is

probably the average fish. A few are smaller, but some are a lot bigger. Harold Sutphen has a 7-pounder mounted and hanging on his wall. He caught it at Buckshot. And the state record was caught a few miles downriver near the White Bluffs.

So remember, when the frost is on the punkin, that's the time to stay by the fire or court girls if you're a young sprout who doesn't hunt ducks. But when the weather is hot and sultry, that's the time to go after bronzebacks at Buckshot.

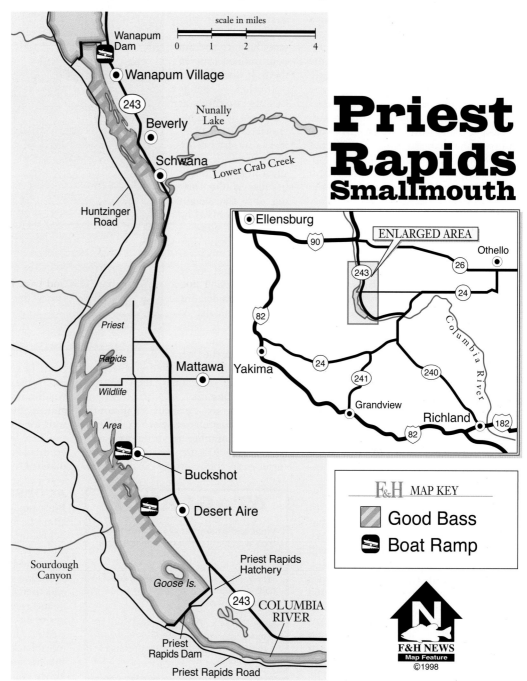

Priest Rapids Smallmouth

F&H MAP KEY

Good Bass
Boat Ramp

N
F&H NEWS
Map Feature
©1998

Potholes sand dunes bass a summertime blast

OTHELLO

by Dusty Routh

Pop-pop-pop. Then I let my topwater plug sit motionless. We could see the largemouth bass in clear, shallow water, his pectoral fins working hard to hold himself steady just beneath and to the side of the popper. The water was so clear I could follow his dark lateral line from his gills to his tail, an asphalt road against the deep green of the rest of his body. Our hearts were racing — mine, my guide Levi Meseberg's and I'm sure the heart of that bass as he considered whether or not to blast the plug that had just popped not 2 feet away from him.

When the stout largemouth finally moved, he seemed to turn away from the popper, but maybe it was just to get a better angle. Quicker than we could cuss he covered that 2 feet and inhaled the lure. Water sprayed everywhere. I didn't need to set the hook on him. He blasted it so hard it took us a few minutes with needlenose pliers to work the hooks out.

A fantastic 2-pounder, taken on topwater by sight fishing. Is anything better?

Poppin' Potholes: We'd left the dock at Mar Don Resort (509-346-2651) around 5 that evening. It was an unsea-

IT DOESN'T GET MUCH funner than sight fishing with topwater baits. Potholes sharpie Levi Meseberg with a typical 2-pound largemouth hooked while fishing the dunes.

AT a GLANCE

What: Hot summertime largemouth bite in the sand dunes section of Potholes Reservoir.

How: Toss weightless Senkos and tubes, spinnerbaits, and topwater chug baits and poppers anywhere you can find current from incoming channels, along solid sand banks and around the beaver huts.

When: Fishing will be good all summer; best topwater action is in August and September when water levels are down.

Launch: There are several launches on the south end of the lake off Highway 262 (Mar Don, Potholes State Park, Blythe, Lind) and on the east side off M SE (Medicare).

Supplies, guides: Mar Don Resort (509-346-2651)

sonably cool afternoon, in the mid-70s, not a cloud and not a breath of wind. Firing uplake in Meseberg's Alumaweld Intruder, it didn't take us long before we'd left the main lake and were snaking our way through the equivalent of one of the Pacific Northwest's only real bayous — the scattered water of the sand dunes section of Potholes Reservoir.

We made our way up Center Channel and into the dunes. Meseberg grew up on the lake, fishing it since he was 3, so he has little difficulty negotiating the sandbars and shallows of the waterway. A former minor league ballplayer in the Tampa Bay Devil Rays farm system, Meseberg is casual, relaxing to be around and a helluva lot of fun to fish with.

Also, he knows where big bass are.

Lay of the land: Potholes is an irrigation reservoir, so water level is one of the key ingredients to understanding fish behavior. During our trip in late June the water was still up high enough to make almost all of the sand dunes section accessible. Even with high water, however, a jet boat makes getting around a whole lot easier than a prop boat. Meseberg also runs an airboat when the

water's low, giving the illusion that you're bass fishing Florida's Miami Canal rather than an irrigation reservoir in the Columbia Basin.

This lake's upper portion is fed by water coming in via three main channels — the Winchester Wasteway to the west, Center Channel in the middle and Crab Creek to the east. In between are sand islands, sandbars, canals, creeks, deep bowlish holes and shallow flats.

Dunes bass: We'd come because of the sand dunes' propensity to hold large numbers of largemouth. Potholes has an excellent smallmouth fishery, but most of that takes place in the main portion of the lake. Up in the warm shallows of the dunes, you'll find tons of strong, aggressive fish that hit eagerly.

We made our way west and started throwing weightless Senkos in areas where there was incoming current from Winchester. Anywhere you find current you'll find bass, and anywhere you find deep sand banks that provide the largemouth with handy ambush points, you'll find bass. It didn't take us long to connect with our first three fish.

As the sun started to slide a bit, we made our way into the middle of the dunes, out of the channels and in amongst the countless little stillwater canals and flats. This is where having an experienced guide like Meseberg comes in handy. Once you're into these areas, you can get turned around a bit, but more so what you're looking for are beaver huts to fish. Because of the huge population of beavers, there are some dandy huts. If you know where they are, you'll catch a lot of fish.

Beaver bass: Meseberg has these beaver huts down cold. He knows where they are, how big they are (many of them are underwater) and where the entrances are. This is important because the huts provide great structure, and baitfish tend to gravitate toward the huts to feed. This in turn brings in the bass.

The best way to work the huts is to throw topwaters and spinnerbaits from a distance, working all areas around the hut. Then, skulk up with your electric motor to within pitching distance and toss a weightless Senko or tube bait. Sometimes the water around the huts seems way too shallow to hold fish, but not so. My biggest fish was in less than a foot of water. Rig your plastic so it's weedless, and throw it into the thickest cover all around the hut.

"If you can throw over a limb or a stick and dance that tube up and down like a puppet, that's one of the best ways to get hit," Meseberg pointed out. And he was right. We caught fish after fish around each hut that we fished.

We also hit fish along solid banks in the area. In such swampy water, if you can find a solid sand bank, especially a solid sand bank loaded with small willows, you'll find bass. These are awesome areas for topwater fishing. Bring a fly rod with an assortment of saltwater-sized poppers for some real sport.

As the sun started to go down, the fishing hit an incredible zenith. I caught five largemouth off one solid bank, all on a chugger. Meseberg hit fish after fish with his weightless tube. Our fish weighed in between 1½ pounds and 3 pounds, nothing huge, but I missed a fish in shallow water off a beaver hut that felt a whole lot bigger.

Summer bite: August and early September can provide some of the best topwater fishing of the whole year, when water levels are low and fish are accessible in shallow water. October can also be a great month as the fish go on the feed in preparation for wintering.

Just remember that Potholes is a popular spot in the summer. As with all of Washington's good fishing lakes, if you can fish it during the week, you'll encounter fewer folks. We fished on a Sunday from 5 p.m. to past dark and had the place almost all to ourselves. Also make sure to bring bug spray.

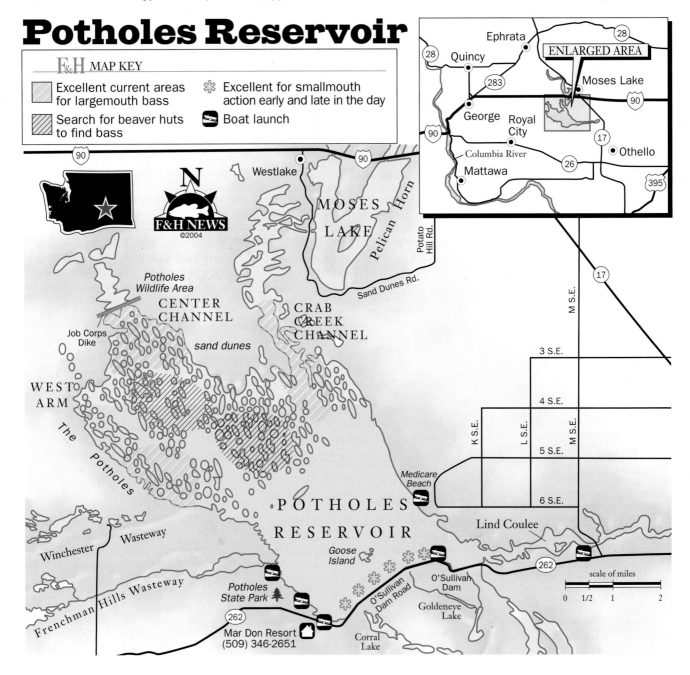

Potholes Reservoir

F&H MAP KEY

- Excellent current areas for largemouth bass
- Search for beaver huts to find bass
- ✳ Excellent for smallmouth action early and late in the day
- Boat launch

Target aggressive smallmouth now at Riffe Lake

————————————————————————————————— **KOSMOS**

by Tim Deaver

Smallies at Riffe Lake are just hitting prespawn and should be on their beds by the first week in May. Get over to the big Cowlitz River impoundment for some fast and furious action.

Where and how, east end: For those of you who are not familiar with Riffe's smallmouth fishery, you'll probably want to start on the east end of the lake at Kosmos Boat Ramp, just off Highway 12 and 3 miles past Morton. The Kosmos area is where 90 percent of the smallmouth fishing takes place, and it has the only real boat launch on the east end. This boat ramp gives access to two prime flats: one on the south side, straight across from the boat launch, and one on the north shore, located at the boat ramp itself.

Traditionally, the south flat has had better fishing than the north, but

SMALLMOUTH BASS like this 2-plus-pound bronzeback are readily available on Riffe's east end, where anglers should endure afternoon wind and chop to target fish feeding actively on stirred-up baitfish.

requires a larger boat to fish it — I would say 16 feet or better due to strong winds and heavy waves, which are almost certain to come up in the afternoon. The good news is that when these waves hit, they churn up the flat, mixing up the baitfish and putting the smallies on the feed.

Although it might be a pain keeping your boat in place, hanging in there and fishing during this heavy wave action should be worth your while.

For lure selection, stick with plastics like Kalin 5-inch grubs in nightcrawler brown, amber hologram and midnight black. Fish these with ⅛- to ½-ounce leadheads, depending on the wind. Also, try reapers and finesse lizards on a Carolina rig with ¼- to ½-ounce brass-and-glass setups.

When fishing the north flat, your lure selection will be a little different since the cover you're fishing there is totally different than that on the south side. The north side is loaded with heavy grass and weeds, so you'll want to fish extremely weedless. Try 4-inch Yamamoto Senkos with no weight and rig them with a 1/0 wide-gap hook. Or fish small 4-inch ringworms in black and purple, rigged Texas style with

about a ¹⁄₁₆-ounce weight. Also, try ¼-ounce white and chartreuse spinner-baits, and don't be surprised if you hit a few largemouth while you're at it.

Where and how, west end: While the east end is where most smallie fishing takes place, it's definitely not the best. Although the bass are a little tougher to find, the west end of Riffe offers good fishing and easy access through the town of Mossyrock. Concentrate your efforts around the Swofford Pond Spillway and the massive flat that surrounds it. Also, hit one of the many creek channels that can be found on both sides of the reservoir.

When looking for smallies on the west end, I like to start with crankbaits. I like a Bill Norman Deep N in crawfish or minnow finish, a bait which allows me to cover a lot of water in a hurry and helps me find good concentrations of smallies. Once I hit a fish or two, I will slow down my technique and finesse fish plastics and grubs.

Riffe's silver lining: Riffe Lake also offers excellent fishing for landlocked silver salmon and Kamloops rainbow trout. Bank anglers should fish the Mossyrock Dam area, both from the Highway 12 and the Mossyrock sides of the dam. Typical rigging should consist of a medium-action spinning outfit and no heavier than 6-pound monofilament. Fish a No. 6 baitholder hook with half a night-crawler, tipped with a piece of white corn, chartreuse Power Bait or a piece of cocktail shrimp under a slip float. The slip float is a must, because these fish can change depth rather quickly. You may start at around 3 feet early in the morning and be as deep as 15 feet by midafternoon.

The dam's silver and rainbow fishery should hold out until late May, at which time anglers should move up to the east end of the lake and fish from

AT A GLANCE

What: Riffe Lake smallmouth and largemouth bass, landlocked coho, rainbow trout, crappie and perch.

When: Smallies are in prespawn mode into May. Best fishing for rainbows and silvers starts in early May and continues into June.

Where: The east end of Riffe is where the majority of the smallie fishing takes place, but there are good smallmouth haunts on the west end as well. Bank anglers can hit silvers and rainbows near Mossyrock Dam and the Kosmos end. Perch are available throughout the lake. Look for crappie in weedy creek channels.

Tactics: Fish crankbaits, grubs and spinnerbaits for smallies. For silvers, toss baits such as nightcrawlers, Power Bait and cocktail shrimp. Perch will hit nightcrawlers. Fish jigs for crappie.

Information: Bob's Sporting Goods (360-425-3870)

the Kosmos boat ramp up to the fishing bridge about 2 miles east of the ramp. Fishing will start out sporadically with nice limits of silvers and rainbows in June, and eventually give way to monstrous catches of silvers that will get up to 20 inches by late July. Boat anglers will want to follow the same migrating pattern but will want to run very different gear. Typical boat gear should consist of flashlight gang trollers followed by a Kokanee Killer or a Wedding Ring spinner tipped with nightcrawler and white corn. Also try running small spinners and spoons such as $\frac{1}{16}$-ounce Bang Tails and $\frac{1}{8}$-ounce Hum Dingers behind gang trolls. When fishing these setups, it's important to note that there aren't any kokanee in Riffe, so rubber

snubbers will not be needed. Also, if you don't have a downrigger, you may want to invest in some color coded triple fish monofilament. This line is color coded every 10 feet so keeping track of your water depth is a snap.

Panfish options: Riffe also has some excellent panfish opportunity. Perch up to 12 inches are very common on the east end around Kosmos boat ramp, starting in late May. Fish off the bank using a 1-ounce sliding sinker with about a 2-foot leader and a No. 4 long-shank baitkeeper hook tipped with a whole nightcrawler on the bottom. This is very productive at night and it's not uncommon to get some nice catfish along the way.

Crappie are also taken on Riffe, although not as readily. One reason is that you have to have a fairly large boat and have to be willing to travel up and down the reservoir looking for dead-end creek channels with stumps and logs. Also, because Riffe is a fairly cold reservoir, the crappie sometimes don't spawn until July. The good news is that if you find them, they usually have lots of buddies and 100-fish days are not unheard of. Also, they are some of the biggest crappies anywhere on the Westside, with fish running into the 1-pound range.

Use 4-pound mono and some $\frac{1}{16}$-ounce black, yellow and white Marabou jigs tipped with a Berkley Crappie Nibblet and fished under a slip float at around 3 to 8 feet for crappie.

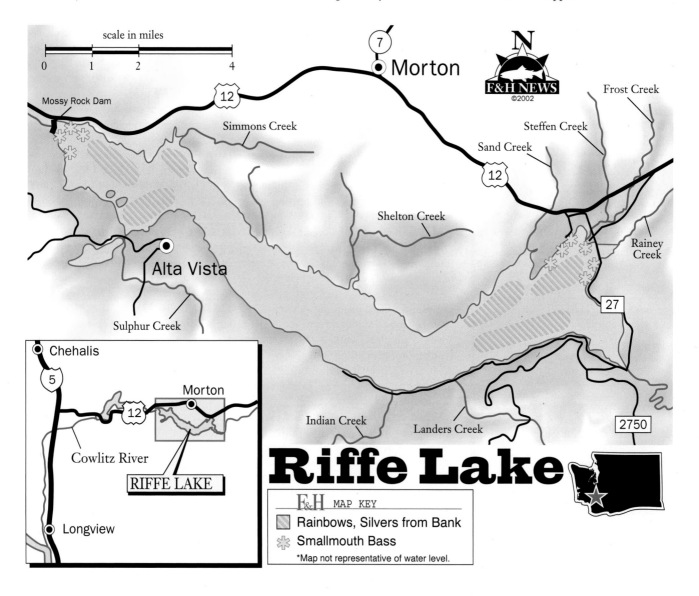

Riffe Lake

F&H MAP KEY

Rainbows, Silvers from Bank

Smallmouth Bass

*Map not representative of water level.

Spring stimulates Silver Lake hawgs

CASTLE ROCK

by Joel Shangle

GUIDE ROGER LUCE stuck this big pig in April on Silver Lake. The fish weighed in at over 9 pounds, indicative of the lake's big fish potential.

This much we know for sure: The Evergreen State's next record largemouth bass lurks in 3 feet of water somewhere. She's a big, old sow, grown huge on a steady food supply, laden with eggs and rendered super aggressive by an approaching spawn. She probably lives in southwest Washington. To be precise, she probably lives in Silver Lake.

"One of the primary choices for the next state record is definitely Silver Lake," says Tim Deaver at Bob's Sporting Goods (360-425-3870). "It's a powerhouse fishery for big fish. If I were to say one thing about Silver Lake, it's that 'I guarantee that it outproduces any other lake in the state for big pigs.'"

Strong words about a fishery that teetered on the brink of extinction three years ago, but Deaver grew up tossing baits into this Cowlitz County hawg factory. He fished it during its "glory years," when double-digit largemouth days were common. He saw it during the dam breach that sucked a lot of water out of the lake and seriously jeopardized both the fish population and their habitat. He knows every square inch of shallow, stained water on the lake, and fishes it religiously 10 months of the year (the other two being occupied by an obsession for duck and goose hunting).

Three years removed from near death, Silver is (in Deaver's words) "second to none for big fish."

"I don't think the dam break hurt the fishery as much as we were afraid it would," he says. "It definitely affected it, though. It's not a spot where you can guarantee a monstrous day. It's not like the old days where two guys could go up there and catch 20 fish, with a lot of 2-pounders. But a guy can still go up there and hit three fish in a day up to 7, 8 pounds. Those big fish are still in there."

March madness: The serious big fish hunting has already started on Silver Lake as gradually warming waters begin to stimulate sporadic spurts of activity in the lake's winterbound bucketmouths. That trend will continue in an off-and-on fashion through March and part of April as weather patterns run from cold to warm to rainy to clear and fish shade closer and closer to the spawn.

"Basically what you have now is skim ice around the edges and on the marshes in the morning, with it heating up by afternoon," says Deaver. "You'll have these southern winds come in and push temperatures up just a little, and it doesn't take much. These fish are used to such cold water in the winter, they'll come up when it warms up a couple of degrees. Any good warming trend will trigger a bite for a couple of days — those fish are laying there in the shadows, and when the sun starts hitting them, they start to get active. It'll be like that for the next couple of months."

Flipping jig-n-pigs to wood and weed cover is the go-to method this month, and Silver has this kind of cover in abundance. The entire perimeter of the lake is dotted with pilings, buckbean (celery) stands, submerged stumps and layover tree structure that reek of largemouth.

"It's a flipping show in March, where you want to fish a jig-n-pig," Deaver says. "There's a ton of wood in the form of dead willows and pilings, and there are more damn Christmas trees out in that lake than you'd believe. Everybody has their secret Christmas tree spot."

The spring topwater bite will also crank up in March (Deaver has caught fish on topwater as early as late February), and it would behoove you to have a Rebel Frog Wee R or some other kind of Kermit imitator in your tackle box.

"Never in my life have I seen this many frogs on the lake," says Deaver. "If you're talking to me on the phone at night, I swear you can hear the damn things. I think there's going to be an outstanding frog bite. We can't have that many frogs in the lake and not have it have some kind of affect on the bite. You can bet that I'll be flipping some jig-n-pigs in green and fishing a lot of Rebel Frog Wee Rs with a size 4 hook with a little meat on it to hold those big pigs."

April action: The fishing on Silver will go from good to mediocre through April, coinciding with high and low pressure systems moving through the area.

"The basic routine is that we'll have warm lows and high pressure cold fronts that'll shut things down for a couple of days at a time until the spawn," says Deaver. "Everybody has this misconception that you want a clear, calm day, but those clear days are crap for fishing. You want it raining and warm, maybe 60 to 65 degrees, moving from high pressure to low pressure. Those are always big paydays for big fish."

Flip Gitzits under docks as they heat up in April, and fan cast shallow divers around submerged wood and along pad field faces. Deaver likes a Norman Deep N; he'll throw it in 4 feet of water, crank down until it hits the mud or bounces off wood, and let it float to the surface. "They'll hit it on the suspend," he says. "I like to bounce it off a stump, let it

come up a little, jerk, and they inhale it."

Deaver will also fish tube baits loaded with BBs and scented with Smelly Jelly, and various combos of plastics, cranks and topwaters until he finds something that attracts a regular bite.

"This lake isn't deep enough for fish to go from a deep pattern to a shallow pattern, so there's no one routine that works for everybody year after year," says Deaver. "You have to try different things, especially now, after the dam breach. You

have to fish different vegetation, different techniques. You have to look at stuff you wouldn't look at, say, five years ago."

May-hem: The spawning cycle will go into June, but most fish will spawn in May, when the weather evens out. Fish outside edges of pad fields for prespawn fish, and inside edges for spawners. "These fish spawn in layers, some up until June, but the biggest spawn is in May," says Deaver.

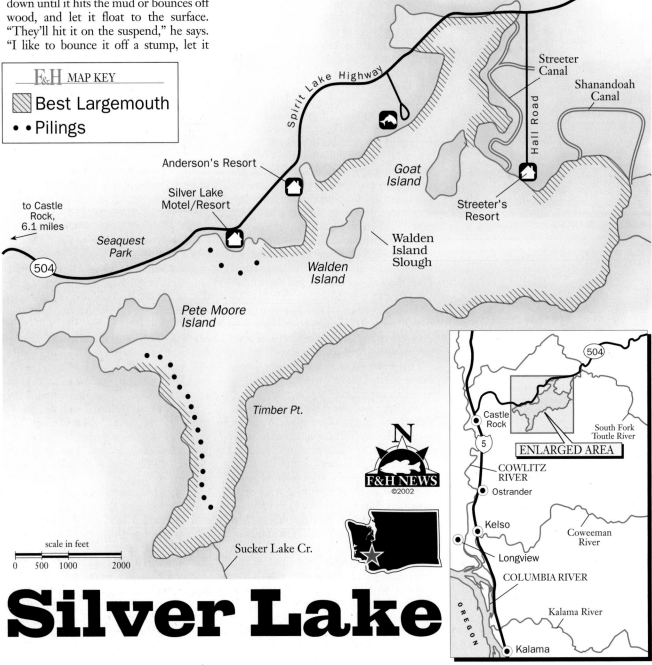

F&H MAP KEY

▨ Best Largemouth

•• Pilings

Spirit Lake Highway

Streeter Canal

Shanandoah Canal

Hall Road

Anderson's Resort

Silver Lake Motel/Resort

Goat Island

Streeter's Resort

to Castle Rock, 6.1 miles

Seaquest Park

504

Walden Island Slough

Walden Island

Pete Moore Island

Timber Pt.

N

F&H NEWS
©2002

504

Castle Rock

5

ENLARGED AREA

South Fork Toutle River

COWLITZ RIVER

Ostrander

Kelso

Coweeman River

Longview

COLUMBIA RIVER

OREGON

Kalama River

Kalama

scale in feet

0   500   1000   2000

Sucker Lake Cr.

Silver Lake

Wail on winter Wanapum walleye, smallmouth

BEVERLY

by Dusty Routh

The Columbia River from McNary Dam on down get tons of publicity for solid walleye and smallmouth bass action. The winter walleye fishery, especially, from McNary downstream past Portland, gets great press. But the lesser-known parts of the upper river can offer amazing fishing too.

One such area is around Vantage, from just below Wanapum Dam upstream to Rock Island Dam. Baking hot summers and hot water temperatures make this area a boater's and skier's zoo in the summertime, and the bar at Crescent is a great place to see all the new styles of bikinis. But come winter, all the Mastercrafts and Jet Skis have vanished, and you're left with tons of some of the best walleye and smallmouth water anywhere.

Late-season smallies: Leave your topwater baits and spinnerbaits at home. Come the November-to-March period, Wanapum's smallmouth will be holding deep on rock structure. You'll need Yamamoto and

AUTHOR DUSTY ROUTH lips a pair of the Wanapum Pool's deep-water denizens. The winter months offer excellent deep-structure fishing for smallmouth, and good bottom-bouncing for walleye.

Kalin grubs on ½-ounce football head jigs, deep-running crankbaits like Luhr Jensen Hot Lips Expresses (in silver/black, fire tiger and crawdad colors), Lucky Craft Pointer 100s (which are deep-running, suspending minnow imitations) in holographic color, and Lucky Craft's Pro-Tune Series LVR D-7s and LVR D-10s (which are Rat-L-Trap-type deep-running baits).

The smallmouth will range from 15 to 40 feet deep. The best spots will be along rock walls that aren't too deep, broken rock sticking up out of the water, rock points and along the rock riprap of the I-90 bridge. If you haven't picked up on it yet, the smallmouth are where the rocks are. There are a lot of sandy flats and shoals in the Wanapum Pool, and while these can be excellent for walleye at night, they are devoid of bass this time of year.

From the boat launch at Wanapum State Park, a good place to start is about a ½ mile downriver. You'll find a series of sandy points and bluffs, then you'll spot the first of several rock walls, points and broken rock scattered around just off the shoreline. The adjoining water will be deep, up

to 40 feet, but there are ledges running as shallow as 15 feet right along the shore. Drop a jig or a Lucky Craft Pointer or run a Pro-Tune, and you'll hit fish.

After that area, head straight across to the eastern shore, and fish your way upriver, working all the broken rock in this area. You'll find broken rock in shallow water that drops off quickly to as deep as 60 feet on this side. It's along these steep edges that the fish are holding, in classic winter pattern.

After that, work both the south and north sides of the rock riprap along I-90. It's noisy, but there's fish to be had. We took four big smallmouth in the same place, right off the southwest point just under the bridge.

Smallie jigsters and spoonsters: Wanapum is an excellent, excellent place to jig a Yamamoto or Kalin jig. The hot colors seem to be brown (176 color for Yamamotos) and root beer. Smoke-and-pepper is also good. Rig these on ½-ounce football jigs. The football shape seems to help reduce getting hung up in the rocks.

Lower your jig right to the bottom, and slowly — very slowly — bump it along. It helps to put your trolling motor on the lowest speed you can and just kind of bump-n-jump the jig along. You don't have to jig it up. Smallmouth are accustomed to sucking up forage right off the bottom. So stay in constant contact with the bottom. You'll feel your jig fall down between big rocks on the bottom. Adjust the length of your line as you work the jig up and down the rocks. In fact, if you're doing it right, you will be making almost constant adjustments to stay in contact with the bottom.

When a smallmouth picks up your jig, all you'll feel is a stop or a hesitation, almost like you've hung up. We found that most hook-sets are through the upper portion of their mouths, probably meaning they're sucking it in and closing their mouths, but not swimming off with it.

On windy days when it's harder to stay on the bottom, try jigging a spoon. Southern bass anglers swear by

AT a GLANCE

What: Smallmouth and walleye on the Columbia near Vantage.

Where: From just below Wanapum Dam upstream to Rock Island Dam.

Why: While the Columbia's lower river is well known and acclaimed by word and print, stretches of the middle and upper river are incredibly productive fisheries as well.

When: November through March, while not the most comfortable months for anglers, can produce both smallies and walleye for anglers who work the pool right.

How: For smallies, fish deep with grubs and deep-running cranks and spoons. For walleye, work humps and wind dams with blade baits and jigs.

Info: Chinook Sporting Goods (509-452-8205) in Selah; Grumpy's S. First Surplus (509-452-0868) in Yakima.

spoons for winter smallmouth, but here out West not too many guys fish them. Yet, they can be incredibly effective. A Johnson weedless spoon in chrome or gold or a Cabela's Weedless Lunker spoon will work, as will most any Hopkins or Kastmaster spoons.

For more on winter spoon fishing techniques, see Marc Marcantonio's Feb. 27-March 13, 2003, column (p. 18).

Walleye too: Wanapum's not as famous as Hermiston or The Dalles for walleye, but it's got 'em. There are plenty of 30- to 40-foot-deep channels and troughs along the west side of Wanapum above the dam, right out of the boat launch. Troll a worm harness and bottom bouncer in a Z-pattern up and down this long trough and you'll hit an 'eye or two.

You'll need to rig four rods for fishing this walleye water: one with a bottom bouncer and worm harness; one with a Whistler jig and a plastic or nightcrawler; one with a blade bait; and one with a plug, such as a Rapala SR Shad Rap, Wiggle Wart or Hot Shot.

Mike Davis, a regional walleye semi-pro walleye tourney angler, also likes the area below Wanapum Dam.

"Wanapum is a cool place," he informs *F&H News*. "We used to fish it mainly in the winter. I never killed them, but we caught fish. I went to college at Central, and my barber in Ellensburg used to hammer them in March."

Davis says the hot spot below the dam is the counter-current right at the boat launch, using blade baits and heavy Whistler jigs.

"Just go around in circles and vary your depth," he says. "The fish can be as deep as 50 feet or shallow near the riprap along the face of the dam. There is

also a point where the two currents meet. This spot is best in the winter at night."

Davis also warns about launching below the dam.

"It can be a very interesting launch," he says. "It's a very, very steep launch with limited dock space, You might want to bring hip waders with felt or spiked soles, and bring a long rope to launch and load. It can be very slick when they drop the water."

Fish humps, wing dams: Davis adds that there is a hump right in the middle of the river just below the dam.

"Look for the water shooting out from the dog leg in the dam, and go back and forth until you find it," he points out. "It's pretty easy to find. Pull silver spinners (worm harnesses) on either side from the deadline, and go down until it shallows way up. Be sure and pull some plugs back up."

The wing dam area is also a hot spot below Wanapum.

"The wing dam on the west side can hold fish at times," Davis confirms. "The west side about a ¼ mile down from the dam also holds fish. Look for the basalt along the shore and fish the current edge in the trench. There's a nice spinner drift just above the bridge on the east side. Look for the inlet and fish the current break."

Caution, caution! Davis is an experienced and capable boatsman, but the water below Wanapum Dam deserves respect.

"Be very careful getting around below the dam!" he warns. "The river shoals up all over the place in the middle and east side. The best way to go to the west side is run straight across from the launch. Putt over the shallow shoal just below the wing dam to the west side, and get in the trench. It'll be a steady 4 to 5 feet deep across the shoal. Once you're down about a mile or so, it gets pretty safe to cross."

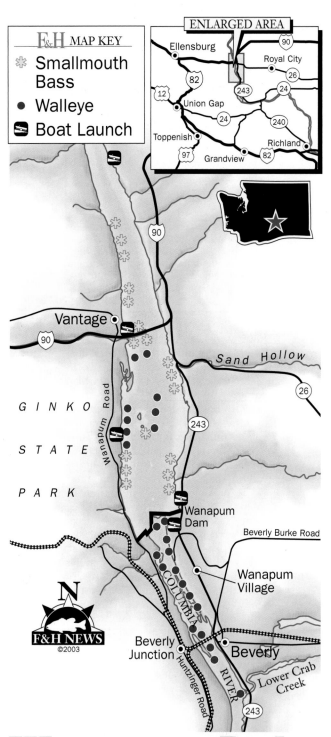

Wanapum Lake

Washougal mouth smallmouth bite turning on

WASHOUGAL

by Dusty Routh

If you're looking for action on Columbia River smallmouth during the first couple weeks of April, point the bow of your bass boat into the lower stretches of the Washougal River.

"You can find a lot of keepers up there sometimes early in the year," says ABA bass pro David Swendseid. "You can find decent fish if the conditions are right. Every once in a while someone will really get on 'em and catch 100 fish out of there. They won't be real, real big, but it's a popular spot."

Reef running: Swendseid says there's a lot of moving water at the mouth, mixing with the strong current coming down Ough Reef from the Columbia.

"You can run up the Washougal with your big motor about 100 yards, then poke your way the rest of the way in with your trolling motor," he says.

"There's a few good gravel bars and mud humps in that area. These can be good early-season holding areas for smallmouth."

Swendseid says to start right at the mouth of the river.

"Cast across the mouth on both sides of it, and fish those little land rises," he advises. "The fish will be nestled up in there. You can also go a little further up, 50 to 100 yards, and find some good fish too."

Swendseid points out that this area is picked over pretty well by walleye anglers in the area, and it's popular with bass fishermen too.

"The area down Ough Reef, and past the boathouse, and across the mouth of the Washougal gets pounded pretty good for both walleye and small-mouth," he says. "Smallmouth will be on that reef all summer."

Get out early: Swendseid says he's expecting an excellent early season this year.

"We might just have one of the best spring years for smallmouth in a long time," he predicts. "It looks like it might be an early spring. The bass didn't have it too bad this winter. There probably wasn't a significant winter kill, and the water temps are really starting to climb."

"If we continue to get good weather and a lot of warm spring days, all of April will be hot fishing."

Contacts/info: Bob's Sporting Goods (360-425-3870) in Vancouver; Fisherman's Marine & Outdoor (503-283-0044) in Portland.

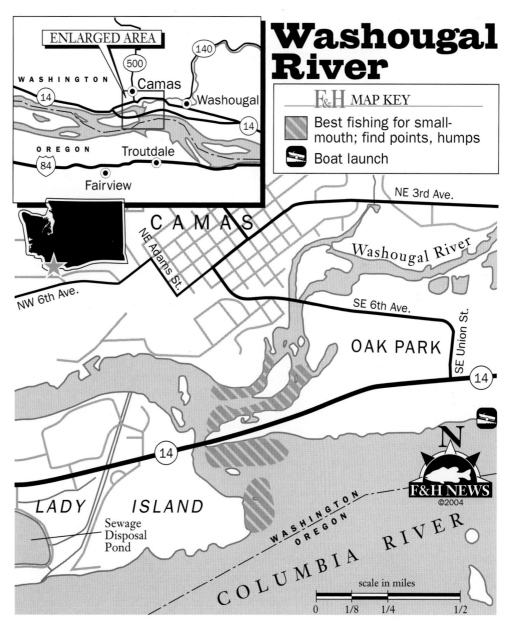

Washougal River

F&H MAP KEY

Best fishing for small-mouth; find points, humps

Boat launch

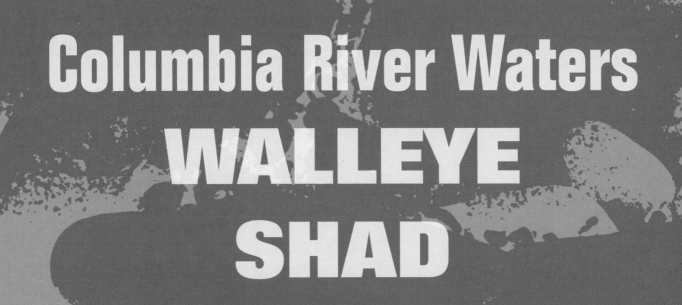

Columbia River Waters
WALLEYE
SHAD

Burgeoning Vancouver walleye fishery hits winter mode

VANCOUVER

by Dusty Routh

WALLEYE THE SIZE of Jeff Warila's massive 16-plus-pound Lower Columbia hawg are possible during winter months. Bring silver and chartreuse blade baits, smile blades, Northland jigs, worm harnesses and crankbaits for the Bonneville-to-Vancouver fishery.

AT A GLANCE

What: Lower Columbia River winter walleye.

Where: From Bonneville Dam downriver to Vancouver.

Why: The lower river's walleye fishery has been building in both popularity and productivity in recent years as Portland- and Vancouver-based anglers discover prime walleye grounds close to home.

Hot spots: Check out Ough Reef, the I-205 Bridge, Government Island, Reed Island and I-5 for starters.

Info: Larry McClintock at Play'N Pos'M Fishing Stuff (503-257-0553).

One thing is for sure: If you fish the lower Columbia River in the winter, you're bound to do some bouncing.

Sure, there can be nasty east winds that will bounce your boat like a basketball from Bonneville Dam all the way down to Clatskanie. But more than that, you'll be bouncing jigs, blade baits, crankbaits and bottom walkers trailing worm harnesses right off the bottom, trying to get warmwater fish to respond in decidedly cold water.

When the Columbia River walleye fishery was just taking off, most of the action and attention was on the upper river, up near Irrigon and Boardman, and on the big upper river impoundments like Roosevelt.

But walleye action on the lower river — defined as from Bonneville Dam down to Astoria — has really picked up the past few seasons.

"They're fishing the Columbia all the way down past Clatskanie now," says Larry McClintock, with Play'N Pos'M Fishing Stuff (503-257-0553) in Portland. "There's a lot more people fishing for walleye there than you'll hear about, because they don't want anybody to know where they're catching fish."

Wintertime catch: You won't catch a lot of walleye in the winter, says McClintock. But the fish you do catch will be big. If you need to hammer a lot of walleye, like 20 or 25 fish a day, that kind of fishing can happen in summer, when the water temperatures are considerably higher. What you're doing in winter is trophy hunting.

McClintock knows his stuff. His company makes specialized walleye tackle, he's on the pro staff for Mack's Lure and he's a competitive walleye tournament fisherman. Most of McClintock's business is with tournament anglers and fishing clubs. (McClintock will be at the Northwest Sportsman's Show Feb. 5-9 at the Portland Expo Center, in case you want to get a look at his specialized walleye tackle).

"We test our products before we carry them," McClintock says. "If they religiously or routinely catch fish, we'll keep 'em in stock, or we won't carry them."

McClintock reports he'll be carrying a customized lure made by David Storm that will debut at the show.

"It's called the Winning Streak," he says. "They're awesome lures. They look similar to the old Hot'N Tots but with a different body shape and new colors."

Understanding winter fish: The most important thing about winter walleye is that their metabolism has slowed to a crawl. That's why smaller fish rarely bite. Only the biggest fish can overcome this sluggishness, and even then most walleye anglers believe the strike comes out of anger and reaction rather than feeding.

Winter fish will be holed up, out of the current wherever possible. Current seams and breaks can be anywhere, including behind rock that's 60 feet down on the bottom. Depth won't be as critical as finding out-of-the-way places protected from current, where walleye are spending the winter.

The time of day (or night) and the moon can also be factors, according to McClintock.

"Three days on either side of a full moon, and three days on either side of a dark moon are the best days of the month," he says.

Some walleye anglers swear by night-fishing for these big bugeyes, but that's a dicey proposition on a big, brawling river like the Columbia unless you know it well.

"You'll want to stay to the edge of channels, watch for barge traffic, keep your boat lights on at all times," McClintock says. "Nightfishing can be very productive, but it's inherently more dangerous."

Top community holes: Anglers who fish the lower river a lot develop their own sneak spots that produce fish. But a number of places that hold fish are well known to the entire walleye angling community.

These include, for example, Ough Reef near Washougal.

"That one's a real good producer," McClintock confirms. "It usually has a lot of walleye. But it can be tough to fish. You can get in trouble on it, with rip currents, lots of rock, and a couple deep troughs on both sides."

McClintock also recommends the I-205 bridge, both the Oregon and Washington sides of Government Island, and the railroad bridge near I-5. Another favorite is Reed Island.

"It's fairly good," he says, which may be an understatement.

McClintock's tournament partner, Cal Burkhardsmeier, pulled 40-some-odd walleye from around Reed Island one blissful summer day, catching them on worm harnesses trolled in only 2 feet of water.

Gear: You can arm yourself with a dizzying array of walleye tackle, but if you're just starting out there are five basic food groups that Columbia River walleye love:

• *Bring the blades:* Silver and chartreuse blade baits, like those made by Heddon, Silver Buddy or Luhr Jensen Ripple Tails, jigged right off the bottom are key to the Columbia's winter fish, the yin and yang of this new art of catching trophy walleye out of cold water. The trick is to fish slowly, and methodically, giving the fish every opportunity to see that blade bait and seize it.

Tie the blade bait directly to your line via a safety snap, usually to the middle hole of the three top holes. Drop the lure until you find bottom, get a tight line, then easy pull it up to make the blade "swim." Then drop it again to lightly contact bottom. Do that until you're crazy. Then do it some more.

What you're waiting for is going to feel like a hang-up on your upstroke. Nothing violent, not like a steelhead or a largemouth slamming a bait. Your blade bait will just stop as you pull it up.

Once you've set the hook, though, these river walleye are incredibly strong from years of living in stiff current. Hang on!

• *Smile when you say that:* "Mack's Lure's smile blades are awesome," McClintock shares. Smile blades are Mylar spinners that can be adjusted for producing tight or wide wobbles on worm harnesses. But they're not just for worm harnesses anymore.

"You can also put smile blades on a jig, above a couple of beads, with a worm, so that you get that spin and wiggle when you're pulling it up," McClintock says.

This may just be the newest thing for whacking walleye. Try the scale chartreuse or sparkle red colors.

• *Get jiggy:* Whistler jigs by Northland Tackle are probably the most popular walleye jigs on the river, adorned with a nightcrawler or a twin-tail chartreuse plastic, like a Yamamoto 4-inch double-tail in the chartreuse with chartreuse flake color. The Rock Dancer by Mack's Lure, which is a hair jig, with a piece of nightcrawler, will also work.

• *Old tried and true:* Popular theory is that worm harnesses are one of the deadliest of all walleye baits. You want to troll these downstream, with the current, behind a bottom walker or, as McClintock uses, hollow pencil lead. You can buy pre-made harnesses, such as Mack's Lure's Double Whammy, or buy components separately and make your own, as a number of walleye aficionados do.

• *'Cranky' winter fish:* The rule of thumb for fishing crankbaits for winter walleye is to troll them well behind the boat, going upstream. The smaller the crankbait, the better, but it needs to dive deep enough to bounce against the bottom. Top crankbaits include Luhr Jensen's Hot Lips. Hot crankbait colors range from blue/silver to fire tiger. The critical thing is size; go with the smallest crankbait you have that will still bang the bottom.

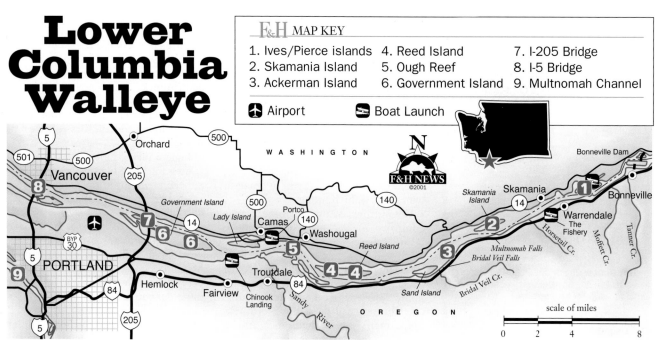

Lower Columbia Walleye

F&H MAP KEY

1. Ives/Pierce islands
2. Skamania Island
3. Ackerman Island
4. Reed Island
5. Ough Reef
6. Government Island
7. I-205 Bridge
8. I-5 Bridge
9. Multnomah Channel

✈ Airport   🚤 Boat Launch

McNary tailrace walleye are winter wonders

PATERSON

by Dusty Routh

BRAWNY, BULKY winter walleye, like this 12-pounder held by guide Bobby Roberts near Irrigon, are your target this month below McNary Dam. February and March represent some of the best times to target trophy fish.

Walleye have a tremendous defensive system to put off both human and aquatic predators. Their weapons include razor-sharp dorsal and pectoral fins, thick, tough-as-nails scales, big sets of gnashing teeth and a fascinating body color scheme that can blend in to just about any underwater surrounding.

But in the winter their most ardent defense against fishermen is the weather rather than their body armor. Fishing in winter isn't for the meek or the casual angler. It requires a steely resolve, a sense of when to say when, and an unwavering belief that today, sometime today, you might catch or at least hook the next world-record walleye (a definite possibility, by the way, on the Columbia River).

Depth control: Winter fishing below McNary Dam is, thankfully, a really rather simple process. You generally won't find the raging current of spring time, or the cloudy or muddy water of summer irrigation releases. The river tends to be in great shape, which means boat control and clarity are in your favor.

You also don't have to do much searching between deep and shallow water. Winter walleye tend to be fairly predictable, in that they prefer to suffer through winter by nosing into the current lying flat along the bottom, by getting slightly out of the current by either going deeper or by dodging in to current seams and hidden flat water. They won't be found, generally, in shallow or even in midrange water.

In fact, most of the walleye you're likely to find in this section of the river will be on 30- to 35-foot flats.

However, there are always exceptions to the rule. Some McNary walleye regulars have found winter fish in as few as 10 feet of water, while others have plugged them in water approaching 50 or 60 feet. But, again, in general, look for water that's ranging in that magic 25- to 35-foot range.

The arsenal: Once you've found the water you're looking for, you'll want to have a number of rods rigged up to put out a solid variety of walleye-getting gear known to provoke big fish to hit.

• **Blade baits:** More Columbia walleye are taken on these goofy-looking metal lures than anything else. You'll have to have ½-ounce models in silver and chartreuse.

• **Spinner harnesses:** Troll these off bottom walkers downstream with a full nightcrawler. Experiment with blade sizes, colors and bead colors. Also experiment with trolling speed. Don't automatically assume that because it's winter dead-slow is the most effective. Big walleye will chase a bait down.

• **Jigheads:** For super-simple bottomfishing, it's hard to beat a round or football jighead adorned with a nightcrawler or plastic bait. Plastics are usually fluorescent or chartreuse, scented with Walleye Feast scent. Bounce, hop or drag on the bottom.

• **Crankbaits:** Troll cranks upstream against the current. In winter your crankbait must be digging into the bottom on a regular basis, so use either deep divers or run your crank off a bottom walker or cannonball sinker. Crankbaits in red, crawdad, fluorescent, chartreuse, and silver/black are favorite colors.

• **Stickbaits:** Rapalas, Yo-Zuris, Lucky Crafts — there's no end to the number of high-quality stickbaits you can use, but these must be fished close to the bottom in winter to be effective. Fire tiger and silver/black are tops.

The where of it all: That part of the Columbia below McNary Dam is officially called Lake Umatilla. There are eight Oregon-side boat ramps below McNary, ranging from right below the dam, to one on the lower Umatilla River, down to one at Irrigon. There's another near Paterson Junction, one near Boardman, another east of Heppner, one at Arlington, and another just east of the John Day Dam near the mouth of the John Day River.

Most of the trophy walleye fishing takes place between Irrigon and McNary. In this stretch, the river is fairly

AT a GLANCE

What: Trophy walleye fishing on the Columbia just below McNary Dam.

When: February and March are the hottest cold-weather times to take your chances to hook into the biggest walleye of your life. Fish into the teens are a definite possibility.

How: Troll worm harnesses downstream, and crankbaits upstream. Jig blade baits and roundhead jigs with plastics and nightcrawlers across long flats and shoals in 25 to 35 feet of water. But don't be afraid to experiment with other depths.

Information: Rod McKenzie, High Desert Marine (541-567-8419).

Guides: Bobby Roberts, Columbia Basin Guide Service, 541-276-0371); Ed Iman (503-658-3753).

broad with long shoals, a deepwater channel, lots of sloughs and creeks (good for crappie, catfish and smallmouth bass) and smaller troughs and shelves.

Most walleye anglers do controlled drifts with the current, working to keep their lines as vertical as possible for blade-baiting and jig fishing. Trollers using harnesses and crankbaits flat-line or leadcore line fish with enough weight to keep their baits and lures in contact with the bottom.

Nightfishing can be really good, even in winter. There's a magic period, from roughly 3 to 7 p.m. in the winter when the fish seem to go on the bite.

Sticks, line and reels: You'll see all kinds of different combinations of rods and reels and lines, but the standard stuff here is a 10- to 20-pound super line (Power Pro or Fireline or something similar) with strong fluorocarbon leaders spooled on baitcasting reels.

Jigging and blading requires a rod with enough oomph to free yourself of the bottom when you hang up, and to set the hook, while still having enough sensitivity to feel the first indications of a pick up. Trolling harnesses, stickbaits and cranks can be done easily with medium-action rods and a quality baitcasting reel.

1. Paterson

2. McNary Dam

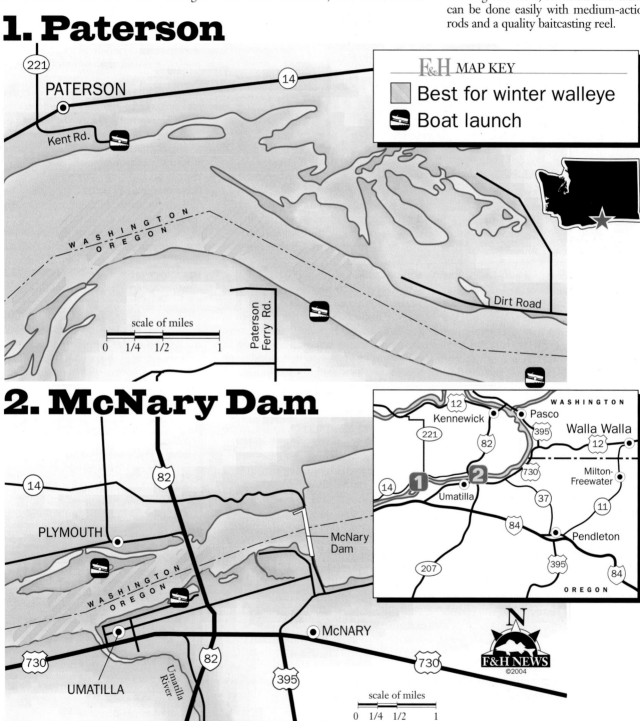

Advanced walleye: apply techniques for McNary 'eyes

UMATILLA

by Louis Bignami

Pros like Jason Schultz, a Snake River guide who fishes below McNary Dam every day for six weeks during prime time for trophy walleye, can raise your fishing literacy to near-Ph.D. levels.

He's quite convinced that this time of year vertical jigging is the way to go, because big trophy female walleyes are lethargic when they wait for night spawning in 25- to 40-foot-deep water convenient to flats.

Schultz keeps gear simple by using ⅜- to ½-ounce chartreuse, black and white jigs like Whistlers or Road Runners, as well as jigs with plastic grubs or twisters. Everything gets tipped with a nightcrawler or dead minnow.

Drift, pull and drop as you move along a depth line and you'll have the chance to feel the sometimes-ultra-light bite of a big walleye.

Flunk "Finesse 101" and you're better off fishing walleye lakes like Roosevelt or Sprague.

Schultz does not troll, as sluggish fish don't chase lures, and he's not interested in the smaller walleyes taken at other times of the year. He doesn't use blades armed with two treble hooks like Silver Buddies or the Bass Pro version, that vibrate when vertically jigged, as he's convinced that "trebles make catch-and-release difficult."

Other, and arguably easier, methods worth considering much of the year are downriver spinner trolling, bottom walkers or crankbaits such as Hawg Bosses that may need extra weight to get down to the bottom.

Of course, vertical jigging with your boat moving down a line of given depth is extremely demanding. Wind blows you one way, and the current tries to move you another. Managing drifts — and some on the Columbia can be a couple of miles long — is difficult, and fine tuning drifts so that you hit the small honey holes tucked away on gravel bars or ledges defines the doctorate needed to consistently take trophies here.

This is why going with a guide who can handle the boat while you handle the jigging is the best bet, and the reason Schultz is willing to share his four prime areas. I've also added other areas from other experts so you can compare and contrast results.

Green Can Hole: This spot near Highway 395 is a lot better bet later in the season when flows slow. It's popular

McNary Walleye

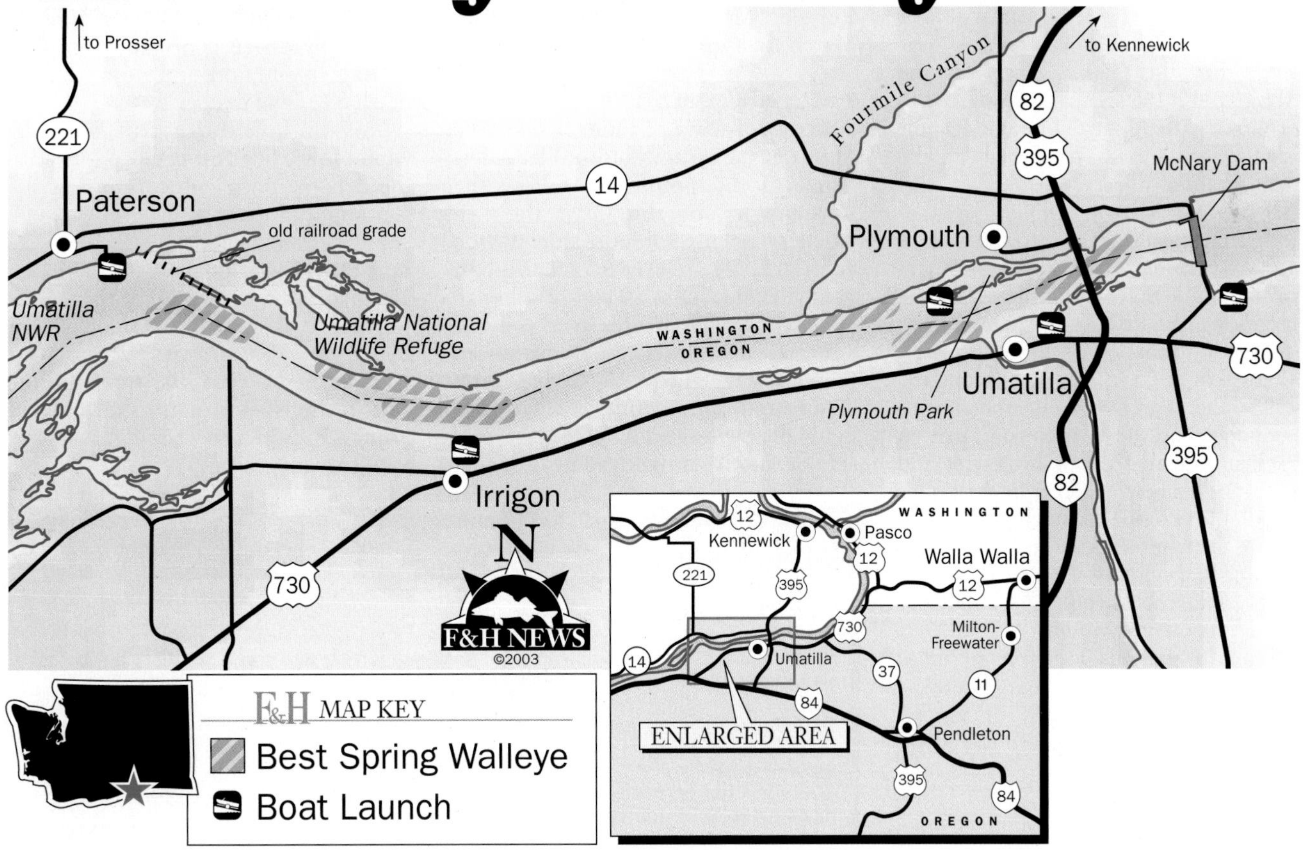

F&H MAP KEY
▨ Best Spring Walleye
⛴ Boat Launch

with blade and plug anglers as well as bait guys. In spring there's usually too much flow here unless you go down with big sinkers or troll with downriggers. Both methods can be very hard on tackle budgets. It's not a bad spot in the fall, however, and this year it could be fishable with more standard tackle because of low waters.

The best water here is the break line at about 20 feet at the edge of the main channel.

County line: The midriver humps on the Oregon side of the main river channel seem to collect more smaller male walleye at the most productive 15- to 25-foot depths than most others, and can be a decent spot for dinner males. The guide's trick is following the hump breaks so you keep a given depth. Watch for small, shallow depressions in the bottom that can collect walleyes too. Bottom walkers and worms work well here.

Hog Line Hole (aka 62 Hole): This is a great spot to start a drifting day. Schultz calls this one Hog Line Hole. It's right out of the Irrigon Park Marina. Immediately to the right is Marker 62, and the drifts start a mile or so upstream at red Marker 64. The ledge that runs from the pylon to the Marker 64 is the spot, and 25 to 35 feet of water is the depth. The underwater island here should be fished on the main channel side.

If possible, start at a given depth — sometimes you'll be able to see walleye on your finder, but sometimes you won't — and stay at that depth all the way down the drift. The channel from the pylon to marker is the spot to fish. Vertical jig in 25 feet of water along the ledge and match current speed with boat speed all the way down. Then go back up, change depth by 5 feet and repeat. This helps keep your drift lines parallel for complete coverage.

The key here is to keep the boat moving at exactly current speed so you keep contact with your jig and feel the sometimes-dainty bites.

The run extends a couple of miles downstream to Marker 62. There's a couple of hundred yards of jigging most miss below that where the island peters out as well.

Oldie Moldy: The most productive 30- to 40-foot depths of a run called Oldie Moldy run deeper than more popular Boulder Alley. It's directly across the river from the Irrigon boat ramp on the Washington side immediately below a rock outcropping with a nifty current break. You can jig the gravel here, but stay further offshore in that 30- to 40-foot band and try to match up current speed. It's possible to stay parallel with Boulder Alley drifters to help maintain depth too. You'll probably need to go to a ¾-ounce jig here.

Boulder Alley: Closer inshore than Oldie Moldy on the Washington side, Boulder Alley can be very crowded during weekends, but the boulders and rough bottom here hold a lot of fish. They extend all the way downstream past Paterson Point and the Umatilla National Wildlife Refuge. Most years it's better in March than in April.

Paterson Point: The point is directly downriver 3 miles from Oldie Moldy at the bottom of Boulder Alley. Start off the point and follow the Washington shoreline past the fish hatchery on the Oregon side. When you see River Marker 57 on the left, use a ½-ounce jig in 30 feet of water in about the middle of the river.

It may take a couple of passes to pinpoint the end of the ledge here. Then hold your depth as this ledge gradually swings back to the Oregon side of the rivers over the next couple

FISH LIKE THIS massive 16-pounder landed by Bob Roberts are the target this spring for bugeye anglers working below McNary Dam.

of miles: You need to lock up on 30-foot-deep water.

By the time you reach Paterson Slough, you'll be almost on the Oregon bank. Schultz thinks this stretch holds the biggest walleye on the river.

Big Blaylock Island (OR side): Big Blaylock Island is about 5 miles downstream from the ramp. Schultz favors the south, or Oregon side, of the island where it drops off into 35 or 40 feet, and notes, "a ½-ounce jig is needed for the deeper water."

This can be a tough drift when the wind blows, but you need to lock into the dropoff until it peters out at the south end of the island.

Big Blaylock Island (WA side): Most locals fish the Oregon side of Big Blaylock down to Glade Creek in 20 to 30 feet of water. After you make several runs, try Schultz's side of the islands or try the "Coyote Humps" between the gravel pit and Boardman.

AT A GLANCE

What: Trophy walleye below McNary Dam.

When: Good fishing from now through April. The further into spring you fish, the better your chances at hooking a monster prespawn fish.

Techniques: Jigs, blade baits are the key methods this time of year.

Information: Jason Schultz, Hells Canyon Sport Fishing (home: 208-750-1100- ; cell: 208-750-6800); High Desert Marine (541-567-8419); Ed Iman (503 685-3753); Columbia Basin Guide Service (541-276-0371).

Moses: Not 'good old days,' but not *bad* by any means

MOSES LAKE

by Leroy Ledeboer

AN IN-STATE DESTINATION fishery, Moses Lake hosts good numbers of bass, trout and walleye. Chad Kennedy, 12, trolled a blue Timber Tiger for this rainbow.

AT A GLANCE

What: Moses Lake spring fishing.

Species: Largemouth and smallmouth bass, walleye, rainbow trout, perch.

When: March through May encompass some of the best fishing of the year on Moses for all species.

Why: Populations are good to improving for almost everything that swims in Moses, including a "rainbow renaissance" boosted by a net-pen program that releases 90,000 fish in the lake through the year.

Techniques: Stock up on Timber Tigers, Needlefish, plastic baits, jigs, Super Dupers, FlatFish, Power Bait — all the basics.

Information: WDFW Ephrata office (509-754-4624)

Talk to some bass anglers and they'll say that our fishing in Moses Lake "ain't what it used to be." But while we haven't seen a return of the thousands and thousands of crappie and bluegill that graced these waters 30 years ago, those bass numbers are still good, perch have made a remarkable recovery, the net-pen project has revitalized the trout, and since the early 1980s we've had walleye.

Without quibbling over whether this latest arrival is our premiere game fish or an undesirable predator, let's look at where to go on Moses for each species.

Bass: As a bass water, Moses went from a predominantly largemouth to a smallmouth fishery over a 20-year span, but last season we saw a remarkable turnaround. Fewer smallmouth were getting hooked south of I-90 and far more largemouth. This even has the local fish biologist stumped, but for the average angler it's irrelevant. Good bass action is fishing at its best.

From late March through early May, cast a shallow-diving plug — such as a DC1 or DC3 Timber Tiger — or a wide assortment of plastics, grubs, lizards, split tails, tubes, etc., into the shallows on any of our rocky shorelines and enjoy the action. Head north from the Connelly Park launch and work around the docks on the east side, the rocks a bit further north, or hit the tree lines directly across and to the south of this launch. If you're into a lot of small bass of either species, switch to that ultralight and a little silver spinner or mini jig.

South of I-90, across from the radio towers, the eastern shoreline as well as right along the freeway holds tremendous possibilities. And don't neglect the shallows around the cattail island, the peninsula point rocks or the south side of Goat Island. As soon as the weather warms the lake a bit, jig the flats and channels all around this island for both bass and walleye, with maybe a big rainbow thrown into the mix.

Walleye: Today walleye may be even more prevalent than bass in this lake,

but anglers looking for steady limits are almost always frustrated. Like the bass, the bugeyes first turn on in the shallow north end, then sometime in late April or May go on a feeding spree off McConnihe Flats, off the peninsula just north and east of Moses Lake State Park boat launch, along much of that western shore and on the flats south of the radio towers. As the heat of summer comes on, try to locate a school of perch in 10 to 25 feet of water and either run diving plugs or spinner/worm/bottom-walker combos around its edge to pick up the hungry predators.

Angler frustration lies in size: The 18-inch-plus class quickly gets cropped off each year, and pretty soon you're catching a dozen undersized fish for every keeper. This won't change on May 1, as Moses Lake has been exempted from the new 16-inch minimum rule until a Washington Department of Fish & Wildlife study is complete.

"We still have very good numbers of big walleyes in Moses Lake," says WDFW biologist Jeff Korth. "We're seeing them all the time in our study — fish that top 24 inches — but for some reason they're not showing up in creel surveys. Almost everyone catches sublegals."

A 5-pound-plus Moses Lake walleye is usually a female and not much for eating, anyway, but if you want the thrill of nailing one, it's time to change tactics. Try a big perch-colored Jointed Rapala, any of the stickbaits or a diving Hawg Boss — a crank that's popular for the lower Columbia River trophies. Or try jigging a blade bait, such as the silver Uncle Walts.

Perhaps more important, when you're into a school, they're usually small. The bigger fish will be along the edges of that school or off by themselves, maybe suspended over deep water.

Perch: Moses Lake's crappie and bluegill numbers are still on the mend but under tight restrictions, so if you're looking for a mess of delicious fillets, think "perch." Again, the Connelly Park boat launch is a good place to start because the little striped-sides frequent the same waters as their predatory

from the lake's crappie numbers to its schools of rainbows. For one thing, although the annually stocked crappie rearing pond north of the railroad trestle always produces thousands and thousands of young-of-the-year, comparatively few reach adulthood. Decent-sized perch, which seemed to be making a real comeback three years ago, have suddenly become difficult to locate.

Thanks to the lake's net-pen project, trout anglers had a half-dozen very good summers, but for the last two summers, catch rates have plummeted. One theory holds that, as the number of their favorite forage fish, perch, have declined, walleye have turned to other prey. It's only those scrappy smallmouth bass that seem to be holding their own against this incursion. Each year, fewer and fewer anglers seem to target the lake's bronze-backs, but they're definitely still around, often snatching up wall-eye baits, more often feeding along the rocky and weedy shorelines at the south end, hanging around docks and brushy overhangs.

Future prospects: Of course every year is different, and maybe '06 will see a rainbow return. Korth is hoping that enough of last year's plants, which the local walleye club transported from net pens to various parts of the lake to avoid concentrated cormorant preda-tion, survive to turn this fishery around. If so, look for them in the deeper water just north of I-90 and east of Moses Lake Park, as well as at the far south end of the lake.

When trout fishing was boom-ing, my partners and I had a lot of fine days trolling the 20- to 30-foot waters that lie roughly from the tip of the peninsula across to the twin outlets and east. Rainbows were always suspended between 5 and 20 feet, and they'd hit anything from cranks to 'crawler-baited Double Whammies or Wedding Rings.

Hopefully, our smaller spinyrays will someday make a major comeback, but with five-fish limits and size restric-

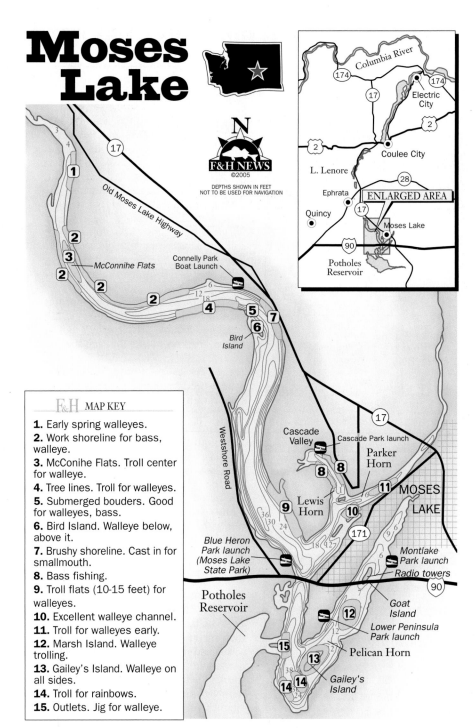

Moses Lake

©2005

DEPTHS SHOWN IN FEET
NOT TO BE USED FOR NAVIGATION

F&H MAP KEY

1. Early spring walleyes.
2. Work shoreline for bass, walleye.
3. McConihe Flats. Troll center for walleye.
4. Tree lines. Troll for walleyes.
5. Submerged boulders. Good for walleyes, bass.
6. Bird Island. Walleye below, above it.
7. Brushy shoreline. Cast in for smallmouth.
8. Bass fishing.
9. Troll flats (10-15 feet) for walleyes.
10. Excellent walleye channel.
11. Troll for walleyes early.
12. Marsh Island. Walleye trolling.
13. Gailey's Island. Walleye on all sides.
14. Troll for rainbows.
15. Outlets. Jig for walleye.

tions, crappie and bluegill aren't worth targeting at present, and this lake needs all the breeders it can get. Our perch may still be in better shape, but I'll be pleasantly surprised if very many of you find huge schools of filletable fish.

Summer '05: Moses Lake might hold a few surprises this summer, but cer-tainly walleye will be its major draw. All the standard techniques will work here, but this is a lake that produces enor-mous bug hatches, and, like predators everywhere, walleye have quickly adapted. So as the water warms, often in late May or early June, use various big flies, mainly leeches and darker Woolly Bugger patterns. They're dead-ly. Basically, troll them or cast them into real shallow water, just off points, around islands, even onto big muddy flats at the north end.

Autumn 'eyes boomin' at Potholes

OTHELLO

by Dusty Routh

It didn't take long. Just as the sun poked a ray or two of pink light down Lind Coulee, the first walleye of the day hit. I was fishing with Brian Henton, one of the walleye "regulars" on the Washington tourney trail. We'd launched at the ramp at Lind Coulee since the low water level made every other ramp an exercise in futility. We ran due west, straight down the coulee, and out to a nice 39-foot water level on the main lake at Potholes Reservoir, where several humps rising to 17 feet are located. Working worm harnesses up the humps, we found our first fish.

It didn't take long for the second, third and fourth fish, either. With water still a walleye-compatible 59 degrees, the fish were feeding aggressively. From roughly 7 a.m. until noon, it was all sharp fins and teeth, nets, bent rods, and whoops and hollers.

Location: Fishing for walleye at Potholes this time of year is not a complicated proposition. Run due west from the mouth of Lind, or start fishing right at the mouth and slowly move west. Stay east of Goose Island, in the lower, southern quarter of the lake. This whole area is Walleyeville in the fall.

To pinpoint the best spots, remember the name of Austin Power's Russian girlfriend: Ivana Humpalott. Flip on your finder and move around looking for any humps indicating change in depth, particularly where there are really pronounced humps. We found several in this general area where the depth changes ranged from a few feet to as much as 20 feet. If you have a GPS, mark these. If you don't, take along plenty of throw-out markers, and drop one whenever you come across a hump.

Once located, either blade bait up, down and around the hump, or troll worm harnesses behind bottom bouncers up the humps, along the tops, sides and down the sides.

We found two humps where every time we made a trolling pass, we got hit. Most of the bottom here is sand/mud, so you won't hang up much. However, there does appear to be some downed trees and rock formations that are grave-

yards for walleye tackle. But, then again, if you're not losing tackle, you're not walleye fishing.

Medicare Beach, the big bluffs adjacent to Lind along the eastern shore, may be better known for great trout fishing than walleye whackin', but this is still a fall hot spot for bugs. Troll crankbaits like Luhr Jensen's Hot Lips Express back and forth, starting shallow and progressively moving out deeper. If you can adjust your line length and the dive of your crankbait so that you're occasional-

DON'T LET the rising water on Potholes Reservoir fool you this month. The big reservoir's walleye, like Bobby Jacobsen's 7-pounder, will stay on the bite as moving water pushes bait around.

ly digging up a little cloud of mud from the bottom, you're in business.

Where's the water? In early to mid-October the water level at Potholes was low like you've never seen. It was a good opportunity to graph channels and mark areas on your map, to remember at full pool. According to Bobby Jacobsen, one of the more accomplished walleye anglers who frequents Potholes, this big

lake will start filling by the end of the month. It may also fill up fast, but that doesn't mean it will hamper the fishing.

"No, not at all," says Jacobsen. "Fishing can get even get better, because you've got all that bait moving around. Plus you've got current, and walleye love current."

Aggressive, toothy predators (aka walleye) like it when bait is on the move, and there's current, and fresh water is coming in, which allows them to move up to new shallow areas that were high and dry a week earlier.

"We've caught them along Medicare Beach right up next to the bank when the water's coming in," Jacobsen reports. "It was amazing. Last December, we were casting blade baits right up into a foot of water and bouncing them back along the bottom, right along the beach, and just nailing the fish."

Moses parts the water: An added benefit of water coming into Potholes is that water is moving out of Moses Lake when they open the canal. That creates current in Moses, congregating the baitfish near the I-90 bridge area.

"Last year was a terrific year for crappie fry on Moses Lake," says Jacobsen. "There were crappie fry pushed down to the bridge when they let the water out, and little crappie were all over the place. The walleye were in there thick, eating up the crappie fry."

Look for Potholes to continue filling in early November, and make sure you hit Moses Lake when it does.

"I take a magic marker and make little black marks on chrome-silver blade baits," Jacobsen shares. "Makes a blade bait look just like a small crappie fry."

'Smile' at 'em: The more you walleye fish, the more you'll appreciate the value of customizing your offerings like Jacobsen does his blades. Henton does the same with his worm harnesses.

"I tie up a ton of them, customizing them in different ways," Henton says. One of his favorites, and hands down one of the most effective I've seen, is his hand-tied worm harnesses with Smile blades from Larry McClintock's Critter-Gitter lure company.

"I use the silver-dot Smile blades, three chrome beads, a day-glo bead, a chrome bead, a couple more day-glo beads, chrome beads, and then either No. 4 or 8 red hooks," Henton says.

This rig sure seemed to work, outfish-ing some manufactured harnesses I'd brought. The day-glo beads seem to make a big difference. To get the best use of the day-glo feature, lay the harness out in the sun and strobe it or hold a flashlight to it before you use it. Henton also changes harness rigs frequently, replacing a used day-glo bead set-up with one that's been sitting in the sun on the dashboard of his boat.

"You need to keep them lit up," he says. Another secret to harnesses?

"Let that second hook hang free," Henton says. "Nose hook your night-crawler on the first hook, and just let that second red hook hang free."

You'll get more hook-ups, and a lot more natural action from your worm.

Blades too: On any given outing at Potholes you'll see roughly a 50/50 split between anglers trolling cranks and worm harnesses, and anglers snap-jig-ging blade baits. In a nasty wind trolling may be your only option, but if you can exercise solid boat control, blades are the way to go. For vertical jigging, Jacobsen "snap jigs" his blade by jerking his rod up violently a few inches, which vibrates the bait upwards. He then lets it free fall on slack line to hit the bottom.

Other times, Jacobsen casts his blade out and away from the boat.

"I let it hit bottom, then I bounce it along the bottom back to the boat," explains Jacobsen.

AT a GLANCE

What: Primo fall walleye fishing on Potholes Reservoir.

Where: Southeast side of the lake (east of Goose Island) in the southern quarter, straight out from Lind Coulee.

When: Should hold up until December.

How: Chrome blades, bottom-bouncers and worm harnesses with day-glo beads.

Expect: Big fish. We saw several 5s and a 7-pounder, all taken in one morning of fishing.

Call: Mar Don Resort (509-346-2651); Mike's Bait & Tackle (509-764-4416).

Potholes Reservoir

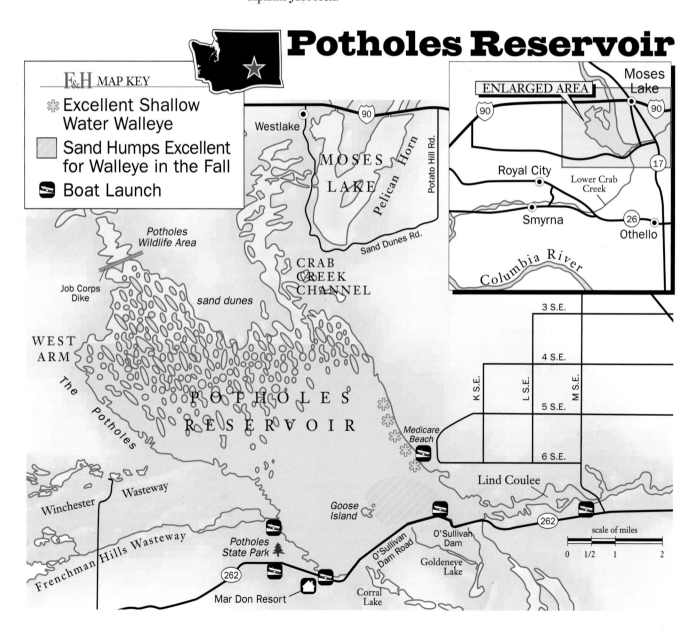

F&H MAP KEY

✳ Excellent Shallow Water Walleye

▨ Sand Humps Excellent for Walleye in the Fall

⬛ Boat Launch

Timing is right for shad just below John Day Dam

———BIGGS, Ore.

by Jim Pearson

The shad are coming, but it's probably a bit early yet. You may be able to catch a few right now, but it'll get better later on. At least that's the way it usually works, although you can't make book on their return dates. They're less predictable than salmon. Sometimes they're early, sometimes not so early. Watch the papers to see when to grab your rod, but remember: the first to show up are the males, and they're smaller than the females.

Transplanted targets: These aliens came to the Columbia River system — probably from the Sacramento River after they had been imported there from the East Coast — and have really taken hold. They move from saltwater into the river to spawn, and they come by the hundreds of thousands. They're fun to catch, they're good to eat and there's no limit. What more could a guy want?

If you get anxious, you can begin down by Bonneville, but I wait until they're closer to home. In this case, below John Day Dam on the Washington side of the river.

Lots of fishing space: It's an easy place to find. Exit off Highway 14 approximately 5 miles north of Biggs junction on the Washington side when

you see the road on the upriver side of the aluminum plant. Drive down along the river until you see some guys fishing either for sturgeon or shad from the rocky shoreline. Usually, they're down close to the Porta-Potty by the only tree along that stretch of river. I don't think they're there because the fishing is better in that spot. I think their choice of spots has more to do with the location of the potty. There isn't much to hide behind along that stretch of river.

When we fished this stretch earlier, a couple guys were sitting in folding chairs with sturgeon rods propped up in the rocks. When we asked for a likely shad-catching spot, they pointed down to the rocks and said, "Anywhere along there." And they were right. It's a long stretch of rocky shoreline providing lots of uncrowded fishing spots.

Shad methodology: My buddy Randy Teague does the fly-fishing bit much better than I. He uses a ½-ounce leadhead jig with the head painted red. It has a gold hook and he ties on six or seven strands of Flashabou, although he doesn't think that is necessary. Eighteen inches up his leader, he puts on a barrel swivel with a BB split shot above that. The leader is attached to 16 feet of No. 8 sink-tip line. He casts slightly upstream so that the fly begins bumping the bottom or is close to it when it's 30 degrees from him as he faces the water.

I was down there last year fly fishing — well, kinda fly fishing. The homemade dart I was using was a miserable thing to cast, but I caught a couple before I gave up the fishing and began taking pictures.

Four people were fishing a hundred yards below me, and I had seen them catch several. I walked down there and met Joe Watkins from Grandview. With him were three teenagers.

"They're just a bunch of waifs I picked up beside the road," he joked, but they were really his grandkids, John Stafford, Derrick Watkins and Jaimie Byrne. They released most of the fish they caught, but they did have a stringer with four tied up in the water,

GRANDPA JOE WATKINS from Grandview shows off a typical shad he's pulled from the Columbia River just below John Day Dam. It's starting to approach peak time now for shad hunters on the big river.

and while I watched, they caught a couple more.

Their gear was simple: medium-weight spinning gear and a chartreuse color curl-tail jig. They cast out slightly upstream and let the jig begin tapping the bottom. They hooked up most often, just as Teague had said, when the jig was at approximately 30 degrees downstream as they faced the water.

Watkins told me that he looks for a slight point running out into the water — it doesn't have to be much of a point — and he thinks the fishing is slightly better in the pocket, but in the long run, it didn't make a lot of difference. He claimed the run was tapering off, and that was June 25, last year.

AT a GLANCE

What: Columbia River shad.

Where: Just below John Day Dam, near Biggs Junction.

When: Beginning right now, but getting better for through the middle of June.

How: Easy fishing here. Your basic routine involves casting from the shore using spinning or fly tackle.

Why: Because they are fun to catch, there is no limit, and they are good to eat

Information: Watch the dam counts for fish moving over Bonneville and The Dalles (*www.fpc.org*).

What to do with a shad

"WHAT DO YOU DO WITH THOSE BONY THINGS once you catch 'em," a guy once asked me.

The answer is simple: I eat 'em. And I've heard an even better answer: "Don't eat the bones." It came from a guy who had a big ice chest full of shad. Shad have a white, delicate flesh and a mild flavor, but how do you deal with the bones? Again, simple: Don't overcook them. In my opinion, overcooking is the mistake most often made when cooking fish. You can also pressure cook them and the bones then become edible and a good source of calcium. Before you go "yuck," remember back to the last time you ate canned salmon.

I like to cut them into chunks small enough to fit inside a pint jar, add a tablespoon or so of olive oil, a couple drops of liquid smoke, and a pinch of salt. Then I pressure cook them for an

hour at 10 pounds. A jar of that, some crackers, mayonnaise and jalapeño peppers often goes along with me on fishing or hunting trips and becomes my lunch.

Many consider shad roe a delicacy. It's OK, I guess, but it doesn't do much for me, so I save it for my buddy, Tom, who fries it in bacon grease or butter. I don't think that fare is recommended for those with a cholesterol problem, but fresh shad roe is a once-a-year opportunity. I cooked them Tom's way, and they didn't do much for me. Then I tried them mixed with scrambled eggs (now that's a cholesterol booster), and they still didn't light any fires in this old body. I rank shad roe right up there with grits — a blah nothing that's OK if you really need something in your stomach and that's what's available. I certainly wouldn't order them in a restaurant even if the price was right.

Some cure or freeze the flesh for sturgeon bait. Years ago, Joe Schneider, a die-hard fisherman who lived in Selah, gave me a jar of shad he had cured. I fooled around and didn't get his recipe before he passed on, but I'm sure it isn't complicated. What I will do this year is cut it into bait-strip sizes, vacuum pack and freeze it.

Some years back, I went after shad below Bonneville Dam. Some people were there with ¾-ton vans and huge ice chests. They were busily filling those chests and taking any fish people didn't want to keep. I asked them what they were doing with so many fish, and they said, "We're eating them."

Maybe, but I'll bet over in the Everett area somewhere, people are being served shad in some exotic dishes. And you know what? I'll bet it tastes just fine.

—J.P.

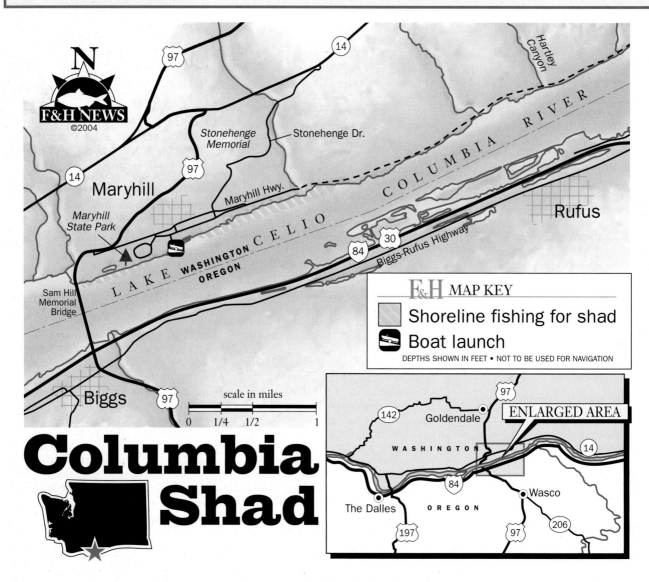

Columbia Shad

Puget Sound Saltwater
SALMON

Shipyard Chinook: Elliott Bay opens July 12

SEATTLE

by Scott Small

BRIGHT KINGS, BIG CITY: Jennifer Enstead caught this big, super-bright king on a trolled cut-plug herring right outside of Todd Shipyard during last year's Elliott Bay fishery. Husband OClaire Enstead II took the photo.

Make a list of major U.S. cities where bosses keep a pair of binoculars on their desk to see who cut out early to go fishing. That's going to be one short list! Where besides Seattle can you find serious numbers of urban Chinook, just spitting distance from downtown high rises?

Switch to a 4-day work week, bring the boss with you, do whatever it takes — this year's short Elliott Bay salmon opening is too good to miss.

Get there: If anything, this fishery is too convenient. A huge cross section of Seattle anglers will be angling for a shot at the Don Armeni boat ramp off Harbor Ave., making it a good place to avoid. If you've got the horsepower, consider launching at Shilshole or even Edmonds, and making the run into Elliott Bay.

Once you're on the water, you won't be alone. Patience and courtesy are your best defense against combat fishing. Try to join the established trolling pattern rather than blazing your own trail, and stay clear when you see someone playing a fish. They'll do the same for you when it's your turn.

Fish here: Our map shows specific areas off Todd Shipyards, Duwamish Head and Pier 90, where Chinook tend to congregate. Fishing is restricted to a specific portion of inner Elliott Bay, so be sure to stay on the east side of the boundary running from Pier 91 to the tip of Duwamish Head.

Try this: This fishery is primarily a trolling show, but certain areas may contain a high enough concentration of salmon to justify killing the motor and mooching or jigging. There's no secret here — successful Elliott Bay anglers employ a variety of techniques.

If you've done some salmon fishing but are new to downtown, just start with the approach that you feel most confident using. All the standard stuff works — a squid, bucktail, spoon or cutplug behind a flasher is a good place to start. Don't be afraid to experiment when the action is slow, and be sure to keep track of the results.

Roll with the changes: The best bites occur at tide and light changes. Elliott Bay is typically an early morning bite, and you'll want to start the day shallow. Tom Pollack of Auburn Sports & Marine (253-833-1440) theorizes that Chinook spend the predawn hours within the top 20 to 25 feet of water, "trying to get their dose of fresh water for their migration up the river." Dawn brings sunlight and boat traffic, chasing the fish down.

Fishing is all about stacking the odds in your favor, so focus your effort on the high-probability time slots. Make sure your presentation is in the water and working properly near sunrise, sunset and tide changes.

"Chinook slow" is the traditional trolling speed, but tradition means squat compared to a fish on the line. If you get more action trolling fast, then by all means do what works.

Nightfishing is also an option, provided that your boat has the required lights. According to Tony Floor of the Washington Department of Fish & Wildlife, "Chinook will feed 24 hours per day, and everything rises at night."

AT A GLANCE

What: Elliott Bay Chinook.

When: Season opens July 12 and closes Aug. 18.

Where: Downtown Seattle.

Regs: Open Fridays, Saturdays and Sundays only; two-king limit.

Launch: Nearest public launch as Don Armeni in Seattle, but prepare for a crowd. Shilshole is another option.

Information Tom Pollack, Auburn Sports & Marine (253-833-1440); Keith Robbins, Spot Tail Guide Service (206-283-6680)

Attractors and lures with glow colors are the norm for nightfishing, and you'll want to add plenty of scent to establish a trail.

But what's Floor's personal take on nightfishing?

"I would rather sleep at night, and fish around the light and tide changes."

Follow the flood: Like some fishermen, Chinook keep on eating long after they really should stop. Habits engrained through a lifetime of chasing bait balls in the ocean are slow to disappear once the salmon enter fresh water. Even on the doorstep of the spawning river, you should fish hard where you see feed. The odds are high that a salmon will be lurking somewhere in the vicinity.

A Chinook may hang around Elliott Bay for several months before it fully matures and heads up the river. Since the fish's behavior changes during that period, it makes sense for anglers to adjust their tactics from "imitation" to "irritation" as the season progresses.

Salmon newly arrived from the ocean tend to keep doing what they've always done, and you can tempt them with a cutplug, an imitation herring like Mack's Bait-Buster or a spoon in herring-like colors. But as the fish adapts to fresh water, favorite foods lose their appeal. That's when you need to get rude.

Finicky fish will strike in anger if you insult them with an obnoxious combination of noise, color and scent. Lure designers have a field day when it comes to targeting mature Chinook. Creative concoctions like the "funky chicken" and "wonder bread" trolling spoon patterns keep showing up in tackle shops, alongside classic sonic irritators like the Buzz Bomb and Sonic Edge.

If doing the funky chicken seems too extreme, some cut-plug artists reportedly make subtle changes in their hook-up and bevel angle to produce a wide spin that mature Chinook especially hate.

Get down to action: Once the morning bite cools off, you'll want to fish closer to the bottom. On that point everyone agrees. But just how close is a matter of debate.

Floor likes to go deep.

"I believe Chinook salmon that are near the bottom are the best biters, while the fish that are upper or middepth tend to be travelers," he says, noting that boats and predators make salmon nervous as they move away from the safety of the bottom. "Seals always attack from the under side."

Some veteran Elliott Bay anglers like to stack their lures at different depths, from 45 feet on down. You can add an interesting twist to this technique by attaching a flasher to the downrigger ball and stacking lines with cutplugs above it. When a fish hits, you'll be playing it directly, with no interference from the flasher. You'll also improve the action of both flasher and bait by preventing them from interfering with each other.

Crystal ball: How big will the 2002 Chinook run be? When will it peak? A month from now, we'll know for sure. Until then, all we can do is guess. Prevailing sentiment holds that the run will start slowly, and peak toward the end of the season in August. But prevailing sentiments change like prevailing winds, and predictions mean squat compared to a fish on the line.

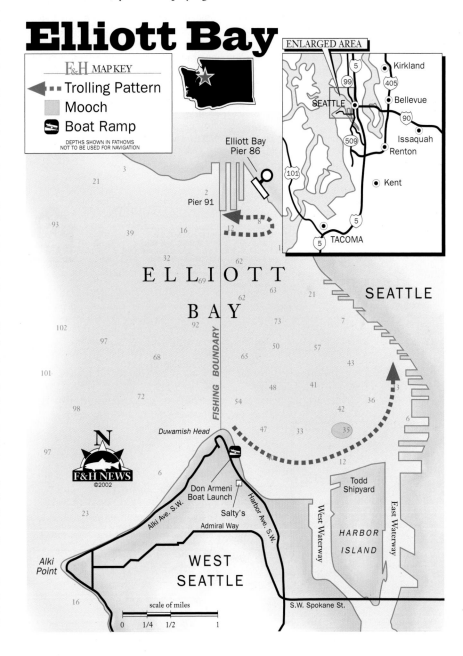

Elliott Bay

F&H MAP KEY
- Trolling Pattern
- Mooch
- Boat Ramp

DEPTHS SHOWN IN FATHOMS
NOT TO BE USED FOR NAVIGATION

Head off to Hat for mid-Sound blackmouth

by John Martinis

Today, the opening day of salmon is the granddaddy of openers in Washington. And even with a one-fish limit on Chinook, the spirit of real fishermen is never dampened.

A GOOD CLOSE-IN SPOT: When the season opens Feb. 16, the weather can still play an important role in whether you leave the dock or not. Other times, the weather will only dictate the distance of travel to the fishing spot on Puget Sound. That leads us to Hat Island (Gedney Island), only 3 miles from the Everett boat harbor and accessible in all but the stormiest conditions.

But I want to point out that the salmon holes around Hat are not second-choice fishing areas. These areas put out excellent Chinook fishing.

There are two primary fishing bars on the south and north sides of Hat Island. Because Chinook are opportunistic feeders, we will explore both areas. Either area may be good depending on the tide or the availability of baitfish.

NORTH HAT: First off let's look at the bar that runs from the northwest corner of Hat to Camano Head. This area has been one of the staple fishing areas for Everett residents for years. While Possession Bar gets the great kudos for being the salmon hot spot, anglers who fish North Hat just laugh when they see the big boats running south. They know that the salmon cruise the bar that runs between the islands. Sometimes the buoy at Camano Head is hot and at other times, closer to Hat Island is hot fishing.

You have to take in the whole bar to get the most out of this area. To start fishing I would plop the downriggers down on the Hat Island side and troll in 90 to 150 feet of water toward Camano Island. The tide runs swiftly across this bar, causing the bait to hug the bottom. Therefore, it is very important to hug the bottom in this area with your downriggers and fishing gear.

Your cue to turn around will be when you approach the buoy at Camano Head.

SOUTH HAT: Another bar skirts the whole south side of Hat Island. This is a rather interesting bar because it has some good curves that hold bait and salmon. This is also one of the few places in Puget Sound where you can catch Chinook suspended from the bottom.

Arriving from the Everett area, I recommend that you start fishing even with the green buoy on the west end of Hat. Actually, you will be south of the buoy in at least 100 feet of water. Follow the bar heading in a westerly direction. When the bar takes a hard northerly turn (about ½ mile), turn around and head back to where you started.

While trolling in this area, vary your depth of fishing from 90 to 180 feet of water. The actual fishing depth should vary also from on the bottom to only three-quarters of the way to the bottom. If you have a good fish finder, you will

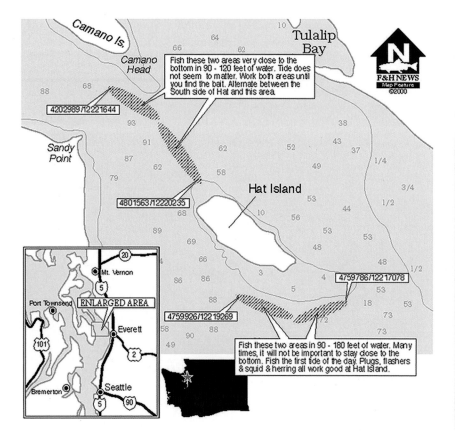

AT A GLANCE

Launches: There are two close-in launches from which you can access the Hat Island blackmouth fishery:
- The Port of Everett (425-259-6001) has an excellent year-round launching ramp at 10th Street and Marine View Drive. Fee is $5. If coming up I-5 from the south, take the Marine View Drive and continue until you get to the boat launch. If coming from the north, take the Everett Avenue exit of I-5 and head west to Marine View Drive. When you get to Marine View Drive head north to the boat launch. Gas and diesel are available at the Port's northern marina, four blocks downstream from the launching ramp.
- The Tulalip Marina (360-651-4999) has a boat ramp that is usable at high tide and is very close to Hat Island. But you have to watch the tides if you plan on getting your boat out of the water. Take I-5 to the Marysville/Tulalip exit. Go west on Tulalip Road to Mission Beach Road. Turn on Mission Beach and drive to the marina.

Charters: Boatless in Seattle and want to do some salmon fishing? Call Tom Young at Tommycod Charters (800-283-8900). Young is also a good source for salmon fishing reports.

Info: Call the author, John Martinis, at John's Sporting Goods (425-259-3056).

be able to determine the correct fishing depth by spotting baitfish either suspended or near the bottom. If you spot bait, keep your downrigger to the upper end of the school of bait and remember to compensate for the downrigger cable angle.

Your blackmouth gear should also include a couple colors of flashers and a variety of spoons and squids. Good flasher colors are green or green with a red stripe. Spoon colors should include green/glow, army truck or nickel/green. Sizes of the most effective salmon spoons are from 3 to 4 inches long. These sizes imitate the average size of herring or candlefish Chinook feed on in the Sound.

If the fish you are catching are feeding on candlefish, fish with more slender spoons like Coho Killers from Silver Horde. If the fish are feeding on herring, fish with the broader spoons like Blue Fox Trixees or Luhr Jensen Coyotes.

Plastic squid should not be forgotten either. Plastic squid are a very effective imitation of the real thing. I like the Gold Star because they are more supple and life-like than other brands. Effective colors are combinations of blue/glow, green/glow and army truck. The most effective size of artificial squid are the Octopus 3.5 inch. Gold Star has also come out with some very attractive twinkle skirts to insert inside the squid. Those colors are double glow green and plain double glow.

FLASHY TACKLE:
I feel that it has been well proven that flashy tackle not only catches the eye of the fisherman but also the eye of the fish. Smell also plays an important role in enticing a salmon to bite on a hook. Standard Chinook tackle includes lures that imitate baitfish. They not only imitate the size of the baitfish but also the swimming action.

Meat up: Head to Hood to fill cooler with silvers

by Joel Shangle

As of Sept. 1, I'm a meathog of the meatiest variety. I want fillets for the 'cue, steaks for the oven and whole sides for the smoker. The no-bonk rule goes out the window, and the fill-my-cooler rule becomes my modus operandi.

That's because Sept. 1, for those of you who have been hovering at the Fred Meyer fish counter, signifies the opening of upper Hood Canal, one of the fishiest (read "meatiest") pieces of water in Puget Sound.

Step away from the fish counter. I repeat: Step away from the fish counter. Instead, get out to Seabeck, get your boat in the water and fill your cooler with limits of rich-fleshed salmonids. Your friends will thank you in a November, when you break out that slab of pepper-smoked coho during your first winter steelhead forays.

Hatchery thick: Ground Zero for upper Hood Canal's annual hatchery coho swarm has actually been fishable since Aug. 16, when the Quilcene/Dabob Bay Salmon Fishery Area (north of Point Whitney, in Quilcene and Dabob bays) opened, with a four-fish limit.

Let me repeat those last three words: *Four. Fish. Limit.*

And this isn't a hard limit to fill. Over the next few months, silvers (and chums) will be thicker than fleas in Quilcene Bay and upper Hood Canal. A bazillion fish, bound for the Quilcene Hatchery (and the circus freakshow that is the Quilcene River fishery) will round Oak Head and make their way into Dabob Bay past Tsutsko

Point, Zalatched Point, Pulali Point, Frenchman's Point and Fisherman's Point, en route to the mouth of the Quilcene.

Concentrated coho: You can realistically nail silvers from dawn to dusk almost anywhere around the Toandos Peninsula this time of year, but let's not screw around here: focus your attention on Dabob and Quilcene bays. That's where the meat (there's that word again) of the runs will be found through September, and that's where you'll make a hero out of yourself with serious poundage of fish flesh.

"The last couple of years have been really, really good for coho," says Mike Smith, owner of Seabeck Marina

(360-830-5179). "There's a lot of fish up there."

This isn't a delicate, touchy-feely fishery: Buzz Bombs are the rule for nine out of 10 boats. You can certainly limit out tossing spinners or trolling spoons from Hazel Point around the Toandos Peninsula into Dabob Bay, but by mid-September, when the joint is really jumping, your best bet is to join the Buzz Bomb Brigade.

Get wet: Launches aren't abundant on the upper Canal. Your best choices are the WDFW public launch at Misery Point (take Seabeck-Holly Road out of Seabeck to Miami Beach Road, hang a right and then a left roughly a half mile later); or the sling at Seabeck Marina ($20 round trip).

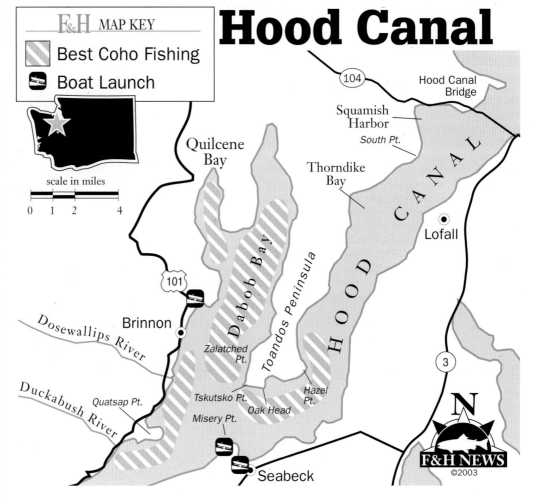

Clean up on fall coho at Jeff Head

by Dusty Routh

Looking for a low-key, mostly uncrowded, productive coho fishery close to home? There are plenty of good opportunities in Puget Sound right now for silvers, but one of the better bets is Jefferson Head.

Locally known as Jeff Head, and officially known as Jefferson Point, this is a darn popular fishery, but the pressure hasn't been all that great this summer. Which is a good thing. There's ample elbow room for trolling and mooching without the combat environment you might encounter at the Tulalip Bubble or on Elliott Bay.

A recent weekday morning sported only about a dozen boats working the water here. Of course, you can expect more company on the weekends, but since Jeff Head is close to home, it's a great saltwater fishery to sneak out to before you have to show up at work.

One of those boats working this water recently belongs to Gary Krein, with All Star Charters (425-252-4188). He's been fishing here regularly, running morning and afternoon trips to put his charter clients into good numbers of silvers, along with the occasional and ever-so-pleasing to catch, hard-fighting kings that are passing through the area. The kings have to be released, but nonetheless they are stubborn fighters and a heck of a lot of fun to accidentally hook into.

"The fishing at Jeff Head has been fantastic this summer," Krein reports. "Most of the action is coming on coho, but we're hooking plenty of kings."

This particular morning, Krein had already caught and released three nice kings. The action on coho isn't the hot, one-right-after-the-other fishing you might encounter at Neah Bay, but it's consistent, Krein reports.

"We're catching silvers anywhere from 35 to 60 feet down," he says.

The best fishing here is almost always at first light.

"The best tides always seem to be that outgoing tide early in the morning," Krein confirms. "We try to get here just at first light, and for the first two hours the fishing can be very,

BREAK OUT THE SQUIDS, spoons and bucktails, boys, it's time to get out early in the morning for coho around Jefferson Head. It's the perfect choice for a "before work" fishery. Ryley Fee nabbed this 14.6-pounder between there and Scatchet last year.

very good."

Afternoon fishing, unfortunately, isn't quite as productive, though there are still some silvers that will hit. But first light is the best time to be here. With sunrise hitting officially around 5:30 a.m., and unofficially it being almost light enough to fish about 45 minutes earlier than that on a cloudless morning, count on getting out early and getting your lines down quickly to nurse as much dawn fishing time as you can.

There is one thing that can put this fishery down, however, and that's a full moon. The big moon we had back in early August all but lock-lipped these fish.

"The fishing at Jeff Head had been very good, from as far back as the first of July," Krein says. "Then we had about a one-week lull, during that full-moon cycle. But ever since then, it's been darn good just about every morning."

Good size averages: A lot of the coho at Jeff Head are resident, nonmigrating silvers, and their size averages will reflect that. Most of the fish taken here are in the 3- to 6-pound range. But migrating silvers are just around the corner, and a few of them are already showing up. You'll know these fish by their larger sizes.

"We're already seeing some ocean coho moving in," Krein says. "They started showing up after that big rain we got back in early August. They'll only keep increasing in numbers, and the sizes already seem to be getting bigger every day."

Krein says the biggest silver to grace his boat from Jeff Head so far this summer has been an impressive 12.7-pounder. But with big fish being reported at Neah Bay and Sekiu, silvers up to 20 pounds, it's just a matter of time until the really big daddies show.

Krein reports that roughly half the

silvers he's hoisting aboard are wild fish, and roughly half are hatchery fish. But in this marine area it's legal to keep both.

Best gear: Krein says the hottest thing you can put in the water here on an outgoing tide is a flasher and Coyote spoon, a Grand Slam bucktail in the white color, or a white squid if you're going to be trolling. White seems to be the hot color, and maybe that's because it approximates the squid that are in the area that the silvers might be feeding on. This is also a good area for winter blackmouth, and that may be because there are good numbers of sandlances on the bottom in this area too.

For mooching, go with 4 to 6 ounces of lead, a 6-foot leader, and a whole, fresh herring. Everyone has a different way of rigging their herring for mooching, but one of the most effective is to use a bait threader to hang the rear hook from the tail, and the front hook through the herring mouth to hold it straight. Jig the herring almost like you would a Dart or Buzz Bomb.

And speaking of which, working a pearl/fluorescent Buzz Bomb along the shoreline early in the morning is a great way to hook into resident coho that are marauding the shorelines looking for baitfish.

Where to fish: Jeff Head is roughly a 3½-mile boat ride across Puget Sound from Shilshole Bay, located just to the east of Indianola, north of Bainbridge Island. The way that it's set up, you can mooch close in to the shoreline, or troll just on the outskirts of it, moving between Jeff Head and Presidents Point as the tide moves in and out. You can run across the Sound from the Seattle side, or launch at Miller Bay to the south or Kingston to the north.

Moving north: Krein says that as of the first of September he'll start fishing a little further north, too, up in Marine Area 8-2, looking for silvers at the Shipwreck along Humpy Hollow. The even-year pinks that dashed through the salt here in July are pretty much out of the salt and up in the Snohomish system, Krein reports.

"We've got a river boat up there and they're catching them," he says.

The even-year pinks run earlier than the odd-year pinks. The even-years came through in early July, while odd-year pinks are usually available to saltwater anglers through late August.

AT a GLANCE

What: Excellent summertime silver fishing for resident and migratory fish close to home at Jeff Head.

Where: Fish between Jeff Head and President Point, directly across from Shilshole Bay.

How: Troll 35 to 60 feet down with white squids, Coyote spoons, or bucktails behind flashers and dodgers. Or, mooch a herring in those same depths. Also toss Buzz Bombs along the shoreline.

When: The first two hours at daybreak (before you have to go to work) is the perfect time.

Who to call: Gary Krein, All Star Charters (425-252-4188); Auburn Sports & Marine (253-833-1440)

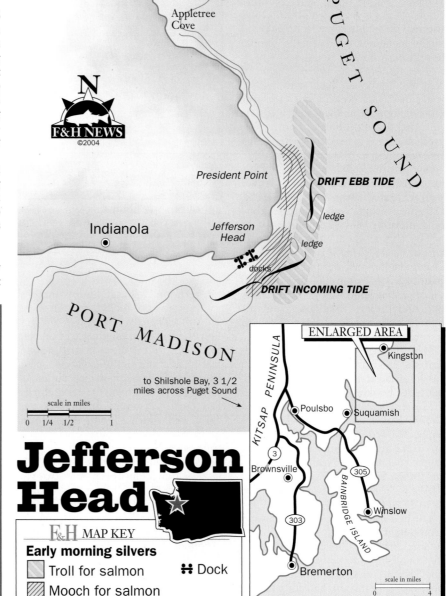

Jefferson Head

F&H MAP KEY

Early morning silvers

Troll for salmon

Mooch for salmon

✛ Dock

Two-Chinook limit for anglers working South Sound

TACOMA

by John Keizer

ord has already started to spread that the South Sound near Point Defiance is *the* place to target trophy Chinook in August. And it's true: this is the kickoff month for returning runs of large ocean-bright hatchery kings headed back to local South End rivers. The Puyallup, Chambers Creek and Nisqually will all see fish returning in August. The limit in Marine Area 11 has even been increased to allow retention of two kings this year, really making the drive south to Tacoma area well worth the trouble.

Where: Try off the Clay Banks and the Slag Pile near Point Defiance, or further east off the mouth of the Puyallup River, where plenty of big fish are nailed by trollers.

• **Puyallup River:** Trolling the 120-foot line with the downriggers set at 30 to 90 feet has accounted for most of my Chinook catches when fishing off the river mouth.

• **Nisqually River:** As we move later into August most large kings will be

AUGUST IS THE KICKOFF MONTH for big kings like this 32-pounder Jennifer Gonzalez caught near Point Defiance while fishing with Puget Sound Salmon Charters (253-565-6598).

taken fishing off the green can in front of McAllister Creek, and off the Nisqually River mouth just south of Anderson Island. The slight depression

on the bottom where the buoy is anchored will hold many Chinook waiting for the right conditions to hit the river.

Also near the Nisqually, troll north from the mouth of the river to Ketron Island on an outgoing tide, and turn it around and troll south along the shoreline on an incoming tide.

• **Chambers Creek:** Plenty of kings — all running 10 to 15 pounds — also show up at Chambers Creek north of Steilacoom anytime around the second week of August. Fishing for these kings is best done trolling south of the railroad bridge or jigging a Point Wilson Dart in the 60- to 90-foot-deep water just north of the bridge.

A few of these fat, hard-fighting fish will run around the 30-pound mark (I had six fatties over the 30-pound mark during August charters last season).

• **Point Defiance:** The most famous spot in the area is the Point Defiance Clay Banks, located just west of Owen Beach Park. This is the top spot to fish on the outgoing tide, and can flat produce fish. Early in the morning (daybreak), mooch or troll the 60- to 90-foot water. Kings move in and feed on

---

AT A GLANCE

What: South Sound kings. Season runs through Dec. 31.

Where: The Nisqually River mouth, Puyallup River mouth, Chambers Creek, McAllister Creek, Clay Banks, Slag Pile, Point Dalco.

Limit: Two salmon a day; coho must have clipped adipose fin south of the Narrows Bridge. The fishery is good now, but it peaks through the middle of August.

Launch: Two-lane launch at Point Defiance Park; one-lane launch with dock at Narrows Marina just south of Tacoma Narrows Bridge; one-lane ramp at Zittle's Marina near Olympia; small ramp in Gig Harbor, with no dock — it's OK for small boats but not much parking.

Gearing Up: Mooching tackle should include sinkers (2 to 6 ounces), light leaders and fresh herring (available at Narrows Marina and Point Defiance tackle shops). For trolling, rig up Hot Spot flashers, Grand Slam Bucktails, B-2 Squids and Kingfisher and Sonic Edge spoons. Also bring along rattle plugs in green-and-white glow.

Lodging: Motel 6 Tacoma (253-473-7100) and Commencement Bay Bed & Breakfast (253-752-8175).

Who to Call: Narrows Marina Tackle Shop (253-564-4222); Point Defiance Boathouse (253-591-5325) and Zittle's Marina in Olympia (360-459-1950). You are also welcome to contact me at Puget Sound Salmon Charters (253-565-6598).

the bait that stacks up in the eddy here.

Trollers, move out and work the 90- to 200-foot water. Run your downriggers at 60 to 90 feet as these are migrating fall king rather than blackmouth. I've done extremely well away from the other boats out in the deeper water.

Just to the east, located in front of the Point Defiance boat ramp, is the Slag Pile, which is another excellent Chinook spot. Deep dropoffs here make great holding water for fall kings. Try 100 to 150 feet of water early in the day. This is also a great coho spot later in the month.

• **Vashon Island:** When tide changes, shift your attack north across to Vashon Island. Troll or mooch from the ferry dock down to Point Dalco. Mooch starting in 60 feet of water off the ferry dock and drift into the deeper water off Point Dalco. Trollers hammer fish straight off Point Dalco itself, trolling the edges of the rip formed by the incoming current.

Mooching setup: The best simple mooching setup is a medium-action rod with a fast tip and a compatible reel, loaded with 12-pound test main line. I like Metzler sliding sinkers, with as little weight as you need (usually 2 to 6 ounces) to maintain bottom contact. The slider allows the fish to pick up the bait without feeling the weight. For hooks I like 3/0 or 4/0 Mustad 92604N Ultra Points on 7-foot leaders attached to a Sampo ball bearing swivel. Rig a fresh cutplug herring with a tight spin and you're set to slay summer Chinook.

Trolling setup: Downrigger fishing

simply outproduces all other methods when the name of the game is hooking fish in numbers. I run up to four electric Scottys on my 26-foot charter boat, the "*Special K.*" Being able to cover lots of water with your tackle at a controlled depth is an extremely effective way to fish.

I use Shimano Calcutta 400 reels and G. Loomis 10½-foot SAR1265C rods. Rig with 20-pound test main line.

If you fish light, go with a cut-plug herring. If you're a hardware fisherman, a large Hot Spot flasher with a mini Glow B-2 Squid, or a green Grand Slam bucktail on a 40-inch leader are consistent producers.

Go with spoons like Silver Horde's Sonic Edge and the Kingfisher — both

of which worked very well last year and have been producing fish through the early summer.

If you like plugs, try a 6-inch green spatterback or all white glow-in-the-dark.

Derby: South Sound's biggest salmon derby, the annual Gig Harbor Puget Sound Anglers Salmon Derby sponsored by Boaters World, will be held on Saturday, Aug. 11.

Prizes include $1,000 for first place, $500 for second, $250 for third, and many merchandise prizes.

Contact your local Boater's World store or Narrows Marina Tackle Shop for more on derby tickets, rules and other information.

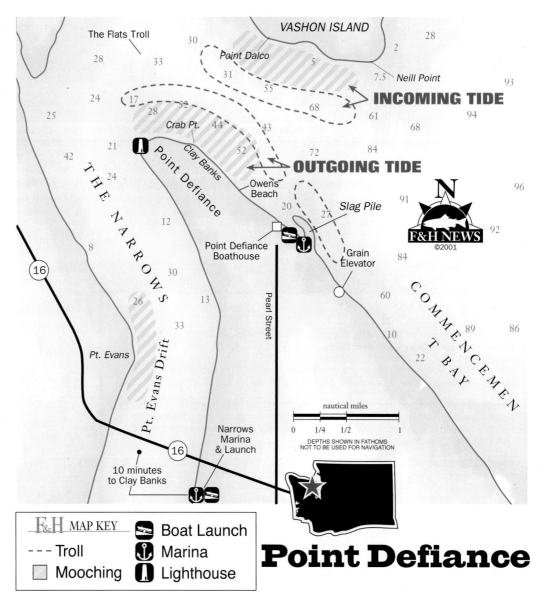

Point Defiance

MAP KEY
- - - Troll
Mooching
Boat Launch
Marina
Lighthouse

Work San Juan passes, tides for winter blackmouth

by Joel Shangle

Perhaps more so than any other salmon fishing region in Puget Sound, the San Juan Islands are all about tides. With water sucking in and around dozens of islands and points, and through dozens more current-funneling passages, hitting the right tides is as important as hitting the right color on the roulette wheel — you pick the wrong one, you're going to lose.

Without a doubt, the San Juans and all of Marine Area 7 will be a hot zone for blackmouth anglers working their way through the February-into-April season. The Islands in late winter are something to behold: scads of bait, tons of biter blackmouth, good fishing. And a handful of fisheries off Rosario Strait, starting north at Point Lawrence and extending south past Obstruction Pass, Peavine Pass, Thatcher Pass and Lopez Pass, are on the A-List for Island anglers looking for a February, March or April score.

But, oh those tides. Timing matters, big time. Not that you absolutely can't catch fish on *any* tide, but maximizing your efforts on the right tide is where the smart money is. Just ask the guys who do this for a living.

"I generally like the morning tides," says Darrell Stacey at Eagle Point Charters (360-966-3334) in Bellingham. "I'm a superstitious fisherman, and I'm into that 'early bird gets the worm' routine, but I'll fish morning tides whenever I can."

Actually, a serious fishing conversation with Stacey is a lesson in the tide book — he books clients around tide schedules, he fishes certain areas around tide schedules, he refers to the push and fall of tides like a scientist refers to the Periodic Table. And with good reason — tides can make or break you, and you're a fool if you don't maximize your time.

Take a look at these Rosario tidal fisheries:

POINT LAWRENCE: One of the best fisheries in Puget Sound on a big flood tide as bait gets pushed around the point into a massive "bait bucket" that stretches along the east shore of Orcas Island south to Sea Acre.

"When you get a big tide, maybe 7, 8, 9 feet, moving off the end of that point, it blows in off the point and makes a huge back eddy that sucks bait all the way down to Sea Acre," says Stacey. "It's basically a big holding area for bait. You get on a line in the 90- to 100-foot range and you can troll that thing back and forth like a freeway."

Staying in the 100-feet-and-shallower range is a key here.

"Don't be afraid to fish it in 75 to 85 feet," suggests Stacey. "The bottom is sandy there, so you don't have to worry about losing gear. Stay on the bottom — your ball will just bounce. You have to stay on that 90- to 100-foot line. As soon as you get off that, you'll find yourself in 150 feet quick. When you make your turn, and this might sound obvious, turn *into* the island. If you turn out, you'll find yourself out there in the deep water and you'll never get back."

OBSTRUCTION PASS: Hot fishing on the flood, and best fished on a smaller tide.

"There's such an enormous current in Obstruction, even on a 2- to 3-foot tide, it just gushes through there," says Stacey. "Even on a small tide, it runs through there hard. It's almost like fishing a river, where you fish up and down in front of the pass."

Stacey likes to skirt the kelp bed around Deer Point and slightly into Obstruction, staying on the Orcas side through the flood.

"When you get into the pass, you hit a series of 'humpty dumpties' that go from 50 to 75 feet deep," he says. "You have to work your downrigger, and you're gonna lose gear. But those fish will sit in those humpty dumpties, and you have to be down on bottom finding them."

PEAVINE PASS: Similar gig, with the flood being the prime tidal influence and the best fishing coming from shallow water on the Blakely Island side.

"My attitude is that if there are fish in Obstruction, they'll be in Peavine," says Stacey.

THATCHER PASS: Another flood fishery, and one where cut-plug herring is the bait of choice. Stick to the 80- to 90-foot zone from Black Rock well into the pass on the ebb. On the Decatur side, fish between the Cable Crossing and Undertaker Reef.

LOPEZ PASS: The earlier the better here because numbers will gradually diminish later in the season as fish migrate. Hang closer to the south side of the pass, trolling east-west toward Kellett Ledge and back in 70 feet of water.

OFF-STRAIT FISH: A couple of areas to target off Rosario include Spring Pass off the west side of Orcas Island and Cattle Point. At Spring Pass, fish from the Orcas side heading toward the Jones side on the ebb or, better yet, hit it right at tide change.

"When things slow down on Rosario in March and April, you'll catch some of those Fraser fish moving through Spring Pass," says Stacey. "That's a fishery where I'll run the boat as hard as I can to

PAY ATTENTION to your tide book for your best shot at San Juan Island blackmouth.

AT A GLANCE

What: Area 7 winter blackmouth.

When: Season runs Feb. 16-April 10. Should see hot fishing from opening day on.

Where: Off Rosario Strait, including Point Lawrence, Obstruction Pass, Peavine Pass, Lopez Pass, Spring Pass.

Tactics: Troll cut-plug or whole herring, glow green squid behind a red/green Hot Spot flasher.

Information: Darrell Stacey, Eagle Point Charters (360-966-3334; eaglepointcharters.com) in Bellingham; Jim Aggergaard at Catchmore Charters (360-293-7093) in Anacortes; Sea Hawk Charters (360-424-1350)

> **"I'm a superstitious fisherman, and I'm into that 'early bird gets the worm' routine, but I'll fish morning tides whenever I can."**
> — *Darrell Stacey at Eagle Point Charters*

get there on the tide change. If I'm at Eagle Bluff and I know the change is coming, I'll pull 'em up and jam over to Spring."

Hit Cattle Point on the ebb, starting at the buoy and working your way back through. And if the weather cooperates, run out to Salmon Bank.

"Those fish are like piranhas out there, man," says Stacey. "The place is just teeming with bait. If the weather is good and you can get out there, the fishing can be really good."

TIMING: First couple of weeks after opener should be ultra productive fishing for blackmouth that have been unpressured and allowed to build for months.

"My best advice the first few weeks is to just go to your old stomping grounds and fish — you'll be good to go, because there'll be plenty of fish around," says Stacey.

The Rosario fishery will hum along through February and March, but by April, Obstruction and Spring will be among the better alternatives.

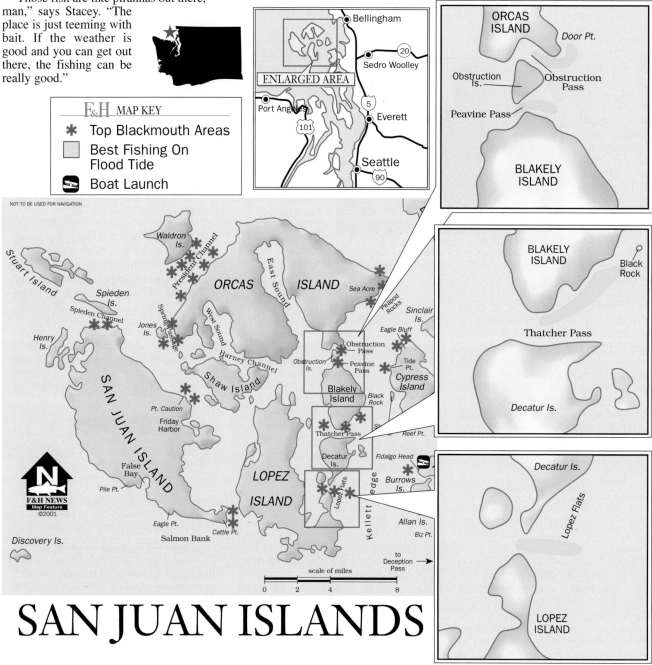

SAN JUAN ISLANDS

Jig inshore, troll offshore for Tulalip Bubble kings

MARYSVILLE

by Tom Nelson

Tulalip Bay. For North Sound king salmon anglers, "the Bubble" is the best, closest and easiest-access Chinook fishery available. Fortunately, there are good numbers of Chinook on tap this year — 6,500-plus to the Tulalip Tribal facility and over 20,000 fly-bys headed to the Snohomish system. Tack on some Stillaguamish kings and a few Skagit strays and *boom*, you have a genuine local king fishery!

There are several ways to get these rapidly maturing kings to bite, but your choice of techniques should be influenced by your location in the Bubble.

Inshore vs. offshore fishing: Tulalip can be broken down into an inshore/bottom-oriented fishery and an offshore/suspended fishery.

Inshore across the bay and on Mission Bar, you'll see jiggers, moochers and sinker/diver trollers all taking Chinook.

Outside, however, downriggers dominate the scene, and rightly so. Sure, you'll see the occasional moocher or jigger out there, but day in and day out, it's very difficult to compete with a good 'rigger man.

So where does the inside fishery end and the outside fishery begin? Good question! For the sake of argument I would put the line at the 100-foot mark. This 100-foot demarcation is somewhat arbitrary, but holds up in light of technique-related depth limitations. Simply stated: It's tough to jig or mooch the bottom

A BIGGER BUBBLE of opportunity awaits North Sound anglers this season, as the Tulalip Terminal fishery opens June 18. Author Tom Nelson and daughter Sophie hoist a typical Tulalip king.

effectively at anything deeper than 100 feet.

Offshore offerings: While the offshore fishery is well attended by the One Depth Society (anglers who lower their gear to a certain depth and keep it there all day), there are many fishermen who work hard at it. You'll have your best success using Hot Spot flasher gear (40- to 60-inch leaders) rigged with Kingfisher or Coyote spoons, squid and bucktails. Silver Horde plugs are a good bet outside, as well as whole herring rigged in a Krippled Herring helmet or a Pro-Troll Roto-Chip bait holder.

So what gives you the edge over all of the other outside trollers? Easy: fish at the right depth.

And how do you know what the "right" depth is? Read your sounder and put your gear at the same depth as fish.

Simple, huh?

But not so fast: Are you still using old black-and-white, low-pixel-count LCD fishfinders? If you are, you're missing out on the whole picture. Lowrance has many high-resolution color sounders available for very reasonable prices. Color's advantage over BW is its ability to vividly depict lower signal strength targets.

In other words you'll see more fish with color fishfinders. If you're seeing more fish and moving the ol' Scotty to the depth of the fish, you're going to catch more fish guaranteed. Color fishfinders used in conjunction with downriggers is the deadliest salmon catching combination there is.

Period.

The inside scoop: While we are targeting suspended (hovering off the bottom) fish in the offshore fishery, once you come inside, the focus shifts to kings hugging the bottom. Even though it's possible to troll the bottom closely with downriggers, the accuracy and effectiveness of bouncing a Pt. Wilson Dart on the bottom cannot be disputed.

The inside troll fishery is definitely more labor-intensive as you must constantly raise and lower the downrigger

Tulalip Kings

ball to accurately track the bottom contour. In addition, the jig fishery actually requires you to — are you sitting down? — *stand up and hold your rod*! I know that we're going to lose a few folks right there, and many are even now signing up for the One Depth Society. Keep in mind that it is very satisfying to be holding the rod when Tyee Von Chinookerson comes a callin'. In fact, there are those who would rather catch one king jiggin' than catch two trolling. You will definitely get your batteries charged when you hook up on a jig.

Think of mooching, jigging and trolling as different "solutions" to your fishing "problem." There are times and tides every day when one technique will outproduce another. Let's look at a couple of examples.

Ebb and flood: High tides, particularly in the morning, will pull kings into the bay. This is a great time to be trolling inside. If you mark a pile of bait, kings or both, pull out the jig rods and drop the darts on their skulls. Naturally, this is tough to do if you don't have a couple of jig sticks prerigged and ready to rock. Daiwa makes a great one-piece jig rod, the SS762, and it will only nick you about 50 bucks. You can't even gas up the boat for that these days!

Once the tide starts to ebb and the sun rises in the sky, the kings have two good reasons to get off the flats — loss of depth/cover and increased light level. Anticipate the kings' desire to bail out of the bay and get to the edges of the bar to intercept them as they flee to the deep water.

Low tides virtually dry up Tulalip Bay as well as Mission Bar. When this occurs during midday, rest assured that it's definitely outside trolling time. The edge of the bar is just too shallow, bright and warm to hold kings in the mood to bite. So look for "pods" of Chinook suspended in the deep water. I've caught Tulalip kings with 250 feet of wire out in over 300 feet of water.

The point is that at this time of day (and tide) they could be about any-

where. However, take heart in the fact that once you find them, there is quite often more that one. Try to stay on top of the school, and if you stop marking them, keep your gear at the depth you last observed fish. This is the classic "put in your time" scenario. When you catch a fish, remember to stay in the general area and depth range and chances are very good that you'll double up!

When the flood begins in earnest, keep in mind that the kings will begin to nose up on the bar. This is a very good jigging/mooching situation, since the kings will certainly be right on the bottom as they sneak into the bay or up on the bar. Pt. Wilson Darts in green/white, plain white or candlefish (green, yellow or silver) in the 2½- or 4-ounce sizes are my favorites.

Use only enough jig to keep your iron close to the bottom and your line angle close to vertical. Jigs are designed to display optimum fish-attracting action on the *drop*. If you start to develop too large of a line angle, it become difficult to give the lure the slack it requires to work effectively.

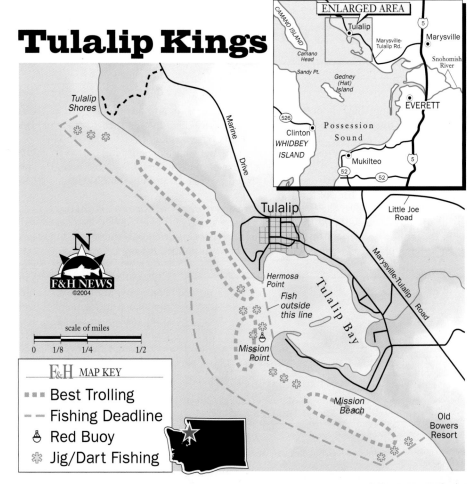

F&H MAP KEY

■ ■ ■ Best Trolling
– – Fishing Deadline
⚓ Red Buoy
❊ Jig/Dart Fishing

Feb. 16 blackmouth opener brings anglers to Area 8-2

by Joel Shangle

CAPT. CRAIG REEDY holds a typical blackmouth, taken on a Les Davis plug just off the Whidbey Island shoreline.

AT A GLANCE

What: West side Whidbey Island blackmouth.

When: Season runs Feb. 16-April 10 in Marine Areas 8-2 and 9. Fishing should be excellent from the opener on.

Limit: One fish, 22-inch minimum.

Where: Areas to target on the west side of Whidbey include Indian Point, Useless Bay, Double Bluff, Mutiny Bay. Across the channel, hit Point No Point and Skunk Bay.

Techniques: Downrigger trolling with plugs, spoons, squid, herring or drift mooching herring.

Information: John Martinis, John's Sporting Goods (425-259-3056); Dave Morgison, Possession Point Charters (360-652-3797); Gary Krein, All Star Charters (425-252-4188); Craig Reedy, AAA Salmon Charters (425-252-8246); Tom Young, Tommycod Charters (800-283-8900); Big King Salmon Charters (425-776-7688); Eagle Enterprise Charters (425-481-4325)

Forget the entrees at The Bistro in downtown Langley — the most appetizing thing on the menu at Whidbey Island from Feb. 16-April 10 is winter blackmouth. When Puget Sound re-opens to salmon fishing in the middle of February, you can bet that the southern half of this sprawling Island County fishery will be swarming with boats hoping to recapture some of the magic of a 2000 season that produced more big fish than any late-winter season in recent memory. You can bet your best trolling rod that *I'll* be in the middle of the mix, working for some more of those 12-pound fish that kept showing up last year through the February-through-April fishery.

"Last year was the most amazing season we've had in years," says *F&H News* North End saltwater columnist John Martinis at John's Sporting Goods (425-259-3056) in Everett. "We saw some of the biggest, most consistent fish I've ever seen around here. Can we repeat that? That remains to be seen, but I'd wager that we can. Salmon seem to be in pretty good shape all over now."

AREA 8-2/9 SPLIT: Marine Areas 8-2 and 9 (including the southern half of Whidbey) are among the most heavily fished pieces of water in Puget Sound, for one reason: the Everett Marina lies in the heart of the area, within minutes of some of the Sound's best blackmouth spots. With easy access to go-to spots on the east side of Whidbey like the Racetrack, Sandy Point, Columbia Beach and Possession Point, the Everett facility serves as our home base to fish this area 99 times out of 100. But there's a whole 'nuther side of Whidbey that doesn't attract nearly the number of salmon boats as those usual east side

favorites, but holds as many biting blackmouth as anything on the Everett side. Starting at Scatchet Head and extending north along the west Whidbey shoreline past Useless Bay, Double Bluff and up past Mutiny Bay, there's an untapped salmon resource just waiting to be exploited by salmon anglers thinking outside the usual mundane Racetrack/Possession box.

"Fishing can be quite good along near Double Bluff and in that general area, but most of the time I won't spend the fuel to get over there," says Dave Morgison at Possession Point Charters (360-652-3797).

And neither will nine out of 10 boats that operate out of Everett. Instead of wasting the time and fuel to run all the way back and forth from Everett, the smart mobile angler will trailer the boat across to Whidbey on the Mukilteo-Clinton ferry and launch at one of the four west shore facilities (see inset) that put them within minutes of Indian Point, Useless Bay, Point No Point, Skunk Bay, Double Bluff, Mutiny Bay and the stretch between Bush Point and Lagoon Point.

...the best fishing starts right at that corner and halfway to the Scatchet Head Buoy.

"It's going to be a little of a wait-and-see approach, but the area over there can be good for fish heading out toward the Strait," says Morgison.

HOW/WHERE TO FISH: Techniques include simple motor mooching with herring or downrigger trolling with plugs, spoons or flasher/bait setups. Locations to consider include:

Scatchet Head to Indian Point: "Not too many salmon anglers fish right at Scatchet Head anymore," says Martinis. "This salmon hole is at the corner where Scatchet Head turns into Useless Bay, and the best fishing starts right at that corner and halfway to the Scatchet Head Buoy. If you try trolling closer to the buoy, the tidal flow will be so great that you won't make any headway as you troll. Besides that, the best fishing is closer to the corner."

Fish this area in 90 to 120 feet of water on an outgoing tide. It's a good place to hit on days tidal intensity is low, because there will be good water flow as the water sweeps across Possession and

Scatchet Head and then flows into Useless Bay.

Useless Bay: Fish at the top of the incoming tide deep inside the bay, on the west side just past Double Bluff.

"You definitely want to stay inside the bay," says Martinis. "Outside, you run into heavier current, and that's not where you'll find the fish."

Double Bluff: Fish right at the buoy, drift mooching on the outgo with herring.

Mutiny Bay: Formerly a local favorite to drift mooch, but not nearly as prolific in recent years.

"You're so close to Midchannel Bank there, most people will just run over to Midchannel and fish," says Martinis.

Still worth a look for moochers working straight out from the launch.

Point No Point: Across Saratoga Passage from Indian Point, mooch Point No Point early in an outgoing tide with *small* herring.

"Point No Point is very good the first hour of the tide," says Martinis. "You have to find small herring for that area, though. If you can find 4-inch herring, you're set. Small bait is a key there."

Skunk Bay: Morgison like to fish this area with plugs in mother of pearl or white, or with Coyote spoons (No. 188).

"If I don't find them at Skunk Bay, I'll fish back toward Pilot Point," he says. "This is not a set-in-concrete thing — sometimes, if you're not catching them, you have to switch up and fish something different. People like to define these fisheries as being a certain way at a certain time and tide, but I find that you'll catch fish almost anywhere, at any time. Fish a location hard, and if there's nothing happening, pull up and go somewhere else."

WHIDBEY ISLAND LAUNCHES

Bush Point Resort
Facilities: Hoist, gravel parking for 30 trailered vehicles, fish cleaning station.
Directions: Take the Mukilteo-Clinton ferry to Clinton and head west on State Route 525 to milepost 19; turn left on Bush Point Road, go 3 miles, and head left at the 'Y' at Scurlock Road. Go roughly ¾ mile and turn left on Main Street to the facility at the bottom of the hill.

Mutiny Bay Launch
Facilities: One-lane concrete ramp, spaces for 25 trailered vehicles, restroom.
Directions: Follow 525 out of Clinton to Fish Road, turn right and go one mile to Mutiny Bay Road. Drive 1.4 mile to Robinson Road, turn right, and drive to the ramp.

Dave Mackie Park
Facilities: One-lane concrete ramp, 30 spaces for trailered vehicles, restroom, public park. Launch is unusable at low tide.
Directions: From Clinton, head west on 525 for 4 miles to Marwelton Road and head south for 5½ miles. The park is on the right.

Possession Beach Waterfront Park
Facilities: One-lane concrete ramp, one loading float, restroom, public park.
Directions: From Clinton head west on 525 for 3 miles to Cultus Bay Road. Drive 5 miles to Possession Road and head east to the entrance of Possession Beach Waterfront Park.

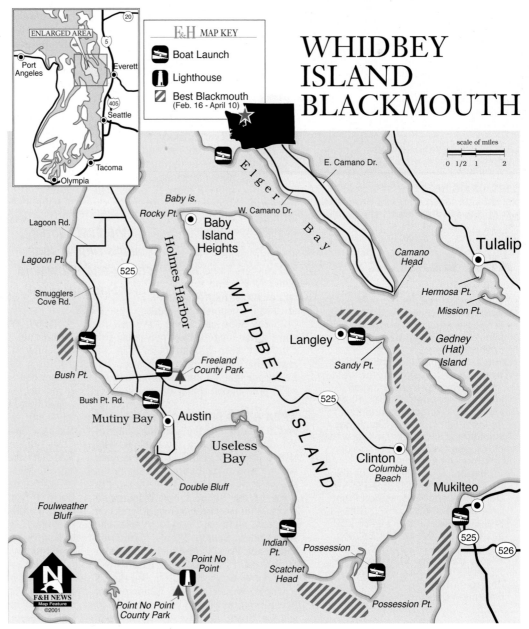

WHIDBEY ISLAND BLACKMOUTH

F&H MAP KEY
- Boat Launch
- Lighthouse
- Best Blackmouth (Feb. 16 - April 10)

Outlook good for Marine Area 8-2 silvers

EVERETT

by Kent Alger

ACTION for Area 8-2 silvers, like this 14-pounder Tristan Costa caught at the Shipwreck last year, should heat up through September for anglers trolling squid, herring, spoons and bucktails.

With a solid number of coho salmon expected to return to Puget Sound this late summer and fall, the fishing should surpass that of the five-year average, and could match the red hot fishing of last season. For a quick refresher, a typical day last summer on favorite North Sound fishing grounds within the area that stretches from Possession Bar through Port Gardner to Camano Head consisted of multiple-fish days, with the best average size anyone had seen in recent years.

With most salmon runs returning about two weeks later than normal, the prime coho fishing is just around the corner. Early reports indicate the majority of the Puget Sound coho are still milling around and fattening up in the Strait of Juan de Fuca, giving anglers some extra time to clean their boats, spool their reels and stock up on favorite coho tackle for the oncoming opportunity.

Timing is everything: With all areas of the central and north Sound now open for coho, it's just a matter of waiting for the bulk of the return to enter our local waters as they begin their migration up the Skagit, Stillaguamish and Snohomish rivers.

By Labor Day, Point No Point and Possession Bar should be fishing very well. The excellent fishing will hold up through the entire month of September and into October. As September passes and October comes, move east and focus on the popular Shipwreck/Humpy Hollow area along the shoreline that runs south of Mukilteo. You will also want to move farther east, closer to the mouth of the Snohomish and Stillaguamish rivers.

Don't give up on October, though. That's when dreams are made for those set on hooking the infamous hooknoses, the largest, strongest and best-fighting coho. Don't be afraid to take a gamble and venture back out to Possession Bar then looking for the last of the ocean-returning coho.

Key areas: Possession Bar is one of the most heavily fished areas in Puget Sound, but it also produces some of the most consistent fishing. The bar is a large shelf that extends about a mile and half into Puget Sound off the southern tip (Scatchet Head to Possession Point) of Whidbey Island and ranges in depth from 30 feet to 180 feet.

It's popular not only because it provides excellent and consistent fishing for coho through August, September and October, but because it also accessible to most boats as long as the weather and water are calm. The easiest and quickest way to reach the bar is to launch at Mukilteo State Park and run west. When you're running across, just focus on the southern tip of Whidbey Island and you'll have no problem finding it on a fogless day. The famous "Green Can" marks the center of the bar.

If you're fishing an outgoing tide, I prefer to fish the west side of the bar; on an incoming tide, focus on the east side. If you have a depth finder or a good navigation map such as those by The Fish-n-Map Company, find and troll along the 90-, 100- or 110-foot marker.

If you're making a run over to the bar at first light, I always make sure to make a quick pass about 300 yards off The Bait Box, a popular beach fishery south of Clinton that is marked by a flashing light. Every year a large number of coho return as adults from juvenile plants by the owners of Possession Bait and Tackle. Because there are always a good number of coho milling of the beach in this area, and because it's on your way out to the bar from Mukilteo or Everett, it's always worth a quick try.

As September progresses, focus on the Shipwreck/Humpy Hollow area south of Mukilteo. Returning coho will begin to stage before entering the local rivers, stacking along the

90-foot line that runs from Mukilteo to the Shipwreck. This is always a productive fishery and is much easier to access for those rough days when getting over to the bar is tough and dangerous for those with smaller boats. Most of those who focus on the area will launch at Mukilteo and begin to fish immediately.

Working the waters from the Mukilteo ferry dock back towards Everett can be productive at times. If you're going to give this area a try, be sure to stay relatively close to shore in 60 to 90 feet of water. Over on the east side of Whidbey Island, Columbia Beach (south of Clinton) and Sandy Point (north of Clinton) are both productive areas, as is the east side of Camano Island just north of Camano Head.

And whatever you do, don't pass up the small bays and points that are situated along the mainland north of Tulalip Bay. This area will literally stack with coho in late September, and it can be quite a spectacle to see hundreds of adult silvers splashing, jumping and milling around. These are fish that are ready to enter to the Stillaguamish and Snohomish rivers and thus can be quite stale. They are by no means easy to catch.

Remember when you are coho fishing, do not stay in one area too long if the fishing slows down — even if the fishing was blistering hot just 20 minutes prior. North Puget Sound coho are notorious for moving very quickly. Look for working birds, bait balls and move between the aforementioned areas constantly and you will be successful.

A quick note on boat launches: The Mukilteo State Park boat launch may be closer to many of the fishing grounds, but it cannot accommodate the amount of boats that the Everett launch off Marine View Drive will. If you decide to launch at Mukilteo, bring plenty of patience and offer a helping hand to your fellow salmon anglers.

Coho gear: When it comes to chasing after coho, I prefer to avoid those oversized downrigger rods and reels loaded with 40-pound monofilament. They are popular and inexpensive, but they take the fight out of a species that — given half a chance — will make quick, long runs and tailwalks. I have a

strong preference for medium-action rods that run from 8½ to 10½ feet and are rated from 8- to 12- to 10- to 20-pound test mono. Fill a 5500, 6500 Abu Garcia or Shimano Bantam 50 or Tr-200 with 15- to 25-pound line and you're ready take these fish on.

The terminal tackle needed to pursue saltwater coho can be quite simple. Talk to a large percentage of salmon fisherman and they will tell you to fish a green/glow squid 31 inches behind a green/glow Hot Spot Flasher 60 feet down. I prefer to keep some variety on my boat because these coho can get picky at times.

Running various green/blue/glow squids 32 inches behind either a

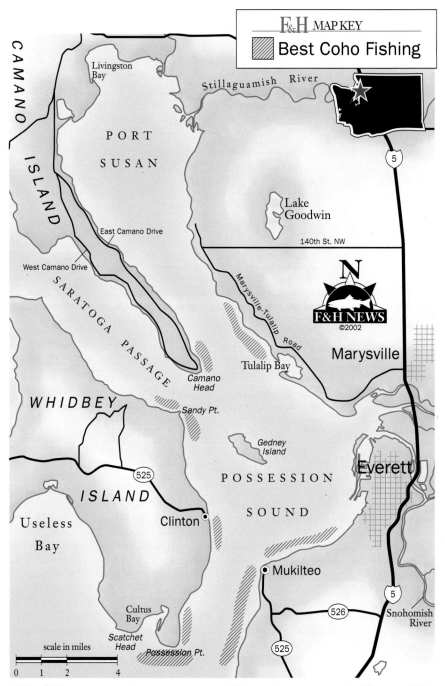

Marine Area 8-2

Puget Sound Saltwater • SALMON

green/glow or red/glow Hot Spot (or like brand) will catch fish, but be sure to have a good selection of spoons to fish when the squids stop catching fish. Must-have spoons are the cop car (top producer last year) and the spatterback green/glow Coho Killers produced by Silver Horde and the 3½-inch Coyote spoons in army truck, cop car, funky chicken and green/glow. Either run the spoons 60 inches behind a Hot Spot flasher or solo.

Another favorite method of mine is to troll any of the commercially available coho flies 18 to 22 inches behind a 0 chrome dodger. I prefer the Grand Slam Bucktails in the 4-inch needlefish green/white, but any of the bucktail flies produced by Whally Whale/Zak Tackle will produce.

At first light, it's possible to catch fish only 20 feet below the surface, but the instant the sun touches the water you'll either have to fish off downriggers or with a diver to reach the depths of 60 to 90 feet, where the coho will be found throughout the day.

If you decide to fish the beaches north of Tulalip Bay, bring along small Krocodile and Kastmaster spoons. As I said, these fish will become very temperamental. It is great fun fishing over hundreds of milling coho, but to be productive, you must change your tactics. Jig small Krocodile, Kastmaster and other spoons, as well as small jigs in fairly shallow water along these beaches. If you stick to your standard trolling methods, you will have an incredibly difficult time getting these stale fish to bite. Launch at Kayak Point Park.

AT A GLANCE

What: Marine Area 8-2 and 9 coho.

Where: From Camano Head and Port Gardner to the north, south to Possession Point. The area includes several key coho fisheries, including Possession Bar, the Bait Box, Humpy Hollow, the east side of Whidbey Island, the bays and points near Tulalip Bay.

When: Silvers will build around Possession through early September before surging further east and north to Humpy Hollow, etc., through the rest of the month into October.

Tackle/Techniques: Troll spoons, flies, hoochies behind flashers, staying close to the surface before first light and then moving gradually deeper through the day.

Information: Three Rivers Marine and Tackle (425-415-1575); John's Sporting Goods (425-259-3056).

Charters: AAA Charters (425-252-8246); Possession Point Charters (360-652-3797); All Star Charters (425-252-4188); Eagle Enterprise Charters (888-594-8393).

Photos Afield

HE ALMOST CANCELLED, but we have a feeling — a 43-pound feeling — that Everett's Dan Bihary (left) is *still* happy he decided to make a high-speed early August run out to the Hoh for kings. He and son Adam were fishing with guide Jim Mansfield when this hog of a Chinook hit a Kwikfish at about 8 a.m. "A 43-pound king from Washington State is nothing to miss out on in one's lifetime," Dan writes. (Eagle Claw Photo Contest entry)

Tune-up for the Everett Derby: 8-2, 9 coho where & how

EVERETT

by Chris Paulson

Anyone who has fished north Puget Sound when the coho are in knows that it can be a frenzy. Literally hundreds of boats school up off places like Edmonds and Humpy Hollow near Mukilteo hoping to get a cut of the action.

Big numbers of silvers will usually show up toward the end of August in Marine Areas 8-2 and 9, staying strong well into September.

These are mainly hatchery fish, mostly running 4 to 7 pounds. Later in September, a shot of larger natives, which can weigh in the teens, move in. These are the fish that'll win the Sept. 20-21 Everett Coho Derby.

Here's more on when and where to catch the whole lot of them:

Trolling: The best time of day to fish for coho is from sunup to midmorning, or roughly 6 to 11 a.m. Trolling the surface with flies or spoons can be good at sunrise. After the sun has been on the water for an hour, it's best to fish down 35 feet or deeper. Keep going deeper as the sun gets higher in the sky until you're down to 80 to 85 feet. There is often a good midmorning bite between 8:30 and 10:30 a.m.

Silvers like a fast-moving bait, and using downriggers and a 12-pound ball allows you to troll at a depth where the fish are while maintaining a speed of around 3.5 mph.

At times, trolling against the tide will catch more fish. It may appear you're going slowly, but as long as your downrigger cable has an angle of 45 degrees or so, your gear should be getting good action.

Fairly light gear can be used for these fish. An 8-foot fiberglass rod works well with downriggers. Use a good levelwind reel, such as a Shimano or Abu Garcia, with 20-pound mainline.

Best set-up for trolling is a flasher and a squid or spoon. A top producer is a 12-inch Hot Spot flasher in dark green, with mirror prism reflectors. These work extremely well with the Golden Bait green squid OG142R trolled 30 inches behind the flasher, or a green-glow Coyote 3.5 spoon 42 inches behind the flasher. Add some Berkley Power Bait Salmon Scent paste to your flasher and lures.

Try trolling surface flies if you get out early enough. A blue/white or pink/white bucktail fly can work well for this. Use a ⅛- to ¼-ounce trolling rudder type weight on a 6- to 7-foot leader.

You may have to use the main motor as you want to troll 5 to 7 mph. It's fun to watch the coho try to jump out of the water to grab the fly.

Trolling paths: While silvers can be taken almost anywhere in 8-2 and 9, there are a few places where they tend to school up. Try trolling off Edmonds Marina close to shore in the early morning.

Midmorning, try farther out in 300 to 400 feet of water between the ferry dock and as far south as Point Wells.

Fishing the riptides on either side of Possession Bar can be good for too.

In 8-2, between the shipwreck and Mukilteo — especially in Humpy Hollow — is a top spot. Trolling north to south here seems to get more hook-ups.

Mooching: Action can also be good mooching herring. Often on a summer morning, lots of bait balls can be seen popping on the surface around north Puget Sound. When you see this, drop a cut-plug herring near a school. That

GET OUT EARLY in the morning during the next two months for your best shot at a limit of Marine Areas 8-2 and 9 silvers. *F&H*'s Andy Walgamott bonked this 9-plus-pounder fishing near Picnic Point with Three River Marine & Tackle's Dave Lee during last year's Everett Coho Derby.

can be just the ticket to a limit.

Use a fairly light salmon rod with a soft tip and a levelwind reel filled with 12-pound test. If you tie your own leaders, run 12-pound fluorocarbon and size 3/0-4/0 Gamakatsu hooks.

Use a sliding sinker set-up, with the lightest keel (banana) sinker you can get away with, and rig your cut-plug herring for a tight spin.

Mooching spots: The riptides around Possession Bar can hold a lot of bait and salmon, making it a good spot to mooch. Around the east corner of Possession Point, the Bait Box area can be good for shallow-water mooching. Also try near the lighthouse at Mukilteo and off the ledge near Apple Cove Point by Kingston.

From the beach: Coho, like steelhead, can often be nabbed from shore as they pass by the Sound's many points. At times, you can beach a limit as easily as a guy can boat one.

A medium-action steelhead rod matched to a levelwind or a spinning reel, such as a Shimano 4000 series, capable of holding 150 yards of 12-pound fluorocarbon, is a good option. If you're fly fishing, go with a 9- to 12-foot rod, 7- to 10-weight line and 9- to 12-pound tippets.

Buzz Bombs in green, chartreuse or pink can work well. Spinners and weighted spoons, such as chrome Krocodiles, also draw hits. Small baitfish-imitating fly patterns in the same colors also work.

Off docks, such as Edmonds Pier, lead jigs pretty much rule, although fishing a small cutplug under a weighted bobber also has taken many fish. Bring a crab ring or other net, with a long rope, which can be lowered from the dock to the water level to land fish.

There are several other shore fishing areas in the north Sound to target. Bush Point, north of Mutiny Bay on Whidbey Island, is a top place to yard a silver in from the surf. The Bait Box, on the island's southeast corner, is another place to toss bobbers and herring. At Mukilteo, cast lures in front of the lighthouse or wade out near Elliot Point just to the south and work a fly. Picnic Point offers shoreline to cast lures or fly fish, as well as fish from a float tube.

Areas 8-2, 9 Coho

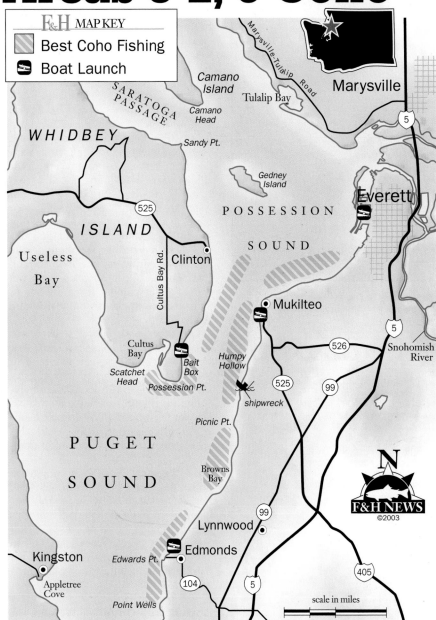

AT a GLANCE

What: Coho in Areas 8-2 and 9.

Where: Between Point Wells and Mukilteo, including hot spots such as off Edmonds Marina, Possession Bar, the Shipwreck and Humpy Hollow.

Timing: Mid-August to mid-October. Peak time is late August through mid-September for large numbers of hatchery silvers.

Limits/regs: Two coho per day in 8-2 and 9. Barbless hooks required.

Who to call: All Season Charters (425-743-9590); Ed's Surplus (425-778-1441); John's Sporting Goods (425-259-3056).

Launch: Edmonds Marina, Kingston Marina, Lighthouse Park in Mukilteo or 10th Street Ramp in Everett.

It's a glow show for Area 10 winter blackmouth

SEATTLE

by Ryley Fee

It's 5:30 a.m. The alarm buzzes, the lights come on. Mumble a few profanities, fill the thermos and fire up the rig to head out for some winter blackmouth. Luckily, you don't have to drive far to find some really good fishing spots here in the greater Seattle area.

Sliding out of Shilshole on a dead calm 36-degree morning, with plenty of hot coffee as company and flat-calm waters through the windshield can't be beat. Knowing exactly where to go helps too, so here's a rundown of some great spots in Marine Area 10:

West Point: This is a well-known fishing spot in central 10, but you don't want to fish it for blackmouth the same way you would for other returning salmon. You have to work the bottom structure here.

First off, in this area I always use a double-glow Silver Horde Flasher and a glow hoochie with a herring strip teaser. For me, only three trolling paths ever produce. The first path begins just south of the West Point Buoy, where you'll find a ledge that runs east to west with 60 to 70 feet of water to the south and 130-plus-foot water to the north. On either tide, you can find blackmouth sitting along this ledge which protrudes for about ½-mile due west-southwest. On an incoming tide, bait will be pushed up from the deeper water coming from the north, and blackmouth lay in ambush along the ledge.

The other path is along the north side of West Point inside Shilshole Bay. On an outgoing tide, bait will tend to congregate inside this protected area. Work the 100- to 140-foot depths here.

The third path can be in the 60- to 80-foot flats south of West Point headed towards Fourmile Rock. Work this area later on during an incoming tide.

The Trees: This area north of Shilshole is offshore from Carkeek Park. During winter there are frequently good-sized bait balls in this protected area, even moreso during higher tidal flows. Work the 100- to 120-foot contour here and look for bait. Drift-mooching herring also produces here.

Appletree Cove / Kingston: Another good place to find herring balls seeking shelter. Troll the whole bay, sticking to the bottom 10 to 15 feet of water in 80- to 120-foot depths. Watch out for ferry traffic!

Jefferson Head: This is one of the top winter producers in central Puget Sound. The two ways I fish this area are to either troll or drift-mooch herring along the outer bar as seen on the map. Similar to other areas, tend to stick to depths of 80 to 130 feet along the outer bar to find fish. However, there is a good chance of bait sitting in shallower water here. If you can mark bait or see it brimming on the surface in the shallow center of the bar, change your depths and/or get a mooched cut-plug in the water under the ball.

Point Monroe: This area also offers good protection for bait. Take a pass or two through this area and look for bait balls. If you can find them, makes some passes while trolling a hoochie, spoon or straight cut-plug.

Yeomalt Point / Eagle Harbor: This area is easy to troll, with a fairly straight north-south 100-foot depth contour that borders some of the deepest water in Puget sound. Fish a B-2 Mini squid here, or a hoochie with a herring teaser. This area is best fished 45 minutes either side of a tide change. You can also drift mooch or execute a shallower troll over the outer parts of Tyee Shoal, again, only if you're marking bait in the area. If the fishfinder screen is barren after a pass or two, move on.

Manchester: Personally, I haven't fished Manchester more than once, and didn't catch anything there, but I've heard from many a blackmouth fisherman that the area produces great fish. Stick to trolling the area between Colchester and Beans Point at the south end of Bainbridge on the incoming tides, and the beaches right off Southworth and Harper during the outgoing tides. I've also heard you can hook up with blackmouth a trolling a little shallower than normal here, try closer to shore in 60 to 80 feet.

GET IN THE GLOW for Area 10 blackmouth, like this Jeff Head fish caught several seasons back.

AT a GLANCE

What: Blackmouth fishing in central Puget Sound.

Where: Marine Area 10's The Trees, West Point, Fourmile Rock, Duwamish Head, Manchester, Yeomalt Point/Eagle Harbor, Point Monroe, Jeff Head and Appletree Cove.

When: Season opened Nov. 1 and runs through Nov. 30. Daily limit two salmon, only one Chinook. Reopens Dec. 16–Feb. 28. Daily limit one Chinook.

Gear/info/guides: Outdoor Emporium (206-624-6550) on 4th Ave. S. in Seattle; Auburn Sports & Marine (253-833-1440); Spot Tail Guide Service (206-283-6680); Eagle Enterprise Charters (888-594-8393); Tight Lines Sportfishing (877-878-1559).

Area 10 blackmouth

Elliott Bay: Fourmile Rock in Elliott Bay has produced some of my best days ever in MA10 when fish are in the area. On a fall day four years ago I caught four silvers and seven blackmouth in one outing in this area. All fish were taken on a glow hoochie. In winter, E-Bay is plum full of squid, so blackmouth will be feeding on them. Troll right off Four Mile Rock in 100 to 120 feet of water with a glow hoochie and herring, or cut-plug if bait is present.

Across the bay to the south, Duwamish Head to Todd Shipyard can also hold fish. Again, look for bait balls in this area, and once you find them, make several passes, changing up gear if whatever you have wet doesn't get a strike.

Increase your hook-ups: Once you've decided on where you want to fish, make sure you're taking all the necessary steps to ensure that you're going to hook up when you get there.

When baiting up or rigging, use surgical gloves or wash your hands prior to rigging. If you have old scent (Bait Butter, Pro-Cure type scents, etc.) on a lure or flasher, clean it up before fishing with it or use something new. Keeping your gear clean and free of human and old scent really makes a difference with these denizens of the deep. Add scent to your downrigger ball and flasher to help mask any possible scents present.

Secondly, use fresh bait if you can obtain it. I truly believe using a fresh herring strip on any trolled lure will double your hookups. Frozen is OK too, but fresh is best. Brine herring the night before use so it holds up better.

Third, use a flash on all glow gear each time you bring it up. Yes, it may be bright where you're standing and you won't see the effect, but once you drop a glow flasher and hoochie to 120 feet, the flash will really help it stand out for Mr. Blackmouth to key in on. I use an old cheap plastic camera to facil-

itate this. Don't we all have a few of those in the garage junk drawer?

Fourth, add something to your bait that will make noise! Blackmouth primarily use hearing and scent to find their quarry. John Abbott (a.k.a "Downriggin'") has a great idea of using a glow-white Spin-N-Glo above a hoochie or squid to add noise.

Keep your eye on the finder! Some days the fish will be suspended off the bottom, or at the depth of their quarry. It's true that you'll catch 90 percent of

your blackmouth in the bottom 15 feet of water, but the other 10 percent are suspended under a bait ball somewhere! Paying attention to your finder can pay big dividends. Fish where the fish are!

Blackmouth derby: Use this map for a blackmouth derby on Nov. 13. Go to *Gamefishin.com/gfboard/default.asp* and click on "Lets go fishing" and "Downriggin's BM derby" for more.

F&H MAP KEY
- Best blackmouth areas
- Area 10 boundary
- Boat launch

Where to bonk North Sound blackmouth

EDMONDS

by Dusty Routh

Summer salmon seasons spoil us. Shirtsleeve weather, calm inland waters, roiling coho in the kelp, deep Chinook in the troughs, and in odd years enough pink salmon to make your arms sore.

But winter salmon fishing is about as distant from summer fishing as you can get. The dang wind and forbidding February temperatures can chill you right down to the bone. The Sound can get rough — real rough — and the tides seem to be running for the hills. And all those once-plentiful salmon that presented such easy pickings? Winter blackmouth salmon can sometimes be a bear to find.

That's not to say that winter blackmouth fishing isn't worth pursuing. It can provide fabulous sport and sometimes easy fish. But in recent seasons the blackmouth have required a fair amount of dedication, stamina, perseverance and determination. What makes the real difference in successful blackmouth fishing, as in a lot of fishing, is locating the baitfish.

AT a GLANCE

What: Winter blackmouth fishing in north Puget Sound.

Where: Look for your friends in all the old familiar places, including Possession, Double Bluff, the Racetrack and PNP.

When: Marine Area 8-2 (Possession Point to East Point at northwest end of Saratoga Passage): Feb. 14-April 10; 8-1 (Deception Pass, Hope Island, and Skagit Bay): Feb. 1-March 31; 9 (Admiralty Inlet to Edwards Point south of Edmonds): Feb. 1-April 15.

How: Get to the bottom and stay there. Troll spoons, herring and hoochies; also mooch and jig.

Information/guides: Dave Morgison, Possession Point Charters (360-652-3797); Craig Reedy, Triple AAA Charters (425-252-8246); Gary Krein, All Star Charters (425-252-4188); Darrell Stacey, Eagle Point Charters (360-966-3334); John's Sporting Goods (425-259-3056).

Best spots in the Sound: The North Sound is considered to be that area extending from the southern tip of the San Juan Islands down through Skagit Bay, Port Susan, Saratoga Passage, Admiralty Inlet, Possession Sound, Possession Point and on southward to the Marine Area 10 deadline running east-west between Apple Cove Point and Edwards Point.

What you're looking for in these northern portions of the Sound are places where baitfish congregate, either willingly or as a result of being pushed against structure during tidal influences. Your primary baitfish search is for herring, candlefish and anchovies.

You're also looking for deep, sandy flats (as in 120 feet or more) where blackmouth cruise the bottom looking to pick off sandlances, one of their favorite dietary supplements. Sandlances dig into the sand during hard-running tides, but then come back out during slack tides.

Here are some spots to target:

• Trolling just above a sandy bottom in deep water at slack tide can often be one of the best ways to connect with a feeding blackmouth. This is why finding the 120-foot contour around Possession Bank, and following it up as far as Double Bluff and Bush Point, is one of the more popular and productive trolls.

• Tide rips congregate baitfish, and there are none better than the awesome rips you'll find at Bush Point in Admiralty Inlet and just to the southwest off Foulweather Bluff. You'll also find bait-magnet areas southeast of Foulweather, in the form of Norwegian

SARATOGA PASSAGE will boot out blackmouth like this one, caught trolling a spoon during the late-winter season last year. Time to tune up the downriggers again for winter blackmouth in North Puget Sound.

Point and Point No Point. As with Possession Point, the rule of thumb in these areas is to fish the east sides as the tide runs out (baitfish pinned against the eastern side), and fish the western side on an incoming tide (baitfish pinned against the western side).

• Another top spot for blackmouth baitfish entrapment is the Racetrack trolling circle between Camano Head and Hat Island. You'll have company here, but it can be productive.

• If you'd like a little more elbow room and still have a shot at fish, try the top end of Saratoga Passage, trolling the deepwater contours that extend northeast into Skagit Bay (near Polnell Point). Or run across from there and work Snakelum Point in 80 to 100 feet of water on the opposite side.

• There's also a ton of structure midway down the east side of Camano Island, near Onamac Point. This spot is very lightly fished — if you can get there at first light on a calm morning, expect a bite or two.

• The area around Baby Island at the north end of Whidbey is another good bet. Fish this during all tides, then swing into Holmes Harbor at high slack to troll over the sandy bottom.

• The southern end of Hat can be quite good, but for whatever reason it's hit or miss. One February morning we fished this and caught four blackmouth in a half hour, all of them gorgeously legal fish. On other trips, this water has been completely empty. Go figure.

Sounds regs: These areas are clustered into Marine Areas 8-1, 8-2, and 9. Blackmouth season in 8-1 runs Feb. 1-March 31; 8-2 runs Feb. 14-April 10; and 9 is open Feb. 1-April 15. In all three areas the limit is one fish per day, minimum of 22 inches.

Strategic notions: The really cool thing about winter blackmouth is that they're predictable. They're not always easy to find, but at least you'll know where to look.

Blackmouth follow the feeding habits of their migrating cousins, in that balls of herring, anchovies, candlefish and bottom-hugging sandlances make up their principal diet. And, like sea-roving Chinook, blackmouth are almost always found deep. Lastly, blackmouth tend to really hug the bottom. Finding fish means staying close to the bottom at all times.

Trolling: The three primary trolling methods that work are flasher or dodger and a trolling spoon, flasher/dodger and herring (either whole or cutplug), or flasher/dodger and a hoochie. Some anglers also use flies and bucktails behind a dodger, and some (me included) fish just a herring with no flasher or dodger.

You could write a treatise longer than *War and Peace* on the relative virtues and drawbacks of whether to deploy a dodger or flasher in any given situation on the Sound. Both will work, though many anglers profess that one or the other has caught a lot more fish. Maybe that's because one or the other spent more time in the water. Hard to tell. But big 000-sized dodgers in chrome with sparkle prism tape are a blackmouth standard. So is a big green/silver Hot Spot flasher. My own preference?

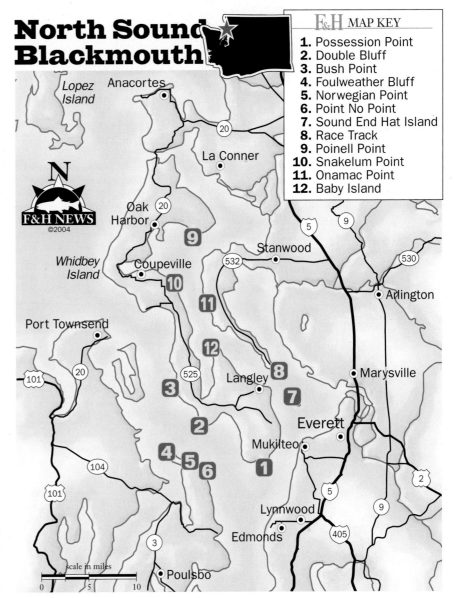

North Sound Blackmouth

F&H MAP KEY

1. Possession Point
2. Double Bluff
3. Bush Point
4. Foulweather Bluff
5. Norwegian Point
6. Point No Point
7. Sound End Hat Island
8. Race Track
9. Poinell Point
10. Snakelum Point
11. Onamac Point
12. Baby Island

Dodgers for spoons and hoochies, flashers or nothing for herring.

Trolling spoons really run the gambit in terms of style and colors, but if you took a survey you'd likely find that Coyote spoons are the most popular for winter fish. They come in a wide variety of colors, so don't think twice about experimenting to see what works best. Also add paste, gel or spray-on scent to your spoon for added appeal and to mask human odors like the onions from your halibut chowder.

Experiment also with speed. On average, trolling speeds for blackmouth tend to be 1½ to 2½ mph.

Chinook find hoochies practically irresistible. From cream, green/white, chartreuse, pink, day-glo, to psychedelic sparkle and combinations of all of the above, hoochies come in an incredible range of colors. They're cheap to buy and easy to use. Add a strip of herring for additional scent. Run these close to the bottom right behind a dodger.

Mooching and jigging: Mooching is also a great way to put the hurt on blackmouth, using up to 5 ounces of banana sinker, a 6-foot leader, and a whole or cut-plug herring. Mooching allows you to really work the water and the bait, and of course you'll feel the strike long before you would on a downrigger. A line-counter reel is handy, or simple drop your rig until the sinker hits bottom and turn up a few cranks. You'll find plenty of dogfish in places, but you'll also potentially find hungry blackmouth.

Puget Sound Saltwater
TROUT

Hood Canal sea-run cutts: 'lions behind an oak tree'

TAHUYAH

by Joel Shangle

WITHIN CASTING DISTANCE of shore, guide Mike Bing shows off a sea-run cutthroat.

There's this pristine little trout pond that we know of, where you can catch and release carnivorous, acrobatic 2-pound cutthroat from dawn till dusk in the company of just your best fishing buddy: yourself. It's within easy driving distance of the heart of Pugetropolis, but largely ignored by 99.9 percent of the metro area's rank-and-file anglers (many of whom believe that a "good" fall fishery must include standing elbow-to-elbow on a river with every *other* member of that 99.9 percent). This fishery is nothing about crowding and all about fishing, and approaching its hottest time of the year.

Oh, you may have to beware of a stray nuclear submarine and an occasional wicked fall wind, but the benefits of this pond far outweigh minor inconveniences provided by the US Navy and Mother Nature.

Welcome to Hood Canal, the "Biggest Little Trout Pond in the West."

Covering well over 100 miles of shoreline from its "mouth" off Admiralty Inlet southeast of Port Townsend to its "foot" in Lynch Cove, southwest of Bremerton, the waters of the Canal represent some of the best fall trout fishing that you've never seen.

"It's that time of year where you go 'which way do I go?' because there are so many good fisheries available, but for my money, the Hood Canal sea-run cutt fishery is right up there with the best of 'em," says Mike Bing at Van Hala Guide Service (206-230-2646). "I love it, I love it, I love it."

Bing, who grew up in Bremerton, has been fishing the Canal since the 1960s, when it was still a catch-and-keep fishery. He was a de facto resident of the Puget Sound Naval Shipyard near Charleston, where in years past you could hike down to the water and wade-fish gravel bars teeming with hungry sea-runs. And while he's graduated from his first Canal ride — an 8-foot homemade plywood pram — to a 19-foot Super V LS decked out with Scotty downriggers and Honda horsepower, the Hood Canal SRC fishery has remained stuck in the '60s.

"I think it's probably just as good now as it was back then," Bing says. "There may not be the sheer number of fish over 20 inches as there used to be, but it's still a great, great fishery."

The 'harvest trout': While it's available 12 months of the year, the Hood Canal SRC fishery blossoms when the air acquires a little more crispness and the leaves start to stack up in the backyard.

"September and October are when (SRCs) are at their best," says Bing. "Old timers call them 'harvest trout,' because back in their day, when the corn was dying in the fall, you went sea-run cutthroat fishing. It's a fall fishery — those fish will be gorging for the winter and the upcoming spawn."

That instinctive aggression is the primer for the explosive catch-and-release fishery that'll take place throughout the Canal over the next two months.

"They can't eat enough during that time," says Bing. "You bring them to the boat to release them and they're spitting out candlefish, basically chomping everything in sight."

Imitate the bait: In an age of high-tech lures and high-dollar gizmo baits, the best offering for SRCs is a simple $2 blast from the past: a two-color spoon.

"Back when I was a kid, all I knew how to fish was a red and white Triple Teazer," says Bing. "Well, you know what I fish with now? Anything that even slightly resembles a candlefish: a Triple Teazer or a Dick Nite. Those fish *love* 'em."

The technique of choice is a slow troll or a slow cast-and-retrieve of a small half-and-half spoon along the shoreline, especially over gravel bars with some surrounding eelgrass cover.

"There's that old adage 'If you can't see the bottom, you're fishing too deep,' and that's accurate, because these fish are shoreline cruisers," says Bing. "Anywhere from 4 to 10 feet of water is ideal, and if you can find gravel bars with eelgrass borders, that's absolutely perfect. Those fish are like lions behind an oak tree, hovering in that eelgrass, waiting for something to swim by so they can attack it."

Fly fishing is another viable option, especially on calm evenings when you can dead drift a Muddler Minnow, Mickey Finn, Skykomish Sunrise or any bright "silver tinsel" streamer along the edges of those eelgrass patches.

"You can either dead drift with the tide

or row a little cartopper and drag your fly along the bottom," suggests Bing. "You're going to hook most of your fish in the lower 2 feet, so a subsurface presentation is the best way to go."

Rig up with a 4- or 5-weight rod loaded with fast sinking tip line and a standard 8-foot tippet.

Best fishing will come on an incoming tide, when bait gets washed close to shore.

Where to fish: About the only places on Hood Canal where you *can't* find SRCs are those that are restricted by the US Navy, a severe ebb tide or the early fall wind that sometimes whips up in the afternoon.

"There's over 100 miles of shoreline on the Canal, and (SRCs) are literally everywhere," says Bing. "Look for points, coves, bays, gravelly stretches of shoreline or anything with structure. These fish are prowlers — they move around a lot. The Canal is kind of intimidating because it looks so big, but I can run from Belfair to Tahuya in 20 minutes. It's no big deal."

Here's a list of hot spots, moving from the foot of the Canal in Belfair to the Hood Canal Bridge:

1) Mouth of the Union River: Dumping into the Canal in Belfair, this area is fishable only at high tide (it turns into a big mud bay on the ebb).

2) Little Mission Creek: The creek empties into the Canal at Belfair State Park, off State Route 300.

"That area is a flyrodders' paradise," notes Bing.

3) Port of Allyn Boat Launch: We'll ignore the fact that this facility is nowhere near the town of Allyn. The launch is located 5 miles west of Belfair off SR 300 (North Shore Road), near the mouth of Stimson Creek. You can fish this area on any tide.

4) Mouth of the Tahuya River: Launch at Twanoh State Park and run across to the tidal estuary at the mouth of the Tahuya.

5) Mouth of the Skokomish River: Don't get caught here on a low tide.

"That thing turns into a huge mud bay," warns Bing. "It completely dries up on a low tide. You get caught out there and you'll be sitting for 12 hours, waiting for the tide to come back in."

6) The Great Bend: Fish around the pilings at the mouth of Redsland Creek, all the way along the gravelly beach that runs north to Dewatto.

7) Mouth of the Lilliwaup River: Best on an incoming tide.

8) Mouth of the Duckabush River: Actually, from the mouth of McDonald Creek (which enters the Canal off the Olympic Loop Highway in McDaniel Cove) north across the mouth of the Duckabush to Quotsap Point.

9) Dabob Bay/Quilcene: "They're looking for any estuary to spawn, so any cove or bay in the Dabob Bay/Quilcene area should be good," says Bing. "Heck, you can basically find them all the way up to the (Hood Canal Bridge), looking to spawn in November and December. The only real limitations are the weather, which can get pretty nasty in November, and the nuclear subs up around Bangor."

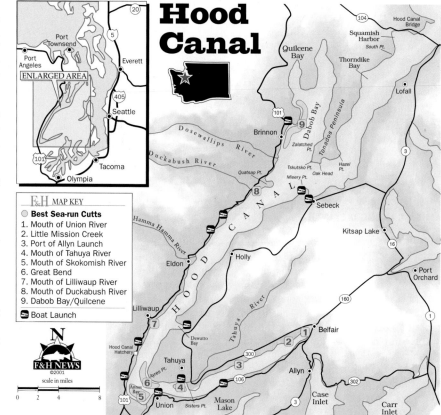

F&H MAP KEY
- ○ **Best Sea-run Cutts**
1. Mouth of Union River
2. Little Mission Creek
3. Port of Allyn Launch
4. Mouth of Tahuya River
5. Mouth of Skokomish River
6. Great Bend
7. Mouth of Lilliwaup River
8. Mouth of Duckabush River
9. Dabob Bay/Quilcene
- ⚓ Boat Launch

AT A GLANCE

What: Hood Canal sea-run cutthroat.

When: Best fishing for SRCs is in September and October, as they start to gorge in preparation for winter and the upcoming spawn.

Where: From the Hood Canal Bridge down to the foot of the Canal in Belfair. Look for shallow, gravelly shoreline with surrounding eelgrass.

Techniques: Slow troll or cast and retrieve small spoons (Dick Nites, Triple Teazers, etc.) in 4 to 10 feet of water; dead drift Muddler Minnows, Skykomish Sunrises or any tinsely leech on a sink tip line.

Launch: Multiple launch sites available throughout the Canal. Good access to the Great Bend/Lower Canal via the Twanoh State Park launch.

Regulations: *Catch and release only.* This fishery is well posted. Pinch your barbs.

Information: Mike Bing, Van Hala Guide Service (206-230-2646)

Lodging/Camping/RV: Mike's Beach Resort (360-877-5324) north of Lilliwaup; Twanoh State Park (360-275-2222); Belfair State Park (360-275-0668); Dosewalips State Park (360-796-4415); Scenic Beach State Park (360-830-5079)

How to fill a winter day? Fish for Puget Sound SRCs

—————————————————————————— WOLLOCHET

by Dusty Routh

Seth Taylor at the Creekside Angling Company in downtown Seattle (206-405-3474) can't believe the complaints he hears from folks coming into his shop, lamenting that there are no good fishing opportunities this time of year.

"What they don't know, or can't seem to remember," Taylor says, "is that we've got a world-class fishery in south Puget Sound that's year-round. It's on a par with Belize, or the flats of Florida, in terms of quality fishing."

Here in Puget Sound? Did we hear right?

Well, he's as right as rain. Just south of the Tacoma Narrows you'll find some of the best sea-run cutthroat trout fishing anywhere, and, even better, the fishery is good 12 months out of the year. But it can be especially good in the winter and spring months, when there are hardly any boats out and the fish are mostly undisturbed. On a calm, windless day, it can be some of the most tranquil fishing you've ever experienced.

"WE'VE GOT A WORLD-CLASS FISHERY in south Puget Sound that's year-round. It's on a par with Belize, or the flats of Florida, in terms of quality fishing," says Creekside Angling Company's Seth Taylor, photographed here working local waters with Capt. Tom Wolf.

AT a GLANCE

What: World-class winter gear and fly fishing for sea-run cutthroat trout out in the salt, along with immature resident coho.

Where: From the Narrows Bridge south, particularly along Colvos Passage, Hale Inlet, and around Fox Island.

How: Fly anglers can ply the waters with clear, intermediate sinking lines and brown Clousers. Gear anglers can throw spoons and spinners. Trolling herring strips will also produce.

When: This is a year-round fishery, but the winter and spring months offer lots of isolated water and undisturbed fish.

Contact: Capt. Tom Wolf (253-863-0711) with Puget Sound Fly Fishing.

Gear: Creekside Angling Company (206-405-3474) in Seattle.

Fishing on a Monday: We recently joined Taylor and sea-run guru Capt. Tom Wolf, of Puget Sound Fly Fishing (253-863-0711), for a day of spectacular sea-run angling. It was a weekday (a Monday, no less). We saw a whopping total of seven other anglers out, all of them fly fishing. The particular stretch we were fishing, just south of Olalla, was empty of any other fishermen.

Haven't fished for sea-run cutts (aka SRCs) before? First, understand that these are anadromous fish. These trout in the South Sound region are born in small adjoining creeks, streams, freshwater inlets and rivers. They then migrate to the salt by their second year and can stay out in the salt for another two years before migrating back. They don't venture too far from their birthplaces, and they tend to hug pretty close to shore. In fact, most sea-runs are caught in less than 10 feet of water.

Size wise, they run from as small as 6 inches all the way up to 22-inch beauties.

SRCs favor near-shore marine areas very similar to what freshwater smallmouth bass prefer — wooded shoreline, rocky or pebbly beaches, grassy points, big boulders, kelp and weedlines. They favor places where there's incoming fresh water, even if it's a trickle. They dine on amphipods, herring, sandlances, crustaceans and fish larvae.

How it's done: Sometimes SRCs can be ridiculously easy to catch. For gear anglers, they'll hit spoons, spinners, Wedding Rings, herring strips, small stickbaits and even topwater poppers. For fly anglers, brown Clousers are killer, and so are color combo Clousers like white/yellow/brown. Reduced Polar Shrimp will also work, as will Comets and just about anything that resembles shrimp, even small coho flies.

But SRCs are not always easy to dupe. On clear, sunny days, they can be very selective and refuse just about everything. And, many times they tend to short-strike, grabbing just at the tail end of a fly or lure, but not enough to get hooked up.

Washington's astute fisheries managers closed catch-and-keep fishing on SRCs back in 1996, to help protect their numbers. So all fishing now is catch-and-release only. Their reputation as a delicacy aside, the real reason to fish for them is the fight: these are notoriously strong, agile fish, as strong or stronger pound for pound than any freshwater trout.

Wading anglers can work their way along rocky beaches on foot, and this can be a very fun way to fish. It's not necessary to wade deep, but casting parallel to shore and quartering out is usually more productive than casting directly out from shore. Angling from a boat, however, offers the advantage of more mobility to find fish, but you increase your chances of spooking them with boat sounds and shadows. Guide Wolf fishes from an open-platform 17-foot Alumaweld Stryker, working oars from the center of the boat to position and maneuver it. When he's fishing, he trims his big engine up to reduce the boat's profile in the water.

TAYLOR SHOWS OFF a nice South Sound SRC.

Whether you like to gear fish or fly fish, the common theme in provoking a sea-run is speed — retrieves and trolls should be quick. Taylor fast-strips his fly line in just as quickly as his fingers will work. They seem to be attracted to fast-moving lures and flies.

Where it's done: The southern reaches of Puget Sound are very much like a huge estuary, characterized by extensive mud flats, shallow bays and coves, lengthy (and rocky) shorelines, lots of grass, and lots and lots of wood. SRCs seem to particularly favor wood structure, as it offers overhead protection from fish-eating birds like cormorants and grebes.

With massive tides that can swiftly swing water levels by as much as 16 feet and produce fast currents, the lower Sound is like a big, well, toilet bowl, that gets flushed out on every tide. This clean, fresh water brings in copious amounts of zooplankton and phytoplankton, which feeds the small baitfish, which provide the diet for the SRC populations. It's a perfect ecosystem to support the sea-run's lifecycle.

Some of the hottest of the SRC hot spots include the west side of Colvos Passage (above Gig Harbor) past Point Richmond and up to Olalla; from Gig Harbor down through the Narrows to the inlet of Hale Passage; the northwest side of Hale; up into Wallochet Bay; and all around Fox Island.

These areas are the best known, and most heavily fished, but SRCs can be found throughout the South Sound, particularly around areas that have freshwater sources nearby. If you can find incoming fresh water, grassy points, rocky beaches and wood structure, chances are you've got the right mixture

for locating fish. Sea-runs are also fond of brackish estuaries.

Coho too: You might be surprised to know that there's also a very viable coho fishery in the South Sound in the winter months. These are Minter Creek Hatchery fish, immature silvers ranging from 10 to 15 inches. They're grouped up usually close to shore in moderate-sized schools, and it's not unusual to catch and release 50 fish in a good morning's out-

ing when you find them. They're pretty obvious too — they'll be breaking the surface, clearing the water, creating foam and tearing around, particularly in back bays and along shorelines.

The day we fished with Wolf, there was a school of immature coho right near the boat launch east of Wollochet Bay. We launched the boat, oared out and caught a handful of them on Polar Shrimp flies. True to form, we worked the school only to have it move on us, then we found it again and were right back into one-right-after-the-other fishing. On one retrieve, six coho followed my fly back to the boat. When I stopped it and just kind of dibbled the rod, one of them took, right at the bow.

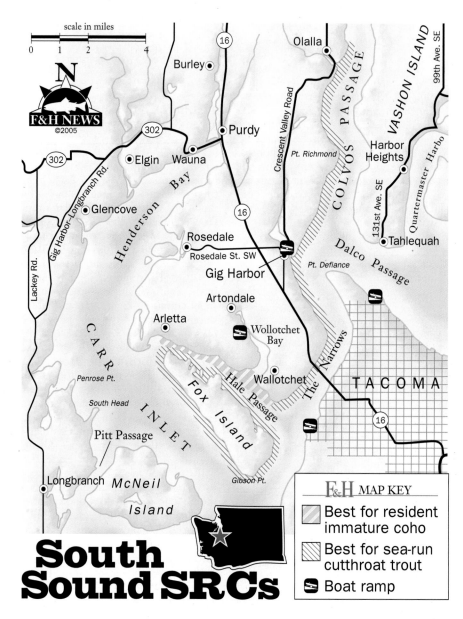

scale in miles

N

F&H NEWS
©2005

South Sound SRCs

F&H MAP KEY

Best for resident immature coho

Best for sea-run cutthroat trout

Boat ramp

Puget Sound Saltwater
HALIBUT
LINGCOD
CRAB

Bounty on the Mutiny, Admiralty bays — halibut

by John Martinis

Salmon has been closed for a month or more in most areas of the Puget Sound. Feeling the withdrawals yet? Don't despair — salmon are child's play — halibut is where it happens.

For my money, halibut fishing is the ultimate in big game fishing in Puget Sound and the Strait of Juan De Fuca. The real die-hard halibut anglers get fish on a regular basis, but you have to get on the water when the season opens. Wait for reports and you risk missing out on the best fish. The best fishing will occur when the halibut season first opens on May 25 in Marine Areas 5 through 13. When the season opens, the halibut are already heading in a westerly migration, so hit 'em hard right from the start.

WHERE TO GO: The two prime areas in Puget Sound to catch halibut are Admiralty Bay and Mutiny Bay, both located on the west side of Whidbey Island. Admiralty Bay is the most easily accessed fishing area in terms of a boat launch nearby — the boat launch is adjacent to the Fort Casey ferry terminal. From the mainland, Mutiny Bay can be reached from the Port of Edmonds or the Port of Everett. In either case, the boat ride is going to be 30 minutes or more. As a practical matter, you could launch at Fort Casey and easily fish both areas the same day.

Admiralty Bay: The beauty of fishing Admiralty is that you are fishing minutes after launching your boat. The good

halibut fishing starts just southeast of the boat launch. I recommend fishing this bay in 90 to 150 feet of water and sometimes deeper if the tide is not running very hard. When the tide is coming in, the bay is sheltered from the intense tidal flow that is characteristic of Admiralty Inlet. Knowing this, I feel you will find the best fishing during this period, regardless of tides — don't try to go fishing by picking the softer running tides, just head out when season opens.

Mutiny Bay: Mutiny, which is closer to the mainland but further by boat than Admiralty, is by far the more comfortable of the two areas to fish. The water is generally smoother and the bottom is free of snags. For those reasons, the boat ride shouldn't discourage you from fishing this area. The halibut fishing area in this bay is across the outside edges of the bay in 90 to 100 feet of water. Again, the best fishing occurs when the tide is coming in.

ROD AND REEL SETUP: One of the beauties of Puget Sound halibut fishing is that you do not have to fish with what I would call your typical halibut rod and reel. You can get by with a heavy salmon outfit as long as the tides are fairly moderate. However, if you go out on a weekend when the tide has a 8- to 10-foot exchange, you will need halibut tackle. For most days, you will need a rod and reel that can handle 10 to 12 ounces of lead. If you get stuck going out on a day when the tides are really booking, your outfit will need to handle 16 to 20 ounces of lead.

If I had to pick one rod and reel to fish halibut, I would suggest the Penn 113H Senator reel and any 5½- to 6½-rod that

CLOSE-TO-DOCK HALIBUT. Mutiny and Admiralty bays out of Everett offer good fishing for 'buts.

can handle heavy leads. If you think you are going to get by with an old reel filled with heavy mono or Dacron, think twice. Your chances of success will be minimal without the right tackle except on the days when the tidal flow is light. Penn and Shakespeare both make standup rods that are very adequate to get the job done.

TACKLE, BAIT: Let's talk tackle. Spectra-based fishing lines are a must! These lines allow you to stay close to the bottom even in the most extreme circumstances, and halibut are not *close* to the bottom . . . they are *on* the bottom. So, it makes good sense to me to keep the bait on the bottom at all times. Something equivalent to 50-pound test Power Pro line will do the job nicely. This line has the diameter of 12-pound monofilament.

AT A GLANCE

What: Puget Sound halibut.

When: Season starts on May 25 in Marine Areas 5 through 13. Fishing for halibut will be best right on the opener.

Where: Mutiny Bay and Admiralty Bay, both located on the west side of Whidbey Island, are two of the best halibut areas in the Puget Sound.

Launch: Launch at Fort Casey, or the ports of Everett or Edmonds.

Limit: One fish. Open Thursday through Monday.

Information: John's Sporting Goods (425-259-3056).

Your choice of artificial or real baits are a matter of preference. I feel that almost all artificial lures work well as long as they are accompanied by bait. Artificial lures that I prefer are the Luhr Jensen 9-inch B-2 squid and the Gold Star Kajiki 9-inch squid. I have used both squid and found them to be superb artificial lures for halibut. Regardless of which squid you use, a filet of herring, octopus or squid is a must. Hungry halibut get very greedy once they get a taste of the real thing.

RIGGING: There are a couple of good ways to rig up these squid. One way involves a wire spreader bar, which not only separates the lead from the leader and bait, but also gives the squid a realistic swimming action. The spreader bar setup should look like this: the lead would be attached to the short arm of the spreader, the leader should 50-pound test or more, 10 to 16 inches long and attached to the long arm of the spreader.

Another rig that many anglers seem to like is running a sinker on a 3-foot chunk of cord. This is what this rig looks like: a swivel is attached to the end of the fishing line and a 3-foot piece of 200-pound test cord (looks like duck decoy line) should be hooked to the swivel. The eye of a cannonball weight is threaded onto the cord and a swivel is attached to the terminal end of the cord. From this point, tie a 10- to 16-inch leader to an artificial squid.

IT'S IN THE MOTION: Once you let the bait to the bottom, you need to move your rod with a vertical movement that is short and slow. This will make your bait look alive. If you get a bite, lower the rod a bit until you feel the fish staying with the bait. Now bring the rod up a little until you feel the line get tight and strike at the fish. If you miss the fish, don't get discouraged — he will come right back if go back to the slow jigging motion.

GET THERE: To reach Fort Casey, take the Mukilteo/Clinton Ferry. Once on Whidbey Island, follow the signs to Fort Casey. Just before entering the park you will see the Fort Casey ferry landing. You are within eyesight of the boat launch. This is a nice launch with a dock. Fuel and moorage are not available at this launch — the nearest fuel and boat moorage is across the channel at Port Townsend.

Mutiny Bay has a cement launch with no dock, and it is consistently sanded in. Don't attempt to launch at this launch. If you are planning a trip to Mutiny, launch at the 10th Street Boat Launch in Everett or at the Port of Edmonds. The closest launch to Mutiny Bay is at Fort Casey.

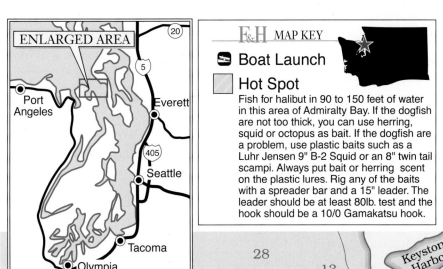

F&H MAP KEY

⬛ Boat Launch

⬜ Hot Spot

Fish for halibut in 90 to 150 feet of water in this area of Admiralty Bay. If the dogfish are not too thick, you can use herring, squid or octopus as bait. If the dogfish are a problem, use plastic baits such as a Luhr Jensen 9" B-2 Squid or an 8" twin tail scampi. Always put bait or herring scent on the plastic lures. Rig any of the baits with a spreader bar and a 15" leader. The leader should be at least 80lb. test and the hook should be a 10/0 Gamakatsu hook.

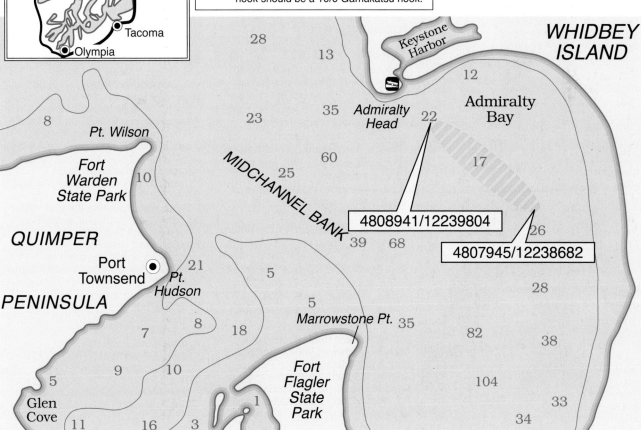

'Insider' info: May 17 means halibut in East Strait

by Joel Shangle

Neah Bay, with its multi-ton quota and access to some of the best flatsider holes off the West Coast of the United States, carries the title of Halibut King for the Evergreen State. Right from the May 1 opener, more poundage of delicate white meat will come out of the waters off Neah Bay than anywhere on the Northwest Coast.

But because of the challenging water conditions off the coast, a relatively small cadre of anglers in *big* boats are

PICNIC TABLE HALI: David Sutor of Marysville latched into this 118-pound fattie fishing out of Port Angeles opening weekend a few seasons back. He used a 6-ounce Pt. Wilson Dart tipped with a squid tentacle.

equipped to motor miles and miles through big tide and wind to tackle the fishery.

"Out there in Neah Bay, you have a couple of things working against you," says Don Frizell at Port Angeles Marine (360-452-3277). "You're out there at the mouth of the Strait, facing that open ocean, and you have a rough tide mix. Plus, a lot of the time when you have those big tide changes, you have the wind to worry about."

But as of May 17, the guys with the smaller craft and big expectations of slabsided fish are officially in the game when Pacific halibut season officially opens from Sekiu to South Sound (Marine Areas 5 through 13).

Best place to be?

The east Strait of Juan de Fuca.

"We certainly don't have the conditions to worry about here that they have in Neah Bay," says Frizell. "Especially here between about Freshwater Bay and the Dungeness Spit, we're a little more protected. We have the mountains to kind of keep the wind down. Plus, we don't have any of those long runs to make — we're going maybe 2 to 3 miles offshore most of the time. The smaller boats can handle that just fine."

WHAT'S 'SMALL?' Tons of adventurous souls have tackled this fishery in itty bitty boats powered by itty bitty motors, but for safety's sake, the typical East Strait halibut ride should be at least a 16-footer powered by 25 horses. Anything bigger and more powerful than that will just make it easier and safer.

"I'd say anything from 16 to 26 feet is OK," says Frizell.

TACKLE THIS: Gear is the same regardless of whether you're standing on the deck of a fully equipped 22-foot Sea Sport or your grandpa's old 16-foot fiberglass runabout: rods with backbone, reels designed to handle a

big payload, braided line, 16 to 48 ounces of lead and baits ranging from jigs to squid. Use hooks from 6/0 to 8/0.

EAST TO WEST: Best fishing in the East Strait starts in Marine Area 6, just off Ediz Hook in Port Angeles, and extends west through Marine Area 5 in Sekiu to the mouth of the Sekiu River. There are literally dozens and dozens of areas in 150 to 300 feet where you can pull a 60-pounder off the bottom, but a handful or areas are worth the extra attention they generally receive during the season.

PORT ANGELES: Your top four bets in the Port Angeles area are:

• **The Rockpile:** Motor out of Port Angeles and head due north of Ediz Hook to an area 6½ miles into the Strait known at The Rockpile. This plateau sits

---

AT A GLANCE

What: Eastern Strait of Juan de Fuca Pacific halibut.

When: Season runs May 17-July 22.

Why: Unlike the wide open waters off Neah Bay, the halibut holes in the Strait are relatively protected and much more accessible for anglers fishing out of small boats.

Boat size: A minimum of 16 feet is safest, preferably with a 25-horsepower motor.

Limit: One fish, no size minimum; open Thursday through Monday.

Where: Marine Areas 6 and 5, from Port Angeles to the mouth of the Sekiu River. Halibut holes to hit in the Port Angeles area include the Rockpile, Freshwater Bay, Crescent Bay to the Lyre River and Deep Creek/Twin Rivers. In the Sekiu area, fish Slip Point to the Coal Mines, the Sekiu and Hoko river mouths and Eagle Bay.

Tackle/Gear: Heavy rods with backbone, reels designed to handle a big payload, braided line like TUF Line or Power Pro, 16 to 48 ounces of lead and baits ranging from pipe jigs to herring to squid. Use hooks from 6/0 to 8/0.

Information: Don Frizell, Port Angeles Marine (360-452-3277); Joe Schmitt at Whiskey Creek Beach Resort (360-928-3489); Chris Mohr or Gary Ryan at Van Riper's Resort (360-963-2334)

in 150 to 160 feet of water, surrounded by a dropoff into 200-foot-plus water. Fish the rocky edges of this plateau.

• **Freshwater Bay:** Start at Angeles Point and fish anywhere in the area that starts at the mouth of the Elwha River and extends northwest across the mouth of this bay just west of Port Angeles. You'll find a series of sandy flats and a ledge that runs northwest in 170 to 190 feet of water.

• **Whiskey Creek:** Actually, the entire area from Crescent Bay to the sandy flats off the mouth of the Lyre River, encompassing 5 miles of water that includes Whiskey Creek, Field Creek and Nelson Creek.

"This whole area is known to the local guys as one of the best halibut beds in the state," says Joe Schmitt at Whiskey Creek Beach Resort (360-928-3489). "These are a little different type of fish than most of the rest of the state. We don't have any of those things that I call 'flyswatter fish.' Our average catch is 50 pounds. We have fish come in in the neighborhood of 200 pounds."

Fish shallow early in the season (60 to 100 feet) for 'buts feeding on crab and small cod, and move deeper (up to 300 feet) as the season progresses and fish move out because of pressure and availability of feed.

Launches in this area are all shallow-water affairs where you have to be willing to motor over a little sand. Put in at Pillar Point or the Whiskey Creek resort launch.

• **Twin Rivers/Deep Creek:** This areas includes 3 miles of sandy flats that extend due north from the mouth of East and West Twin Rivers, and another series of broken up flats northeast of the mouth Deep Creek. Best fishing is between 80 and 150 feet.

SEKIU AREA: The mid-May opening day is a head-scratcher for some long-time Strait halibut hounds, but not one that should negatively affect the fishery.

"We've never fished for them in the middle of May," says Gary Ryan at Van Riper's Resort (360-963-2334). "The opener has always been around

Memorial Day. It's hard to say exactly how the fishery might be that early. But there are always fish moving through here, and always fish around. During the (early April) blackmouth derby, we had a couple of guys who were down in the mouth because they had to throw back a couple of 60-pound halibut they caught mooching for salmon."

• **Slip Point:** Best fishing on the west side of Clallam Bay is between the Coal Mines and Slip Point, in 150 to 240 feet of water.

• **Sekiu River/Hoko:** Fish straight out from the mouth of the Hoko of the Sekiu, on the series of flats that runs 3 miles out. Best fishing is in 150 to 250 feet of water.

"That area is generally called 'The Halibut Hole of Sekiu,'" says Ryan. "You have feed coming out of the rivers, the smaller fish move into feed on that and the halibut feed on *those* fish. The halibut move through here to spawn in deep water. They're in here feeding."

• **Eagle Bay:** Look for the big reef that runs in 130 to 200 feet of water.

STRAIT OF JUAN DE FUCA

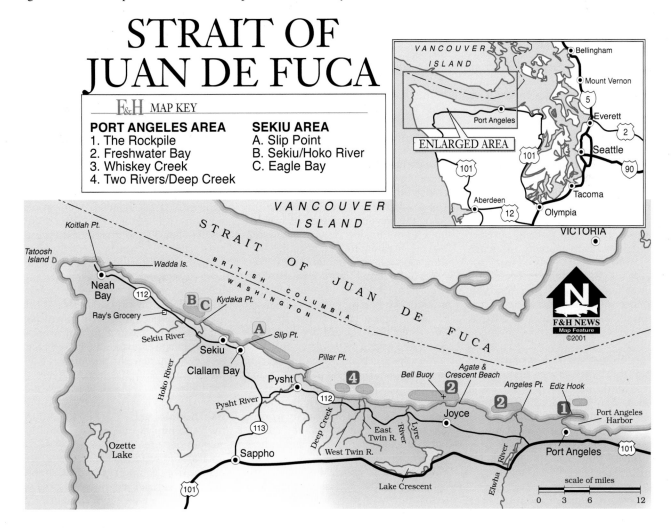

F&H MAP KEY

PORT ANGELES AREA
1. The Rockpile
2. Freshwater Bay
3. Whiskey Creek
4. Two Rivers/Deep Creek

SEKIU AREA
A. Slip Point
B. Sekiu/Hoko River
C. Eagle Bay

May 1 marks Area 9 lingcod opener

EDMONDS

by Chris Paulson

GET ON THE WATER quick for the Area 9 lingcod opener — big gnarly monsters like this one the author stuck don't stick around long.

It's time to catch big uglies again — those aggressive, great-tasting lingcod!

Contrary to popular belief, saltwater lingcod is not actually a cod at all. It's more closely related to rockfish. Its name comes from two sources: similarities in appearance to a fish known as ling on the East Coast; and filets that are very cod-like.

A great thing about lingcods is the fact that they're easy to catch and you almost always land a keeper. Legal sizes in Puget Sound range from 26 to 40 inches. These size fish usually weigh between 6 and 20 pounds.

Knowing where they hang out is the key to consistently bringing lingcods to the table. They tend to hang out near rocky humps, artificial reefs, off points and around kelp beds. Head for Possession Bar, Double Bluff and Foulweather Bluff in Marine Area 9 for some hot spots. You can also nail 'em off places like the jetty and dock at Edmonds.

When to get on the water: The sooner the better is key here. You'll want to hit the water early in the season (it opens May 1), weather permitting, as the most productive areas can get picked over in the first week or two. If the weather is a little rough, say 3- to 4-foot waves, you can still go out for lings, using certain techniques described later.

Don't worry as much about the tides

when fishing for lingcod as you might fishing for salmon. You can use the same techniques described below to overcome hurdles like a fast running tide. So get out early, even if tides don't appear to be in your favor.

Jig it: Use jigs for a no-fuss, no-muss way to catch these toothy guys. Basically, make drifts over an area much the same way you jig for salmon.

There's a variety of gear available for lingcod. The best setup consists of a ½- to 7½-foot rod, with a stiff butt and a fairly soft tip, to give the jig good action. A reel with good cranking power, such as a Penn Jigmaster, allows you to control a hard-pulling fish with ease.

If you don't have bottomfishing gear, a medium-action salmon or steelhead rod will also land you fish.

When you jig off a boat, a levelwind reel is your best option. The line twist that occurs with spinning reels often causes the line to get twisted around your pole tip from the jigging action, making it difficult to reel when you get a hit.

The teeth on these little monsters can cut through lighter monofilament line with ease. Keep that in mind and go with braided lines such as 30-pound Power Pro. No keeper-size lings will be able to break it, but it's light enough for you to snap off if you get snagged up. Also, the smaller diameter of braided lines allows for less drag in the water, making it easier to stay near the bottom, especially in wind or current.

If you're using monofilament line, make sure it's 15- to 20-pound test, or it might just break. It also can be helpful to use a piece of cuttyhunk (braided line often used for halibut and sturgeon) as a leader.

You can use many types of jigs for these fish, but the most productive and popular are the larger rubber worm or scampi-style ones. Use 3-, 4- and 6-ounce jigheads with 6-inch worms. Black or motor oil are standby colors, but root beer, red, white and others also work.

Remember to pinch down the barb and measure the jig against the worm to be sure you thread it so that the

hook is well exposed. Avoid metal jigs with treble hooks, as this will get you snagged in the rocky areas lings favor. Be sure to put on a scent like Butt Juice (anise). It really helps!

Possession Bar and Point: One of the most productive areas is Possession Bar. During the first week of the season, head near the buoy off Scatchet Head on the west side of the bar, as that's where a lot of 'em are traditionally taken. There is a nice hole immediately east of the buoy.

After the first week or two, it becomes more productive to radiate out from this area. Make your way toward the end of the bar, and make drifts across the bar, roughly using the cabins on the beach and the buoy as an east-west border for your fishing area. There are lots of rocky humps here. You shouldn't have to jig in water deeper than 40 to 75 feet.

You'll also be able to hook lingcod near the buoy off Possession Point, on the east side of the bar. There's a sunken ferry about 75 feet deep off the cliffs that face the buoy. It's a quick drift over the wreck, but it can produce some nice fish at times.

Double and Foulweather bluffs: The Double Bluff area is another good choice to target lingcod. Here you'll want to fish along the cliffs inside Useless Bay, just southeast of the western-facing "V," which is the head of Double Bluff. It will be a roughly east-west drift across the rocky peaks and humps, in about 50 to 75 feet of water.

Slightly southwest of Double Bluff, across Admiralty Inlet, is Foulweather Bluff. Concentrate on fishing around the north and east sides, in 40 to 80 feet of water. You may also see anglers fishing in water over 100 feet, just east of the bluff.

Methodology: Here are three productive techniques, depending on the amount of current and wind.

• If lack of wind and current are keeping you from getting a good drift, simply move around and try different spots in an area until you hit a little current.

Area 9 Lingcod

F&H MAP KEY
- ⧄ Good lingcod spots
- ⬤ Good bank spots
- — Area 9 boundaries
- ⛴ Boat launch

• If you have wind waves of a foot or more, try setting the rod in your pole-holder and let the waves give it the jigging action. Just remember to constantly check your rig to keep it between 2 and 6 feet from the bottom.

• If a stronger wind or current is making it difficult to reach the bottom, you can catch lings by "walkin' the jig" — repeatedly casting in the direction the boat is drifting and letting your rig swing down under the boat and out behind you before retrieving it.

Live bait: The most popular live baits are flounders and shiner perch. You can easily pick up a few small flounders by fishing over sand flats with smaller rubber worm jigs or small green/yellow Point Wilson Darts. Get shiner perch off a dock by using a herring jig. Then use a double hook set-up

with live bait to increase your catch. Anchoring up is an option with live bait fishing, as the vibrations of the struggling fish will attract hungry lings.

Land based? Using live bait or jigs can also get you lings from docks like the one at Edmonds Marina. Use a setup that keeps a shiner perch suspended off the bottom by tying your weight to the end of your line and attaching your leader a couple feet above it.

When jigging at Edmonds, cast in a westerly direction, as far off the dock as you can, so you're out over the artificial reef. Let your jig hit the bottom before retrieving it. An adjustable steelhead float can be used as an indicator of depth when casting off the east side of the dock, towards the jetty. You'll be less likely to snag up.

From time to time, you'll take rock-

fish or cabezon using the techniques described above, whether from a boat or dock.

AT a GLANCE

What: Lingcod fishing in Marine Area 9.

Where: Possession Bar, Possession Point, Double Bluff, Foulweather Bluff, Edmonds Marina.

When: May 1–June 15.

Rules: One ling per day between 26 and 40 inches. Barbless hooks required.

Launch: Edmonds Marina, Kingston Marina, Lighthouse Park in Mukilteo, 10th Street Ramp in Everett.

Who to call: All Season Charters (425-743-9590), Ed's Surplus (425-778-1441), John's Sporting Goods (425-259-3056).

Hood Canal the leader of Sound crab production

QUILCENE

by Dusty Routh

IT'S SOME OF THE BEST crab water in the Pacific Northwest. Shelby and Taylor Mercado (far left and right) joined a friend last summer for slam-dunk crabbing in Hood Canal.

Just about everybody who's grown up or spent time in Western Washington has fond memories of Hood Canal. This marine playground offers up a vast assortment of fishing, ranging from Hoodsport dog salmon to Dabob Bay silvers to Seabeck blackmouth to sea-run cutthroat trout and assorted bottomfish like lings and sand dabs.

But what the Canal might best be known for over the years is its excellent crabbing and shellfishing opportunities. Oysters, clams, mussels and crabs from this area have helped provide many a fine evening's seafood dining for countless generations of Washingtonians. And not just here at home either. Imagine my surprise when I was eating at Dock's Restaurant in lower Manhattan and spied "Hood Canal Oysters" on the menu ($32 for a half dozen). Of course, a glass of ice tea was $12 at the Sheraton across the street, so maybe $5 an oyster wasn't such a bad deal.

In the good ol' days, crabbing was simply a matter of throwing a pot or two (or three or four) over the side on your way out to salmon fish, and picking them up on the way back in. Nowadays, however, crabbing at Hood Canal isn't as simple and straightforward as it used to be. Closed seasons, size restrictions, harvest quotas, off-limit beaches and other encumbrances can make crabbing almost as complicated and frustrating as trying to understand the salmon fishing laws.

Staying up to date: Still, crabbing for delicious Dungeness is an important part of life in the Pacific Northwest. The first thing you've got to do to participate is to stay up to speed with the changing regulations that affect this fishery/crabbery. Your best bet? Get to know the sexy voice on the recording machine at the recreational shellfish number managed by WDFW. That number is (866) 880-5431. Before you go crabbing, call to make sure you know where you can go.

You can also stay in touch with changing rules and regs by visiting the WDFW's Web site (*wdfw.wa.gov*). There you'll find important information and emergency closure details, which can happen.

That said, crabbing opened back on June 1 in Marine Area 9 (North Hood Canal, from Foulweather Bluff south to Olele Point) and Marine Area 12, which is the remainder of the Hood Canal area.

Season dates are established based on molt timing, and closed when "harvest shares" are taken. Those closures can happen at any time, so you've got to stay in tune with Johnny Law. We can't say it enough: Call that shellfishing number every time before you go crabbing!

The daily limit is six Dungeness males, measuring at least 6¼ inches in width, or six red rock crab of either sex measuring at least 5 inches across. Only hardshell crabs may be taken. Crabs with soft shells and female Dungeness must be released.

A catch record card is required when you're crabbing. Kids under 15 don't need a fishing license to crab, but they do need a catch record card. According to the WDFW: "Dungeness crab was added to the catch record card system to increase the accuracy of estimating recreational Dungeness crab harvest. Previously, catch estimates for the recreational crab fishery relied on field-based surveys and voluntary returns of logbooks. It was not possible to verify that the voluntary returns were representative of the crabber population at large. Because it does not rely on voluntary returns, the Dungeness Crab CRC will provide a more accurate estimate of recreational crab catch and will include wade, dive, pot, ring-net, and dock fisheries."

So bring a pen and your CRC, or risk a ticket.

Other rules: In Hood Canal, two units of crab gear are allowed per angler (a star trap, one ring net, or one pot is considered one unit of gear). If you leave your crab gear unattended, it must have its own buoy line and a separate buoy that's identified with your first name, last name and permanent address (phone number is voluntary). Buoy lines must be weighted to prevent them from floating to the surface. Buoys cannot be made from bleach bottles, antifreeze containers, paint cans or detergent bottles. They must be half red and half white for crabbing.

Crab pots, star traps and ring-nets may not be tended from a vessel at night (one hour after sunset to one hour before sunrise). There are lots of other rules too about the composition of the buoy line and so forth — enough to make your head spin — so be sure to do your reading before you go crabbing in the new 2004/2005 fishing regs pamphlet.

Where to go: The simple truth about crabbing at Hood Canal is there are really no bad places to crab. Some are more productive than others, but there are crab aplenty throughout the length and breadth of this saltwater fjord.

One of the best spots is at the Canal's lower southern end, in the Great Bend. This area runs from roughly Lilliwaup down to the Hoodsport Hatchery, down to Potlatch State Park, across Annas Bay past the mouth of the Skokomish River and up to Union. What makes this such an attractive area to crab are the relatively shallow depths, tidal influences and big numbers of crab.

You'll see a lot of crab pots here, but you can also toss a ring-net over the side, wait 20 or 30 minutes, and pull up. In fact, the area just off the boat launch near the Tacoma electric plant (Cushman Powerhouse) is one of the best spots.

Further north on the west side, good crabbing is available near Pleasant Harbor State Park, up to Dosewallips State Park and on to Whitney Point. Across the way, you can find excellent crabbing water all around the Seabeck Bay area.

For ring nets, find water that's less than 30 feet deep and toss your ring over the side or out from shore. For potters, you can crab deeper to see if you can find bigger crabs or a higher percentage of males.

How to do it: Just as crabbing is good about anywhere you go in the Canal, just about all kinds of crabbing baits and methods will work too. These crabs are not selective or particular.

But one of the best (and most fun) ways to crab is to catch a bucketful of sand dabs off the bottom first (use a slip sinker and a chunk of herring for bait on a salmon hook), and use these dabs for bait in your trap or ring. Old fish heads will also work, as will the crabbing standby standards such as chicken, a big ol' turkey leg and dog or cat food (although these can be expensive, relatively speaking). Sand dabs are cheap and effective. We cut them into thirds (head, body and tail) and put them in the crab pot bait trap.

AT a GLANCE

What: Summer crabbing in Hood Canal, Marine Area 12.

Why: Get the boiled saltwater and seasoning ready — this is some of the best crabbing in the Pacific Northwest!

How: Ring nets, pots — even fishing for them with a rod-n-reel will work. One of the best baits you can use in the Canal are the resident sand dabs.

When: The season opened on June 1. Pay close attention in case there are emergency/quota closures.

Where: The southern end can be awesome. The western shoreline and the eastern shoreline near Seacrest are also very good.

Regs watch: WDFW hotline (866) 880-5431; Web site: wdfw.wa.gov

Who to call: Seabeck Marina (360-830-5179).

Hood Canal Crabbing

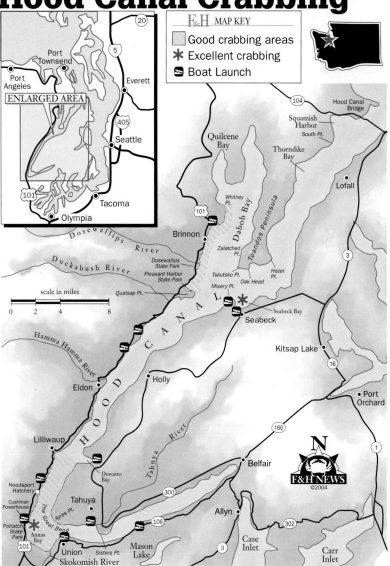

Non-commercial crab zones create prime sport ops

————————————————— EVERETT

by J.D. Wade

PRODUCTIVE CRAB CATCHES can be obtained from the Sound's recreational non-commercial crab zones, such as this ring-trap load pulled in by Amber Wade, 14, from the Chuckanut Bay zone.

Did you know there are crabbing areas within Puget Sound reserved for you, the sportsman, where you won't have to compete with commercial gear? These areas are accessible from beaches, docks or small boats in protected waters and are very productive. Let's take a look at a few:

Port Gardner: This zone was created to serve the popular Mukilteo-to-Everett fishery. Although there are not many accessible public docks within the included waters — which run between Elliot Point, northeast to the Everett Harbor entrance buoy, then south to the beach — it can be easily fished from small boats.

Most people work their crab traps in shallow water here, but there are crab throughout the zone. Water depths range to over 300 feet, and some of the largest Dungeness can be found over 200 feet down. Always use at least 50 extra feet of line (i.e., in 200 feet, have 250 feet of rope). Crab fishing is best an hour before to an hour after every slack tide (high slack being best).

There are numerous launch ramps that serve the area. The closest is the Mukilteo ramp, which is within the zone at the southern boundary. This ramp is next to the Whidbey Island ferry landing. It's a good ramp except at extremely low tides — it ends before it should and trailer wheels can drop off the end. Also watch the currents, because they can make docking a mite tricky. There is a lot of boat and ship travel passing the ramp, so even on a calm day there can be rough water.

The Norton Street ramp, in the Everett Marine Park, is just north of the crabbing zone boundary, and is one of the best launching facilities in the state. The ramp is huge and efficient, handling a tremendous volume of boaters, and there is ample parking.

Possession Point: Nearby to the west, at the southern end of Whidbey Island, lies the southernmost crab zone. It extends from Possession Point south to the Possession Sound entrance buoy then follows the island contour northeast to Glendale, out to a water depth of 50 feet.

Crabbing is quite good here on the gravel bottom, but the shelf drops off sharply beyond the 50-foot mark, so great care must be taken to place traps properly. Due to extreme currents here, it is very important to fish during the slack tides to prevent loss of gear. Besides, the crabs bury themselves in the loose gravel during strong tide runs to prevent being swept away themselves.

The primary access to this zone is through the Possession Beach Park ramp. This is a nice ramp but is exposed to southerly winds.

Holmes Harbor: One of the most popular crab zones lies within Holmes Harbor. There is an excellent ramp at Freeland park and a public fishing dock. Because it's very protected from both tides and winds, this spot can be fished any time any day.

Mukilteo, Possession Point and Holmes Harbor lie within WDFW designated Marine Area 8-2. This area will have an open crab season in 2003 from early May through Aug. 31, then will re-open for the November and December holidays.

Defining non-commercial zones

SPORT CRABBING IS MUCH MORE *productive with the addition of the 27 zones designated non-commercial throughout North Puget Sound. These set aside zones must meet the following criteria:*

1) Traditional or current recreational area that consistently provides reasonable opportunity and catches.

2) Area close to developed access, both public and private (i.e.: marinas, docks, boat launches, shorelines).

3. Waters adjoining or near park shorelines and other accessible public lands.

4. Management regions where there are few or no non-commercial zones to provide reasonable recreational opportunity and catch.

5. Marginal crab production area but of local or regional importance to sport fishers.

6. Sheltered waters which allow recreational boating and crustacean fishing on a regular basis.

7. Area that assists WDFW in meeting the commission policy by region and in overall Puget Sound (i.e.: "maintain a quality recreational fishery").

8. Area or region traditionally closed to state commercial fishing.

9. Three or more of the above should be met before considering any new area. — *J.D.W.*

Utsalady Bay: There are three other crab zones to the north that lie within Marine Area 8.1, one of which is quite unique.

The first is Utsalady Bay at the very northern tip of Camano Island, which is a very productive shallow-water spot. Its borders are from Rocky Point northeast to the red navigational buoy then southeast to Brown Point.

Due to the extreme shallow waters here, the best crabbing is found due north of Utsalady Point, where the muddy bottom drops to 25- to 40-foot depths

There are no docks but the area is served by two launch ramps. To get to the ramp at Utsalady, stay right at the split in the road as you get onto the island, and continue 2.9 miles to Utsalady Road. Stay to the right at Utsalady Point Road and follow the paved road to the beach and ramp. This ramp gets my rating as "just OK," and note the beaches on either side are private.

The better option is Maple Grove. Continue driving on the right split another ⅓ mile to Maple Grove Road and turn right. Follow the paved road down to the beach and turn right into the parking area and ramp. There is more room and the ramp is better.

North Skagit/Similk Bay: The sport crab zone just north is unique in that we share it with the Swinomish Indian Tribe (or, more accurately, they share it with us, exclusively). Noted as the North Skagit Bay/Similk Bay zone, state commercial activity is prohibited here.

This is one of the best crab spots in Puget Sound, without public docks, but all in sheltered waters and accessed by the Deception Pass State Park ramp in Cornet Bay, which is also the last crab zone in this area.

Marine Area 8-1 opens for crabbing June 1 and remains open through Labor Day, then will re-open with area 8-2 for the November-December holidays.

Save these maps and watch this space for details of other zones as the summer progresses and other areas open for crab fishing.

AT a GLANCE

What: Puget Sound crabbing.

Where: Inside recreational non-commercial crab fishing zones which are set aside explicitly for sport fishing during the annual open seasons.

Licences/regulations: A $7.67 shellfish license is required for crab anglers age 16 and up and must be displayed on the outside of clothing during shellfish harvest and transportation. A free catch record card is also required to fish for Dungeness crab.

Zone rules: All crab zones are subject to review each year, and new ones might be added. To enter your input about these areas or to suggest others for consideration, call the Mill Creek WDFW office (425-775-1331) or the Point Whitney Shellfish Lab (360-796-4601).

Timing: The beginning of "major molts" (excess of 20 percent 'softshell' condition in a marine regulation area) or reaching a maximum catch quota in any marine regulation area, will require sudden changes in local fishing regulations.

Information: Call the Shellfish Rule Change Hotline (866-880-5432) for updated information.

Puget Sound Crabbing

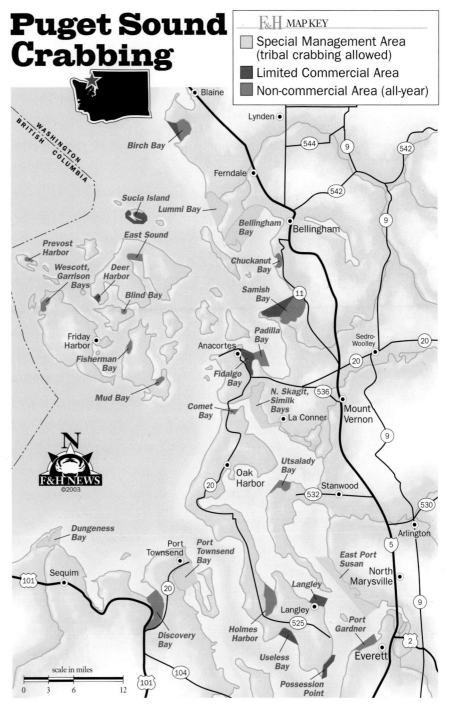

F&H MAP KEY

- Special Management Area (tribal crabbing allowed)
- Limited Commercial Area
- Non-commercial Area (all-year)

Puget Sound Freshwater
SALMON

'Channel' your efforts for Cushman Chinook

HOODSPORT

by Joel Shangle

When it comes right down to it, the landlocked Chinook salmon that inhabit Lake Cushman have no clue what a herring is. Descendants of a run of kings that were cut off from Hood Canal and its herring supply in 1925, Cushman's salmon have only genetic memories of little black and silver baitfish composing any portion of their diet.

But you want proof positive about the power of nature and genetics? Troll a cut-plug herring in front of a Lake Cushman Chinook and get ready to set the hook.

"These fish have never even seen a herring before, but you put one of them in their face and see what happens," says Steve Phillips at Lake Cushman Resort (360-877-9630). "They're land-locked — they shouldn't have any idea what a herring is, but that's what they go after. A flasher and cutplug is the way to catch kings in this lake."

Cushman's kings compose only half of the "landlocked salmon" portion of the lake's fishery, and a quarter of the lake's abundant coldwater opportunity. With a healthy population of kokanee, rainbows and cutthroat (and some Dolly Varden thrown in), Cushman presents West Sound trollers with ample opportunity from spring well into fall.

"The kokanee, rainbow and cut-throat bite usually starts going strong in April and May, and lasts until the end of July, beginning of August," says Phillips. "From about mid-August to early October, the Chinook fishing gets good. Summer and fall are prime times."

TROLL CUTPLUGS for landlocked Lake Cushman king salmon.

Summer simmers: With the kokanee, cutt and rainbow bites already crank-ing at Cushman, anglers on this 4,000-acre impoundment of the Skokomish River should be well occu-pied until the Chinook fishery comes alive later this summer. The chal-lenge for the next month will lie in playing the sun and temperature correct-ly to figure out where in the water column to target kokes.

"Their position really, really, *really* varies," says Phillips. "As it gets brighter and warmer, kokanee will move down to 30, 40 feet. Anytime it's sunny and bright, it starts driving them down deep. But whenever you get a day or two of clouds and overcast, they move up to 10, 15 feet."

Their depth won't be the only thing that changes on a daily basis — because kokanee are generally very nomadic in any system, you can expect to spend significant time searching for schools of fish from one end of the lake to the other.

"You're not going to find them at any one particular place every time you fish," says Phillips. "They could be at any part of this lake at any given time."

Once you locate a school, however, the best technique is to troll a small spinner or fluttering spoon behind a set of dodgers. The flash and vibration of the dodger is key.

"The biggest problem is that these fish have plenty to eat," says Phillips. "They have a kazillion water bugs and things on the surface to feed on. You stick a worm on a hook and just drop it down, they won't give a damn. But as soon as you put some flash in the water to attract them, they'll come over and take a look."

The pattern doesn't vary much for

AT A GLANCE

What: Lake Cushman.

Where: Northern Mason County, just east of Lilliwaup and southern Hood Canal.

Species: Rainbow and cutthroat trout, landlocked Chinook, kokanee, dolly varden, largemouth and smallmouth bass.

Summer fisheries: Kokanee available through early July, trout available until August. The Chinook bite is traditionally at its best in August and September.

Top spots: For Chinook, fish the old Skokomish River channel just off the west shore across from Cushman Lake Resort, or the edge of the old lake site on the north end. For kokanee, move around until you locate a school — they inhabit all parts of the lake.

Techniques: Cushman is a boaters' fishery. Downrigger trolling is the method of choice for all species. For kokanee, drag a dodger/spinner setup. For Chinook, troll a cut-plug herring behind a flasher.

Facilities: Cushman Lake Resort features cabins, 32 RV sites, 45 tent sites, gasoline, convenience store, tackle and a marina.

Directions: Take Highway 119 west from Hoodsport 7 miles to the lake.

Launch: Lake Cushman State Park, Lake Cushman Resort

Information: Steve Phillips, Lake Cushman Resort (360-877-9630)

trout. The basic technique is to troll a spinner or spoon, fishing parallel to shore in the 20-foot range and moving deeper through the summer.

Channel Chinook: The typical Cushman king will run between 8 and 15 pounds, with a top-end fish hitting the 25-pound mark. As mentioned earlier, they're fond of cut-plug herring trolled behind a flasher, but they'll also hit other traditional salmon lures like Silver Horde plugs and Coyote spoons.

Cushman's kings are especially fond of two areas:

1) Close to the west shore, just northwest of Cushman Lake Resort. Head straight across the lake from the resort, turn north (roughly 80 feet off the big landslide on the west shore) and start trolling your cut-plug herring between 80 and 85 feet. Do *not* go deeper — this area is a sunken forest that lies in roughly 300 feet of water.

"The tops of the trees are at about 90 feet, so if you go deeper than the 80-foot level, kiss your gear goodbye," says Phillips.

The prime spot here is above the old Skokomish River channel, which runs north/south between the trees — if you can get into the channel, you're in the middle of the kings' main travel route.

"Those fish like to run the old river channel," says Phillips. "They'll move back and forth along the channel, above the trees and in the channel between the trees. They still stick with the river, even though they haven't had a river to run up into for years and years."

2) Off the east shore on the north end,

along the edge of the old lake site. You want to fish north/south along the ledge that used to define the east shore of the original lake, before it was flooded in 1925.

"It's about 150 feet deep right on the edge of the old lake, and it drops down to 380, 400 feet from there," says Phillips. "That's a nice natural shelf that fish hang on."

> **"These fish have never even seen a herring before, but you put one of them in their face and see what happens."**
> –Steve Phillips

Pretend you're fishing the Sound here — stick your bait within 10 feet of the bottom.

Dollies too: You can only catch and release Cushman's Dollies, but they represent a growing population. Cushman also surrenders the occasional bass, but it's a completely unexplored warmwater fishery.

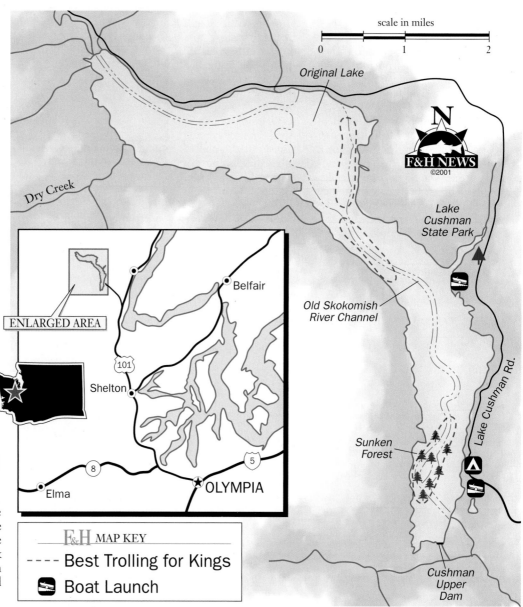

scale in miles

0   1   2

Original Lake

N

F&H NEWS
©2001

Lake Cushman State Park

Old Skokomish River Channel

Dry Creek

ENLARGED AREA

Belfair

101

Shelton

8

Elma

5

OLYMPIA

Lake Cushman Rd.

Sunken Forest

Cushman Upper Dam

F&H MAP KEY

- - - - **Best Trolling for Kings**

Boat Launch

Lake Cushman

Green steel: winter-runs in the heart of Pugetropolis

AUBURN

by Joel Shangle

TYPICAL WINTER CATCH on the Green River will consist of 7- to 10-pound hatchery fish. (*F&H News* photo)

Your best bet for lunch this winter in South Sound doesn't include Ivar's clam chowder or Kidd Valley fries. It includes Pro-Cured eggs, sand shrimp, Fish Doctor jigs, a good shot of crawdad oil and winter steelhead, served up Green River style.

The Washington Department of Fish & Wildlife tells us that the Green River rolls out a modest 600 to 900 sport-caught hatchery winter-runs in a typical November-to-February season, but those numbers don't offer a hint at what makes this river so damn special: it provides miles of streamside access that slashes right through the heart of South Sound suburbia, literally minutes from greater Auburn/Kent's Strip Mall Central and within shouting distance of the SUVs and minivans scooting down Highway 167.

It's about quality steelheading from the bank, minus the highway time to the Olympic Peninsula, North End or Columbia tributaries.

"That's the great thing about the Green River — it's right here in our backyard," says Tom Pollack at Auburn Sports & Marine (253-833-1440). "This is not a river that demands a two- or three-hour drive. If you have a spare hour, you can drive to the river in 10 minutes and start fishing. It has good access throughout the full length of it from the Green River Rearing Ponds down through Kent and Auburn. You can get right to the river, make your two or three or 150 casts and be done. You're fishing, not driving down the highway. You're putting bait in water."

And fresh, nickel-bright winter-runs are attacking that bait with abandon: While the traditional Thanksgiving kickoff of winter steelhead season has yet to come and go, early-season Green River anglers are already tangling with the first waves of fish bound for the Green River Rearing Ponds in Kanasket.

"They're catching steelhead in the river already — we had a couple dozen taken here (in early November)," says Pollack. "We'll see people get out there with enthusiasm in late November because the silvers have gone through, and the chums are in such bad shape you don't know if you want to even fish for them. We're already getting some of that colder water that triggers spawning steelhead to go skittering up the river."

Section by section: The Green is defined by miles and miles of easy bank access, from where it spills out of the lower end of Howard Hanson Lake and continuing downstream through Palmer, Auburn, Kent and Tukwila before it turns into the Duwamish River, and, eventually, the Duwamish Waterway. It features a mix of swift-moving drift water, hundreds of slower, deeper pools that demand a float/bait setup, and several stretches of water that are picture perfect for plunking. It's easily accessed via Green River Road, which parallels the river on the east side between Kent and Auburn, and Green Valley Road, which winds alongside the north bank for several miles above Auburn.

"You have access to all types of water from plunk water to bobber water to drift water," says Pollack. "It's dam controlled, so it doesn't go out even when we get a bunch of rain. On the other side of the coin, if we have a stretch where we get no rain, they can periodically pass some water through the dam and the river will come up."

• **Hatchery to Flaming Geyser:** The upper section of the river, from Kanasket-Palmer State Park down through the Green River Gorge to Flaming Geyser State Park, features tight, steep bankside structure and swift water that calls for finesse presentations of jigs, small egg clusters or bubble gum worms under a float. Because of the gradient and speed of the water, this area is easier to fish in

AT A GLANCE

What: Green River winter-run steelhead.

When: Traditional kickoff of winter season is Thanksgiving, but fish are already being caught on the Green in early November.

Where: Palmer-Kanasket State Park to Kent, including Flaming Geyser State Park, Metzler Park, Highway 18 and the Auburn Golf Course.

Techniques: Drift fish with Corkies/Cheaters and yarn, shrimp or eggs; fish jigs, shrimp, eggs under a float; plunk with small winged bobbers and shrimp or eggs.

Information: Tom Pollack, Auburn Sports & Marine (253-833-1440)

low, slow, clear conditions.

• **Flaming Geyser to Metzler Park:** The river turns into classic Corky/Cheater and yarn/shrimp/egg water as it slips down out of the canyon toward Flaming Geyser Park, which offers wide open access on the south side down to the Flaming Geyser Bridge. Further down, you'll find good drift water and access right below the Whitney Bridge, continuing downstream past the Island to Metzler Park.

• **Metzler Park to Highway 18:** The public access at Metzler Park is a little off the beaten path compared to Flaming Geyser's stroll-on availability, but it puts you onto pristine drift water.

"It's more of a walk than up at Flaming Geyser, but you get into some really good spots at Metzler Park where the fish are *right* by you," says Pollack. "This is an area where you can drift Corkies or Cheaters and yarn, or you can float or swim jigs."

Look for the worn wooden sign and dirt road that leads off Green Valley Road to a parking lot. Follow the clearly marked trail into the woods, where you'll come to a fork in the road. Take the lefthand fork down to the beginning of the Metzler Park Drift. If you go right at the fork, you'll find yourself on the upper end of the O'Grady Drift, which is great for chums but only so-so for steelhead.

You'll find a pair of good drifts below O'Grady, leading into the head of the Neeley Drift just above Neeley Bridge.

• **Highway 18:** The Highway 18 fishery covers a lot of water, but it's easy to move along the bank if you fish opposite the mouth of Soos Creek down to the Car Body Hole roughly a half-mile down. You can either park near the Highway 18 bridge and work downstream, or at the Park & Ride lot near the big pumpkin patch and walk across the field to the Car Body Hole. This section holds mostly swift, drift water.

• **Auburn Golf Course:** References to the "Golf Course" usually encompass the 4 to 5 miles of the east side of the river from the 8th Street bridge downstream to the soccer fields below the golf course. This entire area is easily accessible from Green River Road, and filled with good drift water.

"This is a wide open area that lets people spread out, and it's easy to get to because the road is about 20 feet off the creek," says Pollack. "It's a popular area, but there's enough room for everybody to fish it."

• **Kent:** The lower river, from Kent down, features mostly plunking water.

Driftable? Drift boats could theoretically function between the Whitney Bridge and Highway 18, but fishing from a floating device is prohibited through the winter season. A boat is a great way to access more water, but get your feet on solid land before you start fishing or you'll come home with a fine.

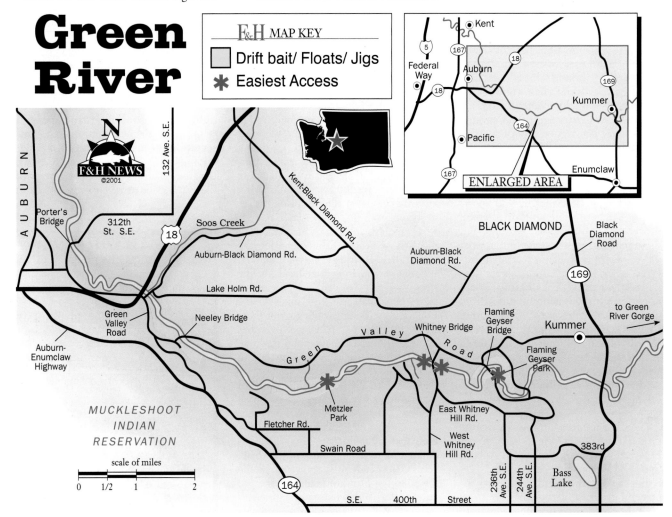

Snohomish River system hosts steelhead, sturgeon, salmon in the heart of Puget Sound

SNOHOMISH

by Joel Shangle

If you can't find Dave Lee and Scott Weedman at their shop, you can easily guess where the co-owners of Three Rivers Marine are: boating fish somewhere on the Snohomish River system.

Two self-professed river rats who cut their teeth on Western Washington's most diverse river system, Weedman and Lee are fixtures on the Snoqualmie, Skykomish and Snohomish, and on smaller tributaries like the Sultan and Wallace.

And for good reason: The Snohomish system provides some of the best fishing, easiest access and diversity of opportunity in the Northwest, all within an hour of downtown Seattle.

"What's not to like about that system?" asks Weedman (425-415-1575). "It has everything: winter-run steelhead, summer-run steelhead, coho, chums, sturgeon, sea-run cutts, humpies. It's loaded with opportunity, year-round."

Snoqualmie River: The smallest of the three main rivers in the system, the Snoqualmie pours over Snoqualmie Falls and meanders down through Fall City, Carnation and Duvall before eventually meeting the Skykomish near Monroe.

"The Snoqualmie has been an emotional favorite for many regulars for years and years," says Mike Bing at Van Hala Guide Service (206-230-2646). "Fish it hard, get to know it. It offers a ton of options to change up, to get creative in order to hook up with hatchery and wild fish."

Translation: It's a challenging, moody river, but the potential rewards include quality late summer/fall coho, summer and winter steelhead, and smaller species ranging from rainbows to whitefish.

TROY SANSOM holds a winter-run steelhead caught out of the Snohomish River system.

WHERE (Boat)
• **Emil Plum launch:** The highest upriver launch for drift boats (jet sleds are limited to a quarter mile below the launch), the Emil Plum put-in lies a quarter mile below Tokul Creek.
• **Raging River:** Launch in Fall City, run upriver to the clay bank and free-drift or pull plugs down past the Two Rivers Golf Course.

"The north side of the river is a beautiful, sloping gravel bar, the south side a riprap slot," says Bing. "(Throw) spoons and spinners on the bar and pull plugs and divers through the slot."

Working down from the Raging, fish plugs or bait divers in the slot underneath the Fall City bridge, into an area known as The Business Drift (where you'll free-drift bait from the flag pole down). Areas to hit as you continue from Fall City to Carnation include the Car Body Hole (pull plugs or toss spinners), Patterson and Griffin creeks, the mouth of the Tolt River (pull plugs or drift bait) and the Swinging Bridge Drift below McDonald Park.
• **High Bridge:** Put in below the bridge and run the extreme lower end of the Snoqualmie, or duck around the corner into the Sky.
WHERE (Bank)
• **Tokul Creek:** The most popular bank fishery on the river, the Tokul

AT A GLANCE

What: Snohomish River system salmonids and sturgeon, including the Snoqualmie, Skykomish and Snohomish rivers.

When: Something to fish for 12 months out of the year. Winter steelhead peaks in December, summer steelhead is at its best in July, fall coho and chums peak in October and November, sturgeon year-round.

Where: Tokul Creek to Carnation Farms on the Snoqualmie; Sultan River to Lewis Street on the Skykomish; town of Snohomish to the mouth on the Snohomish.

Techniques: Free-drift bait, pull plugs, fish bobbers and jigs, fly fish.

Special regs: Catch-and-release on all wild steelhead in the Snohomish River system. Also, system closes to all fishing (except sturgeon below US 2 bridge at Everett) March 1, 2002.

Info/Guides: Scott Weedman, Dave Lee at Three Rivers Marine (425-415-1575), Kyle Ward at Kyle Ward Guide Service (425-334-3988); Mike Bing at Van Hala Guide Service (206-230-2646); Bob Ferris at Ferris & Son's Guide Service (206-362-1894); Ken Pullen at Fish Hard Guide Service (425-334-4664); Sam Ingram at Wilderness Adventures Guide Service (360-435-9311); Mark Heise (206-776-2837); John's Sporting Goods (425-259-3056); Ted's Sport Center (425-743-9505); Sky Valley Traders (360-794-8818); Jerry's Surplus (425-252-1176); Triangle Beverage (360-568-4276); McDaniels Do It Center (360-568-1544)

Creek area can draw a crowd on a good day as bankies target fish running for the Tokul Creek Hatchery. You'll find parking at the Washington Department of Fish & Wildlife access area at Tokul on the north side. Toss spoons/spinners or fish floats with jigs or eggs into The Big Eddy and Cable Hole.

• **Tolt River/McDonald Park:** Foot access available via a county park just below the Tolt River and downriver at McDonald Park (off Highway 203).

NOTES: The Snoqualmie is a great bait river, but check WDFW regulations carefully for bait restrictions ... cutts and steelhead available to flyrodders ... camping available in Fall City and Carnation.

Skykomish River: One of the most prolific rivers on the Westside, the Sky has long been the hub of the North End's hatchery salmon and steelhead network. The stretch of water between Sultan and Monroe gets worked thoroughly by guides and private anglers alike, but it produces as much action year after year as any piece of water in the state. The Sky has been a screaming summer steelhead option the past couple of years, and the 2001 back-to-back-to-back swarm of summer steel, humpies, coho and winter steel *still* has the North End buzzing.

WHERE (Boat)
• **Mouth of the Sultan:** Because it's one of the major tributary destinations for fish running up the Skykomish, the Sultan River is one of your best launch/put-in options, regardless of the season. Drift boaters can launch in Sultan and take out at the Ben Howard launch, hitting traditional downriver hot spots like Taylor Flats, the mouth of Elwell Creek, Thunderbird Hole. Arm yourself with plugs, divers/bait, eggs for free drifting, spoons and spinners, because you'll find places to use 'em all between Sultan and Ben Howard.
• **Ben Howard:** Head east off Highway 203 on Ben Howard Road to this launch, from which you can either fish upstream toward Elwell, or downstream to Monroe and the confluence of the Snoqualmie and Sky.
• **Lewis Street:** Put in by the Lewis Street Bridge in Monroe and fish down to the confluence for the first batches of fish coming up out of the Snohomish into the Sky. (From Lewis Street launch downriver 2,500 feet

closed to boat fishing Nov. 1-April 30.)
WHERE (Bank)
• **Reiter Ponds:** The end of the line for hatchery fish, and the front of the line for many North End bank anglers armed with bait and the need to hook steelhead.
• **Sultan:** Fish either Cracker Bar (across from the mouth of the Sultan River) or along the riprap wall below the mouth of the river.
• **Lewis Street:** Drift bait or fish floats on either side of the bridge.
NOTES: Booted out two world-record humpies in the fall ... good fly fishing in the upper river.

Snohomish River: The big, lumbering mainstem Snohomish doesn't have the personality of either the upper Snoqualmie or Skykomish, but for sheer, fishy productivity, it's the place to start. Both Weedman and Lee ride the Snohomish hard during the course

of the season, hitting the system's freshest fish shortly after they leave the salt and staying with them until they've moved up into the Sky and Snoqualmie. Think about it: All the fish bound for the Sky, Snoqualmie, Wallace, Sultan, Pilchuck and a handful of other streams have to pass through the Snohomish first.

WHERE (Boat)
• **High Bridge on the Snoqualmie:** A short shot above the Sky/Snoqualmie confluence and the mainstem Snohomish itself.
• **Town of Snohomish:** Near the airport, just above Highway 9.
• **Langus Park:** This well-maintained site allows the easiest access to the lower Snohomish's sloughs (Ebey, Steamboat, Union) and their sturgeon fisheries.

NOTES: Best sturgeon fisheries around Priest Point, mouth of Quilceda Creek.

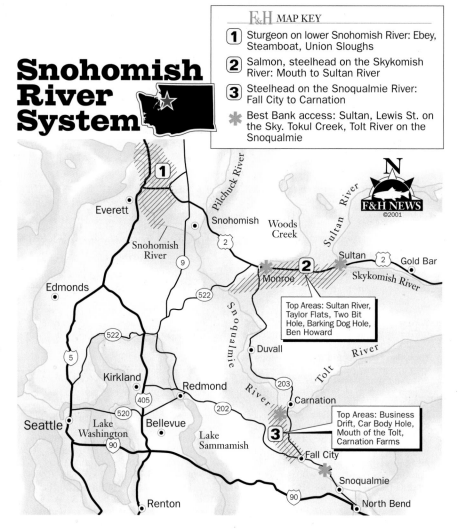

Snohomish River System

F&H MAP KEY

1. Sturgeon on lower Snohomish River: Ebey, Steamboat, Union Sloughs
2. Salmon, steelhead on the Skykomish River: Mouth to Sultan River
3. Steelhead on the Snoqualmie River: Fall City to Carnation
* Best Bank access: Sultan, Lewis St. on the Sky. Tokul Creek, Tolt River on the Snoqualmie

F&H NEWS ©2001

Top Areas: Sultan River, Taylor Flats, Two Bit Hole, Barking Dog Hole, Ben Howard

Top Areas: Business Drift, Car Body Hole, Mouth of the Tolt, Carnation Farms

Snohomish system ground zero for Humpfest 2003

————————————————— SNOHOMISH

by Andy Walgamott

Might as well just call it the Sno-hump-ish River system.

That's because over the next month and a half a massive wave of humpies is gonna swamp the Snohomish River and several tribs as they return to their spawning grounds.

How many jumpin' humpies we talking about? Of the 1.3 million forecasted to return to the Snohomish and Stillaguamish rivers, Curt Kraemer, WDFW biologist for both systems, expects as many as 700,000 to 750,000 to roll up the Snohomish after commercial and saltwater anglers get their share, with the remainder headed to the Stilly.

Champ bloodline: These fish are the progeny of 2001's monster run, a notoriously bite-happy lot that set new state and world saltwater and freshwater weight records and made kajillionaires out of local Dick Nite traffickers.

"It was one of the three biggest runs in the last several decades," confirms Kraemer. He says escapement — that means they got past you, me, Avis and everyone else — in the Snohomish system was 1.1 million pinks, 10 times the usual goal. The slippery little Sultan River alone saw 151,000 return, according to Snohomish County PUD,

THEY'VE GOT HUMPS on their backs, spots on their tail and toothy smiles, and they'll (the fish, not the dude here) be biting up and down the Snohomish-Skykomish system for the next month and a half.

a record in 30 years of data collection.

This go-around, there's again a four-humpy limit. Season opened Aug. 16 on the Snoho, Sept. 1 on the Stilly and Skykomish.

Biters: The best thing about Snohomish pinks is that year in and year out they're good fighters and willing to whack just about anything you throw at 'em. In fact, during 2001's run, it was more difficult to find lures they *wouldn't* bite than what they would. Let's see here: They bit bait, they bit

plastics, they bit hardware. They bit jigs, they bit tiny flickering spoons, they bit tubes. They bit bass gear, they bit crappie gear, they bit steelhead gear.

Heck, they even bit my old dog Blue once, but that's a different story.

I thought I found the only bait a humpy wouldn't bite ... and then I was proven wrong — twice. Floating eggs under a bobber for silvers, I got a take. And then there was the fish which bit a 4-inch green tube better suited for the bass up at Roseiger. Crazy pinkos.

"Pinks have always been good biters in rivers," says Kraemer, but he attributes some of 2001's fantastic bite to just the sheer numbers of returners. That ensured there were always fish moving through, which riled up the older, moodier fish, which kept the whole lot of them snapping at anything drifted in front of their face. Made some of us feel like old humpy pros.

Figure on stoking your smoker from now to about mid-September in the Snohomish, and then get your kicks catching and releasing humpies from mid-September into early October on the lower Skykomish. Let all boots go.

Lower river lures: From the town of Snohomish down, troll or cast spoons and jigs.

"On the lower river, Buzz Bombs just whack them," says Kent Alger at Three Rivers Marine and Tackle (425-415-1575) in Woodinville. On the flood tide, fish bigger pink Bombs, smaller ones on the outgo. If tackle shops are out of pink, buy another color and get yourself some nice nail polish and repaint 'em. I mojoed some fluorescent 2½-inch BBs with Revlon's Passion Punch Shimmer, and they look absolutely breathtaking!

Alger also suggests trolling Dick Nites, jigging leadheads with pink hoochies, fishing smaller pink FatFish, Wiggle Warts and Hot Shots and plunking sand shrimp.

"A pink Wicked Willy is one of the better lures" for trolling on the lower Snohomish, adds John Martinis of John's Sporting Goods (425-259-3056) in Everett.

And there's always the venerable

Search for Son of Humpzilla begins

AVIS PEARSON AND ALEX MINERICH'S *huge pinks in 2001 may not have spread their genes around, but there's always a chance we'll see a few dino-sized humpies moving through this fall.*

Jim Bartz, on the leading edge of the "pink wave" at Curley's Resort in Sekiu, reported in late July that the humpies there were going 10 pounds, and were bigger than the coho. And according to WDFW biologist Curt Kraemer, early test fisheries in the saltwater indicated an average fish size of 5 pounds, analogous to 2001 numbers. Many years the average is just 3½ pounds, Kraemer says, but he wasn't advising putting any greenbacks on a return of fat boys this go-around.

"A betting man wouldn't put money on giants," he said.

However, since we've got a gambling problem, we're putting some kroners down on these whens and wheres for monster freshwater sailfish: late September, the lower Skykomish River.

That's where and when Minerich caught his current record fish and Avis nabbed her cover-shot beast (Oct. 18, 2001). Both were using Dick Nites, Avis a half-and-half; Minerich a silver-with-red-head.

So how'd 2001's massive run come about, anyway? Kraemer attributes good management (naturally), good escapement and a "good marine survival scheme for chums and pinks."

And how'd Humpzilla get so big?

"They continue to hit groceries, they grow at the maximum, and that's clearly what happened in 2001," he says. — A.W.

Humpy Special spoon, Kastmasters and, well, anything pink with a hook.

Upstream setups: From Snohomish upriver, try a Dick Nite rigged steelhead drift-fishing style or a jig or bait under a bobber.

For the former, run a snap swivel and tubing with lead up your mainline, add a bead, then tie on a barrel swivel, 4 or 5 feet of 8-pound leader and a No. 1 half-and-half (50/50) Nite. Cast out, let it drop a bit and then retrieve if there's little or no current. Don't worry too much about keeping your lure near bottom; pinks seem to be spread throughout the water column at this stage of their journey upstream. If ebb tide's sucking water out, cast out and let it

drop until it's quarter downstream, then retrieve slowly.

As for jigs and a bobber, rig up with a bobber stop, bead and a float with a ½-ounce weight just above a swivel. Give yourself 2 to 3 feet of leader and then a bait or jig of some kind — sand shrimp and other shrimp baits will fly as will your steelhead jigs and small pink crappie tubes. For whatever reason steelhead and crappie jigs worked better in relatively faster-flowing pools while bait did best in the slower-moving pools. Toss to the head of the pool and drift through.

Where and when: Basically you want to target pools and inside turns rather than riffles. Here are the better

spots and shore access points from Monroe down:

• Below the boat launch off Tualco Loop Road there's a long pool that's good for back-trolling or casting Dick Nites, or floating jigs or bait. Anchor up near the rock jetties at the end of the hole and toss your bobber towards them.

You can also fish this pool from shore by paying the $2 trespass fee the farm at the end of 177th Ave. (the road past the Monroe prison) charges. It's where Alex Minerich caught his state freshwater record 14.86-pounder. At 300 cfs a friend and I could wade the river and fish from the aforementioned rocks.

• The next hole down has a rock

Snohomish System Pinks

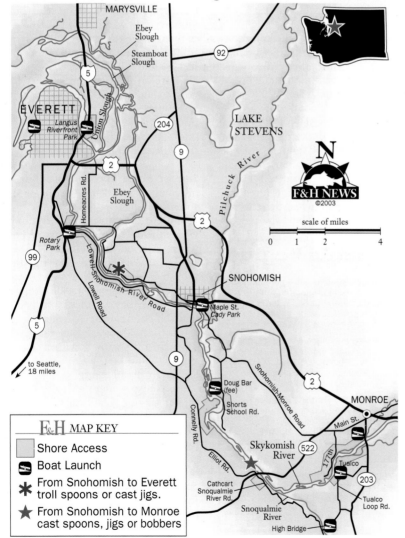

F&H MAP KEY

▨ Shore Access
🛥 Boat Launch
✳ From Snohomish to Everett troll spoons or cast jigs.
★ From Snohomish to Monroe cast spoons, jigs or bobbers

jetty and house on its south side. Anchor about 25 feet or so off the jetty and drift bait or jigs under a bobber. Fish will keg up in this hole. Also back-troll bait or spoons.

• For some odd reason in 2001, bait consistently worked better at the Nordstrom Hole, the next spot down, than jigs, though both fished. (At the hole above, the opposite was true.)

• Below there, the river divides into two channels. The channel on the right is narrow and fast with a 90-degree left-hand turn, but has several deeper spots where you can toss a bobber and jig. At the corner, anchor and back-troll spoons. Remember Humpzilla, Avis Pearson's 14.49-pound *Oncorhynchus gorbuscha giganticus*? He was caught in this general area.

• From the confluence of the Skykomish and Snoqualmie rivers down to the 522 bridge, float jigs, back-troll bait or toss spoons or Kastmasters.

• Below 522, where the Snohomish banks off the bedrock of Lords Hill, drift a bobber through that slick and into the slack.

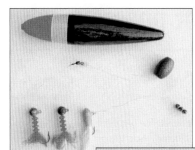

• Down the north bank of the river there are a couple places with deeper water before the main channel switches to the south side.

• Bob Heirman Park, off Connelly Road near Cathcart, offers shoreline access to Thomas' Eddy if you're on the bank. Toss all manner of spoons. If you're running a boat, the river splays out into shallow channels with lots of woody debris.

• Just above Douglas Bar, where you can launch your boat for a $50 fee (talk to Fred Zylstra), there's a deep hole where you can cast spoons or Buzz Bombs, etc. Also, there's shore access off of Shorts School Road.

• Below Doug Bar to Everett things are a tidal show. Anchor up and cast spoons, jigs or plugs, or troll. There's a massive amount of public access in Snohomish, off Lowell-Snohomish River Road and Rivershore Drive, and at Rotary, Riverfront and Langus parks

GET AS GEAR CRAZY as you want for Snohomish River system pinks, or just go simple with a bobber-and-pink-jig or Dick Nite drift rig.

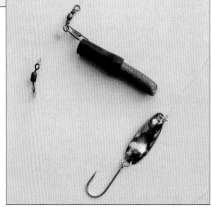

in Everett for tossing spoons, jigs and even floating a bobber and jig.

Gear up for possible Lake Washington sockeye season

————————————————————————————— **SEATTLE**

by Dusty Routh

If you're a Pacific Northwest angler and you fish year-round, you know we've got not only great fishing but also tough, challenging conditions. That may be why so many anglers, hardcore and casual alike, absolutely crave a summer sockeye season on Lake Washington. If there's an easier salmon fishery anywhere, in weather more beautiful with conditions as calm, we'd like to know about it. The relatively simple and straightforward fishing on this lake when the socks are in is a walk in the park compared to some of the other fishing conditions we endure. About the only real downside is the crowds.

Sockeye 101: As of press-time there wasn't any new news about the state of this potential summer fishery. But here's what we do know: Counts are conducted at the Ballard Locks as the fish come into their new freshwater digs. As of late June, the count hovered at 24,314 fish and climbing. That number *should* continue to increase exponentially each day since the bulk of the run (at least 50 percent of it) usually shows up by mid-July.

The escapement goal is 350,000 fish, meaning that at least this many fish must come into the system in order for enough spawning to happen for subsequent runs. If there are fish counts above 350,000 fish, we can expect a season.

WDFW and Muckleshoot Tribe fisheries managers are expecting a run of 480,000 fish, which could conceivably mean 130,000-some fish for sport and tribal harvest.

How it's done: Lucky for everyone, sockeye fishing isn't rocket science (however, for some interesting *new* science on sockeye, see p. 24-16). The standard way to catch these fish is to fish deep and slow. Downriggers are essential, though you could get the job done by using heavy sinkers. You want to get your offering down to 70 feet. Early in the morning during low-light conditions, you can fish as shallow as 45 to 50 feet, but most all fish are taken between 65 and 70 feet. Check out p. 24-12 for three pros' take on how it's done.

To rig up, use a medium-action steelhead or salmon rod, a sturdy baitcasting reel, 17-pound test and a Les Davis chrome dodger with prism tape. Add a 9-inch leader with two red, black, or purple Gamakatsu hooks tied up like you would a plug-cut herring rig. But don't put anything on those hooks. Fish them bare (see p. 24-13 for rigging illustration). Some anglers add a little pink Power Bait, or add some krill scent, but most anglers fish their hooks bare.

Lower the whole works to 70 feet, then troll as slowly as you absolutely, positively can, including throwing your kicker motor into neutral over and over again to slow yourself down. If there's a wind, and there might be, it's better to troll against the wind to slow yourself down rather than letting the wind push you too fast.

Where to fish: If this run is as big as it's predicted, the real question about where to fish will be, "Where will the regulations let us fish?" Sometimes the north end is closed off, for example. So check the regs carefully once WDFW makes them known. Otherwise, the hottest spots season-in and season-out tend to be around the 520 bridge, both sides of the I-90 bridge, on all sides of Mercer Island, and in the "belly" of the lake between I-90 and the mouth of the Cedar River (be aware that the actual mouth of the Cedar is usually closed within 100 yards).

Special attention is usually given to the south end of Mercer Island, and to the deep holes at the northwest end of the I-90 bridge. On the other hand, I've nailed fish at the north end of the island,

IT DOESN'T GET MUCH simpler than Lake Washington sockeye. Danielle Branstetter holds a nice one caught during 2002's fishery.

and in deep-hole areas between the 520 and I-90 bridges. If there's a lot of fish, though, the "where" isn't going to be as important as the "how." If you're not deep enough and slow enough, your chances of having fresh sockeye on the grill after your day on the water won't be quite as good.

Dealing with the crowds: The Lake Washington sockeye fishery is wildly popular, no doubt about it, so you've got to expect a lot of company and be willing to deal with it.

Everybody with anything that floats gets out for these fish. In seasons past I've seen people trolling from yachts to tiny rubber rafts to even Jet Skis. It's a madhouse.

The last statistic I heard from the last time this fishery was open was something like 5,000 boats came out for it. That's absolutely a ton of people.

But if you keep a good attitude and don't let salmon fever enslave you, once you're on the water it's not that big a deal. Courtesy and patience are going to be the best things to have in your boat as you set out in search of fish.

Lake Washington

Launching 101: If you have friends on the lake, it's a good idea to launch your boat ahead of time and leave it on the lake for the duration of the season.

But if you don't, the earlier you can get to the boat ramps the better, in order to be out at first light when the season opens up. Or, if you can stomach the wait, give it until 8 a.m. when all the boats are already out, then go launch. Any way you do it, however, retrieving your boat almost always takes twice as long as launching.

There are a lot of ramps on Lake Washington. In my experience, the ramp at Magnusson Park at the north end of the lake seems to handle the volume reasonably well; there may be fewer boats going out of there than at Mercer Island, Coal Creek, Gene Coulon Park or even Kenmore. But every ramp will be crowded.

A few pointers:

• Make sure your engine will start (a test run before the season is a good idea)

• Have all your gear and rods ready before you leave the house

• Get your boat launch- and water-ready while you're waiting in line so you can launch quickly

• Make sure you carry extra vehicle and boat keys. Also be sure to have your Vehicle Access Permit on your rig — WDFW will be checking for that this year.

For the retrieval, for the love of God, please make sure the person getting the rig knows how to back a trailer down the ramp. Every season there are massive hold-ups as people try to back a trailer they've never backed before.

AT a GLANCE

What: WDFW and tribal preseason projections showed 480,000 sockeye through the Ballard Locks, but it's still up in the air. Escapement goal is 350,000.

When: Announcement of a season (or not) should be made in early July. The sportfishing season could happen anytime thereafter. Monitor WDFW's Web site (*http://wdfw.wa.gov/*).

How: Fish deep and slow. Troll as slowly as you can at 70 feet with a chrome dodger and two bare red hooks on a 9-inch leader.

Where: Hit the bridges and the south and west sides of Mercer Island, as well near the mouth of the Cedar.

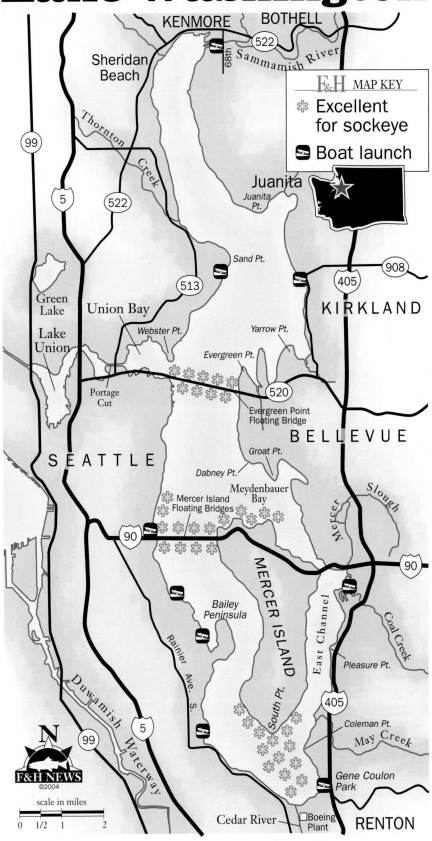

F&H MAP KEY

❋ Excellent for sockeye

⛴ Boat launch

scale in miles
0   1/2   1   2

Puget Sound Freshwater
STEELHEAD

Relearn the turbid Sauk for big metalheads

DARRINGTON

by Joel Shangle

The definition of the word "enigma" is as follows: one that is puzzling, ambiguous or inexplicable.

The definition of "world class steelhead" is a little more black and white: anything over 20 pounds.

If there's one North End stream that perfectly fits both definitions, it's the Sauk River. This tributary of the Skagit is legendary for its massive wild steelhead, but it's just as well known for a fickle nature that makes it one of the most volatile, challenging winter fisheries in the state. Tumbling out of the Cascades through a drainage whose physical composition changes dramatically from year to year, it's next to impossible to pattern, even in typical water years. And once you think you have it figured out, Mother Nature turns it all

AT a GLANCE

What: Big, wild winter steelhead.

Where: The Sauk River in eastern Snohomish and Skagit counties. The river tumbles out of the Mt. Baker-Snoqualmie National Forest then flows through Darrington, where it parallels Highway 530 downstream to its confluence with the Skagit near Rockport.

Why: The Sauk is the definition of a "big fish river" — fish to 20 pounds are caught here on a yearly basis.

When: This is normally a February and March fishery, but recent flooding guarantees that you won't be fishing it until at least early March.

Rules/regs: Catch-and-release with selective gear between the mouth and Darrington, March 1 through April 30. The upper mainstem closes Feb. 28, re-opening June 1. The forks are also closed until June 1.

How: Pink worms, jigs and plugs are your go-to techniques.

Who to call: Tom Nelson, Skagit River Outfitters (425-238-2013); Rob Endsley, Pacific Northwest Sportfishing (360-676-1321); Andy Moser, AM Guide Service (206-367-6094).

upside down with a flood or two, as she's done the past couple of years

"The river changes every year to a great degree, but with the floods, it's changed to an even greater degree" confirms Tom Nelson of Skagit River Outfitters (425-238-2013), who grew up fishing the Sauk. "Nobody has even seen the doggone thing yet this year because it's been blown out, so what you're going to find in regards to favorite holes is a total crapshoot. I'll tell you one thing, though: It takes a commitment and years of time to figure that river out, and even then, you never really know what kind of conditions you'll be dealing with."

Muddy waters ahead: One thing you can unfortunately predict this year on the Sauk is water clarity running from stained to mud brown. Don't expect it to be even remotely fishable before March.

"It was mud last year until early March, and then it cleared up enough to fish down low," says Rob Endsley at Pacific Northwest Sportfishing (360-676-1321). "We had another slide with the last flood that really wrecked it, so it's going to be awhile for that one to come down again."

Water watching: If and when the Sauk falls back into fishable shape, the most valuable asset you can have is an ability to analyze the conditions.

"What you need is an ability to read water," Nelson says. "You need to be able to decode what the river is telling you. If I'm going up there for the first time, I'm looking for areas out of the main body with broken surface. I'm looking for boulder gardens and current seams where old mossback steelhead might be holding."

If you can break that code, though, the potential rewards are as good as you'll find in any river in the world.

"You can get that once-in-a-lifetime fish on the Sauk," Nelson says. "It'll take you back to the roots of this sport: scenery, solitude and big steelhead."

Sectioning the Sauk: The Sauk can be broken down into three very definitive sections: the upper mainstem from the Whitechuck River to Darrington;

KEVIN RAINES releases a Sauk River native, one of seven hooked while fishing with guide Andy Moser on an early spring day last year.

Darrington to the Suiattle River; the Suiattle to the Sauk's confluence with the Skagit near Rockport.

1) Whitechuck to Darrington: The upper mainstem closes Feb. 28. It's a small, tight, pockety, rocky stream with scattered public access via Forest Road 22, but it's capable of producing big fish.

"The brush is close to the creek and there's a lot of private property up there, but steelhead spawn all the way up into the Whitechuck," Nelson says. "That part of the river is one of the last frontiers in this area. It's labor intensive, but you could be rewarded for that work with a big, big fish. There are some huge Dollies there, too, and they're there for a reason: they're feeding on eggs and smolts."

2) Darrington to Suiattle: The Sauk's most well-known drift starts at the launch next to the mill in Darrington, under the Sauk Prairie Road Bridge. Between there and the take-out just below the mouth of the Suiattle, you'll typically find a mix of rocky pockets and gravelly slots that are picture-perfect holding spots for big metalheads.

"If the water allows, that drift from Darrington to the Suiattle is the one drift where you should concentrate your time," Nelson says. "It's a lot like some of the Peninsula streams there — you have some classic steelhead water there, and

Sauk River

you don't have to deal with the added turbidity of the Suiattle. Some of the best holding water in the river is on that middle section."

Start the drift by plugging the water on the mill side, near the riprap, a slot that's produced the biggest North End fish in Nelson's career.

"My Uncle Dale Olson and I pulled a 26-pounder right there, on a No. 25 silver Hot Shot with a black bill," Nelson says. "Before you even start your drift from the bridge, *stop!* Put the plugs out immediately and work that riprap."

Moving further down, break out the floats and jigs and let them run through the seams and pockets between the mill and a point in the river that Nelson refers to as "Splitsville," a three-pronged channel that provides your first major challenge on the oars (take the channel furthest to the right).

"You can anchor drop and back your floats through the seams before Splitsville, but take your time," he says. "If you get in a hurry and don't work this stuff over well, you're doing yourself a disservice. Some of the best boulders and pockets in the state are in that part of the river."

Below Splitsville, the river settles out into a slower flat not unlike Wallace Flats on the Skykomish. This is a great place to break out Jake the Snake and spend some time floating through the seams and pockets between there and the Suiattle.

"Right below Splitsville, the river comes back together into a nice flat, slow pool that's pink worm city," Nelson confirms. "From there down you can cast or float onto the seams, or back a couple of pink worms through kinda like you would with plugs. Adjust them so they're about a foot off the bottom and let them dance right into the back eddies. That's not a real good fast-water technique, so you have to pick your spots."

3) Suiattle to Skagit: Once you've passed the Suiattle, you get into a neutral section of water that steelhead will usually blow right through en route to the middle and upper section.

"Once you have the influence of the Suiattle, you get a lot more sand," Nelson says. "Steelies won't hold in that very much. They'll hold down in the Skagit because they're still trying to figure out 'Right or left?', but once they commit to that home water response and then hit the sandy stuff in the lower Sauk, they just keep right on trucking."

F&H MAP KEY

Darrington to Suiattle River
Fish pockets, flats, runs with floats and jigs, pink worms, plugs. Water may be turbid because of slides.

Suiattle to Skagit
Sandier bottom composition. Fish selectively. Transitional water where steelhead won't hold.

Boat launch

Very rough boat launch

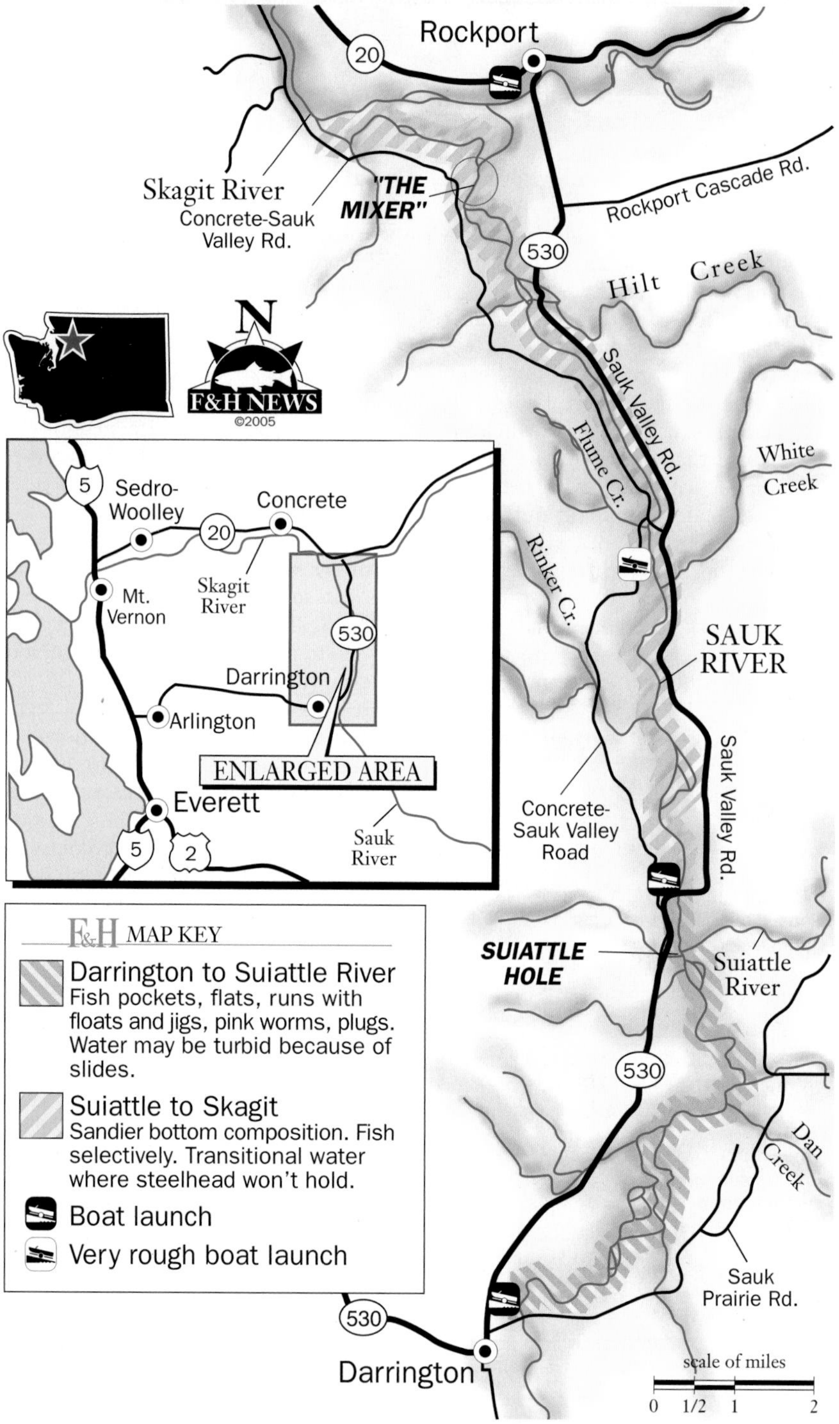

Holding grounds in the lower section include Rinker Creek and Hilt Creek, but from there down, you're better off pushing on your oars and scooting down to the Sauk Pool and the river's confluence with the Skagit.

"I don't get very excited about the water below Hilt Creek," Nelson says. "It's just not a place to spend a lot of time."

This section might be worth a little more time, though, if the slides further upriver are pumping mud through the middle section.

Skagit River having its moments for wild fish

CONCRETE

by Dusty Routh

HE WASN'T SO SURE about float fishing before, but after landing this high-teens buck on the Skagit, Sunny Lee was more of a believer. He used a pink-and-white jig to fool the Marblemount-area fish.

Early and mid-February on the Skagit River was a slow, transitional period for this big, brawling steelhead river. With hatchery fish mostly long gone, and its famous wild March monsters yet to show up in thoroughly good numbers, anglers were left with a fairly typical onesy-twosy experience on the river.

A typical example: "We were out on the river today. We went 1 for 3," said guide John Koenig, with John's Guide Service (360-853-9801) after he finished up a day on the water in early February. "Early in February, the Skagit can have its moments, but it's not super dependable."

That one fish, however, was a 15-pound native, so that can certainly make up for an otherwise slow day. Plus — and this is fairly typical too — Koenig reported some excellent incidental action on the Skagit's big resident Dollies that day. The aggressive nature of these char and their propensity to hit steelhead gear can help keep even the slowest steelhead day interesting.

"We landed and released two Dollies over 20 inches," Koenig reported back then. Anywhere else, these would be considered darn near trophy Dollies. On the Skagit, they don't even raise an eyebrow.

This too shall pass: But the slow, transitional steelhead period on the Skagit is bound to come to an end. And if this year is like most years, that passing will take place by the time we get to the end of the month, and into the first couple of weeks of March. Then, the Skagit comes alive with some of the best wild steelhead fishing in the universe.

"You don't come here for anything in late February and early March except for the big hawgs," Koenig says. "These wild fish are really big. Twenty-pounders. Some of the biggest steelhead you'll catch and release in your life. We're hopeful the big natives will be in and showing good by the end of the month."

Net 'scape: If there's a bummer factor to the Skagit's wild run of big natives, and it's a helluva bummer at that, it's the tribal netting that goes on in the lower portions of the river. Even though these are wild fish and anglers aren't allowed to keep even one a year, the tribal netting of course continues, and the carnage continues with it.

The tribal netting schedule from now until March 15 will run from Sundays to Tuesdays. That means if you want a good weekday fishing trip, Thursdays and Fridays might be your best bets, allowing Wednesday for new fish to move into the system. If you're looking for the best weekend day, Saturdays are typically what you want.

Best drifts: The entire Skagit River system can be good for wild fish at the end of February and early March. But if you're a betting man and you want to play the percentages, then stick to fishing the high percentage areas.

"The best drift, I think, is going to be from Rockport on down," Koenig says. "Depending on how much water you want to work if you're in a driftboat, for example, you can drift from Rockport down and take out at Concrete. That's about 8 miles of pretty darn good water. But it'll depend of course on the clarity of the Sauk. If the Sauk is dumping mud, then the better drift is from Marblemount on down to Rockport."

The wild fish coming into the Skagit are going to one of two places: they're either heading to the very upper reaches of the Skagit to spawn, or they're heading up to turn into the Sauk River to spawn. For those fish heading to the upper Skagit, the drift from Bacon Creek down to Marblemount is the drift to take.

Bigger everything: The rule of thumb for changing tactics between hatchery fish and wild natives is one of size: gear up everything for the wilds.

"I always go with bigger gear for the natives," Koenig says. "Bigger plugs, bigger jigs, bigger, brighter stuff like Corkies and cheaters."

Koenig likes to fish yarn flies and Glo Bugs too, with pencil lead weights and 24-inch leaders.

"I'll fish those all day sometimes," he says. "You'll pick up steelhead as well as Dollies with those."

Time of day can be a factor with wild fish too, says Koenig.

"It can really depend on the sun, or the lack of the sun," he explains. "When we have those cold, bright, sunshiny days in the winter, the best bite is almost always first thing in the morning, before the sun hits the water. Once the sun comes out, I think it puts them off a little."

Koenig says that on overcast and rainy days, time of day is much less important a factor.

Upper Skagit River
steelhead drifts

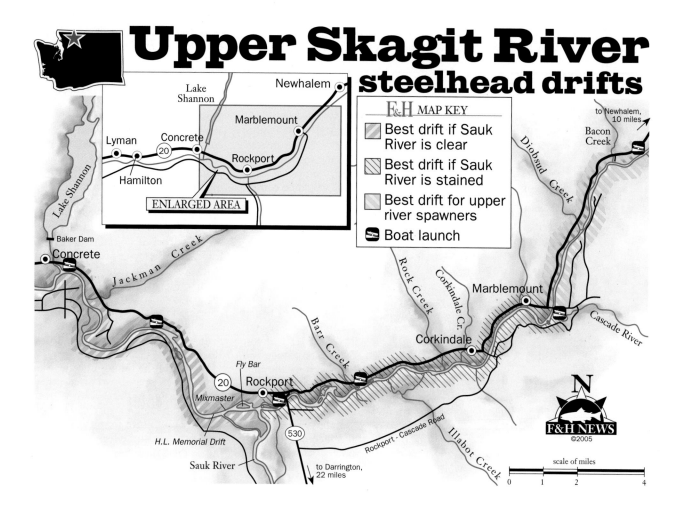

F&H MAP KEY

- Best drift if Sauk River is clear
- Best drift if Sauk River is stained
- Best drift for upper river spawners
- Boat launch

ENLARGED AREA

N

F&H NEWS
©2005

scale of miles
0   1   2   4

Sauk criticial: Another critical factor, though, is the Sauk. When this tributary stream is running off-color, it can really affect the fishing.

"If there's a slide or something on the Sauk, and that discolored water is coming down and into the Skagit," says Koenig, "it can really put the fish down."

But when the water is good, that stretch of the Skagit just below the Sauk can be phenomenal water.

"Just below the mouth of the Sauk," Koenig says, "it seems like they really stack in there, from Rockport on down. What you have is a mix of fish that are both Skagit River fish, and Sauk River fish."

Fly time: Koenig says that he believes the Skagit is one of the best rivers around for angling with a fly for metalheads.

"It's a great fly fishing river," he says. "There's not much better in the state. The fly bars can be fishing real good down below Rockport. And there are new fly bars pretty much all over the place since the big rains we had back in January rechannelized and moved the river around some."

Rules, rules, rules: The Skagit is one of those rivers that's really on the radar of the WDFW in terms of rules and enforcement. For example, after March 15 you can't fish for steelhead while you're under power (no electric motors, no kicker or main engines running while you're fishing.). "That's why you see so many of these Skagit River scows with oars," says Koenig. "The fishing around mid-March can be very good, but you can't be fishing while you're under power."

Koenig says the river has a new enforcement officer from WDFW, Troy McCormick, out of the LaConner WDFW office (360-466-4345 ext. 221) who lives up on the river.

"He's a good enforcement officer," Koenig says. "He's real into it. I think he's going to be real good."

AT a GLANCE

What: That time of year again for giant native metalheads on the Skagit River.

When: Expect action to be tops by the end of February, with the first two weeks of March potentially as good as it gets.

Where: Drift from Rockport to Concrete, about 8 miles of terrific water. If the Sauk is dumping mud, drift from Marblemount down to Rockport. For upper river fish, drift from Bacon Creek to Marblemount.

How: Pencil lead with yarn flies on 24-inch leaders are tough to beat, plus you'll get Dollies galore. Or pull big plugs.

Caution: Web boards warned of nails dumped at the Marblemount boat launch late last month.

Guides: John Koenig (360-853-9801); Tom Nelson (425-238-2013); Rob Endsley (360-676-1321); Andy Moser (206-367-6094); Wayne Ackerlund (206-218-3362).

Hit Skagit River hatchery steelhead above Concrete

SEDRO-WOOLLEY

by Joel Shangle

We fish Blue Creek on the Cowlitz because that's where the hatchery fish are bound. We hit Tokul Creek on the Snoqualmie for the same reason. We target the Hatchery Drift on the Bogachiel because it's the water closest to the rearing ponds.

Follow that same line of thinking this month on the Skagit River as fish bound for the Cascade River and their hatchery home waters blast upriver to Concrete, Rockport and several good slots in between.

"All those hatchery fish are headed up to the Cascade," says Cal Stocking at Cause for Divorce Guide Service (360-428-5038; *www.fishmonitor.com/guides/calstocking*). "Any time we get some higher water, like we're having now, those fish will blow from the mouth to the upper river in four, five days easy. When the water starts to drop again, they'll start to stack up in there below Rockport, and that'll be the place to go after those 8-pound hatchery runs."

The drifter: If ever there was a river that demands eggs, yarn, shrimp and Corkies, it's the Skagit. This massive, plodding river drops out of Ross Lake in the North Cascades before eventually spilling into the salt at Skagit Bay below Mount Vernon. From top to bottom, it's defined by big stretches of relatively flat, unimaginative water that might drawn yawns from those of you accustomed to fishing the rock gardens of the Olympic Peninsula.

"The Skagit is such a great river to boondog," Stocking asserts. "There's so much wide, featureless water out there that it's a real key not to stay in any one place for a long time. It's important to cover as much water as you can out there — you want to hit as many seams and trough edges as you can in a day, until you find some stacked fish."

This time of year, the best piece of river to find those hatchery fish is between Rockport and Concrete, specifically from the launch at Howard Miller Steelhead Park to Jackman Creek, roughly a half-mile above Concrete.

"I'll usually cover that area in a day, boondogging first," says Stocking. "If for some reason we're not doing anything in the morning with that, we'll go back up and concentrate on the tailouts

SKAGIT BOONDOGGER Vic Rogers holds a 12-pound steelhead caught out of the *Escape Pod*. Photo by Barak Rabel.

of some of the slots with spoons and spinners. (Between Rockport and Concrete) is probably some of the best holding water we have on this river — it gives you a good variety of water to fish with just about every technique imaginable if you want."

> **"The Skagit is such a great river to boondog."**
> — guide Cal Stocking

Winter sledding: Stocking's 20-foot Alumaweld Super V with 150-horsepower Mercury is standard issue for sledders on the Skagit. Launch at Howard Miller Park (it's a busy launch when fish are in), and hit these slots:

• **The Flats:** Fish from straight out of the launch down to a big tailout that's visible when the water's up. You can toss No. 3 Vibrax blue/silver spinners right up against the riprap that runs along the campsite side of the river for fish holding close to the bank in high water, or boondog down through the Sand Hole right into the

AT A GLANCE

What: Skagit River winter steelhead.

Where: Upper river, between Concrete and Rockport.

Why: Hatchery fish will move upriver quickly on high water, bound for the Cascade hatchery. This is some of the best holding water on the river.

How: Boondog with Corkies and eggs or sand shrimp, toss spoons and spinners.

Hot spots: 1) The Flats near Howard Miller Steelhead Park at Rockport; 2) Sauk River; 3) The Mixmaster/Fly Bar; 4) Leaning Cedars; 5) Faber's Landing; 6) Jackman Creek.

Information: Cal Stocking, Cause For Divorce Guide Service (360-428-5038); Rob Endsley, Kulshan River Excursions (360-676-1321); Wade Erickson, Fish On! Guide Service (360-652-2359); Holiday Market (360-757-1221); Dave Hambright at Rockport Country Store (360-853-8531).

Sauk Drift.

"It's good all the way from the launch down to the Sauk when the water's up," says Stocking. "I'll start at the bridge and drift 300 to 400 yards down toward the Sauk with Corkies and eggs. If it's slow, I'll throw on a sand shrimp and switch to green-, pink- or clown-colored Spin-N-Glos."

• **Sauk River:** Fish the south side of the river below the Sauk, boondogging along the edges of the seams in 4 to 8 feet of water.

• **Fly Bar/Mixmaster:** The Fly Bar, according to Stocking, "probably holds as many fish as anywhere." You'll find some big boulders strewn throughout the holes on the north side of the river, in 2 to 4 feet of water, but Stocking will work both sides of the river here. You'll drop over Fly Bar into the Mixmaster, where you want to work the south side if water is low and clear and the north side if the water's up.

• **Leaning Cedars:** Staying on the south side of the river out of the Mixmaster, the best fishing starts at a small creek that enters the river near the trees from which this spot derives its name, and extends roughly 250 yards downriver to some houses on the south shore.

• **Faber's Landing/The Dutchman:** Boondog all the way down from the

> ## "When the water starts to drop, they'll start to stack up in there below Rockport, and that'll be the place to go after those 8-pound hatchery runs."
> — Stocking

end of the slot at Leaning Cedars, through Larson's Bar down below Faber's Landing to the Dutchman — stay to the right above Jackman Creek when the river splits below the Dutchman.

• **Jackman Creek:** "There are some huge boulders piled in there at Jackman Creek, probably 3 feet in diameter," says Stocking. "Below Jackman, the river takes a cut and then falls into a chute on the south side that you can fish all the way down to the Baker River."

From the bank: Areas to target from the bank include:

• **Cascade River:** Drift anglers have been thumping hatchery fish up there since early November, fishing rocket red or pink Corkies and eggs from below the creek down through three good drift holes on the Cascade.

"The Cascade is *the* place to work on hatchery fish," says Stocking. "It's fishy from the creek down through three really good holes. The tailout of the second hole is also a good place to throw spoons and spinners."

• **Swift Creek:** Offers 300 yards of easy access just above Rockport. Fish spoons and spinners from the head of the hole and work it clear down through the tailout."

• **Jackman Creek:** Fish below the creek with spoons and spinners.

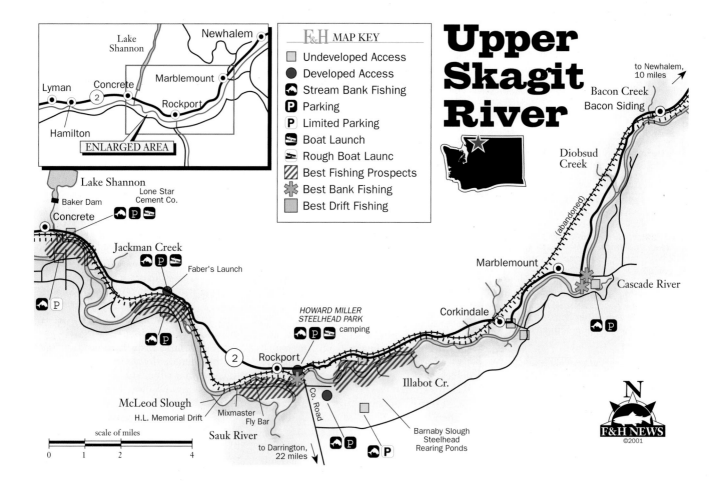

Summer on the Sky: steelhead, some Chinook

SULTAN

by Joel Shangle

RUN EGGS for Skykomish River kings and steelhead. The river opens June 1 for both species. Guide Andy Moser shows off a nice Sky king.

You'll have to pardon us for being a little gunshy about predicting fish runs. Still a little sore over the "Great Columbia Springer Debacle of 2005" (not to mention the "Great Columbia Springer Debacle of 2004") we've decided to err on the side of caution in regards to the summer-run steelhead and Chinook season on the Skykomish River.

Perhaps there may possibly be a number of fish which could enter the river system at some point.

OK, so that's a bit overboard, but the point is, instead of competing with Mother Nature and mercurial creatures like migrating fish, we'll first stick with what we know as gospel:

• The season opener on June 1 — even though it's on a Wednesday — will see puh-lenty of jet sled traffic below Sultan and a flotilla of drift boats between Gold Bar and Startup, but a fair number of North End river rats will shift their opening-week attentions further north, to the concurrent Skagit River Chinook opener.

• If we're fortunate enough to connect with a bright Chinook in early June, we'll be able to keep him this year ('Nooky season didn't open until the middle of June last year).

• Water conditions will likely vary between marginal-to-high, to scraping-the-bottom low, all within the space of a month.

• OK, so there *will* be fish to catch. We just ain't saying how many.

Eye on the Sky: The first bit of advice about steelhead and Chinook on the Sky is to forget the very recent past on the Columbia system and pay attention to the indicators that drive the Snohomish system's Chinook and steelhead fisheries.

"You can't draw any conclusions about anything that's gone on with the salmon runs so far this year," says Tom Nelson at Skagit River Outfitters (425-238-2013; *fishskagit.com*). "The Columbia springer runs and Snohomish system runs are absolutely two different things. From what I hear, there are fish out front already. The early reports from commercial test fisheries are very, very positive, and if we get good early returns to Tulalip Bay, we should also see good early returns to the Sky. Those two runs are, for all intents and purposes, one and the same."

One more little reminder about the Sky's relation to Tulalip: Remember the last few days of the recent blackmouth season in Marine Area 8-2? It was a pretty well-kept secret, but the handful of sharpies who worked the Tulalip area hard in April caught more honest-to-God springers than resident blackmouth.

Water we going to do? The summer season of 2004 was pretty well defined by razor-thin water, which severely limited the Chinook hunters in the crowd (more on this later). The first few days of the '05 season, though, could see significantly more water in the Sky: NOAA's long-range forecasts for Western Washington call for rains throughout the end of May, which could/should translate into higher

water and lower visibility than early-season '04.

"Rain is the wild card, but if the rain and cool spring continues, I'd expect marginal to slightly high water on the opener," says Nelson. "Last year, we had a large snowpack and no precipitation in May. This year, it's no snowpack

> **"You can't draw any conclusions about anything that's gone on with the salmon runs so far this year. The Columbia springer runs and Snohomish system runs are absolutely two different things. From what I hear, there are fish out front already."**
> — **Tom Nelson a Skagit River Outfitters**

and a wetter late spring. Of course, this will all change rapidly if (we) get a dry June. By July, bring a gallon of water to the river if you come."

Fish it and they will come: If you're part of the circus at the Sultan launch on the opener, you're likely stocked up on well-cured eggs. If you're not, you should be, because the Sky's kings will bite eggs as readily as plugs.

"The No. 1 option, Plan A, if you're fishing out of a sled platform, is to swing eggs," Nelson advises. "The most successful dudes will be the ones who hit the water with bait right off the bat. You have to remember, there's some overlap of steelhead and Chinook water on the Sky — you'll find steelhead in shallow riffles early and the kings will be more in the gut of the holes, but there are plenty of places on the Sky where those two water conditions are side by side. The species you're targeting will be more a func-

Skykomish Chinook, steelhead

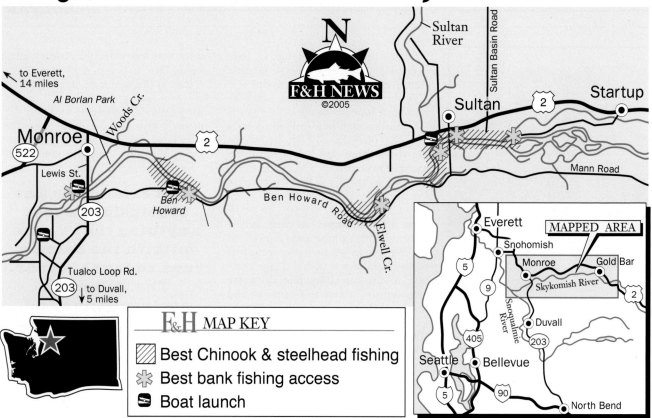

F&H MAP KEY

▨ Best Chinook & steelhead fishing

✳ Best bank fishing access

🚤 Boat launch

tion of the kind of water you fish rather than your technique, because the Sky's kings are egg biters."

On the flipside, the Sky's steelhead will bite a plug too. That means that the driftboat-backing brigade should consider a combination of FatFish or Hot Shots and some form of bait on at least one rod.

"If I was backing a drift boat down the Sky, I'd have a couple of fire tiger FatFish out, but I'd also tie on a Hot-N-Tot with a 6-foot leader and a gob of eggs. Multi-tasking, my friend!"

King for a day: The Skagit's king hunters will likely be rolling out the big banana plugs when that fishery opens this year for the first time in years, but those big Kwikies and FlatFish are much less likely to entice a Skykomish king into biting.

"For whatever reason, those big plugs aren't a great choice on the Sky," Nelson says. "The big, loud banana plugs aren't a top-shelf choice on that river. I'll run FatFish, but I seriously doubt I'll roll out any of the Magnums.

If there's any issue with visibility early in the season, I'll slow down the presentation and add some bait. Bait divers are dynamite ways to catch both steelhead and Chinook, but I'd keep the big plugs in the box."

The friendly Sky: Back to those predictions: "There will always be

steelhead in the Sky on opening day," says Nelson. "It doesn't matter what else is happening out there, the dudes who know what they're doing will catch fish."

Places those dudes will hit hard: Taylor Flats, McCoy Creek, Elwell Creek, Ben Howard flats, the Stilt Hole.

AT a GLANCE

What: Skykomish River summer steelhead and Chinook

When: Season opens June 1 for both species.

Where: Jet sledders can run from Sultan all the way down to Monroe (and farther, if they want), but the pressure center on this fishery is between Sultan and Ben Howard. You'll find mixed bank access (Cracker Bar, Ben Howard Road, Monroe, etc.) up and down the river.

How: Eggs, eggs, eggs. Plugs and bait divers are standard choices if you're backing a drift boat, but the jetsled brigade will unload a ton of eggs in the Sky's first month.

Info: 3 Rivers Marine (425-415-1575; 3riversmarine.com; Jim Stahl, J&J Guide Service (425-347-1615); Tom Nelson, Skagit River Outfitters (425-238-2013); Eli Rico, Hot Shot Guide Service (425-417-0394); Andy Moser, AM Guide Service (206-367-6094).

Maximize time on Snoqualmie: hit best spots

CARNATION

by Joel Shangle

If the crowd of boats lined up near Carnation on a recent Saturday was any indication, many of you are spending a ton of your precious fishing time and money on the Snoqualmie River. The last time I drove down Highway 203 on a weekend — granted, it was a picture-perfect Saturday morning and the river was in good shape — I could have probably crossed the river without getting my feet wet. There were that many boats.

But much like the neighboring Skykomish, which the Snoqualmie joins near Monroe, catch rates on the Snoqualmie have been consistently low. There's a whole lot of fishing, and not a whole lot of catching.

"A lot of the guides are calling it 'the toughest game in town,' for good reason," says Mike Bing at Van Hala Guide Service (206-230-2646). "The hatchery thing is over and done, so you're looking for big natives. There's just not a whole lot of fish being caught right now."

Oh, but there's always the specter of a thick-shouldered Snoqualmie wild fish lurking somewhere below Fall City, and a couple of 20-plus-pounders have already shown up on the Sky. Yep. It's that time again.

"These fish are those big, beautiful Snoqualmie River natives, usually in the 15-pound range," says Bing. "They're nice, nice fish, but there are very few being caught."

We picked Bing's brain for information on the spots to hit on the Snoqualmie for a shot at a burly catch-and-release wild steelie. His first bit of advice: Ignore the area from Carnation Farm Bridge down to the Sky.

"There's nothing there but frog

A TYPICAL SNOHOMISH-system wild fish like you'll find now making the trip toward the Raging and Tolt rivers on the Snoqualmie. Mike Rodriguez of Smokey Point landed this nickel-bright hen fishing with guide Sam Ingram.

water," he says. "Everything you want to fish is basically between Fall City and Carnation. There are only a few places where I know people are catching fish, and they're all from just below Carnation up."

Here's a rundown of Bing's top five areas on the Snoqualmie.

RAGING RIVER: For drift boaters, the float down the Snoqualmie should start at the mouth of the Raging River and end at the foot of Neal Road.

"You don't want to drift all the way down because, No. 1, it'll take all day, and No. 2, it runs into frog water further downriver," he says. "The drift from the Raging to Neal Road is a pretty low-key deal. There's one chute right after Fall City that moves pretty fast, but it's pretty straightforward if you haven't drifted the river before. Just stay on the Fall City side."

The Raging dumps in on the Fall City side, just above the Highway 202 bridge over the Snoqualmie. What you'll find here is a large tailout at the end of the mouth of the Raging, graduating toward the bridge. Launch on the upriver side of the Raging and fish

the chute that extends all the way underneath the bridge.

"It's a fast chute down to the bridge, about 50 yards long," Bing says. "It's between 8 and 12 feet deep on the far side, across from the ramp. You can just anchor up and wait for fish to come by, heading for the Raging."

This is a spot where Bing likes to drop a plug or rig a Tadpolly with a 4-foot leader to a 1/0 hook and a sand shrimp — the old diver and bait routine.

BUSINESS DRIFT: Just below Fall City, extending just below a spot known as the Flag Pole Hole. Deeper on the Fall City side, but a drift where you can head right down the middle, casting out in either direction and free-drift bait.Official Guide Hint: "The guys who are lucky enough to have fresh steelhead eggs are doing better than the ones without," says Bing. "Sand shrimp will work, but those fresh eggs are a key."

CAR BODY HOLE: Roughly 100 yards upstream of where Neal Road joins Highway 203, and easily identifiable because of the hulks of three old cars that sit on the side of the river. A gravel bar runs along the car side of the river — fish bait or toss spinners (Mepps No. 3 or 4 rainbow blade) up tight against the car side.

"You want to get as close to the car bodies as you can," says Bing. "This area is extremely good for spinners."

The Stink Hole and Richter's are also spots to hit in the vicinity of the Car Body Hole. All three are just upstream of the Neal Road launch.

PATTERSON/GRIFFIN CREEKS: Patterson Creek dumps in just before a series of cutbacks that eventually lead you to Griffin Creek and Tall Chief, just barely below Griffin Creek. Fish Tall Chief on the west side, sticking tight to the bank.

THE BIG T: The mouth of the Tolt River, commonly referred to as the "Big T," is easily one of the most heavily fished spots on the river. For good reason — it produces fish.

"This is a good drift fishery," says Bing. "It's a fairly fast slot. You can toss across the T to the riprap on the other side when you have the visibility or use a bronze Hot'N Tot flatlined 50 feet behind the boat (and) juiced with shrimp oil. But it's definitely a bait fishery right where it dumps in."

A great way to fish the Big T is to anchor up above the chute, which starts almost straight out from the boat launch on the Tolt side, and drop your plugs. The water above the Tolt is usually dead calm, leading into the chute that extends roughly 100 yards below the ramp. Blue and green Wiggle Warts or chrome/green/blue Hot Shots are good choices.

The Big T tails out into Schaeffer's Bar, well within reach of bank anglers taking advantage of the easy access via the park on the downriver side of the Tolt.

"This is a wonderful place to slip on the waders and fish the downstream side of the Tolt," Bing says.

Drifting bait is the way to go here.

SWINGING BRIDGE DRIFT: Spinner territory, starting just above McDonald Park and extending down almost to the Carnation Farm Bridge. This is one of the best bank fisheries on the river, with access via a number of short footpaths from the park.

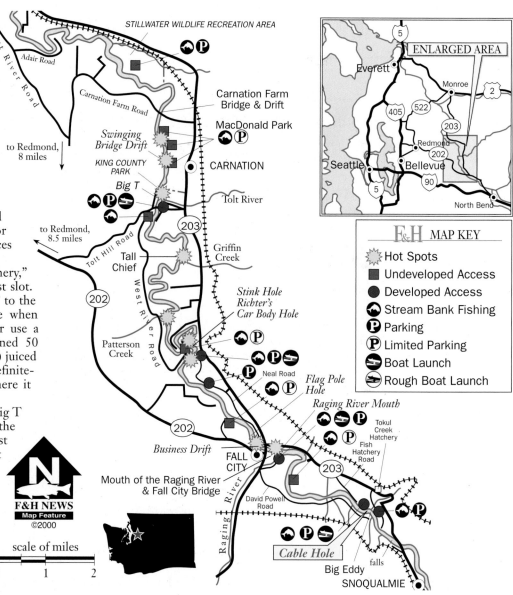

F&H NEWS
Map Feature
©2000

scale of miles

0   1   2

AT a GLANCE

What: Snoqualmie River steelhead.

When: Catch and release wild fish now through March.

Where: Between Fall City and Carnation. The mouths of the Raging and Tolt rivers are two of the best fisheries on the Snoqualmie, but the Car Body Hole, Business Drift and Swinging Bridge Drift can also be productive.

Why: Wild fish. Big ones, running well into the high teens.

Techniques: Fresh steelhead eggs are your first choice for drift fishing, but sand shrimp will work. Lots of good plugging water (Hot'N Tots, Wiggle Warts, Hot Shots) and spots where a Tadpolly rigged with a 4-foot leader to bait is effective. Drift-fishing bait from the bank below the Tolt. Hammered brass Mor-Tac spoons or No. 3 Mepps with rainbow or pink blades are also good choices.

Information: Van Hala Guide Service (206-230-2646); Washington Fishing Adventures (360-653-5924); Buffalo Bill's (425-392-0228); Sky Valley Traders (360-794-8818).

Puget Sound Freshwater
TROUT

American Lake rainbows: as American as apple pie

LAKEWOOD

by Dusty Routh

If you're looking for an overlooked trout lake close to home, take a good gander at American Lake just south of Tacoma near Lakewood. This is a beauty of a fishery, a scenic 1,100-plus-acre piece of wondrous water smack-dab in the middle of a sprawling metropolis. While you'll hear a little of I-5 if you're fishing the southwest corner of the lake, the

Big, or main American Lake, is nearly 1,000 acres. The upper, northeast portion of the lake sports lakeshore homes and there's an island about a third of the way up the lake that has weekend cabins on it. You'll find some depths in the main lake to 90 feet, with tons of ridges and humps, shallow muddy flats, and a smattering of rocky flats. It's a cornucopia of excellent water to explore.

if you're a bass fan.

More to the point, however, American was planted in 1996 with broodstock, landlocked steelhead. With all the small fish in the lake from repeated spring hatchery trout plantings, these big boys have grown really big. Our biggest fish was a 10-pounder caught by John Montsebraten in November this past fall. Other anglers such as American Lake regular Josh Bond have hooked and boated fish ranging from 5 to 12 pounds.

Getting a 12-pound steelhead while you're trolling around with trout gear can only be described as something worthy of a trip to this terrific lake.

With such a good variety of fish available, the where-to and how-to should be considered by species. Here's a quick thumbnail guide:

WHEN WE SAY that some of the trout in American Lake are big, we're not joking. This 8-plus-pounder, hooked by Anuhea Freitas (left), is an example of the size of fish this South Sound fishery holds, though most, of course, are smaller. Anuhea was fishing there in February with friend Kellie and Kellie's parents.

majority of this pretty water is quiet, fairly wooded and full of good fishing.

Little versus big: American Lake is actually two lakes in one. Little American can be found at the southwestern corner of the big lake, connected by a small, shallow (about 5 feet deep) waterway opening into a cool little mini-lake of about 30 acres. Little American offers shallow shoreside fishing, with a few deep holes that plunge to nearly 40 feet. There are also a number of ridges and humps in Little American, and a few 20-foot flats that are perfect holding areas for big trout.

Fishy stuff: For trout enthusiasts, American is underfished and underutilized but the fish are definitely oversized. For starters, the lake sports a good population of scrappy cutthroat that run the gamut from 8-inchers up to fat and sassy 3- and 4-pounders. There are also resident rainbows, with fish running from 12 inches up to the occasional monster 5-pounder. Definitely the stuff of dreams for an urban fishery.

There are also kokanee galore. They run small but it's not unusual to find some lunkers by kokanee standards going 14 and 15 inches.

There's also smallmouth in American

Cutthroat: American's cutts are spooky and paranoid. If you want to tangle with them, stealth and deceit are your best weapons. The water in is crystal-clear and noise travels a long ways.

For starters, fish the shorelines from as early as you can get on the lake (the gate at the public ramp is unlocked each morning at 7 a.m.) for the first two hours of the day. Either troll close to shore with an electric motor, or cast to shore like you're bass fishing.

If you're casting, go with small ⅛- or ¼-ounce black Rooster Tails.

If you're trolling, use perch-colored stickbaits like Rapalas and Cultivas. Troll well behind the boat as close to shore as you can get.

All around little American, and the east and west shorelines of the main lake are productive.

Once full daylight is on the lake, switch to figure-8 and S-curve trolling 15 to 20 feet offshore, including out toward the middle of both lakes. Troll shallow-running stickbaits over humps, ridges, mud and rock flats and shallow water; go with deeper-diving Cultivas or other stickbaits for deeper water. You can also troll thin trolling spoons like fire tiger Needlefish off downriggers in the first 35 feet of water over deeper water.

American Lake

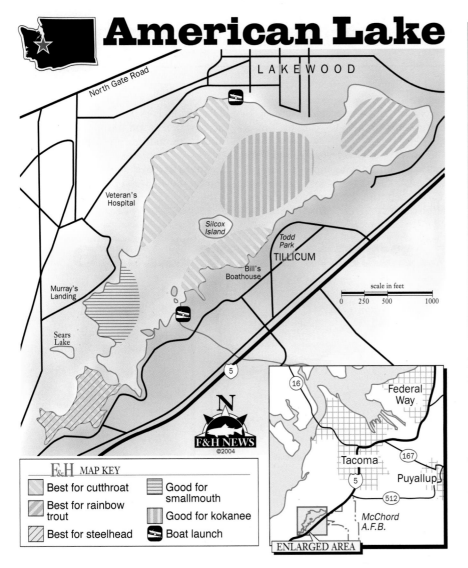

LAKEWOOD

North Gate Road

Veteran's Hospital

Silcox Island

Todd Park

TILLICUM

Bill's Boathouse

Murray's Landing

Sears Lake

scale in feet
0   250   500   1000

N

F&H NEWS ©2004

F&H MAP KEY

- Best for cutthroat
- Best for rainbow trout
- Best for steelhead
- Good for smallmouth
- Good for kokanee
- Boat launch

16

Federal Way

Tacoma

167

5

Puyallup

512

McChord A.F.B.

ENLARGED AREA

Rainbows: The lake's resident rainbows tend to hug bottom and structure. Fishing with traditional trout bottom gear (slip sinker, leader, and nightcrawlers/marshmallows or Power Bait) should score.

If you have good electronics, look for bottom depressions, weedbeds and wood in the water. The points of the lake including the islands are good bets too. If you find deep water adjacent to shoreline, which is common on the upper lake, bounce your bottom gear from shore out to the deeper water to score on rainbows stacked along the contours.

Smallmouth: A few bass guys stationed at Fort Lewis ply American for smallmouth, but the lake isn't famous for being prolific smallie water. Still, there are some excellent places to intercept fish once the water warms up. Because this is a big, deep lake, the smallmouth can be sluggish until late April and early May.

At that time, look for fish preparing for the spawn and warming themselves by fishing any shallow water you find that's adjacent to deeper holes. The huge bay straight across from the public boat launch at the lower end of the lake is one of the best spots.

White spinnerbaits, crawdad-colored crankbaits, black and brown grubs on leadhead jigs, and, particularly, Carolina-rigged creature baits will all score.

If you can get on the lake during a weekday when the water's undisturbed, throw a small yellow Torpedo topwater along the wood and rocks of the lake's bountiful shoreline.

Kokanee: American's plentiful kokes can all be found north of the main island in the midsection of the big lake over the deepest water. You can see them plain as day on your fish finder. Troll 000-sized dodgers and red Wedding Rings tipped with white corn. You can also chum and still fish with a pinch of prawn and a red salmon egg, or jig a small Gibbs Minnow.

Steelhead: Ah, big 'ol landlocked steelhead. There's nothing quite like them. The 10-pound fish that Montsebraten boated hit a salmon-sized spinner thrown into tree limbs in little American.

These are aggressive fish, but they're shy. Target them either by casting to shore (pick the gnarliest, nastiest, most tackle-grabbingest spots you can find) or you can troll for them.

Go with big silver/black or rainbow-colored stickbaits trailed far behind the boat close to shore early and late in the day.

We've also experimented with big plugs but without success.

Stalking stockers: American is usually blessed with plants of sacrificial hatchery trout in the spring, usually by mid- to late April. You can catch these little devils on small Kastmasters, flies and worms-and-bobbers in the lower third of the lake.

Troll, strip big Buggers, leeches for Cranberry browns

CORNET

by Jeremy Thurston

Cranberry Lake receives most of its pressure in spring and summer when campers fill up every available space at Deception Pass State Park. But flyrodders who abandon this lake after Labor Day are missing a good opportunity for rainbow and some big brown trout.

Many of the 8,000 rainbows planted last spring either ended up in the frying pan or a cormorant's belly. The ones that survived have grown to a respectable 15 inches. You can fish from shore near the boat launch and have a reasonable chance at the rainbows.

The most popular offerings are salmon eggs, worms and dough baits fished off the bottom.

Nearby Pass Lake is known for its big brown trout, but the Germans grow large in Cranberry too.

"Most of the browns are around 2 pounds," park ranger Jim Aggergaard says. "The biggest one I know to have come out of there was 12 pounds."

Trolling tech: Every angler has their preferred method for targeting the browns. Some use trolling gangs, others FlatFish or Kwikfish. Spoons with a rainbow or brown trout finish are also good producers. Remember the adage big lure equals big fish, and fish sizes larger than you would for the rainbows.

For browns, concentrate on the lake's south end near the point. Most anglers troll perpendicular from the point.

On the fly: When fly fishing, use some of the same tactics you do at Pass. Fish big Woolly Buggers and rabbit strip leeches in black or olive. Weighted white Zonkers stripped in erratically can draw a violent strike. Cranberry isn't real deep. The south end is only 10 to 15 feet, so a slow to medium sink-tip will work nicely.

You shouldn't come to Cranberry expecting a fish on every cast this time of year, but if your idea of a day well spent includes rowing around a

quiet lake with a good chance of picking up enough fish for dinner, this is the place to be.

Cranberry is open year-round with statewide limits. Gas motors are prohibited.

To reach the lake, drive west on Highway 20 from Burlington to Deception Pass State Park. The 125-acre water is on the Whidbey side along the main campground road.

Information: Deception Pass State Park (360-675-2417), Skagit Anglers (360-336-3232).

Cranberry Lake

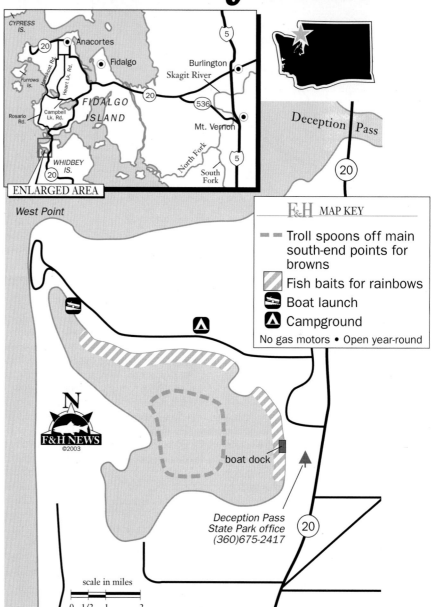

MAP KEY

- - - Troll spoons off main south-end points for browns

Fish baits for rainbows

Boat launch

Campground

No gas motors • Open year-round

Five Emerald City lakes for trout, bass

by Randall Peters

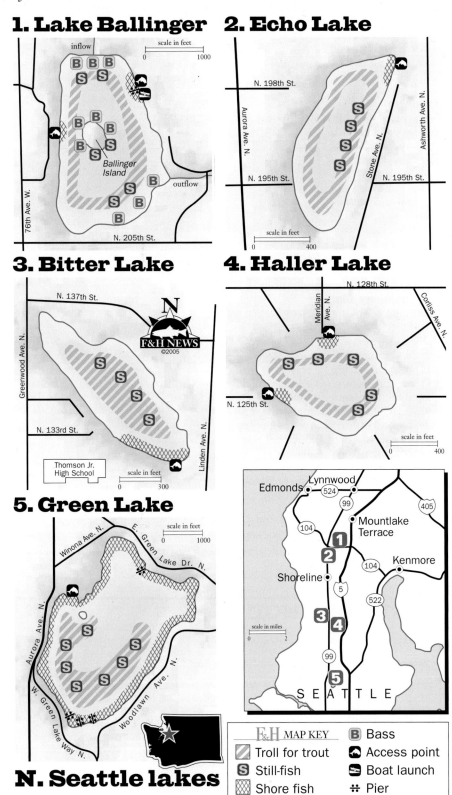

1. Lake Ballinger

2. Echo Lake

3. Bitter Lake

4. Haller Lake

5. Green Lake

N. Seattle lakes

F&H MAP KEY

- Troll for trout
- Still-fish
- Shore fish
- B Bass
- Access point
- Boat launch
- Pier

If the price of gas and traffic is keeping you from venturing out of Seattle for your trout fishing, no worries. The north end of town has plenty to offer. Five lakes, all along or just off the Aurora Avenue corridor, dot the landscape from Woodland Park up to the King-Snohomish county line. All offer plenty of trout action and all are open year-round. Here's a rundown on where they are and what they offer:

Green Lake: This can be your 255 acres of bank-fishing paradise. There are ample opportunities to step off the walking path and fish from shore. You can also use several docks located around Green Lake.

In addition to the generous trout plantings prior to opening day, Green Lake was planted with 4,000 surplus triploid trout in mid-May, so this urban lake is capable of kicking out fish that you'll measure in pounds, not inches. Expect to catch a good stringer from the bank, using floating baits tipped with salmon eggs, or worms plunked off the bottom.

For boaters and float tubers, troll small lures like Dick Nites, Triple Teasers, and F3, F4 and F5 FlatFish or Kwikfish in similar sizes. Casting small Rooster Tails and Kastmasters will also induce strikes.

Green Lake also contains tiger musky, but catching one with the 36-inch minimum size could prove very difficult. If you do, don't hesitate to take photos and let us know!

Haller Lake: Because of its size, Haller is perfect for a float tube or a cartopper. At 15 acres, it's less susceptible to high winds and choppy waves because it's surrounded by houses and numerous trees. There's always a piece of flat water no matter which way the wind is blowing.

Fly fishermen take heed: It's a great lake to practice on. Haller was planted in March with 1,400 rainbows, and it has continued to produce. Access is limited at this tiny lake, however. There's an access point on Meridian Avenue North, and another on North

125th Street, with the later being the better of the two for bank anglers.

I've seen several fishermen with nice stringers caught with Power Bait-and-worm and marshmallow-and-worm combos fished 3 or 4 feet off the bottom.

I prefer to fish Haller by s-l-o-w-l-y trolling an F4 FlatFish about 50 feet behind my float tube. I use 4-pound-test line, an ultralight rod, no weight and no swivel. This produces enough action on the lure to keep it 1 or 2 feet under the surface, which is ideal action. If you fish it properly, the FlatFish (or Kwikfish) should produce a slight pulsating throb to your rod tip. Every color seems to get strikes, I prefer greens, olives and yellows.

On recent outings in the evenings, I've had the place virtually to myself, a nice bonus when you're fishing in a city of 572,600.

Bitter Lake: This 12-acre lake is sandwiched between Aurora and Greenwood avenues and is seldom fished. The south end is the only access point, and the many baseball and softball games during the spring and summer months may turn anglers away.

Bitter was planted with 1,200 catchables this year and should continue to produce into the summer months. Access the lake from Aurora by turning west onto North 130th Street until you get to Linden Avenue North. Take a right. The lake will be on your left.

Echo Lake: No, this is not the one in Snohomish County near Maltby. Referred to as Echo on "99," it is located just east of Aurora, in Shoreline. From Aurora, travel east on North 200th Street and turn right onto Ashworth Avenue. The lake and the limited parking will be on your right.

At only 12 acres, you can easily cover Echo thoroughly from a pontoon boat or float tube. Standard trout offerings should get you trout in the 8- to 10-inch range, but, as always, hold on tight for holdovers pushing 14 inches or more.

Lake Ballinger: Located just north of the King-Snohomish county line, 104-acre Lake Ballinger has much to offer. Decent plants of trout have kept the lake viable year-round, and local bass fishermen have pulled nice largemouth out in recent years.

If you're trolling, use Pop Geer, Wedding Rings tipped with worms and even small plugs like Rapalas and FlatFish to entice trout pushing 12 inches, and holdovers into the teens. If you're still-fishing with a scented marshmallow and worm and/or salmon egg combos off the bottom, you'll have a recipe for success.

If it's bobber fishing you like, fish the same worms and eggs you would use for bottomfishing, but remove the buoyant marshmallows. Use a 3- to 4-foot leader and standard baits when fishing from the pier for good, consistent trout yields as well.

On the bass front, many fishy-looking areas around Ballinger deserve a glance. On the north end, an extensive lily pad forest, split by an in-flowing creek, should hold largemouth (watch out for errant golf balls). The numerous private docks that line the west shoreline offer plenty of cover and should warrant a cast or two.

On the south shore, several downed trees and numerous submerged logs look rather daunting and snaggy, but may offer the necessary cover for large fish. The same can be said of the island in the center of Ballinger. It's been known to kick out its share of largemouth as well.

Pack small crankbaits, rubber worms

NO NEED TO max out the gas card to find fish, Emerald City anglers. From about 65th and Aurora north to Ballinger Way, you'll find five lakes that hold trout, bass, perch and even tiger musky. Aidan Boyle, 9, shows off a 2-pound trout he caught off the southwest shore of Green Lake May 21. He used two marshmallows and an egg.

and small spinnerbaits in your tacklebox when you target Ballinger's bass.

As the summer progresses and water temperatures increase, fish worms for perch along the east shore near the golf course.

AT a GLANCE

What: Seattle-area trout and bass lakes.

Where: Green, Bitter, Haller, Echo and Ballinger lakes.

Why: Spend more time on the water catching fish and less time filling up and traveling.

How: For trout, dunk the standard float-and-bait rigs right off shore, or troll around with small banana-type plugs or spinners. For bass, work small cranks, plastic worms and spinnerbaits around cover.

Info/gear: Try Outdoor Emporium (206-624-6550) for tackle and info, and Fred Meyer's along Aurora or on N. 85th just west of Greenwood for gear.

Stevens kokes: not hot yet, trout the main game

──────────── LAKE STEVENS

by Lou Bignami

The biggest problem on 1,021-acre Lake Stevens is getting away from the aquatic action during the summer, when dawn and dusk visits are realistically the only way to go.

Right now, however, the water's still cold so the skiers are ashore. And while the kokanee have barely started, rainbows, cutthroat, perch and crappie are hungry.

Best of all for Everett-area anglers, it's close to home.

Stevens boat show: Shorefishers can try the city park off Vernon Road, working from the ends of the buoyed beach, or the fishing pier at the boat ramp at Wyatt County Park. However, this is a boat-fisher's lake and, later in the year, you may need downriggers to hit the prime spots.

Trollers can, of course, follow their electronics to the fish, which often lay along the steep east bank north of the county ramp.

The usual Cowbells with worms, Dick Nite spoons (produced, incidentally, just down the road in Machias) or Triple Teazers are the usual choice for trout. We usually fish trout-finish minnow or banana plugs this time of year, working just off the boat docks to take cutthroat and some bass.

Bubba bassin': Casting tube lures and plastic worms up along the docks below the trophy homes on both the east and west shores produces decent bass. Crankbaits work well, but a lot of the docks

are shallow and consequently have brush and such around as summer comes on — lost lures can be a problem that jigs nicely solve.

This submerged brush can hold schools perch and crappie. Worms, jigs under floats and small spinners and spoons work for panfish and the odd trout or bass.

Get there: Head east from Everett on Highway 2 and stay to the right when 2 veers left onto State Route 204 (you'll be on 20th St. NE). Follow this past Highway 9 to the Tom Thumb convenience store and turn left. Follow the road for roughly ¼

mile before turning left onto North Davies Road, which parallels the west shore to Wyatt County Park. You'll

> **We usually fish trout-finish minnow or banana plugs this time of year, working just off the boat docks to take cutthroat and some bass.**

find a public pay launch with two loading floats and a fishing pier there.

Information: River Otter Guide Service (425-422-9616); Greg's Custom Rods (425-335-1391).

Lake Stevens

Winter options to explore for Lake Washington trout

RENTON

by Dusty Routh

You may occasionally see a boat as you drive over the 520 floating bridge or I-90 with a million other commuters. A lone boat, bobbing around in the gray winter chop. Most times it will be raining, and the boat's canvas will be closed up. You won't see anybody. Just a boat, off by itself, like some kind of ghost vessel bouncing around on the cold winter water of Lake Washington.

When you see it you might wonder, "What's a boat doing out on the lake in this kind of weather, at this time of year?"

But if you could see it closer, you'd know the reason. A telltale downrigger boom will be out over the water, perpendicular to the stern, with a hard-bent rod pulled down to the cable.

Fishing, that's what that boat is doing out there. Fishing.

And fishing for what?

How about for trophy-sized rainbow and cutthroat trout?

Sound crazy? Not necessarily. There's a hardy group of core fishermen who target these fish, and with good reason. Some of the trout that are caught in Lake Washington in the winter can approach legendary status. Like the monster, state-record 14.9-pound cutthroat caught two years ago near Juanita Bay.

AT a GLANCE

What: Winter fishing on Lake Washington for cutthroat and rainbows.

When: Some of the best fishing is from November to March.

Where: High percentage spots are south and north of Mercer Island, both sides of both floating bridges and near Juanita Bay.

How: This is deep-water trolling with Needlefish spoons and small herring.

Information: Mike Bing, Van Hala Guide Service (206-355-7133); Curt Welch, Special Moments Guide Service (425-226-6327);.Outdoor Emporium (206-624-6550).

Not for everyone: This isn't the kind of fishery where you can go out and catch a limit. Far from it. Even the best, most experienced core anglers get skunked regularly, or come back from an outing having had only one or two take-downs and maybe one or two hook-ups.

These are spooky, wary, hard to catch, non-schooling fish. The big cutts in Lake Washington, particularly, seem to be lone-wolf predators and are often few and far between. The rainbows can be equally elusive. But the average size of one of these fish can be enormous by trout standards, with cutts usually over 18 inches (2 to 3 pounds) and 'bows that tip the scales at over 5 pounds. If you're looking to fill your freezer, you'll have to fish elsewhere. But if you're willing to put in your time, be patient, work hard and fish smart, you can catch big trout.

The 'fish smart' part: Lake Washington is a big lake. Really big. Over 22,000 acres. Which is one reason that's it hard to fish. This is a lot of water to cover, and it makes for a lot of water where the fish can hide where you'll never find them. The best way to narrow it down is to eliminate non-productive water, and concentrate on the best known, most productive spots.

But, keep in mind that the "productive" areas are places where anglers who've caught fish return to fish again and again, trip after trip. In a lake this big it would seem that there are bound to be other productive areas that no one's discovered yet. So it doesn't hurt to explore in search of your own new, undiscovered hot spots.

The unproductive areas that you can probably eliminate right off the bat seem to be the middle of the lake between the two floating bridges, midlake north of Bailey Peninsula, the middle areas of the East Channel, and the area northeast of the Cedar River.

The high-percentage, best known locations are around the mouth of the Cedar, the southern and northern ends of Mercer Island, both sides of

BRIGHT, BEAUTIFUL CUTTS like this are your target during the winter months on Lake Washington. This metro fishery, despite its potential as a trophy trout fishery, is extremely underfished.

the floating bridges and the area around Juanita Point. Less known areas that still have a reputation for producing include the southwest side of Mercer and Groat, Dabney and Evergreen points.

Fish diet: While most trout are famous for eating bugs, who wants to eat an insect when they can have succulent seafood instead? Trout love to fish (just like you do), and feast on what they catch. Whether it's shad fry (yes, there are shad fry in Lake Washington), mysis shrimp, or salmon and trout fry, trout go after smaller fish more readily than they do the lake's infrequent bug hatches. Trout even feast on baby crappie.

In other words, cutthroat and rainbow in Lake Washington eat fish, so if you can concentrate your efforts where there's fish available for dinner, you'll up your chances of scoring.

That's why the floating bridges are so productive. As Mike Bing of Van Hala Guide Service (206-355-7133) once pointed out to me, the bridges have their own kind of food chain going on. They grow algae and other vegetation on the floats which attracts bugs which attracts shrimp which attracts baitfish which attracts big trout.

Understanding the diet of these big lunkers is key to knowing not only where to fish, but what to put in the water to catch them.

The catching part:
In my 12 years of fishing the lake, I don't believe I've ever seen anyone fishing it for trout who wasn't trolling. That's not to say that jigging, throwing a spoon or spinner, fishing off the bottom or still-fishing with a float won't work. But for higher percentages, this is the place for deep-water trolling, from 30 to 110 feet down. It's a deep lake and the baitfish are deep and so the fish are deep.

You can use weights, but downriggers are the way to go because you can then use much lighter lines and leaders. These fish are notoriously leader-shy, so be stealthy. Your best bet is a 6- or 8-pound-test leader. Fluorocarbon is ideal, but a stealthy mono like Stren Magnathin will work just as well.

You can pull a string of blades or use flashers and dodgers, but you don't need to. This is crystal-clear water and trout can see and sense a long way. In fact, I have a theory that blades, flashers and dodgers are actually counter-productive, serving to shy fish away instead of attracting them.

You can troll all kinds of offerings, and many anglers do. Some swear by Jointed Rapalas in rainbow and fire tiger. Some troll big Panther Martins and Rooster

Tails. Some troll worm harnesses with nightcrawlers. But my favorites are Needlefish spoons, and herring.

For Needlefish, use 8-pound main line and 6-pound leader. Use a leader that's at least as long as your fishing rod. Connect main line and leader with a high-quality ball bearing swivel, like a Sampo. If the Needlefish has a flutter tail, remove it. You want it to look just

like a minnow to the fish. Tie the Needlefish directly to your leader. Use a No. 2 or No. 3 Needlefish in fire tiger or the red head/brass body color. Vary your trolling depth, speed and pattern. Don't be afraid to fish too deep, even in winter. Remember that more fish are caught at 60 feet than at 30 on this lake.

Now, it may sound weird to use herring for trout in freshwater, but believe me it's incredibly effective (refer back to the fish's diet, above). Trout are less suspicious of a trolled herring and will hit it with a lot of velocity. They may take a subtle poke at a Needlefish spoon, but they will absolutely inhale a herring. Use orange or yellow label herring. You can plugcut it, but you don't need to. Tie a two-hook snelled leader, just like you do for salmon fishing, with 8-pound Stren Magnathin (fluorocarbon is too delicate for snell tying and tends to fray). Go with two No. 2 Gamakatsus.

Once tied, take the first hook and put it through the left nostril of the herring and poke it down through and out the lower jaw. Let the second hook hang free, roughly two-thirds of the way to the tail. You'll notice that you get a terrific spin using a whole herring this way. Trout will notice too. As with your Needlefish, you don't need anything else — no dodgers, flashers, or blades.

Put your spoon or herring well behind the boat so that your down-rigger cable and ball don't spook these wary fish. Set your clip for light release, and be prepared to do battle with a big fish if your rod goes off.

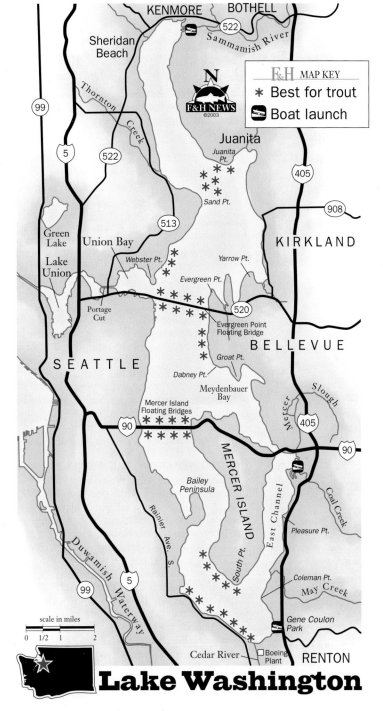

Lake Washington

The big lake's winter trout fishery: 'This place is like a ghost town'

LAKE WASHINGTON isn't just a summer bass fishery, and it's not just for sailboating with Biff. No, the big lake has a winter trout fishery that's all but unknown. Jim Smith knows about it, though — he landed this 7-pound, 24-inch 'bow while angling for perch in mid-November.

by Joel Shangle

The concept of being alone in the middle of a city of half a million people is completely incomprehensible to most people. Tranquility within spitting distance of the morning Highway 520 commute? Impossible!!! Rubbish!!! Not so. The fact of the matter is that a very small corps of anglers who make their winter/spring homes on the waters of Lake Washington have all told themselves this at one time or another: "This lake is all *mine!*"

Seattle's big metro lake is grossly underutilized by anglers in the height of the summer, and almost completely ignored from December until March, when the bass crowd finally starts to return for the season. You fish the big lake in the wintertime, and you *define* being alone. There's more untapped opportunity awaiting Puget Sound trout, panfish and bass fishermen in Lake Washington than in any other water on the Westside, and it's high time to kick this mother out. Over the next two issues, we'll take a hard look at the big lake's wintertime trout and bass options. We're spending the winter fishing with the experts, and we're taking notes on "where, how, why and when." Grab a Thermos and a snowmobile suit, and join us as we examine the metro monster.

GETTING TO KNOW THE FISHERY: The truckers who honked from the I-90 bridge as they sped by two lone Lake Washington fishermen slowly moving along the bridge's north-side buoy line? *They* know. The cormorants lazily milling around N buoy, fat and content after a breakfast of shad? *They* know. Guide Mike Bing, shaking his head, smiling, lowering a worm harness into the depths on a brisk, calm November morning? *He* definitely knows.

The other 4 million residents of the Seattle/Puget Sound area? Most of 'em don't have a clue about the winter trout fishery on Seattle's sprawling metro lake.

"Man, this place is like a ghost town in the winter," says Bing, owner of Van Hala Guide Service (206-230-2646). "There's a small group of regulars who know about this fishery and fish it hard in the winter, but, most of the time, there's nobody here."

Not that Bing tries to keep the fishery a secret — it can get lonely out there sometimes, with 22,000 acres of water all to yourself.

"Heck, I wouldn't mind if more people fished this, just so I could wave at somebody every now and then," Bing laughs.

But the winter trout fishery on Lake Washington is no laughing matter. Matter of fact, it's one of the most unknown, unappreciated opportunities on the

Westside — where else can you launch a small boat at 8 a.m. in January, troll for three hours, catch a couple of 3-pound fish, and still make your noon business lunch?

"It can be a wonderful opportunity," says Bing. "You get out here in the morning, you fish basically by yourself, and you have the potential to hook some *nice* fish. It amazes me that more people don't do it."

BIG WINTER TROUT: The last time I fished Lake Washington with Bing, the action was typical: three or four hits in three hours. Not fast action, by any means, but at this time of the year, each hit carries the potential of turning out to be a fat, bright, beautiful fish.

"Normally, you'll boat a couple of big fish on a morning's fishing" says Bing. "The typical size of fish out there is in the 18- to 20-inch bracket, but there's potential for fish in the 5-, 6-pound range. Usually, the bigger fish will be cutthroat, but in the winter, the catch is much more prone to be a rainbow."

The pressure was typical too: one windsurfer, a bunch of cormorants and truckers honking as they crossed the bridge.

"Rainbow and cutthroat on Lake Washington sometimes seem untouchable," says Bing. "One day they're nailing your favorite rig, and the next they appear to have left town. But they're there."

TROUT HOT SPOTS: The first step in finding wintertime trout digs on this massive lake is in understanding the habits of your quarry.

...that's where you'll find the fish...

"(Do) steelhead hang behind rocks and logs, and Chinook hide under kelp beds and along rocky shorelines by chance?" asks Bing. "Hardly. Fish seek shelter so they don't expend any more energy than necessary in search of their protein requirement."

With that in mind, Bing will spend much of his time fishing areas where current and water flow are broken up by structure.

"Larger bodies of water with islands and irregular shorelines, tributaries and the like have currents that are overlooked or not even thought of by many anglers," Bing says. "Fish the points — inside 'em, outside 'em, the backside.

During the months of January and February, Bing fishes four general locations: 1) The buoys north of the I-90 bridge; 2) The southwest end of Mercer Island; 3) The Bellevue waterfront, including Meydenbauer Bay; 4) The mouth of the Cedar River. All of them are defined by some manner of current break, structure or other definitive fish-holding factor.

I-90 bridge: Launch at Stan Sayres

Park in Seattle, and within 5 minutes you're motoring under the east span of the I-90 bridge between Mercer Island and Seattle, and ready to fish the buoy line that parallels the bridge on the north side. Running from the beginning of the east span to the beginning of the west span, the line includes 17 big red-and-white-striped buoys, labeled in alphabetical order from west to east (starting with Buoy A and ending with Buoy Q). Start trolling straight out in front of the east span, before you even get to Buoy Q — the water here runs around 80 feet — and head due west, right along the line. As you pass Buoy Q and Buoy P, you'll notice the bottom slowly climbing from 80 to 70 to 60 feet. By the time you're at Buoy O, you'll be fishing in roughly 50 feet of water. Trout territory.

"The bottom gradually comes up to about 40 feet on a submerged island at the third (O) buoy," says Bing. "That's where you'll find the fish."

The island quickly slopes off past Buoy M, falling off to 200 feet for the length of the buoys on the western half of the line. Once you pass the island and the bottom starts falling off, turn around and troll the island again (as long as you're marking fish) until you've fished any bite out.

South Mercer Island: Starting on the southern tip of Mercer and moving west along the shoreline across from Rainier Beach and Atlantic City, fish the 40- to 90-foot depths inside the 8 mph buoy line. The bottom here drops noticeably along a series of shelves, and there are current breaks in the form of small points that lead around the westernmost point below Bailey Peninsula. This area is also worth fishing if the wind is blowing out of the north — tuck in on the lee side of the island and fish as far west into the lake as you want.

"That's cutthroat spawning territory," says Bing. "It's very rocky and steep."

Cedar River: Just a two-minute motor out of Gene Coulon Park and you're at the mouth of the Cedar River, staring smack into the face of

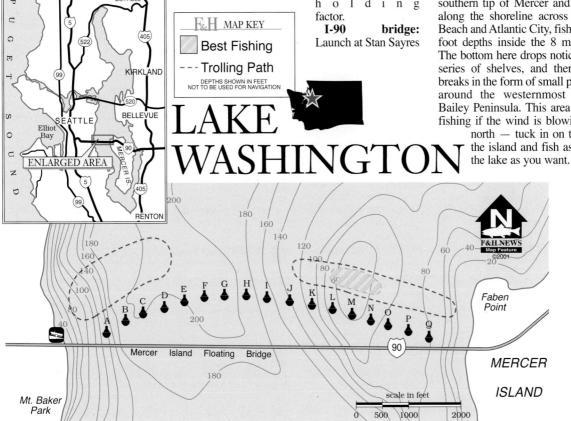

F&H MAP KEY

Best Fishing

- - - Trolling Path

DEPTHS SHOWN IN FEET
NOT TO BE USED FOR NAVIGATION

LAKE WASHINGTON

aircraft blasting off from the Renton Boeing facility.

This area features a natural "amphitheater" contour directly off the mouth, where Bing will troll in a triangular pattern over the shelves and bottom breakup brought in by the river's current.

"There are times where you can definitely feel the current moving in there," says Bing.

"The natural 'bowl' shape of the amphitheater is where I find most of my fish here."

Bellevue waterfront: Includes Meydenbauer Bay on the mainland side of I-90, and Luther Burbank Day Park on the northeast shore of Mercer Island. Fish the southern point of the mouth of Meydenbauer (not Groat Point — more on that next issue).

OTHER AREAS, SOUTH: 1) The Atlantic City waterfront; 2) Barbee Mills, in the east channel between Coleman Point and Pleasure Point; 3) Coulon Park dock, for shorebound anglers; 4) Stan Sayres Park Beach, another bank fishing area.

OTHER AREAS, NORTH: 1) Webster Point to Sand Point; 2) Juanita Bay, along the backside of the bay where Juanita Creek dumps in; 3) Champaign Point, along the shoreline from the entrance to Juanita Bay around the point.

"If you live on the north end, get to know that area," says Bing. "I personally live near the south end, and I've been fishing it for 20 years. I know people who have excellent success from Renton to Bothell,

---

AT A GLANCE

What: Lake Washington winter trout.

When: Now through March, when water temperatures bring trout to the surface of this massive, deep lake.

Species: Cutthroat, rainbow trout.

Where: North of the I-90 bridge, troll along the buoy line past O buoy and the sunken island that rises up to 50 feet there. Also hit the southwest end of Mercer Island, the mouth of the Cedar River, the Bellevue waterfront, Atlantic City, Barbee Mills, Luther Burbank Day Park, Meydenbauer Bay, Juanita Bay, Champaign Point, Webster Point, Kenmore.

Why: Blissful solitude, and the chance at hooking a fish ranging over 4 pounds.

Information: Mike Bing, Van Hala Guide Service (206-230-2646); Tom Pollack, Auburn Sports & Marine (253-833-1440)

---

but it's usually in one (specific) area or other — 20,000 acres takes time."

TECHNIQUES: Trolling is the name of the game throughout the winter, and finding the right depth is a key. Generally, you'll want to fish from 10 to 20 feet down, but you'll hook them at much greater depths as well.

"Cool weather puts fish near the surface," says Bing. "Surface temps of 47 to 55 degrees seem to be ideal. Good quality fish finders will show you a thermocline too."

You could catch fish on Lake Washington with a thousand different presentations, but here are a few of the setups that have been among Bing's wintertime arsenal.

• The good old 'crawler hauler: A nightcrawler threaded on No. 2 hooks, trolled behind Sep's Mountain Lite, or behind a Wedding Ring, or behind any of your favorite spinner/Pop Geer setups.

• Needlefish: Probably the most widely used presentation on the lake for trout, a No. 2 rainbow trout Needlefish trolled behind a small dodger. Other spoons/lures like Dick Nites, Triple Teazers, Sparkle-fish will work just as well.

• Flies: Natural-colored Muddler Minnows or Sep's Trolling Flies trailed about 2 feet behind a small dodger.

• Plugs: A bright red No. 50 Hot Shot trolled fast on the surface is one of Bing's favorite methods for scaring up an occasional big fish.

LAKE WASHINGTON LAUNCHES

Magnuson Park
Launch Type: 4-lane concrete ramp, three loading floats.
Facilities: Restrooms, beach access, barbecues, picnic tables.
Parking: 120 spaces.
Fees: $4 to launch, $6 for overnight parking.
Directions: North on Montlake Blvd. NE, which becomes 45th St. then Sand Point Way NE; right on 65th St. NE at park entrance.

Kirkland Marina Park
Launch Type: 1-lane concrete ramp, one loading float.
Facilities: Restrooms, fishing pier, boat moorage.
Parking: No parking for vehicles with trailers; car parking limited to 2 hours.
Fees: None.
Directions: In Kirkland, go west on NE 85th St. (which becomes Central Way NE); left at Market St., look for the ramp on right.

Day Street Park
Launch Type: 1-lane concrete plank ramp; mainly a cartopper launch.
Facilities: Fishing dock, trails, restrooms.
Parking: 10 spaces, no trailer parking.
Fees: None.
Directions: From Seward Park in Seattle, north on Lake Washington Blvd. S. for 3 miles; continue north on Lakeside Ave. S. another quarter mile, directly under I-90 bridge; turn right at entrance to park.

Stan Sayres Park
Launch Type: 8-lane asphalt ramp, two loading floats.
Facilities: Restrooms, water available, paved trails.
Parking: 35 paved spaces for vehicles with trailers.
Fees: $4 launch fee, $6 overnight parking fee.
Directions: Take I-90 to southbound Rainier Ave. (right); left on Genesee St. a half mile; left on 43rd Ave. S. for 0.4 miles; right on Lake Washington Blvd.; left at park entrance.

South Ferdinand Street Park
Launch Type: 1-lane gravel ramp; cartop or hand-carry launch only.
Facilities: Trash.
Parking: 20 paved spaces.
Fees: None.
Directions: From Rainier Ave. S., go east on Orcas St. to the end at Seward Park; turn north on Lake Washington Blvd. and go a half mile to launch.

Atlantic City Park
Launch Type: 8-lane concrete ramp, three loading floats.
Facilities: Restrooms, trash, water, picnic tables.
Parking: 20 paves spaces; 35 trailer spaces.
Fees: $4 to launch, $6 for overnight parking.
Directions: In Renton, north on Rainier Ave. S for 2 miles; right on Seward Park Ave. S a quarter mile; right at ramp.

Mercer Island Launch
Launch Type: 2-lane concrete ramp, one loading float.
Facilities: Restroom, water, trash.
Parking: 57 paved spaces for trailers.
Fees: $4 to launch.
Directions: From Seattle, head east on I-90; take Exit 8; right on Mercer Way and then a quick left at "Mercer Island Boat Launch" sign; follow the road downhill under I-90 bridge to the launch.

SE 40th Street Ramp
Launch Type: 2-lane concrete plank ramp, one loading float.
Facilities: Restrooms, fuel at nearby marina.
Parking: 60 paved spaces for trailers.
Fees: $4 to launch,
Directions: Take I-405 to Exit 13A in Bellevue and head west 1 block on 8th St.; go left on 11th Ave. NE a half mile; right on Main St. 2 blocks; right on 114th Ave. SE, which becomes 118th Ave. SE; right on SE 40th St. to launch.

Gene Coulon Park
Launch Type: 8-lane concrete ramp, two loading floats.
Facilities: Restrooms, fishing dock, moorage,
Parking: 96 paved trailer spaces.
Fees: Seasonal launch fees, $2.25 for parking at launch.
Directions: From the north, go south on I-405 to Exit 5 (Sunset Blvd); right on Park Drive; quick right on Lake Washington Blvd. to stop sign at park entrance.

Snoqualmie forks offer good fly fishing for cutties

by Dusty Routh

It takes a lot to get Seth Taylor of Creekside Angling Co. in Issaquah (425-392-3800) excited when it comes to fly angling for trout. After all, he lives and breathes the sport day in and day out from behind the counter, and on the water as a fly fishing instructor and coach. His passionate pursuit of fish with a fly extends to all manner of freshwater trout, sea-run cutts out in the salt and winter and summer steelhead.

But if there is one thing that consistently pushes his button, it's the good trout fishing on the upper Snoqualmie River. Yep, that's right. The lowly, often ignored, mostly overlooked and infrequently fished Snoqualmie above the falls and out past North Bend.

Taylor practically gushes when it comes to talking about the wild cutthroat residing in both the South and Middle forks of this river.

"The Middle Fork harbors a bigger population of trout than the South Fork," Taylor says. "The trout may not be larger, but there are more of them. The Middle Fork is a bigger river, it drains a wider area — the whole thing

is a bigger watershed. I've been most taken with those Middle Fork cutts, just in terms of sheer beauty. They are amazing looking fish, just beautiful, full of color. The cutthroat from the South Fork are nice fish too, but they're more silvery, a little less colorful."

Say what? You didn't know there was a top-caliber trout stream so close to Pugetropolis? Figured you had to run to the Peninsula or over the mountains to the Yakima for blue ribbon fishing? The upper Snoqualmie might help to reshape your where-to-go strategy, especially if you've only got a few hours before or after work to spare.

The South and Middle forks offer good action for wild cutthroat trout, with an occasional odd rainbow showing up every now and then. There is plenty of fish, great access and easy-to-wade water. If there's a drawback, it's the relative size of the fish, says Taylor.

"On the Middle Fork, a 16-inch fish means calling all your friends to tell them what you caught," Taylor admits. "Most of the South Fork fish are going to run even smaller, around 8 to 10 inches. And you may catch an odd rainbow. But it's mostly all wild cutthroat. They're pretty cool. They're not jumbos — 10 inches is what I consider to be a really nice one, but the average fish is going to be around 8 inches. Still, they're scrappy. They'll break off a 5X tippet if you're not careful."

So you may not break any world line-class records, but that's OK. You'll still have tons of action, and you won't have to drive for hours to get to it.

Cutty coulee: One of the real treats of the upper Snoqualmie is you won't

THEY'RE NOT TROPHIES in size, but the colors of the Snoqualmie's wild cutts make up for it. This fishery, despite being right on the outskirts of Seattle, is one of the most underutilized fly fisheries on the Westside.

need a drift boat, pontoon, belly boat or raft. Both forks offer superlative access and fairly easy wading.

"I go up there all the time," says Taylor. "My access point for the South Fork is kind of a weird one. The best way to describe it is the Exit 32 (heading east on I-90) bridge. You can walk downstream right from there, and during low water you can wade well upstream, picking your way up, fording and wading. Downstream, there's a trail, a public trail system that goes almost all the way to North Bend, to the end of the River Bend housing development."

Taylor points out that on some evenings there will be other anglers on the river.

"When that happens, if one gravel bar is taken, I just go to the next one. There's plenty of places to fish."

You can also access the South Fork below where it tumbles out of the Cascades from Olallie State Park, south off Exit 34.

To fish the larger, more cutthroat-

AT a GLANCE

What: Good summertime fly fishing for wild cutthroat trout close to Seattle on the South and Middle forks of the Snoqualmie River.

How: Fish Woolly Buggers and subsurface dropper nymphs as snowmelt flows wind down. Then switch to throwing dries imitating caddis and mayflies. A small Stimulator is one of your best bets.

Where: There's good public access on both forks of the river in the North Bend area, or take Exit 34 off I-90 and go north for the Middle Fork or south for the South Fork. Bring a pair of chest waders with felt soles for rambling up and down the river.

When: Prime time is early July, but June can be excellent too.

Information: Creekside Angling Co. (425-392-3800).

heavy Middle Fork, take Exit 34 and turn north.

"There's a well-marked sign along Lake Dorothy Road," Taylor says, "just as the residential area peters out. The road changes to gravel, and you'll see a big state-park colored sign."

The rough road up the Middle Fork goes for many, many miles.

How it's done: Early in the season, like in early June, both forks are liable to still hold cold snowmelt water. If that's the case, fish Woolly Buggers in the deeper pools. Or go with subsurface flies.

"When there's still that last little bit of snowmelt, go subsurface," Taylor confirms. "But don't go full-bore nymphing with strike indicators and split shot and all that. Just go with an all-purpose weighted fly, like a Beadhead Prince Nymph."

For this rig, Taylor adds a wet fly up top, something with fairly skimpy hackle to use as the indicator and to see if he can draw a rise.

"You can skip the indicator," he repeats. "These fish hit hard. It's a real take. You'll know it."

Taylor rounds out his offering with a 3X tippet to the first No. 12 or 14 nymph, and a 4X tippet tied to the second fly, which is a No. 16 or 14. He throws a floating line and a 9-foot leader.

While the water is still cold, Taylor says you're looking for deeper water.

"I know that sounds funny, but when the water's cold the fish have to rest because of the cold water," Taylor says. "They can't fin in the current and make a living at the same time. So they'll munch and rest in the deeper water."

Come summertime, both forks drop and warm up considerably.

"That's when you'll be looking for fish in the faster water, faster than you'd think would hold fish," Taylor explains. "You're looking for knee-deep riffles that are high in oxygen content, because in the summer the flows really calm down and the river can get oxygen poor. Look for where the bubbles mix."

Prime time: Taylor says if you're looking for the very best fishing on the Snoqualmie, wait until just after the Fourth of July.

"You can set your clock by that," he says. "That's when it's really, really good. Days in late May and June can be good too, but right there in early July is when it's best. July is gangbuster up there."

What makes it so good, Taylor says, is that the dry fly hatches are so consistent late in the evenings (as late as 10).

"It's purely dry fly action then," he says. "You'll have caddis all day long plus there's a mayfly up there. The best imitation is a light Cahill, a kind of cream-colored mayfly. Might even be like a kind of pale evening dun. There's also yellow sally stoneflies, which can best be imitated by an orange or Yellow Stimulator. And in the fall, there's an October caddis that's sensational."

The other component that makes this such a good fishery is that the fish seem to be very forgiving.

"The cuts never really get all that picky," Taylor says. "When it's time to feed and the water's the right temperature, they're less selective."

Laws and such: The North and South forks from Snoqualmie Falls upstream are open to trout angling June 1-Oct. 31, with selective-gear rules and a daily limit of two fish over 10 inches. It's open for CNR angling from Nov. 1-May 31. The Middle Fork is open year-round, CNR only, selective-gear rules.

Upper Snoqualmie Cutthroat

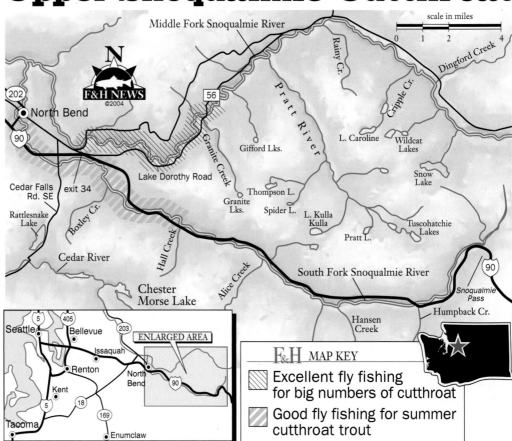

174

Puget Sound Freshwater
BASS
CRAPPIE
PERCH

Lake Cassidy bass, crappie: fish slow, methodically

MARYSVILLE

by Dusty Routh

The great thing about small lakes is that you can cruise around with your electronics on and see all there is to see in a matter of hours instead of days. Rather than having to guess which hemisphere the fish might be holding in, you can partition them into five or six nautical sections, and thoroughly fish each one with a variety of lures and presentations based on your findings before the day is out.

Such is the water presented by Lake Cassidy, located just north of Lake Stevens. This 125-acre water has an excellent reputation for productive crappie fishing. The lake's largemouth bass, while sometimes difficult to coax up, nonetheless grow to good sizes. While my personal best from Cassidy has only been a 3½-pounder, I've missed on bigger fish and a few of my buddies have taken fish to 6 pounds.

On a recent trip in late March, I hung a Yamamoto jig in some underwater brush in 4 feet of water at the northeast corner of the lake. Using the electric motor to go fetch it, I saw an amazing swirl and a big tail that spooked out of the brush. Of course all fish look bigger in the water, but still I believe that fish might have been a 7- or 8-pounder.

Cassidy logistics: To get to Cassidy, head east on Highway 2 out of Everett. Once over the trestle, take Highway 204 to Lake Stevens and then head north on Highway 9. At the Lake Cassidy Road sign, turn right. Proceed up and down the hill there. You'll see the lake and ramp which will be on your left.

The ramp isn't really a ramp per se. It's a sand launch and there's no dock. Cassidy is perfect for small boats like cartoppers, canoes, float tubes, drift boats and catarafts. If you have 4-wheel drive, however, you can get a bass boat in (and back out) from the sand launch,

but bring hip boats or waders. There is a restroom facility and gravel parking area on the other side of the road from the launch. An 8-mph speed limit on the lake keeps the Jet Skiers and water skiers from degrading the place.

The lay of the lake: Cassidy lies north-south. It's ringed with brush, wood, trees, grass and marsh. There are a number of small inlets and shallow, weedy bays. If you like to work

MOST BASS IN North-End lakes will run 2 to 3 pounds, like this one caught by **F&H**'s Andy Walgamott last spring, but hooking occasional fish to 5, 6 even 7 pounds is possible during the spawn.

shoreline cover, there's plenty of it, including a lot of wood in the water.

The deepest part of the lake is at the southern end, with depths from 15 to 27 feet. Much of this, however, is flat and featureless. Like a lot of these kinds of lakes, Cassidy is basically a big bowl. At the northern end there are extensive of 7- and 8-foot flats. Along the eastern shoreline there is deep water (10 to 15 feet) adjacent to shallow shoreline cover. The lake is also quite dark in color.

Fishing Cassidy: A fair number of regulars can be found on Cassidy, par-

ticularly once warm weather comes on. The lake is planted by WDFW with trout, so you'll find plenty of trollers and plunkers. Power Bait and worms on the bottom will take fish. For trolling, just about anything will do the trick, but a black or olive Woolly Booger is a pretty consistent producer.

Once the trout fishing hubbub dies down, most people who know this lake well target black crappie. Once hot weather comes on, usually starting in June, these crappie are famous for coming to the surface for an hour or so each evening to hit bugs.

It's really quite a phenomenon. That is, rising crappie aren't exactly a common occurrence in the Pacific Northwest, but it's a sight to behold. Most of the action is along the shoreline on the southern end of the lake. By June there are lots of lily pads. The crappie will rise along the outside edge of the pads. If you're a fly angler, any small black fly will do the trick, but so will a small Stimulator. Gear fishermen throw floating jigs adorned with maggots or a pinch of worm. It's not unusual to hook into 20 or so crappie during this magic hour. The action usually starts up a half hour before dark.

Until the weather warms up, however, Cassidy's crappie are bashful and tough to get. Your best bet is to rig up with an ultralight slip bobber, a single small split shot and a small bait hook sporting two or three live maggots. Adjust the bobber so the spikes are just off the bottom, and then cast-and-retrieve this rig into likely areas — wood in the water, emerging lily pads and docks.

Bass hunting: Cassidy's bass are smart and spooky. This isn't the place, unfortunately, to catch 10 or 15 on an outing. If you can catch one or two, you've done well.

Early in the season, a jig-n-pig fished around wood and docks can produce.

Carolina-rigging creature baits along the extensive shallow flats will also work. Once the lily pads are fully emerged and the water's warmed up quite a bit, a white spinnerbait pulled through the pads is a very consistent producer and my favorite (and most productive) way to score on these fish.

We've also found bass on this lake by fishing white/blue Slug-Gos and white/black flake Senkos. It may be that the lighter color shows better in that dark, dark water.

AT a GLANCE

What: Lake Cassidy, just north of Lake Stevens in Snohomish County.

What: Good to great crappie fishing, solid trout in April and May, and work-for-'em largemouth once waters warm.

When: Trout plants in April. Crappie will start their evening bug feedings by mid-June. Bass fishing gets good from late April on through summer.

How: Crappie love maggots and nightcrawler pieces, along with tiny leadhead plastic jigs; also try black chironomids or small Stimulators. Also toss floating jigheads with a nightcrawler. Trout here love Woolly Buggers. For bass, try jig-n-pigs or white spinnerbaits through the pads.

Info: Angler's Choice (206-364-9827); John's Sporting Goods (425-252-3056).

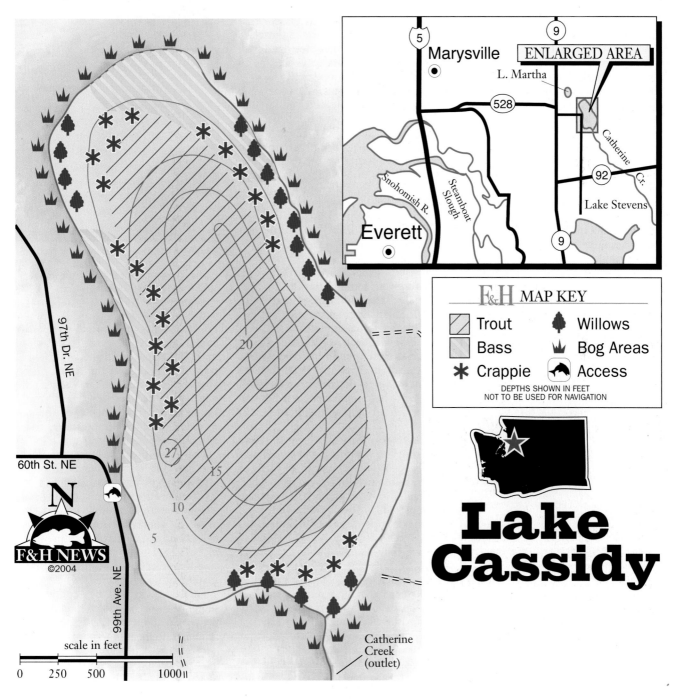

F&H MAP KEY

Trout   Willows
Bass   Bog Areas
Crappie   Access

DEPTHS SHOWN IN FEET
NOT TO BE USED FOR NAVIGATION

Lake Cassidy

Warming brings Sammamish spawning bass shallow

ISSAQUAH

by Jamie Parks

Every winter I hear it from my fishing buddy at the other end of his green Ranger: "I can't wait for May and the spawn," St. Croix pro staffer Paul Hall mutters as we drag in deep water praying for one bite.

Well, the spawn is on at Lake Sammamish.

A mild winter and some incredibly sunny days have put fish in shallow since late April. But a hot streak in the first two weeks of May pushed males in to sweep beds. The females are right behind them.

Lake Sammamish is blessed with a great population of smallmouth. What most people don't see are the large numbers of bucketmouths that can be caught here as well.

There are a ton of fish in this lake, and there really isn't any secret to finding them in late May and early June. But there are a couple of keys to keep in mind when you hit the water.

First, keep an eye on the thermometer. You'll want to see the surface temperatures rise over 55, preferably 57, degrees and stay there for a little

while. In mid-May, the top 20 feet of water had temperatures holding over 55 degrees, and fish were up shallow and at various stages of spawning.

Second, don't hit the water without a good pair of polarized sunglasses. While Hall swears by Hobies, you don't have to spend a ton of money. Just get a decent pair of glasses that are polarized. This will cut the glare off the water a great deal and will allow you to see bottom as deep as 20 feet if conditions cooperate.

Third, be patient. Take your time moving along the shoreline and docks. Look carefully for beds, and then watch carefully for fish. They won't always be sitting right on the bed, rather lingering off to the side, trying to stay out of sight. Make plenty of casts. Try different angles and different lures. Sometimes fish won't mind a little worm or jig moving through, but a lizard or a tube bait may send them into a frenzy.

If a fish swims off, back off and wait. Try fishing from a little farther away. Try throwing a crankbait over the bed.

Finally, take good care of these fish. While this is a great time to get out and catch fish, it's important that you get these fish back in the water quickly and as close to their bed as possible.

It's also an especially great time to get new anglers on the water, as you'll be able to help them catch a lot of fish and teach proper fish handling.

Locations: Spend a lot of time cruising the shoreline and docks and you'll see bass. Stay within 30 yards of the shore anywhere on the lake, checking out structure like docks, stumps and big rocks, but you'll see them on open, gravelly shorelines too.

Start your search at about the third dock on the right heading out of the boat launch. The following string of docks runs around a series of points and coves out into the main lake. Along the way, you'll see tons of white-looking spots on the bottom where smallmouth are holding.

Typically, once the shoreline makes a hard turn north and the lake opens

GREEN WITH ENVY: St. Croix and McCoy Line pro staffer Paul Hall shows off a dandy 5-pound largemouth caught off a bed at Lake Sammamish.

up, beds thin out for a bit. When the shoreline cuts back to the east to make a couple of little bays, you'll start seeing a good bunch of gravel shorelines. You'll start seeing the number of beds pickup again. You'll notice that if it's difficult for the sun to shine on a stretch of water, there will be fewer beds.

There are great stretches of docks and gravel in the northern end of the lake where you're sure to catch fish, but let's head to the western shoreline.

Combine an incredibly long stretch of gravel shoreline from the big bay halfway up the western shoreline south to Vasa Park with day-long sun exposure and you have the best spawning smallmouth area on the lake.

You'll also do well by scouring the shoreline from the sunken forest west to the purple house and the first few docks heading into the southernmost bay.

Largemouth are, obviously, a little bit of a different quest. While I have heard stories about largemouth

AT a GLANCE

What: Spawning smallies and bucketmouths at Lake Sammamish.

When: Now! Bass are shallow and holding tight to swept beds. Temps hit the mid-50s in late April, the top of the water column was prime in mid-May; bite should last till mid-June.

Where: Lake Sammamish is located just north of I-90 at Issaquah. Take Exit 15 or 17 off I-90 and follow signs to the lake. The launch is off East Lake Sammamish Parkway.

How: Sight fishing is key. Have jigs and plastics tied on. Pitch them out past the bed and hop your offering into the bed. Watch closely; when a fish picks it up or your line jumps, set the hook.

Who: Angler's Choice (206-364-9827); Auburn Sports & Marine (253-833-1440); Outdoor Emporium (206-624-6550).

hanging on a few docks around the lake that you wouldn't expect, your best bet is to think weeds. Find the weeds, particularly lily pads, and you're in the area.

There are a few fish caught each year in the lily pads both east and west of the boat launch. It won't hurt to spend a few minutes here, especially if you have a smaller boat. Another place to check is the lily pads south and west of the swimming area at Lake Sammamish State Park.

Best place for largemouth is the far northern end of the lake. The pilings in the northeastern corner are always a good bet. Lily pads will be all over the place. Move slowly and watch carefully. Pick your way around the north end of the lake plying the lily pads with your favorite spawning bait.

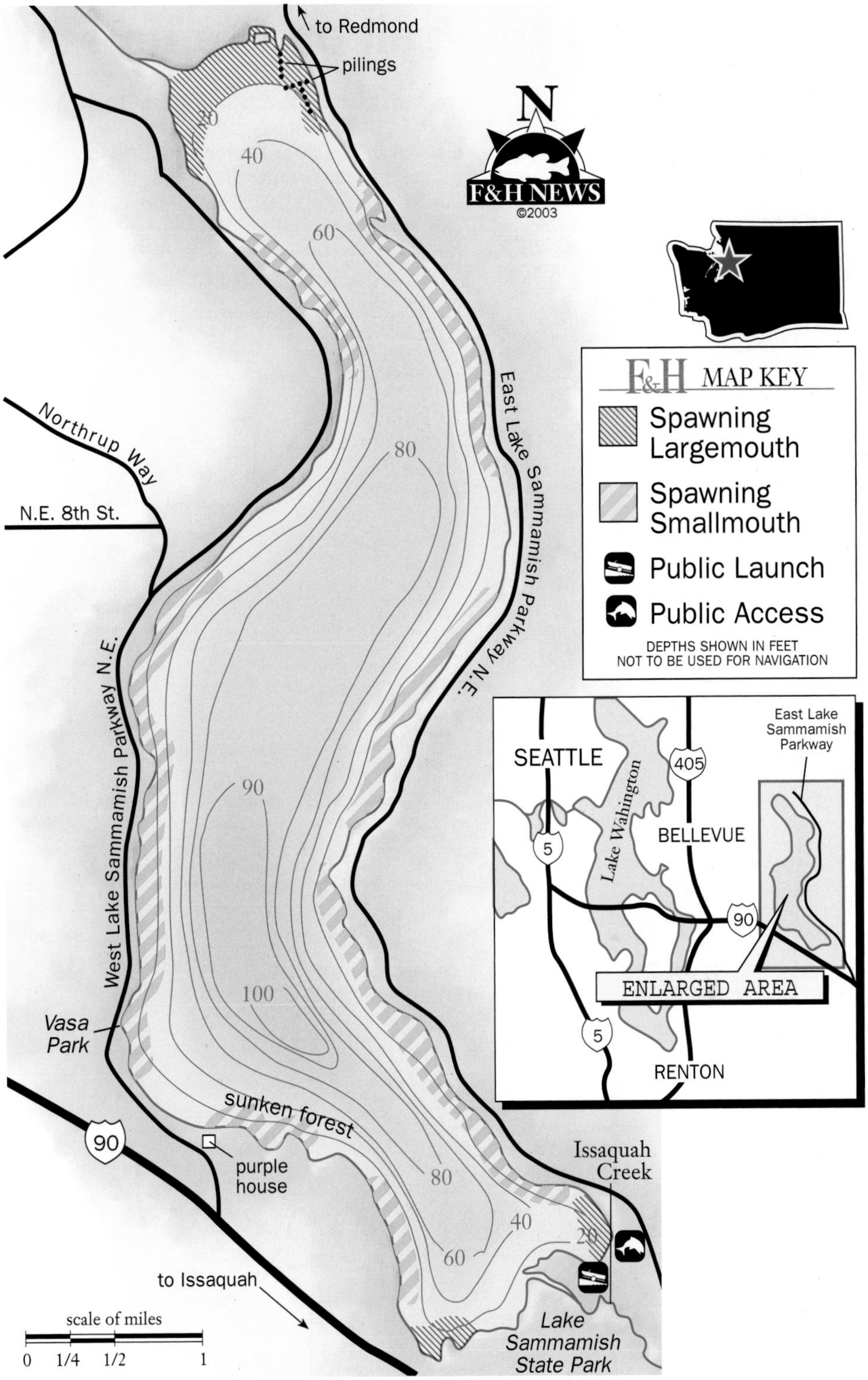

Gearing up: Catching spawning bass is more a function of watching and reacting than what bait you fish. While there are times when a lure will make a difference, it's more important to focus on watching your lure and line. Seeing is key; use light-colored baits like yellow, white or chartreuse. June bug is also a good bet, as it tends to show up well in the sunlight.

Hit the water with a few different rods ready to roll:

• A flipping stick: Have a ⅜- to ½-ounce jig tied on. A dark black and blue color is a good choice. Put a pork or a plastic craw trailer on. This will be a great choice for flipping up into a bed and hopping it like a crawdad.

• Spinning rods: Rig one with a tube bait on a jig head. This is perfect for skipping back under a dock at hard-to-reach beds. It's also quite effective on just about any spawning bed. Have a couple rigged up with different plastics like worms and lizards. That will give you a couple of easy options if a fish doesn't respond to one bait. Also, you'll be able to cast these further to beds that you can't get close to.

• Cranking rod: Have a shallow-diving crankbait or a twitchbait ready to go too. Sometimes you'll have a hard time drawing a fish off a dock, but they'll chase a hard bait. They can also be effective when conditions don't allow you to see as well.

Map

to Redmond

pilings

N

F&H NEWS
©2003

40

60

80

Northrup Way

N.E. 8th St.

East Lake Sammamish Parkway N.E.

West Lake Sammamish Parkway N.E.

90

100

Vasa Park

sunken forest

90

purple house

to Issaquah

scale of miles
0   1/4   1/2   1

F&H MAP KEY

- Spawning Largemouth
- Spawning Smallmouth
- Public Launch
- Public Access

DEPTHS SHOWN IN FEET
NOT TO BE USED FOR NAVIGATION

SEATTLE

405

East Lake Sammamish Parkway

Lake Wahington

BELLEVUE

5

90

ENLARGED AREA

5

RENTON

Issaquah Creek

80

40

20

60

Lake Sammamish State Park

Bass, kokes, trout all on fire now at Lake Stevens

by Joel Shangle

It's one of those suburban lakes that has something to satisfy every urban fisherman's requirements: 1) Serious North End bassers can flip and crank to their hearts' con-tent, searching out smallmouth up to 5 pounds; 2) Kokanee anglers can troll up a storm in search of a bonus limit of 10 of the sweetest-eating little freshwater bullets in the world; 3) Trout aficionados can go after rainbows that grow to lunker proportions.

Located 5½ miles east of Everett just off of Highway 9 and within 40 minutes of downtown Seattle, Lake Stevens is the Rich Little of the North End fishing scene: it's nothing if not versatile.

"Lake Stevens is a real good fish-eries," says Gordon Rose at Anglers Choice Pro Tackle (206-364-9827). "It's one of those places where a guy can hit

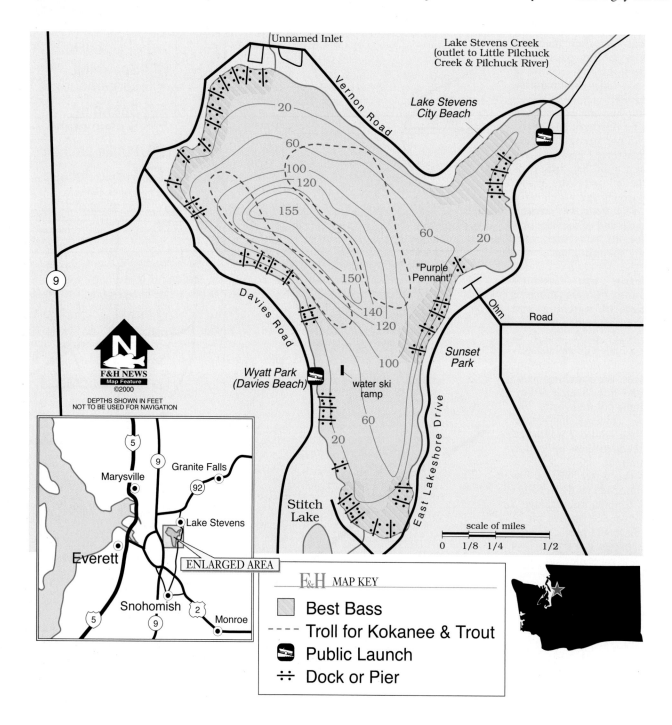

DEPTHS SHOWN IN FEET
NOT TO BE USED FOR NAVIGATION

ENLARGED AREA

scale of miles
0   1/8   1/4   1/2

F&H MAP KEY

Best Bass
Troll for Kokanee & Trout
Public Launch
Dock or Pier

it for a few hours after work because it's so close. It gets hit plenty hard."

But it can take the pressure. The three primary species — smallmouth bass, kokanee and rainbow trout — are all strong and healthy in this year-round lake, and the summer onslaught of personal watercraft users and waterskiers is still far enough away to allow you some quality fishing time. If you get out now, you'll be in the middle of a peak for all three fisheries — bass are phasing into prespawn, kokanee are getting active and trout are patrolling shallow.

BASS: The lake contains both smallmouth and largemouth, but the marquee black-eyed fish in these waters is the smallie. You'll find them ranging from 1½ to 5 pounds, with an average catch running 2½ pounds.

"You see quite a few 4-pounders caught in that lake," says Rose, a tournament angler who has been fishing Lake Stevens for 10 years. "It holds some very nice smallmouth — I've personally caught quite a few 4-pounders, and they run up to 5 pounds."

Prespawn activity is just getting underway at Stevens, and the best bass fishing on the lake will come toward the end of May and into early June.

"It's just starting to pick up right now," says Rose. "Guys have been catching a few here and there, but it takes a little while for that lake to warm up. It's a fairly deep lake, and it doesn't warm up as quickly as some of the smaller lakes in the area. The best fishing is still to come out there."

There are three primary bass areas on Lake Stevens. Those include:

• **Northeast corner:** The bay that tucks into East Lake Stevens Drive, right next to downtown Lake Stevens, is probably the hottest year-round producer for bass on the lake. You can start to fish about midlake on the east side, flipping lizards and working crankbaits around the multitude of docks, and working your way north along the shore to the bay. On the right-hand side entering the bay, you'll find a shallow, rocky flat that juts up to just below the surface — it drops to 3 to 4 feet deep in the back, and plunges down to 20 to 30 feet in the front.

"You can fish all the way around that flat," says Rose. "It's a perfect transition area for bass. You can work your way all the way around the bay to the shallow north point that sticks out just before you enter the bay."

• **Northwest corner:** Docks aplenty in the northwest corner of the lake, most in shallow water that hits a gradual, gentle, grassy bank. Start fishing at the public boat ramp off of Davies Road about midway down the west shore and work your way north along the docks into the northwest corner.

• **Southeast corner bridge:** Fish right along the pilings and into the pads that build at the bridge on the very southeast tip of the lake.

The shoreline is literally filled with docks up and down both sides, so there are several other places to target bass moving shallow.

KOKANEE: The kokanee bite is just on the verge of kicking into high gear, and anglers looking for a high-quality landlocked-sockeye fishery on the Westside should head straight to Stevens. This fishery it thriving, with loads of fish, a generous 10-fish limit and relatively light pressure.

Look fairly shallow for these scrappy little salmon early in the season, but remember that they'll almost always suspend over deeper water as the weather heats up.

"Kokanee basically graze," says *F&H News* columnist and kokanee expert Sep Hendrickson at Sep's Pro Fishing (www.sepsprofishing.com). "They move into an area until the available food supply is gone. They relate more to points and deepwater holes, but they'll generally move up and down between 40 and 60 feet — they're just looking for plankton."

Hendrickson, who was instrumental in

ONE OF THE STATE'S BEST kokanee fisheries, Lake Stevens, will be a good bet for landlocked sockeye like this from mid-May on.

the development of the Loomis GL Series of light trolling rods, recommends the following equipment setup: A Shimano 50 Calcutta or Penn 955 International reel loaded with 6-pound test; a 7-foot, medium/slow rod, specifically the Loomis CR841 or CR842; a bead chain swivel and a set of copper/pink dodgers; a 7- to 8-inch leader hooked to a Kokanee Kandy, Bite Me Bug, No. 1 Needlefish, or whatever small, flashy lure you prefer; a set of flashers on the stacked release 3 feet above the downrigger ball, and another lure of choice trailed behind that.

"These fish see that setup whipping up a storm coming through the water and it gets their attention," says Hendrickson. "They have a highly competitive, schooling nature that pushes them to go after something like that."

TROUT TOO: Very rarely will you see such a quality rainbow fishery take a back seat in any lake, but Stevens' rainbows are grossly underfished — and thanks to a steady food supply of kokanee, they can grow to bragging-size proportions.

For the next month, troll within the top 20 feet of water parallel to the west shore, straight out in front of the boat ramp. As the summer progresses, move out further, over the dropoffs in the center of the lake that feature elevation changes of over 100 feet. Similar elevation changes across the lake toward the city limits provide prime trout-holding areas too.

Troll deeper and deeper through the summer with Needlefish, Dick Nites, Z Rays, Triple Teazers and similar lures.

AT A GLANCE

What: Lake Stevens.
Species: Smallmouth and largemouth bass, kokanee, rainbow trout.
When: All species are on the bite now.
Where: Bass haunts include the northeast, northwest and southeast corners of the lake. Kokanee will move around the entire lake in search of food. Rainbows will be found along the ledges and dropoffs along the west shoreline.
Launch: Wyatt Park on Davies Road on the west shore features a fabulous launch, restrooms and a fishing pier.
Information: Gordon Rose, Anglers Choice Pro Tackle (206-364-9827); John Martinis, John's Sporting Goods (425-259-3056).

Slumbering giant stirs: Lake Washington bass awaking

SEATTLE

by Jamie Parks

It's not just a fad or super-secret society anymore. Bass fishing in Washington, more specifically Seattle, has become one of the best and most consistent opportunities in the area.

Sure, BASS has a stop every so often on the Columbia River, but Lake Washington is, by far, the place to be.

Why? It's easy.

It's an easy fishery. It's easy to find a place to fish. Gearing up is easy. And it's an easy drive for many.

For bass fisherman, the diversity of the lake is key. You can fish for both largemouth and smallmouth, and they're often not that far apart.

Structure and cover provide diverse habitat and fishing challenges. You can fish rocky flats, sharp drop-offs and vertical structure, weedlines, lily pads and docks all over the lake.

One thing that isn't as diverse is fish size. Sure there are a few smaller fish in this lake, but you don't see too many peanut-sized fish weighed during bass tournaments here. In fact, five-fish limits often tip the scales over 20 pounds. On several occasions anglers have weighed smallmouth over 6 pounds. That's hard to beat.

In early April you'll see water temperatures in the upper 40s or hopefully the low 50s. That means you should look for fish in the 15- to 25-foot depths. Find rock piles and docks that relate to these depths and work them over well.

Trying to tell you where to fish is both easy and difficult. There are so many places to put your boat, but I also don't want to get a visit from the local bass fishing mafia. Let's start in the East Channel. It's a good bet that 60-plus percent of the bass caught from Lake Washington come from this area. We'll start at the south end of the channel and work north.

Coleman Point: Across the channel from the southern end of Mercer Island. This area used to have ton of log booms that drew fish from all over the lake. Now most of the log booms are gone but there are still a ton of pilings and wood structure on the bottom. It's a popular spot among the tournament guys, who'll

THE BIG LAKE doesn't hold many peanut bass — witness Jeff Terrana's pair of chunky smallies caught out of Lake Washington last spring.

fish a lot of plastics. A Carolina or drop-shot rig is going to be most popular.

South end of Mercer Island: Stick to the eastern half. In fact, as you head east, you'll find a lot of humps off the last few docks that are great to fish. Then, as the shoreline becomes more brushy and turns north, you start hitting some brush piles that are absolute gold mines. You'll see a lot of boats here drop-shotting small plastics.

Pleasure Cove: Also called Pleasure Point, this may be one of the most popular fishing areas on the lake. It's about halfway up the channel on the east side. There is a bigger point that sticks out a bit south of I-90, and the cove below it is Pleasure Cove. The area produces fish year-round. You'll find good fishing in shallow all the way out to 50-plus feet.

Spend a lot of time here. There are a lot of contours, drop-offs and wood cover that hold fish. Cast football heads and grubs, drop shot or just Carolina rig some plastics.

Western shoreline: The entire western shoreline of the East Channel is covered with docks. Also, there is a good number of humps and ridges that will hold fish. This isn't a top producer, but you shouldn't ignore it.

Newport Shores: One of the hottest fisheries in recent years has been the canals just south of the Newport Marina. Try to avoid heading back in the canals as it's important to respect the privacy of the residents. On the other hand, don't be afraid to sit outside and throw crankbaits and plastics over the sandbar created by the creek that dumps in here.

Newport Marina: Actually the cover just to the northeast is a little-known largemouth spot. It hasn't been as productive in recent years, but there have been a few nice fish come from here. Be patient and work the cover thoroughly.

I-90 Bridge: A lot of anglers will spend all day here. There is a lot of rock, concrete and who knows what else all over the place down below. And just north and south of there are big rock piles and more structure to fish. You can drop-shot the bridge pilings. Cast plastics all over the place. Some anglers even have luck throwing crankbaits and twitchbaits in shallow starting in early May.

Once you get north of I-90, things scatter a little bit. I'll mention that there are a lot of scattered rock piles and structure that hold on both shorelines. But there are some bigger, more important spots to cover as we head out of the east channel and into the main lake.

North end of Mercer Island: As you pass the north end of the island, there are a lot of flats and rock humps from the eastern edge all the way back into the big cove. These areas range from 15 out to 45-plus feet. It's a great spot throughout the year.

Meydenbauer Point: The submerged point here is a fabulous winter spot and in the spring if you move up shallower and fish up along the shoreline, you'll get into fish. Plastics are great here. This time of year, a Carolina rig or football head and grub work great.

Webster Point: The big point on the north side as you head into Union Bay might be the second-most popular spot to fish on the lake. There is scattered rock on this point and a variety of depths.

Sand Point: Head north from Webster until the shoreline makes a western turn. This is a unique fishery. The bottom drops off very quickly from rock riprap. You don't hear anglers talk about it much, but there are fish scattered all over it.

Three Points: There is a series of three points and three bays just northeast of the 520 bridge. Yarrow Bay may be the most well known. There are a lot of points, ledges, channels and docks that provide habitat for a ton of fish. The bays produce well in mid-May, so the fish are likely a little deeper right now.

Gearing up: A good 7-foot medium or medium-heavy spinning rod is most important.

Due to the lake's water clarity, it's important to use smaller baits in natural colors. Three to 5 inches is plenty, and go with browns and greens. Crawdad colors are big — green pumpkin might be the best color on this lake.

Lizards work great here as do crawdad imitations. Success has come recently on a local hand-poured bait by Sniper Lures, the Sniper Snub in dark brown with copper flake or green pumpkin. Fish it on a drop-shot rig.

Crankbaits should start to produce over shallow humps and along docks in the coming weeks. Try first thing in the morning and later in the evening now. Look for a crankbait bite to start in early May.

AT a GLANCE

What: Lake Washington spring bass.

Where: Located right in the heart of Pugetropolis. There are numerous launches around the lake, including: Gene Coulon at the southeastern end of the lake; the I-90 launch at exit 8 off I-90; and the launch at Newport Marina off Coal Creek Parkway.

When: It's a year-around fishery, but best fishing is still ahead. Things should really heat up in the next few weeks. Look for the spawn in mid- to late May.

How: Plastics are tops. Lizard, worms and craws are all good. Throw them in natural brown and green colors.

Info: Auburn Sports & Marine (253-833-1440); Angler's Marine (253-548-2232); All Marine (360-923-9535).

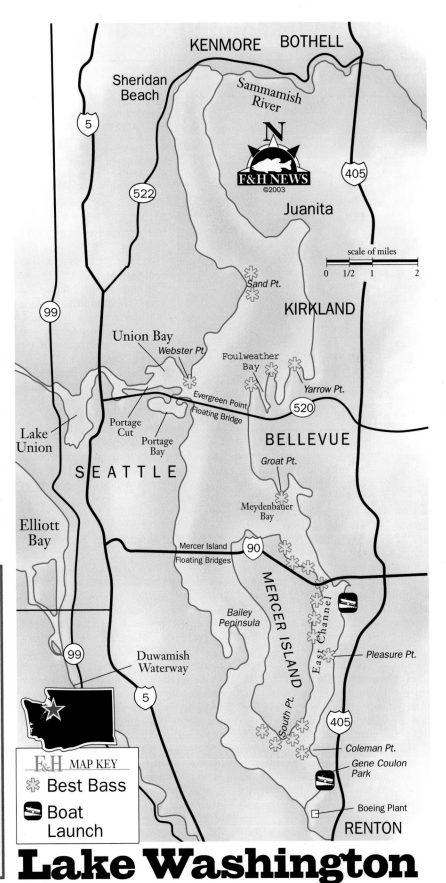

Lake Washington

Fish Lake Washington for bruiser bronzebacks

SEATTLE

by Marc Marcantiono

YOU'D THINK that with how good the fishery is and how many anglers surround the water — think summer sockeye — Lake Washington would be crowded with bassers, but it just isn't so. The author shows off a Lake Union smallie.

At last! For the past seven months, if you wanted to catch a trophy smallmouth bass, you had to fish deep. Those days are over! May is the magical month where big, hungry smallmouth invade the shallows in search of nourishment and spawning gravel. If you want to have your string stretched by an angry smallie more than 5 pounds, then you'd better call in sick to work this week and recuperate on Lake Washington. No other time produces more trophy-size bronzebacks for more anglers.

Big-city bassin': When you think of Seattle, you conjure images of kings jumping from the Sound or being tossed in Pike Place Market. Who would expect that, in the midst of Latte-Land, the water hides a near world-class bass fishery? Yes, Lake Washington is loaded with bruiser bronzebacks, and many of the hundreds of thousands of residents surrounding the lake have no idea.

Big-city bassin' is now at its best, and while the highways are congested with traffic, the water is wide open. The few boats that you do encounter in May are likely to have names like "Skeeter" instead of "Bayliner." Entering a bass tournament on Lake Washington this time of the year? If you don't have a limit of five bass that weigh more than 20 pounds, you might as well kiss your entry fee goodbye.

What could be better than having huge smallmouth bass waiting for you in shallow water *and* having the lake to yourself? Smallmouth inhabit every part of the lake, from the Cedar River to the Ballard Locks. You could be roping in 5-pound smallies within sight of the Space Needle — even a largemouth or two.

Lake Union clue in: Between I-5 and the Montlake bridge is Lake Union, an often overlooked area, even by those who ply Lake Washington waters regularly. The docks and small backwaters along the shoreline are inhabited by both smallmouth and largemouth. The entire shoreline along Gas Works Park holds many bass, particularly in the early part of the year. Occasionally these bass will disappear in late summer, if saltwater intrusion from the locks drives them away, but in the spring you can expect to hook into some really nice bass here.

Bodacious bronzebacks are normally difficult to fool with artificial lures, but consider that these fish have just stirred from a long slumber. It's been months since they've been chased by artificial lures, and they have a strong hunger that demands satisfaction. Their dark backs absorb the warming rays of sunlight, motivating them to move towards spawning grounds in shallow water. There's just enough time for a quick feeding spree before turning their attention to procreation. A Lucky Craft Slender Pointer, fished on a Lamiglas cranking stick, is a sure bet for enticing a trophy bronzeback in Lake Union.

Union Bay play: Further east along the ship canal is Union Bay, in the shadow of Husky Stadium. This area probably contains the largest population of largemouth bass, but it is also chock full of bronzebacks. The closer you get to Webster Point, the better the fishing will be for smallies. There are always trophy smallmouth visiting Webster Point, and a well-placed tube, drop-shot minnow or worm, is sure to get their attention. Crankbaits, like a crawdad-color Lucky Craft Flat CB deep or medium runner, can be dynamite right at the tip of the point. Also try this along the docks north of Webster Point.

Westside ride: The entire Lake Washington shoreline up to Sand Point has nice gravel that attracts bass both for feeding and spawning, making this a high-percentage area to fish. If you're looking for a launch, Magnuson Park Ramp is located here.

East-shore galore: On the east side from Webster Point, three bays are also favorite shallows for bruiser bronzebacks. Fairweather Bay, Cozy Cove and Yarrow Bay are high-percentage areas, particularly wherever you find rock or gravel near the shore. My favorite tactics here include slow-rolling white spinnerbaits and drop-swimming Basstrix Bait Fry with a 3/16-ounce QuickDrop drop-shot sinker.

Moving south along the east shoreline brings you to Groat Point, which is always an excellent spot to hook into a huge smallie, especially along the scattered rocks in 8 feet of water. This is also an excellent crankbait and jerkbait location.

If you continue south to Calkins Point, at the northeast end of Mercer Island, you'll find underwater boulders and smaller rocks which attract staging smallies, and make great ambush spots for getting that last meal before spawning. This is another of my favorite spots. You might even see me there this week in my sparkly new Skeeter ZX250 bassboat.

East Channel handle: The entire East Channel between Mercer Island and Bellevue is dynamite for big smallmouth, and is probably one of the best areas of the entire lake. Virtually every inch of shoreline on the mainland and on Mercer Island could produce a lunker at this time of year, so be sure to cover a lot of territory. Use a fast-paced reaction lure like a jerkbait. Just don't make the mistake of fishing it too fast. The best retrieve is one in which you frequently pause the lure. Nothing triggers a strike faster than to pause a jerkbait (or crankbait) in the face of the following bass, especially when the water is still cold.

Further south, you'll reach Pleasure Point and Coleman Point. As is typical in spring, main-lake points are prime staging areas that attract feeding bass before they move to the spawning beds. Both of these points are textbook locations — entice big smallies on crankbaits or on Yamamoto Twin Tail hula grubs that imitate the prolific crawdads of the region.

Launch: At the extreme southeast end, in Renton, is the best launch ramp on Lake Washington. It's located in Gene Coulon Park and is an improved ramp with eight lanes. There are also a large parking lot and facilities.

AT a GLANCE

What: Superb spring smallmouth fishing in the middle of a million people.

Where: Lake Washington, specifically Lake Union, Union Bay, Webster Point, Sand Point, Fairweather Bay, Cozy Cove, Yarrow Bay, Calkins Point, Groat Point, Pleasure Point, East Channel and Coleman Point.

Baits: Tubes, drop-shot minnows, plastic worms and grubs, jerkbaits, crawdad-colored deep- or medium-diving plugs, white spinnerbaits.

Contacts: Marc Marcantonio (LimitBy9@aol.com); Outdoor Emporium (206-624-6550); Auburn Sports & Marine (253-833-1440).

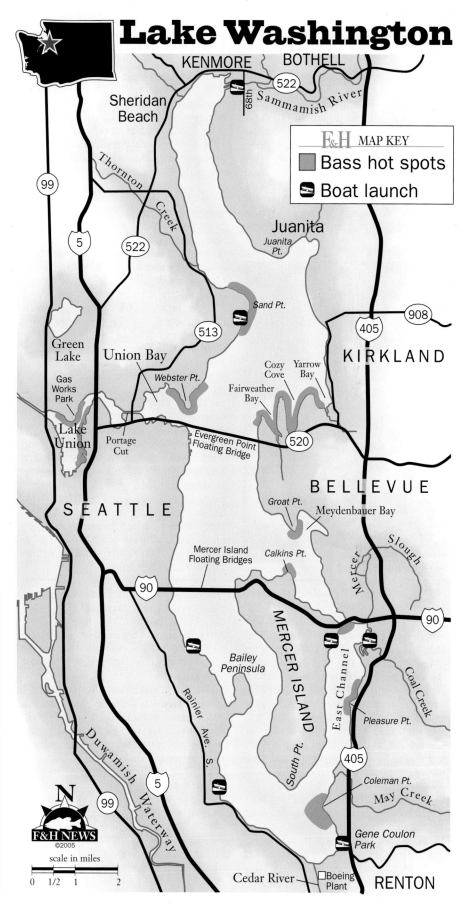

Lake Washington

F&H MAP KEY
Bass hot spots
Boat launch

Cold water surrendering Westside crappie

by Mike Schoby

You're a little cold. You're a lot wet. You're borderline miserable. There's nobody else on the lake, you haven't had a bite for a long time, and there's a good chance that you're going to get skunked. You ask yourself, "Why am I out here?" You're there because you have spring fever.

PAUL SCHOBY pulled this pretty crappie out of the cold water during a late winter trip to a favorite King County lakes.

You're tired of watching fat men with an accent dressed in t-shirts kissing bass on television. You're also there for a chance at the largest crappie of the year, maybe the largest you ever caught in your life, possibly even the largest you've ever seen. Can the fishing be slow? You bet! Slower than a conversation with your dentist. But you just keep telling yourself you're having a good time and stick with it.

COLD FISH, BIG FISH: Finally! There it is! The very lightest of bites. It's what an old fishing buddy of mine calls an "imagination" bite. Or was it really a bite? After a light set of the hook, a good solid struggle confirms that there really is life under the water before May. A

beautiful big crappie is eased toward the boat and suddenly it's a good day. Will you catch very many? Not likely. But the ones you get can be big enough to give you a thrill and make you proud!

Of course, crappie aren't the only thing you may catch. Fish are quite gregarious in their cold-water hideaways, with many species occupying the same spots. It's normal to also catch some very large perch, with their bellies so grossly extended with roe they look ready to explode. Sunfish are common. A few trout are no surprise. Occasionally bass or even whitefish will show up. On one memorable cold day, a friend and I caught seven different species of fish while anchored in one spot over deep structure.

IT AIN'T EASY: Early spring fishing for spinyrays is inherently difficult. Water temperatures are low, fish are lethargic and feed very little. I've caught fish after breaking kim ice for a 100 yards between the boat ramp and open water, but it wasn't very fast. Surprisingly, there are oodles of feed in the cold water. I've never been on an unfrozen lake when there wasn't a hatch of some kind coming off, with lots of empty pupae cases floating on the surface. With the exception of an occasional trout, surface feeding is not evident. But you know the depths are loaded with larvae and nymphs. Lots more than enough to satiate meager appetites.

Here are a few tips that can improve your chances in this cold-water game. First, do yourself a favor and pick a nice day. Flat calm windless days are best. Even a light breeze makes fishing unpleasant and the necessary slow deep presentation with light gear is almost impossible.

Fish deep: On the smaller lakes that I prefer, this usually means at or near the deepest spot in the lake. On larger waters like Washington or Sammamish, fishing at depths of 50 to 60 feet or more is common. A good depth finder is essential. Watch for anything unusual at or near the bottom and fish on it. Schooled fish resting close to the bottom don't always show up individually. They can look like clutter, structure or baitfish. If it really is structure, all the better. I get most fish on or very near the bottom. Scattered suspended fish often show on the depth finder, but I find them almost impossible

to catch. If you break the code on this problem, clue me in.

Fish slow: Warmwater fish can be very inactive and selective in cold water. They will watch and ignore a bait for a long time before taking it. I try to stay in position over a likely spot and work it thoroughly. If I get a bite or catch a fish, I often anchor both ends of the boat and fish straight down under it. Think of it as ice fishing without the ice.

Fish light: Summer-sized lures will sometimes take winter fish, but I have a lot more luck by downsizing my tackle. The weeds aren't prevalent yet, and most of the time the fishing is in deep water away from shoreline hazards. Light lines are adequate and are easier to use with small lures in deep water. This is a good place to use your ultralight rod with 2- to 4-pound test line. One-sixteenth-ounce jigs may work, but I often use $\frac{1}{64}$- or even $\frac{1}{100}$-ounce jigs. Tiny ice fishing lures and spoons are also good.

> **Spicing up your offering with a little raw meat helps a lot.**

Spicing up your offering with a little raw meat also helps a lot. A tiny piece of worm, mealworm, wax worm, maggot or a bit of shrimp is great. If these aren't available at the local bait shop, try a pet supply store. It's sometimes amazing what will grab these little items.

One winter day seven bass came up on a No. 12 hook and an almost invisible piece of worm. Go figure!

WHERE TO GO: Almost any lake that has other spinyray fish will also contain crappies. I like the smaller ones because they are easier to explore and are less exposed to the wind. A few good prospects are identified below. There are many others that are equally good.

Lake Sawyer: A popular King County lake northwest of Black Diamond, Sawyer has a great variety of freshwater fish including crappie. Try the deep water between the east shoreline and the large islands. Another good bet is in the large bay north of the public access off of Covington-Sawyer Road.

Spring Lake: This lake southeast of Renton has trout, perch, and bass in

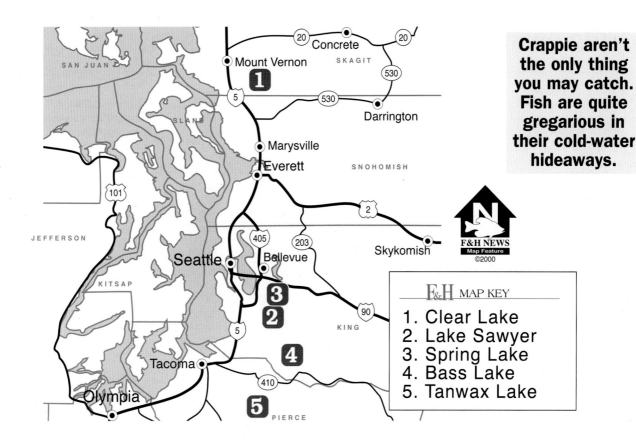

Crappie aren't the only thing you may catch. Fish are quite gregarious in their cold-water hideaways.

F&H MAP KEY
1. Clear Lake
2. Lake Sawyer
3. Spring Lake
4. Bass Lake
5. Tanwax Lake

addition to large crappie. A public boat ramp is available on the northeast corner of the lake, but no gasoline motors are allowed. The deeper water is in the center of the lake to the left of the ramp as you go out.

Bass Lake: A small lake north of Enumclaw, Bass has a shallow narrow access on the east side suitable only for small boats and cartoppers. It also contains perch, sunfish and bass as well as crappie. Look for deep water in the middle of the lake.

Clear Lake: This popular Skagit County lake south of Sedro Woolley has almost everything in it. The deepest area is straight out from the boat ramp toward the east.

Tanwax Lake: This lake near Eatonville has large crappie along with perch, bass and trout. The deepest area is in the center toward the east end just past the two main points.

Almost any lake that has other spinyray fish will also contain crappie. I like the smaller ones because they are easier to explore and are less exposed to the wind.

AT A GLANCE

What: Cold-water crappie in Western Washington.
Where: Almost any lake with spinyrays. Try lakes Sawyer, Bass and Spring in King County; Tanwax and Ohop in Pierce County; Clear and Big in Skagit County.
Equipment: Depth finder, light spinning gear, 2- to 4-pound test line, ⅟₁₆- to ⅟₁₀₀-ounce jigs, ice fishing lures, worms, mealworms, wax worms, maggots.
Bonus: Perch, trout, bass.
When: Through April.
Information: G. I. Joe's in Issaquah (425-961-2000); Priced Less Sporting Goods (888-347-4441); Auburn Sports & Marine (253-833-1440).

SLAB-SIDED CRAPPIE are the catch of record for cold-water anglers hitting select King, Pierce and Skagit county lakes through April. (*F&H News* photo by Mike Schoby)

Wile away the winter with Washington perch

SEATTLE

by Dusty Routh

You might not get all that excited about the idea of perch fishing. But you should know that one of the best perch lakes in the universe is located right here at home, in the form of dear old Lake Washington.

On a recent winter outing with local perch expert and guide Curtis Welch of Special Moments Guide Service (425-226-6327) and a few friends, we managed to scratch out 112 yellowbellies. We did it fishing banker's hours (9 a.m. to 3 p.m.), and had one of the most relaxing days on the water you could imagine.

School zones: You don't have to run far on Lake Washington to get into big schools of perch. Launch at either the Coal Creek launch (Bellevue side of the East Channel; officially known as the Mercer ramp) or at the Mercer Island launch over on the island side. Pay the ransom to launch or park ($7) or risk a ticket — even in winter, the black boots are out checking to make sure you've paid.

From either launch, run north to Groat Point, which is just above and to the northeast of the north end of Mercer Island. This is a long, pronounced point. The water drops from 20 feet close to shore out to 140 feet at the ends of the point. It's a wide point too, very easy to identify with your electronics. Zigzag up and down and across the point with your finder on bottom zoom.

When you've located a school of perch (also very easy to identify, as the schools are large), throw a marker over the side. Use your electric or kicker to stay with the school. You'll be tempted to anchor up, but Welch believes it's best to stay mobile and right over the school

CURT WELCH of Special Moments Guide Service is one perch-catching machine. However, you don't have to be a pro to stack 'em on Lake Washington.

as much as possible.

You'll know if you've lost the school, because the action will diminish or stop altogether. And you'll know when you've found them again, for the opposite reason.

Another hot spot is right in the middle of the East Channel area, from the I-90 bridge south to about parallel with Pleasure Point (which is the first major point south of the Coal Creek boat launch on the east side of the channel). You may see other boats in this area doing the same perch thing. On the day we were out, a half-dozen perch jerkin' boats were working schools in the East Channel. Depths here range from 40 to 80 feet.

It's so easy: This is kick-back, laid-back, gunny-sack fishing at its finest — not nearly as complex as steelheading, nor as elbow-busting as smallmouth fishing. There's no downriggers required like cutthroat trout fishing, and no intense mental focus like busting winter walleye.

Once you've located a school, you can either use white plastic curl-tail jigs smeared in Smelly Jelly, or strips of perch meat. To rig up, start with a light-action spinning or baitcasting rod. It really helps to spool up your light-action reel with something like Berkley Fireline (10-pound-test variety) so you can feel the light-biting winter perch. They are very, very light hitters in cold water, so you need that extra sensitivity.

Slide up a small egg sinker, then a glass bead, then a barrel swivel. Tie a short (8 inches or so) leader to the swivel, and add a No. 6 or No. 8 Gamakatsu hook.

The leader should be 8- to 10-pound mono. Gamakatsu makes pre-tied leaders (available at Auburn Sports and Marine) that Welch trims down to 8 inches. The short length helps prevent the leader from twisting around the mainline when you dump your rig down 45 to 55 feet to hit the bottom.

If you go the jig route, the best jigs are white curl-tail Kalin's, in the 1½-inch size. Smear liberally and frequently with mojo. You can also fillet a perch and cut the white meat into thin strips. Thread one of these on the hook like you would a nightcrawler.

Either cast your rig out from the boat and let it fall to the bottom, or just lower it over the side. You'll want to make sure you keep it on the bottom once it gets there, because that's where the fish are.

Lake Washington

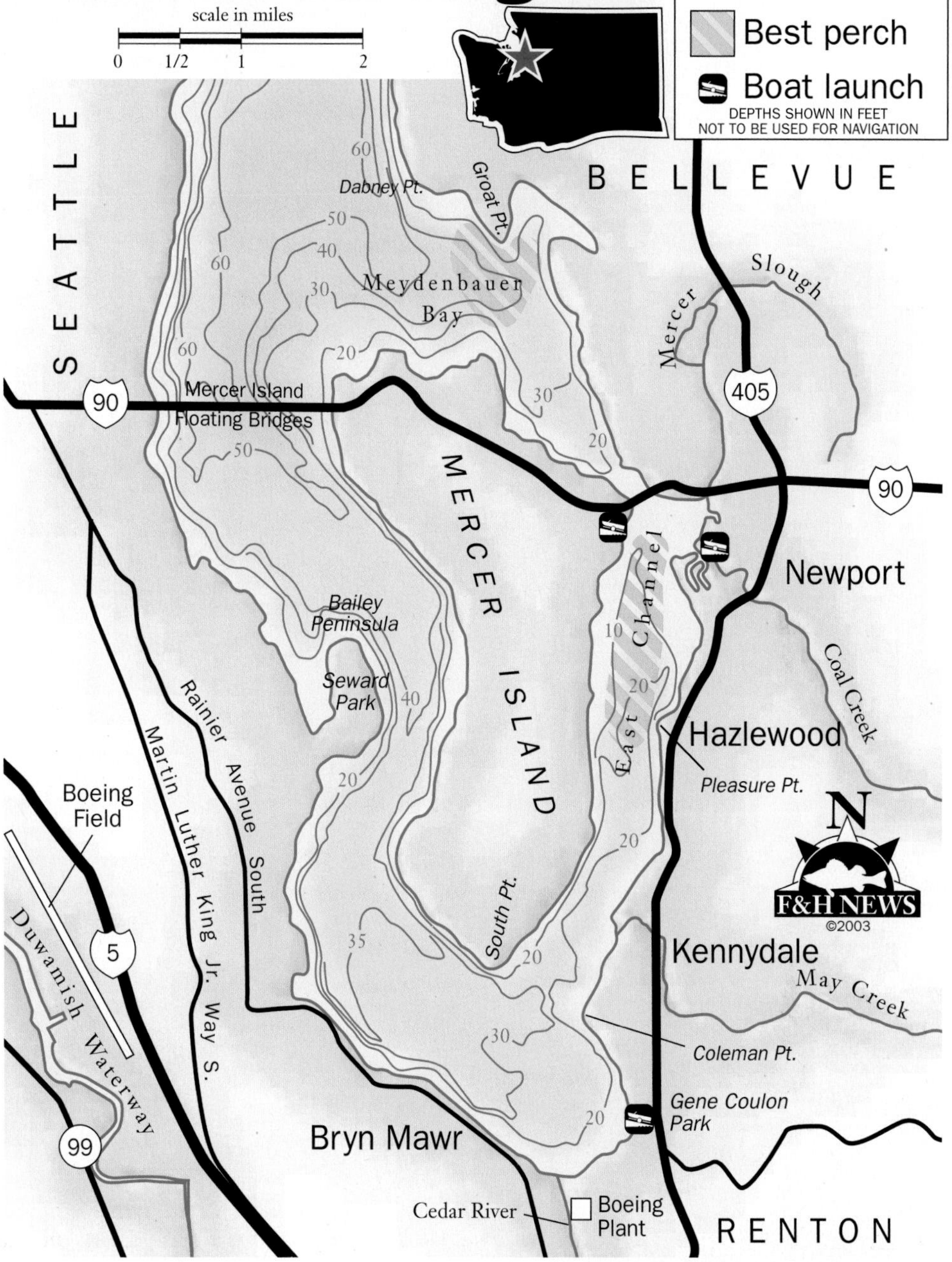

scale in miles
0   1/2   1   2

F&H MAP KEY
Best perch
Boat launch
DEPTHS SHOWN IN FEET
NOT TO BE USED FOR NAVIGATION

(map labels: SEATTLE, BELLEVUE, Dabney Pt., Groat Pt., Meydenbauer Bay, Mercer Slough, 405, 90, Mercer Island Floating Bridges, MERCER ISLAND, East Channel, Newport, Bailey Peninsula, Seward Park, Hazlewood, Pleasure Pt., Coal Creek, Boeing Field, 5, Rainier Avenue South, Martin Luther King Jr. Way S., Duwamish Waterway, 99, Kennydale, May Creek, Coleman Pt., South Pt., Gene Coulon Park, Bryn Mawr, Cedar River, Boeing Plant, RENTON, N F&H NEWS ©2003)

A slight, gentle jigging helps attract bites. When a perch takes it, you'll feel a super-light tap-tap-tap. After you've missed and caught 20 or so, you'll know exactly when to set the hook.

In deep winter water (we found all our perch around 45 feet deep), it's tough to catch and release these fish, as their swim bladders expand and protrude from their maws. We kept most of our fish, releasing those that did not have the swim bladder protruding. But the rest you'll have to toss in your bait bucket and take home to eat.

Seasons and depths: Perch are pretty easy to dial in. In the winter, look for these little devils to be in the 45- to 90-foot range. In spring, they start moving up, 35 to 45 feet. In summer, you'll find perch anywhere along weedlines from 5 to 20 feet. And in fall, 20 to 45 feet is just about right.

Great treat for kids: If you've got youngsters you want to treat to a day of non-stop fishing action, perch are the way to go. Once you're in a school you'll know it, because they eat anything you put on the bottom and you can keep the kids entertained all afternoon. Be careful of youngsters handling perch, however, since perch have very sharp scales and fins. A fish glove is definitely recommended if kids are going to be handling fish. Otherwise, you could do worse than to spend your day baiting hooks and dehooking fish.

Time to feast: Most anglers who eat perch make the argument that these fish are just as tasty as walleye (and that's tasty), only smaller. Perch can be prepared for the table in just about any old way that you prefer. They can be breaded and pan-fried or deep-fried. They can be baked. They can be sautéed, or used in any fish soup recipe calling for white meat. And they are delicious in the smoker, either smoked as fillets or deheaded and gutted. Welch likes to soak his perch in a beer batter and deep fry them, or soak them in a brine overnight and toss into the smoker.

If you've got an electric knife (or a lot of time), you can fillet perch for some excellent, boneless eating. Or you can dehead and gut 'em and cook them like that. You don't necessarily need to scale them, either. The scales are packed tight. Simply remove the skin after cooking.

AT a GLANCE

What: Great winter fishing for Lake Washington perch.

How: Fish right on the bottom in 45 to 90 feet of water with 1½-inch white curl-tail Kalin grubs smeared with scent or strips of perch meat.

Where: From Groat Point, just north of Mercer Island, down the entire length of the East Channel (between Bellevue and Mercer Island).

Info: Curt Welch, Special Moments Guide Service (425-226-6327).

Olympic Peninsula & Coastal Waters
SALMON

Grays Harbor opener brings you a shot at a pig

by Joel Shangle

BAY OF PIGS: Fattie Chinook like this beefy slab hooked by Rich Mercado will bottle up in Grays Harbor, waiting for rains to pull them into the Humptulips, Wynoochee and Satsop rivers.

where, and in the case of the Satsop, 'Nooch and Hump, that "somewhere" is Grays Harbor.

"Grays Harbor is definitely a 'big-fish' fishery," says Rich Mercado at Rich's Northwest Guide Service (253-535-0403), who has fished the harbor on his own time for the past seven years. "It feeds those big kings that run into the Satsop, 'Nooch and Hump. They all have to come through Grays Harbor to get to those rivers."

The Marine Area 2.2 king fishery was a no-go last year because of low run size, but preseason projections for the 2000 fishery are good, with a Sept. 1 opener and an Oct. 31 closure in effect.

TRANSITION SPOT: Think of Grays Harbor as the blood vessel that leads to some of the best big-king river veins in the Pacific Northwest — as the fall spawning instinct kicks into high gear for kings bound for the Satsop, 'Nooch and Hump, they pour into Grays Harbor and wait for weather and water conditions that jump-start their trips up their respective natal streams. The bay is like the Renton S-curves on a Friday at 4 p.m., but with big, bright Chinook milling around instead of a plodding line of SUVs and minivans.

It's high-drive time.

"Mid-September to about mid-October is the time that I'll be there," says *F&H News* saltwater columnist John Keizer at Puget Sound Salmon Charters (253-565-6598). "To me, that's always been the period when the bigger kings start showing up. You can catch fish right from the opener, but some of the best fishing I've ever seen there is in the first week of October."

HOW BIG IS BIG?: Both Keizer and Mercado have boated 42-pound Grays Harbor pigs — the 40-pound marker is realistically the top end of anything that'll be pulled out of the shallow water here this season, but most of your catch will range anywhere from 20 to 30 pounds.

"There have been a few 50-pounders caught in there in the past," says Keizer. "A 40 is a real big fish now, but 30-pounders are fairly common."

WHERE TO FISH IT: Nine out of 10 boats that fish Grays Harbor will concentrate on the trough area straight out of the mouth of Johns River, in front of Ocean Spray company land and the Johns River Wildlife Area on the south side of the bay. The bay is routinely sandy and shallow, so any kind of breakup on the bottom (ledges, dropoffs, depressions, etc.) you can find will be worth a look.

AT A GLANCE

What: Grays Harbor kings.

When: Season opened Sept. 1, closes Oct. 31. Best fishing is traditionally from mid-September to mid-October. The first week of October is often lights out for big fish.

Why: Big kings destined for the Humptulips, Satsop, Wynoochee rivers all have to come through Grays Harbor to get to their natal rivers. They'll stack up in the bay until weather and water conditions trigger their move upriver. Fish will routinely range from 20 to 30 pounds, but you'll see occasional 40-plus-pound hogs come out.

Limit: No more than two adult fish, release wild coho.

Hot spot: Straight off the mouth of Johns River, on the south side of the bay. The majority of the fishing pressure concentrates in this area.

Techniques: No downriggers needed in this shallow-water (15 to 30 feet) fishery. A dropper with 4 to 8 ounces of lead and big cut-plug herring is all you'll need. Troll with the current to cover more ground, and look for breakups in the shallow, sandy bottom. Fish the contour of any ledges that you can find in the bay.

Regulations: Single-point barbless hooks required. Charter licenses required.

Launch: Easy launch at Coast Guard ramp in Westport, which is a 5-mile run to the fishery. Boats 18 feet and under can launch in Johns River.

Information: Puget Sound Salmon Charters (253-565-6598); Rich's Northwest Guide Service (253-535-0403); Washington Department of Fish & Wildlife Region 6 office (360-249-4628).

The Humptulips River is a big-fish river. The Satsop River is a big-fish river. The Wynoochee River is a big-fish river. Any one of those three drainages is a good bet to boot out a 30-pound Chinook when the fall runs start coming in.

All those beefy kings have to transition from the salt to the river some-

"You can basically fish all over out there, but wherever you go, you need to fish structure," says Mercado. "There are a few spots in there that are a little better than others, but I spend most of my time fishing the trough in front of Johns River."

WHEN TO FISH IT: Tides play a tremendously important role in the Grays Harbor fishery. Your best action will come if you fish it on the morning tide, about an hour before the change and an hour into the new tide, but any tide change leading up to a low can be productive. Once the tide is out, you're better up packing it up for the day.

"It's a tidal fishery all the way," says Mercado. "You can be out there all day and maybe scratch up a fish, but once the tide change comes into play you get into some really good fishing. There's always a morning bite. If you

"Mid-September to about mid-October is the time that I'll be there. To me, that's always been the period when the bigger kings start showing up."
— F&H News saltwater columnist John Keizer

hit it in the morning, at the right tide, you'll be in the fish."

HOW TO FISH IT: "Grays Harbor is really similar to Willapa," says Keizer. "They're almost identical fisheries."

That means a basic setup that requires no downriggers — rig up a double swivel with 4 to 8 ounces of dropper lead and a cut-plug herring and troll fast enough to get a good roll on the bait.

"A deep spot in that fishery is maybe 30 feet," says Keizer. "Most of it is 10 to 15 feet deep. It's pretty simple fishing in shallow water."

Keep your bait close to the boat and pretend you're fishing Buoy 10.

"I fish right behind the boat," says Mercado. "There are too many boats in there. If you put your bait out way behind your boat, somebody's always going to be running over it."

Troll with the current when you can to cover more ground.

BIG BAIT, BIG FISH: Keizer is a firm believer that bigger bait catches bigger fish in this fishery. "The bigger herring you can find, the better," he suggests. "I'll bring some of the black label herring, the purple stuff you fish for halibut. I want my bait to be pretty sizable here."

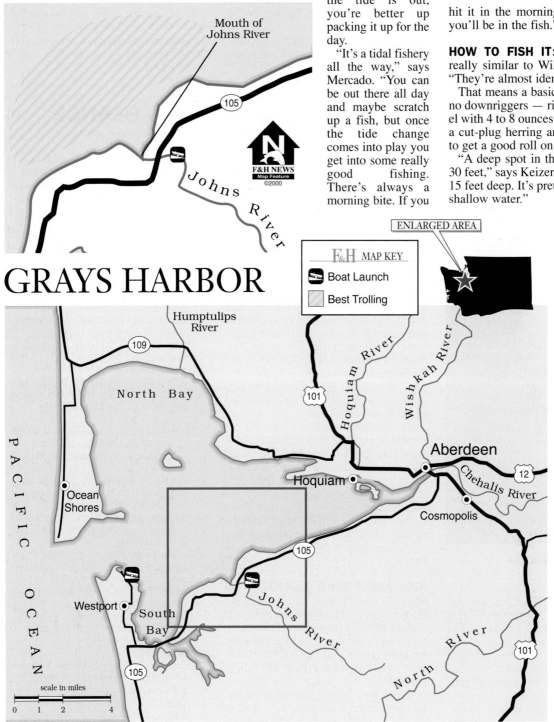

Mouth of Johns River

Johns River

105

F&H NEWS
Map Feature
©2000

GRAYS HARBOR

ENLARGED AREA

F&H MAP KEY
Boat Launch
Best Trolling

Humptulips River

109

North Bay

Hoquiam River

Wishkah River

101

PACIFIC OCEAN

Ocean Shores

Aberdeen

12

Chehalis River

Hoquiam

Cosmopolis

105

Westport

South Bay

Johns River

North River

101

105

scale in miles
0   1   2   4

Water levels key to Humptulips salmon

COPALIS CROSSING

by Dusty Routh

It may sound obvious, but it's a truism nonetheless: The key to hitting combinations of kings and silvers coming in from the Pacific and into Grays Harbor — and then running into the myriad of area tributaries like the Humptulips, Chehalis, Satsop, Wynoochee and Johns — all depends on water levels. And water levels, of course, depend on how much rain the area receives.

September was one of the wettest in recent memory, and it moved up the timetable for a lot of fish. To them, when they got here in early- to mid-September, it must have seemed more like mid-October, and they came right in. That meant that fishing in Grays Harbor was hot when it opened on Sept. 16, and remained solid through the end of the month. How the fishing will be in October is a big question mark, but the betting money says it will die off or at least slow down significantly in the bay as these fish squirt up their rivers fairly quickly.

That leaves anglers with the option of hitting the rivers in order to find the hottest fishing. One of the best of these for drift boaters is the amazing Humptulips.

Getting to know the Hump: The

FISH EGGS or plugs for Humptulips kings. Steve Russell caught his backbouncing last Halloween. Friend Murray Smith of Olympia sent the pic.

Humptulips is shaped from waters coming out of the Olympic National Forest in the form of the West and East forks of the river. They come together about 5 miles upstream from the small town of Humptulips. The river drains about 130 square miles of land; water levels are greatly influenced by rainfall (as opposed to glacial or snow runoff), and can fluctuate wildly. For example, between the end of August and the end of September, the river ran as low as just under 200 cfs, and as high as 4,000, depending on how much rain was hitting. In some dry summers, the Hump can be a trickle. But that wasn't the case this year.

"It's really going to depend on what the level is," says guide Rich Mercado of Rich's Northwest Guide Service (253-376-8004), who fishes the Humptulips solidly every year, where and how you should fish depends on what that water's doing to the river. "Everything on the Humptulips fluctuates. If the water is high, they'll be up high in the river. They'll go right up. If it's been high for a week or so, they'll

push their way in from the lower river all the way up to the hatchery. So that's where you have to be."

On the other hand, if we hit a dry spell between now and when the river opens (Oct. 16), look for better fishing and more fish to be centered at or near the lower portion of the river closer to the confluence with Grays Harbor.

"If the water gets low and stays low," Mercado says, "you can count on those fish being down in the lower river. I'll fish it then from the Rainier Bar, from there on down."

It's kind of a hit-or-miss deal, says Mercado, depending on what the weather does before the opener. "You just won't know where the fish are going to be until the week before it opens up," he says. "Especially, you want to watch the weather the two days before it opens."

How-to: The Humptulips will have a mix of kings and silvers in it through fall. Some of the silvers, particularly, can get ridiculously kegged up in the holes, and anglers can sometimes enjoy

AT a GLANCE

What: Good to great fishing for kings and silvers in the Humptulips River.

When: Opens Oct. 16. Usually stays fishable to the end of the month, but depending on rainfall levels.

How: Toss Dick Nite spoons on three-way rigs and float eggs under bobbers for the silvers. Pull sardine-wrapped Kwikfish and float eggs/bobber for kings.

Where: If there's a lot of water, fish up high, closer to the hatchery. Of water levels are low, fish the lower river closer to Grays Harbor.

Who: Rich Mercado, Rich's Northwest Guide Service (253-376-8004)

near one-after-the-other catching.

A three-way rig for the silvers — a dropper weight and a leader leading off to a Dick Nite spoon — is absolutely a killer presentation that will capture the attention of any nearby silvers. Fishing with Mercado a couple of seasons ago, a buddy and me hooked and released more than 30 silvers out of one deep hole using this rig. Position yourself on the shallow side of the river and cast into the hole, letting the pencil weight reach bottom, fluttering the spoon down. If there are fish in the hole, the spoon won't make it to the bottom.

For the kings, Mercado likes to pull sardine-wrapped Kwikfish if there's enough water in the river to allow him to adequately pull plugs. FlatFish in similar sizes also work. Another way to work this river for its kings is to back-bounce eggs, or even bobber fish with eggs.

In terms of the bookends of the season, Mercado says he'll fish it from the opener until the rainfall makes it unfishable later in the season.

"I'm there from the opener to when it can't be fished anymore," he says. "Once you fish this river and see how good it is, you come back year after year. I'll fish it at least until the end of the month, or until it blows out. If the water stays good, I'll just keep fishing it. But it'll usually blow out by the end of the month."

Where-to: The Humptulips can be fished by driftboat or on foot. A sled is not advisable. "The locals will have a fit," says Mercado. "This is a drift boat fishery."

You can launch at the Highway 101 bridge near the hatchery and float down to the ramp near the Powerline hole, or do the Powerline/Weyerhaeuser ramp float, or the Weyerhaeuser to the Rayonier launch. There are lots of footpaths up and down the river from the launches for wading.

Expect company. This can be a popular wading fishery for a lot of the locals.

Hump regs: From Oct. 16 to Nov. 30, from the mouth to the Highway 101 Bridge, daily limit is six fish, of which no more than two adults may be retained, and one may be an adult king. Release wild adult silvers. From Dec. 1 to Jan. 31, release kings too.

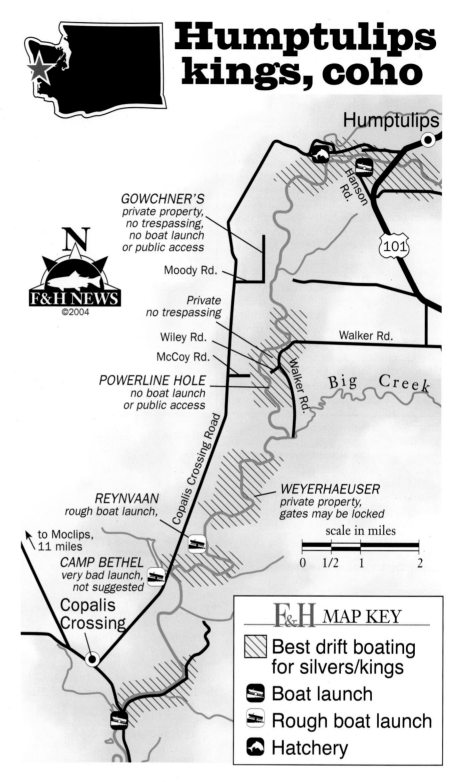

Humptulips kings, coho

F&H NEWS
©2004

Humptulips

Hanson Rd.

101

GOWCHNER'S
private property,
no trespassing,
no boat launch
or public access

Moody Rd.

Private
no trespassing

Walker Rd.

Wiley Rd.

McCoy Rd.

POWERLINE HOLE
no boat launch
or public access

Walker Rd.

Big Creek

Copalis Crossing Road

WEYERHAEUSER
private property,
gates may be locked

scale in miles

REYNVAAN
rough boat launch,

to Moclips,
11 miles

CAMP BETHEL
very bad launch,
not suggested

Copalis
Crossing

0   1/2   1   2

F&H MAP KEY

- Best drift boating for silvers/kings
- Boat launch
- Rough boat launch
- Hatchery

Fishing the bay: Even though the bite may not be as hot later in the fall as it was earlier, Grays Harbor itself can still be a good place to get into big kings. Fish this water just like you would at Buoy 10, using stout rods, divers and Fish-Flashes, and blue- or green-label herring on 5/0 hooks with 40-pound leaders. The harbor is open until Nov. 30. Daily limit is six fish, minimum of 12 inches, only two adults may be retained, and only one may be a king.

Lightly fished La Push a productive salmon center

LA PUSH

by Dusty Routh

Most attention given to saltwater salmon off the Washington coast tends to go to Westport and Neah Bay. But sandwiched in between these two is the tiny burg of La Push, located at the mouth of the Quillayute River.

Not nearly as well known, and not nearly as crowded, in recent years La Push has nonetheless very quietly become one of the best places in the Lower 48 to fish for salmon, lings, halibut and assorted bottomfish. Still, not many anglers fish here. If you haven't given it a try, you might want to put it on your list this summer, particularly given how big some of the salmon are that hit the docks in July and August.

No pressure — why?

Because of its remote location, lack of facilities in past years and the contentious push and pull between tribal fishing interests and recreational fishers, La Push nearly fell off the salmon fishing charts over the past couple of decades. The fact that all the amenities and the marina are tribally owned may have turned off some recreational anglers as well.

As the saying goes, however, that was then and this is now. Those past days are behind La Push, and fishing here can now be considered a real treat. There's a reliable marina, fair to good facilities and at least two charter operators. Best of all, the fishing can be ferocious, the setting is gorgeous and you won't find the crowds like at Westport, Ilwaco or even Neah Bay. Charter rates are also very reasonable.

One of those charter operators is Randy Lato, of All-Ways Fishing Charters (360-374-2052), who takes anglers out aboard *The Shelbie Tessa*, a 27-foot Olympic. Another is Jim Richeson, with Top Notch Ocean Charters (888-501-5887). Richeson's operation also offers cabins for rent, and Richeson guides on the local rivers as well.

Where and how: As season opened at the end of June and progressing into July, most of the good action is centered around that area known as Umatilla Reef, roughly an 18-mile run north of La Push and 18 miles southwest of Cape Flattery (or 6 miles

BIG KINGS and relatively light pressure — what are you waiting for? Marine Area 3 and 4's season is under way, and approaching the peak time for big fish lurking along the coast. Rick Palumbo hooked this 43-pounder out of La Push two seasons back.

southwest of Cape Alava). Trolling is the best method early in the season when the fish are still somewhat scattered. As the season moves forward into later summer, however, mooching can be fantastic and a lot more fun.

Also, as the season progresses, the fish move closer in to shore. That's when the "Rockpile" turns on, which is a very short run from the protected waters of La Push. The Rockpile is rough 7 miles offshore.

Fish deep for big kings early in the season, Richeson says, from 100 to 250 feet down. Focus on finding big concentrations of bait balls. The salmon won't be far away.

As July inches closer to August, the big kings (and hordes of silvers) will move up in the water column, roughly to within the top 50 feet. This is when you can have an absolute heyday mooching herring.

Last year, Richeson reports several kings were caught by his clients in the 30-, 40- and over-50-pound range, and they had lots and lots of days when 30 to 40 fish an outing was common. Unlike the bigger (and more crowded) charter boats to the south, Richeson concentrates on fishing smaller groups (six anglers or less), and he allows catch-and-release angling.

Salmon regs: La Push is in Marina Area 3, and offers early and late salmon seasons. First season runs June 27-Sept. 19. Wild coho must be released. Daily limit is two fish, only one being a Chinook. Minimum size is 26 inches for kings, 16 inches for silvers.

Late season runs Sept. 25-Oct. 10, and might very well be worth checking out for getting into bigger silvers. The late-season area is restricted to an area roughly 3 miles offshore.

Umatilla Reef is in Area 4; season also runs June 27-Sept. 19. Same size and bag limits as Area 3.

Caution, big water: While the fishing can be terrific in this area, the conditions don't always cooperate. La Push was the scene of a very tragic accident three seasons ago when a grandfather and his grandsons capsized and drowned while heading out for a day of fishing. If you don't know this water, go with a charter to learn it. If you're taking your own boat, sea trial your vessel and make certain you have all the necessary safety equipment, VHF marine radio, GPS and that the boat is in sound mechanical condition. Heavy fogs are notorious here in the late summer, so avoid going out when a nasty fog has come in.

Seasickness is also a strong possibility in the open ocean, especially on windy days. The best advice: Avoid drinking the night before (you can do that afterwards), get plenty of sleep, eat what you would normally eat for breakfast and take a non-drowsy Dramamine an hour before heading out.

La Push Marina: The only marina in town is the La Push Marina

(360-374-5392). The boat ramps are good on all tides except low-low tides. They do offer full fuel service, and moorage on a first-come/first-service basis. Don't expect much in the way of info and advice like you might at Olson's in Sekiu or Zittle's on Puget Sound.

Lodging, mooring, etc.: La Push Ocean Park Resort is the way to go if you're planning to stay for a few days or if you need to stay overnight to catch an early charter the next morning (360-374-5267). They offer motel

rooms, one-, two- and three-bedroom cabins on the water, and pets are allowed in special units. If you're RVing, try Lonesome Creek R.V. Park and Grocery Store (360-374-4333). They also offer tent sites. The grocery store opens at 6 a.m.

If you need to catch an early breakfast before heading out on a 5 a.m. charter, you might be in trouble. The closest restaurant is the River's Edge (360-374-5777). They're open at 7 a.m. However, they do make box lunches to go, so you can order and pick up the night before.

AT a GLANCE

What: LaPush (Marine Area 3) and Umatilla Reef (Area 4) Chinook fishing.

Why: Outstanding ocean fishing for kings and silvers in July and August.

Where: Umatilla Reef, roughly 18 miles outside of La Push, turns on first. "The Rockpile," 7 miles from La Push, turns on later.

How: Troll deep early in the season, 100 to 250 feet down for the biggest kings. Later on, mooch in the top 50 feet of water for a mix of kings and silvers.

When: The season's open now and runs to Sept. 19, but could close if subquotas are caught earlier.

Who to call: Randy Lato, All-Ways Fishing Charters (360-374-2052); Jim Richeson, Top Notch Ocean Charters (888-501-5887).

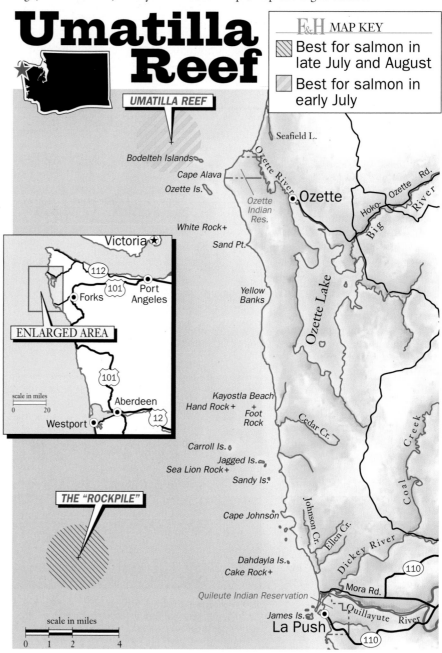

Umatilla Reef

F&H MAP KEY

Best for salmon in late July and August

Best for salmon in early July

Switch channels for *big* Willapa Bay kings

by Joel Shangle

If you're not reading this in the passenger's seat of a truck-and-trailer rig heading across Highway 12 or State Route 6 toward Raymond, then you're missing out on some of the best big fish potential in the Pacific Northwest. As a matter of fact, about the time you plunked down your $3.79 for this magazine and strolled out of your local 7-Eleven, somebody else was pulling a 30-pound Chinook out of Willapa Bay.

Here are two things you need to know right now: 1. Willapa Bay is still one of the best big fish fisheries in the state; 2. The time to fish for those fattie kings is *right now*.

AT A GLANCE

What: Willapa Bay salmon.
Species: Kings and coho. Kings will average around 20 pounds, but a few 40-plus-pound hogs will show up during the season.
When: Season started Aug. 16. Traditional peak is Labor Day. Good king fishing can extend well into September.
Where: Inside Willapa Bay, from Washaway Beach to the mouth of the Willapa River. Primary fishing area is in the main channel and at the intersection of the channels running out of the Willapa and North rivers.
Technique: Six-ounce mooching sinkers and cut-plug herring. No downriggers needed. Because it's protected, this is a viable small craft fishery.
Launch: Tokeland Marina (at Toke Point off Highway 105) can handle any trailerable boat ($5 fee). The South Bend ramp is OK for small boats. The launch in Raymond is OK for larger craft on high tide.
Lodging: Contact Beth Oman at the Chamber of Commerce (360-875-5900) for a detailed list of hotel, B&B and camping options available.
Bait & Tackle: Available at Dennis Co. (360-942-2427) in Raymond and Bud's Lumber (360-875-5900) in South Bend
Information: Tokeland Marina (360-267-2888); Port of Willapa (360-942-3422); WDFW Montesano office (360-249-4628).

"Labor Day is considered the traditional peak of this fishery, plus or minus a couple of weeks," says David Lewis, a Willapa local who spends as much time on this fishery as anybody in the state. "You have silvers coming in behind early kings. As the fall progresses, the silver percentage climbs and the king percentage drops, but last year my last king was on Sept. 15."

There are no dates set in stone to define the timing of the Willapa king fishery — it all depends on Mother Nature — but the first couple weeks of September should be highlighted in bright red on your calendar. And the more it rains, the smaller your window of opportunity becomes.

"It all has to do with rain," says Lewis. "If the flow out of the Willapa River is slow, the fish will just stay down in the bay and not go anywhere. If it starts to rain, they'll start just *booking* up that river, especially if it's been really dry for a few weeks. The best case is if it rains for a couple of days and then stops for a couple of days. Then we'll have a nice, steady flow of fish up into the river."

SIZE MATTERS: Tons of boats have converged on the Willapa king fishery since its Aug. 16 opener for exactly one reason: big fish potential. This is one of the few spots in the state where you can realistically expect an occasional 40-pound king to come out of the water.

"This place is known for having big kings," says Lewis. "I wouldn't claim that *all* the kings are going to be big — the biggest on my boat last year was 26 pounds — and I wouldn't guarantee anybody that they're going to catch a 40-pounder. But they're certainly in there. The biggest fish caught last year was 56 pounds."

Read that again. Fifty-six. While the average Willapa king will hover around 20 pounds, the prospect of a 40-plus-pound behemoth should be reason

KING ME: The Willapa Bay king rush will tail off in the middle of September, but until then, this fishery is one of your best choices for a shot at 20-pound kings like this beauty. Fish in the 40-pound range are available at Willapa for anglers fishing the main channel in the bay.

enough for you to fish here this month.

TIDAL INFLUENCE: How important are tides in this fishery? Most Willapa anglers will tell you that fishing on the incoming tide is the way to go, but, just like any fishery, you can find action at virtually any stage of the tide.

"I've caught fish at all times during the day, but on the incoming tide, you're bringing saltwater in, and they're going to come with it," says Lewis. "When the tide is out, it pushes all the fish into a pretty limited space in the channels, so it's pretty easy to figure out where they are."

CHANNEL YOUR ENERGY: For years, Washaway Beach was *the* place to fish Willapa, but erosion of the surrounding shoreline has altered the nature of that fishery in recent years. Angler effort has now shifted deeper into the bay, and now the main channel that runs through the bay from the Willapa River is *the* place to target fish.

"The sport fishery has changed," says Washington Department of Fish & Wildlife biologist Lorna Wargo. "The erosion at Washaway has changed the lay of the land. We're seeing a shift in effort into the bay, eastward into the vicinity of where the Willapa River channel meets the North River channel. The catch rates have been better there than anywhere else in recent years."

The bay itself is uniformly shallow, especially on low tide when the mud flats become clearly visible, but the main channel is dredged and clearly marked — it runs along Washaway Beach, adjacent to Tokeland and then diagonally across the bay until it meets another channel along the south side of the bay.

"The bulk of the channel is around 38 feet, but there are some holes off of shelves that drop off deeper than that," says Lewis. "You kind of have to think of it along the lines of a river — there are edges to the channels, and I tend to think that the fish will do the exact same thing in there that they would in a river. They'll move along the ledges and into the holes."

TECHNIQUE: Tie on a 6-ounce mooching sinker, a cutplug herring and motor mooch along the channel. Simple as that.

"I suppose you can tie on flashers and spoons and other stuff, but I like just a banana sinker and a cutplug," says Lewis. "Bring frozen bait — green or blue label."

RUN SIZES: Forecasts called for 23,000 Chinook, 25,000 coho and 70,000 chums to pass through Willapa Bay this season.

"That's not a good preseason forecast," says Wargo. "I'd classify it as poor, or at least on the low end of average. It's definitely not a strong run."

That said, the 23,000-king forecast is significantly better than the 15,000 forecast for last season, and it *could* turn out to be a lowball figure.

"What we're finding out this year is that the forecasts may be on the conservative side because, apparently, ocean conditions have turned around a little bit," says Wargo. "There are no hard numbers yet, other than the success of the ocean fishery."

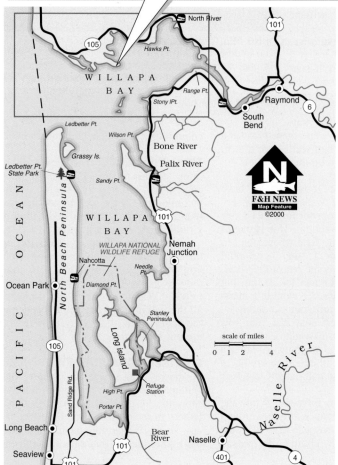

WILLAPA BAY

F&H MAP KEY

- Follow Channel
- Motor Mooch

N
F&H NEWS
Map Feature
©2000

scale of miles
0 1 2   4

Olympic Peninsula & Coastal Waters
STEELHEAD

Olympic alternatives to N. Sound steelie closures

by Joel Shangle

Come March 1, thousands of steelhead anglers used to fishing northern Puget Sound rivers are going to be looking for places to wet a line. With the Washington Department of Fish & Wildlife's recent announcement of system-wide closures throughout the North End's favorite wild steelhead streams, it's time to turn your eyes to different alternatives. Say goodbye to the Skykomish, Snoqualmie, Sauk, Stillaguamish, Snohomish and Skagit (to name a few), and say hello to some of the hundreds of other metalhead rivers across the Westside.

Think of it as an opportunity to explore. Think of it as a chance to break new ground. Think of it as a way to ease your pain.

Over the next three issues, we'll map out some choices that we think will help dull the pain of losing the North End's wild steelhead season. We'll explore the map from British Columbia to the Columbia River in search of the oppor-

AT A GLANCE

What: Olympic Peninsula wild steelhead.

Where: Sol Duc, Bogachiel, Hoh, Clearwater rivers.

When: Wild fish in now, building to a March peak and holding into April.

Why: Where else are you North End anglers gonna go? Especially to catch big wild fish.

Timing: The Hoh, Bogie, Sol Duc, Queets and Clearwater see their biggest numbers in March, building from about mid-February on. The Calawah (see Dec. 7-Jan. 4 issue for more) comes on in late January and February.

Information: Mike Price (360-374-5873); Jeff Woodward, River Inn (360-374-6526); Bob Kratzer, Angler's Guide Service (800-577-8781); Dean Swearin, Venture Northwest Guide Service (360-374-5247); Don Kinsey, Don Kinsey Guide Service (253-631-6739); Bob Ball, Piscatorial Pursuits (360-374-2091); Brad Shride, Onco Sportfishing (877-483-0047); Mike Schmitz (360-374-2602); Olympic Sporting Goods (360-374-6330)

tunities that best suit you. Time to log some hours of road time, and even more hours of learning new fisheries.

Time to go on the road for a touch of wildness.

OLYMPIC PENINSULA: Peninsula businesses are looking at the upcoming wild fish season as a boon. Local anglers, however, are more than a little leery of the effect that thousands of extra hours of angling pressure will have on their steelhead rivers this spring.

"Our wild runs are generally in good shape, but I'm afraid of what's going to happen to them when we get all those people over here, hammering on these rivers day after day," says guide Mike Price (360-374-5873).

It's a valid concern — if you choose the Peninsula this spring, you'll be choosing the closest, easiest alternative . . . and the one with the most intense pressure. Still, it's impossible to overlook the draw of fish that have made the Peninsula synonymous with huge steelhead. Numbers will continue to build in rivers like the Bogachiel, Hoh, Sol Duc, Clearwater, Calawah and Quillayute, peaking about the time the North End gets shut down.

"Wild fish are in," says guide Jeff Woodward (360-374-6526). "From mid-January on, we'll see increasing numbers of wild fish, with a big push in mid February. It'll last until early April."

BOGACHIEL RIVER: Expect the lower Bogachiel, from the Hatchery down to Lyendecker Park, to absorb the majority of the Peninsula's dispersed North End pressure. You may have to wait in line, but the following holes/slots are worth fishing on this stretch:

• Tall Timbers: Roughly a quarter mile run below the hatchery, defined by a

choppy top end and a nice, medium-speed section of water that runs 5 to 7 feet.

• Forks Hole: The confluence of the Calawah and Bogachiel. Boily at the top, running 4 to 6 feet, and then pushing over a fine gravel bottom into some nice water in the tailout.

• Ice Box: A big, slow slot where the

WILD PENINSULA STEELHEAD runs will likely draw more than a few Puget Sound anglers looking for opportunities in the wake of closures there. Jerry Wright of Port Angeles holds a nickel-bright Olympic river fish.

top end and tailout are your best bets. The middle section of Ice Box is deep — 10 to 15 feet. What you're looking to do here is go into the riffle on the right (south) side, on the opposite side of the river from the big boulder breakup, and throw to the far side.

• Goodman Mainline: A long, medium-speed run, uniformly 4 to 6 feet deep from top to bottom. Good tailout fishing.

• Wilson Access: More of a salmon hole, near the Wilson Access ramp, but good steelhead fishing at the top.

The section of river above the hatchery, from Highway 101 down, is also prime wild fish water.

"There are some really nice riffles, some nice, big chutes and slots that are excellent drifts," says Price.

SOL DUC RIVER: Most pressure and earliest fish will come from the hatchery down.

"There's some good water in that section," says Woodward. "Some of it's a

200

little rougher, but it's pretty uniform from 3 to 7 or 4 to 8 feet deep."

• Hatchery to Maxfield Road: Roughly 6 miles of medium-difficult water, defined by nice pocket water and well-defined tailouts and slots.

• Maxfield to Whitcomb Dimmell Road: Four miles of good steelhead water, starting with the Shuwah drift (top and tailout) and extending past the Culvert Hole, an area of medium/slow water where fish will lie in 3 to 6 feet of water under some overhanging trees.

The upper river, from Klahowya Campground down to Bear Creek, is a fair bet for early fish, and your best alternative in high water.

HOH RIVER: Late February and early March are the best times to hit the upper Hoh for wild fish.

• Olympic National Park to Coon's Bar:

Small canyon water, filled with logjams and tight, small slots and runs.

• Coon's Bar to Morgan's Crossing: "A lot of logjams and rockpiles in that section," says Woodward. "You'll be fishing a lot of rip rap and overhanging trees.

• Morgan's Crossing to Allen's Bar: Includes a take-out at Oxbow Campground (near Highway 101).

"It changes out there every day, but from Oxbow down you're talking about easy, self-explanatory stuff," says Woodward. "You want to fish the root-wads and brushpiles . . . basically, any obstruction in the river."

CLEARWATER RIVER: Sleeper river that is basically empty until the runs comes. It doesn't last long, but when the fish are in, you'll be hard-pressed to find better wild fish water.

"The Clearwater is a hell of a river," says Price. "I've never, ever kept a fish out of that river. It's not a major river — it's very hit and miss. It doesn't have a lot of fish, but they're *big*. I had a three-day stretch on the Clearwater where we had a 24½, 25 and 28½. Pretty amazing."

• Copper Mine Bottom to Groves Bridge: Accessible off the Clearwater Road mainline. Primitive put-in, but fairly easy water down to the bridge, a run of about 7 miles.

"It's pretty classic steelhead water," says Price.

"There's a lot of rocks, which create pools, some nice tailouts. It's a little grabby, but not bad. You definitely need to go with lighter tackle when it's in shape — it's very driftable, but it's a small stream."

The Clearwater is very temperamental — slides in the upper river will push it out of shape in a hurry with significant precipitation.

OLYMPIC PENINSULA STEELHEAD

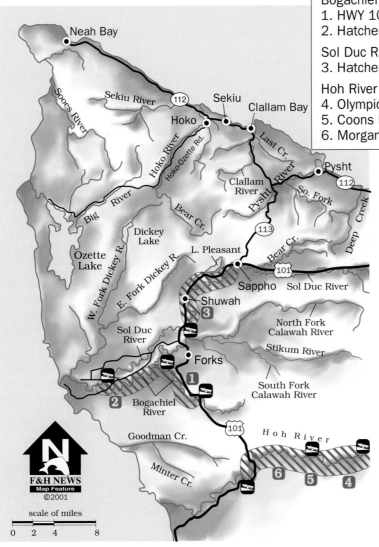

F&H MAP KEY

🛥 Boat Launch
▧ Best Steelhead

Bogachiel River
1. HWY 101 to Hatchery
2. Hatchery to Lyendecher Park

Sol Duc River
3. Hatchery to Whitcomb Dimmol

Hoh River
4. Olympic N.P. to Coons Bar
5. Coons Bar to Morgans Crossings
6. Morgans Crossing to Allens Bar

Forks winter steelhead: here's lookin' at you, Bogey

FORKS

by Dusty Routh

This is that incredibly magic time of year when we shift gears from salmon in the salt, sea-run cutts, big doggie chum and tomato-can silvers, and purify our fishing lives again. This, my angling brethren, is winter steelhead time.

There may be no more classic a river in the Lower 48 in which to pursue these big, gorgeous fish, than the Bogachiel. Starting up near Bogachiel Peak in the Olympics, the Bogey runs due west down past Green Peak. There it's joined by the North Fork. It then flows past Tumwata and Hades creeks, to near the South Bogachiel Road, then close to Undie Road, past Bogachiel State Park, along Highway 101, and on to the Bogachiel Hatchery. Just below there the Bogey is joined by the Calawah River.

AT a GLANCE

What: Hot time in cold weather for Bogachiel River winter steelhead. Glory, glory hallelujah.

When: Expect the hatchery brats to be in the river from Thanksgiving to Christmas. The bruiser wild fish, some going 20 to 25 pounds, will be landing in January. You can expect February-April to be prime months.

How: For a kick-in-the-pants experience, you can't go wrong with floats and pink/white marabou jigs. Plugs, Corky-and-yarn, diver-and-shrimp, and spoons work too.

Why: Because if you have any Northwest blood in you, you were born for winter steelheading. It's your destiny, and you can't deny your destiny or you'll burn in hell.

Info/guides: Mike Zavadlov, Bob Kratzer, Angler's Guide Service (360-374-3148); Olympic Sporting Goods (360-374-6330); Jeff Woodward, Jeff Woodward Guided Sportfishing (360-374-6526); Randy Lato, All-Ways Fishing (360-374-2052; *alwaysfishing@centurytel.net*); Jim Richeson, Quillayute River Guide Service (888-501-5887; *jimr@olypen.com*); Andy Moser, AM Guide Service (206-367-6094; *amguideservice@comcast.net*).

The river then runs southeast of La Push Road, through a series of switch-backs past Maxfield and Murphy creeks, and finally underneath La Push Road bridge and on to Leyendecker Park.

At Leyendecker, the Bogachiel is no more, as it's joined by the Sol Duc from the north. Together they form the Quillayute, which has a well-deserved reputation as a steelhead freeway for fish that are shooting up to the rivers above.

Run timing: The Bogachiel comes on early, especially in comparison with the Sol Duc. You can expect a good supply of hatchery fish by late November, and the peak of the hatchery run to be in the water throughout the month of December. Traditionally, Thanksgiving is the kick-off month and Christmas break is the touchdown.

The Bogey will stay consistent for hatchery fish some years clear into March. But what every steelheader lives for are the wild fish, which start showing up in January. These big brutes will come in to the river slow at first, then will really stack up with the winter rains so that February, March and April are absolute peak months.

Metalhead methodology: There are no closely guarded secrets or myster-ies for hitting fish on the Bogachiel. All steelhead standards will work here, with some either being slightly more effective or, as is more often the case, slightly eas-ier to do with less frustration on the angler's part. Case in point: the Bogey can be snaggy, and the steelhead have a contemptuous habit of stacking up in some of the snaggiest of the snag-laden stretches. That's why float-and-jig fish-ing is so popular, and so effective.

Just ask Mike Zavadlov of Angler's Guide Service (800-577-8781) in Forks. Zavadlov is one of the best guides in the region, and he knows the Bogey coming and going. He also knows steelhead, and when he's not guiding for winter-runs he's up north in the summer in Alaska helping to run a salmon camp. In other words, he fishes almost every day of the year (except when he's elk hunting in Idaho) and he's tried just about every method you can think of to catch winter

BOGACHIEL STEELHEADING will warm up with Thanksgiving's hatchery run, and keep puffing into late winter as wild fish roll up the West End river. Guide Bob Kratzer holds a nickel-bright Bogey fish.

steelhead. And he likes the float-and-jig approach.

"Float fishing with jigs is really just sight fishing," he points out. "And there's something about sight fishing that's just really cool. I personally like watching that float go down. There's nothing like it, it's so much fun.

"But it's practical too. You can fish so much water, you don't get hung up, and the fish always seem to be stacked up in places that are really, really snaggy. If you fished through those places some other way, you'd get all messed up."

Float fishing is as simple as can be.

"I like to use foam steelhead floats, the Dink floats are the best, I think," Zavadlov says. "I don't use slip floats. I use a fixed float, because you're never fishing more than 5 feet down at the most anyway."

Underneath the float, Zav likes a pink-and-white marabou jig. He ties his own, but good commercial versions include Beau-Mac's line of steelhead jigs. Go with the pearl/pink, or the pink/white.

Or, if you're a Corky man, drift pink or pearl Corkies with pink yarn, off a three-way rig with pencil lead. Use a 4- to 5-foot 8- to 10-pound leader.

Pullin' plugs is also mighty effective, with the standard being a pink Hot Shot 30 or 35. Heddon Tadpolly plugs are also a great way to get the attention of a massive metalhead, with the tickled pink (533) color a hot choice.

Zav is also a fan of divers-and-shrimp.

"They work really well," he confirms. "I use a Hot'N Tot plug with the hooks removed as the diver, and a natural-colored sand shrimp, either a tail with a Puff Ball, or a whole shrimp."

All the usual steelhead fly patterns can work here. You can also throw spoons, and a lot of guys do, but you have to have clear water or you'll be wasting your elbow energy.

"If the water's clear, a steelhead will come a long way to hit a spoon," Zav says. "But if it's clouded up, spoons just don't work."

Popular drifts: The steelhead highway on the Bogey is from the launch at the hatchery down to the Wilson Access (4 miles of river), near La Push Road. More adventurous drifters can drift all the way down to Leyendecker. Bank anglers can be shoulder to shoulder from the hatchery to the mouth of the Calawah.

If you're drifting a boat and don't feel like driving two rigs over, there's a rep-utable shuttle service available on the Bogachiel, Sol Duc and other local rivers. Roadrunner Shuttle Service (Ted Miller, 360-374-5195) is the way to go. Call a few days ahead of time if you can.

Going with a guide: If you haven't fished the Bogachiel before, or you're in the mood for concentrating on the fish and not on boat handling or wading, booking a trip with a guide can be one of the most fun things to do in the winter outside of getting hammered and watching the Super Bowl.

If you're coming from Seattle or other points east, it's best to drive to Forks the night before. A good place to stay is at the Miller Tree Inn (360-374-6806). They'll give you a good deal if you're fishing with Zavadlov or one of the other guides at Angler's. You'll have a big breakfast at the Forks Coffee Shop around 5:30 a.m., and be fishing by 7 or so. The Coffee Shop also supplies a boxed lunch. Bring a thermos of coffee or cocoa, dress warm, definitely bring your rain gear, hat, gloves and knee-high boots or hip waders (helps for getting in and out of the drift boat).

Zav's boats have forced-air heat, which is a hell of a nice luxury if you're fishing in December, January, February and even March, when it's damp, cold (really cold) and/or raining.

It helps if your schedule can be flexi-ble weather-wise, since a day or two of rain can blow out Peninsula rivers like a candle.

"They shut down when it rains hard," Zav says, "and we have to move dates around to accommodate the weather."

But the upside? Every time it rains, more fish move in.

The regs: From the mouth to the 101 bridge, the minimum size is 14 inches and the daily limit is two. One wild steelhead can be retained per day Dec. 1-April 30. From the 101 bridge to the Olympic National Park boundary, selective gear rules apply Dec. 1-April 30, and the daily limit is two.

Bogachiel River

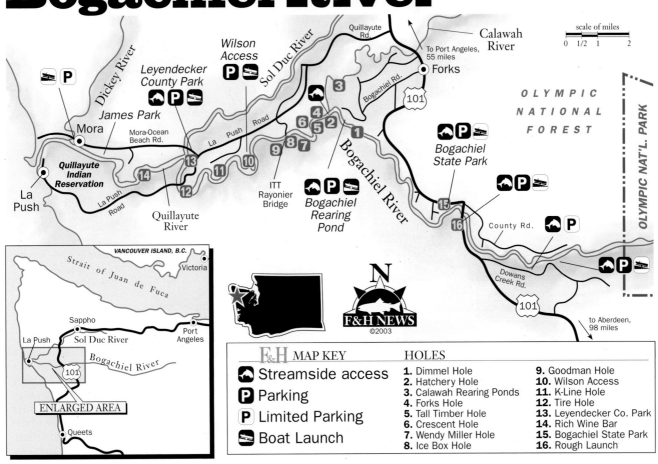

F&H MAP KEY

 Streamside access
P Parking
P Limited Parking
 Boat Launch

HOLES

1. Dimmel Hole
2. Hatchery Hole
3. Calawah Rearing Ponds
4. Forks Hole
5. Tall Timber Hole
6. Crescent Hole
7. Wendy Miller Hole
8. Ice Box Hole
9. Goodman Hole
10. Wilson Access
11. K-Line Hole
12. Tire Hole
13. Leyendecker Co. Park
14. Rich Wine Bar
15. Bogachiel State Park
16. Rough Launch

Expect Grays to color up with hatchery, wild steel

ROSBURG

by Terry Otto

Washington's Grays River was full of winter steelhead, but the bright afternoon sun had them hiding in the deep pools and under the many logjams of the little tributary of the lower Columbia. They were definitely in a defensive, non-aggressive mood, and the few takers that I had gotten quickly shook themselves free of the hook.

Sunny days in December are a rarity, but the sun was starting to slant low over the hills, and about 3:30 that after-noon their shadows fell over the river. The schools of steelhead immediately pulled out of the deep water and schooled up in the runs and tailouts. The metalheads also began snatching at anything that floated by, including the pink Corky I was putting on their noses. For about two hours it was a steelheader's dream, and I hooked fish after fish.

Somewhere after releasing about a dozen steelhead I lost count. The fish were running between 6 and 10 pounds, and they were definitely fired up. They put up a good tussle, with lots of hard runs and some fine aerial displays. I finally did keep a nice bright 7-pound hen right before the end of fishing hours, putting a nice conclusion on one of the best days I've ever spent fishing for winter steelhead.

That trip to the Grays last year may just be a sign of what's in store for the river this winter. According to Dan Rauding of the Washington Department of Fish and Wildlife, there are reasons for optimism. "The good ocean conditions that brought us last year's run's still exist," he says. "As long as that's the case, we should continue to see good returns."

Numbers and timing: Hard numbers on hatchery steelhead returns to the river are hard to come by, since none of the adults returning to the hatchery are trapped or collected. About 30,000 to 40,000 juvenile steelhead are moved to the hatchery for acclimation and release every year. These fish return at a rate of 1 to 3 percent, which means that in the good years, more than a thousand steelhead will crowd into the holes near the hatchery on the lit-tle river. Most of these fish are from 5 to 8 pounds, but a few three-salt fish return every year, giving anglers a chance at steelhead to the midteens.

The hatchery steelhead are a Chambers Creek stock, and they return much earlier than the wild com-ponent of the run. The biologists do this so that when

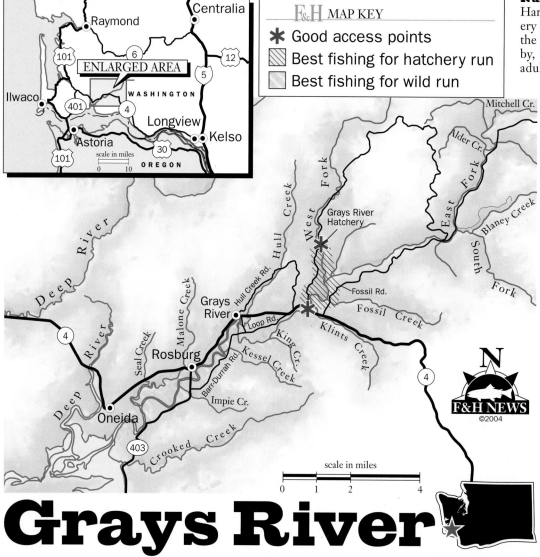

F&H MAP KEY
* Good access points
▨ Best fishing for hatchery run
▧ Best fishing for wild run

Grays River

the wild steelhead return to the river in February and March there are few hatchery fish left in the river to inter-spawn with the wild steelhead. The first hatchery fish will show up about Thanksgiving, and the run will peak in late December and early January. By the end of January most of the fish are dark and in spawning condition.

Where to angle: Best fishing for the hatchery winters can be found between the Highway 4 Bridge and the state-run hatchery. Top spot is at the hatchery itself. There is plenty of access here, so anglers can really spread out. On that day last December there were only a few others fishing near me, and often I was fishing alone.

The water is easy to fish by wading, or from the bank. There are good pools as well as good fast water to fish here. There is no deadline, so you can fish above the hatchery or below. However, the numbers of steelhead thin out quickly above the hatchery. The numbers stay strong as you move below the facility, but the best fishing is still found right at the hatchery.

Best method seems to be drifting, but the water also lends itself to hardware and floating jigs or bait. Your usual winter steelhead colors and baits work here, so bring red, pink, and orange Cheaters, and yarn of similar colors. Bait such as sand shrimp and salmon roe are effective, especially when the fish get finicky.

The area near the hatchery is also a good stretch of water for fly fishing. There are good stretches with plenty of room for a backcast, and the runs and glides are a good depth for a fly presentation. The first choice for baits would be any of the single-egg patterns such as the Glo Bug. Egg-sucking Leeches will also draw strikes.

There's also some good access at the Highway 4 bridge. This water is a little bigger and slower than the hatchery reach, and it fishes well with hardware. Stee-Lees are always a good bait on these lower Columbia River tribs, with blue and green being the best colors. You can also take fish on silver-bladed spinners such as Bud's Spinners or the Blue Fox Vibrax. This reach also fishes very well with bobber and jigs. Red, pink, purple and black are good colors. Best fishing in this reach for the hatchery steelhead will be when the river first starts to drop into condition following some hard rains.

Good wild run too: The Grays also gets an excellent wild run of winter steelhead. However, they can be negatively affected when the returning steelhead bump into the salmon nets in the lower Columbia. State biologists see a direct relationship between the amount of time the commercial netters are allowed to fish, and the numbers of spawning steelhead in the Grays. Timing your trip so that the nets have been out for a while increases your chances of success.

These are the big steelhead of the Grays, averaging almost 10 pounds. There are lots of fish in the midteens, and even a few four-salt monsters. Unlike the hatchery fish, these wild ones tend to spread out throughout the system. The fish tend to bite better in the lower river, and the area around the Highway 4 Bridge can be very good. This is also a great place to fish for wild fish with a fly rod.

These wild brutes start to show up in the river in mid-February, and their numbers start to really increase in March. The stream closes to steelhead fishing on March 15 to protect the wild spawners, but the first half of the month can be the best time of year to hang a really huge wild winter steelhead. The

THE AUTHOR holds a Grays River steelhead Fish start to trickle into the river right around Thanksgiving, and peak in December or early January.

same methods that work for the hatchery run also work for the wild fish.

Like all small streams near the coast, the Grays will blow out from time to time during the winter. However, the stream will come back into shape pretty quickly, and usually the water is running very clearly. For this reason, approach the stream with some caution. The steelhead in the shallows are easy to spook, so keep low and avoid wearing brightly colored clothes.

AT a GLANCE

What: Steelheading one of southwest Washington's lesser-known streams.

Where: The Grays River, in Wahkiakum County along Highway 4.

Best fishing: Of course, at the hatchery for clipped fish. Lower down, below Highway 4 for wild runs.

When: Hatchery fish begin to trickle in around Thanksgiving, with the peak in December/early January. Wild fish begin to arrive in mid-February and fish well until the March 15 closure.

How: Standard steelie methods — drifting red, pink or orange drift bobbers with yarn or bait, tossing spoons or spinners, floating bobbers-and-jigs of fly fishing with egg-sucking leeches, Glo Bugs, etc.

Contact: Grays River hatchery (360-465-2446).

Hoh in Feb.: 'Best river in the state'

FORKS

by Joel Shangle

Imagine, if you can, hotwiring your cerebral cortex's ability to process reality and logic while a steelhead measuring 40 inches in length is ripping 12-pound-test mainline out of an Ambassadeur reel like it were a Duncan yo-yo.

After you've returned from that little trip into Fishing Fantasia, try to bend your mind around a half-hour of run-

HATCHERY STEELHEAD, like Amber Keehn's 9-pound Hoh River fish, are on the wane in the big West End river, but keep on it as fishing for wild steelies picks up in February and March. Port Orchard's Keehn took this fish drifting an egg cluster and Spin-N-Glo in late December.

and-gun with a steelhead running 44 inches in length and several ungodly inches in girth.

The official arcana of formulas and equations tells us that those two fish would weigh exactly too damn much for mere mortals to even comprehend, but they were both hooked, battled, tamed and released within the space of three mind-boggling hours last year on the Hoh River by a couple of clients of Mike Price at Grizzly Charters (360-374-5873) in Forks.

Two very, very, very happy clients.

"Those were two 30-pound fish, in one day — awesome," says Price, a master of understatement. "That's the Hoh, though. I love that river during the catch-and-release part of the season, when the big fish are in."

The land of the giants: In an area that reads like a roll call of America's Best Steelhead Rivers, the Hoh could very well stake a claim as *the* best place in the Pacific Northwest to fish for 20-pound winter-runs over the next two months. For Price's money, anyway, the Hoh stands out just enough over the Quillayute, Sol Duc, Calawah and Queets to garner almost all of his angling attention as we approach February, and the most prolific "big fish time zone" of the year.

"It's the best river in the state at that time of year," he says. "There's no doubt about it — if it's in shape, it'll have fish, and it's almost like a 20-pounder a day. It's not totally uncommon to go up there for four or five days straight and land eight or nine fish in the 20-pound class."

Spilling out of the Olympic Mountains and Olympic National Park south of Forks and eventually emptying into the Pacific Ocean midway between LaPush and Queets, the Hoh is the moodiest of the Olympic Peninsula's big steelhead rivers. It's the first to go sideways during winter rains, and could very well spend the majority of the next two months out of shape and unfishable. But it's that same gusher flow quality that makes the Hoh such a big-fish vacuum.

"The Hoh is always the very first river to go out of shape here, and it has a huge volume," says Price. "Mother Nature really takes good care of her. She blows

her to smithereens — there's a lot of water coming through there, and there are always fish coming in."

Changing, rearranging: After consecutive mild winters on the Peninsula, December came in like a rabid lion — double-digit rainfalls pushed every single stream in the area out of shape, and, in the case of the Hoh, changed the face of several components of its fishery.

"The last couple of years have been really mild, but we're paying for that now," jokes Price. "Mother Nature is laying a licking on us. We had that big storm in December, where we got 10 to 11 inches of rain, and it just flat blew the Hoh completely out. There are some major changes in the channels. You're going to be looking for new fishing water, but you just want to go where there's the most water. It's nothing that's going to hurt anything or get you into major trouble."

The major points of change include a couple of lower river access areas that are now different, or completely unusable. They are:

1) Oxbow Campground: The bottom end of the drift from Morgan's Crossing,

AT A GLANCE

What: Hoh River steelhead.

When: Hatchery runs will be over by the end of January, when the first significant runs of big wild fish start to hit the river. Prime time for big fish on the Hoh is February and March. The river closes April 15.

Where:: The upper river — from Oxbow Campground to the boundary of the Olympic National Park — is almost always more fishable during this time frame than the lower river. Drift from the park boundary to Morgan's Crossing, or from Morgan's to Oxbow.

Why: Selective gear regulations and catch-and-release of wild fish makes the upper Hoh one of the best trophy steelhead opportunities in the Pacific Northwest. This river is capable of kicking out a 30-pounder.

Access issues: A December blowout changed the composition of the river, especially on the lower river, where it wiped the Cottonwood Campground access completely out.

Lodging: Several hotels and bed and breakfasts are available in and around Forks. Places to try include the Mill Creek Inn (360-374-5873); Hoh River Resort (360-374-5566); Westward Hoh Resort (360-374-6657)

Information: Bob Gooding, Olympic Sporting Goods (360-374-6330)

Guides: Mike Price, Grizzly Charters (360-374-5873); Bob Kratzer, Angler's Guide Service (800-577-8781); Bob Ball, Piscatorial Pursuits (360-374-2091); Jim Mansfield (360-374-9018); Adventure Northwest Guide Service (360-374-5247); Jeff Woodward, River's Inn (360-374-6526); Randy Lato, All-Ways Fishing (360-374-2052); Tom Lines, Tight Lines Guide Service (877-878-1559)

the put-in/takeout is heavily silted in, but still usable with a 4-wheel drive.

2) Cottonwood Campground: Gone. Bye bye. December's blowout wiped this northbank campground and accompanying fishing access right out of the picture.

"Cottonwood Campground is really wrecked," says Price. "That thing got completely taken out of there. I was shocked as hell that it hit Cottonwood so hard. We've been able to finagle ourselves in there for years, but it's undoable now. You *might* be able to put a boat in. Maybe."

The drifts: Every inch of the Hoh — from the plunking water at Nolan's Bar near the bottom, to the walk-in fly fishing access inside the National Park boundaries at the top — offers big fish potential, but the lower half (below Oxbow) is often out of shape and unfishable during the winter.

"The water clear first up high," says Price. "The lower end is the place to be when the hatchery runs are going, and then again really late in the season. The upper river will get hot, and then gradually taper off after March or so. April is a *fine* time to steelhead on the Hoh, and

on the Peninsula in general."

• **Mount Tom Creek to National Park Boundary:** You can't fish from a boat inside the boundaries of the National Park, but if you're a flyrodder, the upper reaches of the Hoh are designed for you.

"You can fish all the way up into the park, up to Mount Tom Creek, and find some phenomenal fly fishing," says Price. "There's some tremendous fly water up there, all walk in."

• **Park Boundary to Morgan's Crossing:** The put-in at the park is still usable after the December deluge, but the composition of the upper Hoh will seem like the face of the moon for everybody but the legion of Forks-based guides who make their living on this river.

"Traditionally, that section has been a lot of shallow, flat water that leads into deeper pools and some nice runs, but there's been a lot of 'fingering' in the river," says Price. "It's very flat — nothing but long gravel bars up there — but the river goes all over the place. It's easy to boat, but you have to really be aware of sweepers and blockages in the river, which will happen after big waters. You'll have all these 7-, 8-foot spruce trees in the water. Best thing to do is get on the phone with Bob Gooding at Olympic Sporting Goods (360-374-6330) to get the word on some of those conditions."

• **Morgan's to Oxbow:** This is 8 to 9 miles of the best steelhead water in the

Lower 48, encompassing tried-and-true producers like Willoughby Creek, an area long known as the Clay Bank, and the Canyon. Except for a rapid just above Oxbow that requires a little extra care, it's an easy float where you can spend the entire day pitching Spin-N-Glos, bouncing pink worms along the bottom, fishing rags, or pulling single, barbless-hook plugs (it's selective gear only from Oxbow up).

"Because it's all wild-fish release, that section is just filled with guys fishing to have some fun," says Price. "You won't find some of that stuff that goes on in the 'Kill Zone.' It's nice and pleasant."

• **Oxbow to the mouth:** The lower river — from Highway 101 down — provides three major takeouts: Allen's Bar, Nolan's Creek and G & L Mill. This section is stuffed with bank access, and can be incredibly productive when water conditions allow.

"Below Oxbow, the river has changed so damn much, there aren't really any names for most of the holes anymore," says Price. "There are just lots of fish, and the best access for bank fishermen of all the rivers on Peninsula. Every road that goes toward river usually ends up there. There are several gravel bars that guys can camp on — the access to Nolan's Bar has changed down at the bottom, and the bottom end of Barlow Bar is closed now, but there are a good couple of miles of gravel bar between those two areas for guys to fish."

Net sched: Self regulation by the Hoh tribe means that the Hoh isn't netted nearly as heavily as other Peninsula rivers. Through February, the schedule is usually Monday noon to Wednesday noon, switching to a Monday-to-Tuesday schedule in March.

Hoh River

BEST DRIFTS
- Park to Morgan's Crossing
- Morgan's Crossing to Oxbow Campground

F&H MAP KEY
- ■ Undeveloped Access
- ● Developed Access
- Stream Bank Fishing
- P Parking
- P Limited Parking
- Boat Launch
- Rough Boat Launch

1. Park Bar
2. G & L Shake Mill
3. Nolan's Creek
4. Cottonwood Campground (unusable)
5. Allen's Bar
6. Oxbow Campground
7. Hoh River Resort
8. Morgan's Crossing
9. National Park Access

Winter-run alternatives: consider Satsop, 'Nooch

ELMA

by Joel Shangle

In these days of late runs and funky weather patterns that push rivers around like schoolyard bullies, it pays to have alternatives. Especially if you want to fish for steelhead. The Cowlitz, the Kalama, the Skykomish, the Hoh, the Bogachiel . . . you can't go wrong with any of them. But keep your eyes and ears open for news out of Elma, because the Satsop River is an alternative that you should have on your list of winter steelhead streams.

Falling out of the Olympics and pouring into the Chehalis River just south of the small town of Satsop in Gray's Harbor County, the Satsop River has long been one of those streams with a mystique. It's like Sasquatch for most steelheaders: they suspect it's there, they want to see it . . . but they don't take the time to pursue it. The river's big-fish mystique — bolstered by production of state-record-size steelhead back in the 1970s — is only fanned by the locals' close-mouthed attitude toward the fishery. Getting somebody to talk about the Satsop is like convincing Linus to give up his blanket: nobody's surrendering a thing.

So all the secrecy must mean that somebody's hiding a world-class fishery, right? Not necessarily. But the

FISH WITH ALL OF THEIR FINS will be making their way into the Satsop from now through March. Greg Nelson exalts over a big wild fish caught on a glob of eggs.

river is nothing to sneeze at, especially if possibly catching and releasing 15- and 16-pound wild-runs are your bag.

"The Satsop can be a pretty good river," says Rich Bogle at Rich's Guide Service (360-983-3608). "As long as it stays clear and the flows don't get above 2,000 cubic feet per second, it'll be a decent bet."

EXPECT COMPANY: This river is fished religiously by a substantial group of locals and a handful of guides. When the nearby Wynoochee is out or when runs are in strong, you'll be lucky to buy a spot in the parking lot. Fish it midweek if possible.

WILD THINGS: If you're looking for fin-clipped keeper fish, skip the Satsop and hit the neighboring Wynoochee — maybe 1 in 10 fish moving up the Satsop is of hatchery origin. The rest are scrappy wild-runs, many well into the double digits in size.

"What makes the Satsop great is that there are some nice, big fish in there," says Bogle. "It's probably 85 to 90 percent native fish. You rarely ever catch a hatchery fish in there. It's a good river to fish if you don't mind

AT a GLANCE

What: Satsop River steelhead.

When: Wild fish moving into the river now. Best fishing won't come until the end of February. Will last through March.

Wild runs: The majority of the Satsop's runs are wild fish, ranging upwards of 15, 16 pounds.

Techniques: Jet sleds applicable to lower river, below the confluence. Drift boats above that. Drift eggs and Corkies/Cheaters, pull Hot Shots, Wiggle Warms, Tadpollies, toss Vibrax spinners. Bank anglers, plunk with Spin-N-Glos and eggs.

Access: Launch below the Highway 12 bridge and run downriver to the mouth or upriver to the confluence of the forks. Bank access is limited almost exclusively to the lower river.

Directions: Take I-5 to Olympia and head west on Highway 12 to Satsop. Get off at Satsop (East Satsop Road) or Brady (Middle Satsop Road).

Information: Rich Bogle, Rich's Guide Service (360-983-3608); Clancy Holt, Clancy's Guided Sport Fishing (360-262-9549); John Robarge, JR's Guide Service (360-262-9584); Raleigh Stone, Raleigh's Guide Service (360-864-6009); Bob Balcombe, Balcombe's Rod & Reel Service (360-249-6282).

turning wild fish loose."

RUN TIMING: The best fishing on this river will come from now through the end of March as wild runs start to pile in out of the Chehalis. According to Bob Balcombe at Balcombe's Rod & Reel Service (360-249-6282) in Montesano, sporadic pushes of fish have been in the river through January.

"They're catching fish now, but in no great numbers yet," he says. "The numbers won't start to show up until February — that's when you'll start looking for more fish in the 15- to 16-pound range."

The Satsop isn't necessarily a numbers river, but 4-fish days are common enough.

"It can produce 3 to 4, or even 5 to 6 fish a day, and that's pretty good fishing in my book," says Clancy Holt of Clancy's Guided Sportfishing (360-262-9549).

WHERE AND HOW: This ain't the Skagit or the Cowlitz, and you won't be skirting up and down miles and miles of water in your 21-foot sled. The Satsop is defined by fairly small, intimate water in all but the lower main stem. Anglers running jet sleds will launch at the Twin Bridges at Highway 12 and run upriver as far as the confluence of the West Fork and about a mile downriver of the bridge. Above the confluence, the river is a lot tighter and much more applicable to drift boaters.

"A 17-foot sled on the Satsop works superb," says Bogle. "I wouldn't go any bigger than that. I'd say that 18 feet would be about the maximum, and then you'd be looking at some problems turning around in some spots."

Holt fishes the Satsop out of a 16-foot Zodiac mounted with a 60-horsepower Mercury and oars.

"I can go where a lot of the sleds can't," he says. "But the confluence is about as far as you want to go in a sled."

Starting from the Chehalis, some of the best fishing areas include:
• Willis' Gravel Bar: Also known as Worman's Bar, this stretch is located roughly 160 yards upstream of the Chehalis. It runs along the west side of the river, roughly 100 yards long.

• Twin Bridges: Where Highway 12 crosses the river. You'll be fishing above the railroad bridge, continuing under the bridge below the launch. This is also a good bank fishing area. On the east side, park in the lot by the bridge and simply walk down to the river. On the west side, you have to park along the highway. Follow the fence line down to the river and fish near the dikes.

From here on up, bank access cuts off because of private ownership. Boaters, however, will do well from the confluence down, drifting bait, pulling plugs (blue pirate Mini Wiggle Warts or Hot Shots) or fishing with bobbers and jigs.

• The S Curves: Just below Shafer State Park on the East Fork. Crowded conditions will apply here.

THE 'NOOCH: If you have to keep a fish, get into the Wynoochee's hatchery runs. Access is along Wynoochee Road, with a launch near Black Creek, drift-boat put-in near Shafer Creek Hit Elk Bar, just below Highway 12 off of Devonshire Road, for bank access.

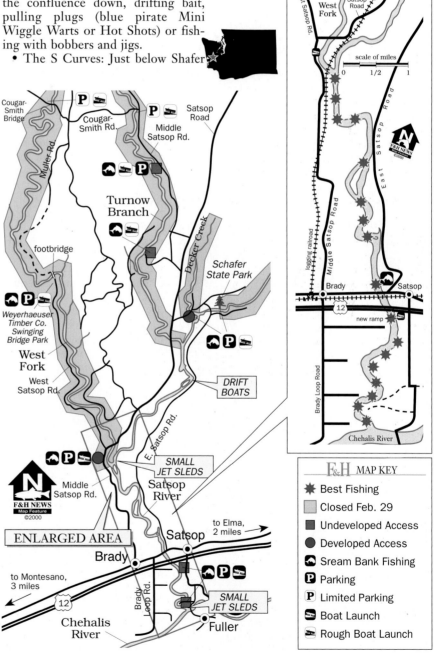

Upper Sol Duc hot spot for November silvers

FORKS

by Dusty Routh

If you're looking for an Olympic Peninsula river where incoming silvers are stacked up in the holes like cordwood, look no further than the upper stretches of the Sol Duc River. This incredible fishery is as dependable as it gets come November for big incoming coho that can get as large as anything you'd encounter up in Alaska.

"These are really big fish," confirms guide Jim Richeson of Quillayute River Guide Service (888-501-5887). He pounds this water throughout the winter starting in November, spending as many as 100 days a season putting the hurt on big silvers, kings and steelhead

The Duc is not only reliable for putting up numbers and big fish, it's reliable because it takes a lot more rain to

GUIDE JIM RICHESON hoists 20-plus pounds of Olympic Peninsula hooknose. Fish of this caliber are on tap this month on the upper Sol Duc.

blow it out than other Olympic Peninsula rivers such as the Hoh and Bogachiel.

"The Sol Duc can take a lot more rain and stays fishable," Richeson says.

And did we mention there are lots and lots of big fish to catch? The hatchery on the Sol Duc, according to Richeson, is doing an amazing job.

Thick with big fish: "Silvers in the Sol Duc are about as big as you can find anywhere. I can only think of a couple places in Alaska that produce such big silvers," Richeson points out. "The hatchery produces silvers as big as any wild fish I've caught."

These big coho come blasting through the Quillayute first, fresh from the ocean. This is the main-stem river that the Bogachiel to the south and the Sol Duc to the north flow in to. You'd think then the Quillayute would be the place to fish first, but more often than not these fish will shoot right through before they settle down in the deep holes of the Bogie and Sol Duc.

"During steelhead season I won't fish the Quillayute because the steelhead fly through there and don't hang in," Richeson says. "Plunkers can get them sometimes. During salmon season, especially early in the season, the salmon can get thick in the Quillayute if we don't get a lot of rain. But once the rains start up, the salmon just like the steelhead will shoot on through and end up in either the Bogachiel or the Sol Duc."

Timing: Rain is the greatest influencer for river fishing on the Peninsula.

"We're getting more rain

than we did last year, so there have been some huge pushes of fish," Richeson points out. "November is going to be an awesome month. Mid-November should offer the best fishing. If it's like last year, there will be so many fish piled up from the hatchery on down, the holes get so full, you can't fit another fish. From one hole on down to the next and the next and the next, the fish are incredibly thick."

Fisheries managers anticipate such a good year this year that they've raised the limits. Last year it was two salmon in any combination. This year it will be three salmon, with a daily limit of two wild fish from the hatchery down.

"I think the hatchery was so overwhelmed with fish last year, they had to raise the limit for this year," Richeson says.

Start here: Naturally, just below the hatchery on the Sol Duc is one of the hottest places to start fishing.

"Up above the hatchery, it's all catch-and-release for wild fish," Richeson reports. "I like to drift from the ramp at the hatchery down to Whitcomb-Dimmel Road in mid-November. Or launch at the hatchery boat launch, and drift to the next launch down which is Maxfield Road. Next launch after that is Whitcomb-Dimmel. Or you can fish all the way down to the next launch, which is Rayonier. The one after that is Leyendeckers where the Sol Duc and Bogachiel come together. That can be a great location too."

What you're looking for are deep holes where the silvers and kings are stacked up.

"Sometimes there's so many fish piled up from the hatchery on down, you'll just be amazed," Richeson says.

How to hook 'em: For silvers, your tackle selection is amazingly simple. Start with a quality, 9-foot light-action steelhead rod like a G.Loomis or Okuma. Use a decent baitcasting or spinning reel (Shimano and Okuma are good choices) spooled up with 15-pound Maxima Ultragreen.

"You can go lighter than 15-pound

test for silvers," Richeson points out, "but every now and again you're going to get hit by a big king and you're going to need that extra strength."

For the silvers, throw spinners like the No. 3 or No. 4 Blue Fox Vibrax. Or attach a little weight and throw marabou jigs down through the holes.

"Silvers really go after those marabou jigs, especially in marabou orange," Richeson says.

You can also back-troll big banana plugs, which is probably the single-most effective way to hook into both silvers and kings when the river's running hard.

"If the water's dirty, if we get rain, run Kwikfish. As the water clears, the most productive fishing will be with spinners and jigs," Richeson says.

Kings: While you can expect some thumb-burning, rod-bending action on wild and hatchery silvers, don't discount the big kings that lay in the Duc.

"The kings are pouring in real heavy," Richeson reports. "They may be older, but they're still in great shape and very catchable."

Boat show: The Sol Duc is tough to fish without a drift boat.

"There seems to be limited bank access," Richeson says. "On some of the best holes I don't see bank anglers because there's not too much access. The locals know a few places where they can get to the river, but it's rare to see bank guys below the hatchery."

Richeson fishes out of a 16-foot Willie drift boat, and fishes while drifting as well as anchored up.

"I'll position the boat above a good hole and anchor up and throw spinners or drift jigs down through the hole," he says. "Or we'll back-troll plugs down into the holes."

Hoh, Hoh, Hoh: While the Sol Duc is your best bet, particularly if the weather stays wet, don't overlook the upper Hoh above Oxbow if it's not blown out.

"If the river's in good shape," Richeson says, "the upper Hoh will be red-hot.

Same with the upper Bogachiel. And on the Bogachiel, fish from Highway 101 down to Wilson's boat ramp. That drift should be great."

Be flexible: If you're going to book a trip, it's best to have some calendar flexibility to account for squalls and big rains which can blow any of the Peninsula rivers to smithereens for a day or two and sometimes up to a week. Most of Richeson's clients stay the night in Forks and fish all the next day. If you ferry over from Seattle on the Edmonds/Kingston ferry, Forks is 113 miles from Kingston.

AT a GLANCE

What: Silvers and occasional kings stacked up thick in the Sol Duc River.

When: Mid- to late November is one of the hottest times of the year, particularly for the big hatchery coho.

How: Back-trolling banana plugs, drifting marabou jigs, and throwing Blue Fox Vibrax spinners.

How many: Limit's been raised to three salmon a day, no more than two of which can be wild.

Guides: Jim Richeson, Quillayute River Guide Service (888-501-5887; jimr@olypen.com); Bob Kratzer, Angler's Guide Service (800-577-8781; anglersguideservice.com); Jeff Woodward, Jeff Woodward Guided Sportfishing (360-374-6526); Randy Lato, All-Ways Fishing (360-374-2052; alwaysfishing@centurytel.net); Andy Moser, AM Guide Service (206-367-6094; amguideservice@comcast.net).

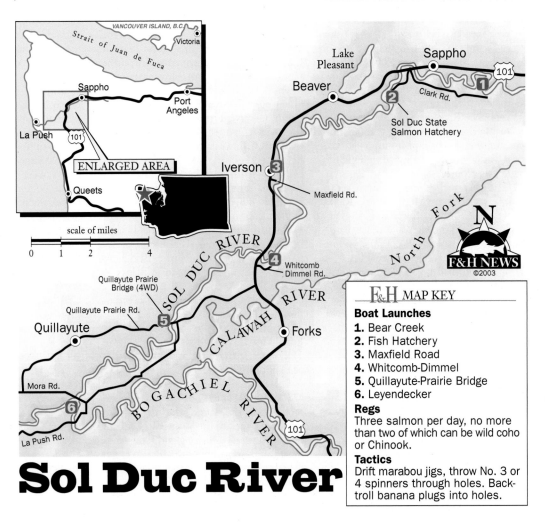

F&H MAP KEY

Boat Launches
1. Bear Creek
2. Fish Hatchery
3. Maxfield Road
4. Whitcomb-Dimmel
5. Quillayute-Prairie Bridge
6. Leyendecker

Regs
Three salmon per day, no more than two of which can be wild coho or Chinook.

Tactics
Drift marabou jigs, throw No. 3 or 4 spinners through holes. Back-troll banana plugs into holes.

Sol Duc River

The Nooch: drift high ... jet low ... for steelhead

MONTESANO

by Joel Shangle

RUSS WYMAN prepares to release a burly Wynoochee River wild winter-run, landed pulling plugs below White Bridge.

It's not the least-pressured steelhead river in the state. It's not the best big-fish steelhead river in the state. And it's not the best numbers steelhead river in the state. But even though you can't attach one definitive "Best Of" label to the Wynoochee River, you have to recognize it for offering an intriguing combination of conditions that shape it into one of the best winter steelhead opportunities in the state this month.

"The Wynoochee is just a nice river to fish," says Rich Mercado at Rich's Northwest Guide Service (253-535-0430). "You go through a lot of farmland, and you have some hill country on one side — it's quiet and it's pretty. Plus, it's a good river to fish if you're a novice drift boater. It's generally pretty easy to float."

Oh, and it has a nice mix of hatchery and wild fish that start pushing into the river through January and into March.

"Typical hatchery fish on the Wynoochee are 8 to 9 pounds; natives are up to 15 to 18 pounds," says Mercado. "They're there through February. The 'Nooch had a push of fish in late January, but generally February is the best time to fish it."

COASTAL INFLUENCE: More so than the dam-controlled rivers in the southwest and the inland rivers throughout north Puget Sound, the Wynoochee is a stream whose steelhead runs are heavily influenced by weather — it falls under a definite "coastal river" pattern of sucking fresh batches of fish in on a rain and gradually slowing down shortly thereafter through drier weather.

"February seems to be the month you want to hit the Wynoochee, but it really depends on the weather," says Mercado. "Everything hinges on rain. If it rains and brings fish in, it can be really good. It can go well into March, but how long it lasts beyond February really depends on how much rain it gets over the next month."

DRIFT THE RIVER OR JET: Pouring out of Wynoochee Lake and winding south through the Wynoochee Valley in Grays Harbor County before emptying into the Chehalis River east of Montesano, the Wynoochee offers several miles of fishable water between Schaefer Creek and the Chehalis. The upper stretches of the river — from Schaefer Creek down to about Caldwell Creek — are defined by tight, shallow runs that are accessible only from a drift boat. The lower river, mainly from Black Creek down, is much more open and available for anglers running small jet sleds.

The drift boat water can be broken down into three runs: 1) Schaefer Creek to White Bridge; 2) White Bridge to Crossover Bridge; 3) Crossover Bridge to Gravel Bar.

All of them will see their share of attention.

"Oh, the 'Nooch gets pounded pretty heavily," says Mercado. "You'll see 10 to 15 boats out there on any given day. It can get pretty busy."

UPPER DRIFT: The least-fished section of the river, the drift from Schaefer Creek to the White Bridge boat ramp is several miles long and semi-technical, and, consequently, doesn't get fished as much as the 10-plus miles below White Bridge.

"That's a long run," says Mercado. "You have to fish it pretty fast because it's so far from Schaefer Creek. You go through one big rock garden and a few spots where it gets pretty bumpy. You have to know what you're doing on the oars or you're going to bang your boat up pretty good."

MIDDLE DRIFT: Roughly 5 miles of water, defined by a nice mix of slick plug water and seamy drift water. The White Bridge to Crossover Bridge drift isn't very technical, with the exception of some rootwads that can be tricky when water conditions aren't good.

"The whole river is pretty easy to drift, but there are a few spots from White Bridge to Crossover Bridge that are tricky when the water gets low," says Mercado.

Mercado will sometime pitch eggs in this section off a Loomis 1141, and sometimes pull Hot Shots and Tadpollys off a Loomis HSR 930 — both techniques are effective, depending on the water level.

"You can just boondog it all the way down if you want," he says. "It's a good place to just drift and pitch bait, but there are some nice places to pull plugs too."

To get to the White Bridge launch, take Wynoochee Road off Highway 12 just west of Montesano. Take Wynoochee Road north past Black Creek for several miles until you get to a fire station. Take a left at the station to the launch.

LOWER DRIFT: Another drift of roughly 5 miles, and very similar to the water from White Bridge down. The Crossover Bridge to Gravel Bar drift features good bait-drifting water and some nice plug water that eventually blends into some rougher spots the closer you get to Gravel Bar.

"You start to see more logjams and rootwads the further down you get," says Mercado. "You have to pay attention as you get closer to Gravel Bar."

The Crossover Bridge launch isn't marked by signage — watch for the yellow house on the right-hand side coming up Wynoochee Road and take the next left toward Wishkah-Wynoochee Road.

BLACK CREEK DOWN: The lower

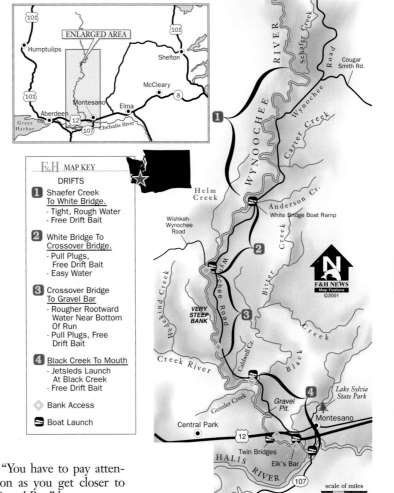

WYNOOCHEE RIVER

Wynoochee can get pretty crazy on a weekend — it's usually loaded with jet sleds from Black Creek down to the mouth, just as the parking lot is usually loaded with trucks and trailers.

"It gets a lot of pressure," says Mercado. "That parking lot is always full."

The launch is roughly three miles up Wynoochee Road from Highway 12. You're limited to a relatively short stretch of water above Black Creek before you get into water that's too tight for a sled, but from there down you have almost five miles of water leading into the mouth of the river.

"That's boondoggin' water," says Mercado. "You're drifting bait."

MIDDLE DRIFT: Roughly 5 miles of water, defined by a nice mix of slick plug water and seamy drift water. The White Bridge to Crossover Bridge drift isn't terribly technical, with the exception of some rootwads that can be tricky when water level conditions aren't the best.

"The whole river is pretty easy to drift, but there are a few spots from White Bridge to Crossover Bridge that are tricky when the water gets low," says Mercado.

Mercado will sometime pitch eggs in this section off a Loomis 1141, and sometimes pull Hot Shots and Tadpollys off a Loomis HSR 930 — both techniques are effective, depending on the water level.

"You can just boondog it all the way down if you want," he says. "It's a good place to just drift and pitch bait, but there are some nice places to pull plugs too."

To get to the White Bridge launch, take Wynoochee Road off Highway 12 just west of Montesano. Take Wynoochee Road north past Black Creek for several miles until you get to a fire station. Take a left at the station to the launch.

LOWER DRIFT: Another drift of roughly 5 miles, and very similar to the water from White Bridge down. The Crossover Bridge to Gravel Bar drift features good bait-drifting water and some nice plug water that eventually blends into some rougher spots the closer you get to Gravel Bar.

"You start to see more logjams and rootwads the further down you get," says Mercado.

"You have to pay attention as you get closer to Gravel Bar," he warns.

The Crossover Bridge launch isn't marked by signage — watch for the yellow house on the right-hand side coming up Wynoochee Road and take the next left toward Wishkah-Wynoochee Road.

BLACK CREEK DOWN: The lower Wynoochee can get pretty crazy on a weekend — it's usually loaded with jet sleds from Black Creek down to the mouth, just as the parking lot is usually loaded with trucks and trailers.

"It gets a lot of pressure," says Mercado. "That parking lot is always full."

The launch is roughly three miles up Wynoochee Road from Highway 12. You're limited to a relatively short stretch of water above Black Creek before you get into water that's too tight for a sled, but from there down you have almost five miles of water leading into the mouth of the river.

"That's boondoggin' water," says Mercado. "You're drifting bait."

MAP KEY

DRIFTS

1. **Shaefer Creek To White Bridge.**
   - Tight, Rough Water
   - Free Drift Bait

2. **White Bridge To Crossover Bridge.**
   - Pull Plugs, Free Drift Bait
   - Easy Water

3. **Crossover Bridge To Gravel Bar**
   - Rougher Rootward Water Near Bottom Of Run
   - Pull Plugs, Free Drift Bait

4. **Black Creek To Mouth**
   - Jetsleds Launch At Black Creek
   - Free Drift Bait

◆ Bank Access

🚤 Boat Launch

AT a GLANCE

What: Winter-run steelhead fishing on the Grays Harbor County's Wynoochee River.

When: Now. Best fishing on the 'Nooch is in February, when both hatchery and wild fish are in the river. Best fishing is shortly after fresh rain.

Where: Drift boaters can float from Schaefer Park down, but the most popular drifts are between White Bridge and Gravel Bar, with Crossover Bridge in between. Jet boaters fish from the Black Creek launch down to the mouth.

Techniques: Drift eggs and shrimp with Cheaters or Corkies, or pull plugs such as Hot Shots or Tadpollies on the upper river; drift bait from Black Creek down.

Information: Rich Mercado at Rich's Northwest Guide Service (253-535-0403); Clancy Holt at Clancy's Guided Sportfishing (800-871-9549); Harvey Van Brunt at Rip Some Lips Guide Service (888-750-8707)

Olympic Peninsula & Coastal Waters
HALIBUT

Hali season continues in Canadian waters

NEAH BAY

by Doug Edelstein

For halibut this summer, the grass is really greener on the other side of 48 degrees North. Canadian halibut! They're plentiful and on the move into this area, and now's the time. They'll go 15 to 50 pounds. At the current Canadian exchange rate, that's, uh, 10 to 35 pounds, American, right? But there've been fish to over 140 pounds this year from the waters of the Pacific off Neah Bay, and there's a 60- to 70-pounder caught every week or so up here. And that means a chance for something huge, that will truly — I mean, really — bust your gut.

Go for it now, while the getting's still good. You can fish Canadian-side halibut all summer out of Neah Bay, and if you don't want the struggle of securing a B.C.-side fishing license, you can fish US-side halibut, plus rockfish, long as the 15,000-pound US-side halibut quota lasts. The way the effort is going, that could hold up the rest of summer, too.

What's it feel like to fight a small halibut? Tough enough to make you appreciate what it takes to boat a big one. The fish that veteran fisherman Bob Lindeman and I caught on a recent trip ranged from probably 12 pounds, to a solid 35. Not big halibut, by any stretch.

But after just one fish, we were wiped out — arms heavy, out of breath, giddy and wobble-kneed with adrenaline rush, flopping around the careening cockpit like the fish themselves. Then we were onto another fish, and another fight, with barely time to steady our legs. We're exhausted, by the end of that. Then, the whole thing again — and this time, Bob was hooked up with a 14- to 17-pound yelloweye rockfish, which beat him up with sheer stubborn resistance.

Halibut fishing's just simply great right now on the Canada side, if you get the decent weather. The halibut population is healthy — rare news these days! You can limit in a half-hour or less, depending on what kind of physical shape you're in, and how fast you can winch a 25-pound slab of

BOB LINDEMAN hoists a 25-pound hali caught in Canadian waters off Neah Bay. Deckhand Steve Connally (left) gives him a hand.

struggling meat out of 400 feet of water. Two halibut is the bag for Canadian waters. Count 'em — one halibut more than you can catch in the US. After a three-hour boat ride out to 30 miles in the Pacific, the fast fishing might seem like an anti-climax. But somehow you can pack a whole lifetime of adrenaline into just those few minutes of mayhem.

Neah Bay offers two saltwater charter trips right now through the rest of summer that you really ought to consider, if you're looking for the next thing to a sure thing for halibut. One trip is for Canadian-side halibut, with its lure of a two-fish limit. The other is a combo halibut/rockfish trip well out into the Pacific on the American side, with a one-fish halibut limit and the usual stateside ocean rockfish limits. That combo will produce big yelloweye to 17 pounds or better, plus lingcod, canary and black rockfish. These trips are not cheap at $135 and $130, respectively,

but you can be almost certain that if the weather cooperates, you will go home with a bag heavy with filets when it's all over.

Bob and I took the bait for the Canadian side halibut trip, lured by the two-fish limit.

We fished with Big Salmon Charters (866-787-1900) out of Neah Bay, and stayed in Sekiu, 17 miles east down the road, at Herb's Motel (360-963-2346). Both were good choices. Ron Pennington at Big Salmon runs a tight ship, and the folks at Herb's couldn't be more charming or accommodating to the needs of fishermen. One word to the wise: When you charter out of Big Salmon, give them plenty of notice if you have a cancellation. One member of our party had to cancel, and that cost half a charter fee. That stings.

Our skipper on the 56-foot *Advantage* was Geoff Grillo, who is all you want from a charter skipper — low-key, professional, affable, tolerant of mistakes, dedicated to his clients catching fish and having a great time. Call 1-800-356-0323 for details.

Charter skippers out of Neah Bay have a host of hot spots on the Canada side that are literally loaded with halibut. Grillo says he's not missed a boat limit in seven years on the Canadian side. He finds the spots with his electronics — GPS, Loran numbers, etc., plus a little bit of dead reckoning and Kentucky windage. He scouts for new locations like a freshwater bass fisherman looking for fish-holding structure. Halibut migrate, but hold on certain types of bottom structure. Look for them on bottom shelves where hard gravel bottom meets up with sand. Also on underwater humps, rises, drop-offs and other depth changes. The skippers scout with depth finders, echo sounders and charts, looking for bait patterns, and other clues to contours where a gravel bottom changes to sand.

Several place names have emerged as the hot spots lately, but the reality is that skippers won't tell exactly where they fish. Generally, we found plenty of fish in 350 to 410 feet of water, around 29 miles from the Cape Flattery beaches. Expect to take a boat ride of at least

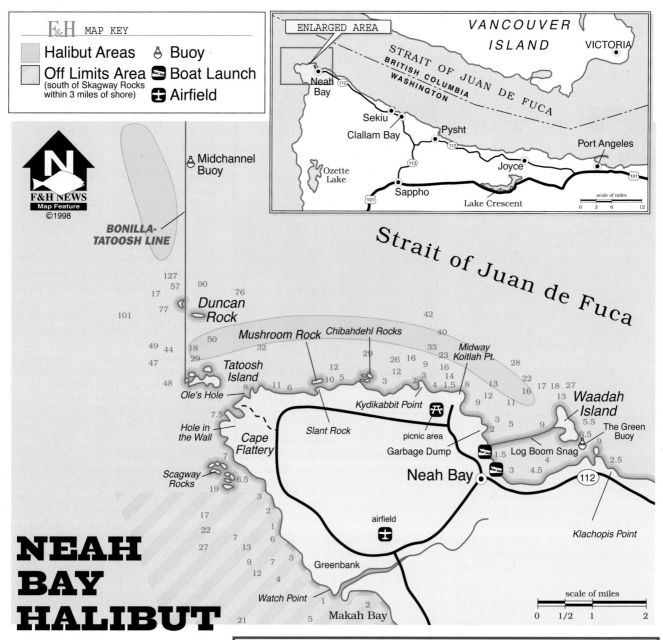

MAP KEY

Halibut Areas   Buoy
Off Limits Area   Boat Launch
(south of Skagway Rocks within 3 miles of shore)   Airfield

ENLARGED AREA

VANCOUVER ISLAND   VICTORIA

STRAIT OF JUAN DE FUCA
BRITISH COLUMBIA
WASHINGTON

Neah Bay

Sekiu
Clallam Bay   Pysht
Ozette Lake   Joyce   Port Angeles
Sappho   Lake Crescent

scale of miles
0   3   6   12

F&H NEWS Map Feature ©1998

Midchannel Buoy

BONILLA-TATOOSH LINE

Strait of Juan de Fuca

Duncan Rock

Mushroom Rock   Chibahdehl Rocks

Midway Koitlah Pt.

Tatoosh Island

Ole's Hole

Kydikabbit Point

Hole in the Wall

Slant Rock   picnic area

Cape Flattery

Garbage Dump

Waadah Island

The Green Buoy

Log Boom Snag

Neah Bay

Scagway Rocks

Klachopis Point

airfield

Greenbank

Watch Point

Makah Bay

scale of miles
0   1/2   1   2

NEAH BAY HALIBUT

two and a half hours to get to the fish, on both the American and the Canadian sides. You'll fish for as long as it takes to catch your fish — then relax and watch the spectacular show of scenery on the way back.

Fishing tips? All it takes to catch halibut is to keep your bait on the bottom. You'll just drop lines and drift. Let out line, or take up slack, to keep contact with the bottom. When your rod tip dips, don't strike on the first nibble. Wait a few seconds for the fish to Bogart that bait. Then snap the rod tip up, hard. You'll feel that heavy solid weight that means you're, er, hooked on halibut.

AT a GLANCE

Location: Canadian waters off Neah Bay

Species: Halibut, average 15-30 pounds, occasional 40-70, largest to over 150 pounds.

Season: All summer on Canadian side for halibut. American side now under a 15,000-pound quota since July 1.

Bag limit: Two, with three-fish possession limit, on Canadian side. American side limit is one fish.

License: Canadian saltwater license required. One-day license, around $6.50 American.

Facilities: Motels, groceries, gas, moorage available in Sekiu/Clallam Bay and Neah Bay communities.

Charters: Big Salmon Resort (866-787-1900) offers charters on both the Canadian and American sides, in 6-, 8- and 12-angler boats.

Everything you wanted to know about Neah Bay halibut, and more

NEAH BAY

by John Martinis

No matter what kind of fishing you do, in general it is fun, relaxing, and often times exciting. I don't know about you but my taste buds really start acting up when I start to think about fresh halibut at the dinner table. I've had more than one customer return for another charter just because their taste buds couldn't do without bottomfish or halibut cooked that special way. Why didn't they just go to the store you ask? (And I'm glad you did.) Here are some reasons:

Yes, it is the challenge, the adventure and the taste of fresh halibut that brings people out time and time again. Although, if this isn't enough, then what about the great memories you make with friends and loved ones. Furthermore, when was the last time you caught a glimpse of an orca, humpback or grey whale? It's not just about going out on some boat to catch a fish.

Halibut and bottom fishing is one of my favorite things to do. Fishing out of Neah Bay and off Cape Flattery is one of the best places to do it. Just out of Neah Bay and west of Waadah Island about 2 to 3 miles are a couple of spots that produce a lot of halibut. The area (4A) which is affectionately referred to as The Garbage Dump, is fished by many anglers each year. This area yields a number of halibut in the 100-pound range annually, and most of the fish are in excess of 30 pounds.

SPECIFIC SPOTS TO FISH are no secret, because one can see them on a NOAA chart of Neah Bay. Many anglers fish what is called The Finger in about 250 feet. The area here tends to be a little less lumpy or windy because it is closer to shore. Another spot you can locate on the chart is approximately 1 mile east of Duncan Rock and another mile

LESLIE WRIGHT caught this halibut in early May of '97 while fishing out of Big Salmon Resort in Neah Bay.

Northwest of The Finger. I call this spot the "Patch." It is a very small area, which comes up to about 300 feet. You have play the tide and the wind right here in order to fish it. This hole has some snags, so be ready and willing to lose some gear. If you remain diligent, you will catch some nice fish.

GEAR: Since there are few dog fish, especially early on, I use a combination of octopus and herring for bait. Although, the pearl/silver flake B-2 squid works well too. I'm using 65-pound Power Pro fishing line on a Penn 340 reel with a medium action Penn Standup Slammer rod. You can use either a long-arm spreader bar or a 2-foot length of 200-pound tuna leader and 3 pounds of weight. They both work well; however, the tuna leader is less complex, less expensive, and less likely to foul. I use 200-pound monofilament leader from the end of the spreader bar or tuna leader to either the cutbait or squid. Go prepared to catch a big fish. You'll need a flying gaff or a harpoon with float to deal with the really big ones.

OFFSHORE: The really wide open fishing for halibut is offshore. The most common areas are Swiftsure, 72 Square, and U.S. or Canadian Blue Dot. I am sure there are many more just waiting to be found.

Swiftsure is 9 to 13 miles west of Cape Flattery, depending on whether you fish U.S. or Canadian waters. When I go to Swiftsure, I enjoy fishing a spot called the Cod Hole. I've gone to basically the same waypoint numbers every time I've gone for the last three seasons, and have not yet experienced any down turn in numbers. As a matter of fact, the '98 season turned out a higher average, 35 to 40 pounds. I fish for halibut pretty much the same way wherever I go. Usually the further out in the ocean you travel, the less effect the currents have — although, the current at Swiftsure can still be pretty difficult to deal with at times.

NEAH BAY Halibut & Rockfish

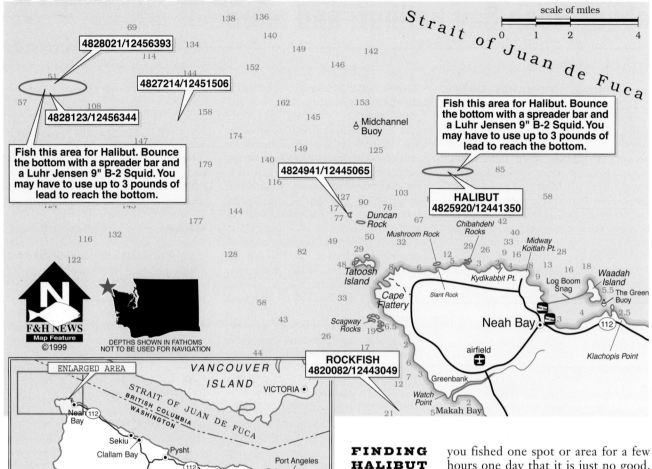

Strait of Juan de Fuca

scale of miles

4828021/12456393

4828123/12456344

4827214/12451506

Fish this area for Halibut. Bounce the bottom with a spreader bar and a Luhr Jensen 9" B-2 Squid. You may have to use up to 3 pounds of lead to reach the bottom.

Fish this area for Halibut. Bounce the bottom with a spreader bar and a Luhr Jensen 9" B-2 Squid. You may have to use up to 3 pounds of lead to reach the bottom.

Midchannel Buoy

4824941/12445065

HALIBUT 4825920/12441350

Duncan Rock

Mushroom Rock

Chibahdehl Rocks

Midway Koitlah Pt.

Tatoosh Island

Kydikabbit Pt.

Log Boom Snag

Waadah Island

The Green Buoy

Cape Flattery

Slant Rock

Neah Bay

Scagway Rocks

airfield

Klachopis Point

F&H NEWS Map Feature
©1999

DEPTHS SHOWN IN FATHOMS
NOT TO BE USED FOR NAVIGATION

ROCKFISH 4820082/12443049

VANCOUVER ISLAND

VICTORIA

Greenbank

Watch Point

Makah Bay

ENLARGED AREA

STRAIT OF JUAN DE FUCA
BRITISH COLUMBIA
WASHINGTON

Neah Bay

Sekiu

Clallam Bay

Pysht

Port Angeles

Ozette Lake

Joyce

Sappho

Lake Crescent

OFFSHORE TACKLE: I like to use a 6-ounce jig head with an 8-inch pearl/silver flake curl tail when I am fishing at Swiftsure Bank. I fish this up to 300 plus feet. With the exception of Canadian Swiftsure, nearly all the places you fish for halibut will be at least 300 feet deep. The 6-ounce jig head works well for halibut and also the occasional rockfish or lingcod. Of course, other heavier jigs like the pipe jig or diamond jig work very well. I don't believe I've ever gone on a halibut trip without pipe jigs on board. Remember these jigs also work well for bottom dwellers other than the halibut. Offshore the dogfish can be a real problem. I use a combination of cut bait and artificial lures early in the season. When dogfish move in, I go to all artificial lures.

FINDING HALIBUT HAUNTS: With regard to finding an area that may hold halibut, I look for any place where the bottom comes up from very deep to about 45 to 80 fathoms. You may begin this process by carefully studying charts for the areas you are going to fish. As you travel to and from these areas, keep a careful eye on your depth finder. I have been fortunate enough to find a few spots that fit the above parameters which are not clearly marked on charts. For the most part, we have been able to catch nice fish consistently at no deeper than around 370 feet. Actually, fishing at 370 feet with the right equipment is not as bad as it sounds. These 40- to 85-fathom plateaus can be a couple of hundred yards up to several miles in diameter. The halibut will come up and lay on top of them along with other bottom-fish. Be patient. Don't think because

you fished one spot or area for a few hours one day that it is just no good. A different day, and or an incoming versus an outgoing tide can make a huge difference. For the most part it takes a lot of time and patience to find a good fishing hole offshore.

SEASON: It's always best to check with the Department of Fish and Wildlife (360-902-2200) before you go fishing. With this in mind, halibut fishing west of the Bonilla-Tatoosh line will open May 1 and probably go to at least July 4. There is a one-fish limit with no size restriction. Halibut fishing out of Neah Bay is outstanding.

GETTING THERE: Neah Bay is located at the far northwest corner of Washington's Olympic Peninsula. Here is how to get there: From Edmonds, take the Edmonds-Kingston ferry to Kingston and follow the signs to Hood Canal and Port Angeles (Hwy. 104). Highway 104 leads into Hwy. 101 before you get to

Port Angeles. When you leave Port Angeles you have two choices, you can either take Hwy. 112 through Joyce or stay on Hwy. 101. If you stay on 101 you will go past Lake Crescent. When you come to Sappho you will see the sign to Neah Bay and Clallam Bay on Hwy. 113, turn right. From Clallam Bay there is only one road to Neah Bay. Most folks think the route around Lake Crescent is easier, but it is about a half hour longer.

From Aberdeen, take Hwy. 101 North through Forks. Going this way you will pass the town of Beaver and make a left onto Hwy. 113 at Sappho. You will see the sign to Clallam Bay Neah Bay.

FACILITIES: At Neah Bay, there is a state-of-the-art marina available for any size boat and plenty of room for the sportsman who brings their own boat. A launch ramp is available for trailered boats. There is a launch fee, so please check with Big Salmon upon your arrival.

CHARTERS: For charter reservations you can call Tommycod Charters (1-800-283-8900) or Big Salmon Fishing Resort (866-787-1900) . You need to call as soon as possible because dates are going fast. Big Salmon does have a number of options for boats from 24 to 55 feet. These boats take from 4 to 14 people depending on the boat size. If you fish the U.S. side you can purchase your license at Big Salmon.

Most boats leave the dock at about 5:30 a.m. and usually do not return until afternoon. This means that you will probably want a lunch and/or snacks with you, and something to drink. Some boats will have hot coffee on board. Breakfast and lunch items are available for purchase at the Big Salmon office. The weather on the ocean in the Neah Bay area can be warm, sunny and delightful, but it also can be very cool and often wet, so be sure to bring clothing that will keep you both warm and dry. Rain gear and boots will almost always come in handy, and we will all be delighted if you don't need them.

You will be provided with rod, reel, and all tackle needed to catch your fish. Be sure to check in at the Big Salmon office when you arrive in Neah Bay. They are open until 10:00 p.m. You will need to get your boarding pass, find out your specific boarding time, and be shown where to board your boat.

CANADIAN LICENSES: If you are going to take a Canadian trip you must purchase your license in Canada before coming to Neah Bay. Here is a list of possible sources for your Canadian license:

1. Campbell River Store (1-604-538-2454) across border at truck crossing in Blaine.

2. Robinson's Sporting Goods (1-250-385-3429) Victoria BC, 6 blocks from ferry.

3. Hub Sports (1-604-859-8316) 22719 Essendine Ave., Abbotsford, BC.

ACCOMMODATIONS: The following is a list of options for accommodations while you are in Neah Bay:

1. The Cape (360-645-2250): Motel, RV and camping with full hook-ups.

2. Hilden's Motel (360-645-2306).

3. Silver Salmon Motel and RV (360-645-2388).

4. Tyee Motel and RV (360-645-2223).

LAST, but not least, you'll need a great recipe for cooking your fish when you get home. The one I'm going to give you is primarily for halibut, but you could use it for other fish as well.

In a bowl stir, but do not blend, the following ingredients:
2-3 jalapeno peppers, diced
1/2 cup fresh green or white onion, diced
3 cups sharp cheddar cheese grated
3-4 cups sour cream
2 cups real mayonnaise

Optional items can be added depending upon your tastes: black olives, chopped bell peppers, mushrooms and a variety of cheeses.

In a casserole dish, place one or two thicker portions of halibut. These fillets should be 4 or 5 inches wide, 11/2 to 2 inches thick and 8 to 9 inches long. Sprinkle these with seasoning salt, and pepper lightly. Spread the paste made from the ingredients above over the fish evenly. Lastly, sprinkle some grated cheese over the top of this. Bake in the oven at about 350-375 degrees for 20 to 40 minutes. This can also be prepared on a cookie sheet on an outdoor gas grill.

Just one word of warning: make sure everyone has a portion on their plate before you allow anyone to taste it or a fight may break out over what remains. This stuff will keep you halibut fishing for the rest of your life.

INFORMATION, EQUIPMENT: You can purchase any of the equipment I've mentioned at John's Sporting Goods in Everett (425-259-3056). Also, if you have any questions about halibut or bottom fishing; please give me a call at Tommycod Charters (800-283-8900).

AT a GLANCE

What: Halibut fishing out of Neah Bay.

When: Season begins May 1 and should continue through at least July 4.

Where: The Finger, Duncan Rock and the Patch are close-in spots. Offshore there's Swift Sure, 72 Square and U.S. or Canadian Blue Dot.

Tackle: Deeper, 300 feet of more, use a 6-ounce jig head with an 8-inch pearl/silver flake curl tail. In more shallow areas, use a combination of octopus and herring for bait, or the pearl/silver flake B-2 squid.

Information: Tommycod Charters (800-283-8900); John's Sporting Goods (425-259-3056); DFW in Olympia (360-902-2200)

May 1 halibut: get your sea legs under you

by Joel Shangle

Sea legs or Dramamine. If you don't have one, you better have the other when halibut season opens May 1 in Marine Areas 1, 2, 3 and 4.

Those of you who can't wait till the May 27 inside halibut opener should prepare yourself like you're heading into a prizefight. This isn't gentle, placid, protected, tucked-away fishing on the lake-flat waters of the Puget Sound. It's rigorous, rocking-and-rolling, out-before-daylight-back-after-dark fishing, miles and miles away from shore.

We're not talking playtoy 18-foot boats here — if you're not driving a 24-plus-footer, don't even think about it.

"I expect to have a limit of fish every day — that's the way it was last year," says Milt Gudgell of Pacific Salmon Charters (800-831-2695) in Ilwaco. "It should be a good fishery as long as it lasts. But where we're fishing, I wouldn't advise any small boats to try to go out that far."

THE BIG BLUE: If you have the experience, knowledge, equipment and desire to run three hours one way to the fishing grounds, the early-May openers in Areas 1 to 4 are surefire hali on the grill. Run out to the fish, catch the fish.

"We'll take up to 15 on some charters, but we'll only fish six at a time," says Gudgell. "It doesn't make sense to get a bunch of lines in the water because they'd get tangled when everybody hooks up. As soon as you get down, you're hooked up."

If you *don't* possess the experience, knowledge, etc., then stow the egocentric posturing and book one of the

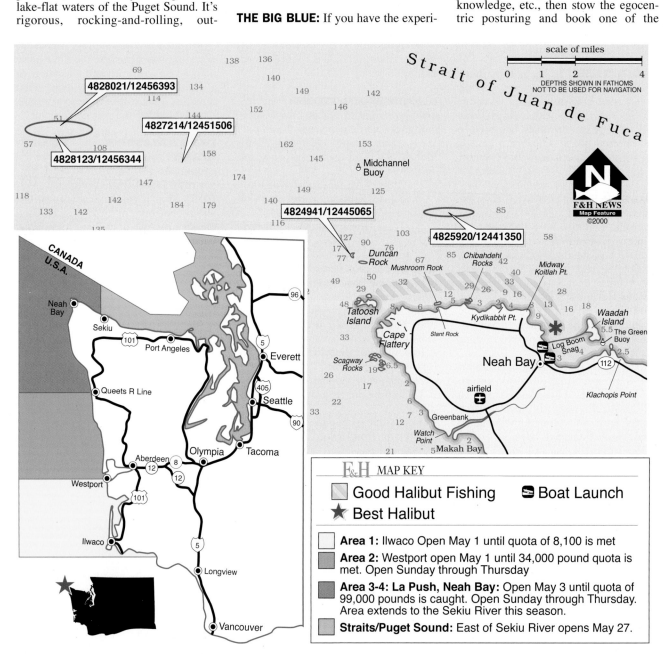

F&H MAP KEY

▨ Good Halibut Fishing   ⬓ Boat Launch
★ Best Halibut

Area 1: Ilwaco Open May 1 until quota of 8,100 is met

Area 2: Westport open May 1 until 34,000 pound quota is met. Open Sunday through Thursday

Area 3-4: La Push, Neah Bay: Open May 3 until quota of 99,000 pounds is caught. Open Sunday through Thursday. Area extends to the Sekiu River this season.

Straits/Puget Sound: East of Sekiu River opens May 27.

FLATTIES averaging 25 pounds will be worth the 30-mile run for anglers fishing aboard charters after the May 1 opener in Marine Areas 1, 2, 3 and parts of 4. Reader Shaun Perin landed this typical halibut.

charters operating out of Ilwaco, Westport or Neah Bay or hit the fisheries close in to Neah Bay (see inset box). Either way, get your butt out after some 'but.

AREA 1 ILWACO: Some of the biggest fish on average on the Pacific Northwest coast are the attraction for boats crossing the bar from the mouth of the Columbia River and heading out into the depths of Area 1.

"We averaged 30 pounds last year," says Gudgell. "This area has the largest average weight year after year on the Oregon/Washington coast."

The quota of 8,100 pounds is the smallest of the four areas, but the fishery isn't highly pressured by private boaters because the best fishing is roughly 25 miles due west of the mouth of the Columbia, in up to 600 feet of water.

AT A GLANCE

What: Pacific halibut season.
When: Starts May 1 in Marine Area 1 (seven days a week) and Marine Area 2 (Sunday through Thursday), opens May 2 in areas 3 and 4 (Tuesday through Saturday).
Limit: One fish per day, 32-inch minimum in Marine Area 1.
Info: Ilwaco: Pacific Salmon Charters (800-831-2695); Westport: Ocean Charters (800-562-0105), Deep Sea Charters (360-268-9300), Coho Charters (800-572-0177); Neah Bay: Tommycod Charters (800-283-8900), Big Salmon Resort (360-645-2374).

Gudgell, who has paid attention to the growing halibut fishery for the last seven years, plans on hitting it only on premium tides to maximize the opportunity.

"I won't fish it every day," he says. "I've gone through the tide books and picked the days that looked the best — little tides, not those big, gushing tides. That way we get a good number of days for a limited number of fish. It's much more meaningful for us if we maximize the days and preserve the season as long as we can."

The days that Gudgell has pegged as good-tide days are May 13-14 and 26-28, June 9-11 and 23-25, July 1-9 and 21-23. Gudgell charges $130 plus tax and license for a charter.

AREA 2 WESTPORT: Open Sunday through Thursday until a quota of just over 34,000 pounds is reached, Westport's halibut fishery is defined by a 25-pound average and occasional slabs weighing upwards of 80 pounds.

"We had a fish that weighed 149 pounds two years ago," says Larry Geisse at Deep Sea (360-268-9300). "The top end is about 80 pounds, but we saw a lot of fish in the 50-pound range last year."

The hot halibut fisheries (the Hot Spot and the Near Spot) are 35 and 25 miles away, respectively, in water ranging from 450 to 750 feet. The Hot Spot will be closed to start the season, but will be reassessed early in May for a possible later opener. Deep Sea's charters run $147.50.

Ocean Charters (800-562-0105) runs charters for up to 12 people for $135 plus tax. Book now for Sunday trips.

Coho Charters (800-572-0177) runs charters aboard a 43-footer for $125 a person.

AREAS 3, 4 LA PUSH/NEAH BAY: Open May 3 Sunday through Thursday until Sept. 30 or until the 99,000-pound quota is met.

Flat out, this is Hali Heaven, starting with Swiftsure Bank and an area on the southeast end of the bank known as the Cod Hole.

"If my clients fishing on the American side want to just get their halibut and get back in, I head straight to Swiftsure," says Tom Young at Tommycod Charters (800-283-8900). "You're almost always going to get something weighing 25 to 35 pounds. The last four years, we've limited every single time we've gone out there. It's that good."

The American side of Swiftsure is roughly 15 miles due west of Neah Bay, routinely running 300 feet deep. Tides and wind can combine to create some tricky conditions at Swiftsure, but drifts will usually be east or west on the tide. Other outside areas to hit out of Neah Bay include the Blue Dot (25 miles) and 72 Square (33 miles).

Coordinates for some of Neah Bay's best outside spots are: 4828123/12456344, 4828021/12456393, 4827214/12451506.

Close-in fishing for *big* 'buts

NEAH BAY HAUNTS are about to open for spring action on this state's biggest flatfish. It's the challenge of hooking into a giant halibut that brings anglers back here year after year.

Neah Bay, located at the farthest northwest tip of Washington, is where the current state-record 288-pound halibut record is held. The term "barn door" fits these fish like a glove, and you don't necessarily need a 27-footer to target some of the biggest fish in the area.

INSIDE SPOTS TO FISH: The closest halibut hole is just out from the entrance of Neah Bay off Waadah Island. Running north out into the Strait of Juan de Fuca can produce fish, and is a great fishery for small-boat anglers, as it's a quick run back into the harbor if the wind kicks up. Waadah also provides some good early action on lingcod.

The Garbage Dump, the most famous inside halibut location in the state, is located just northwest of Neah Bay and provides lots of action for inside anglers. This area yields fish in the 100-pound range, and a large number in the 30- to 40-pound class. Most of the fishing here takes place in 300 to 400 feet of water.

TACKLE: The No. 1 all-time favorite bait for these fish is large horse herring (Black Label Size) off a spreader bar with 12 to 24 ounces of lead. Second would be Tentacle Jigs by John Youngquist — these have proven very deadly on halibut for me. They can also really save the day when the dogfish go on the bite. Let's just say I don't go offshore without them.

For line, stick with a super braid like Power Pro or TUF Line — the thin diameter and zero stretch these lines provide are the only way to fish halibut in deep water.
— *John Keizer*

Central Washington Waters

TROUT

BASS

WALLEYE

KOKES

Alpine Lakes Wilderness full of hike-in trout waters

SKYKOMISH

by Andy Walgamott

Gaze to the east of Seattle on a sunny day. There, out in the blue distance, you'll see the Cascades rising out of the foothills. But the hacked-over mountains on the horizon are just a front range to another rampart beyond, and another beyond that. At the heart of all the uplift and erosion is the Alpine Lakes, a 615-square mile federally protected wilderness that comes by its name honestly. It's studded with hundreds of diamond-beautiful lakes of every sort, everything from massive, deep and island-dotted Dorothy to 7,200-foot-high Ida perched above the Icicle Creek valley to house-sized potholes.

Often ringed by woods and slopes of granitic talus, many of the high lakes are reachable by some sort of trail, maybe not always a maintained Forest Service trail, but a path nonetheless up through the blueberries, into the big timber, across a stickleback ridge and down to a clear, cold pool where rings mark trout rises. Since high school, friends and I have been hiking into lakes like this throughout Washington's central Cascade Range. Always we bring a spinning or fly rod and a tiny tackle box loaded with flies, lures and clear plastic bubbles. And almost always we catch brookies, cutthroat or rainbows.

Special resource: Make no mistake, the Alpine Lakes' namesakes are not your lowland put-n-take fisheries, they're not a resource that will take abusing. Leave Uncle Stringer Filler and cousin Stompon Theprettyflowers at home. While some alpine lakes have naturally reproducing fish populations, state and various groups only occasionally plant certain lakes.

"We plant about 300 lakes in the region on a regular basis," says Mark Downen, a WDFW inland fisheries biologist at the Mountlake Terrace office. By "regular basis," he means a lake may be planted once every four to five years. The state coordinates stocking with groups such as Washington Hi-

Lakers and the Trailblazers, and some larger lakes can be planted by plane.

THE CASCADE RANGE east of Seattle offers a plethora of hike-up trout fishing opportunities for family anglers and hardcore bushwhackers alike. This pretty cutthroat, caught at a lake above 6,000 feet, bit a fly for Greg Olenik.

"What we try to do is plant enough lakes that a person going to a lake is likely to find fish. The Alpine Lakes is a good example," says Downen.

"Meaty" won't describe most fish up here — where there's an overpopulation (and I use that word loosely) their heads are large and out of proportion with their bodies. Most range in size from 5 to 10 inches.

But that's not to say they're all runts. The further back you can get, the bigger the fish. That 14-inch cutt in the photo above came from an Alpine Lakes water above 6,000 feet,

we've cast for a brute that pushed 2 feet at another, and pools of one creek held foot-long cutthroats.

Downen says the most-planted fish nowadays is the Mt. Whitney rainbow trout strain, a subspecies which doesn't reproduce well, if at all, under mountain conditions. By planting this strain and limiting the amount of trout stocked, a lake may grow larger fish.

"You can grow a 4- or 5-pound rainbow up there ... and you can grow them in smaller bodies of water," says Downen.

Another factor in how big fish grow is a lake's geology, Downen says. If the lake bed is granitic, it will have a lower productivity than one with a sedimentary substrate, which is more nutrient rich. Another is how long a lake is ice covered. Most high lakes should be completely open by mid- to late August, especially in this low-snowpack year. A June 9 hike with my girlfriend to Talapus (3,270 feet) and Olallie (3,780 feet) lakes near Snoqualmie Pass found both completely open with fish rising.

"The end of August and September is the peak of alpine lakes trout fishing," says Downen.

High mountain areas are fragile environments. Please stay on trails as much as possible and pack out your litter.

Where to go: By one count there's 600 lakes in the Alpine Lakes Wilderness. And while it's a wild, rumpled stretch of country, proximity to Seattle means it's also well trailed. That's good and bad for mountain anglers. Good because of access. Bad because of access. You and every other Tom, Dick and Harry can hike to Dorothy Lake and be fishing from shore or rubber raft in an hour thanks to well-maintained trails, decent forest roads and paved highways. But the trail to

> **"You can grow a 4- or 5-pound rainbow up there ... and you can grow them in smaller bodies of water."**
> **–Mark Downen, WDFW**

Dorothy can serve as a jumping-off point to other lakes. That's where you, the competent cross-country hiker, can get yourself into some fishy waters.

A valid concern of the state's is how to manage information on high lakes trout fishing — too much publicity might overwhelm a particular lake. In that vein, I'm going to present info on an overwhelming number of lakes in hopes of keeping pressure dispersed.

The following is broken down by river valley. It *includes* lakes to the north of the Alpine Lakes proper.

• **Main Branch Skykomish:** Two big lakes spring out from the map — Wallace (access it via Wallace Falls State Park, a 7-mile hike in for brookies, etc.) and Lake Isabella. The latter is one I'd like to float plane a boat into. Way back in the Sultan Basin above Spada Lake are two more to consider: Big Greider and Boulder. The former is 2 switchback-intensive miles in, and the latter's an easy 3.5. Both have eastern brook, and, according to Downen, Big Greider's got goldens. Boulder fished well last summer for myself and hiking partner Eric Bell — we found lots of hungry brookies at the inlet end of the lake. Packing a float tube into Greider is a viable option. Up in Olney Creek is Lake Stickney.

• **North Fork Sky:** There's Blanca in the headwaters of Troublesome Creek. Survive the trail's near-terminal case of switchbackitis for rainbows and excellent scenery.

• **South Fork Sky:** Barclay Lake is an easy hike in, but a better fishing lake is Eagle, accessible off the sometimes-difficult-to-find trail that leads straight up to the left (north) from Barclay's inlet. Eagle offers lots of shore access and a trail through the aptly named Paradise Meadow, among the most beautiful of lower-elevation meadow strolls.

• **Miller:** An easy-to-reach lake, Dorothy sits practically off the end of

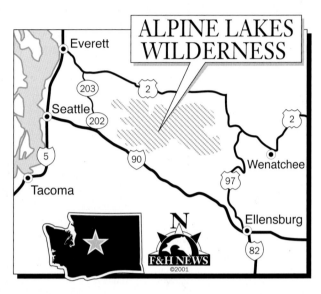

the Miller River Road. A short hike and you're at the 1.5-mile-long lake. Plenty of shoreline here. Step off the trail before the outlet and hug the west shore until you reach the creek-draining Lake Pugsley. Strike up through the woods to this remote lake for brookies.

• **Foss:** Maloney, Evans, Top, Rock, Panorama and Purvis lakes are all accessible via maintained and other trails off Forest Road 6840 south of Skykomish off Foss River Road. A three-in-one hike would take you from road end up a ridge and down into Rock, back up gulches and over a pass to Panorama, and then up an even higher pass under Malachite Peak to Purvis. Tough cross-country work, but it could be worth it. Further up the West Fork Foss River valley is a string of large lakes — Malachite, Copper, Big Heart, Little Heart, Angeline, Azurite, Otter, etc. — and in the East Fork's headwaters is the lake-rich Necklace Valley.

• **Tye:** Fisher Lake holds decent brook trout, and nearby are the Ptarmigan Lakes chain. The easy Surprise Lake Trail takes you four miles to said lake; Glacier Lake is a short ways beyond. A side trail near Surprise's mouth heads up to Trap Lake on the other side of the Cascade crest. Small lakes dot the mountains near Stevens Pass.

• **North Fork Snoqualmie:** With a Weyerhaeuser pass, you've got road access to Calligan and Hancock off the Spur 10 gates north of North Bend. Further up the North Fork road, hike in to Sunday Lake.

• **Middle Fork Snoqualmie:** Just a quarter-mile past where pavement gives out is a gated logging road that leads into the basin containing Upper and Lower Granite lakes (follow old logging tracks down to Upper where there's plenty of shore access). Off the Taylor River trail and up a valley is Marten Lake. The state mentions Hardscrabble Lakes as a planted lake, but if you go, take your buddy's rig — the Middle Fork Road beyond Dingford Creek can be rough.

• **South Fork Snoqualmie:** The trail past Talapus Lake leads up into a cornucopia of waters, including Ollalie, Mason, Island, the Tuscohatchies, Pratt, Kulla Kulla, Thompson, etc. Fly fish off the peninsula at Talapus's inlet end. You'll be with company here —

the whole area gets a lot of use by day-hikers and overnighters.

And here's a general tip: Fish any decent-sized pool below a waterfall/steep pitch of water (like the one just above where Marten Creek crosses the Taylor River Trail). If there's fish in the pool, they'll get smart in a hurry to your lures, but the fun can be well worth the time.

NOTEBOOK

What: High-mountain trout lakes.

Where: East of Seattle, in the Alpine Lakes Wilderness and nearby sections of the Mt. Baker-Snoqualmie National Forest, Wenatchee National Forest and state and private lands.

Species: Rainbow, cutthroat and eastern brook trout. Chance at Mackinaw and golden trout.

Tackle: Clear plastic bubble bobbers, light leader, flies (Carey Specials, midges, nymphs, mosquitos), small lures (Panther Martins).

Access: The Alpine Lakes Wilderness proper is encircled by an asphalt ring comprised of Highways 2, 97, 90, 202 and 203. Numerous gravel forest service or county roads branch off the highways, following most major stream valleys up. Trailheads are everywhere.

Fees: To park within a quarter-mile of any USFS trailhead requires a Northwest Forest Pass ($5 for the day; $30 for the season). Three good spots to get day permits on your way into the national forest include North Bend Texacos (downtown near the post office, Ken's Truck Town) and the espresso stand a half-mile east of Index on the right off US-2. They are also available at Jerry's Surplus in Everett and REI stores. State trailheads, such as those to Greider and Boulder lakes, do not at this time charge parking fees.

Trail conditions: As of early June, some trails at elevation are already snow-free. A good resource for trail reports is the Mt. Baker-Snoqualmie Web site (www.fs.fed.us/r6/mbs/); click on "Trail Conditions." Another is www.wta.org.

Contact: Mt. Baker-Snoqualmie NF Skykomish ranger station (360-677-2414), Leavenworth station (509-763-3103), North Bend station (425-888-1421; Swede's (425-487-3747), Creekside Anglers (425-392-3800)

Tackle: If fishing partner Eric Bell could only take one lure with him into the mountains, he says it would be a green Carey Special. Of course he'd want about a dozen of the flies because high lakes fishing can be tricky with the lake-side brush and snags in the water.

Fishing partner Greg Olenik scoffs at the Carey, saying it's fine if you want to catch runt fish. He touts a black-bodied Panther Martin with yellow-dotted blade and spreads his hands a bit wider to show what size fish it'll catch. Personally, I take both lures up.

Other general patterns to consider: Mosquitoes, leeches, streamers, nymphs, beadheads.

A great high-lakes rig is a clear plastic bubble above a barrel swivel, 4 or more feet of light leader and a fly. Fill the bubble to your liking with water, cast and retrieve. You might consider fishing this rig at night. Bell did so at Little Heart Lake in the headwaters of the West Fork Foss a few years back, catching quite a few smaller fish. And though he admits to partaking of some spirits that eve, he claims it also triggered "a huge hit ... and snap!"

"Damn, I would've liked to have seen how big that one was," he mutters to this day.

Regardless, leaders should be light because of water clarity.

Preparations: To get started, you should have a hiking trails book. If you don't have one (or several), go to your local library or book store — they'll have an extensive selection. After that, you'll want good quality maps. Green Trail maps are nice, but I prefer USGS 7.5-minute-series maps — they're better for off-trail work. REI has both kinds. Next, get ahold of a "Lakes of Washington" book — these are like gold with their size, altitude and depth data as well as aerial and shoreline lake pictures.

In your pack include a knife, compass, rainjacket, extra clothes, food and water, water purification tablets or pump, matches, bug spray, a mini first aid kit, mirror and camera. As much as it pains me to write this, you might even bring a cell phone.

Always let someone know where you're going, hike with a partner and know your limit — when the contour lines get close, things get steep and hairy. Turn around and ask yourself, "Are my knees ready for going back down?"

And keep valuables out of plain sight in your vehicle at the trailhead.

Banks Lake winter trout a solitary pursuit

COULEE CITY

by Dusty Routh

The first thing you notice as you drive from the southern end of Banks Lake over Dry Falls Dam into Coulee City is that no one is here. If you vacation here in the summer, maybe doing a little walleye fishing or smallmouth chasing, you know that massive Banks Lake is a real fun-in-the-sun hot spot, replete with water skiers, campers and tons of bass and walleye boats.

ON the SCENE

But in the chilling months of winter, the whole area is a ghost town. There's just nobody here, and that in itself is an alluring feature.

As you drive up the lake along Highway 155, you also notice that Banks is eerily calm. Famous for stiffly fierce winds in spring and summer, in winter the upper Grand Coulee impoundment might have a slight afternoon breeze. But most of the time it's as flat as a pancake and calm as glass.

And why fish Banks in the winter, besides the aesthetics that it offers? All the lake's spinyrays are locked up in cold-water lockjaw, after all. But Banks also has trout in it, mostly unmolested, untargeted trout, that no one really bothers to fish for. And that's a crying shame, because these are some of the biggest, most beautifully colored trout you'll catch anywhere in the state. Best

of all, you'll have these fish all to yourself all winter long.

Getting down to business: There are seven boat launches on Banks: Two at the southern end (one in Dry Falls Junction, and one in Coulee City), two at roughly the mid-section of the eastern shore (known as the Million Dollar Mile portion of the lake), and the rest at the far north end. One of these is at Steamboat Rock State Park, and the other is in the same vicinity but on the mainland shore just north of there. The other ramp is at the far north end of the lake in Electric City, at Coulee Playland.

At press time, south- and north-end bays had ice cover, so you'll want to call Coulee Playland (509-633-2671) and Big Wally's (509-632-5504) for the latest before trailering your boat here.

The lake's resident rainbows are scattered from one end of the lake to the other. The big rainbows don't school, so it's difficult to get into real numbers at any one time. However, in the winter they can be found pretty close to the surface, and trolling is the best way to pick these solitary fish off.

On a recent trip to Banks we started our four days of fishing by pulling in at the Million Dollar Mile to work the significant rock walls and cliffs that Banks is so noted for. This can be a fantastic place to fish, so long as the wind is down. When the wind's up, fishing the northern end is safer and more comfortable, particularly in the rock-protected bays and coves around Steamboat Rock.

Both middle-lake ramps along the Million Dollar Mile are rough launches. There are no docks, no places to tie up. It's a good idea to have a 4-wheel-drive vehicle, particularly if you've got a big boat or if it's been snowing or it's

PULL SPOONS either off a downrigger or leadcore for Banks Lake trout.

icy. My 17-footer slid in just fine, and came out just fine, with a little 4-wheel-drive assistance. Given the absence of a dock, it's a good idea to have waders or hip boots.

Get some 'bows: Interestingly, there's a really significant first-light bite on Banks. All our big fish came before 9 a.m. The fishing slowed between 9 a.m. and 1 p.m. but picked up again as the sun was going down.

You can fish with downriggers, anywhere from 10 feet down to 40 feet, and find fish. We also pulled leadcore, and spoons were hot. Fire tiger Needlefish, red/brass Needlefish, and chrome/gold Gibbs spoons were excellent. We also caught plenty of fish on a jointed fire tiger Rapala, as well as on a small fire tiger blade bait flat-lined as our third rod (one leadcore rod, one downrigger rod, and one flat-line rod).

What's really incredible is how colorful these trout are, and how big they are on average. We didn't catch any fish under 2 pounds, and all were chrome bright with amazingly red gill plates and sides.

Banks' water is clear this time of year, and we got the sense the fish

AT a GLANCE

What: Winter trout fishing in the northern Basin.

Where: Banks Lake's midsection and north end. Fish the vertical cliff walls along the Miracle Mile at the lake's mid-section, then troll around the rock islands at Steamboat.

How: Troll three rods: a leadcore rod with spoon, a flat-line rod with anything fire tiger-colored, and a downrigger rod with a brass/red Needlefish or chrome/gold Gibbs spoon.

Tackle and info: Coulee Playland (509-633-2671) on the north end; Big Wally's (509-632-5504) on the south end.

Banks Lake

were easily spooked. Executing lots of turns, stopping and starting, and putting lines well behind the boat seemed to help.

Up to Steamboat:
While the Million Dollar Mile rock walls on the eastern shore, and the towering cliffs and points directly across and south from there on the other side of the lake produced good fishing, it wasn't until we hit the Steamboat area that we really got into fish. Launching from the state park, we started trolling right away in the rock cauldron of this area, and picked up good fish right at first light. The bite seemed to stay on pretty good throughout the day. The number of fish wasn't exceptional, but it was steady, and we released everything, so we weren't really fishing for limits. Still, we easily would have limited out by noon each day.

At Steamboat we put the downrigger away — most of the water in this area is no more than 50 feet deep. We ran two leadcore rods with long mono leaders and brass/red spoons, and trailed a fire tiger blade bait and jointed Rapala on the flat-line rod — these were the really productive baits. An angler we talked to at Coulee Playland said that he fished at the far north end of the lake and hit limits each day by trolling pink Apexes.

Our trolling speed ran the gamut, from dead slow to super quick. Speed, however, didn't seem to be near as critical as stop-and-start and turning motions with the kicker.

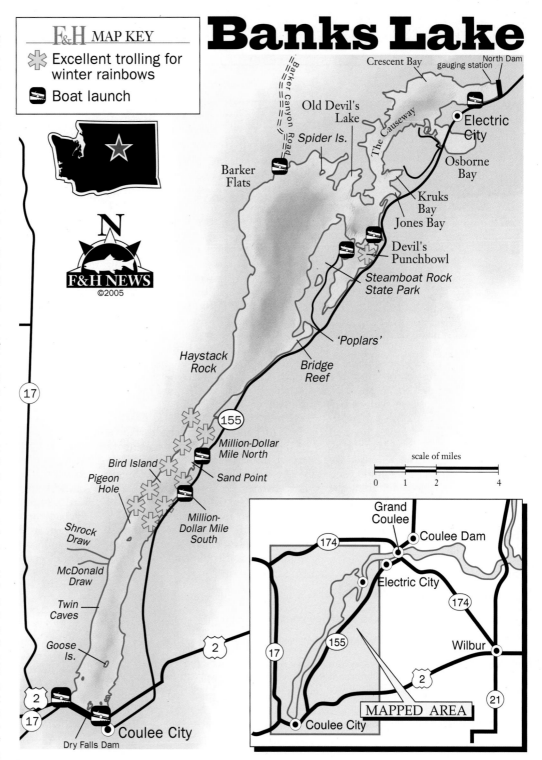

MAP KEY
✳ Excellent trolling for winter rainbows
🚤 Boat launch

F&H NEWS ©2005

Contact information: For tackle, fuel, fishing information, RV and camping sites, and good advice and help when you need it, Coulee Playland is the place. They're open all winter. For lodging, there are a number of motels in the area, including Center Lodge Motel (509-633-0770), Trails West Motel (509-633-3155) and the Sky Deck Motel (509-633-0290). The best place to get breakfast in Grand Coulee early in the morning is Flo's Café (check out their collection of coffee mugs), and the best place to get a burger-n-beer is Stuck's Bar and Grill, right on Spokane Way in Grand Coulee.

Best Banks Lake walleye, bass days coming up

— COULEE CITY

by Leroy Ledeboer

ABUNDANT SMALLMOUTH and good numbers of walleye make Banks Lake a great spot for sport and fillets.

Once water temperatures climb into the mid- to high 50s, there isn't really a bad time to fish for smallmouth bass on Banks Lake. Some of you may still consider late May and all of June prime time. You can also take walleye throughout the summer and into the fall, but June is definitely the apex of that fishery. The walleye spawn is over, the postspawn bite is on, and young-of-the-year forage fish aren't yet as plentiful as they'll be in late summer.

North end: Banks Lake smallmouth have now proliferated to the point where they may soon be subjected to more liberal harvest rules, and its walleye are definitely making a real comeback after a few somewhat down years. A recent WDFW netting study turned up surprisingly good numbers in many of the back bays.

"Up at the north end, you have all kinds of good walleye bays that turn on in late May or early June," says expert angler Gordie Steinmetz at Big Wally's (800-632-5504). "Osborne Bay, Brian's Bay, Jones Bay, Kruks Bay, the Devil's Punchbowl, Old Devil's Lake, inside Steamboat Rock — they're all walleye havens at that time of year, especially when a steady southwest wind is blowing. If you can

locate the old roadbed, right off the southern tip of Steamboat Rock, it's a good place for both walleye and bass."

It takes a decent-sized boat and some expertise, but Banks Lake walleye regulars know that a pretty stiff breeze means these fish will get active in a hurry. A pounding surf disorients their forage fish, allowing the big predators to move in for an easy meal.

"Yeah, let the wind be your friend," Steinmetz says. "Don't take unnecessary risks, but if you can handle a pretty good chop, you're going to catch more walleye than if you're always looking for calm water.

"Start in close, maybe in 10 to 12 feet of water," Steinmetz says. "Then, if you're not hitting fish, work your way out to 20 feet or so. Trolling spinners and 'crawlers behind bottom-walkers is always a good way to begin, but if you're fishing over grassy or weedy areas that make that tough, go to cranks, maybe a No. 5 Rapala for 9 to 10 feet, a No. 7 for 12 feet or a No. 8 for 15 feet. A lot of colors might work, but I like perch and clown patterns."

Although there might be a few walleye on the big part of Osborne Bay, east of the highway, this is primarily bass territory. It also holds good numbers of perch and crappie.

There are some dandy points and inlets further north, particularly on the west side, where I've seen the bass pros yarding in smallmouth, and where I've had pretty fair walleye fishing success.

Just across the lake from Steamboat Rock lies a huge span of water called Barker's Flats. It's appropriately named, because one "flat" seems to stair-step into the next. You can start on the really shallow shelves and gradually work your way out. I've been on Barker's when the walleye were at 6 to 8 feet, and I've hit it when you had to go to a heavier bottom bouncer and troll the 35-foot stretches.

These bays also hold plenty of smallmouth, which you'll often nail on your walleye gear. To target them specifically in early and mid-June, work the shoreline riprap with plastics, lizards, tubes, Senkos, spinner-

AT a GLANCE

What: Walleye and smallmouth bass fishing in northern Grant County.

Where: Banks Lake, between Coulee City and Electric City.

North-end hot spots: Osborne Bay, Brian's Bay, Jones Bay, Kruks Bay, Devil's Punchbowl, Old Devil's Lake, Steamboat Rock, road bed off Steamboat, Barker's Flats, Haystack Rock, Rose Bush, Million Dollar Mile North, Sand Point, McDonald Draw, Twin Caves.

South-end hot spots: Goose Island, dam riprap, sunken islands and reefs.

Walleye how-to: It's tough, but you may have better luck fishing on choppy days. Start fairly shallow and troll spinner-'crawlers combos behind bottom-walkers, or, depending on water depth, try No. 5, 7 or 8 Rapalas in perch and clown through spring. As water warms, try more crankbaits and troll slightly faster for more aggressive fish.

Bass how-to: Work the shores and rocky rubble with plastic worms, lizards, tubes, Senkos, spinnerbaits and crankbaits.

Contacts: Gordie Steinmetz at Big Wally's (800-632-5504; bigwallysfishing.com) in Coulee City; Coulee Playland Resort (509-633-2671; couleeplayland.com) near Electric City.

Banks Lake

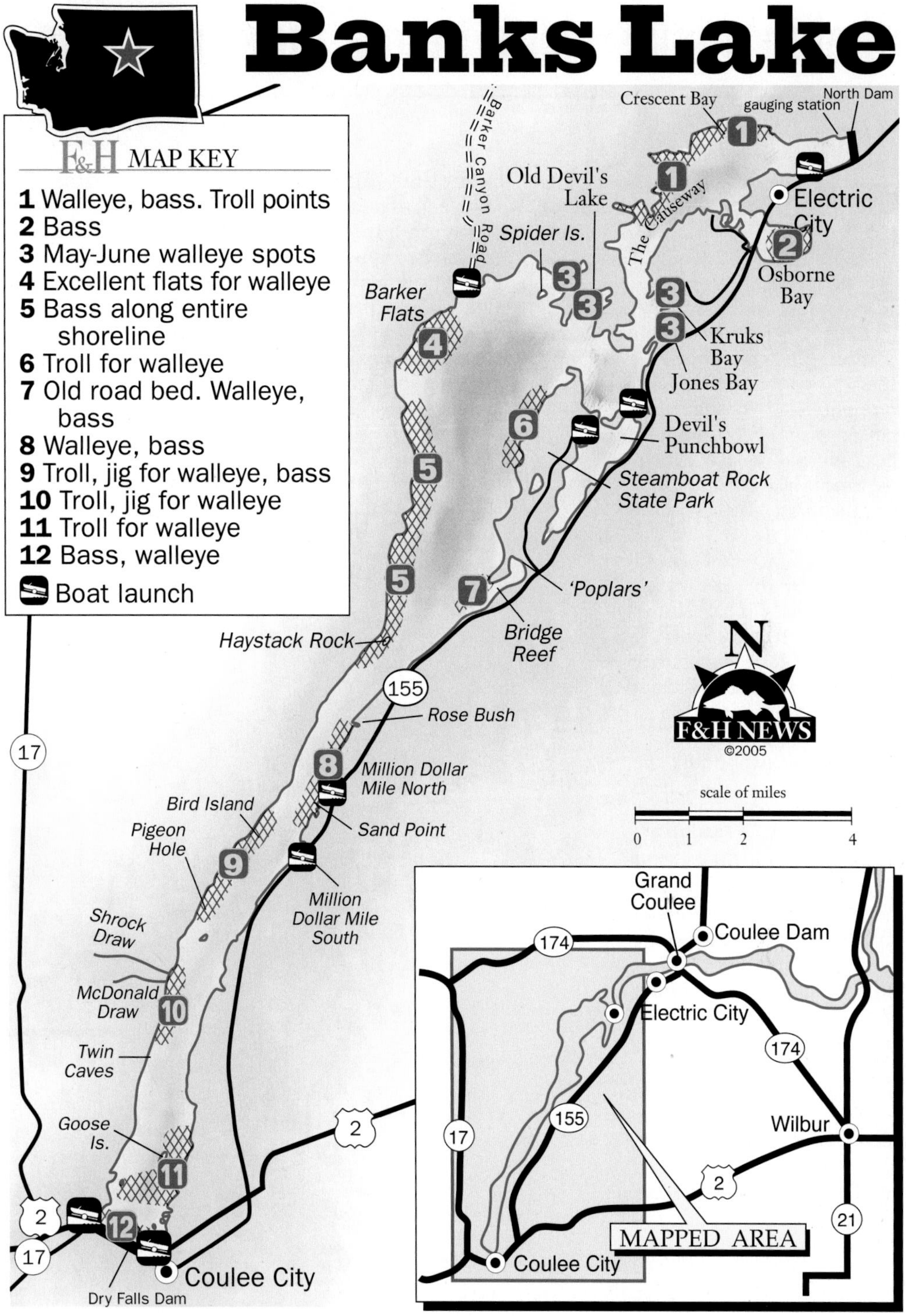

baits and cranks. Often, they'll be right up in the shallows, particularly in the early morning, and again an hour or so before sundown.

"Barker's Flats holds plenty of bass too, and from there you can work your way south along the shoreline, all the way to below Haystack Rock, and find bronzebacks," Steinmetz says. "Well, actually, you can now find smallmouth just about anywhere along that western shoreline."

Midlake: "Just below Haystack, you can cross back to the east shore and have almost a 3-mile stretch of good bass and walleye water," Steinmetz says, "everything from above Rose Bush, all the way past the Million Dollar Mile North boat launch to Sand Point. Around Rose Bush, you'll find boulder fields. As its name indicates, Sand Point features nice sandy flats that, at times, hold plenty of fish."

"From there, you can again cross the lake and work your way south," Steinmetz says, "from above Bird Island down to the Pigeon Hole, for both species. After that, say near McDonald Draw and the Twin Caves, you again have real nice walleye flats, 20 to 25 feet deep."

South end: Probably no one knows the far south-end waters better than Steinmetz does, but this area has so much walleye structure that he's hesitant to single out specific reefs and points. Obviously, the ridges off Goose Island and the riprap near the dam are good places to start, but this area holds so much more.

"Get yourself a good map that shows all the sunken islands and reefs and just start working them, marking up your GPS wherever you get action," he says. "A lot of anglers are afraid of this part of the lake because of all those rocks, but if you're careful until you know your way around, it's a good place to find walleye."

"Early on, you're probably going to catch most of your walleye on those spinner-'crawler combos, but as we move into summer, spend some of your fishing hours running cranks, and even with your spinner rigs, pick up your trolling speed," Steinmetz says. "As the water warms and the fish get more aggressive, it can be much more effective than the traditional, slow walleye speeds too many anglers never abandon."

F&H MAP KEY

1 Walleye, bass. Troll points
2 Bass
3 May-June walleye spots
4 Excellent flats for walleye
5 Bass along entire shoreline
6 Troll for walleye
7 Old road bed. Walleye, bass
8 Walleye, bass
9 Troll, jig for walleye, bass
10 Troll, jig for walleye
11 Troll for walleye
12 Bass, walleye

Boat launch

Crescent Bay
North Dam gauging station
Electric City
Old Devil's Lake
Spider Is.
The Causeway
Osborne Bay
Barker Canyon Road
Barker Flats
Kruks Bay
Jones Bay
Devil's Punchbowl
Steamboat Rock State Park
'Poplars'
Bridge Reef
Haystack Rock
155
Rose Bush
Million Dollar Mile North
Bird Island
Sand Point
Pigeon Hole
Shrock Draw
Million Dollar Mile South
McDonald Draw
Twin Caves
Goose Is.
Coulee City
Dry Falls Dam
17
2

N
F&H NEWS
©2005

scale of miles
0   1   2   4

Grand Coulee
Coulee Dam
174
Electric City
174
155
17
Wilbur
2
MAPPED AREA
21
Coulee City
2

Chelan's lakers and kokes: best days lie ahead

by Leroy Ledeboer

When I joined guide Craig Martin of Mountain Dew Guide Service (509-884-3582) for a morning on the crystal-clear waters of Lake Chelan in early April, our weather changed hourly, everything from sporadic clouds and a nippy wind to bright balmy sunshine. We fished the midlake flats almost straight out from the Mill Bay Boat Launch. We caught lake trout, but not with the speed Martin's accustomed to.

"The barometer's been all over the place this past week," he explained. "That always makes these fish less active. If we'd have had steady weather for the last couple of days, we'd be nailing more lakers, plus some lings."

For about two hours we tried jigging up these two species, using 2-ounce bullethead jigs with white or green skirts and baited with pikeminnow fillets. Either the fish didn't like my green skirt or I was holding my mouth wrong, but Martin pulled four lakers ranging from 3 to 5 pounds out of that 200-foot water.

When we went to trolling, using big 00 flashers trailed by hoochies, again baited with pikeminnow fillet, we were only targeting the lakers. We'd set our downriggers within 10 or 15 feet of the bottom, and Martin kept up a slow troll with his electric. Our strikes were steady, about one every 10 minutes or so, and we did make several hookups, but again the lakers were lethargic, often giving our baits an initial tug, then disappearing.

"May and June are absolutely our best months," Martin says. "The weather is better, and they've dumped enough water over the dam to pull most of the baitfish down here to the south end of the lake, so of course all the predator fish are here too. That's when I can run two upper lines for kokanee, my two downriggers for lake trout and have almost constant action."

Kokanee coming: I was there a bit early for kokes, but these delicious little salmon give me a good excuse to go back in May. Troll with Pop Geer or flashers, trailed by Wedding Rings baited with corn. Martin, though, says he gets better action by using the smaller Mack's Lures Kevlar Flashlights, trailed by his home-made spinners baited with a small chunk of white foam soaked in Pro-Cure shrimp oil. "Corn or even maggots may be just as good at attracting strikes, but with the foam you're spending way less time rebaiting and more time fishing," Martin explains.

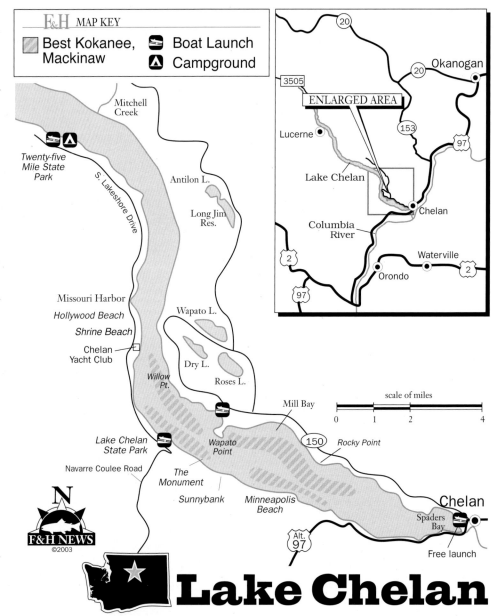

Jig for Chelan's massive winter Mackinaw

MANSON

by Dusty Routh

Ever dragged up a 20-plus-pound lake trout from over 200 feet of water? Now's your chance.

The winter months at Washington's premier lake trout factory, Lake Chelan, represent the best time of the entire year to get over these deep char and jig a tempting morsel in front of their snappy maws.

You can troll for lake trout too, and a lot of anglers do. But chances are pretty good that you'll be outdone by those laker seekers energetic and dedicated enough to jig for these bottom-hugging, deepwater residents rather than troll around for them.

One of the key elements to lake trout that calls for a jigging strategy is that they lay right on the bottom and cruise for forage very close to it. The contours at the bottom of Lake Chelan range from deep flats and bowls to very abrupt up-and-down ridges and shelves and rock formations. Those contours rapidly transition when you're trolling, making the objective of keeping your rig close to the bottom either a real chore or a definite impossibility. But by jigging, you can hit bottom on every bounce.

AT a GLANCE

What: Excellent winter fishing for lake trout and freshwater lings on Washington's Lake Chelan.

How: Jig 2-ounce leadhead jigs with northern pikeminnow, herring or plastics in water ranging from 100 to 250 feet deep.

Where: The entire southern third of the lake holds fish. Wapato Point is one of the best places to start.

When: Anytime you can get there. Winter's a great season for these coldwater critters.

Guides: Terry Allan, Allan's Fishing Guide Service (509-687-3084; 670-0411); Anton Jones, Darrell and Dad's Guide Service (509-687-0709).

Lodging info: Go to *lakechelan.com*.

YOU CAN GO either high tech (electronic downriggers) or low tech (leadhead jigs) for Mackinaw this winter on Lake Chelan. Either way, you'll be in the running for a big laker.

"You want to do about an 18-inch jig motion," says lake trout guide and Lake Chelan expert Terry Allan with Allan's Fishing Guide Service (509-670-0411) in Manson. "On the drop, you want to hit bottom every time."

That kind of regularly-in-touch-with-the-bottom strategy equals putting your offering in front of Mr. Big Char a whole lot more often than you could ever hope to do by trolling.

That is, unless your boat is equipped with electronic downriggers tuned to your bottom finder. Some boats do have this technology (these are very popular set-ups, for example, on Idaho's Priest Lake, and on the Great Lakes), but without this kind of expensive, specialized gear, you're better off wrist-jamming to get at these fish.

"Even in the tournaments you'll find that guys jigging will outfish the trollers by a huge margin," Allan reports.

He's been fishing Chelan for 16 years, and guiding on it professionally for six years. Allan also fishes the Columbia River for salmon and walleye, and Rufus Woods for triploids.

"So far this winter jigging for the lake trout has been really good," Allan reports. "We had that real hard cold spell in early January that made it hard on the equipment, but other than that it's been a great winter of fishing so far."

Mack daddies: For those who aren't familiar with Lake Chelan as a winter fishing destination (maybe you know it best via a beer-induced haze, faintly recalling a blazing hot bikini fest of water- and Jet-skiing in the summer months), this big Eastside lake offers one of the best spots — if not the best spot — in Washington for nailing a big lake trout. Allan's boat has produced two state-record Mackinaw, a 33.65-pound laker and the current record, a 35.7-pound fish taken in December 2001.

There are no daily limits or size restrictions on the lakers. This doesn't set well with Allan, who feels the lake trout are getting a bad rap.

"We try to catch-and-release as much as possible," Allan says. "But the problem is, they killed off all the good Chinook salmon fishing by derby fishing and by a lot of pressure when the salmon fishing wasn't so good on the west side of the state. Now they blame it on the lake trout. The next thing you know they're going to kill off the lake trout the same way, by allowing all this derby fishing and not having any limits or size restrictions."

Lake Chelan used to offer trophy-class freshwater Chinook fishing similar to what anglers can find at blue-ribbon Coeur d'Alene Lake in Idaho. But, says Allan, "Chelan's salmon are pretty much fished out now. I think the fisheries managers and the sportsmen's association out here let that fishery get fished out."

February/March fishing: During these two terrific months of the year for lakers, one of the best ways to induce a Mackinaw bite is to fish with a 2-ounce leadhead jig adorned with a northern pikeminnow.

"You can also use herring," says Allan, "or a Mad Max Crayfish. I've also used some Storm Crawdads with a rattle, and Exude crawdads."

Whichever you choose, fish your jig between 100 and 250 feet of water, bouncing it right on the bottom on every drop. That kind of action is sure to get the attention of one of the thousands upon thousands of lakers lurking near the bottom.

If you split your bait open or switch it with chicken livers, get ready for some outstanding burbot action. Burbot are pretty homely looking, but on the grill or deep-fried they're every bit as good as a saltwater lingcod.

No need to run uplake: Though Macks are scattered throughout Chelan, and a potential record is probably swimming around somewhere up in the unpressured northern part of the lake, the southeastern end has more food fish to offer and the water's somewhat warmer. Another factor driving most anglers to fish the lower end is that conditions on Lake Chelan can turn viciously bad rapidly, making the place a raging sea.

"The fishing is just as good close to home as it is if you were to run way up the lake, so why make such a long drive?" Allan offers.

He usually fishes his clients right at daybreak, and fishes six to eight hours or until they hit self-imposed limits of five burbot and five lake trout.

"On an average day we're picking off 20 to 25 fish," for catch-and-release, he says.

Fighting big lakers: A key piece of counsel Allan gives his clients is to patiently work these fish up from the bottom, particularly from really deep water.

"If you bring them up too fast, their air bladder will expand and we won't be able to release them," he says. "Plus it takes the fight out of them. If you bring them up more slowly, that air bladder doesn't expand and they'll fight you the whole way up to the boat."

Hot spots: Anywhere in the lower third of the lake can hold fish. Reliable time-after-time hot spots, however, include Mack Bar, Wapato Point and Party Point.

"Also," says Allan, "that first deep hole out of Chelan, about in line with the Chelan Shores Condos, straight out from that, where the deep water first begins, that's a great place."

Start by finding water around 100 feet deep and work your boat around that contour. Then move out deeper in a very gradual, flat "Z" pattern, working progressively deeper on every turn, jigging the whole time. The take from a deep-water Mack in late winter won't

be aggressive. Your line will simply stop, that's about it, and you'll have to set the hook on a deep fish.

This is when using a non-stretch super braid line becomes an absolute must. Allan uses PowerPro spooled on Shimano 300 Corsair reels. He deploys a 10-foot leader, the leader made up of 15- to 20-pound Maxima Ultragreen monofilament.

For deep-water jigging rods, Allan utilizes a medium-heavy action Shakespeare Intrepid. "You need a stiff rod with a stiff tip," he says. "You don't want a club, just a heavy steelhead-type rod with a stiff tip."

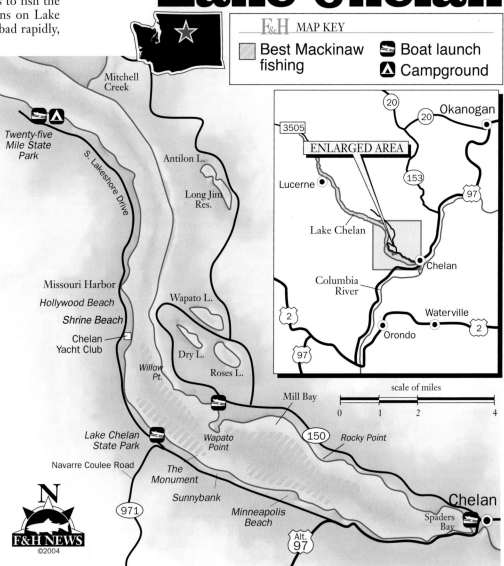

Lake Chelan

F&H MAP KEY

Best Mackinaw fishing   Boat launch   Campground

Fish Lake lives up to its dazzlingly fishy name

PLAIN

by Dusty Routh

Sometimes you're amply rewarded by the fish gods. And when you are, it sets your whole life straight. The nonsensical makes sense, the sky is bluer, all is right with the infinite universe, and everything falls in to place just as the winds of fate surely must have somehow decreed.

Such is your mindset when you can catch limits of scrappy trout within minutes. Such is your life when everything you throw in the water catches fish. Your ego grows to unimaginable proportion and you think to yourself, "Damn, I am a really good fisherman."

That's the experience you can expect when you travel U.S. 2 and launch your boat off the little dirt boat ramp at Cove Resort (509-763-3130) on Fish Lake, just north of Leavenworth.

Fishing with my trout bum pal James Seno, we set speed records by scoring limits of scrappy trout within 20 minutes of commencing fishing one evening recently. The next day, we ventured back out with our buddy Wally Walker and caught and released 70-something fish on barbless hooks throwing rainbow and chrome Kastmasters at the far end of the lake.

Get to know the lake: Fish Lake isn't huge or intimidating, and that's a big part of its attractive charm. While the wind can howl across the water delivering moderate whitecaps, with morning breezes coming from the east and afternoon gales coming down the Cascades from the west (bringing cold air off the remaining snow right down to the lake), at other times it's dead-flat calm and as gorgeous and emerald as any mountain lake you've ever seen.

Fish Lake is located just to the north of the eastern tip of Wenatchee Lake. To get there, take U.S. 2 to Coles Corner and turn north on Highway 207. Follow the signs to Cove Resort. There you'll find moorage slips, boat launch, convenience store, bait and tackle. It, as well as nearby Lake Wenatchee State Park (509-763-3101), have campsites. Cascade Hideaway Resort (509-763-5104) on the lake's north side also features a boat launch, fishing dock and lodging, though you'll need to be a member for access.

At roughly 500 acres, Fish Lake is the perfect size for most anything that floats. You'll see cartoppers, runabouts, float tubes, fish/ski boats and all manner of fishing craft on the water. If you have a small boat, this is a perfect place to fish.

There are no speed limits on the lake, so if you have a big outboard, be mindful of the canoes, cartoppers and float tubers that may have difficulty with your wake.

All about the fish: Most of what you'll find at Fish Lake are trout. Scads and scads of them in the form of scrappy, feisty, highly cooperative rainbows running from 8 to 12 inches. They are everywhere in the lake. Most anglers troll for them, either under power of electric or kicker motor, or simply by turning their boats sideways to the wind and drifting from one end of the lake to the other.

You'll find that trout respond mightily to a green Wedding Ring tipped with a chunk of nightcrawler. Or a red Wedding Ring. Or a fly. Or a Kastmaster. Or a Super Duper. Or a small Needlefish. Or just about any trout gear you'd care to put in the water. The hottest bite happens early and late in the day, but the action is pretty much non-stop no matter what time it is.

You don't need downriggers. My favorite rig is a small 000 dodger and a green Wedding Ring tipped with a chunk of 'crawler, fished 65 pulls behind the boat. Get your offering out and away from the boat to increase your catch rate. We trolled with our electric on moderate speed and cleaned up. We also noted that on just about every sharp turn we hit a fish.

REPEAT AFTER ME: "I'm a great fisherman, I'm a great fisherman." That's what you'll think if you take time to hit aptly named Fish Lake, where Wally Walker landed this nice brown.

One of the best ways to fish the lake is to run to the eastern end and troll north-south from shoreline to shoreline. You can also do the same thing at the western end of the lake. We caught fewer fish on the north and south shorelines than we did at the east and west ends.

Fish Lake also has some brooders and we've heard rumors of triploid plantings, so don't be surprised if something big hits in between the hundreds of bites you'll get from the 8-inchers.

In addition to the rainbows, you also might hit a German brown trout or two. Of our 10 fish the one evening and 70 fish the next day, we hit one 2-pound brown. There are larger browns in the lake, however. If you want to target them exclusively, get on the water early-early or late-late in the day and troll the shoreline with jointed Rapalas or large streamers.

Fish Lake is also famous for perch. Drop a night-crawler to the bottom just about anywhere and you'll clean up.

By the fly: If you like to fly fish, this is a terrific spot to do it, particularly when the wind lays down. Any wet fly or streamer will do the job. Dry fly action can be expected later in summer when bug activity in the mountains hits its hot-weather peak, usually from June on. If you're camping, expect mosquitoes starting in June too.

For browns, fish a sink tip line and streamer on an extra long leader off the brush and grass along the shoreline. The key is to get on the lake early or fish it at dusk when the browns tend to be the most active. Expect fish in the 2- to 5-pound class, though bigger ones have been caught.

Miscellany: The lake is a perfect place to take kids and/or a spouse who must have constant action in order to enjoy a fishing trip. This is a very kid-friendly place. Remember to put a life vest on 'em. If you don't have a boat, you can rent one from Cove Resort, or fish on their oversized public fishing dock.

If fishing in the wind bothers you, you can get out of it somewhat by fishing at the end of the lake in the direction of where the wind is blowing (fish the west end of the lake when the wind is blowing from the west, for example).

AT a GLANCE

What: Incredible trout action at Fish Lake near Leavenworth. If you want a hot bite, this is the place.

When: Spring and early summer are the very best times, but the lake fishes well all summer into early fall.

How: Troll all the standard trout gear, from Wedding Rings to spoons. Or simply cast and retrieve a rainbow-colored Kastmaster (replace the treble with a single hook).

Where: The east and west ends of the lake seem to produce the best.

Camping: Lake Wenatchee State Park (509-763-3101)

Who to call: Cove Resort (509-763-3130); Cascade Hideaway Resort (509-763-5104).

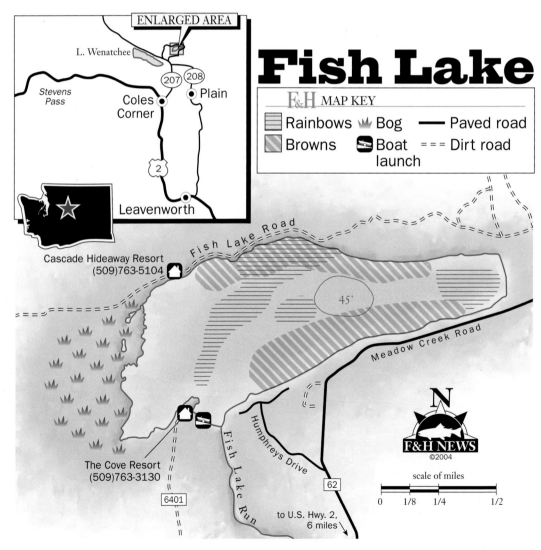

Mineral Lake perfect for easy fishing, easier limits

ELBE

by Dusty Routh

Occasionally you get lucky and find yourself on a certain body of water where you can measure the fishing in minutes, rather than in inches and pounds. Meaning, how many minutes once you're on the lake before you get your first strike, and how many fish can you catch with your fishing buddy during friendly 15-minute mini-tournaments. That's how you measure the fishing at Mineral Lake.

On a recent trip here the week after the season opener in April, we had our first strike two minutes after we put a line in the water. We had four subsequent pokes before we finally hooked up. During one quarter-hour mini-tournament, my fishing buddy for the day, son Nicky Routh, won with a score of two fish to one. The next 15-minute tourney he won too, three fish to two.

Other lakes may be more challenging, but not many will be more productive than Mineral Lake. This 360-acre natural lake in the shadow of Mount Rainier just south of Elbe in Lewis County is about as trustworthy and reliable for easy limits of trout as any body of water in the state.

It may not be the quietest or least crowded of lakes, but Mineral more than makes up for its popularity with the quality of its fishing. On our weekday spent here, we counted 16 boats on the water, all of them catching fish. On the weekends, expect a lot more boats. But there's plenty of fish to go around, including some big ones.

Fish factory: As Kenna Bergstrom at Mineral Lake Resort (360-492-5367) will tell you, the lake is an ongoing experiment for WDFW biologists.

"I think they're earning their doctorates on this lake," she jokes. "They've done a lot of experimenting and a lot of planting."

That planting includes 100,000 rainbow fingerlings last year, along with

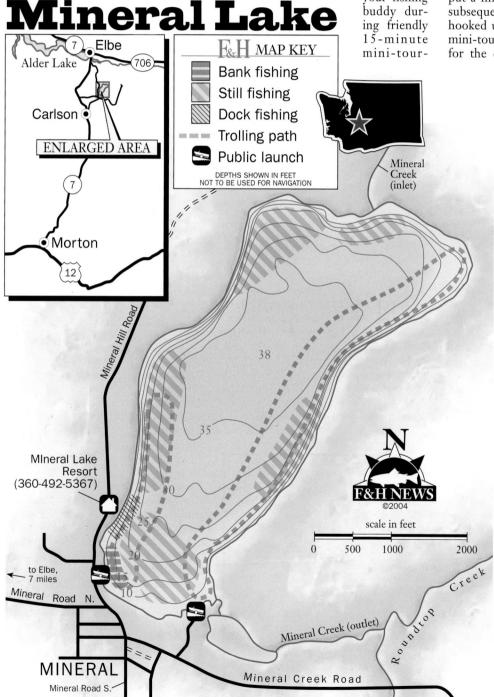

Mineral Lake

Elbe
Alder Lake
Carlson
ENLARGED AREA
Morton

F&H MAP KEY
Bank fishing
Still fishing
Dock fishing
Trolling path
Public launch

DEPTHS SHOWN IN FEET
NOT TO BE USED FOR NAVIGATION

Mineral Creek (inlet)

Mineral Hill Road

38
35
30
25
20
15
10

MIneral Lake Resort (360-492-5367)

to Elbe, 7 miles
Mineral Road N.

MINERAL
Mineral Road S.

Mineral Creek (outlet)
Mineral Creek Road
Roundtop Creek

N
F&H NEWS
©2004

scale in feet
0   500   1000   2000

5,000 brown trout, plenty of brooders (some of which grow to astonishing 10-plus-pound proportions), and enough 3-pound triploids to keep you hopeful all day long. On our trip, one of the local RVers fishing from the resort's public dock managed to haul in a 3½-pound triploid fishing orange Power Bait right on the bottom.

As with many trout lakes, the early bite is the best, from dawn to about 8 or 9 a.m. We experienced a lull between 9 and 10 a.m., then the fishing got hot and heavy again from 10 a.m. until we took a lunch break at noon.

Top to bottom: If you fish Mineral on a weekday, you definitely will have enough elbow room to troll. The shoreline opposite the resort is the hot trolling area, as is the water just off the resort's docks. While we were eating our shoreside lunch at one of the resort's picnic tables, we watched a boat out front catch 10 trout by trolling back and forth.

The lake's scrappy rainbows like red-and-green Wedding Ring spinners with corn or nightcrawlers, along with lake trolls and small chrome trolling spoons.

If you like to fly fish, we captured a number of 'bows and a couple of browns by dragging a maroon-colored Woolly Bugger behind the boat.

ROLAND BROWN rolled down to Mineral Lake from Tacoma, hooking up with this 7½-pound bruiser while fishing a minnow imitation.

Seth Taylor at Creekside Anglers (425-392-3800) in Issaquah first introduced me to that maroon color. So far this season it has outfished black and olive big time, and put all my green Carey Specials to shame. I'm not sure why the trout are loving that maroon color, but they definitely have been pouncing all over it.

You'll also see a lot of anglers still-fishing here, and with good reason.

Most of the bigger fish seem to be right on the bottom. The lake isn't deep, about 40 feet at the deepest point, with plenty of water ranging from 10 to 35 feet. Rig up with a slip sinker, bead, swivel and a 12- to 15-inch leader.

Hands down, Power Bait is the No. 1 choice here for fishing on the bottom, in the orange color.

Marshmallows and worms will also catch you plenty of fish.

Good still-fishing can be found just about anywhere on the lake. Most anglers that we saw catching fish this way were stationed around the lake's shorelines, and at the northeast end.

Everything you need: WDFW has put in a new concrete ramp on the lake. It's a beautiful ramp, but it doesn't have (at least not yet) an extended dock, so bring your waterproof boots and bow line. Mineral can accommodate all sizes of boats, though of course this is a pretty small water, so you might not want to launch your 34-footer here lest you be seen as pretentious. Instead, it's perfect for canoes, cartoppers, drift boats, rafts and belly boats.

Beware the wind, however. Being this close to Mount Rainier, there are some nasty sheer winds that can blow down off the mountain from the east, and incoming storms from the Pacific mean pretty healthy west winds on occasion too.

Mineral Lake Resort has everything you need to fish. There's a covered public dock to fish from, a bait and tackle store, RV sites, fishing and pontoon boat rentals (perfect and easy for fishing with a group of your friends), picnic sites, and lots of free advice on how to catch the big ones. The atmosphere here is friendly and congenial, with lots of banter between anglers about the fishing.

AT a GLANCE

What: Good fishing for rainbows, browns, brooders and triploids at Mineral Lake south of Eatonville.

When: The lake is open now till the end of September. The early bite is the best for the hottest action, but you'll catch fish all day here.

Where: From Seattle, go south on Highway 167 to Highway 161 and follow it south. Watch for signs to Elbe as you go through Eatonville, which will put you on Highway 7 at Alder Lake. Head south on 7 until you reach Mineral Road North. It's well marked with a sign indicating the lake and resort. Turn left there, and follow the small road to the lake. From Vancouver or Yakima, take Highway 12 to Morton and head north on 7 to Mineral Road North.

How: Trolling flies and Wedding Rings works wonders for trollers; still-fishermen use orange Power Bait and marshmallows/nightcrawlers.

Information: Mineral Lake Resort (360-492-5367).

Palmer offers potential off-beaten-track trophy smallies

TONASKET

by Leroy Ledeboer

Think "Okanogan fishing" and you probably envision rainbows, either those pansize critters that get harvested out of the county's many put-n-take lakes or maybe a Lake Chopaka brute ripping away at your fly rod.

Then there's 2,000-acre Palmer Lake, virtually on the Canadian border. It's most noted as home to some fine kokanee fishing, but it also has a solid smallmouth and perch population.

"I wouldn't go up to Palmer expecting 30-fish days like you might see on Banks Lake or the Potholes, but it does hold a fair number of real quality smallmouth, up to 5 pounds, or even a little better," says Kirk Truscott, WDFW Okanogan fish biologist. "You have to remember, though, that this is much more of a cold-water environment than you're going to see in your Basin lakes, so the growth rates up here are a lot slower. Plus, year to year, Palmer won't get the high juvenile recruitment you can get in warmer bass waters."

> ## "It does hold a fair number of real quality smallmouth, up to 5 pounds, or even a little better,"
> — Kirk Truscott, WDFW biologist

Translation: *catch and release* is critical to maintain this bronzeback opportunity.

Spawn staging: By far the most popular time to fish Palmer smallies has been the prespawn staging and the spawn itself. That's when the fish are up in the shallows, in no more than 8 feet of water, and massing along every available rocky ledge or rocky shoals that lead up to the gravel spawning beds. Come a little later, though, and you could have miles of good bass habitat almost entirely to yourself.

"Yes, after the spawn it seems like most of the bass guys go somewhere else to fish, but obviously you can still catch smallmouth in Palmer," Truscott observes. "It might take a little more searching to find where they're feeding, and you might have to get out a little deeper, particularly during the hotter part of our day. Even then, though, I'd be looking at no more than our 12- to 15-foot depths, particularly anywhere you have some vegetation, such as the Sinlahekin Creek inlet, or try the riprap shorelines and the shoals with submerged boulders."

Facilities, info: Palmer does have one small resort at the upper end, a couple of rough public campgrounds and adequate launching facilities, but for RV hookups, cabins or other amenities, you'd have to stay at nearby Spectacle Lake Resort (509-223-4141) or Sun Cove (509-476-2223) on Wannacut Lake.

Call Dick Caryl at Cascade Outfitters (509-826-4148) in Omak for info.

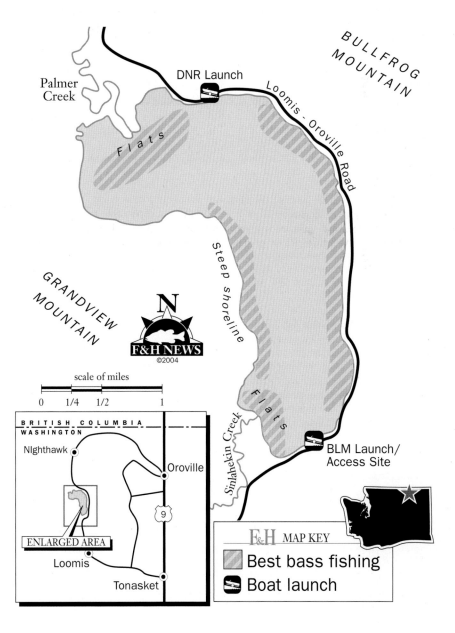

scale of miles
0   1/4   1/2   1

BRITISH COLUMBIA
WASHINGTON
Nighthawk
Oroville
9
ENLARGED AREA
Loomis
Tonasket

F&H MAP KEY
Best bass fishing
Boat launch

Palmer Creek

DNR Launch

BULLFROG MOUNTAIN

Loomis - Oroville Road

Flats

GRANDVIEW MOUNTAIN

N

F&H NEWS ©2004

Steep shoreline

Flats

Sinlahekin Creek

BLM Launch/ Access Site

Kokes, trout, walleye on tap at Rufus Woods

by Leroy Ledeboer

AL BROOKS of Manson hooked this 6-pound triploid at Rufus Woods in mid-January. The big Columbia impoundment also offers solid kokanee and walleye fishing.

Ever since at least the mid-1990s, it's been those lunker triploid rainbows around the netpens and the walleye in its upper reaches that have attracted most of the attention at Rufus Woods Reservoir. But in truth, this 50-plus-mile impoundment of the Columbia River holds fishing opportunities all the way from just above Chief Joseph Dam to the fast water a few miles below Grand Coulee.

Lower reservoir kokes, 'bows: Let's start with that big deep pool above Chief Joseph. From late winter right through summer, this is an excellent place to troll for both kokanee and rainbows. In winter these two species can be right on the surface, but at times a good sonar and adequate downriggers are essential. Spot your quarry, get to the right depth and you're in business.

"This winter we've been fishing right up by the cans, or buoys, and taking everything from triploids to kokanee," says guide Anton Jones (509-687-0709), who has been making the trip over from Chelan along with his partner Joe Heinlen. "Once in a while you'll hit a real monster triploid, but on average they're going to run 4 to 7 pounds. Our kokes have been coming in two age classes, one right at 16 inches, the other

at 20 to 22 inches, which is really a beautiful fish."

"We're doing a real slow troll, no more than 1½ mph, running kokanee flies tipped with shoepeg corn behind a flasher about 150 feet back. We find that soaking the corn in anise oil definitely improves the bite."

Jones says that on some days they've had to run the 'riggers, "but we've never had to drop more than 30 feet. A good cloud cover does help bring the fish up, but on any day it seems you have some dead time, then a red-hot bite, followed by more dead time, so you have to be patient. The real thrill up there is that every strike can produce anything from a 10-inch rainbow to a 20-pound triploid. Until you set your hook and start doing battle, you just won't know."

Douglas County-side bays: Brewster's Bob Fately, who runs a tackle shop out of his Triangle Shell Station (509-689-3473), and his partners prefer heading upriver a few miles and fishing the little bays.

"We've been sticking to the Douglas County side, mainly because it has more nice bays," Fately says. "These start about 4 miles upriver, and we rarely go more than 10 miles, simply because that stretch gives us all the fishable water we need."

"This time of year both the native

rainbows and the triploids are usually in the top 10 to 20 feet of water, but if we mark them deeper, we'll sure go down after them," says Fately. "We always have at least one rod set up with a Double Whammy and a 'crawler, because that combo will catch anything from a triploid to the occasional big walleye. And we use a lot of No. 3 Dick Nites or Needlefish behind a two-bladed Mack's Flashlite. Oh, and we tip those spoon hooks with corn or maggots, simply because it increases your strikes."

Although Fately acknowledges that even bigger triploids might await if he ran the 20-plus miles to the commercial net pens, he doesn't feel the need. "Even the native rainbows we've been catching are running 2 pounds or better, and we're getting triploids up to 10 pounds," he says. "So we simply don't feel the need to burn up more gas running that far

Midlake netpens: Of course, those three commercial net pens — the first just above Bensen Spring, the other two near Nespelem Bar — do have their advantages. For one, this is where most of the 80,000 triploids the Colville Tribes purchase annually to replenish this entire system are first released. Many of these fish stick around for at least the first year, growing rapidly, and it's around the pens where our state records have been smashed in recent years.

Second, the uppermost net pen area is accessible by road, dropping down from Highway 155 at the Colville Tribes Agency, and it accommodates shore anglers who must purchase a tribal license.

Shore anglers use everything from spinners to flies, but by far the most common method is plunking, often using a slip sinker. Because the triploids are staying close to those net pens to scarf up excess feed that washes through,

Rufus Woods Lake

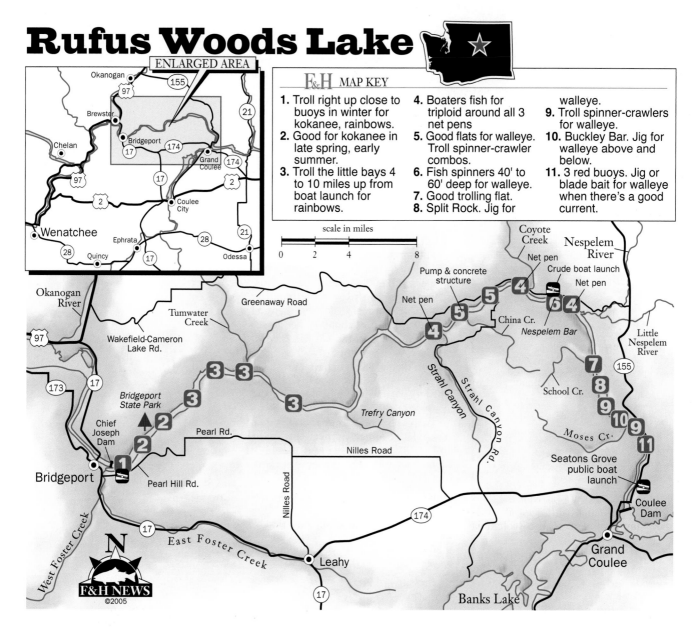

ENLARGED AREA

F&H MAP KEY

1. Troll right up close to buoys in winter for kokanee, rainbows.
2. Good for kokanee in late spring, early summer.
3. Troll the little bays 4 to 10 miles up from boat launch for rainbows.
4. Boaters fish for triploid around all 3 net pens
5. Good flats for walleye. Troll spinner-crawler combos.
6. Fish spinners 40' to 60' deep for walleye.
7. Good trolling flat.
8. Split Rock. Jig for walleye.
9. Troll spinner-crawlers for walleye.
10. Buckley Bar. Jig for walleye above and below.
11. 3 red buoys. Jig or blade bait for walleye when there's a good current.

Power Bait pellets that simulate this feed have become popular. If shoreline space allows it, the regulars will use just enough weight to get down but not anchor their bait, because a slow drift with the current triggers a better bite.

Boat anglers also hit the pen areas, some coming upriver from Chief Joseph, others downriver from Seatons Grove, a few now trailering smaller craft to the rough boat launch near the pens. Once on the river, they can cover more water, pulling plugs such as Fat Fish, Hawg Bosses, and Hot Lips upstream, drifting baits or working small bucktail jigs tipped with 'crawlers or leeches.

Bugeyes all over: Walleye have also discovered that suitable habitat exists

from one end of Rufus Woods to the other, but for this popular game fish it's the upper reaches that get the most attention, particularly in fall, winter and early spring.

For years noted walleye angler Gordie Steinmetz at Big Wally's (800-632-5504) in Coulee City has been launching at Seatons Grove and carefully searching out some of the river's top spots.

"Any time there's a pretty good current flowing, I'll start fishing just above the launch, generally jigging or blade baiting near those three red buoys," Steinmetz says. "Then from just above these buoys to way beyond Buckley Bar you can find good 20- to 40-foot deep stretches where you can drag spinners and 'crawler rigs. On the Colville side across

from Buckley Bar, there's a big tree with birdhouses nailed onto it, which makes a handy visible marker."

"Start out trolling in 20 feet, but if you're not picking up walleye, don't stay in there all day," Steinmetz says. "Drop deeper, anywhere from 40 to 60 feet, where you might need 3-ounce bottom bouncers to get down, because sometimes that's where the fish are hanging. At that depth you might not get a normal walleye bite. You'll feel your rig suddenly feeling heavier, and it's time to set the hook. Not real hard, just with a nice sweeping action."

"Jigs are most effective wherever you have any kind of break in the river's flow, such as above and below Buckley Bar, or around Split Rock and up around Nespelem Bar," Steinmetz says. "I like to use the lightest jighead that will let me maintain good bottom contact. For jig bodies you can go with any of your old walleye favorites — split tails, curl tails, whatever — and try a variety of colors because at times they'll all work. I always add a chunk of worm to my hook, and

AT a GLANCE

What: Rainbow, triploid, kokanee and walleye fishing in north-central Washington.

Where: Rufus Woods Reservoir, from Chief Joseph Dam on upriver past Bensen Springs, Nespelem Bar and Seatons Grove.

How: For kokanee, troll slowly and drag a flasher and kokanee fly tipped with corn soaked in anise oil; Double Whammy-and-'crawler combos for triploids and walleye; No. 3 Dick Nites or Needlefish tipped with bait off a Mack's Flashlite for trout; tossing spinners, flies, etc., or plunking Power Bait pellets from shore, pulling Fat Fish, Hawg Bosses and Hot Lips, drifting baits or working small bait-tipped bucktail jigs for triploids. Jig or blade bait in currents, or drag spinners and nightcrawlers in deeper areas for walleye.

Regs: Rufus Woods walleye fall under overall state guidelines, but kokanee and rainbow have a combined two-fish limit.

Contacts: Guide Anton Jones (509-687-0709); Gordie Steinmetz at Big Wally's (800-632-5504) in Coulee City; Bob Fately at Triangle Shell Station (509-689-3473) in Brewster.

sometimes I just skip the plastic and go with a whole 'crawler."

From Split Rock down to the Little Nespelem River, Steinmetz has mapped out another excellent trolling flat along the Colville side of the river, and one of his favorites is the Nespelem Bar, right across from the uppermost net pen.

"Nespelem Bar is at least a mile long," Steinmetz says, "and it almost always holds walleye, though here again you want to be ready to experiment with your depth. Particularly in winter when the water is a lot colder, those 40- to 60-foot waters just seem to attract a lot of fish."

Although many of the walleye anglers who start out from Seatons Grove make Nespelem Bar their final destination, Steinmetz says he's had some fine days trolling the various flats from there all the way to Pump 8, about 6 miles downriver, primarily on the Colville side of the river.

"Don't quickly bypass an area because your sonar shows you're in 100-foot water," he says. "Try moving in towards the shoreline, because in a lot of places you'll find there's a real abrupt ledge, quickly moving up onto a 20- or 30-foot shelf. That makes ideal walleye habitat, where they can move back and forth easily."

"Walleye fishing is a lot like hunting upland birds," Steinmetz says. "You have to know what kind of habitat they're most likely to be in, then spend your time hunting that habitat, finding out where they are on that particular day."

Eastern Washington Waters

STEELHEAD
TROUT
BASS
CRAPPIE
WALLEYE

'Sneaky Snake': Fish between Clearwater confluence, Heller Bar for low-pressure steelhead action

CLARKSTON

by Louis Bignami

Ever wonder why everyone always heads up the road/trail/stream to the most remote, inaccessible fishing or hunting Nirvana when they could fish or hunt more — and walk or drive less — to improve results? Consider that each and every Snake River steelhead and salmon passes the Clearwater confluence between Lewiston and Clarkston on the way to spawning grounds. Some locals fish here with lighted plugs and floats and jigs, but most head up to Heller Bay to jet boat far up into the Salmon or Snake where "you can catch twice as many fish per hour."

Fortunately for those who neither own gas stations to fuel jet boats for the upstream haul nor want to spend most of there time getting there and back, there's a sneaky section of the Snake River along Snake River Drive between the confluence and Heller Bar.

YOU'LL FIND PLENTY of similar-sized metalheads between the Clearwater confluence and Heller Bar on the Snake River.

Washington licenses are good for bank and boat action, but Idaho residents have to fish from a boat or boat across to their wading side of the river. That's a small price to pay for what natives like Trent Brown consider "some of the best steelhead fishing in the river. Besides, I can go before or after work."

You aren't limited to power: We launch drift boats at Heller Bar or beach launch them down by Buffalo Rapids to drift down to the Idaho side ramp at Hells Gate State Park.

Confluence to Hells Gate SP:
The river looks slow here, but it flows faster than it looks, so power's handy when you head upstream. Launch prop-powered boaters in Lewiston or Clarkston, or upstream at Hells Gate State Park. During daylight hours some troll where the Snake and Clearwater rivers join, but more fish brown, purple or black jigs under floats along the edges of drift lines. After dark, trolling lighted plugs improves results.

Water's Edge (509-758-2474) in Clarkston, Traditional Sportsman (208-746-6688) and The Guide Shop (208-476-3531) in Lewiston have specialized gear needed for the nocturnal action.

Drift and skiff anglers can put in at Hells Gate SP and fish down to the confluence. Anchoring and still-fishing bait, plugs or jigs is popular with

the oar-and-paddle set too.

Shorefishers do well by walking or biking along the levees and looking for sometimes subtle riffles that give away holding waters. Roe, shrimp and other baits under floats are the ticket. There's decent fly casting on the Idaho side along the park. On the Washington side, better spots wait upstream.

Hells Gate to Tenmile Rapids:
Road access ends at Hells Gate SP for Idaho anglers. Washington anglers have a solid set of shore spots in holes above and below riffles that are easy to spot from the frontage road; boaters find few hazards here. Jigs and floats seem the best approach in the deep holes. The mouth of the unnamed Idaho stream just downstream from Tenmile Rapids is worth special attention, and the mouth of

During daylight hours some troll where the Snake and Clearwater rivers join, but more fish brown, purple or black jigs under floats along the edges of drift lines. After dark, trolling lighted plugs improves results.

nearby Tenmile Creek is another hot spot. Watch for the clump of rocks just below Tenmile Rapids — it's easy to miss from upstream at certain water levels, and death on lower units on props.

Tenmile to Buffalo Rapids:
At most flows it's possible to get a prop boat up and over Tenmile Rapids, but few prop-powered anglers take advan-

---

AT A GLANCE

What: Snake River steelhead.

Where: Between the confluence of the Clearwater River and Heller Bar.

Why: Thousands of steelhead bound for the Clearwater and Snake's many feeder streams pass through the confluence area. Fishing between the confluence and Heller Bar provides several miles of good steelhead water close to both Lewiston and Clarkston.

Techniques: Drift yarn and bait, pull plugs from a sled or drift boat, fish float and bait or cast big flies from shore.

Information: Water's Edge (509-758-2474) in Clarkston; Traditional Sportsman (208-746-6688) in Lewiston; The Guide Shop (208-476-3531) in Lewiston; Aardvark's Adventures (509-758-0108); Black Sheep (208-746-8948) in Lewiston.

tage of this long section. Creek mouths at Tenmile Canyon, Couse Creek and the long hole below Graham's Landing are the hot spots here.

As elsewhere up to Heller Bar, a day spent watching the guides from the frontage road pinpoints the action. The key for shore fishers is to get to the water at dawn and cast to the shallows before cautiously wading out to cover deeper water. There's another hot period: the last half hour of sunlight (dusk comes early in the canyon).

Since the river gradient is lower here, this is an exceptional stretch of river to either fish from the bank or to learn drifting and boating skills.

Buffalo Rapids to Captain Lewis Rapids and Heller Bar:
This section gets less pressure than most, although some locals launch at Heller Bar and fish down to Captain Lewis Rapids early in the season. Most realize that it's always a good idea to fish upstream from your launch point. The hot spot is the long pool below the mouth of Captain John Creek and the deeper Idaho side of the two holes on the bend to the west immediately downstream. Waters run a bit faster here, and bait fished off a pencil lead is the method of choice save in the low pools where float methods shine.

Upstream from the mouth of Captain John Creek, the Washington side of the river is the best choice for shore fishing. Flyrodders have at least six good riffles available from the Washington side. We take a cataraft or pram across to the Idaho wader's spots too. Bank bait anglers may find sideplaners a good choice where the deep water's on the Washington side.

Above Captain Lewis Rapids the river gets more visitors. Most put in at Heller Bar. Each season a number of good steelhead are taken just downstream from the bar and off the Washington where the river loops west to the top of Captain John Rapids. Most years the channel splits here and at some flows the shallow channel holds decent steelhead. Watch the rocks and check out the holding water on the Idaho side just below the rapids.

Logistics: There's a good RV Park behind Costco in Clarkston and more camping in Hells Gate SP. Lewiston and Clarkston both have all sorts of motels, hotels and restaurants.

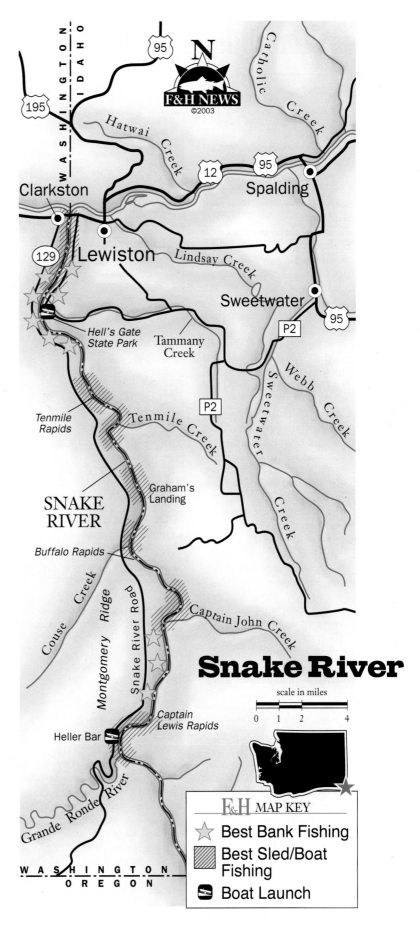

Get set for chilly weather steelies on the Snake River

CLARKSTON

by Dusty Routh

During the dog days of summer, fishing on the Snake River is all about catfish and smallmouth. The Snake has ample numbers of both of these warmwater fish, and a lot of anglers spend their days under the blazing sun yarding them in. But when the days get short and the hills pick up their first light dustings of snow, all attention turns to coldwater fish. In this case, that means it's time to ply the Snake for steelhead. Just because it's getting cold out doesn't mean it's time to hang up your fishing sticks.

Stu Waters at Waters Edge (509-758-2474) in Clarkston sums it up best: "Heck, it's un-American not to fish in the winter."

Got fish? Waters confirms that this season is already looking pretty good and steelheaders are scoring fish regularly.

"We're expecting about 130,000 fish up here. I think the counts at McNary, there's about 190,000 fish. We get about 75 percent of the fish between McNary and Lower Granite Dam. So we should easily get 150,000 fish."

Waters says these fish are a combination of A- and B-run steelhead.

"The typical A-run steelhead this year seems to be between 6 and 10 pounds," Waters says. "And your real true B-runners, those big Clearwater fish, are showing up as 12 to 13 pounds to start, though we've had one 21-pounder caught already."

Red hot/white cold steelheading: Waters points out that the quality of the fishing seems to rise and fall with water levels and current flows.

"The fishing up here was red hot until about eight to 10 days ago," he says. "Then they backed the whole system up, from Lower Granite on up, and the water level came up about 4 feet. Then they reduced the dams to minimal flows, partially to protect the salmon spawn on the Snake, to protect the smolts. As I understand it, the smolts feed and grow faster with minimal flows."

But those minimal flows designed to help the salmon smolts can wreak havoc

BAIT'S FISHING BEST now for Snake steelhead, but be prepared to switch over to plugs if that bite fades. Bill Stanley of Spokane caught this 37½-incher at Wawawai early last December on a jig and shrimp.

on guys trying to get steelhead to hit.

"When the currents get cut down to minimum, the fish get a lot less aggressive," Waters says. "It makes fishing a lot tougher. But that will change. Current flows should get back to normal in time."

Understanding steelhead behavior: Keep in mind that steelhead coming up the Snake do not behave like salmon. The salmon are on a one-track mission to get up the river, establish their spawning redds, spawn and expire. But these steelhead won't be spawning until next March or April, so they have six to seven months to lollygag around in the river.

"Some of these fish have been in the river since the third week of July," Waters says. "They get up here and I

call them almost nomadic, because they'll move around so much. They have a lot of time to get acclimated, and they move a lot. You have to find them."

For starters, if you're in water that's more like a moving lake than it is a river, like the main body of the Snake as opposed to the mouth of the Grande Ronde or the confluence with the Clearwater and the lower Clearwater, position yourself in relatively deep water.

"These steelhead like to be in deeper water," Waters says. "We're catching fish in November in water that's 18 to 24 feet deep. The steelhead are suspended down there."

As you move into faster moving water, you'll be able to locate steelhead on the edges of the back eddies, in places where you'd typically look for salmon.

"A steelhead is like a salmon in the ways that it moves in faster water," says Waters. "Steelhead are a very efficient fish. They'll find places where they have the least current to deal with, but they won't be in dead-still slack water. They'll be tucked behind rocks, or down in depressions and holes. That way, they expend the least amount of energy. So you have to be looking for that type of area."

How and where it's done: Waters says bait is the No. 1 steelhead-catching methodology right now. A lot of anglers resort to bobber fishing, drifting shrimp in the main Snake or drifting eggs in faster water in the rivers.

"The plug fishermen haven't done as well this year as bait fishermen," Waters says. "Bait is king, at least for now. But it tends to even up as we move along into the winter."

Back-trolling bait into likely-looking current seams and edges is also popular and productive. But don't overlook how well plugs can work at times, too.

"Under these conditions, I'll tell you, I sent some guys from Montana up to the Asotin area. And they got two really nice ones, a 12- and a 14-pounder, trolling. They caught them on fluorescent pink-with-black-bill FlatFish. That's one of my favorite plugs."

Waters says the hot spots continue to

be centered around the confluence water between the Clearwater and the Snake. The lower Clearwater is also producing, Waters says, and the fishing has been good at the Heller Bar area at the mouth of the Grande Ronde.

Derby doings: This year's Snake/Grande Ronde/Clearwater winter steelhead season officially gets under way with a couple of derbies in the area. The first, slated for Nov. 6 and 7, is the Colton Knights of Columbus Steelheader Derby. Headquarters for this event is at The Waters Edge, with proceeds benefiting the Knights' charity work.

"They do some wonderful work for kids," Waters says. "And it's a fun derby. Well, it's as much fun as it is serious fishing."

This derby usually attracts between 100 and 125 steelhead anglers.

The second derby is much bigger, put on by the Lewiston Chamber of Commerce (*lewistonchamber.org*; (208) 743-3531). It's called the Great Snake Lake Steelhead Roundup, and it runs Nov. 20–27. More than $10,000 will be awarded to winning anglers. Entry fees are $20 for adults and $10 for kids under 12. Twenty-four-hour weigh-in is available at North Lewiston Dynamart and Albertson's, as during business hours at Camp, Cabin and Home, Riverview Marina and Les Schwab.

Over 800 anglers participated in the derby last year.

AT a GLANCE

What: Winter steelhead season on the Snake River.

Where: In the Clarkston area, between Lower Granite Dam and Heller Bar.

Where: Fishing is already getting good and should hold up well into February.

How: Bait is king right now (shrimp and eggs), and FlatFish are producing. Fish deep in the main river, and look for current seams and edges in faster water.

Info: Waters Edge (509-758-2474) is open 7 a.m. to 5:30 p.m. Tues.–Sat.; 7 to 10 a.m. on Sun.

Guides: Mike Kelly (509-243-3474); Aaron Echternkamp (509-766-6791).

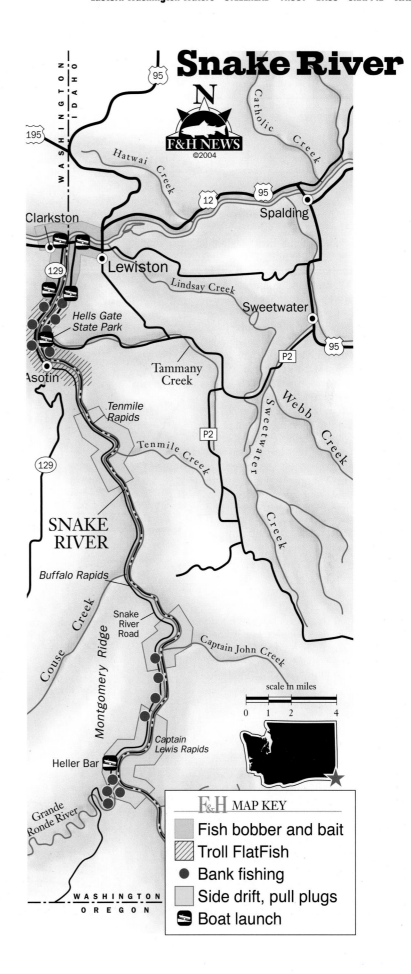

Snake River

F&H NEWS ©2004

F&H MAP KEY

- Fish bobber and bait
- Troll FlatFish
- Bank fishing
- Side drift, pull plugs
- Boat launch

Rock Lake rounding into April peak

EWAN

by Louis Bignami

It's six miles from Rock Lake's inlet to its outlet, where the primitive boat launch is.

I know. I've rowed back when the motor quit, and just barely made it home after fishing on a day more suited for windsurfing. The water splashing over the side of the boat was cold too. How cold? Cold enough so bodies don't float when unprepared boaters drown. Cold enough so you don't want to even consider float tubes until July, or perhaps August.

So why would you fish this lake, where the winds blow you off the lake and agricultural runoff can change the deep, clear blue waters to cocoa? Some cite the bass and panfish, but I fish Rock for the nice rainbow and brown trout in the foot to 18-inch range. Rock should peak in April.

Methods here seem less important than does runoff. If a lot of rain and muddy runoff turns the lake to cocoa, head over to Sprague Lake or up to Williams or Amber lakes, which clear faster. But if April waters are clear and reasonably calm, turn off I-90 at Sprague and head on down Highway 23 to Ewan and up the road to Rock.

You need not go all the way up the long lake to the inlet, either. The aluminum chair set favors the relatively sheltered cove at the boat ramp, and the usually posted stream on the south side of the bridge seems popular with tubers.

Trolling remains the local's choice. Toplined rigged worms, Panther Martins and other spinners, small minnow plugs, flies and Kastmasters all produce in clear water conditions anytime from October until late in April.

Temps keys results: When the water's less than 55 degrees, I fish the middle of the day. Once the water warms, the shaded side of the lake near the cliffs kicks out more photophobic browns than the sunny side where rainbows are more common.

I prefer to simply motor along the bank and cast up tight to the rocks on the cliff side with lures like small motor-oil fat Gitzits that produce all species. Small spinners and small spoons work too. Worms under floats work all year and depth increases as water warms.

Fly fishers aren't left out. You can catch bass, rainbows, browns or panfish on successive casts. Move along an easy cast from shore and toss in No. 10 streamer, Woolly Buggers with or without rubber legs and most anything else that suits a hand twist retrieve, and you can do well on top before the light hits the water and after it leaves. Once hatches start in late April or early May fling No. 12 to 14 Stimulators, Parachute Royal Wulffs and other flies you can see. Otherwise those tiny nymphs like Brassies work.

Since there are no services at the lake, call nearby Fish Trap Lake Resort (509) 235-2284. It's a place to stick an RV or tent, and has a ramp and decent fishing. Otherwise, Rich Bluhm at the Sprague Chamber of Commerce (509-257-2444) can help with fishing reports.

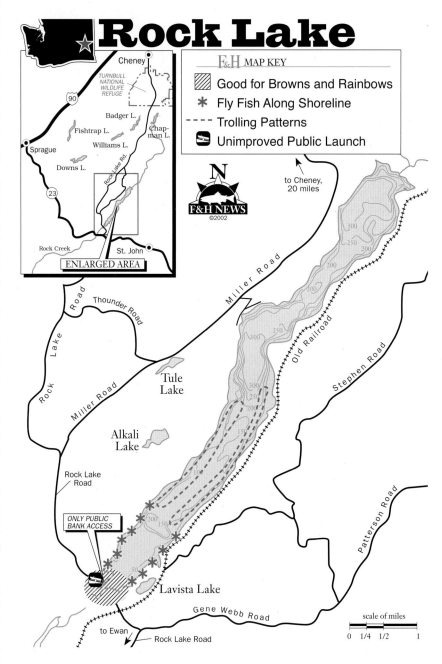

Rock Lake

F&H MAP KEY

- Good for Browns and Rainbows
- * Fly Fish Along Shoreline
- - - - Trolling Patterns
- Unimproved Public Launch

Cheney

TURNBULL NATIONAL WILDLIFE REFUGE

90

Badger L.

Fishtrap L.

Chapman L.

Williams L.

Sprague

Downs L.

23

Rock Lake Rd.

Rock Creek

St. John

ENLARGED AREA

F&H NEWS ©2002

to Cheney, 20 miles

Miller Road

Old Railroad

Stephen Road

Rock Lake Road

Thounder Road

Tule Lake

Alkali Lake

Rock Lake Road

ONLY PUBLIC BANK ACCESS

Lavista Lake

Patterson Road

Gene Webb Road

to Ewan

Rock Lake Road

scale of miles

0   1/4   1/2   1

Drag Princes, Buggers, plugs for Rock browns

by Lou Bignami

It could be the lousy ramp, the unlovely and unimproved south end access, the muddy agricultural runoff or the way the lake dumps unwary boaters every few years when wind whistles up the cliffs, but one thing is certain: few Eastern Washington lakes offer such good brown trout fishing and enjoy so little fishing pressure as sprawling Rock Lake. Only Bonnie Lake, with even more limited access just upstream on Rock Creek comes to mind.

The key to Rock Lake is timing unless you want to troll or deep all summer. Catching fish, after you survive the ramp, isn't difficult early and late in the year. There is both a spring and a fall window each year and an early and late hatch most days. The spring window is open now, as it usually lasts until mid-May. Right now, for example, you can simply troll small spoons or spinners along the rocky sections starting at the ramp and going up along whatever is the lee side of the lake.

Realize that spring winds can kick up ferocious steep waves here, so bring your safety gear and carefully consider your boat choice. For example, we use a 20-foot jet boat to transport float tubes and catarafts up to the head of the lake. You can, of course, always beach a boat and wait out the wind.

Once we get to the upper basin (there are two that divide the long lake roughly in half) we space out along the shore and cast in tight to the bank where the shore's steep, but you have some brush. As a rule, you can expect four or five browns in the 13- to 16-inch range per half-day in the spring, with bonus rainbows and some decent bass as the water warms.

Productive lures include small spinners like and spoons, tiny plugs like Shad Raps or Wee-R's or small Rapalas, and the usual trolling rigs. Fly fishers can score with Woolly Buggers, big nymphs, our favorite trolling flies behind Wiggle-Fins, chironomids, etc. The key is finding fish that seem to be in pods rather than singletons, and determining the correct depth to fish. This time of year it's less than 20 feet,

so I use a Fishing Buddy depth- and sidefinder.

If you don't have one, try dragging an olive size 10 Woolly Bugger with a Beadhead Prince on a dropper behind a sinking line over the side.

It's also important to fish away from your boat, or the bank in the launch area — most of the shore is private otherwise — as browns seem rather boat shy. Sideplaners should work. We use 12-foot-long British bait rods as mini outriggers when trolling instead. Casting with a light steelhead stick and

4-pound test seems to improve catch rates and casting distance.

Prime spots include the launch side cliffs, the outlet cove, the inlet or Rock Creek and areas where shallows meet the edges of cliffs. However, if the lake looks like cocoa, as can happen shortly after spring rains, I'd head over to Sprague for some walleye action.

Information: Sprague Chamber of Commerce (509-257-244); Northside Fishing and Outdoor (509-483-8500).

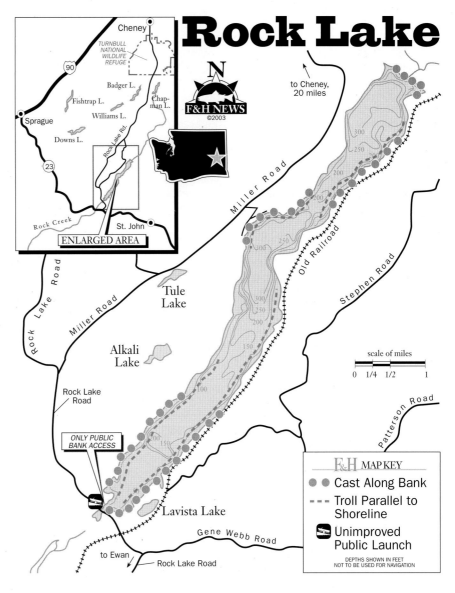

Sullivan Lake: Worth the trip for big browns, 'bows

METALINE FALLS

by Dusty Routh

The woman from the Sullivan Lake Ranger District said it best.

"You're not from around here, are you?" she asked. She knew right away that I wasn't, from my question about whether or not there was a guide who works on Sullivan Lake, and where I might find a sporting goods store close by.

"There are no guides out here," she pointed out. "And there are no sporting goods stores. What we have out here are a few *small* — well, make that *tiny* communities — and some trout, and some grizzly bears. And that's about it."

Ha ha. Pretty funny. But she was spot-on. Sullivan Lake, located in the far northeast corner of Washington is definitely one of the roads less traveled in the state for anglers, other than for a handful of locals and a few visitors from Spokane who occasionally come up to fish.

The fact that Sullivan Lake is a long way from the beaten path adds to its mystery and allure. This lake of roughly 1,300 acres, plunging to depths of over 312 feet, is a picture-perfect place for beauty, isolation, wilderness and ruggedness. No stores, no resorts, no fuel docks and darned

few people. There are two campgrounds at either end of it (Sullivan Lake and Noisy Creek campgrounds), and that's about it.

So why make a trip here? Why drive so far? Because Sullivan Lake at one time gave up the Washington state German brown trout record, a massive brown that went 22 pounds even, yarded in by R.L. Henry in May of 1965. This oversized *Salmo trutta* still stands as the unbeaten brown trout record in the state.

Just to the south of Sullivan in Bead Lake, the new state record burbot was caught earlier this year. But you don't need to go to Bead for burbot, because Sullivan has some incredible burbot fishing in its own right, too. The Latin name for burbot, by the way, is *Lota lota*, and that's what you'll find at Sullivan, particularly if you fish through the ice during their winter spawn.

Waiting out a brown: If you've heard that fishing for giant brown trout in lakes is a time-intensive endeavor, you've heard right.

"The way I would characterize brown trout fishing in Sullivan Lake," says Karen Honeycutt, fisheries biologist with the Colville National Forest (509-684-7224), "is you've got to put in your time. But there are some big, big browns in Sullivan. And it doesn't get much pressure."

Honeycutt ought to know what's in Sullivan. She snorkels the lake frequently, and has seen first-hand what's down there in all that cold, crystal-clear water.

"There are some big rainbows," she reports, "along with whitefish and some cutthroat. There are some really, really big kokanee in Sullivan, too. Most are 12 to 14 inches, but there are also some very nice ones up to 16 inches."

But what stuns Honeycutt the most are the browns she's seen.

"They seem to be light sensitive," she reports. "They are never out in the open. The ones I've seen are up under ledges, and under logs. I've seen browns up to 36 inches. I've seen them in the lake and I've seen them swimming up Harvey Creek under

TOP LURES for big fall browns include stickbaits and heavy metal jigs.

the bridge to spawn. These are large, very large, browns. But there aren't a lot of them."

Honeycutt says seeing one of these big brown trout is a thrill.

"They're huge browns," she says again. "They're as big as salmon. But they are not easy to catch. When we see them, they're hunkered under a log, like I said, not out in the open. The best opportunity to catch one is going to be at the bookends of the day or at night. I saw one once; he had just torn up a rainbow trout. The rainbow was missing some fins and an eye."

Honeycutt again points out that the overall density of browns in Sullivan is low.

"But the fish are big, and they're deep. Very deep," she reports.

Browns vs. kokanee: Honeycutt explains that while Sullivan's browns feast on other trout and on kokanee, it's the lake's big population of kokanee that are having the last laugh on the browns.

"Both species compete for spawning areas," she says. "The browns spawn first, then the kokanee follow them and wreck their redds and eggs."

Up and down: October is a prime month to fish Sullivan, particularly the creek inlets and outlets, as browns prepare for autumn spawning. But there is a small dam on the lake, and the water is dropped every fall about 20 feet. This makes having a healthy riparian section around the lake almost impossible, and reduces the lake's overall productivity.

Sullivan's prevailing forage fish for browns are pygmy whitefish (minnows), insects, and smaller trout and kokanee. Deepwater trolling should be done at dawn and dusk along rock ledges, using leadcore line or downriggers. Top lures for browns include big jointed Rapalas, especially in the German brown color, an A.C. Plug and big Cultiva Rip'n Minnows or Lucky Craft stickbaits with holographic finishes. You can also jig for these monsters with big metal jigs like Buzz Bombs and Crippled Herrings.

Creek and river browns too: If deepwater trolling and jigging for bigger lake browns isn't your thing, no worries. Nearby Sullivan Creek is home to a healthy population of creek browns.

"The browns in the creek run 16 to 22 inches," Honeycutt tells us. There are also browns in the nearby Pend Oreille River. "You can catch browns out of the river by fishing where the creeks come into it," she says. The creek also has bull trout (Dolly Varden) that must be released.

Brown rules: Honeycutt points out that it's legal to fish in Sullivan Creek until Oct. 31, using unscented flies and lures/single barbless hooks only. No bait. Sullivan Lake is open year-round, and usually has a good lid of ice in the winter for burbot bopping.

For more information: Contact the Sullivan Lake Ranger Station (509-446-7500) or the Colville National Forest (509-684-7224). Watch for grizzlies in the area. Honeycutt warns there's been a grizzly around Sullivan Creek that was spotted in September.

Get there: Sullivan Lake is located just east of Metaline Falls off Highway 31. The nearest "large" town is Colville.

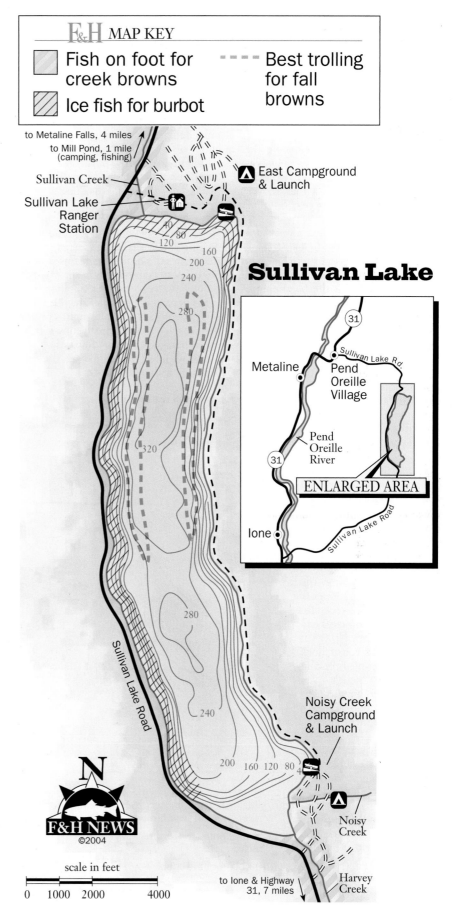

Rehabbed Williams back on track, with 'Loops to boot

CHENEY

by Pat Hayett

What can you realistically expect from a lake that was rehabbed last fall? I expected Williams Lake to be on the recovery stage at least for the first year, but that's definitely not the case.

In years past, Williams always produced big fish over the first six to eight weeks of the season, with several Kamloops rainbows weighing 6 pounds and above caught at the beginning of the year. This year, Williams Lake Resort owner Jerry Klinkenberg (509-235-2391) took a little different approach. He has a permit through WDFW to purchase fish at his own expense for the lake. In years past he would purchase fish that weighed 1 to 3 pounds, 4 to 6 pounds, and 7 pounds and above. His thinking this year is, instead of releasing one fish that weighs 9 pounds and making one angler happy, why not purchase three 3-pounders for the same price and make several people happy?

It's apparently working. Klinkenberg says that in all his years in owning the resort, this April's opener was the most successful ever. On opening weekend alone, there were 2,100 fish caught off the resort dock or from people renting boats. That doesn't even take into account the fisherman at the public launch or from Bunker's Resort (509-235-5212).

The notable fact in all of this is that 80 percent of those fish weighed over a pound each.

Williams' whales: Jerry purchased a total of 5,000 of these hybrid Kamloop rainbows and planted them before the season started, mixing them with the 3,500 rainbow triploids that WDFW unloaded before the opener. Before the end of May (if not already), Klinkenberg will have purchased another 5,000 Kamloops to be transplanted off the end of his dock.

How to catch 'em: Both the smaller stocker rainbows and the Kamloops are feeding in the shallows, 15 feet or less. According to Klinkenberg, this is not a hit-the-water-at-sunrise lake. At this time of the year the best time for fishing is between 8 and 11 a.m.

Williams' fish will bite light-colored patterns — green and yellows. Use Needlefish, FlatFish, Rapalas, Dick Nites, Triple Teasers or a Muddler Minnow with a mealworm.

After 11 a.m., the fish seem to head for the deeper water (around 45 feet).

If you troll the shallows early, keep your lure above 15 feet for best results. If you're trolling later in the day, try using three to four colors of leaded line with a leader of at least 10 feet.

Get updated info: Before you make the trip, give Klinkenberg a call and he'll tell you honestly how the fishing is before you head out. He also has everything you'll need, including a complete baitshop, an excellent restaurant, plenty of room to keep your boat, plenty of space for dock fishing, tent and RV sites, boats and motors for rent, plus paddle boats for the kids.

Williams Lake

scale in feet

0   500   1000   2000

N
F&H NEWS
©2004

Williams Lake Resort
(509-235-2391)

Mullinix Road

Bunker's Resort
(509-235-5212)

Rock #14

Deep Hole

Dr. Davis' Fly Bay

105

65

45

25

25

Myrtle's Hole

Tree #11

Jack Lloyd Island

Jack Lloyd Reef

Twin Pines

BB Rock

The Narrows

Rock #20

Cove

outlet

CHENEY

90

904

TURNBULL NATIONAL WILDLIFE REFUGE

Mullinix Rd.

Dover Rd.

Cheney Plaza Rd.

Pine Grove Rd.

Badger Lk. Rd.

Cossalman Road

Cheney Plaza Road

Williams Lk. Rd.

ENLARGED AREA

F&H MAP KEY

Still-fish, troll shallow (15 feet or less) in morning	Fishing dock
Troll deeper water in afternoon	Resort
Public boat launch	Reef
	Grass & weeds

DEPTHS SHOWN IN FEET
NOT TO BE USED FOR NAVIGATION

Long Lake: fishy water not to ignore

SPOKANE

by Joel Shangle

Searching for firsthand fall and winter fishing information about Long Lake? Good luck.

This impoundment of the Spokane River is fished consistently by Spokane anglers through the spring and summer, but about the beginning of October, the angling crowd disappears in a fashion that would make Harry Houdini jealous.

Too bad, because few lakes in the state serve up the mix of opportunity that comes from the water between Nine Mile and Long Lake dam.

Bass: Look for largemouth hovering off the edges of the pad fields and around the abundant underwater structure between Nine Mile and Forshees Resort (509-276-8568) in Tumtum.

"There's a lot of brush hanging over in the water in that section and a lot of lily pads, which should be good until the first major frost," says Kelly Moody at White's Outdoor (509-535-1875) in Spokane. "You'll find some really good sandy edges, a lot of docks, and a ton of underwater structure. They've had a number of restoration projects where people have put manmade structure in the lake when the water's down."

Toss Carolina-rigged 4-inch ringworms just off the edges of the pad fields, or jig a tube down into the deeper structure in the middle of the lake.

You can expect a fall/winter drawdown of the lake for power generation, but the lake's plethora of manmade structure will provide cover even when the water's significantly low (like this spring, when it was 16 feet down).

"There will be fishable structure, no matter what," says Moody. "There's structure even way out in the center of the lake. It's going to be hard to launch, but you can get to structure in a float tube or small boat because there's just so much of it out there."

You'll find smallies around "The Islands" straight out from Forshees, and along the scattered rock west of there. Fish cranks and grubs.

Crappie: Because the water in Long Lake is warmer than usual, the crappie bite should last well into fall. They'll suspend in deeper water (30-plus feet), but if you can find a school of them, drop a tiny crappie jig under a bobber.

Trout: Troll plugs for German browns between Long Lake Dam and Riverside Park (509-456-3964).

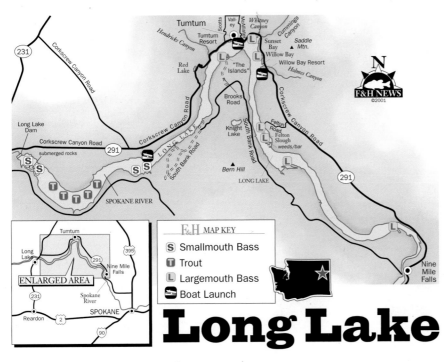

MAP KEY
- **S** Smallmouth Bass
- **T** Trout
- **L** Largemouth Bass
- ▬ Boat Launch

Long Lake

Fish early, late for Twin Lakes bass, trout

by Pat Hayett

Inchelium's Twin Lakes are providing anglers with some consistent rainbow and brookie fishing. I've been fishing the lakes consistently the past few weeks, landing nothing smaller than 12 inches, with quite a few upwards of 15 (weighing between ¼ to 2 pounds)

Green Power Bait tipped with a worm is working well for still-fishermen. During early morning and evening, fish are suspended from 15 to 30 feet, and during midday activity, they've been holding from 25 to 35 feet. If you're trolling, try a Muddler Minnow tipped with a worm.

Areas to concentrate on are Mallard Bay, Split Rock, Mels Point and Pine Tree Point, all of which are on South Twin.

Boomin' bassin': The bass fishing has been just as good in both lakes, with a large number of 4-pounders caught recently, as well as one 6-pound, 10-ounce lunker. A lot of the bass are being caught in the evening after 6 p.m. or early in the morning before 9 a.m. Nightfishing is an option here, because there is still plenty of light from the resorts and docks to fish safely.

Work the docks hard, as bass are holding tight. I have found that if I make several casts in the same area I tend to have better success. My philosophy is that during this hot time of the season, bass don't like to bothered. When you cast to the same spot three or four times, it has a tendency to annoy them and they tend to strike a plug or lure. I like using a large Rapala (around 5¼ inches) in either silver or perch patterns, or even a Jitter Bug or Hula Popper.

Work the channel between the two lakes early in the morning, when there's no traffic between them. If you try to fish the channel late in the evening, the water still tends to be pretty churned

up and it's difficult to catch fish. I try to hit the water no later than 5 a.m., after the water has settled and the bass aren't so reluctant to bite.

Also, hit Mud Flat, which is located at the southern end of South Twin. There are lily pads there that provide cover for the bass. Again take your time, making several casts in the same spot to work the area over thoroughly.

Rules, regs: A state fishing license is not required here. All that is need is a reservation fishing license, which can be purchased at any of the resorts on the lake.

Who to call: Rainbow Breach Resort (509-722-5901) on North Twin; Log Cabin Resort (509-722-3543) on South Twin.

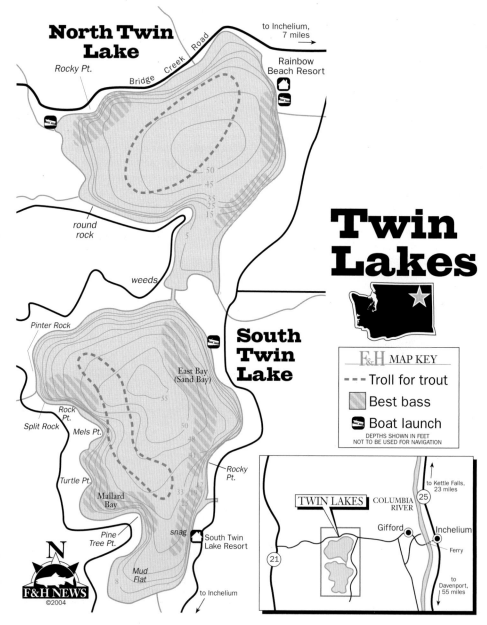

Keep it simple for Twin Lakes bass, trout

by Pat Hayett

Y ou know the old phrase "Keep it simple, stupid"? Well, this is pretty much all you need to know to catch Twin Lakes trout.

There's no reason to try an outsmart the fish at these two joined lakes northwest of Spokane on the Colville Indian Reservation. Instead, go with the old-fashioned basics.

The fishing at the Twins has been more consistent this summer than the majority of the lakes on the Eastside. Both are producing some large trout; a 6- and an 8-pounder were recently caught early in the same morning.

Techniques: The method of choice for those two big fish was nothing fancy — just fishing down below the thermocline where the water changes temperature. Both of those chunky rainbows were caught between 28 and 32 feet of water using green Power Bait and a worm. Look to the coves around the perimeter of both lakes for good still-fishing spots.

Many of the two lakes' old timers have been trolling slow, around 1½ miles per hour, fishing three colors of leadcore line out, using a fly (Woolly Bugger, Royal Coachman, Muddler Minnow) and catching 12- to 15-inch rainbows and brookies. Parallel the shoreline along the east bay of South Twin, and across the mouth of Mallard Bay. Stick to the deeper north end of North Twin.

Twin bass: The bass in these lakes are not particularly large in size, three-quarters of a pound to a pound and a half, but they are providing anglers with plenty of action. And every once in awhile, though, someone catches a 4- or 5-pounder, so there's potential for nice largemouth.

Use a good old fashioned No. 2 or 3 Mepps or a nightcrawler on a weedless hook. You'll want to work the shoreline, pads and what few docks are on the lake. If you can pull yourself out of bed early in the morning (just before sunrise), this seems to be the time they are feeding the heaviest.

Get there: There are two different ways to get to Twin Lakes. You can take Highway 21, north out of Odessa, and take the Keller Ferry (it's free) across Lake Roosevelt. Head north about 20 miles to Bridge Creek Road, and then head due east approximately 15 miles until you run into the North Twin. Follow the signs.

Another way is to take Highway 395 north out of Chewelah about 5 miles to Blue Creek West Road, take a left and go 7 miles until you come to a T in the road. Make a right hand turn and you'll run into Cedonia-Addy Road. Turn right and go less than a third of a mile, take a left turn onto the Addy-Gifford Road. Follow it about 11 miles until you come to the Gifford Ferry (it's free). After you've crossed the river by ferry, head east and follow the signs, for about 10 miles.

Info: Rainbow Beach Resort (509-722-5901); Log Cabin Resort (509-722-3543).

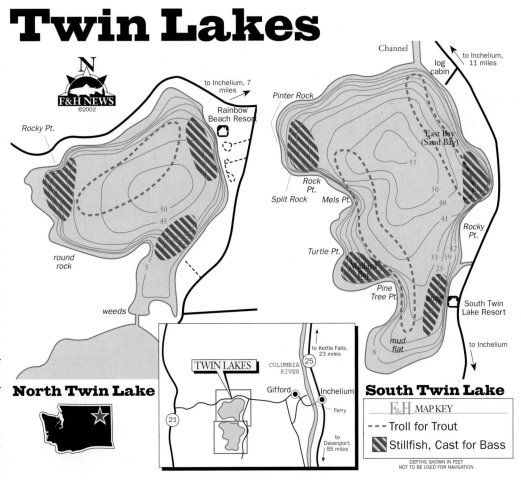

Upper Ronde features good summer mix of trout, bass

ANATONE

by Lou Bignami

Sometimes being cheap helps. Years ago when fishing the Grande Ronde River on the Washington side of the line, I lost so many spinners that I switched to more affordable tube lures and started to catch smallmouth. In the years since, I've found smallmouth all into Oregon while the lower reaches offer a reliable spin and fly fishery all summer and well into fall.

Not that anyone bothers with smallmouth when the steelies arrive.

We fish the Grande Ronde most often on the Washington side of the line. The canyon section upstream holds a few smallmouth, as does the nice, short section of river from the Troy bridge down to Grouse Creek Road, which is the upstream extent of our fishing. Shortly below that, you're in Washington with much better road access, but shorter smallmouth. The guys up at the Joseph Fly Shop (541-432-4343) insist that "It's too cold for smallmouth upstream in the canyon, but there's plenty of trout."

In any case, think "brown trout" and you've got smallmouth licked. We do very well fishing hopper patterns morning and evening. During the day, Muddlers, Spuddlers and bunny-strip leeches all work in dull colors in sizes from 4 down to 12.

Remember that, except for the section near the river's mouth, the Ronde is selective gear for all species, so salted or flavored plastics are off limits. The mouth area goes selective Sept. 1.

If you don't mind catching steelhead smolts, trout flies such as Parachute Adams, Humpies, Yellow Sallies, Hair Wing Royal Coachmen and the like offer more, if smaller, fish.

Spin fishing — replace all treble hooks with single barbless siwash hooks to ease catch and release on smolts — is easy too. Water depth determines lure selection. Bright spinners work in riffles and shallows when the light's not on the water and black, copper or darker-painted blades suit smallmouth early

and late in the day. Black and copper spoons such as Hopkins, Kastmasters, etc., suit deeper pools. If smolts are a problem, small fat plugs work too.

There is decent road access for bank fishers along the road to Troy and wise anglers ford the river and fish from the far bank. However, the roadless sections still offer the best bet for steelhead and trout. Overnight floats are the key on this easy Class II water. Our choice is an inflatable kayak and we usually start up on the Wallowa at Minam for upstream trout and steelhead and take out at Troy.

Several companies offer trips and this is an ideal river for family trips. The best trips use a support raft to tote gear and put you into individual or two-person inflatable kayaks. "On your own" kayaks most call "rubber duckies" let you set your pace, pick your fishing spot and, best of all, are light enough to portage back upstream for instant reruns of prime water. Just watch for snakes on the bank and bring plenty of sunscreen.

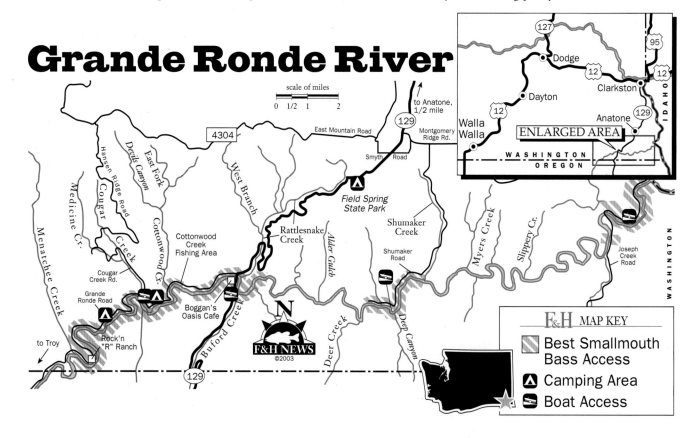

Patrol lower Spokane River to tap into bronze bonanza

FORT SPOKANE

by Jim Pearson

If you have a boat and you like to catch smallmouth, head for the last few miles of the Spokane River.

Last September, I spent several days exploring the upper reaches of Roosevelt Lake. That's what the Spokane River flows in to, and that's when I discovered some wonderful smallmouth. I launched my boat at Lincoln and headed upstream, a move that proved to be unwise later that day. I would have done better to have launched at Fort Spokane or Porcupine Bay. I could also have launched at Seven Bays 4 miles upstream from Lincoln. I didn't need to run so far to get into the Spokane River smallmouth fishery.

Pick your spot: I didn't get far upriver before finding "just Chuck" with his boat anchored while he caught smallmouth. He was sitting near a point 3 miles upstream from the bridge at the mouth of the Spokane River, casting a curl-tail grub in motor oil color and retrieving it in jerks after it hit the bottom in 20 feet of water. The point has a navigation marker, so it's easy to find, but if you will see a campground on the north shore with big signs saying you're not welcome unless you're a Spokane Indian, you've gone too far. Cross to the south shore and retreat downstream a mile.

Just Chuck (I think he didn't want his

ALL THE SMALLMOUTH you care to tackle await on the lower Spokane River.

wife to know he was fishing) said that smallie fishing was also good in February and March just upstream in the bay on the south shore.

Upstream approximately 6 miles, I talked with a man and woman who were successfully jigging for smallmouth along the south shore. They had recently moved to Washington because of the great fishing offered in the Spokane River. "It's never crowded," they added.

Upstream another 4 miles is Porcupine Bay. It is a popular spot that can get busy in the summertime, so don't stop there. Head on upstream looking for a rocky shoreline or points projecting into the water. Smallies love rocks, and rocky points are even better.

Approximately 6 miles upstream from Porcupine Bay, you will see a cabin setting on a flat on the north shore. That too is a good spot for smallmouth.

How to hook 'em: If the water is warm, smallmouth will slam a variety of offerings. Early in the morning, I like a small, topwater popping plug. I use a grey-bodied one with a silver head that Yakima Bait sells, but I'm not sure the color or the type of plug is important as long as it floats and makes a chugging sound when you twitch the rod tip. Since Bill Roberts, local bass fishing pro, told me about it, I'm making sure my plugs have some red on the bottom even if I have to paint them myself. I think surface plugs make

them mad, and they want to beat up whatever it is. Lacking hands, they do the best they can with their mouth.

Later in the day as the sun gets higher, I go to a spinner. They will slam a variety of offerings, but my all time favorites are Rooster Tails in flame coachdog, or the sonic Rooster Tail with a sliver spinner and a black body. I'm also fond of the Mepps Black Fury. That's the one with the black blade with yellow spots.

When I was a kid growing up in the Okanogan, we caught bronzebacks on F-4 FlatFish in a variety of colors — frog, orange with black spots, and I forget what else. Knowing what I do now, I would choose one with some red spots. Bill has truly made a believer out of me.

Bigger plugs will work, of course. I've caught smallmouth in the Columbia River on Magnum Wiggle Warts in fluorescent orange color. I was trolling for salmon and got in a bit too close the rocks along the shoreline, but I don't think plugs that big are best.

When the water is cold and the smallmouth are off their feed, try a nightcrawler. Is there a fish that doesn't like a nightcrawler? I cast only the weight of the worm from a long and limber spinning rod. The line is chartreuse Fireline because it floats and because I can see it easily. For whatever reason, worms don't make smallies angry. They usually pick it up slowly, sometimes dropping it and coming back later. The bite reminds me of a little old lady nibbling a pear. She isn't really hungry, but she knows it's good for her. Eventually, though, if they haven't felt the hook, they will decide it's time to eat that piece of protein, and that's when I set the hook.

Sometimes, I rig the worm behind a small spinner on a two-hook setup. That's a cast-and-retrieve set-up, and the action can be good. If they get a taste of the worm without being hooked, they often come back and hit it a second or even third time. Those repeated strikes are often the difference between a plain spinner and a spinner with bait. Normally, though, I don't use bait unless the water is cold and the action is slow.

AT a GLANCE

What: Smallmouth fishing near the mouth of the Spokane River, on Lake Roosevelt.

When: Virtually the year around, but better when the water is 50 degrees or warmer in spring and early summer.

Where: Along the south shore from the mouth upstream in selected spot for approximately 18 miles.

How: Spinners, spoons, bottom bouncers, nightcrawlers and plugs.

Who to call: White's Outdoor (509-535-2422) in Spokane; Fort Spokane Store (509-725-5783)

255

As for rubber worms, I'm not qualified to talk about them. I know they take fish, and I'm pretty sure I could catch smallmouth on them, but, frankly, I've never used the things. It's a void in my fishing experience I plan on filling this summer.

If bronzebacks are spawning and guarding their beds, I don't think it makes a lot of difference what you throw to them. They will hit it. It's their way of saying, "Get the hell out of my territory *now!*"

If my enthusiasm for these feisty illegal immigrants to our state doesn't show up in what I've already written, it's because I'm a poor writer. Trust me,

when the water warms a few more degrees, I'll be out there chasing them, and I won't feel guilty about keeping a few for dinner that night.

Take enough fuel: In the opening paragraphs, I mentioned that I would have been smarter to have launched closer to Lincoln, where I had the camper parked. Here's why: Coming back, I was motoring along the shoreline of the Colville Indian Reservation still several miles from the camper when I spotted two bears headed toward a camp on the shore. I turned around to tell the campers to get all their food put away, but no one was

home. I did get a good picture of one of the bears vainly trying to find berries in a tree directly behind the camp, though.

I turned the boat around to continue my journey when the Evinrude pump coughed and died. I was in trouble because the Honda kicker runs off the same tank. In a few minutes, a wheat farmer from Almira and his wife came by. I flagged them down and they towed me back to the dock at Lincoln and refused payment for their gasoline.

I had started with a full tank of gas that morning, so I figured the jet pump was delivering 3 miles to the gallon. Good thing I don't go touring with that motor often.

Spokane River Smallmouth

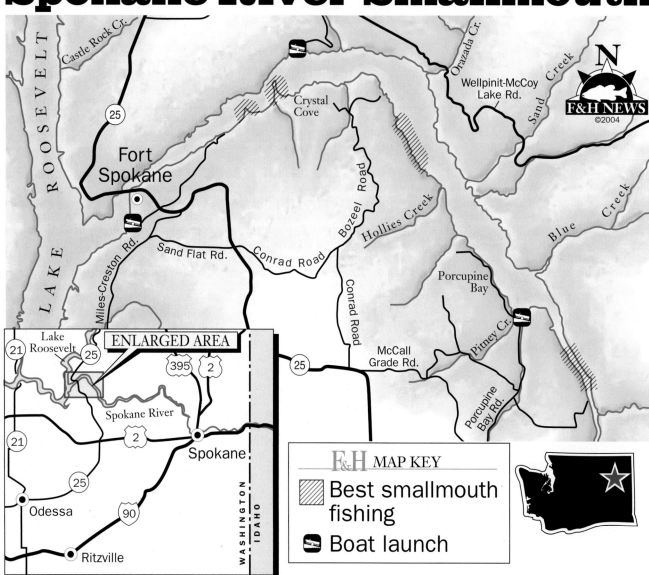

Work out on Spokane's upper arm for March walleye

by Leroy Ledeboer

Head upstream from the Porcupine Bay launch to chase down walleye finning into the upper Spokane Arm these next five weeks. Thousands upon thousands of the tasty fish will be moving upstream towards the moving waters just below Little Falls Dam as they prepare to spawn. But you'll want to go soon: The entire arm closes to walleye fishing April 1–May 31.

It's all good: When you head upriver, selecting likely waters is easy because from Porcupine on up, the entire arm holds one nice walleye cove, gravel flat and rocky point after another. A few of these top spots have names among the local walleye guys, but for the most part their monikers aren't based on the kind of easy landmarks you'll find on places like Banks Lake or even Roosevelt's mainstem.

"Knowing a few names of good holes really isn't significant because when you get into March that entire upper arm is all good," expert walleye angler John Carruth says. "All anyone has to do is get above Porcupine and immediately start looking for your typical walleye structures, like around any of the many points that jut out or in those little breaks. Unless the weather is really wild this spring, you're most likely going to find your fish in 20 to 35 feet of water, but maybe even a little deeper at times. Or you can just look for a concentration of boats and know where the walleye are."

Upper arm keys: Once you leave that Porcupine boat launch, the Spokane Arm quickly turns into a relatively narrow river for several miles, and it's tempting to fly through this section to get to the wider bays above it. But it's a real mistake to ignore this stretch entirely because it always holds plenty of walleye. Along its western shore you'll find everything from trollable sandy and rocky flats to sharp rocky drop-offs where jigs work best. Across the river you have several nice stretches of submerged rocks, good waters for a slow drift.

Essentially, any technique that catches walleye in other places will work up in this part of the arm, but Carruth and several other regulars stick exclusively to their jigs and plastics, some tipping their hooks with small chunks of 'crawler, at times flipping them out over rocky ledges, then making slow retrieves, steadily twitching their rods for more action.

Along a productive walleye flat, they might also cast and retrieve or else vertically jig it, using either the current or their electric to cover more ground.

A few arm anglers like to use spinner-'crawler rigs trolled behind bottom walkers along those flats, at

BUZZER BEATER: Just before the Spokane Arm closed a couple years back, Robert Spellman of Marysville tied into this 13½-pound walleye in the Spokane River. He was using a leadhead jig and worm while fishing with R/C Guide Service.

least until they've located a school of fish, dropped their markers or punched that spot in on their GPS unit. Then they might go back to their jigs so they can stay right on top of the school.

Little Falls: My partners and I have even caught March walleye in the fast current just below Little Falls Dam. We'd anchor up, then flip straight 'crawlers behind heavy slip sinkers out and wait for a bite. This is a good lunch hour break that works, but be prepared to lose some gear to the rocks, and you're probably going to be battling at least as many pikeminnows as walleye.

Because the upper arm is essentially a river with sporadic sunken logs along its bed, trolling cranks can get a little pricey at times, but they definitely work. In fact, a few seasons ago I had a very good morning trolling perch-colored DC-13 Timber Tigers along a couple of those rocky straights a mile or so above that Porcupine Bay boat launch

Unfortunately, this isn't the good

AT a GLANCE

What: Upper Spokane Arm walleye.

Where: From Porcupine Bay upstream to Little Falls.

How: Cast and slowly retrieve jigs and plastics tipped with worm chunks, or vertically jig the 20- to 35-foot waters in coves, gravel flats and rocky points. Also troll worm harnesses or crankbaits on flats.

Regs: Open through March 31 for walleye, daily limit five, no more than one over 18 inches. Reopens June 1.

Info/gear: WDFW (509-892-1001), White's Boots Inc. (800-541-3786) and Sportsman's Warehouse (509-891-1900), all in Spokane.

ol' days of the late '80s and early '90s when my buddy, LeRoy Johnson, and I would spend a week in late March camping out at Porcupine Bay and catching plenty of walleye. The marble-eyes we caught weren't necessarily huge, but they sure were plentiful, and back then we had the advantage of facing minimal competition. Only a solid week of near-freezing daytime temperatures and raw March winds ever stood between us and some perfect outings.

Popular fishery: It's been at least a dozen years now since this fishery was discovered by the masses. The weather is still pretty touch-and-go this time of year and the walleye are as plentiful as ever, but the big change is that now anglers from across this state and even from Idaho and Montana will be heading for the Spokane Arm this spring.

"Yeah, on any given day from late February right up until that end of the March walleye closure on the entire arm, it's no longer uncommon to see 150 or more boats out there plying those narrow channels and little bays," Carruth says. "The word has definitely gone out in recent years. In fact, I now avoid fishing up there during March because I just don't like that much boat traffic, and I know I can always find enough walleye out in the mainstem. The action might not be as fast in other places, but to me the fishing is a lot more enjoyable."

However, if you're willing to put up with a crowd, tons of Roosevelt walleye will once again be heading upriver, everything from thousands of those 12- to 17-inchers to some 8-plus-pound females.

This is a no-minimum-size, one-walleye-over-18-inches-fishery, so quick limits can be pretty common in March. In fact, most of the regulars use slightly faster hook-sets up there so they can release all the

Upper Spokane River Arm Walleye

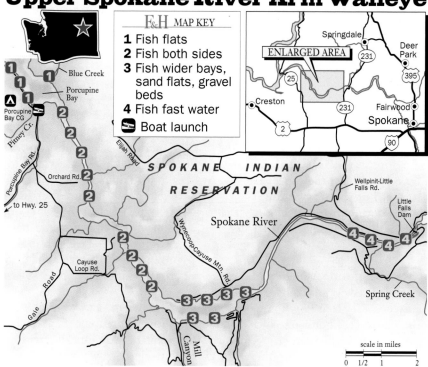

F&H MAP KEY
1 Fish flats
2 Fish both sides
3 Fish wider bays, sand flats, gravel beds
4 Fish fast water
Boat launch

really tiny fish, as well as the roe-filled female heavyweights, unharmed.

Other options: If the upper arm's too crowded, work out on its elbow, particularly from just below Porcupine Bay to a mile or so down from Crystal Cove. The shallows off both edges of Blue Creek as well as all those little rocky points and broken rock flats just downriver should still be reasonably productive, but the best action is going to be upriver, where faster water flows and more river-like conditions will

pull in far more walleye, including all those big prespawn females.

CPR, please: Unless you pick up a walleye that's going to eventually decorate your wall, please save your memories of that big female with a couple of quick photos, then get her back in the river so she can do her job. She's up in that fast water for one purpose: to lay thousands of eggs that will insure a future generation of Roosevelt walleye.

June reopener good too

If the crowds and low temps keep you away, wait until early June to fish the Spokane Arm of Lake Roosevelt. Then you'll find warmer weather, good facilities — a big public campground or nearby Two Rivers Casino and the top-notch boat launch — and walleye all right near the confluence of the lake and arm.

With a fast boat you'll have the option of making the long run to the faster waters below Little Falls Dam, then gradually working your way back. But by June plenty of hungry, spawned-out walleye will have spread throughout this system, so there's little reason to spend an hour running or burn that much fuel.

— L.L.

Experiment for Sprague Lake's abundant walleye

SPRAGUE

by Leroy Ledeboer

A GOOD CROP of walleye is hitting legal size at Sprague Lake, a fishery that's good enough to pull anglers across state lines. John Walz of Orofino and Frank Triano of CDA show off their limits, caught in late March. (Photo courtesy of Four Seasons Campground, *fourseasonscampground.com*)

Check out the photo board at Four Seasons Campground and the first thing that pops out is Coeur d'Alene anglers John Waltz and Frank Triano hoisting a dandy stringer of Sprague Lake walleye.

The most surprising thing about that double limit of hefty walleye is that it was taken on March 25, when very few anglers were even venturing out on Sprague.

"John and Frank have been willing to try different methods, to search out our walleye," says Four Seasons (509-257-2332) owner Scott Haugen. "They took those by casting tubes up in the shallows. Too often our walleye anglers spend all their time trolling baited spinners and bottom-walkers across the flats. That works fine when that's where the walleye are feeding, but at times they're up around the rocks, along the shoreline or on a weedline."

"A couple of years ago we found suspended walleye by running 'crawler-baited Rooster Tails behind a gang troll," says Haugen. "Later in the summer the trolled spinner/bottom-bouncers started to work, but you had to experiment with colors.

Last year Shad Raps worked well and at times Floating Rapalas cast up into the shallows were effective."

The bottom line is experimentation, both with lure choices and water depths. Both can change by the week, depending mostly on food supply. In Eastern Washington, walleye have adapted to massive aquatic insect hatches. Sprague's are busy cramming their bellies with chironomids, making them more likely to suspend over deeper water. As the new crops of spinyray and bullhead fry come on in the late summer, they're just as likely to work rocky points or even those long flats. In recent years the crawdad population seems to be down, but walleye will still hit crawdad patterns.

Sprague 'loaded': WDFW biologist Chris Donnelly agrees that Sprague walleye anglers might have to change tactics.

"That lake is absolutely loaded," he says "We can put out our gillnets anytime and anywhere, and we come up with walleye. But too often anglers want to head out at 10 a.m. and come in the early afternoon, which isn't a walleye's prime feeding hours."

"I've anchored off various rocky points just at dark, and while I go after channel cats with cutbaits, my wife fishes a worm below a bobber and caught walleye. You simply have to check out your depths, then throw out marker buoys so you know approximately where you want to fish and how deep to set your slip bobber so your bait is close to the bottom. Sprague has lots of walleye in every age bracket, but right now there's a huge class of two-year-olds, many of which will be hitting a legal 16 inches by June."

Catfish: Take another look at Four Season's photo board and there's Spokane's Bill Blosser with his 19-

---

AT a GLANCE

What: One of the Basin's richest walleye lakes, which also happens to host rainbows, catfish, crappie and bass.

Where: Sprague Lake, alongside I-90 southwest of Spokane.

Why: To quote the local biologist: "Sprague has lots of walleye in every age bracket, but right now there's a huge class of two-year-olds, many of which will be hitting a legal 16 inches by June." Yabba-dabba, daddy-o. Also good numbers of big channels and rainbows.

How: Just because there's a lot of walleye doesn't mean they're easy to catch — experimentation is key. For catfish, plunk worms, packaged catfish baits, chicken livers along the shorelines. Still-fish bait after dark, or troll brighter colors for trout.

Contact: Scott Haugen, Four Seasons Campground (509-257-2332).

pound channel cat.

While Sprague's catfish are far more elusive than its walleye, Donnelly and Haugen both say they're well worth pursuing. In 1999 WDFW planted 9,000 channels, and it looks as if a fair number have survived and are propagating.

"Some guys have figured out how to catch cats here, not only at night but in the daylight hours too," Haugen says. "But overall they haven't been targeted that much, so this could be a fantastic summer for them. You won't see many of those 19-pound monsters, but the mature cats are now running in the 6- to 14-pound range. Different anglers use everything from worms to packaged catfish baits and even chicken livers, but the main thing is to find where they're prowling, often right here near the resort, in the shallows of the south end or along either shoreline."

Rainbows: Nobody expects Sprague's rainbows to return to their glory days of the mid- to late 1980s, shortly after the lake's rotenoning and before its spinyrays reached predatory proportions. Once that happened, trout fingerling plants quickly turned into walleye fodder, so for the last few years it's mainly that occasional whopper 'bow, a fish that can easily top 5 pounds, that draws attention.

However, this spring WDFW planted 35,000 catchables, which should turn that fishery around. Even by midsummer these trout will have added length, girth and flavor thanks to the lake's billions of chironomids. By next spring they'll top 2 pounds.

"Our big trout usually get caught after dark with baits still-fished off the bottom," Haugen says, "but now with this many catchables in the lake I'd

expect to see more rainbows taken by trollers. Traditionally our trout have gone for bright colors."

Spinyrays: When the decision was made to manage Sprague as a warmwater fishery, the goal was to provide anglers with opportunities to catch everything from crappie and perch to walleye and catfish. However, it's the walleye that are now taking too much of a toll on the smaller spinyrays.

"It's always a balancing act," Donnelly says, "and starting out we may have been too protective of the walleye. Now we definitely want to see more of them harvested so the smaller spinyrays can make a comeback. Recently we've seen more perch in our net surveys, but with all

those walleye you have to wonder how long they'll last."

The lake's crappie are now protected by a 9-inch minimum size and 10-fish limit. Consider using some restraint if you do hit a big school of perch.

"Our smallmouth situation is kind of an unknown right now because in the last couple of summers we haven't had the clubs here — the guys who know what they're doing and concentrate on bass," Haugen says. "Almost no one is targeting them."

Still, it's Sprague's walleye that Donnelly says need a whole lot of harvesting. In fact, if the situation doesn't change drastically, don't be at all surprised to see that 16-inch size restrictions lowered by '06.

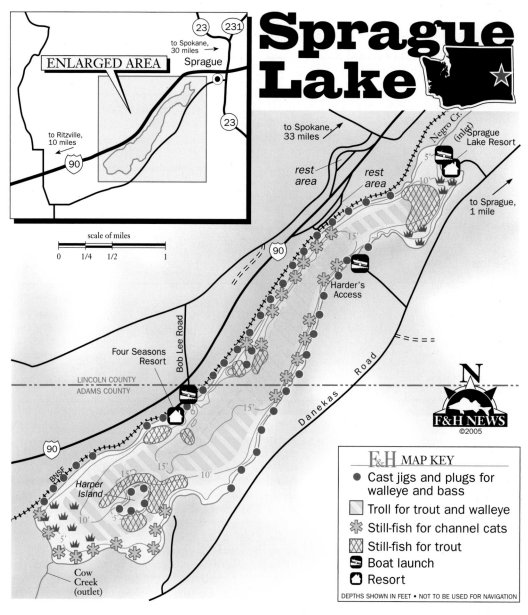

Canada Waters

STEELHEAD

Northern BC steelhead: Land of the giants

KITIMAT, BC

by Joel Shangle

The mere mention of their names causes the hair on the back of your neck to stand on end: Skeena, Kalum, Kitimat, Babine, Kispiox, Nass, Copper, Sustut.

If you're a steelheader, that is.

If there's such a thing as the Holy Grounds of steelhead fishing, it lies in the remote northern reaches of British Columbia, between Prince Rupert Sound and the Continental Divide. It's wild, rugged territory, with wild, rugged fish that carry an almost mythical status among the Pacific Northwest steelheading world.

"Wild runs of big fish," Buzz Ramsey says simply. "The biggest fish I ever caught was 30.4 on the Thompson, but those kinds of fish are caught and released over (in northern BC) every year. There are plenty of those that nobody even hears about. A guy will catch it, release it, and not even think twice about it."

And that's not an Americanized version of reality. The God's-honest truth about the rivers in this part of the province is that they produce some of the biggest steelhead in the world.

"Well, that depends on what you define as 'big', I guess," says Randy Murray at Northcoast Anglers (250-635-6496) in Terrace. "Fifteen pounds? Oh, no, that's not big. We think of 25 pounds as big. I've seen hatchery fish here to 20 pounds, so, yeah, if you think a 15-, 16-pound fish is big, we get some *really* big fish."

An upward trend: The steelhead runs of the Skeena and neighboring systems have gone through boom and bust cycles like many fisheries in the Pacific Northwest, but the Skeena and Nass of 2005 are significantly healthier than the runs of the 1980s, when over-harvest of wild fish pushed many of the rivers around Terrace and Kitimat into a depressed danger zone.

"About 20 years ago, there were really not a lot of fish," Murray says. "They started coming back about 10 years ago, after many of the rivers were put under catch-and-release regulations. The numbers now are much better than they had been historically."

Wild, wilder, wildest: The hatchery component that drives most steelhead fisheries in both Washington and Oregon is mostly nonexistent in the northern reaches of BC. The Kitimat River hatchery services its namesake system and the nearby Dala and Kildala rivers, but the rivers of the Skeena system are all wild-fish only, where catch-and-release is the rule rather than the exception.

"We've proven that catch-and-release works," says Murray. "A lot of guys up here like to catch a lot of fish in a year, but they know (the fish) won't last if they catch and kill them. We're OK with releasing our fish."

Such is the nature of steelheading in this part of the province, where the fish are treated with protective care by most of the locals. You think it's tough to get

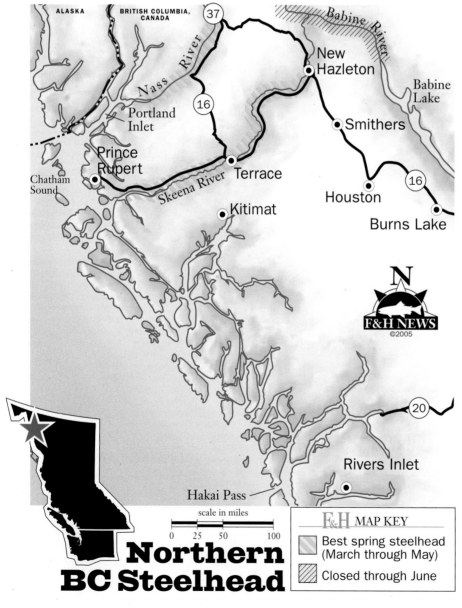

Northern BC Steelhead

scale in miles

0   25   50   100

F&H MAP KEY

Best spring steelhead (March through May)

Closed through June

the straight scoop from the Olympic Peninsula? You've never tried to pry information out of some of the guides who operate out of Terrace, Kitimat, Smithers, Hazelton and the other small towns in the area.

"The real avid fishermen feel very protective," Murray says. "None of them want to see it return to the way it was 20 years ago."

Tricky timing: Washington or Oregon anglers planning a run to the north need to keep a couple of things in mind: Run timing is different than rivers in the US, and some of the rugged inland tributaries of the Skeena (the Kispiox and Babine, to name a couple) are closed from January to July.

On the rivers most easily accessed via Terrace — the lower Skeena, Kalum and Copper — the best winter/spring fishing starts in March and continues through April and sometimes into late May.

"January and February are really the only two months when the fish really don't move much in those local rivers," Murray says. "Fish will start coming into the Skeena in late February and March, and it peaks around April and into May. You can catch fresh fish into the first part of June sometimes, depending on the water temperatures."

The summer runs start filtering in shortly thereafter, and by the time the Kispiox, Babine, Bulkly, Maurice, etc., reopen in July, it's time to gear up for the biggest fish of the year.

"The summer-runs are the biggest fish," Murray says. "If you're looking for truly big fish, August, September and October are the best times. It's not uncommon to still get fish over 30 pounds then."

How, where, why: Of the streams open for spring fishing, the Kalum and Skeena are the biggest and, generally, most productive, but the Copper and Kitimat runs get cranking around April too. Both of the first two are fishable via a sled and drift boat, while the Copper is easily fished from the bank.

"You can cover everything on the Copper on foot," says Murray. "It's an easy enough river to walk, but you have to be up on the regulations. There are parts of it that close in the winter, but there are still plenty of places to fish it year-round."

The mainstem Skeena is also where you'll likely find the biggest fish.

NORTHERN BC offers big, beautiful rivers with big, beautiful steelhead. Woodburn, Oregon's, Leroy Miller and Bob Engle show off a fly-caught Skeena River hawg.

"The whole system has big fish in it, and there's really no rhyme or reason to it, but the Skeena itself has the biggest," Murray says. "The Kispiox and Babine and all those smaller rivers certainly have their big fish too, but they're not present in the numbers that they are on the Skeena. The Skeena's fish are just *big.*"

Rules/regs: Leave the barbed trebles at home. Everything here is single barbless hooks, and you can't fish bait on several of the streams in the area.

The nuts and bolts of it all: Unlike the easily accessible streams of lower mainland BC and Vancouver Island, the rivers in the northern part of the province demand some travel. Hawk Air (*hawkair.net*) and Air Canada (*aircanada.ca*) both fly from Vancouver to Terrace (it's roughly a 90-minute direct flight), and you can also ride the VIARail (*viarail.ca*) from Vancouver to Terrace.

Don't bother with trailering a boat up — book with a local guide to fish the bigger waters of the Skeena and Kalum, and don't even think about trying to figure out the regulations and access restrictions on the Kispiox, Babine, etc., on your own.

AT a GLANCE

What: Steelheading in northern British Columbia.

When: March through May is the best winter/spring fishing, but summer season starts shortly thereafter: July through September.

Why: Quite simply, the biggest steelhead in the world swim in the waters of the Skeena, Kalum, Nass, Kispiox, Babine, Kitimat and several other streams in the area.

Where: Using the towns of Terrace, Hazelton and Kitimat as your bases, you'll find all of the above rivers in a relatively compact zone between Prince Rupert Sound and the continental divide.

Travel: Hawk Air (*hawkair.net*) and Air Canada (*aircanada.ca*) fly direct from Vancouver to Terrace.

Information: Northcoast Anglers (250-635-6496) in Terrace; Outdoor Experience (250-847-9233) in Smithers; Tracey John Hittell, Steelhead Heaven (250-632-9880) in Kitimat; Kispiox Adventures (877-842-5911) in Hazelton.

Lodging: Northern British Columbia Tourism Association (*NorthernBCTravel.com*); *BCFishing.com*; Babine Steelhead Lodge (250-577-3108; *fishbabine.com*).

Border crossing equals world-class steelhead

ABBOTSFORD, B.C.

by Joel Shangle

Editor's note: This is Part 1 of a three-part series on B.C. steelheading. Parts 2 and 3 will look at upper mainland and Vancouver Island streams.

What is it about an international border that prevents more Western Washington steelheaders from pursuing winter runs on the rivers and streams of lower mainland British Columbia?

It certainly isn't distance, because several B.C. steelhead rivers lie as close to the Seattle metro area as most Columbia River tribs, and are easier to reach than the streams on the Olympic Peninsula. It's definitely not access, because several of those same B.C. streams offer miles and miles of public bank fishing. And it's absolutely not for lack of fish, because seasonal catch rates on some streams in the province (specifically the Chilliwack/Vedder) rival those of the mighty Cowlitz.

Yep, it has to be the border crossing. Get over it.

Get your passport, invest the $80 (Canadian!) in an annual non-tidal fishing license, stock up on floats, pink worms, jigs and yarn, and take a crash course on the steelhead culture of lower mainland B.C.

CLOSER THAN YOU THINK

Plenty of Washington anglers have already discovered the wealth of winter steelhead opportunity that lies just over the border, but I'd wager that 90 percent of the Westside's steelhead crowd doesn't fully understand just how close some of the lower mainland's rivers really are. Let me put it to you like this: If I drive south on I-5 from the Mercer Street exit in Seattle, I have roughly 135 miles of road ahead of me before I reach the banks of the Kalama. If I head north from that same exit, I'm standing on the banks of the Chilliwack/Vedder after 138 miles, and I don't have to deal with the Seattle/Tacoma/Olympia traffic cluster.

CHILLIWACK/VEDDER RIVER

Those tricky Canucks! If you didn't know better, you'd think that the Chilliwack and Vedder were two different drainages, but they're not. This is actually one river with two names: it's the Chilliwack from the headwaters at Chilliwack Lake to Vedder Crossing, and the Vedder from there to the

BIG WINTER STEELHEAD — like this Vedder River beauty hooked by Peter McPherson on a bubble gum worm — are the drill on several lower mainland B.C. streams. Some of the province's best winter steelhead fisheries lie within two hours of Seattle.

Vedder Canal, which eventually empties into the Fraser.

Whatever you call it, this system should be especially attractive to Puget Sound anglers for three reasons: 1) It has one of the strongest hatchery runs in B.C., boosted by a broodstock program that pushes the average-sized steelhead into the 12-pound range; 2) It offers roughly 20 miles of fishable water, all accessible from the bank; 3) It's within 140 miles of downtown Seattle.

The system has several distinct personalities, and much of the fishery is influenced by five slides that can flip the clarity from steelhead green to chocolate brown overnight.

"The reality of this river is that it's totally weather related as far as its fishability is concerned," says Fred Helmer at Fred's Custom Tackle (604-858-7344) in Chilliwack. "The Chilliwack Valley is made up of a lot of clay, and we have a little bit of a historical problem when we get snow followed by a Chinook and some rain. If that happens, the river can come up 6 to 7 feet and turn to crap. The good news is that the watershed has been worked on a lot over the past few years, to give some stabilization to some of the problem areas. But it can still change on a day-to-day basis."

AT a GLANCE

What: Two of lower mainland British Columbia's better winter steelhead rivers, the Chilliwack/Vedder and the Chehalis.

Where: The Fraser River Valley, east of Vancouver.

Why: There are dozens of excellent steelhead options in the lower mainland, and they're all within two to three hours of downtown Seattle. Rivers like the Chilliwack/Vedder offer some of the best bank access for steelhead in the Pacific Northwest, and they're easily reachable from Puget Sound.

When: Fish began showing in early December, but the best fishing in most rivers in the Fraser Valley is in January, February, March and April

Best rivers: The Chilliwack/Vedder is lower B.C.'s steelhead superstar, thanks to an excellent hatchery run. Other nearby options include the Chehalis, which is a good bet when the Chilliwack is blown out, the Fraser and the Stave.

Licenses: Annual non-tidal (freshwater) license is $80 Canadian. You can buy a one-day license for $20 and an eight-day license for $50.

Information: Fred's Custom Tackle (604-858-7344) in Chilliwack; Anglers West Fly & Tackle (604-874-3474) in Vancouver.

Vedder River Steelhead

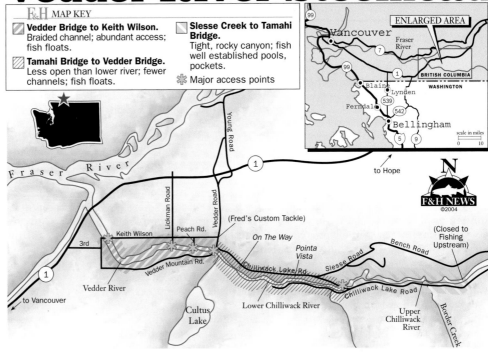

F&H MAP KEY

▨ **Vedder Bridge to Keith Wilson.** Braided channel; abundant access; fish floats.

▨ **Tamahi Bridge to Vedder Bridge.** Less open than lower river; fewer channels; fish floats.

▨ **Slesse Creek to Tamahi Bridge.** Tight, rocky canyon; fish well established pools, pockets.

❋ Major access points

ENLARGED AREA

Vancouver

Fraser River

BRITISH COLUMBIA

WASHINGTON

Blaine

Lynden

Ferndale

Bellingham

scale in miles

0   10

to Hope

N

F&H NEWS ©2004

Young Road

Lickman Road

Vedder Road

Peach Rd.

(Fred's Custom Tackle)

Keith Wilson

On The Way

Pointa Vista

(Closed to Fishing Upstream)

Bench Road

3rd

Vedder Mountain Rd.

Chilliwack Lake Rd.

Slesse Road

Chilliwack Lake Road

Border Creek

Vedder River

Lower Chilliwack River

Upper Chilliwack River

to Vancouver

Cultus Lake

Fraser River

Helmer's advice for Pugetropolites planning a run across the border: Check the Bellingham weather forecast the night before you plan to fish, and call his shop after hours for a recorded report of river conditions.

"We usually get Bellingham's weather about a half day later, so it's a good idea to take a quick peek at it before you come up here," he says. "There are so many mountains and valleys in the Fraser Valley it's really hard to predict the weather, but the Bellingham forecast is usually pretty close."

When: Winter runs began filtering into the Vedder in early December, but the best fishing is yet to come: January, February and March are your best bets for hatchery fish, and you can catch winter fish well into April.

How: Floats and jigs/yarn (peach, orange, pink and light purple) or pink worms are the go-to baits here, but you can also throw spoons and spinners, drift eggs or fly fish with leech patterns.

Where: Divide the Chilliwack/Vedder into three sections:

1) Lower river: The stretch from the Vedder Bridge downstream is defined by lots of braided water, side channels and easy access via Peach Road, Lickman Road and the Keith Wilson access. The best way to tackle this section — which sees the highest amount of angling pressure — is to treat it like a trout stream: "Get out and cover ground," advises Helmer. "Fish and move on. The lower river changes every time the water comes up, but it's a fantastic place to fish. When fish first come in, it's their first stopping grounds. They're very aggressive."

2) Middle river: The midsection, from Vedder Bridge upstream to Tamahi Bridge, is a transition zone. There aren't as many braided channels, and the topography is a little more restricted than the wide-open lower river.

"You're getting into a fairly adventurous part of the river there," Helmer says of the midsection. "What you're doing there is driving up (Chilliwack Lake Road), stopping, and walking a

mile or two along one section. You're bushwhacking a little, but it's not nearly as heavily fished (as the lower end)."

3) Upper river: You'll notice a definite gradient and topography change as you follow Chilliwack Lake Road to the upper section, from Tamahi Bridge upstream to the deadline at Slesse Creek. The river narrows here through a series of canyons, where you'll find large boulders and well-established pools and pockets.

"That's more an area where you'd fish specific pockets and spots," advises Helmer. "The elevation and gradient change a lot, but the spots don't change like they do on the lower river. The big boulders and rocks stay where they are, so you have a lot of established spots to fish."

Get there: Take I-5 north to Highway 542 in Bellingham and head north/east to Highway 9. Head north, taking the Sumas crossing as 9 becomes Sumas Way. From there, merge onto Provincial Route 1 East toward Hope for roughly 17 miles to the Sardis/Cultus Lake exit. Take a slight right off the exit onto Vedder Road, which leads through Vedder Crossing. From there, you can head upstream on Chilliwack Lake Road, or follow lower-river access roads like Peach Road, Lickman Road, the

Railroad Bridge, etc.

Who to call: Fred's Custom Tackle (604-858-7344; *freds-bc.com*).

CHEHALIS RIVER

Canada's Chehalis is 180 degrees removed from Washington's Chehalis. Unlike the big, slow water of the Evergreen State version, the B.C. stream is defined by water that tumbles out of Chehalis Lake through several miles of rugged, narrow, rocky canyons before spilling into the Harrison. And while the Chehalis' bank access is miniscule compared to the Vedder's, this drainage is often fishable when the Vedder is blown out.

When: January through April.

How: Floats with jigs/worms, eggs/shrimp, Corkies and yarn, blades or spoons.

Where: Easiest access lies below the upper canyon, from the hatchery on Morris Valley Road down.

Why: Upper canyon challenging. Access on Hemlock Valley. Only one road it.

Get there: Take I-5 north to Bellingham and take the Sumas crossing onto Highway 1 toward Mission. From Mission, drive east on Highway 7 to the Hemlock Recreation Area.

Who to call: Anglers West Fly & Tackle (604-874-3474).

Vancouver Island's steelhead just a ferry ride away

VICTORIA, B.C.

by Joel Shangle

Editor's note: This is part two of a three-part series on BC steelheading. Part three will look at upper mainland streams.

The only place I'd ever move to if I were to renounce my American citizenship is Vancouver Island, BC. It has everything an outdoorsman could want: It's one of the most mind-numbingly beautiful places in the world, it's uncrowded and uncluttered, and the monolithic "EverythingMart" warehouses are rare, replaced by Mom & Pop's tackle shops. And with well over 200 steelhead-bearing rivers and streams lacing the island between BC's capitol city and the wild, wooly north island coast around Port Hardy, a steelhead junkie could easily spend the rest of his days under the Maple Leaf, happily pursuing world-class metalheads.

Fortunately for red-blooded Evergreen Staters like me, there's no need to turn in my Social Security card. Access to some of the best steelhead streams on the south and central portions of Vancouver Island are just a ferry or short plane ride away.

CLOSER THAN YOU THINK

I mentioned last issue (p. 12, Dec. 30-Jan. 13 issue) that most American anglers suffer from a severe case of the yips when they think about British Columbia steelheading. Maybe it's the international border, but a whole bunch of you treat the province as though it were located clear across the globe, instead of right next door.

It's even worse with Vancouver Island. Despite incredibly easy access via several ferries that make the Seattle-to-Victoria run daily, and a handful of airlines that shuttle passengers back and forth from Seattle/Tacoma/Portland to portals like Victoria, Tofino and Campbell River, the majority of the Washington and Oregon steelheading public will never make the hop across the Strait of Juan de Fuca.

I'm here to tell you, it's not as difficult as you think.

Here's a brief look at some of southern and central Vancouver Island's most well-known winter steelhead options. My advice to the potential American angler who's considering a little island hopping: Hook up with the guides and sources listed under each river. Let them decode the Canadian regs for you. Let them educate you on the river in question. After that initial crash course, the island is simply this: an excellent place to pursue winter steelhead

SOUTH ISLAND

Draining more than 20 miles from its headwaters in Lake Cowichan to its outlet in Cowichan Bay near the town of Duncan, the Cowichan River is regarded as a premier destination for trout-hunting flyrodders, but you'll also find a good run of winter steelhead in the river from January to April.

Two things you need to know about this river: 1) Much of it is fly-fishing or selective gear only; 2) It can blow out quickly, and for long periods of time. However, if you're keen on flinging flies or fishing pink worms, Colorado blades, Corkies and yarn, etc., and can catch it when it's not sideways, the 89 named pools and runs of the Cowichan are worth a three-day weekend.

"If you're coming up for a two- or three-day

Vancouver Island steelhead

F&H MAP KEY

South Island: Cowichan, Tasis, San Juan, Sooke rivers

West Coast/Central: Stamp, Sproat, Somas, Gold, Heber rivers

East Coast/Central: Campbell, Salmon, Oyster, Nanaimo rivers

Port Hardy

Vancouver Island

Esperanza Inlet — Tahsis

Nuchatlitz Inlet

Nootka Sound

Clayoquot Sound

Tofino

Ucluelet

Barkley Sound

Campbell R.

19

Vancouver

BRITISH COLUMBIA
WASHINGTON

5

Victoria

Everett

N

F&H NEWS
©2005

scale in miles

0   20   40   80

fish, I recommend that you just go drive the river for a couple of hours when you get here," says Calvin Kennett at Bucky's Sports Shop (250-746-4923) in Duncan. "Spend the first half-day getting to know the spots and you'll save a whole day of fishing."

The basics: Easiest access is below the Silver Bridge (Trans Canada Highway 1) in Duncan. Fish this area from the bank on an incoming tide. The Cowichan is fly-fishing only from Stanley Creek to the 70.2 Bridge, and hardware only from there to Silver Bridge.

Who to call: Scott Blewett, eX-Stream Guide Service (250-474-3619; *ex-stream.com*); Craig & Fred Harman, Bright Waters Guide Service (250-715-1189/748-5558; *brightwatersfishing.com*); Bucky's Sports Shop (250-746-4923).

Other options: Nitnat River, Sooke River.

WEST COAST/CENTRAL

The Stamp-Somas is one of the Island's most dependable systems, with a mix of hatchery and wild metalheads to 15 pounds and up. Why is it so dependable? Simple: It's the site of the famed Robertson Creek Hatchery, which supplements many of the West Coast's salmon and steelhead hatchery streams.

The basics: The Stamp pours out of Great Central Lake and turns into the Somass below its confluence with the Sproat. In all, you'll find just over 11 miles of water open to fishing. Unfortunately, it's an access headache, with private land covering the bottom 2 miles of the Stamp, and the entire stretch of the Somass. You'll find more public land in the middle and upper Stamp, but the access points aren't obvious to newbies. Stop at Gone Fishin' Shop (250-723-1172; gone-fishinshop.com) on River Road in Port Alberni for a map.

"The Stamp is an early stream: Dec. 1 through March 1 is typical," says David Murphy at Murphy Sportfishing. "Fish were here in November this year, so they're early. I usually think that an early run is a big run."

Who to call: David Murphy, Murphy Sportfishing (250-723-2772; 877-218-6600; *murphysportfishing.com*); Jay's Clayoquot Ventures (888-534-7422; *tofinofishing.com*); Gone Fishin' (250-723-1172).

Other options: Sproat River.

Gold River: Emptying into Muchalat Inlet (the easternmost finger of Nootka Sound), the Gold is one of west/central BC.'s most historically significant wild steelhead fisheries. The run isn't supplemented by a hatchery, and big, beautiful wild fish are part of the mystique — but they're rare. The Gold is coming off a depressed year, so local guides and outfitters are keeping their fingers crossed for a resurgent run in 2005.

The basics: The mouths of the Heber and Ucona rivers attract a lot of attention, but the entire lower section of the canyon offers plenty of spots to fish floats and jigs, worms or yarn.

Who to call: The Lodge at Gold River (250-283-2900; *thelodgeatgoldriver.ca*); David Chard, Profish Adventures (250-923-6335/203-4773; *profish.bc.ca*).

Other options: Heber River, Stamp River.

EAST COAST/CENTRAL

The plunging fortunes of steelhead rivers on the East Coast of the island have been well documented over the past several years, but the Campbell River is still the most viable option. And if it was good enough for Roderick Haig-Brown, it's good enough for me. Canada's most beloved fishing scribe considered the runs and pools of the Campbell his home waters, and you'll find constant reminders of Haig-Brown throughout the region, from the Haig-Brown Institute to Haig-Brown Provincial Park.

But although Haig-Brown's writings may have brought this East Coast river to the attention of anglers throughout

THE GOLD RIVER and others make Vancouver Island a productive place to steelhead.

the region, it'll take a whole lot more than book study to decode the winter steelhead fishery. It's a big river to start out with, and with dwindling runs of fish, every hookup is precious here.

The basics: You'll find access points spread along the Campbell Highway, on the south bank, but the best winter fishing is from the mouth of the Quinsam River downstream. You can fish bait from the powerline crossing (Pump House Hole) down, but it's fly fishing only from there upstream to the John Hart power station.

Who to call: River Sportsman Outdoor Store (250-286-1017; *riversportsman.com*); Curtis Smith, Coastal Wilderness Adventures (250-287-3427; 866-640-1173; *coastwild.com*).

Other options: Gold River, Oyster River, Salmon River.